Open Questions

Readings for Critical Thinking and Writing

Open Questions

Readings for Critical Thinking and Writing

CHRIS ANDERSON

Oregon State University

LEX RUNCIMAN

Linfield College

BEDFORD/ST. MARTIN'S

Boston ◆ New York

For Bedford/St. Martin's

Developmental Editor: Stephen A. Scipione
Production Editors: Stasia Zomkowski and Deborah Baker
Production Supervisor: Yexenia Markland
Senior Marketing Manager: Rachel Falk
Editorial Assistant: Amy Hurd
Copyeditor: Mary Lou Wilshaw-Watts
Text Design: Anna Palchik
Cover Design: Donna Lee Dennison
Cover Art: The Poet, by Richard Piloco. Eleanor Ettinger Gallery; private collection.
Composition: Macmillan India Ltd.
Printing and Binding: R.R. Donnelley & Sons Company

President: Joan E. Feinberg
Editorial Director: Denise B. Wydra
Editor in Chief: Karen S. Henry
Director of Marketing: Karen Melton Soeltz
Director of Editing, Design, and Production: Marcia Cohen
Managing Editor: Elizabeth M. Schaaf

Library of Congress Control Number: 2004112284

For information, write: Bedford/St. Martin's, 75 Arlington Street, Boston, MA 02116 (617-399-4000)

ISBN: 0–312–41635–0
EAN: 978–0–312–41635–5

Acknowledgments

Elmaz Abinader. "Profile of an Arab Daughter." From *Al Jadid* by Elmaz Abinader. Copyright © 2001 by Elmaz Abinader. Reprinted by permission of the author.

Scott Adams. "Dilbert." By permission of United Media.

Kofi Annan. "Nobel Lecture." © The Nobel Prize. Courtesy of The Nobel Foundation.

Acknowledgments and copyrights are continued at the back of the book on pages 710–14, which constitute an extension of the copyright page. It is a violation of the law to reproduce these selections by any means whatsoever without the written permission of the copyright holder.

Preface for Instructors

As teachers of college composition, we know that our challenge involves more than teaching grammar or paragraphing or the subtleties of the semicolon—however genuinely important those concerns are. Perhaps the first challenge is simply how to conceive of the course itself. What questions will constitute the locus of inquiry? What will you read and discuss? What will prompt the deep engagement from which lively discussion, patient thinking, and good writing might result?

In many different ways, this book asks students a question at once time-less and very much of the moment: "how should we act?" We all read the papers and watch the news. We hear about and see what's going on in our neighborhoods and communities. CEOs cook the books, coaches break recruiting rules, politicians fudge the truth, teachers or police betray those who trust them. We see scandals and abuse, uncertainty and fear. And we're uneasy about what seems like a general decline in courtesy, respect, and regard for complexities, particularly in public language about values and policies. Our age appears increasingly strident and antagonistic, and this can sometimes seem true on campus, too. Does the plagiarism we see come from ignorance, willed dishonesty, or a simplistic assumption that integrity doesn't matter to anyone anymore? Is celebrity really better than achievement? How should we act in a world that sometimes treats us arbitrarily or unfairly?

And what does it mean to live in communities? How should we think about this? And on the basis of such thoughtfulness, how should we act?

Why would we, as teachers of writing, want to embrace such questions? Perhaps because composition courses have long sought to encourage in our students the excitement, passion, probity, and precision of the intellectual life. We want to help our students become better readers, thinkers, writers—better prepared to face the intellectual challenges of academia—but also, ideally, better able to lead examined lives as informed citizens, more capable of making a positive difference in the world. Our effort has always been to foster the values of the intellectual life as we impart its skills, and this, by its nature, has profoundly ethical dimensions.

WHY THIS ORGANIZATION?

If the purpose of a composition course is to encourage ecumenical inquiry, critical thinking, and persuasive writing that will serve all students, whatever their ethical heritage, how could a reader support such goals? How could ethics be a part of such a course?

As we thought about this issue, we hit on the idea of organizing the book around a series of "open questions." We'd been moving towards an open-ended approach, as we selected readings and started trying to group them together, and we wanted to engage students immediately with the kinds of everyday ethical dilemmas that we all face—dilemmas that are genuinely perplexing, genuinely complicated. Usually in these situations there isn't a clear-cut answer at all, no one right way, and that, we realized, was the key. That was the reason to make ethical issues the focus of a composition reader: because the readings reveal rich and layered and complicated issues, issues that require exactly the kind of critical thinking skills that all university education relies upon and affirms.

The reason to do a composition reader on ethics is to open the questions, open them wide. Thus, each chapter in the book begins with a brief scenario that bears on the question of the chapter title, a scenario in which a choice or judgment has to be made. For example, in Chapter 2, "Are We Responsible for Others?" the opening scenario asks students what they would do if they discover a friend has a drinking problem. Should the student intervene? If not, why not? If so, why—and how? From this specific situation that many students may already have encountered (*What did they do, and why?*), the chapter moves on to present students with readings that complicate and open up different and larger issues of responsibility, examining them first from one point of view, then from another, proposing one solution, then a variant or opposite, and sometimes wondering whether action is even possible. That is, each chapter in *Open Questions* encourages students to examine their underlying assumptions, recognizing them *as* assumptions, as interpretations and choices, not absolute truths. The result is to suggest how even a small, everyday concern is caught up in the great truths and the great dilemmas. Our lives bear on great things.

We soon realized, too, that we didn't have to organize chapters by conventional topics (business ethics, environmental ethics, and so on), but that we could group the readings around larger questions involving various, overlapping fields of inquiry. Real life doesn't follow conventional categories. In any given situation we have to think about business ethics *and* environmental ethics and a whole variety of related kinds of ethics, all at once. By making the chapter titles into questions, we realized that we could further emphasize the open-endedness of this kind of thinking and living—the kind of thinking and living we all struggle with and do.

Although the chapters and readings in the book can be assigned in any order, depending on the preferences and interests of instructors and students, we have organized them in what seems to us to be a logical sequence, beginning with the question that we generally ask when we meet someone for the first time: "Where Are You Coming From?" In other words, what is your background? What are your values? Once we arrive on campus, from all our various places, differences arise and conflicts begin. The individual comes into relation with other individuals and so communities form, or fail to form, or struggle, or grow, or all of these. Thus the next logical question is "Are We Responsible for Others?" which is to say, how am I related to the others I find myself living with? What are my obligations? This leads us to several topics having to do with relationships and communities—all ethics have to do with community—including questions of violence, the body, and the challenge and nature of honesty. Overall, the chapters in the book move outward, from the dorm room to the board room and beyond, towards increasingly broader concerns. In "What Is This Worth?" for example, several selections engage students in thinking about the relationship between environmental and business concerns. In "Why Change Your Mind?" the readings and apparatus encourage students to step back and to think about their thinking, to examine the intellectual movement that may or may not have happened in earlier chapters as they did the readings and started to complicate their thinking.

The final chapter asks the next logical question: "What Should You Do?" Given all of this complexity and nuance, what actions can we take or should we take in order to make the world a better place? What have others done?

WHY THESE READINGS?

Whether by design or default, the composition course often also functions as an introduction to the intellectual life of higher education. With class size kept relatively small, our courses offer the possibility of genuine, intense, open-ended intellectual inquiry—the foundation for all critical thinking. We know that while good teaching and good thinking do not guarantee good writing, they make it more likely; students deeply engaged in the issues care more about what they say and how they say it.

For *Open Questions,* we've chosen readings that have pushed us to such thoughtfulness. Some of them—Adrienne Rich's "Claiming an Education," Martin Luther King Jr.'s "Letter from Birmingham Jail," and George Orwell's "Politics and the English Language" for instance—we've chosen on the basis of long acquaintance. Others claimed a place here because they offered such rich opportunities for provocative discussion—Sallie Tisdale's "We Do Abortions Here," Stephen Carter's "The Best Student Ever," Milton Friedman's "The Social Responsibility of Business Is to Increase Its Profits," for example. Still others were chosen based on their timeliness: Chris Hedges's essay on war, for example, and Elmaz Abinader's "Profile of an Arab Daughter." But this listing hardly scratches the surface. The great challenge—and joy—of making this book has been to choose readings that in declaring their views ask us to reply.

We have chosen readings that seem to us to matter—to address fundamental concerns about how we hear others, how we declare ourselves, how we decide what to do, and how we rethink as we encounter new experience, new ideas, and new understandings. We've chosen readings that represent intellectual life as dynamic, thoughtful, sometimes unsure, always important—and always with language at its vibrant center. Thus, our assignments become, we hope, more than mere homework, and the composition course becomes more than a hurdle to be cleared. Instead, students and teacher collaborate to make composition the central course of the term, and students understand reading and writing—and the actions that result—as the fundamental ways we are and become.

WHY THIS FORMAT?

Open Questions begins with an introduction that orients students to the book and asks them to start doing some of the thinking that the composition course itself will emphasize. Thus, while the introduction identifies several systematic modes of ethical thinking, it also stresses the central importance of reading carefully and listening attentively. Students are offered straightforward suggestions for reading and discussion. The introduction's two central examples—music downloading and gay marriage—also stress the ways that this course takes for granted that higher education inevitably must connect with the world outside school itself.

Each of the readings in *Open Questions* is prefaced with a brief headnote that gives authorial information and so places the selection in some human context. Each reading is followed by a series of questions in three categories that try to broaden the students' inquiry, making it wider and wider, more and more open. The first set of questions, "What Did She [or He, or They] Say?" stresses a student's first reading of a piece, helping him or her to some initial clarity about its meaning and structure. In effect, these are comprehension questions for use at home, though they can of course be used in the classroom for class discussion, too. The second set of questions, "What Do You Think?" we intend to be particularly useful for class discussions. Now that students are relatively clear about what the piece is saying, we want them to start bouncing ideas off each other, expanding and complicating their thinking through their interactions with each other. The third set of questions after each piece, "What Would They Say?" widens the discussion even further by including other authors, often in other chapters of the book. Again the categories break down. Lance Armstrong or Wendell Berry may be in this or that chapter addressing this or that issue, but all issues bear on each other.

It's not that we're on the side of dithering or simplistic relativism. It's (again) that we're on the side of intellectual curiosity and humility because that's where ethical behavior must begin, with these recognitions—that each of us as an individual is not enough, that we live with other thoughtful people in the world and that they have lives too, lives deserving of our attention and respect. In fact, what we're ultimately on the side of is action in the world, action outside the classroom, the kind of action that results (we hope) when students begin to abandon their first biases and make contact with the complexities of the world as it is. That's why we end each chapter with questions and projects emphasizing community research and service. Finally, however necessary, talk is cheap; even reading can be cheap. In our view and in the view of many others in our field and profession, for education to matter it must move beyond textbooks and beyond campus and make a difference in real lives.

ANCILLARIES

Teachers adopting *Open Questions* would do well to consult Anna Harrell's instructor's manual, *Resources for Teaching OPEN QUESTIONS*. In addition to sample syllabi and concise commentary on every reading, the instructor's manual provides useful discussions of teaching pedagogy, including "Using Small Groups," "Using Listening Exercises," "Requiring Journals," and "Grading Concerns and Formal Assignment Design." The book also has a companion Web site <bedfordstmartins.com/openquestions>, where instructors can find an online version of the instructor's manual, and students will find resources for additional reading and research.

ACKNOWLEDGMENTS

Certainly the two of us have grown and changed in the course of writing this book. Our notions about ethics have evolved in ways we could not have predicted. Our own classroom practices have been challenged and deepened. And as on earlier projects, we've experienced the ways in which collaboration enriches and rewards the mind—how two heads *are* better than one, how a project takes on a compelling life and voice of its own. We've ended up, we think, with a book that can make our teaching better—our classes less predictably rote, more thought-provoking, and the papers we read more engaged and engaging.

We want to thank, then, all those who have shared in this process and collaboration. At Bedford/St. Martin's, we thank Joan Feinberg, Denise Wydra, and Karen Henry, who supported our enterprise; Elizabeth Schaaf, Stasia Zomkowski, and Deborah Baker, who produced the book; and Karen Melton Soeltz, Jane Betz, and Rachel Falk, who marketed it. Leasa Burton had a preliminary conversation with Chris Anderson about the idea of this book, and Nancy Perry and Steve Scipione expanded on the idea in a meeting with

Lex Runciman. We want to thank Dominic LeFave, formerly of St. Martin's, for his insight, expertise, and enthusiasm in the early development of the book. Along the way, it's been editor Steve Scipione who kept egging us on and raising the bar, who never said he liked something when he didn't, who read what we sent with a keen critical intelligence, and who kept urging us to greater deftness and precision and nuance. When Steve finally *did* say that he thought something was good, we believed him. We could not hope for better editorial collaboration and support.

Without our assistant, Anna Harrell, the book would be years away from being done. She gathered reams of material, then sorted that material, then gathered more, then filled in holes as the book started taking shape, then helped us by writing the headnotes to the readings and later a fine instructor's manual. With us, she worked to hold the whole book in mind. We salute her true collaboration on this project.

We thank Oregon State University and Linfield College and our trusted colleagues for giving us each a stable base. We thank our students, former and present, who grant us—and their fellow students—the privilege of seeing their minds at work. We have chosen readings we hope will provoke reaction in them, as they continue to do in us. We thank all the people who commented on two drafts of the book in progress, particularly those who either resisted the whole idea or who loved it and gave specific feedback: Timothy Barnett, Northern Illinois University; Anne Beaufort, Stony Brook University; Michael Benton, University of Kentucky; Shane Borrowman, Gonzaga University; Genevieve Coogan, Houston Community College–Northwest; Regina Clemens Fox, Arizona State University; Lynee Gaillet, Georgia State University; Hank Galmish, Green River Community College; Michael Mackey, Community College of Denver; Tom Montgomery-Fate, College of DuPage; Lisa Wilde, Howard Community College; and Heidi Wilkinson, California Polytech State University, San Luis Obispo.

We thank our families, too, for their patience, though this time around, with our kids mostly grown and gone, no one really seemed to notice. Our wives are used to this process by now; they tolerate and support it in ways we could never fully acknowledge. And we thank each other, on this third project we've done together: for the trips up and down Highway 99, for the phone calls, e-mails, lunches, rewrites, disagreements, and agreements—and for a continuing and uncommon friendship. It's rare in a collaboration when each person does what he says he will do and does it consistently well, at such a high level. That's happened again. And again, the result is something neither of us could have or would have written on our own; something much better. What a fascinating, satisfying process.

Chris Anderson

Lex Runciman

Preface for Students

We often hear that the world is smaller than it was. And we *are* more connected: news travels the globe in seconds. We can e-mail anyone with a computer and Internet access. But there are also more of us than ever before. And our new abilities to tap information can also make us aware of how little we understand each other. As citizens, workers, and individuals with private lives, we are busier than ever, with less and less time to hear the stories of others or to understand their viewpoints, values, and reasons for acting. Sometimes our divisions and many distractions alienate us from others. It begins to be easy to be selfish, eager to fulfill our own needs and secure individual happiness. In such a climate, common rules or guidelines can seem not to matter very much. So what if I cheat a little bit on my taxes? Everyone does. What does it matter if I take a pen or two from my employer? I'm not getting paid enough anyway.

This book is interested in helping us reconnect. It hopes to do that by offering many stories and much food for thought. It hopes that you will react to what you read; talk with each other about your reactions; think hard about the stories, viewpoints, and advocacies they assert; consider carefully the values and premises that underpin them; and then write clearly and thoughtfully about what new understandings—and new questions—result. We will call this kind of discussion—sometimes very personal, sometimes personal and analytical, always shared—civic rhetoric. We hope that together you will make a community of critical and ethical thinkers, listening to, respecting, and pushing each other just as you listen to, respect, and think deeply about the readings themselves.

Imagine for a moment the world as a crowded bus. Everyone on the bus—every one of us—has known real hurt and wants happiness; each carries inside a wealth of stories (complicated, spoken, unspoken); each knows weariness and elation, desperation and calm, frustration and occasional success, and has limits of patience, experience, and cash; each has loved ones; each feels sometimes lost, sometimes sure. No two people's lives are exactly alike, yet each is a human person with the right to make choices. But what choices? If you sit down, will someone else have to stand?

Civic rhetoric is difficult to conduct on a bus. It's easier in a class setting. We hope that your practices in this course will lead you to self-knowledge and civic participation—that is, to thoughtful, articulate, and personal interaction in many communities of many sorts, in classrooms and outside of them, thus helping us all to achieve fuller lives.

Contents

"I didn't notice the green car drive up and stop right next to me as I walked. The border patrol interrupted my daydreaming: 'Where are you from?' "

"If you were passing by the house where I grew up during my teenage years and it happened to be before Election Day, you wouldn't have needed to come inside to see that it was a house divided."

"Later I learned about *profiling*, the new system that was installed at airport security to stop terrorists. I read about security guards being trained in what a terrorist is likely to *look like* as they pass through security. But not any kind of terrorists: ones with dark hair, aquiline features, deep eyes. By the end of the article, my entire family was indicted."

"He twice wrote to his recruiter, describing how he was getting his 'ass kicked' so hard he'd lost twenty-eight pounds, but also to thank him for helping him 'fulfill a life long dream, being AN AMERICAN SOLDIER!!!'"

"The meaning of the evolution of civilization is no longer obscure to us.... It must present the struggle between Eros and Death, between the instinct of life and the instinct of destruction, as it works itself out in the human species."

"Are we, forever, to be torn in two different directions, cruel in one instance, kind the next? ... My observations of the apes offered at least a glimmer of an answer."

4. Are We Our Bodies?   *275* ●

"'Josie, you haven't eaten anything, have you? That's very disappointing: you know the rules. You remember what the doctor said.' 'I'm not hungry,' I say."

"That first encounter, and those that followed, signified that a vast, unnerving gulf lay between nighttime pedestrians — particularly women — and me."

"How should a man look at women?"

"What has caused American men to fall into the beauty trap so long assumed to be the special burden of women?"

5. Is Honesty the Best Policy? *375* ●

hug. I hug her back. I am still not comfortable touching her, and I am still not comfortable having her touch me, but I know it's better if I let it happen."

"You might suppose that the concept of integrity ... would apply in a rather straightforward way to letters of recommendation: the writer should reach an honest evaluation of the applicant. ... But that is not what happens."

"We believe ... that America's institutions of higher education need to recommit themselves to a tradition of integrity and honor."

"In the following remarks, I want to explore some of the ways in which we can respond to the moral challenges posed by ease of plagiarism on the Web."

"They deserve to be printed because they are great pictures, breathtaking pictures of something that happened. That they disturb readers is exactly as it should be."

"After all, how many Americans could reasonably be expected to pay a twelve-thousand-dollar premium for what was essentially a dressed-up truck?"

"If the beauty myth is not based on evolution, sex, gender, aesthetics, or God, on what is it based?"

"The great enemy of clear language is insincerity. When there is a gap between one's real and one's declared aims, one turns as it were instinctively to long words and exhausted idioms, like a cuttlefish squirting out ink."

"In the higher cultures the standardization of custom and belief over a couple of continents has given a false sense of the inevitability of the particular forms that have gained currency, and we need to turn to a wider survey in order to check the conclusions we hastily base upon this near-universality of familiar customs."

"[T]he community of truth . . . can never offer us ultimate certainty—not because its process is flawed but because certainty is beyond the grasp of finite hearts and minds."

8.   What Should You Do?   *639*

"Terrorism forces us to make a choice. We can be afraid. Or, we can be ready."

"[T]he fact that the poor are dying of illnesses for which effective treatments exist is, like many global facts of life, unacceptable to Farmer. Indeed, to him it is a sin."

"Raw humanity offends our sensibilities. We want to protect ourselves from an awareness of rags with voices that make no sense and scream forth in inarticulate rage."

"Now you, too, have the information you need to save a child's life. How should you judge yourself if you don't do it?"

"It *is* a stretch to think about Mexican prison labor while contemplating Victoria's Secret lavender lace boy-cut panties."

"If we want to put local life in proper relation to the globe, we must do so by imagination, charity, and forbearance, and by making local life as independent and self-sufficient as we can—not by the presumptuous abstractions of 'global thought.' "

"How could you not have known? What more evidence did you need that your lives, your comfortable lives, would do so much damage to ours?"

"Injustice anywhere is a threat to justice everywhere. We are caught in an inescapable network of mutuality, tied in a single garment of destiny. Whatever affects one directly, affects all indirectly."

"My choice to volunteer came easily—I have always been fascinated by different cultures. It is inspiring to me to see just how similar people actually are, despite our obvious outer differences."

"[L]istening is a magnetic and strange thing, a creative force."

Introduction
Critical Thinking, Reading, and Writing

WHAT WOULD YOU DO? THREE SCENARIOS

○ You are a first-year student in a course that requires you to write a paper. It's a course you enjoy, and you've participated consistently in the discussions. However, the paper for the course is due the same week as two other papers, and you've caught a cold. At the last minute, you decide to check the Internet for sources that might help you think about the topic for your paper. But when you get to the Internet, you discover whole sentences and paragraphs that you decide to use as the foundation for your paper—without citation. As a result, your three-page paper gets turned in on time, although you understand that two-thirds of it is composed of the words of others.

Your professor finds out. What should your professor do?

○ You have two friends who don't like each other. You like them both, and in an effort to make yourself look good to friend number one, you write an e-mail that criticizes friend number two. You don't entirely mean what you've written. You've exaggerated for effect. Later that day, for reasons of her own, friend number one decides to forward your e-mail to friend number two, with a brief note. The friend you've criticized is understandably upset.

What should you do? If you write another e-mail, to whom do you send it and what do you say? If you don't write an e-mail, what do you decide to do or not do?

○ In your student newspaper, you read the following letter from a student: "Last week was Gay Pride Week on campus and I was outraged and disgusted. How dare this misguided minority force its own values onto us—especially since homosexuality is always wrong? There can be no debate about this. There are simply moral absolutes in this life, and if you don't know what they are, you're ignorant. Public displays such as Gay Pride Week ought to be banned. Like it or not, some things are wrong, regardless of anyone's ability to explain why, and whether we admit it or not, we all understand this in some way or another."

How do you respond? Would you respond?

Suppose someone over lunch at the commons reads this letter aloud. Do you join the discussion? What would you say?

ETHICAL THINKING IS CRITICAL THINKING

Every day, in our personal lives, we face questions and formulate answers. When we do this—consciously or not—we are engaged in ethical thinking. *Ethics* can be defined as an effort to study the reasons why we decide to take the actions we do. This effort moves us beyond what we take for granted and pushes us to inquire into the source of these values: Where do they come from? How are they articulated? Who articulates and teaches these values? What other possible values might make sense to us? How can we persuade others and how can we search for common ground in the midst of disagreement?

And these are not just personal questions. Ethics is a matter of community and national concern as well. Every day, when we open the paper or turn on the television, we confront still another scandal.

- An athlete is suspected of taking illegal, performance-enhancing drugs.
- A health-care worker ends the life of a terminally ill patient in severe pain.
- A doctor's office is picketed because the doctor offers legal abortions.
- A CEO is shown to have fudged the books.
- A professor harasses a student.
- A coach is fired after partying at a strip club and then allegedly paying a prostitute to visit his room.
- A woman's husband sues to have her feeding tube removed following more than a decade of her life in what he regards as a vegetative state, and the court agrees. The state legislature then disagrees and intervenes by passing a new law.
- A business executive goes on trial for allegedly having cheated stockholders of billions of dollars.

How should we think about these stories? How can we respond? What can we do? *Civic rhetoric* is the language we use to articulate our views about scandals like these and the questions they provoke—difficult questions, open questions. What it requires exactly is the ability to keep the questions open, to ask them and to keep asking them.

> **ACTIVITY.** Focus on one of the three "What would you do?" scenarios mentioned in the introduction and write at least two paragraphs of response. Write these paragraphs even if you're undecided. Write one paragraph that gives an answer, even if you're not sure how strongly you believe in it. Take a stand. Write another paragraph in which you reflect on the assumptions and values behind your response. What are you assuming is true? What are you assuming is valuable? Where do these assumptions originate in your own experience or education—from parents, from a religious tradition, from encountering similar situations in the past?

In writing the second paragraph in this activity, you have begun the effort to think ethically—that is, to think clearly and with self-awareness, providing reasons for your answers.

A CASE STUDY: DOWNLOADING MUSIC FROM THE INTERNET

Let's look at an example of how ethical thinking is critical thinking.

Randy Cohen is the writer of a weekly column in the *New York Times* Sunday magazine and author of *The Good, the Bad, & the Difference*, a book that collects many of his newspaper pieces. Here is a letter written by a college student seeking advice about a personal choice, a letter that Cohen uses to raise a larger issue about technology and society.

> I am a college student who listens to music I download from the Internet. This is probably illegal and in a sense it is stealing. However, I do not want to buy CDs just to listen to one or two songs. Can I continue to do it, just as many ethical people jaywalk? Or is this akin to walking into a store and stealing something?
>
> —ANONYMOUS, New Jersey

> *ACTIVITY.* *Before reading Cohen's response, play the ethicist yourself. Take the questions seriously and write your own brief reply. Now, as you did before, step back from your reply and ask yourself what in your own experience and education led you to answer as you did. Write at least one paragraph about the origin of your beliefs. We realize that you might not have thought about your ethical and moral premises in this conscious way very often. You might not be entirely clear about what you think yet. Or certain ideas may seem self-evident to you. You may discover conflicting ideas and positions. Good. The goal here isn't to establish one right answer but to think ethically, exploring the complications and half-hidden assumptions that prompted your answer.*

Though developments in technology and recent legal decisions have already somewhat dated Cohen's reply, the underlying issue that he addresses is still very much to the point. Here's what he says:

> To download music from the Net illegally is theft, depriving songwriters, performers, and record companies of payment for their work. It is not so iniquitous as tossing a canvas sack over Elton John's head and swatting him with a stick until he sings "Candle in the Wind" (or stops singing it, depending on your taste), but it is dishonest, and you should not do it.

Your temptation is understandable. In a perverse kind of social progress, the Internet makes it easy to steal songs right in your own home while you're still in your pajamas. You might almost make a case that it is unethical of Napster, say, to tantalize honest music lovers beyond human endurance. This is a ticklish line of reasoning, however; perilously close to blaming the victim. That is, even if I sashay around town in a sport coat made of hundred-dollar bills, your robbing me is unethical. Unethical, but understandable.

Yours is an intriguing sort of mischief, less likely to be deterred by calls for individual rectitude than by technological innovation. What stops many people from photocopying a book and giving it to a pal is not integrity but logistics; it's easier and inexpensive to buy your friend a paperback copy. Similarly, technologies will soon be in place to encrypt music so it can't easily be stolen and that make it convenient to pay for just the songs you want.

This is a cogent and reasonable response, it seems to us, but what's more important is that Cohen doesn't stop there. Rather, as a good ethicist, he invites another person to offer his own responses, creating in the process the sort of dialogue—the kind of civic rhetoric—that allows various principles and beliefs to surface. The counterargument comes from Siva Vaidhyanthan, a professor in the Department of Culture and Communication at New York University:

Contrary to conventional wisdom (and the efforts of media companies), copyright is not property. It's the result of a complex series of deals that publishers have made with the American people over the past 210 years. We allow them to set monopoly prices and create false scarcity for a product for limited purposes and limited times. This creates an economic incentive to publish that might not exist under perfect competition. This is very different from property. Copyright is a state-granted limited monopoly.

When I was fourteen years old, a friend played for me his copy of the Clash's album *London Calling*. I loved it. I put a tape in his deck and recorded it. I listened to it for about a year. When I turned fifteen, I earned a bit more money. So I bought the album and recorded over my tape. Is this theft? Is it unethical?

This is also a reasonable and cogent argument, we think, and by including it Cohen is doing the work of ethical thinking. He is opening the question. And he keeps opening it, recording the rest of a very interesting conversation, a back-and-forth discussion. Perhaps most admirable is that Cohen even gives his dialogue partner the last word in the discussion.

COHEN'S REPLY: If you phrase your argument as impoverished young hipster versus bloated parasitical record company weasel, well, it's hard for me to type with my eyes so clouded with tears. But if you acknowledge that the music you're downloading is by the very emerging and cutting-edge artist you champion, it looks a little different. It may indeed be in their interest to have you do so, but that's their decision, not yours.

VAIDHYANTHAN SAYS: When Sheryl Crow released her second album, many of the cuts received substantial airplay on FM radio and VH1. I liked all the songs I heard and enjoyed hearing them for free. But I never bought the CD. I enjoyed the music enough for free, and felt no urge to pay eighteen dollars for them. This is private, noncommercial use. I paid nothing. Is this theft? Is it unethical?...

COHEN REPLIES: Here's the difference: the band gives its permission for the airplay...but they've not given you permission for the download. I'm a big, big fan of the artist having control over his work. If he wants to give it away, fine. Quibble all you want about the word, but when you take someone's work without his permission, stealing seems a serviceable term....

VAIDHYANTHAN SAYS: I do not mean to glorify or even encourage the further exploitation of artists by anyone—consumer or corporation. What I meant to do with my examples was to complicate your analysis....It is a mistake to see the rise of tech and its use by young people as exclusively exploitational. It depends on the use, the extent, and the context.

"What I meant to do with my examples," Vaidhyanthan says, "is to complicate your analysis." Yes. This is the point.

ETHICAL SYSTEMS: FIVE EXAMPLES

Over the centuries, various philosophers have reflected on ethical problems, inquiring into the nature of their own experience just as this book asks you to do. They've then gone on to organize their reflections into different schools, or systems, of ethical thought; systems that may have influenced your own thinking, whether you're aware of them or not.

- In *divine command* or *biblical ethics*, moral behavior is seen as dictated by God. We know what is right and we know what is wrong because sacred scripture or some other vehicle of revelation has told us so. For example, murder is wrong because the Bible says it is wrong.

- In the *natural law ethics* of the Greek philosopher Aristotle (384–322 B.C.E.) and the medieval philosopher Thomas Aquinas (1125?–1274 C.E.), the human person is understood to be endowed with certain "virtues," certain natural qualities and tendencies. An action is moral or ethical if it advances or supports such tendencies, wrong if it interferes with them—if it is somehow "unnatural." For example, it is the nature of the human person to live and grow. It is therefore wrong to kill.

- The German philosopher Immanuel Kant (1724–1804) formulated a principle of right action that he called the *categorical imperative*. In this theory, something is simply right or wrong, regardless of the circumstances or the consequences. The idea can be summarized in two related propositions:

  Always act so as to treat humanity, whether in yourself or in another, as an end and never merely as a means.

  Act only according to the maxim whereby you can at the same time will that it become a universal law.

  As the first proposition implies, for Kant human beings have certain basic rights that must be respected. Thus, killing is wrong because it fails to respect the intrinsic dignity of the human person. The second proposition expands the notion to encompass universally ethical behavior: killing is wrong because the world would be a terrible place if everyone felt free to take a life.

- *Utilitarianism* is an approach to ethics developed by two English thinkers, Jeremy Bentham (1748–1832) and John Stuart Mill (1806–1873). Its premise is that action is moral or ethical if it achieves the greatest good for the greatest number. If something will help eight people and hurt two, it's more moral than something that will help two people and hurt eight. What follows from this, too, is the idea that the ends can justify the means—that something "bad" in itself may be necessary and right if in the end it serves to advance the common good. For example, killing one person could be justifiable if such an act saved the lives of others.

- In the *land ethics* of ecologist Aldo Leopold (1887–1941), right action depends on relationship, in human behavior as in ecosystems. Just as a forest depends on the complex relationships of various species and forces, society depends on the relationships among people and between people and their environment. An action is right if it contributes to the ecology of those relationships, wrong if it causes those relationships to break down. "All ethics so far evolved rest on a single premise," Leopold says, "that the individual is a member of a community of interdependent parts" (ch. 6, p. 531). In this notion of ethics, furthermore, human beings are not the only beings regarded as having rights. The idea of rights must be extended to nature as well. Rocks and birds and trees and other things are valuable in and of themselves, apart from their human uses.

Of concern in all of these systems of thought is the central question of whether moral values are *subjective* or *objective*, something we've made up and can change or something outside of us and so always true. Many modern philosophers think morality is subjective. The anthropologist Ruth Benedict

(1887–1948), for example, claims that moral values change from culture to culture and so can't be considered universally true (see "The Case for Moral Relativism," ch. 7, p. 619). Political philosopher John Rawls (1921–2002) builds on an idea called "social contract theory" to argue that moral behavior is simply a set of rules that we all agree to follow. One group can follow one set of rules and another a second, as long as everybody in each group understands those rules and freely accepts them.

This is complicated and tricky stuff, and we don't pretend to have mastered it. We don't think you need to have mastered it either. Our purpose is to help you think critically and write ethically in first-year writing classes and beyond, not to give you a systematic introduction to ethics. But at their heart, each of these philosophical systems is doing what we're asking you to do: think about thinking, inquire into the nature and premises of actions in the world. Knowing a little about these theories in a general way can deepen and complicate your own intellectual process.

> ACTIVITY. Think about your reactions to the exercises and scenarios presented in light of the five ethical systems we've summarized. Where does your thinking fit? Which premises match up with your premises? Does your thinking fit into more than one system? Are there contradictions in your reasons for saying what you've said and writing what you've written?

AN ETHICS OF LEARNING

"I understand truth," Parker Palmer says in "The Community of Truth" (see ch. 7, p. 627), "as the passionate and disciplined process of inquiry and dialogue itself, as the dynamic conversation of a community that keeps testing old conclusions and coming into new ones."

Think of a sport or an activity or a subject that has held your attention for some time—something you're interested in to the extent that you can tell the difference between novice and professional performance or between simple understanding and sophisticated awareness. This could be anything from swimming to chess to football to photography, meteorology, cooking, a foreign language, a video game—you get the idea. Chances are you've acquired a solid understanding about this field or interest, and in the process you've no doubt done a good bit of research, study, and reflecting on what you've learned. Research, study, and reflection are the basis of ethical thinking.

Here's how we'd explain the traits of mind that make this kind of thinking possible and allow it to flourish:

- a fundamental eagerness to ask questions,
- a routine willingness to try,

- an open curiosity about the responses of others whether they are agreeable or contrary, and

- an unshakable understanding that the process is always incomplete.

You've no doubt already experienced those moments when you suddenly realize how little you know and how much more there is to investigate and practice. We all have. And it's this awareness of partial knowledge and partial understanding, this humility, that makes education possible. The ethics of learning requires from all of us the routine acknowledgment that our certainties are always subject to revision as prompted by new experience and new understandings.

In practical terms, we see an ethics of learning as broadly divided according to the two most common tasks college students face: reading and writing.

CRITICAL READING AS LISTENING AND ANALYZING: LOGOS, ETHOS, AND PATHOS

Let's start with reading, though it may seem a little crazy for us to start at such a basic level. We do so because virtually every course and subject you study in college depends to some extent on the ability to read and understand material new to you and sometimes unsettling, challenging what you already think or believe.

Think of it this way: reading is a kind of conversation you construct in your head. What you're reading amounts to a voice talking to you. Your task as a good reader is first to hear that voice in your head and then to listen in an effort to understand it thoroughly. Consider these opening paragraphs to Lindsy Van Gelder's 1984 *Ms.* magazine essay, "Marriage as a Restricted Club." This issue has hardly gone away.

> Several years ago, I stopped going to weddings. In fact, I no longer celebrate the wedding anniversaries or engagements of friends, relatives, or anyone else, although I might wish them lifelong joy in their relationships. My explanation is that the next wedding I attend will be my own—to the woman I've loved and lived with for nearly six years.
>
> Although I've been legally married to a man myself (and come close to marrying two others), I've come in these last six years with Pamela, to see heterosexual marriage as very much a restricted club.... Regardless of the *reason* people marry—whether to save on real estate taxes or qualify for married student housing or simply to express love—lesbians and gay men can't obtain the same results should they desire to do so. It seems apparent to me that few friends of Pamela's and mine would even join a club that excluded blacks, Jews, or women, much less assume that they could expect their black,

Jewish, or female friends to toast their new status with champagne. But probably no other stand of principle we've ever made in our lives has been so misunderstood, or caused so much bad feeling on both sides....

One example of inequity is our inability to file joint tax returns, although many couples, both gay and straight, go through periods when one partner in the relationship is unemployed or makes considerably less money than the other. At one time in our relationship, Pamela—who is a musician—was between bands and earning next to nothing. I was making a little over $37,000 a year as a newspaper reporter, a salary that put me in the 42 percent tax bracket—about $300 a week taken out of my paycheck. If we had been married, we could have filed a joint tax return and each paid taxes on half my salary, in the 25 or 30 percent bracket. The difference would have been nearly $100-a-week in our pockets.

Around the same time, Pamela suffered a months'-long illness which would have been covered by my health insurance if she were my spouse. We were luckier than many; we could afford it. But on top of the worry and expense involved (and despite the fact that intellectually we believe in the ideal of free medical care for everyone), we found it almost impossible to avoid internalizing a sense of personal failure—the knowledge that *because of who we are, we can't take care of each other.*

ACTIVITY. *While reading these paragraphs, you might have had a visceral response to agree or disagree. But we want you to set that aside for the moment and ask yourself some questions instead.*

- *So far as you can tell in these paragraphs, who is Lindsy Van Gelder and what seems surest about her perspective?*
- *What is she saying exactly? Where in the excerpt can you most clearly understand that message?*
- *What values or shared understandings does she assume readers will also have?*

In short, the first element of ethical reading requires you to listen carefully and to reread, ponder, and interrogate what you're hearing. This resolve may not always be easy, but the postponing of judgment—so that you can inquire first—makes understanding possible.

Aristotle's terms *logos, ethos,* and *pathos* can be helpful tools as you try to analyze any reading or any argument. Some speakers or writers try to make their case by logical argument, or *logos.* Van Gelder does this when she draws the comparison between a ban on homosexual marriage and a ban on blacks or Jews. Her effort here is to make a logical comparison. She's also appealing to reason when she notes the inequity of the tax situation. Some speakers or writers also call attention to their own character and trustworthiness, or *ethos;* sometimes they try to persuade readers by evoking strong emotions (*pathos*).

Van Gelder establishes herself as someone who has been married before (to a man) and as someone who is now, as a lesbian, denied that possibility. By identifying herself in these ways, she establishes some of her own credentials; she's pointing to her own *ethos*. She does some of the same thing when she includes in parentheses the information that she and Pamela believe in free health care for all. And at the end of the excerpt, she begins to invoke emotions (*pathos*) — those "misunderstandings" and "bad feelings" as well as that internalized sense of failure, which she emphasizes by putting it in italics.

Here are some additional questions that you can apply to almost any text. If you keep a reading journal, any of these questions might serve as a useful prompt for an entry.

- What is this writer's subject, interest, objection, or ideal? Where in the text can you find this most clearly stated?
- What evidence, examples, or explanations seem essential to what this text says?
- Can you see clear use of logic (*logos*)?
- Can you see where the writer aims to establish his or her own credentials and qualifications (*ethos*)?
- Can you see where the text appeals to your emotions (*pathos*) in an effort to deepen your understanding or agreement?
- How would you explain this evidence or these examples in your own words?
- What words, sentences, or paragraphs simply stump you now?
- What questions, if answered, would make this text clearer to you?
- What parts of this reading seem clear and well understood?
- What response would partially agree with this text or this author and partially disagree?
- How does this text connect to other texts you've read?
- What personal experience, if any, can you bring to the set of questions that this text discusses?
- What aspect or complication does this text leave out or treat as unimportant?

ANNOTATING YOUR TEXTS
AND KEEPING A READING JOURNAL

Given the complexities of college courses, you'll rarely understand a reading assignment the first time through. Your first impulse, then, might to be skip over what you don't get, and that's a good first impulse so long as you remember to circle back, identify, and phrase the questions that come to mind at particular points as you read.

Writing in the margins of your own book is one quick, effective way to keep track of what's clear and what's not. If you have a system for making such notes, use it. If not, consider this one: use underlining or double lines in the margin to indicate material you know is important or central to what an author wants you to understand; use a squiggly line to mark those places that seem unclear. (We don't find simple highlighting very useful, unless you decide on one color for the clear, important parts and another color for those you don't quite follow.) Here's an annotated version of the Van Gelder excerpt:

> Several years ago, I stopped going to weddings. In fact, I no longer celebrate the wedding anniversaries or engagements of friends, relatives, or anyone else, although I might wish them lifelong joy in their relationships. My explanation is that the next wedding I attend will be my own—to the woman I've loved and lived with for nearly six years. *Why not?*
>
> Although I've been legally married to a man myself (and come close to marrying two others), I've come in these last six years with Pamela, to see heterosexual marriage as very much a restricted club....Regardless of the *reason* people *Why do people marry?* marry—whether to save on real estate taxes or qualify for married student housing or simply to express love—lesbians *Are these the only reasons?* and gay men can't obtain the same results should they desire to do so. It seems apparent to me that few friends of Pamela's and mine would even join a club that excluded blacks, Jews, or women, much less assume that they could expect their black, Jewish, or female friends to toast their *Sounds reasonable.* new status with champagne. But probably no other stand of principle we've ever made in our lives has been so misunderstood, or caused so much bad feeling on both sides....
>
> One example of inequity is our inability to file joint tax returns, although many couples, both gay and straight, go through periods when one partner in the relationship is unemployed or makes considerably less money than the other. At one time in our relationship, Pamela—who is a musician—was between bands and earning next to nothing. I was making a little over $37,000 a year as a newspaper reporter, a salary that put me in the 42 percent tax bracket—about $300 a week taken out of my paycheck. If we had been married, we could have filed a joint tax return and each paid taxes on half my salary, in the 25 or 30 percent bracket. The

difference would have been nearly a $100-a-week in our pockets.

Around the same time, Pamela suffered a months'-long illness which would have been covered by my health insurance if she were my spouse. We were luckier than many; we could afford it. But on top of the worry and expense involved (and despite the fact that intellectually we believe in the ideal of free medical care for everyone), we found it almost impossible to avoid internalizing a sense of personal failure—the knowledge that *because of who we are, we can't take care of each other.*

2nd example

appeal to emotion

Keeping reading notes in a reading journal is another very effective method. To do this, read with your journal open. Copy phrases or sentences that will help you remember what you've clearly understood in your reading and what still stands out as puzzling.

Notice that we've not yet said anything about your opinions—your agreements or disagreements with what you presume is an author's argument. We're asking you to postpone such reactions and to focus first on listening to and paying close attention to what you read.

PARTICIPATING IN THE CONVERSATION

Once you've started to read something, you've begun a conversation with that author and an investigation of what that author says. That's important but incomplete. In fact, you will find that many courses meet in classrooms (or online) precisely in order to give students the chance to talk seriously about their understandings and questions as a result of their private reading, their individual listening to a text.

Class discussion becomes a way to learn from and with each other. It seeks to take advantage of every intelligence in the room (when classes are small enough to let this happen). We believe that class discussion ought to focus first on understanding what a text says, on how we might summarize it or say it in our own words, and on where the text seems unclear or our understanding shaky. Here, annotations or journal notes become useful: they indicate the contributions you can make and the questions you can raise.

Here, too, the ethics of reading become also an ethics of discussion. That is, good discussion involves the same kind of careful listening we've suggested earlier and the same identification of what's clear and unclear. Class discussion means not just asking questions of the text itself; it also means asking questions when some part of the discussion becomes unclear to you. The aim in class discussion is not to dominate or silence others. This is not a game of winning or losing. The aim, especially early in the discussion, is to open up the inquiry in order to find out what other people understand a text to say and what questions other people have. Sometimes, you might have answers to their questions and vice versa. Thus, a class discussion builds a community of individuals who share a common effort.

CONTRIBUTING TO CIVIC RHETORIC: MAKING CLAIMS

Education begins with questions about facts and then proceeds to advocacy based on those facts. To advocate means to declare oneself, to say "I think _____ is true" or "I think _____ ought to be done" or "I think _____ ought to be investigated further." That is, careful listening, questioning, and discussion about texts and about what they mean or try to say is all meant to help us find our own relationship to those texts and their arguments. The ultimate point of study is not merely to understand complexities but also to declare ourselves in response to them. And, of course, we make such declarations in every choice we make: from what we say, to what we wear, to where we work or go to school, and so on. Each choice says, "this is who I am, this is what I understand, and this is what I affirm as worthy or true."

College essay assignments will often ask you not merely to summarize but also to analyze critically. Such assignments essentially ask you to talk back, to formulate a response that shows you have understood some text or position or argument: you've heard it thoroughly, understood it, and have this to say in response. Thus, you make your contribution to the conversation and to the community of people who have also thought hard about the same questions and come to their own understandings.

The key to making such claims in a persuasive and ethical way, in life and in the university, is providing the reasons for these claims. It's not enough to assert. It's not enough to generalize. When Van Gelder makes the *claim* that lesbians should be allowed to marry, she goes on to explain her reasons: the unfair application of the tax system and the unfair granting of health benefits. But notice that there's one more logical assertion being made in Van Gelder's argument: she's arguing that we ought to be fair. This assertion—that we ought to be fair—is a *warrant*. We could summarize Van Gelder's logical argument this way:

- *Claim*: Marriage and its benefits ought to be extended to all committed couples.
- *Reason*: Right now, health-care benefits and tax rules grant benefits to heterosexual couples that are not granted to gay or lesbian couples.
- *Warrant*: The law ought to be fair and equal in its treatment of committed couples, be they straight or gay.

Evidence is often in dispute, as are the conclusions we draw from it. For example, some people might challenge the warrant above, namely, that the law ought to be fair in its treatment of committed couples. They would view the warrant as a claim that itself needs reasons and warrants. As you see, complicated questions can provoke much discussion, and that is our point. The world is a complex place, and people of good will can disagree. But much unethical thinking and unethical writing proceeds from claims offered without reason or warrant. Egregious examples include statements like "women are inferior to men" or "people of color are inferior to white people." We may think such things out of ignorance, in which case the challenge is to learn. Or we may think such things out of a willed ignorance—a reluctance to admit the faultiness of our reasons and warrants—or perhaps even a conscious dishonesty. In either case, we would be thinking and writing and acting unethically. The "great enemy" in our public discussions, George Orwell says in "Politics and the English Language" (ch. 5, p. 461), is "insincerity." The great enemy is abstraction without concreteness, cliché without thought, claim without reason or warrant.

COMMUNITY, INTEGRITY, AND COMPROMISE: AN APPROACH TO ARGUMENT

Facts are questions with single or dependably repeatable answers. At sea level, what is the boiling point of water, as expressed on the Fahrenheit scale? 212 degrees. Education deals relatively easily with facts, and often we absolutely require knowledge of facts in order to stay safe and make good decisions. It's useful to know how to recognize which mushrooms you could pick and eat and which ones would kill you. But many of our understandings remain partial, just as our human experience is always limited. So an ethics of reading asks us to remember that there is always another text to consider, always another voice waiting on a page or a computer screen. The paradox of education is that it seeks, on the one hand, to make self-knowledge and self-declaration possible, while, on the other hand, it also cautions us against closing off the process.

This notion of education leads us, finally, to the characteristics of what can be called an ethics of argument. Too often the term *argument* becomes synonymous with *battle*—or some other notion based more on war as a guiding analogy—rather than conversation, negotiation, or discussion. If education genuinely is a sort of large, multifaceted, various, and ever-evolving conversation, then its values are not the values of war or conquest. War always assumes the utter rightness of one's cause; to go to war is to assert that someone else is so powerfully wrong that only killing them can successfully stop their actions or blunt their ideas. If we think of argument as warlike, then to silence someone else would be to win, to succeed. Education and argument do go together, but the result should not be silence but rather new conviction and a willingness to discuss your change of mind. Studs Terkel's interview of former Ku Klux Klan member C. P. Ellis (ch. 7, p. 568) is a prime example. "The whole world was opening up," Ellis says, "and I was learnin' new truths that I had never learned before."

In the same way, we admire the civility of Cohen's exchange with Vaidhyanthan on the subject of downloading. Cohen writes with vividness and wit—"it's hard for me to type with my eyes so clouded with tears"— but also with respect for his colleague and what he has to say. If he didn't respect his colleague, he wouldn't have included his arguments at all. Vaidhyanthan follows suit, acknowledging the validity of Cohen's logic even as he disagrees.

The conversation that is education always benefits from passionate belief, but it never benefits from willful ignorance, intolerance, or an effort to merely silence those with whom we disagree. Our ethics of argument tells us that in order to safeguard our own integrity, we must work to recognize and safeguard the integrity of those with whom we dispute or whom we believe to be in error. Parker Palmer's image is of all of us sitting around a banquet table, each in his or her own chair, seeing from our point of view the great truths in the middle ("The Community of Truth," ch. 7, p. 627). At such a banquet "ultimate certainty" is never possible, he says, not because the conversation is flawed or inadequate "but because certainty is beyond the grasp of finite hearts and minds."

On this basis of mutually acknowledged integrity, communities can be made and successfully sustained. On the basis of such integrity, communities can welcome disagreement in the knowledge that the resulting discussions will teach all involved. Compromise is no enemy of conviction, no enemy of anyone's closely held values or beliefs.

As you read the pieces in this book, as you discuss them, and as you write about them, we do not ask you to compromise your values or beliefs. We do ask you to consider them anew, in light of what you read and given what you hear in discussion. You will likely not agree with everything you read—in this course or any number of others. But education asks you to choose between absolute conviction on the one hand and the acknowledged possibility that you might learn something on the other. If an inflexible, unquestionable certainty is your choice, then you have said *no* to education. In this book, we hope and presume that you will say *yes*.

1.

Where Are You Coming From?

WHAT WOULD YOU DO?
SPEAKING UP FOR A FRIEND

One of the three scenarios we discussed in the introduction involved a student letter to the campus paper protesting Gay Pride Week. "There are simply moral absolutes in this life," the student had written, "and if you don't know what they are, you're ignorant." For this student, homosexuality is wrong. End of discussion.

Let's say that the writer of this letter is a high-school friend of yours, someone you grew up with and like and still see a lot at college. Let's say, too, that one day in your favorite class (a first-year writing class, of course), your favorite teacher uses the letter your friend has written as an example of close-minded thinking and badly argued writing.

What would your reaction be? What would you do?

Would you speak to the teacher? Why or why not? What would you say and how would say it?

Would you speak to your friend? Why or why not? What would you say and how would say it?

Each of the pieces in this section tells the story of where the writer is coming from: the writer's family background, the color of the writer's skin, the writer's landscape and culture and place. Each invites us to look beyond the surface to the complicated reality underneath, the real flesh and blood human being. The point is that our moral values come from somewhere, too. Moral values are never simply out there, for all to see. We are born into them, we are taught them, they are rooted in our gender and ethnicity, our cultural heritage and economic class, and so they can vary widely from person to person. What is true for Maxine Hong Kingston, as a second generation Chinese American woman, may not be true in the same way, or true at all, for Benjamin Saenz, a Hispanic American man, or Sarah Vowell, a white woman who grew up in Montana.

And so the readings in this section invite you to complicate your thinking—not to abandon your values necessarily but to see that they are not self-evident or beyond discussion. You're already aware of this, of course, as an intelligent human being, but we hope that thinking about the question of origins in more detail will begin to change both the way you approach ethical problems and the way you talk about these problems with others.

Opening the Question

After reading and discussing several of the selections in this chapter, return to the situation above. **Now** *what would you do? Write an essay answering this question, drawing on at least two of the selections. You don't need to have changed your mind, but you do need to demonstrate how the reading has complicated your thinking.*

BENJAMIN SAENZ
Exile: El Paso, Texas

W<small>E START THE BOOK</small> with a piece that frames the chapter's question in terms at once ethnic, political, and personal. Benjamin Saenz (b. 1955) was a graduate student studying in El Paso when he was stopped and asked "Where are you from?" by the U.S. Border Patrol, an incident that informs the selection reprinted here.

Now teaching English at the University of Texas at El Paso, where he is a member of the Chicano Studies Research Program, Saenz has written two collections of poetry, two novels (including The House of Forgetting, *1998), a short-story collection, and two children's books. "Exile: El Paso, Texas" is an excerpt from* Flowers for the Broken *(1992).*

That morning—when the day was new, when the sun slowly touched the sky, almost afraid to break it—that morning I looked out my window and stared at the Juárez Mountains. Mexican purples—burning. I had always thought of them as sacraments of belonging. That was the first time it happened. It had happened to others, but it had never happened to me. And when it happened, it started a fire, a fire that will burn for a long time.

As I walked to school, I remember thinking what a perfect place Sunset Heights was: turn of the century houses intact; remodeled houses painted pink and turquoise; old homes tastefully gentrified by the aspiring young; the rundown Sunset Grocery store decorated with the protest art of graffiti on one end and a plastic-signed "Circle K" on the other.

This was the edge of the piece of paper that was America, the border that bordered the University—its buildings, its libraries; the border that bordered the freeway—its cars coming and going, coming and going endlessly; the border that bordered downtown—its banks and businesses and bars; the border that bordered the border between two countries.

The unemployed poor from Juárez knocking on doors and asking for jobs—or money—or food. Small parks filled with people whose English did not exist. The upwardly mobile living next to families whose only concern was getting enough money to pay next month's rent. Some had lived here for generations, would continue living here into the next century; others would live here a few days. All this color, all this color, all this color beneath the shadow of the Juárez Mountains. Sunset Heights: a perfect place with a perfect name, and a perfect view of the river.

After class, I went by my office and drank a cup of coffee, sat and read, 5 and did some writing. It was a quiet day on campus, nothing but me and my work—the kind of day the mind needs to catch up with itself, the kind of uneventful day so necessary for living. I started walking home at about three o'clock, after I had put my things together in my torn backpack. I made a mental note to sew the damn thing. *One day everything's gonna come tumbling out—better sew it.* I'd made that mental note before.

Walking down Prospect, I thought maybe I'd go for a jog. I hoped the spring would not bring too much wind this year. The wind, common desert rain; the wind blew too hard and harsh sometimes; the wind unsettled the desert—upset things, ruined the calmness of the spring. My mind wandered, searched the black asphalt littered with torn papers; the chained dogs in the yards who couldn't hurt me; the even bricks of all the houses I passed. I belonged here, yes. I belonged. Thoughts entered like children running through a park. This year, maybe the winds would not come.

I didn't notice the green car drive up and stop right next to me as I walked. The border patrol interrupted my daydreaming: "Where are you from?"

I didn't answer. I wasn't sure who the agent, a woman, was addressing.

She repeated the question in Spanish, *"¿De dónde eres?"*

Without thinking, I almost answered her question—in Spanish. A reflex.   10
I caught myself in midsentence and stuttered in a nonlanguage.

"¿Dónde naciste?" she asked again.

By then my mind had cleared, and quietly I said: "I'm a U.S. citizen."

"Were you born in the United States?"

She was browner than I was. I might have asked her the same question. I looked at her for awhile—searching for something I recognized.

"Yes," I answered.   15

"Where in the United States were you born?"

"In New Mexico."

"Where in New Mexico?"

"Las Cruces."

"What do you do?"   20

"I'm a student."

"And are you employed?"

"Sort of."

"Sort of?" She didn't like my answer. Her tone bordered on anger. I looked at her expression and decided it wasn't hurting anyone to answer her questions. It was all very innocent, just a game we were playing.

"I work at the University as a teaching assistant."   25

She didn't respond. She looked at me as if I were a blank. Her eyes were filling in the empty spaces as she looked at my face. I looked at her for a second and decided she was finished with me. I started walking away. "Are you sure you were born in Las Cruces?" she asked again.

I turned around and smiled, "Yes, I'm sure." She didn't smile back. She and the driver sat there for awhile and watched me as I continued walking. They drove past me slowly and then proceeded down the street.

I didn't much care for the color of their cars.

"Sons of bitches," I whispered, "pretty soon I'll have to carry a passport in my own neighborhood." I said it to be flippant; something in me rebelled against people dressed in uniforms. I wasn't angry—not then, not at first, not really angry. In less than ten minutes I was back in my apartment playing the scene again and again in my mind. It was like a video I played over and over—memorizing the images. Something was wrong. I was embarrassed, ashamed because I'd been so damned compliant like a piece of tin foil in the uniformed woman's hand. Just like a child in the principal's office, in trouble for speaking Spanish. "I should have told that witch exactly what I thought of her and her green car and her green uniform."

I lit a cigarette and told myself I was overreacting. "Breathe in—breathe 30 out—breathe in—breathe out—no big deal—you live on a border. These things happen—just one of those things. Just a game…" I changed into my jogging clothes and went for a run. At the top of the hill on Sunbowl Drive, I stopped to stare at the Juárez Mountains. I felt the sweat run down my face. I kept running until I could no longer hear *Are you sure you were born in Las Cruces?* ringing in my ears.

School let out in early May. I spent the last two weeks of that month relaxing and working on some paintings. In June I got back to working on my stories. I had a working title, which I hated, but I hated it less than the actual stories I was writing. It would come to nothing; I knew it would come to nothing.

From my window I could see the freeway. It was then I realized that not a day went by when I didn't see someone running across the freeway or walking down the street looking out for someone. They were people who looked not so different from me—except that they lived their lives looking over their shoulders.

One Thursday, I saw the border patrol throw some men into their van—throw them—as if they were born to be thrown like baseballs, like rings in a carnival ringtoss, easy inanimate objects, dead bucks after a deer hunt. The illegals didn't even put up a fight. They were aliens, from somewhere else, somewhere foreign, and it did not matter that the "somewhere else" was as close as an eyelash to an eye. What mattered was that someone had once drawn a line, and once drawn, that line became indelible and hard and could not be crossed.

The men hung their heads so low that they almost scraped the littered asphalt. Whatever they felt, they did not show; whatever burned did not burn for an audience. I sat at my typewriter and tried to pretend I saw nothing. *What do you think happens when you peer out windows? Buy curtains.*

I didn't write the rest of the day. I kept seeing the border patrol 35 woman against a blue sky turning green. I thought of rearranging my desk so I wouldn't be next to the window, but I thought of the mountains. No, I would keep my desk near the window, but I would look only at the mountains.

Two weeks later, I went for a walk. The stories weren't going well that day; my writing was getting worse instead of better; my characters were getting on my nerves—I didn't like them—no one else would like them either. They did not burn with anything. I hadn't showered, hadn't shaved, hadn't combed my hair. I threw some water on my face and walked out the door. It was summer; it was hot; it was afternoon, the time of day when everything felt as if it were on fire. The worst time of the day to take a walk. I wiped the sweat from my eyelids; it instantly reappeared. I wiped it off again, but the sweat came pouring out—a leak in the dam. Let it leak. I laughed. A hundred degrees in the middle of a desert afternoon. Laughter poured out of me as fast as my sweat. I turned the corner and headed back home. I saw the green van. It was parked right ahead of me.

A man about my height got out of the van and approached me. Another man, taller, followed him. "*¿Tienes tus papeles?*" he asked. His gringo accent was as thick as the sweat on my skin.

"I can speak English," I said. I started to add: *I can probably speak it better than you,* but I stopped myself. No need to be aggressive, no need to get any hotter.

"Do you live in this neighborhood?"

"Yes."   40

"Where?"

"Down the street."

"Where down the street?"

"Are you planning on making a social visit?"

He gave me a hard look—cold and blue—then looked at his partner. 45
He didn't like me. I didn't care. I liked that he hated me. It made it easier.

I watched them drive away and felt as hot as the air, felt as hot as the heat that was burning away the blue in the sky.

There were other times when I felt watched. Sometimes, when I jogged, the green vans would slow down, eye me. I felt like prey, like a rabbit who smelled the hunter. I pretended not to notice them. I stopped pretending. I started noting their presence in our neighborhood more and more. I started growing suspicious of my own observations. Of course, they weren't everywhere. But they *were* everywhere. I had just been oblivious to their presence, had been oblivious because they had nothing to do with me; their presence had something to do with someone else. I was not a part of this. I wanted no part of it. The green cars and the green vans clashed with the purples of the Juárez Mountains. Nothing looked the same. I never talked about their presence to other people. Sometimes the topic of the *Migra* would come up in conversations. I felt the burning; I felt the anger, would control it. I casually referred to them as the Gestapo, the traces of rage carefully hidden from the expression on my face—and everyone would laugh. I hated them.

When school started in the fall, I was stopped again. Again I had been walking home from the University. I heard the familiar question: "Where are you
from?"

"Leave me alone."

"Are you a citizen of the United States?"   50

"Yes."

"Can you prove it?"

"No. No, I can't."

He looked at my clothes: jeans, tennis shoes, and a casual California shirt.
He noticed my backpack full of books.

"You a student?"   55

I nodded and stared at him.

"There isn't any need to be unfriendly—"

"I'd like you to leave me alone."

"Just doing my job," he laughed. I didn't smile back. *Terrorists. Nazis did
their jobs. Death squads in El Salvador and Guatemala did their jobs, too.* An unfair
analogy. An unfair analogy? Yes, unfair. I thought it; I felt it; it was no longer my
job to excuse—someone else would have to do that, someone else. The Juárez
Mountains did not seem purple that fall. They no longer burned with color.

In early January I went with Michael to Juárez. Michael was from New York,   60
and he had come to work in a home for the homeless in South El Paso.
We weren't in Juárez very long—just looking around and getting gas. Gas
was cheap in Juárez. On the way back, the customs officer asked us to declare
our citizenship. "U.S. citizen," I said. "U.S. citizen," Michael followed. The
customs officer lowered his head and poked it in the car. "What are you bringing over?"

"Nothing."

He looked at me. "Where in the United States were you born?"

"In Las Cruces, New Mexico."

He looked at me awhile longer. "Go ahead," he signaled.

I noticed that he didn't ask Michael where he was from. But Michael   65
had blue eyes; Michael had white skin. Michael didn't have to tell the man in
the uniform where he was from.

That winter, Sunset Heights seemed deserted to me. The streets were empty
like the river. One morning, I was driving down Upson Street toward the
University, the wind shaking the limbs of the bare trees. Nothing to shield
them—unprotected by green leaves. The sun burned a dull yellow. In front
of me, I noticed two border patrol officers chasing someone, though that
someone was not visible. One of them put his hand out, signaling me to slow
down as they ran across the street in front of my car. They were running with
their billy clubs in hand. The wind blew at their backs as if to urge them on,
as if to carry them.

In late January, Michael and I went to Juárez again. A friend of his was in town, and he wanted to see Juárez. We walked across the bridge across the river, across the line into another country. It was easy. No one there to stop us. We walked the streets of Juárez, streets that had seen better years, that were tired now from the tired feet that walked them. Michael's friend wanted to know how it was that there were so many beggars. "Were there always so many? Has it always been this way?" He didn't know how it had always been. We sat in the Cathedral and in an old chapel next to it and watched people rubbing the feet of statues; when I touched a statue it was warmer than my own hand. We walked in the marketplace and inhaled the smells. Grocery stores in the country I knew did not have such smells. On the way back we stopped in a small bar and had a beer. The beer was cold and cheap. Walking back over the bridge, we stopped at the top and looked out at the city of El Paso. "It actually looks pretty from here, doesn't it?" I said. Michael nodded. It did look pretty. We looked off to the side — down the river — and for a long time watched the people trying to get across. Michael's friend said it was like watching *The CBS Evening News.*

As we reached the customs building, we noticed that a border patrol van pulled up behind the building where the other green cars were parked. The officers jumped out of the van and threw a handcuffed man against one of the parked cars. It looked like they were going to beat him. Two more border patrol officers pulled up in a car and jumped out to join them. One of the officers noticed we were watching. They straightened the man out and walked him inside — like gentlemen. They would have beat him. They would have beat him. But we were watching.

My fingers wanted to reach through the wire fence, not to touch it, not to feel it, but to break it down, to melt it down with what I did not understand. The burning was not there to be understood. Something was burning, the side of me that knew I was treated different, would always be treated different because I was born on a particular side of a fence, a fence that separated me from others, that separated me from the past, that separated me from the country of my genesis and glued me to the country I did not love because it demanded something of me I could not give. Something was burning now, and if I could have grasped the source of that rage and held it in my fist, I would have melted that fence. Someone built that fence; someone could tear it down. Maybe I could tear it down; maybe I was the one. Maybe then I would no longer be separated.

The first day in February, I was walking to a downtown Chevron station to pick 70 up my car. On the corner of Prospect and Upson, a green car was parked — just sitting there. A part of my landscape. I was walking on the opposite side of the street. For some reason, I knew they were going to stop me. My heart clenched like a fist; the muscles in my back knotted up. *Maybe they'll leave me alone. I should have taken a shower this morning. I should have worn a nicer sweater.*

I should have put on a pair of socks, worn a nicer pair of shoes. I should have cut my hair; I should have shaved . . .

The driver rolled down his window. I saw him from the corner of my eye. He called me over to him—*whistled me over*—much like he'd call a dog. I kept walking. He whistled me over again. *Here, boy.* I stopped for a second. Only a second. I kept walking. The border patrol officer and a policeman rushed out of the car and ran toward me. I was sure they were going to tackle me, drag me to the ground, handcuff me. They stopped in front of me.

"Can I see your driver's license?" the policeman asked.

"Since when do you need a driver's license to walk down the street?" Our eyes met. "Did I do something against the law?"

The policeman was annoyed. He wanted me to be passive, to say: "Yes, sir." He wanted me to approve of his job.

"Don't you know what we do?"   75

"Yes, I know what you do."

"Don't give me a hard time. I don't want trouble. I just want to see some identification."

I looked at him—looked, and saw what would not go away: neither him, nor his car, nor his job, nor what I knew, nor what I felt. He stared back. He hated me as much as I hated him. He saw the bulge of my cigarettes under my sweater and crumpled them.

I backed away from his touch. "I smoke. It's not good for me, but it's not against the law. Not yet, anyway. Don't touch me. I don't like that. Read me my rights, throw me in the can, or leave me alone." I smiled.

"No one's charging you with anything."   80

My eyes followed them as they walked back to their car. Now it was war, and *I had won this battle.* Had I won this battle? Had I won?

This spring morning, I sit at my desk, wait for the coffee to brew, and look out my window. This day, like every day, I look out my window. Across the street, a border patrol van stops and an officer gets out. So close I could touch him. On the freeway—this side of the river—a man is running. I put on my glasses. I am afraid he will be run over by the cars. I cheer for him. *Be careful. Don't get run over.* So close to the other side he can touch it. The border patrol officer gets out his walkie-talkie and runs toward the man who has disappeared from my view. I go and get my cup of coffee. I take a drink—slowly, it mixes with yesterday's tastes in my mouth. The officer in the green uniform comes back into view. He has the man with him. He puts him in the van. I can't see the color in their eyes. I see only the green. They drive away. There is no trace that says they've been there. The mountains watch the scene and say nothing. The mountains, ablaze in the spring light, have been watching— and guarding—and keeping silent longer than I have been alive. They will continue their vigil long after I am dead.

The green vans. They are taking someone away. They are taking. Green vans. This is my home, I tell myself. But I am not sure if I want this to be my home anymore. The thought crosses my mind to walk out of my apartment without my wallet. The thought crosses my mind that maybe the *Migra* will stop me again. I will let them arrest me. I will let them warehouse me. I will let them push me in front of a judge who will look at me like he has looked at the millions before me. I will be sent back to Mexico. I will let them treat me like I am illegal. But the thoughts pass. I am not brave enough to let them do that to me.

Today, the spring winds blow outside my window. The reflections in the pane, graffiti burning questions into the glass: *Sure you were born . . . Identification . . . Do you live? . . .* The winds will unsettle the desert — cover Sunset Heights with green dust. The vans will stay in my mind forever. I cannot banish them. I cannot banish their questions: *Where are you from?* I no longer know.

This is a true story.

85

WHAT DOES HE SAY?

1. Benjamin Saenz's essay begins as a narrative: it tells a story. What are the bare bones of his story, as you understand them? Make a list of the crucial facts.

2. What's the significance of the questions the border patrol asks Saenz as he walks down Prospect Street, and why do these questions shake him?

3. Of course, the border patrol officers in this essay are merely doing their job. What is that job? Why do they so frequently ask Saenz "Where are you from?"

4. The base of the Statue of Liberty carries an inscription that reads, in part, "Give me . . . /Your huddled masses yearning to breathe free." Discuss the extent to which immigration is the best thing that has happened to America or one of the worst. Think about this first in terms of your own family's history.

5. Explain how you, too, have been understood or judged merely on the basis of where you're from or how you appear. Were the judgments accurate? Positive or negative? How much did those who judged you actually know about you as a person?

WHAT DO YOU THINK?

6. What assertions about freedom and citizenship do you think that Benjamin Saenz would make? Would he agree that people born across the river in Juárez ought to be treated differently than people born on the U.S. side? Whatever assertions you believe he would make, explain them carefully and back them by citing evidence from Saenz's essay. End by discussing the reasons that you would agree or disagree

with them. Include in your discussion some explanation of how your own experiences matter (or do not matter) in your analysis.

7. Discuss your own idea of home—what it is, how it's identified in terms of family, culture, community, government, and so on. Include whatever seems important. Use Saenz's essay and your own experience to explain how and why your idea of home makes sense to you.

8. Write about your experience crossing a border and finding yourself on the other side, in unfamiliar territory. Did you change simply because you had crossed that border? Did people's opinions of you change once you were on the other side? Compare your experiences and reactions to those you see in the Saenz essay. Then explain how the Saenz essay helps you better understand the effects that borders have on those who cross them or live on the "wrong side" and those who benefit by living on the "right side."

WHAT WOULD THEY SAY?

9. After completing Benjamin Saenz's essay, read Sarah Vowell's "Shooting Dad" (p. 29) and Winona LaDuke's "Voices from White Earth" (p. 72). Assume that all three essays are responses to the question, "Where do you come from?" How do LaDuke's and Vowell's answers overlap with or seem different from the responses and answers you see in Saenz's essay?

10. Read Bernard Cooper's "A Clack of Tiny Sparks" (p. 314) together with Saenz's essay. Clearly, both Saenz and Cooper feel uncomfortable in settings they wished were more welcoming. How do their experiences significantly differ? What dilemmas or choices do they face as each author seeks to be at home where he is?

SARAH VOWELL
Shooting Dad

*M*ᴜꜱᴛ ᴡᴇ ᴀꜰꜰɪʀᴍ ᴇᴠᴇʀʏᴛʜɪɴɢ *about where we've come from? Sarah Vowell (b. 1969) doesn't. Witty in tone but serious in subject, this essay addresses the possibility that one might substantially disagree with one or both parents. Thus, where one is coming from might not be the same as what one chooses to affirm.*

Vowell's essays have appeared in Esquire, GQ, *and the* Village Voice. *A contributing editor for National Public Radio's* This American Life, *she has published two essay collections,* Radio On: A Listener's Diary *(1998) and* Take the Cannoli: Stories from the New World *(2001), from which "Shooting Dad" is excerpted.*

If you were passing by the house where I grew up during my teenage years and it happened to be before Election Day, you wouldn't have needed to come inside to see that it was a house divided. You could have looked at the Democratic campaign poster in the upstairs window and the Republican one in the downstairs window and seen our home for the Civil War battleground it was. I'm not saying who was the Democrat or who was the Republican—my father or I—but I will tell you that I have never subscribed to *Guns & Ammo*, that I did not plaster the family vehicle with National Rifle Association stickers, and that hunter's orange was never my color.

About the only thing my father and I agree on is the Constitution, though I'm partial to the First Amendment, while he's always favored the Second.

I am a gunsmith's daughter. I like to call my parents' house, located on a quiet residential street in Bozeman, Montana, the United States of Firearms. Guns were everywhere: the so-called pretty ones like the circa 1850 walnut muzzleloader hanging on the wall, Dad's clients' fixer-uppers leaning into corners, an entire rack right next to the TV. I had to move revolvers out of my way to make room for a bowl of Rice Krispies on the kitchen table.

I was eleven when we moved into that Bozeman house. We had never lived in town before, and this was a college town at that. We came from Oklahoma—a dusty little Muskogee County nowhere called Braggs. My parents' property there included an orchard, a horse pasture, and a couple of acres of woods. I knew our lives had changed one morning not long after we moved to Montana when, during breakfast, my father heard a noise and jumped out of his chair. Grabbing a BB gun, he rushed out the front door. Standing in the yard, he started shooting at crows. My mother sprinted after him screaming, "Pat, you might ought to check, but I don't think they do that up here!" From the look on his face, she might as well have told him that his American citizenship had been

29

revoked. He shook his head, mumbling, "Why, shooting crows is a national pastime, like baseball and apple pie." Personally, I preferred baseball and apple pie. I looked up at those crows flying away and thought, I'm going to like it here.

Dad and I started bickering in earnest when I was fourteen, after the   5
1984 Democratic National Convention. I was so excited when Walter Mondale chose Geraldine Ferraro as his running mate that I taped the front page of the newspaper with her picture on it to the refrigerator door. But there was some sort of mysterious gravity surge in the kitchen. Somehow, that picture ended up in the trash all the way across the room.

Nowadays, I giggle when Dad calls me on Election Day to cheerfully inform me that he has once again canceled out my vote, but I was not always so mature. There were times when I found the fact that he was a gunsmith horrifying. And just *weird*. All he ever cared about were guns. All I ever cared about was art. There were years and years when he hid out by himself in the garage making rifle barrels and I holed up in my room reading Allen Ginsberg poems, and we were incapable of having a conversation that didn't end in an argument.

Our house was partitioned off into territories. While the kitchen and the living room were well within the DMZ, the respective work spaces governed by my father and me were jealously guarded totalitarian states in which each of us declared ourselves dictator. Dad's shop was a messy disaster area, a labyrinth of lathes. Its walls were hung with the mounted antlers of deer he'd bagged, forming a makeshift museum of death. The available flat surfaces were buried under a million scraps of paper on which he sketched his mechanical inventions in blue ball-point pen. And the floor, carpeted with spiky metal shavings, was a tetanus shot waiting to happen. My domain was the cramped, cold space known as the music room. It was also a messy disaster area, an obstacle course of musical instruments—piano, trumpet, baritone horn, valve trombone, various percussion doodads (bells!), and recorders. A framed portrait of the French composer Claude Debussy was nailed to the wall. The available flat surfaces were buried under piles of staff paper, on which I penciled in the pompous orchestra music given titles like "Prelude to the Green Door" (named after an O. Henry short story by the way, not the watershed porn flick *Behind the Green Door*) I starting writing in junior high.

It has been my experience that in order to impress potential suitors, skip the teen Debussy anecdotes and stick with the always attention-getting line "My dad makes guns." Though it won't cause the guy to like me any better, it will make him handle the inevitable breakup with diplomacy—just in case I happen to have any loaded family heirlooms lying around the house.

But the fact is, I have only shot a gun once and once was plenty. My twin sister, Amy, and I were six years old—six—when Dad decided that it was high time we learned how to shoot. Amy remembers the day he handed us the gun for the first time differently. She liked it.

Amy shared our father's enthusiasm for firearms and the quick-draw   10
cowboy mythology surrounding them. I tended to daydream through Dad's

activities—the car trip to Dodge City's Boot Hill, his beloved John Wayne Westerns on TV. My sister, on the other hand, turned into Rooster Cogburn Jr., devouring Duke movies with Dad. In fact, she named her teddy bear Duke, hung a colossal John Wayne portrait next to her bed, and took to wearing one of those John Wayne shirts that button on the side. So when Dad led us out to the backyard when we were six and, to Amy's delight, put the gun in her hand, she says she felt it meant that Daddy trusted us and that he thought of us as "big girls."

But I remember holding the pistol only made me feel small. It was so heavy in my hand. I stretched out my arm and pointed it away and winced. It was a very long time before I had the nerve to pull the trigger and I was so scared I had to close my eyes. It felt like it just went off by itself, as if I had no say in the matter, as if the gun just had this *need*. The sound it made was as big as God. It kicked little me back to the ground like a bully, like a foe. It hurt. I don't know if I dropped it or just handed it back over to my dad, but I do know that I never wanted to touch another one again. And, because I believed in the devil, I did what my mother told me to do every time I felt an evil presence. I looked at the smoke and whispered under my breath, "Satan, I rebuke thee."

It's not like I'm saying I was traumatized. It's more like I was decided. Guns: Not For Me. Luckily, both my parents grew up in exasperating households where children were considered puppets and/or slaves. My mom and dad were hell-bent on letting my sister and me make our own choices. So if I decided that I didn't want my father's little death sticks to kick me to the ground again, that was fine with him. He would go hunting with my sister, who started calling herself "the loneliest twin in history" because of my reluctance to engage in family activities.

Of course, the fact that I was allowed to voice my opinions did not mean that my father would silence his own. Some things were said during the Reagan administration that cannot be taken back. Let's just say that I blamed Dad for nuclear proliferation and Contra aid. He believed that if I had my way, all the guns would be confiscated and it would take the commies about fifteen minutes to parachute in and assume control.

We're older now, my dad and I. The older I get, the more I'm interested in becoming a better daughter. First on my list: figure out the whole gun thing.

Not long ago, my dad finished his most elaborate tool of death yet. A 15 cannon. He built a nineteenth-century cannon. From scratch. It took two years.

My father's cannon is a smaller replica of a cannon called the Big Horn Gun in front of Bozeman's Pioneer Museum. The barrel of the original has been filled with concrete ever since some high school kids in the '50s pointed it at the school across the street and shot out its windows one night as a prank. According to Dad's historical source, a man known to scholars as A Guy at the Museum, the cannon was brought to Bozeman around 1870, and was used by local white merchants to fire at the Sioux and Cheyenne Indians who blocked their trade access to the East in 1874.

"Bozeman was founded on greed," Dad says. The courthouse cannon, he continues, "definitely killed Indians. The merchants filled it full of nuts, bolts, and chopped-up horseshoes. Sitting Bull could have been part of these engagements. They definitely ticked off the Indians, because a couple of years later, Custer wanders into them at Little Bighorn. The Bozeman merchants were out to cause trouble. They left fresh baked bread with cyanide in it on the trail to poison a few Indians."

Because my father's sarcastic American history yarns rarely go on for long before he trots out some nefarious ancestor of ours—I come from a long line of moonshiners, Confederate soldiers, murderers, even Democrats—he cracks that the merchants hired some "community-minded Southern soldiers from North Texas." These soldiers had, like my great-great-grandfather John Vowell, fought under proslavery guerrilla William C. Quantrill. Quantrill is most famous for riding into Lawrence, Kansas, in 1863 flying a black flag and commanding his men pharaohlike to "kill every male and burn down every house."

"John Vowell," Dad says, "had a little rep for killing people." And since he abandoned my great-grandfather Charles, whose mother died giving birth to him in 1870, and wasn't seen again until 1912, Dad doesn't rule out the possibility that John Vowell could have been one of the hired guns on the Bozeman Trail. So the cannon isn't just another gun to my dad. It's a map of all his obsessions—firearms, certainly, but also American history and family history, subjects he's never bothered separating from each other.

After tooling a million guns, after inventing and building a rifle barrel boring machine, after setting up that complicated shop filled with lathes and blueing tanks and outmoded blacksmithing tools, the cannon is his most ambitious project ever. I thought that if I was ever going to understand the ballistic bee in his bonnet, this was my chance. It was the biggest gun he ever made and I could experience it and spend time with it with the added bonus of not having to actually pull a trigger myself.

I called Dad and said that I wanted to come to Montana and watch him shoot off the cannon. He was immediately suspicious. But I had never taken much interest in his work before and he would take what he could get. He loaded the cannon into the back of his truck and we drove up into the Bridger Mountains. I was a little worried that the National Forest Service would object to us lobbing fiery balls of metal onto its property. Dad laughed, assuring me that "you cannot shoot fireworks, but this is considered a fire*arm*."

It is a small cannon, about as long as a baseball bat and as wide as a coffee can. But it's heavy—110 pounds. We park near the side of the hill. Dad takes his gunpowder and other tools out of this adorable wooden box on which he has stenciled "PAT G. VOWELL CANNONWORKS." Cannonworks: So that's what NRA members call a metal-strewn garage.

Dad plunges his homemade bullets into the barrel, points it at an embankment just to be safe, and lights the fuse. When the fuse is lit, it resembles a cartoon. So does the sound, which warrants Ben Day° dot words along the lines of *ker-pow!* There's so much Fourth of July smoke everywhere I feel compelled to sing the national anthem.

I've given this a lot of thought—how to convey the giddiness I felt when the cannon shot off. But there isn't a sophisticated way to say this. It's just really, really cool. My dad thought so, too.

Sometimes, I put together stories about the more eccentric corners of the 25 American experience for public radio. So I happen to have my tape recorder with me, and I've never seen levels like these. Every time the cannon goes off, the delicate needles which keep track of the sound quality lurch into the bad, red zone so fast and so hard I'm surprised they don't break.

The cannon was so loud and so painful, I had to touch my head to make sure my skull hadn't cracked open. One thing that my dad and I share is that we're both a little hard of hearing—me from Aerosmith, him from gunsmith.

He lights the fuse again. The bullet knocks over the log he was aiming at. I instantly utter a sentence I never in my entire life thought I would say. I tell him, "Good shot, Dad."

Just as I'm wondering what's coming over me, two hikers walk by. Apparently, they have never seen a man set off a homemade cannon in the middle of the wilderness while his daughter holds a foot-long microphone up into the air recording its terrorist boom. One hiker gives me a puzzled look and asks, "So you work for the radio and that's your dad?"

Dad shoots the cannon again so that they can see how it works. The other hiker says, "That's quite the machine you got there." But he isn't talking about the cannon. He's talking about my tape recorder and my microphone— which is called a *shotgun* mike. I stare back at him, then I look over at my father's cannon, then down at my microphone, and I think, Oh. My. God. My dad and I are the same person. We're both smart-alecky loners with goofy projects and weird equipment. And since this whole target practice outing was my idea, I was no longer his adversary. I was his accomplice. What's worse, I was liking it.

I haven't changed my mind about guns. I can get behind the cannon 30 because it is a completely ceremonial object. It's unwieldy and impractical, just like everything else I care about. Try to rob a convenience store with this 110-pound Saturday night special, you'd still be dragging it in the door Sunday afternoon.

I love noise. As a music fan, I'm always waiting for that moment in a song when something just flies out of it and explodes in the air. My dad is a one-man garage band, the kind of rock 'n' roller who slaves away at his art for no reason other than to make his own sound. My dad is an artist—a pretty

---

Ben Day: A system of color printing devised by printer Benjamin Day (1838–1916); the colored dots or patterns are especially obvious in comic books if the images are looked at under a magnifying glass. [All gloss notes are the Editors'.]

driven, idiosyncratic one, too. He's got his last *Gesamtkunstwerk*° all planned out. It's a performance piece. We're all in it—my mom, the loneliest twin in history, and me.

When my father dies, take a wild guess what he wants done with his ashes. Here's a hint: it requires a cannon.

"You guys are going to love this," he smirks, eyeballing the cannon. "You get to drag this thing up on top of the Gravellies on opening day of hunting season. And looking off at Sphinx Mountain, you get to put me in little paper bags. I can take my last hunting trip on opening morning."

I'll do it, too. I will have my father's body burned into ashes. I will pack these ashes into paper bags. I will go to the mountains with my mother, my sister, and the cannon. I will plunge his remains into the barrel and point it into a hill so that he doesn't take anyone with him. I will light the fuse. But I will not cover my ears. Because when I blow what used to be my dad into the earth, I want it to hurt.

WHAT DOES SHE SAY?

1. Sarah Vowell says her home was a "Civil War battleground." Why does she say so? Make a list of the issues and preferences about which she and her father argue.

2. Clearly Vowell and her father disagree. Do they also hate each other? How can you tell? (One idea: consider this essay's title and explain how we should understand it.)

3. Vowell says at one point that she's "interested in becoming a better daughter." What does that mean to her? How does she go about it? Where can you most clearly understand this in her essay?

4. What do Vowell and her father have in common that keeps them from simply fighting all of the time? Find two places in the essay where you can see these things clearly.

5. Discuss a time when you've had a serious disagreement with a family member about some issue of policy or morality. What were the reasons for your disagreement (assuming that you could understand them)? How does reading Vowell's essay help clarify your experience?

WHAT DO YOU THINK?

6. Using Sarah Vowell's essay and some of your own experience, discuss the ways that you think children ought to respect their parents and the extent to which children should agree with their parents' views. Look at it from the parents' perspective too: should parents expect that their children agree with them? Finally, end by explaining

---

Gesamtkunstwerk: German for "total work of art."

to what extent—or not—you are happy, troubled, or confused about your own disagreements across generational lines.

7. The opening scenario to this chapter (What Would You Do? Speaking Up for a Friend, p. 18) quotes a letter that says, in part, "There are simply moral absolutes in this life." Would Vowell agree? Would her father agree? If they disagree, on what grounds do they do so?

8. Use the following question as the basis for an essay. How has your race or ethnicity mattered to other people and to you as you've thought about "where you've come from"?

WHAT WOULD THEY SAY?

9. Consider Sarah Vowell's essay together with Benjamin Saenz's "Exile: El Paso, Texas" (p. 20). How do questions of race, ethnicity, or family cultural heritage affect each writer as she or he tries to tackle questions about home and belonging? Do the differences and similarities you see seem significant? Why or why not?

10. Discuss the ways that Vowell and Judith Ortiz Cofer ("The Story of My Body," p. 323) differ in terms of what their essays indicate as significant in their childhoods. Do you see any important similarities? Using these two essays as examples, explain how you would answer the question, "Where are you coming from?"

ELMAZ ABINADER

Profile of an Arab Daughter

*T*HE EVENTS OF SEPTEMBER *11, 2001, produced grief and fear in many people. And they raised questions about how one's country of origin can become important. In spare, imagistic prose, this piece gives us a snapshot of a dutiful and fearful Arab daughter after September 11.*

Elmaz Abinader (b. 1954) is a memoirist, poet, and performance artist. Her collection of poems, In the Country of My Dreams *(1999), won the 2000 Oakland PEN Josephine Miles Award, and she has been awarded a Fulbright Senior Service Scholarship for study in Egypt. "Profile of an Arab Daughter" was first published in the Fall 2001 issue of* Al Jadid: A Review & Record of Arab Culture and Arts.

Mother has fallen and fractured her pelvis. She was reaching for a jar in her kitchen and lost her balance. This is not her first fall. She has two artificial hips and was just recovering from the last time her foot gave way—that time, her toe caught on the edge of the carpet. Every tumble, slip, slide, and collapse, we are called. Each one of my mother's six children tenses a little, not because she has fallen, again, but because we cannot turn back the clock, we cannot avoid these repetitive reminders that my mother is getting older and that one cannot recover from old age; reminders, too, that we are getting older.

This time, when she stretched her arm up to the cabinet over the refrigerator, this time, when she tried to reach the peanut butter, it was September 11, 2001. It was just after two jets crashed into the World Trade Center, about the time the towers collapsed and thousands and thousands of people died and thousands went missing, and the nation's and the world's faces knotted from fear or opened in shock or closed in sorrow.

So in the midst of this tragedy, we did not know of my mother's fall until later. The silence of the phone gave no hint; no one knew my mother was in the hospital. Instead, my older sister, Selma, and I were desperately trying to reach our youngest sister, Geralyn, in New York, shaking our phones like rattles, hoping for something other than the sound of empty air. We recited her route to work as best we could remember and tried to judge where her husband would be: tower, tunnel, train, bus....

My mother is curled in a ball, my father says, on the downstairs couch, unable to move. The sadness courses in his voice like a slow river. He has driven her again and again to Montgomery County Hospital, fall after fall: up the stairs, over the threshold, losing her balance standing or sitting. At eighty-seven years old, my mother is worn out by her own fragility. Her body sinks in on itself, drying up. Now at ninety pounds, this tiny fortress endured childhood hunger, escape, field labor, emigration, three businesses, five relocations, fifteen pregnancies, nine births, six children. She does not recite these events, as her own mother did, sucked into a tunnel of memory. Her old age confuses her; she did not predict her own feebleness.

My mother's voice rattles hollow when she speaks to me. What can we do? People fall. Things fall. My mother tumbled at the same time another jet burst into the Pentagon, dangerously close to where she lives in Maryland. She lay on her side, my father running frantically toward her. She wept into the carpet, scared that she would never get up again. My ninety-one-year-old father pulled her by her armpits, leaned her body against his, and took her to the car. He drove, his vision foggy, to the emergency room.

The day of my mother's fall, my parents' grandchildren were sent home to Chevy Chase from their school in Washington, D.C. Alone in the house, my nephew and niece were transfixed by the television. Slow-motion footage of the second tower falling suspended their breathing for a minute.

As the children flipped through the news coverage, they spotted their father, my brother Jean, who works for an Arab advocacy institute. He sat at a table with a newscaster and other experts, speaking, calming, trying to make sense of the devastation in discussions laced with words like "backlash," "retaliation," "revenge."

My nephew and niece did not hear their father's words. They saw his name below his face, the title of his job, the organization he worked for, all printed clearly against his blue shirt and brown jacket. We aunts and uncles tried to reach them: land lines, cell phones, Internet. Finally the New York sister reaches them. My brother's son asks my sister, "Do you think someone will try to kill my dad?"

My mother doesn't know these things as her heels numb, her shoulder electrifies her with spasms, and she shifts and shifts again on the couch, trying to relieve the pain radiating in her hip and lower back. The television flashes at her but she can take the pictures only in small doses, the doses of horror much stronger than the painkillers that don't seem to reach the fire in her body. My father recites the rosary with her, sitting on the edge of the couch, watching her body ripple as she prays. My mother mumbles each decade until the drugs put her to sleep.

My mother gave me a picture of herself that she kept in the back of her diary. She is sixteen in the picture and has a closed-mouth smile. Her hair is in tight curls close to her head. Her face is open, her gray eyes bright, even in black and white; her nose is long and slightly hooked, and her cheeks are wide.

That is my face, the one I grew into. The one that causes all the trouble. They caution, when you travel, try not to look so...
    Arab?
    Yes, Arab.

My mother never considered herself an Arab. "We're Lebanese, descendants of the Phoenicians." Stories of our forefathers include their sailing ships to every continent carrying the wisdom of language, arts, and mathematics around the world. These were our ancestors.

In Profile

Six girls faced sideways, all our noses pointing to the right. Mrs. Smoothe, the Girl Scout leader for the junior troop, inspected our forms, adjusted our shoulders, and pushed our chins so we would be perfectly sideways. I stared at the back of Jeannie Ostich's dishwater-blond hair in front of me. It fell easily into a Miss America flip. Mrs. Smoothe stepped back and pulled a shade off a living room lamp, opening the light so that it sprayed around us. Suddenly, bathed in the glow of the bulb, we saw our faces appear on the white papers hanging beside us. "Oh," we glanced sideways, but quickly righted ourselves when Mrs. Smoothe cleared her throat.

"We are going to make silhouettes of your profile." Mrs. Smoothe walked toward us with her pencil raised.

I was the last in line, so I watched while Mrs. Smoothe drew the outline of the other Girl Scouts' faces. Everyone stood perfectly still, our green uniforms pressed, our badge sashes crossing our chests diagonally. The other girls had gentle lines of faces, silky hair, slender noses. Mrs. Smoothe's hand could quickly trace their images without pausing, rendering their beauty easily. Debbie's blond hair was pulled back with a white stretchy band, Renee removed her glasses from her green eyes, Marcia pulled a spit curl around into a big C. My knees softened watching them, my body slumped, and I wanted to bolt, out of the cafeteria of All Saints School in Masontown, Pennsylvania, down Main Street where my father sold shoes, to our house not far from the auto parts store.

When Mrs. Smoothe approached me, I straightened and stared out be- 15 yond the other girls who were already cutting out their profiles to paste on black paper. "Hmm," Mrs. Smoothe paused, her pencil raised. "Those braids are a bit difficult." I could feel the weight of my mother's hands as she pulled my bushy hair into three sections and crossed the tresses over and under, over and under—first on the right, then on the left. After every row, she pulled tighter and tighter, tearing my hair away from the perfectly drawn part down the middle of my head. Her hand scooped a wad of Vaseline, and she slathered the stray curls that insisted on popping up around my face.

Mrs. Smoothe lifted my braids and threw them behind my shoulders. I quivered briefly. I imagined the profile she would draw—the only one with a hook nose, a sharp chin. It couldn't disguise the chaos of my thick curly mop, it couldn't hide my "large bottom" or cover my dark hairy arms. When everyone saw the portrait, they would say "sand nigger," like Dave Lupinsky on the playground. My mouth will pout like Darlene Pardy's mouth did when she pulled down her lip into a swell imitating full African lips. Somewhere in the construction-paper portrait, my dark eyes would be revealed and my life would be uncovered. A door would open on the chaos of my home life with nine family members shouting in two languages, eating raw lamb, and trilling their tongues when the excitement rose into a frenzy.

PROFILED

The first time I was ever stopped at an airport in the United States was on a layover in Denver before a flight to New York. My husband was carrying a laptop, a CD player, a bag of food, and a briefcase. People waited behind us as he unstrapped and untwisted his cases and placed them on the belt. After he walked through the security gate, his belongings tumbled from the scanner onto the little ramp.

Every trip we took together through airports, I sucked in my breath as he fumbled with all his equipment. Always highly conscious of the people behind me, always afraid of missing the plane, always aware of how big I was at any given moment, I believed in traveling light. One purse with a book, a notebook and pen, a bottle of water, and some cosmetics. As I followed my husband through the gate, a security guard raised her hand. "Go over there." She pointed to an empty low table against the wall staffed by another security guard. His uniform hung just a little too large on him. Without speaking, he motioned for me to place my purse down and then raised his hand in a halt. He waved, and I obediently took one step back. Two women joined him and proceeded to take my purse apart. As they poured my checkbook, lipstick, pick, wallet, tissues, sunglasses, and makeup case onto the table, I felt a burning in my legs. I have traveled all over the world; I've been inspected, searched, frisked, and scanned—but here I am in Denver, an airport with pizza stands and coffee shops, the standard newsstands and shoeshine chairs.

They turned my purse inside out and x-rayed it. One guard picked every credit card out of my wallet and held it to the light. They flipped through my notebook, shook out my magazines. I stayed in my position, staring with fury. No one else is being asked to stop. What is this about? What could I be transporting from Oakland to New York that should cause all this scrutiny? The man finally asked me for my coat.

I handed it over, speechless. Behind me, others beeped through the 20 gates and headed to their flights unchecked. Finally, the man poured my water into the garbage can. He replaced the cap and offered me the empty bottle. Soon they shoved everything toward me and left the table. I glanced down at the contents of my purse lying scattered on the brown Formica. "Is this crazy or what?" I asked my husband. "What the hell was that about?"

Later I learned about *profiling*, the new system that was installed at airport security to stop terrorists. I read about security guards being trained in what a terrorist is likely to *look like* as they pass through security. But not any kind of terrorists: ones with dark hair, aquiline features, deep eyes. By the end of the article, my entire family was indicted.

My mother, whose face I inherited, would never believe I have been profiled over and over. She talks about Arabs as *them*, the other population in Lebanon, her home country. They are Muhammadans, not Catholic, like us. *Them*—despite our common looks, language, music, politics, food, customs. Our sympathy with Palestinians.

And on September 11, 2001, when the country grieved the losses in New York and Washington, my mother and father prayed extra rosaries, my mother's lips dry from painkillers, her body limp against the brushed velvet of her sofa. The television reminded her again and again that the world she traveled through so doggedly to make a home for her family was not safe.

BRANDED

A week after the destruction and devastation in New York and Washington, D.C., one news station took a poll and discovered that most Americans think that Americans of Arab origin should carry identification cards. They think that capturing our faces, pasting them flat on a card with our names and addresses, will somehow lessen the dangers.

I do not want to believe this poll. I do not want to believe that suddenly 25 we are all suspects and apart from everyone else, people who need to be feared and named. History is a poor teacher—tattooed numbers flash across my arm, and internment camps grow in the desert of my imagination. My eyes darken.

I try to picture how I would lead my mother and father from their suburban town house to some government office to have their picture taken. "Why are we doing this?" my mother would ask. She has told the story of her mother entering Ellis Island in 1921 and having her name changed by some unschooled clerk.

When I take my parents for their Arab IDs, we will have to decide if my mother needs her walker or a cane. They have been in the United States for sixty-three years, they have attended Catholic church every week of their lives, but they speak Arabic and originate from a troubled region. My mother's legs will wobble under her. She will complain to my nearly deaf father that they are Christian. Doesn't anyone understand? Because they don't realize how poor their hearing is, their Arabic will echo all around them. It will echo off the marble pillars of the government building, float through the air, and crash into the walls.

"We are Phoenicians," my mother will plead. And she will still say rosaries for the dead, for the missing, for her son whose children worry for his life. In her mind, she, like me, will sail away, following the Phoenicians, carrying wisdom with her, tucked inside the fractures in her pelvis, where she will ache and ache.

WHAT DOES SHE SAY?

1. Even before you begin to read this essay, react to the title. Write a paragraph or two that discusses what comes to mind as you see "Profile of an Arab Daughter" rather than "Profile of a Daughter" or "Profile of an American Daughter."

2. As you read, note any fact or detail that somehow runs counter to any stereotype of "Arab" and any that seems to confirm the stereotype. Then write a paragraph explaining why you think we have stereotypes, how they persist, and when and how they fall away.

3. Underline two places where you can clearly see this essay's most important points. Then write a few sentences explaining why you've underlined these two places in particular and what seems most important about them.

4. Discuss the ways that your own experience of September 11, 2001, affects your reading of this essay.

WHAT DO YOU THINK?

5. When have you been profiled—that is, judged solely on some exterior characteristics (your age, your gender, your clothing or appearance)? What does it feel like? What responses does it provoke in you later on as you think about it? What convinces you—or doesn't yet convince you—about the legitimacy or illegitimacy of profiling in order to anticipate or prevent unwanted behavior?

6. If you were to write a letter to Elmaz Abinader about her essay, what would you want to say to her? What do you think it would be important for her to understand about your thinking in response to what she has written?

WHAT WOULD THEY SAY?

7. Obviously, we are not all equal. Some of us are taller, others shorter. Some are born to wealthy families, others to poverty. Consider Elmaz Abinader's essay together with Brent Staples's "Just Walk on By: Black Men and Public Space" (p. 289) or with Benjamin Saenz's "Exile: El Paso, Texas" (p. 20). How do these essays help you understand the complexities of what the Declaration of Independence terms "created equal"?

8. Read Andrew Sullivan's "The Pursuit of Happiness: Four Revolutionary Words" (p. 217). How does it combine with Abinader's essay to help you understand the complexities of responding to the events of September 11, 2001?

LANGSTON HUGHES

Theme for English B

HOW DO WE REPRESENT OURSELVES? What becomes important for others to know? The speaker in "Theme for English B" asks if the color of his skin affects his writing. This poem raises race questions—and questions of location and personal freedom— and resolves them in its own way. It also raises the question of what is "true," a question returned to many ways in this book.

A prominent figure in the Harlem Renaissance and winner of the NAACP Springarm Medal, Langston Hughes (1902–1967) wrote sixteen books of poetry, as well as novels, plays, short stories, and two autobiographies.

The instructor said,
 Go home and write
 a page tonight.
 And let that page come out of you—
 Then, it will be true.   5

I wonder if it's that simple?
I am twenty-two, colored, born in Winston-Salem.
I went to school there, then Durham, then here
to this college on the hill above Harlem.
I am the only colored student in my class.   10
The steps from the hill lead down into Harlem,
through a park, then I cross St. Nicholas,
Eighth Avenue, Seventh, and I come to the Y,
the Harlem Branch Y, where I take the elevator
up to my room, sit down, and write this page: 15

It's not easy to know what is true for you or me
at twenty-two, my age. But I guess I'm what
I feel and see and hear, Harlem, I hear you:
hear you, hear me—we two—you, me, talk on this page.
(I hear New York, too.) Me—who?   20
Well, I like to eat, sleep, drink, and be in love.
I like to work, read, learn, and understand life.
I like a pipe for a Christmas present,
or records—Bessie, bop, or Bach.
I guess being colored doesn't make me *not* like   25
the same things other folks like who are other races.

So will my page be colored that I write?
Being me, it will not be white.
But it will be
a part of you, instructor.   30
You are white—
yet a part of me, as I am part of you.
That's American.
Sometimes perhaps you don't want to be a part of me.
Nor do I often want to be a part of you.   35
But we are, that's true!
As I learn from you,
I guess you learn from me—
although you're older—and white—
and somewhat more free.   40

This is my page for English B.

WHAT DOES HE SAY?

1. You can tell at a glance that this is a poem. What has been your experience of reading poetry? Write about that for a paragraph. Then read the poem out loud, slowly, and write another paragraph about how this poem is or is not like the others you've read.

2. What would "let that page come out of you" mean to you if a teacher told you to write in that way? Why does the speaker in this poem wonder "if it's that simple"?

3. Where does this poem get a little bit complicated or tricky to understand? What's confusing? Write about this for a paragraph.

4. As you read this poem, do you identify with the person who's talking, the person who says "I"? Do you identify with the instructor? Do you identify with "American"? Explain.

WHAT DO YOU THINK?

5. Focus centrally on these lines:

   Being me, it will not be white.
   But it will be
   a part of you, instructor.
   You are white—
   yet a part of me, as I am part of you.
   That's American.

Explain how you read them. What does "it" refer to? How does "it" somehow become "part of you"? What are the relationships here? Can you draw any conclusions about how reading this "page for English B" might have an effect?

6. Write an essay that takes as its opening the same as in this poem:

The instructor said,
> Go home and write
> a page tonight.
> And let that page come out of you—
> Then, it will be true.

Don't let the essay run longer than a page, but do try to have it "be true" in ways similar to the poem. Then, on a second page, write about how you and Langston Hughes share or do not share the same viewpoints.

WHAT WOULD THEY SAY?

7. Consider "Theme for English B" together with "Shooting Dad" (p. 29), by Sarah Vowell. Both essays speak directly of personal experience, yet only Hughes's poem speaks of race. Why is that? If you were to write your own page so that it would "be true," would your page include mention of your race or ethnicity or family heritage? Why are these issues so complicated for Americans?

8. Read "Theme for English B" together with Jenefer Shute's "Life-Size" (p. 279). Assume that their narrators are actual people and that each wants to speak truthfully. Write your own essay explaining how these two speakers complicate or confuse what's meant by "the truth."

MAXINE HONG KINGSTON
No Name Woman

IN THIS ESSAY, Maxine Hong Kingston (b. 1940) asks a series of probing questions as she works to understand her own origins, both cultural and familial. This piece is also concerned with the uses of the story—especially the one told to her in order to make a strong point about what constitutes right behavior.

Maxine Hong Kingston's The Woman Warrior: Memoirs of a Girlhood among Ghosts (1976), from which "No Name Woman" is taken, won the National Book Critics Circle Award. She has also received the American Book Award and the 1997 National Medal for the Humanities. She is currently a senior lecturer at the University of California, Berkeley.

"You must not tell anyone," my mother said, "what I am about to tell you. In China your father had a sister who killed herself. She jumped into the family well. We say that your father has all brothers because it is as if she had never been born.

"In 1924 just a few days after our village celebrated seventeen hurry-up weddings—to make sure that every young man who went 'out on the road' would responsibly come home—your father and his brothers and your grandfather and his brothers and your aunt's new husband sailed for America, the Gold Mountain. It was your grandfather's last trip. Those lucky enough to get contracts waved good-bye from the decks. They fed and guarded the stowaways and helped them off in Cuba, New York, Bali, Hawaii. 'We'll meet in California next year,' they said. All of them sent money home.

"I remember looking at your aunt one day when she and I were dressing; I had not noticed before that she had such a protruding melon of a stomach. But I did not think, 'She's pregnant,' until she began to look like other pregnant women, her shirt pulling and the white tops of her black pants showing. She could not have been pregnant, you see, because her husband had been gone for years. No one said anything. We did not discuss it. In early summer she was ready to have the child, long after the time when it could have been possible.

"The village had also been counting. On the night the baby was to be born the villagers raided our house. Some were crying. Like a great saw, teeth strung with lights, files of people walked zigzag across our land, tearing the rice. Their lanterns doubled in the disturbed black water, which drained away through the broken bunds. As the villagers closed in, we could see that some of them, probably men and women we knew well, wore white masks. The people with long hair hung it over their faces. Women with short hair made it stand up on end. Some had tied white bands around their foreheads, arms, and legs.

"At first they threw mud and rocks at the house. Then they threw eggs   5
and began slaughtering our stock. We could hear the animals scream their
deaths—the roosters, the pigs, a last great roar from the ox. Familiar wild
heads flared in our night windows; the villagers encircled us. Some of the
faces stopped to peer at us, their eyes rushing like searchlights. The hands flat-
tened against the panes, framed heads, and left red prints.

"The villagers broke in the front and the back doors at the same time,
even though we had not locked the doors against them. Their knives dripped
with the blood of our animals. They smeared blood on the doors and walls.
One woman swung a chicken, whose throat she had slit, splattering blood in
red arcs about her. We stood together in the middle of our house, in the family hall with the pictures and tables of the ancestors around us, and looked
straight ahead.

"At that time the house had only two wings. When the men came back,
we would build two more to enclose our courtyard and a third one to begin a
second courtyard. The villagers pushed through both wings, even your
grandparents' rooms, to find your aunt's, which was also mine until the men
returned. From this room a new wing for one of the younger families would
grow. They ripped up her clothes and shoes and broke her combs, grinding
them underfoot. They tore her work from the loom. They scattered the cooking fire and rolled the new weaving in it. We could hear them in the kitchen
breaking our bowls and banging the pots. They overturned the great waist-high
earthenware jugs; duck eggs, pickled fruits, vegetables burst out and mixed in
acrid torrents. The old woman from the next field swept a broom through the
air and loosed the spirits-of-the-broom over our heads. 'Pig.' 'Ghost.' 'Pig,'
they sobbed and scolded while they ruined our house.

"When they left, they took sugar and oranges to bless themselves. They
cut pieces from the dead animals. Some of them took bowls that were not
broken and clothes that were not torn. Afterward we swept up the rice and
sewed it back up into sacks. But the smells from the spilled preserves lasted.
Your aunt gave birth in the pigsty that night. The next morning when I went
for the water, I found her and the baby plugging up the family well.

"Don't let your father know that I told you. He denies her. Now that
you have started to menstruate, what happened to her could happen to you.
Don't humiliate us. You wouldn't like to be forgotten as if you had never
been born. The villagers are watchful."

Whenever she had to warn us about life, my mother told stories that ran   10
like this one, a story to grow up on. She tested our strength to establish realities. Those in the emigrant generations who could not reassert brute survival
died young and far from home. Those of us in the first American generations
have had to figure out how the invisible world the emigrants built around our
childhoods fits in solid America.

The emigrants confused the gods by diverting their curses, misleading
them with crooked streets and false names. They must try to confuse their

offspring as well, who, I suppose, threaten them in similar ways—always trying to get things straight, always trying to name the unspeakable. The Chinese I know hide their names; sojourners take new names when their lives change and guard their real names with silence.

Chinese-Americans, when you try to understand what things in you are Chinese, how do you separate what is peculiar to childhood, to poverty, insanities, one family, your mother who marked your growing with stories, from what is Chinese? What is Chinese tradition and what is the movies?

If I want to learn what clothes my aunt wore, whether flashy or ordinary, I would have to begin, "Remember Father's drowned-in-the-well sister?" I cannot ask that. My mother has told me once and for all the useful parts. She will add nothing unless powered by Necessity, a riverbank that guides her life. She plants vegetable gardens rather than lawns; she carries the odd-shaped tomatoes home from the fields and eats food left for the gods.

Whenever we did frivolous things, we used up energy; we flew high kites. We children came up off the ground over the melting cones our parents brought home from work and the American movie on New Year's Day— *Oh, You Beautiful Doll* with Betty Grable one year, and *She Wore a Yellow Ribbon* with John Wayne another year. After the one carnival ride each, we paid in guilt; our tired father counted his change on the dark walk home.

Adultery is extravagance. Could people who hatch their own chicks and 15 eat the embryos and the heads for delicacies and boil the feet in vinegar for party food, leaving only the gravel, eating even the gizzard lining—could such people engender a prodigal aunt? To be a woman, to have a daughter in starvation time was a waste enough. My aunt could not have been the lone romantic who gave up everything for sex. Women in the old China did not choose. Some man had commanded her to lie with him and be his secret evil. I wonder whether he masked himself when he joined the raid on her family.

Perhaps she had encountered him in the fields or on the mountain where the daughters-in-law collected fuel. Or perhaps he first noticed her in the marketplace. He was not a stranger because the village housed no strangers. She had to have dealings with him other than sex. Perhaps he worked an adjoining field, or he sold her the cloth for the dress she sewed and wore. His demand must have surprised, then terrified her. She obeyed him; she always did as she was told.

When the family found a young man in the next village to be her husband, she had stood tractably beside the best rooster, his proxy, and promised before they met that she would be his forever. She was lucky that he was her age and she would be the first wife, an advantage secure now. The night she first saw him, he had sex with her. Then he left for America. She had almost forgotten what he looked like. When she tried to envision him, she only saw the black and white face in the group photograph the men had had taken before leaving.

The other man was not, after all, much different from her husband. They both gave orders: she followed. "If you tell your family, I'll beat you.

I'll kill you. Be here again next week." No one talked sex, ever. And she might have separated the rapes from the rest of living if only she did not have to buy her oil from him or gather wood in the same forest. I want her fear to have lasted just as long as rape lasted so that the fear could have been contained. No drawn-out fear. But women at sex hazarded birth and hence lifetimes. The fear did not stop but permeated everywhere. She told the man, "I think I'm pregnant." He organized the raid against her.

On nights when my mother and father talked about their life back home, sometimes they mentioned an "outcast table" whose business they still seemed to be settling, their voices tight. In a commensal tradition, where food is precious, the powerful older people made wrongdoers eat alone. Instead of letting them start separate new lives like the Japanese, who could become samurais and geishas, the Chinese family, faces averted but eyes glowering sideways, hung on to the offenders and fed them leftovers. My aunt must have lived in the same house as my parents and eaten at an outcast table. My mother spoke about the raid as if she had seen it, when she and my aunt, a daughter-in-law to a different household, should not have been living together at all. Daughters-in-law lived with their husbands' parents, not their own; a synonym for marriage in Chinese is "taking a daughter-in-law." Her husband's parents could have sold her, mortgaged her, stoned her. But they had sent her back to her own mother and father, a mysterious act hinting at disgraces not told me. Perhaps they had thrown her out to deflect the avengers.

She was the only daughter; her four brothers went with her father, husband, and uncles "out on the road" and for some years became Western men. When the goods were divided among the family, three of the brothers took land, and the youngest, my father, chose an education. After my grandparents gave their daughter away to her husband's family, they had dispensed all the adventure and all the property. They expected her alone to keep the traditional ways, which her brothers, now among the barbarians, could fumble without detection. The heavy, deep-rooted women were to maintain the past against the flood, safe for returning. But the rare urge west had fixed upon our family, and so my aunt crossed boundaries not delineated in space. [20]

The work of preservation demands that the feelings playing about in one's guts not be turned into action. Just watch their passing like cherry blossoms. But perhaps my aunt, my forerunner, caught in a slow life, let dreams grow and fade and after some months or years went toward what persisted. Fear at the enormities of the forbidden kept her desires delicate, wire and bone. She looked at a man because she liked the way the hair was tucked behind his ears, or she liked the question-mark line of a long torso curving at the shoulder and straight at the hip. For warm eyes or a soft voice or a slow walk—that's all—a few hairs, a line, a brightness, a sound, a pace, she gave up family. She offered us up for a charm that vanished with tiredness, a pigtail that didn't toss when the wind died. Why, the wrong lighting could erase the dearest thing about him.

It could very well have been, however, that my aunt did not take subtle enjoyment of her friend, but, a wild woman, kept rollicking company. Imagining her free with sex doesn't fit, though. I don't know any women like that, or men either. Unless I see her life branching into mine, she gives me no ancestral help.

To sustain her being in love, she often worked at herself in the mirror, guessing at the colors and shapes that would interest him, changing them frequently in order to hit on the right combination. She wanted him to look back.

On a farm near the sea, a woman who tended her appearance reaped a reputation for eccentricity. All the married women blunt-cut their hair in flaps about their ears or pulled it back in tight buns. No nonsense. Neither style blew easily into heart-catching tangles. And at their weddings they displayed themselves in their long hair for the last time. "It brushed the backs of my knees," my mother tells me. "It was braided, and even so, it brushed the backs of my knees."

At the mirror my aunt combined individuality into her bob. A bun 25 could have been contrived to escape into black streamers blowing in the wind or in quiet wisps about her face, but only the older women in our picture album wear buns. She brushed her hair back from her forehead, tucking the flaps behind her ears. She looped a piece of thread, knotted into a circle between her index fingers and thumbs, and ran the double strand across her forehead. When she closed her fingers as if she were making a pair of shadow geese bite, the string twisted together catching the little hairs. Then she pulled the thread away from her skin, ripping the hairs out neatly, her eyes watering from the needles of pain. Opening her fingers, she cleaned the thread, then rolled it along her hairline and the tops of her eyebrows. My mother did the same to me and my sisters and herself. I used to believe that the expression "caught by the short hairs" meant a captive held with a depilatory string. It especially hurt at the temples, but my mother said we were lucky we didn't have to have our feet bound when we were seven. Sisters used to sit on their beds and cry together, she said, as their mothers or their slave removed the bandages for a few minutes each night and let the blood gush back into their veins. I hope that the man my aunt loved appreciated a smooth brow, that he wasn't just a tits-and-ass man.

Once my aunt found a freckle on her chin, at a spot that the almanac said predestined her for unhappiness. She dug it out with a hot needle and washed the wound with peroxide.

More attention to her looks than these pullings of hairs and pickings at spots would have caused gossip among the villagers. They owned work clothes and good clothes, and they wore good clothes for feasting the new seasons. But since a woman combing her hair hexes beginnings, my aunt rarely found an occasion to look her best. Women looked like great sea snails—the corded wood, babies, and laundry they carried were the whorls on their backs. The Chinese did not admire a bent back; goddesses and warriors stood straight. Still there must have been a marvelous freeing of beauty when a worker laid down her burden and stretched and arched.

Such commonplace loveliness, however, was not enough for my aunt. She dreamed of a lover for the fifteen days of New Year's, the time for families to exchange visits, money, and food. She plied her secret comb. And sure enough she cursed the year, the family, the village, and herself.

Even as her hair lured her imminent lover, many other men looked at her. Uncles, cousins, nephews, brothers would have looked, too, had they been home between journeys. Perhaps they had already been restraining their curiosity, and they left, fearful that their glances, like a field of nesting birds, might be startled and caught. Poverty hurt, and that was their first reason for leaving. But another, final reason for leaving the crowded house was the never-said.

She may have been unusually beloved, the precious only daughter, 30 spoiled and mirror gazing because of the affection the family lavished on her. When her husband left, they welcomed the chance to take her back from the in-laws; she could live like the little daughter for just a while longer. There are stories that my grandfather was different from other people, "crazy ever since the little Jap bayoneted him in the head." He used to put his naked penis on the dinner table, laughing. And one day he brought home a baby girl, wrapped up inside his brown Western-style greatcoat. He had traded one of his sons, probably my father, the youngest, for her. My grandmother made him trade back. When he finally got a daughter of his own, he doted on her. They must have all loved her, except perhaps my father, the only brother who never went back to China, having once been traded for a girl.

Brothers and sisters, newly men and women, had to efface their sexual color and present plain miens. Disturbing hair and eyes, a smile like no other, threatened the ideal of five generations living under one roof. To focus blurs, people shouted face to face and yelled from room to room. The immigrants I know have loud voices, unmodulated to American tones even after years away from the village where they called their friendships out across the fields. I have not been able to stop my mother's screams in public libraries or over telephones. Walking erect (knees straight, toes pointed forward, not pigeon-toed, which is Chinese-feminine) and speaking in an inaudible voice, I have tried to turn myself American-feminine. Chinese communication was loud, public. Only sick people had to whisper. But at the dinner table, where the family members came nearest one another, no one could talk, not the outcasts nor any eaters. Every word that falls from the mouth is a coin lost. Silently they gave and accepted food with both hands. A preoccupied child who took his bowl with one hand got a sideways glare. A complete moment of total attention is due everyone alike. Children and lovers have no singularity here, but my aunt used a secret voice, a separate attentiveness.

She kept the man's name to herself throughout her labor and dying; she did not accuse him that he be punished with her. To save her inseminator's name she gave silent birth.

He may have been somebody in her own household, but intercourse with a man outside the family would have been no less abhorrent. All the village were kinsmen, and the titles shouted in loud country voices never let kinship be forgotten. Any man within visiting distance would have been neutralized as a lover—"brother," "younger brother," "older brother"—one hundred and fifteen relationship titles. Parents researched birth charts probably not so much to assure good fortune as to circumvent incest in a population that has but one hundred surnames. Everybody has eight million relatives. How useless then sexual mannerisms, how dangerous.

As if it came from an atavism deeper than fear, I used to add "brother" silently to boys' names. It hexed the boys, who would or would not ask me to dance, and made them less scary and as familiar and deserving of benevolence as girls.

But, of course, I hexed myself also—no dates. I should have stood up, 35 both arms waving, and shouted out across libraries, "Hey, you! Love me back." I had no idea, though, how to make attraction selective, how to control its direction and magnitude. If I made myself American-pretty so that the five or six Chinese boys in the class fell in love with me, everyone else—the Caucasian, Negro, and Japanese boys—would too. Sisterliness, dignified and honorable, made much more sense.

Attraction eludes control so stubbornly that whole societies designed to organize relationships among people cannot keep order, not even when they bind people to one another from childhood and raise them together. Among the very poor and the wealthy, brothers married their adopted sisters, like doves. Our family allowed some romance, paying adult brides' prices and providing dowries so that their sons and daughters could marry strangers. Marriage promises to turn strangers into friendly relatives—a nation of siblings.

In the village structure, spirits shimmered among the live creatures, balanced and held in equilibrium by time and land. But one human being flaring up into violence could open up a black hole, a maelstrom that pulled in the sky. The frightened villagers, who depended on one another to maintain the real, went to my aunt to show her a personal, physical representation of the break she had made in the "roundness." Misallying couples snapped off the future, which was to be embodied in true offspring. The villagers punished her for acting as if she could have a private life, secret and apart from them.

If my aunt had betrayed the family at a time of large grain yields and peace, when many boys were born, and wings were being built on many houses, perhaps she might have escaped such severe punishment. But the men—hungry, greedy, tired of planting in dry soil—had been forced to leave the village in order to send food-money home. There were ghost plagues, bandit plagues, wars with the Japanese, floods. My Chinese brother and sister had died of an unknown sickness. Adultery, perhaps only a mistake during good times, became a crime when the village needed food.

The round moon cakes and round doorways, the round tables of graduated size that fit one roundness inside another, round windows and rice bowls—these talismans had lost their power to warn this family of the law: a family must be whole, faithfully keeping the descent line by having sons to feed the old and the dead, who in turn look after the family. The villagers came to show my aunt and her lover-in-hiding a broken house. The villagers were speeding up the circling of events because she was too shortsighted to see that her infidelity had already harmed the village, that waves of consequences would return unpredictably, sometimes in disguise, as now, to hurt her. This roundness had to be made coin-sized so that she would see its circumference: punish her at the birth of her baby. Awaken her to the inexorable. People who refused fatalism because they could invent small resources insisted on culpability. Deny accidents and wrest fault from the stars.

After the villagers left, their lanterns now scattering in various directions 40 toward home, the family broke their silence and cursed her. "Aiaa, we're going to die. Death is coming. Death is coming. Look what you've done. You've killed us. Ghost! Dead ghost! Ghost! You've never been born." She ran out into the fields, far enough from the house so that she could no longer hear their voices, and pressed herself against the earth, her own land no more. When she felt the birth coming, she thought that she had been hurt. Her body seized together. "They've hurt me too much," she thought. "This is gall, and it will kill me." With forehead and knees against the earth, her body convulsed and then relaxed. She turned on her back, lay on the ground. The black well of sky and stars went out and out and out forever; her body and her complexity seemed to disappear. She was one of the stars, a bright dot in blackness, without home, without a companion, in eternal cold and silence. An agoraphobia rose in her, speeding higher and higher, bigger and bigger; she would not be able to contain it; there would be no end to fear.

Flayed, unprotected against space, she felt pain return, focusing her body. This pain chilled her—a cold, steady kind of surface pain. Inside, spasmodically, the other pain, the pain of the child, heated her. For hours she lay on the ground, alternately body and space. Sometimes a vision of normal comfort obliterated reality: she saw the family in the evening gambling at the dinner table, the young people massaging their elders' backs. She saw them congratulating one another, high joy on the mornings the rice shoots came up. When these pictures burst, the stars drew yet further apart. Black space opened.

She got to her feet to fight better and remembered that old-fashioned women gave birth in their pigsties to fool the jealous, pain-dealing gods, who do not snatch piglets. Before the next spasms could stop her, she ran to the pigsty, each step a rushing out into emptiness. She climbed over the fence and knelt in the dirt. It was good to have a fence enclosing her, a tribal person alone.

Laboring, this woman who had carried her child as a foreign growth that sickened her every day, expelled it at last. She reached down to touch the hot, wet, moving mass, surely smaller than anything human, and could feel that it was human after all—fingers, toes, nails, nose. She pulled it up on to her belly, and it lay curled there, butt in the air, feet precisely tucked one under the other. She opened her loose shirt and buttoned the child inside. After resting, it squirmed and thrashed and she pushed it up to her breast. It turned its head this way and that until it found her nipple. There, it made little snuffling noises. She clenched her teeth at its preciousness, lovely as a young calf, a piglet, a little dog.

She may have gone to the pigsty as a last act of responsibility: she would protect this child as she had protected its father. It would look after her soul, leaving supplies on her grave. But how would this tiny child without family find her grave when there would be no marker for her anywhere, neither in the earth nor the family hall? No one would give her a family hall name. She had taken the child with her into the wastes. At its birth the two of them had felt the same raw pain of separation, a wound that only the family pressing tight could close. A child with no descent line would not soften her life but only trail after her, ghostlike, begging her to give it purpose. At dawn the villagers on their way to the fields would stand around the fence and look.

Full of milk, the little ghost slept. When it awoke, she hardened her 45 breasts against the milk that crying loosens. Toward morning she picked up the baby and walked to the well.

Carrying the baby to the well shows loving. Otherwise abandon it. Turn its face into the mud. Mothers who love their children take them along. It was probably a girl; there is some hope of forgiveness for boys.

"Don't tell anyone you had an aunt. Your father does not want to hear her name. She has never been born." I have believed that sex was unspeakable and words so strong and fathers so frail that "aunt" would do my father mysterious harm. I have thought that my family, having settled among immigrants who had also been their neighbors in the ancestral land, needed to clean their name, and a wrong word would incite the kinspeople even here. But there is more to this silence: they want me to participate in her punishment. And I have.

In the twenty years since I heard this story I have not asked for details nor said my aunt's name; I do not know it. People who can comfort the dead can also chase after them to hurt them further—a reverse ancestor worship. The real punishment was not the raid swiftly inflicted by the villagers, but the family's deliberately forgetting her. Her betrayal so maddened them, they saw to it that she would suffer forever, even after death. Always hungry, always needing, she would have to beg food from other ghosts, snatch and steal it from those whose living descendants give them gifts. She would have to fight the ghosts massed at crossroads for the buns a few thoughtful citizens leave to decoy her away from village and home so that the ancestral spirits could feast unharassed. At peace, they could act like gods, not ghosts, their descent lines providing them with paper suits and dresses, spirit money, paper houses, paper automobiles, chicken, meat, and rice into eternity—essences delivered up in smoke and flames, steam and incense rising from each rice bowl. In an attempt to make the Chinese care for people outside the family, Chairman Mao encourages us now to give our paper replicas to the spirits of outstanding soldiers and workers, no matter whose ancestors they may be. My aunt remains forever hungry. Goods are not distributed evenly among the dead.

My aunt haunts me—her ghost drawn to me because now, after fifty years of neglect, I alone devote pages of paper to her, though not origamied into houses and clothes. I do not think she always means me well. I am telling on her, and she was a spite suicide, drowning herself in the drinking water. The Chinese are always very frightened of the drowned one, whose weeping ghost, wet hair hanging and skin bloated, waits silently by the water to pull down a substitute.

WHAT DOES SHE SAY?

1. This essay begins by relating a story that the author was admonished she "must not tell anyone." What are the main events of this story? If you're not sure, where do you lose track? Try making a quick timeline of the story (first this happened, then this, and so on).

2. Why does the narrator's mother tell this story to her daughter?

3. Make a list of facts that you know about this narrator and her family's history. Also make a second list of the questions that the narrator struggles with.

4. Locate two important sections in this essay where you see the narrator imagining what her aunt's life might have been like. Write a paragraph about why these two places seem important.

WHAT DO YOU THINK?

5. Is this essay the narrator's story or is it her aunt's story? Why does the narrator work so hard to understand what might have happened to her aunt?

6. How important are family expectations and cultural ties in this story? How do they work? In the case of the aunt's life, how and why would such cultural expectations and the actions they produce be seen as praiseworthy?

7. What is the narrator's attitude toward the traditional Chinese culture of her aunt's time? How can you be sure?

8. Explain how you know that family and cultural expectations can be hard to confront. Then discuss how this knowledge helps you understand what Maxine Hong Kingston is trying to do in this essay.

9. Ask your mother or father or other older family member to tell you a story about someone in the previous generation—some story that was embarrassing or

suppressed. Why was it suppressed? In hearing the story, what do you learn about that family member, about that time, about anything else?

WHAT WOULD THEY SAY?

10. Much in this essay circles around the issue of what can and cannot be said or ac-knowledged. Read James Frey's memoir, "How Do You Think It Makes Your Mother Feel?" (p. 378). In what ways does Frey echo or remind you of the narrator of "No Name Woman"? How do they differ?

11. Read "No Name Woman" together with Elmaz Abinader's "Profile of an Arab Daughter" (p. 36). Discuss the ways that these essays deal with how our actions can be influenced by the ways others judge us or expect us to act. What differences and similarities do you see in the conclusions or implications of these two essays?

PETER STEINER

"You can be anything you want to be—no limits."

A FORMER PROFESSOR OF GERMAN at the University of Pittsburgh, Peter Steiner (b. 1940) sold his first cartoon to The New Yorker in 1980. Since then, more than 250 of his cartoons have appeared in that magazine.

"You can be anything you want to be—no limits."

WHAT DOES HE SAY?

1. Write a paragraph that discusses what's funny about this cartoon.

2. What experience or time of your life do you recall hearing something close to the same sentiments the cartoon parent says here? Write a brief description of the incident.

WHAT DO YOU THINK?

3. How would you make the translation between the cartoon setting of a parent fish speaking to a child fish and a human parent speaking to a human child? That is, to what extent (or not) is the cartoon's fishbowl an accurate metaphor for the human experience of limits?

4. Can you recall a time in your own life when some authority figure essentially told you the opposite of "you can be anything you want to be"? Discuss this. Was it a difficult situation? Did you hear what you wanted to hear? Did you hear what you needed to hear?

5. What should parents tell their children about what to hope for or what to strive for? Why?

6. Do you believe your own future is unlimited? Explain your position, making sure to do justice to its complexity.

WHAT WOULD THEY SAY?

7. Compare the sentiments of this cartoon with those of "The Earth Charter" (p. 158). Do you find any overlap? Or are these two things so disparate that they really have nothing to say to each other? Explain your reasons.

8. Consider this cartoon together with William Stafford's poem "Traveling through the Dark" (p. 172) or John Daniels's "The Authentic Trail" (p. 87). How do they contrast with or complement each other?

ROBERT COLES

I Listen to My Parents and I Wonder What They Believe

A RESEARCHER WHO HAS long worked with children, Robert Coles (b. 1929) here writes an essay that comments on the personal narratives that precede it and reports the moral and ethical questions that children ask. This essay also reasserts the ways that childhood is partly a time of stories received (from parents, from one's culture) and partly a time during which we ponder large questions.

Coles received the U.S. Presidential Medal of Freedom in 1998. The author of more than sixty books, his work has been recognized with the Pulitzer Prize, and he is a past recipient of a MacArthur Foundation Award. A research psychiatrist for Harvard University Health Systems, he is a professor of psychiatry and medical humanities and Agee Professor of Social Ethics at the Harvard Graduate School of Education. "I Listen to My Parents and I Wonder What They Believe" was first published in the February 1980 issue of Redbook.

Not so long ago children were looked upon in a sentimental fashion as "angels" or as "innocents." Today, thanks to Freud and his followers, boys and girls are understood to have complicated inner lives; to feel love, hate, envy, and rivalry in various and subtle mixtures; to be eager participants in the sexual and emotional politics of the home, neighborhood, and school. Yet some of us parents still cling to the notion of childhood innocence in another way. We do not see that our children also make ethical decisions every day in their own lives, or realize how attuned they may be to moral currents and issues in the larger society.

In Appalachia I heard a girl of eight whose father owns coal fields (and gas stations, a department store, and much timberland) wonder about "life" one day: "I'll be walking to the school bus, and I'll ask myself why there's some who are poor and their daddies can't find a job, and there's some who are lucky like me. Last month there was an explosion in a mine my daddy owns, and everyone became upset. Two miners got killed. My daddy said it was their own fault, because they'll be working and they get careless. When my mother asked if there was anything wrong with the safety down in the mine, he told her no and she shouldn't ask questions like that. Then the Government people came and they said it was the owner's fault—Daddy's. But he has a lawyer and the lawyer is fighting the Government and the union. In school, kids ask me what I think, and I sure do feel sorry for the two miners and so does my mother—I know that. She told me it's just not a fair world and you have to remember that. Of course, there's no one who can be sure there won't be trouble; like my daddy says, the rain falls on the just and the unjust. My brother is only six and he asked Daddy awhile back who are the 'just' and the 'unjust,' and Daddy said there are people who work hard and they live good lives, and there are lazy people and they're always trying to sponge off others. But I guess you have to feel sorry for anyone who has a lot of trouble, because it's poured-down, heavy rain."

Listening, one begins to realize that an elementary-school child is no stranger to moral reflection—and to ethical conflict. This girl was torn between her loyalty to her particular background, its values and assumptions, and to a larger affiliation—her membership in the nation, the world. As a human being whose parents were kind and decent to her, she was inclined to be thoughtful and sensitive with respect to others, no matter what their work or position in society. But her father was among other things a mineowner, and she had already learned to shape her concerns to suit that fact of life. The result: a moral oscillation of sorts, first toward nameless others all over the world and then toward her own family. As the girl put it later, when she was a year older: "You should try to have 'good thoughts' about everyone, the minister says, and our teacher says that too. But you should honor your father and mother most of all; that's why you should find out what they think and then sort of copy them. But sometimes you're not sure if you're on the right track."

Sort of copy them. There could be worse descriptions of how children acquire moral values. In fact, the girl understood how girls and boys all over the world "sort of" develop attitudes of what is right and wrong, ideas of who the just and the unjust are. And they also struggle hard and long, and not always with success, to find out where the "right track" starts and ends. Children need encouragement or assistance as they wage that struggle.

In home after home that I have visited, and in many classrooms, I have   5
met children who not only are growing emotionally and intellectually but also are trying to make sense of the world morally. That is to say, they are asking themselves and others about issues of fair play, justice, liberty, equality. Those last words are abstractions, of course—the stuff of college term papers. And there are, one has to repeat, those in psychology and psychiatry who would deny elementary-school children access to that "higher level" of moral reflection. But any parent who has listened closely to his or her child knows that girls and boys are capable of wondering about matters of morality, and knows too that often it is their grown-up protectors (parents, relatives, teachers, neighbors) who are made uncomfortable by the so-called "innocent" nature of the questions children may ask or the statements they may make. Often enough the issue is not the moral capacity of the children but the default of us parents who fail to respond to inquiries put to us by our daughters and sons—and fail to set moral standards for both ourselves and our children.

Do's and don'ts are, of course, pressed upon many of our girls and boys. But a moral education is something more than a series of rules handed down, and in our time one cannot assume that every parent feels able—sure enough of her own or his own actual beliefs and values—to make even an initial explanatory and disciplinary effort toward a moral education. Furthermore, for many of us parents these days it is a child's emotional life that preoccupies us.

In 1963, when I was studying school desegregation in the South, I had extended conversations with black and white elementary-school children caught up in a dramatic moment of historical change. For longer than I care to remember, I concentrated on possible psychiatric troubles, on how a given child was managing under circumstances of extreme stress, on how I could be of help—with "support," with reassurance, with a helpful psychological observation or interpretation. In many instances I was off the mark. These children weren't "patients"; they weren't even complaining. They were worried, all right, and often enough they had things to say that were substantive—that had to do not so much with troubled emotions as with questions of right and wrong in the real-life dramas taking place in their worlds.

Here is a nine-year-old white boy, the son of ardent segregationists, telling me about his sense of what desegregation meant to Louisiana in the 1960s: "They told us it wouldn't happen—never. My daddy said none of us white people would go into schools with the colored. But then it did happen, and when I went to school the first day I didn't know what would go on. Would the school stay open or would it close up? We didn't know what to do; the teacher kept telling us that we should be good and obey the law, but my daddy said the law was wrong. Then my mother said she wanted me in school even if there were some colored kids there. She said if we all stayed home she'd be a 'nervous wreck.' So I went.

"After a while I saw that the colored weren't so bad. I saw that there are different kinds of colored people, just like with us whites. There was one of the colored who was nice, a boy who smiled, and he played real good. There was another one, a boy, who wouldn't talk with anyone. I don't know if it's right that we all be in the same school. Maybe it isn't right. My sister is starting school next year, and she says she doesn't care if there's 'mixing of the races.' She says they told her in Sunday school that everyone is a child of God, and then a kid asked if that goes for the colored too and the teacher said yes, she thought so. My daddy said that it's true, God made everyone—but that doesn't mean we all have to be living together under the same roof in the home or the school. But my mother said we'll never know what God wants of us but we have to try to read His mind, and that's why we pray. So when I say my prayers I ask God to tell me what's the right thing to do. In school I try to say hello to the colored, because they're kids, and you can't be mean or you'll be 'doing wrong,' like my grandmother says."

Children aren't usually long-winded in the moral discussions they have 10 with one another or with adults, and in quoting this boy I have pulled together comments he made to me in the course of several days. But everything he said was of interest to me. I was interested in the boy's changing racial attitudes. It was clear he was trying to find a coherent, sensible moral position too. It was also borne in on me that if one spends days, weeks in a given home, it is hard to escape a particular moral climate just as significant as the psychological one.

In many homes parents establish moral assumptions, mandates, priorities. They teach children what to believe in, what not to believe in. They teach children what is permissible or not permissible—and why. They may summon up the Bible, the flag, history, novels, aphorisms, philosophical or political sayings, personal memories—all in an effort to teach children how to behave, what and whom to respect and for which reasons. Or they may neglect to do so, and in so doing teach their children *that*—a moral abdication, of sorts—and in this way fail their children. Children need and long for words of moral advice, instruction, warning, as much as they need words of affirmation or criticism from their parents about other matters. They must learn how to dress and what to wear, how to eat and what to eat; and they must also learn how to behave under X or Y or Z conditions, and why.

All the time, in 20 years of working with poor children and rich children, Black children and white children, children from rural areas and urban areas and in every region of this country, I have heard questions—thoroughly intelligent and discerning questions—about social and historical matters, about personal behavior, and so on. But most striking is the fact that almost all those questions, in one way or another, are moral in nature: Why did the Pilgrims leave England? Why didn't they just stay and agree to do what the king wanted them to do?...Should you try to share all you've got or should you save a lot for yourself?...What do you do when you see others fighting—do you try to break up the fight, do you stand by and watch or do you leave as fast as you can?...Is it right that some people haven't got enough to eat?...I see other kids cheating and I wish I could copy the answers too; but I won't cheat, though sometimes I feel I'd like to and I get all mixed up. I go home and talk with my parents, and I ask them what should you do if you see kids cheating—pay no attention, or report the kids or do the same thing they are doing?

Those are examples of children's concerns—and surely millions of American parents have heard versions of them. Have the various "experts" on childhood stressed strongly enough the importance of such questions—and the importance of the hunger we all have, no matter what our age or background, to examine what we believe in, are willing to stand up for, and what we are determined to ask, likewise, of our children?

Children not only need our understanding of their complicated emotional lives; they also need a constant regard for the moral issues that come their way as soon as they are old enough to play with others and take part in the politics of the nursery, the back yard and the schoolroom. They need to be told what they must do and what they must not do. They need control over themselves and a sense of what others are entitled to from them—cooperation, thoughtfulness, an attentive ear and eye. They need discipline not only to tame their excesses of emotion but discipline also connected to stated and clarified moral values. They need, in other words, something to believe in that is larger than their own appetites and urges and, yes, bigger than their "psychological drives." They need a larger view of the world, a moral context, as it were—a faith that addresses itself to the meaning of this life we all live and, soon enough, let go of.

Yes, it is time for us parents to begin to look more closely at what ideas   15
our children have about the world; and it would be well to do so before they become teen-agers and young adults and begin to remind us, as often happens, of how little attention we did pay to their moral development. Perhaps a nine-year-old girl from a well-off suburban home in Texas put it better than anyone else I've met:

"I listen to my parents, and I wonder what they believe in more than anything else. I asked my mom and my daddy once: What's the thing that means most to you? They said they didn't know but I shouldn't worry my head too hard with questions like that. So I asked my best friend, and she said she wonders if there's a God and how do you know Him and what does He want you to do—I mean, when you're in school or out playing with your friends. They talk about God in church, but is it only in church that He's there and keeping an eye on you? I saw a kid steal in a store, and I know her father has a lot of money—because I hear my daddy talk. But stealing's wrong. My mother said she's a 'sick girl,' but it's still wrong what she did. Don't you think?"

There was more—much more—in the course of the months I came to know that child and her parents and their neighbors. But those observations and questions—a "mere child's"—reminded me unforgettably of the aching hunger for firm ethical principles that so many of us feel. Ought we not begin thinking about this need? Ought we not all be asking ourselves more intently what standards we live by—and how we can satisfy our children's hunger for moral values?

WHAT DOES HE SAY?

1. As you're reading, make a list of each new moral or ethical question that a child raises.

2. According to Robert Coles, how do children develop moral understanding and moral values? Do his views and examples ring true to your experience? Do they seem representative of children other than the ones that Coles quotes? Write a paragraph discussing this.

3. Go back to the introduction to this book and review the section titled Contributing to Civic Rhetoric: Making Claims (p. 13). Identify a claim, a reason, and a warrant that combine to make one part of Coles's argument and write them down.

4. Copy two sentences from this essay that come close to summarizing Coles's argument as you understand it. Then write a paragraph about what you think of this argument.

5. What personal experience does this essay call to mind about when you had similar questions as a child? What adults made a difference or had an influence on you then? Write for ten minutes about this.

WHAT DO YOU THINK?

6. Coles argues that parents have an obligation to give their children moral guidance. Should schools also be teaching moral and ethical values? Do they do so?

7. Coles's essay does not cite data. Rather, it offers examples that he has chosen to make his points. Is this an effective strategy? How does it work to make you think?

8. Explain how Coles's essay uses children's words to criticize their parents. What kinds of lives are the parents living in these children's examples? Are there differences between the moral outlook and understandings of the children and the moral outlook and understandings of the adults?

9. In the opening scenario to this chapter (What Would You Do? Speaking Up for a Friend, p. 18), the letter writer claims that there are "moral absolutes" which are simply and always right. Sometimes children are believed to think in similar absolute terms. Does the evidence that Coles presents in this essay support the assumption that children think of ethics in terms of absolute right and wrong, or does that evidence support the assertion that children see ambiguities and nuances as they try to understand moral choices and the actions they see others—especially their parents—take?

WHAT WOULD THEY SAY?

10. Based on what this essay helps you understand of Coles, how would he react to Maxine Hong Kingston's essay "No Name Woman" (p. 45)? What would he recognize and understand? What would he say about the moral or ethical world of the old China as it is presented in "No Name Woman"?

11. Read Coles's essay and then read the Studs Terkel interview with C. P. Ellis (p. 568). How does the Ellis interview complicate Coles's call for parents to help their children develop moral awareness? What new questions are raised by it?

●

○

BARBARA KINGSOLVER

Stone Soup

*W*HAT CONSTITUTES GENUINE SUCCESS *must surely be an ethical question. But this essay asks readers to consider what constitutes familial success, especially when it comes to families that do not fit our cultural stereotype.*

An essayist and short-story writer, Barbara Kingsolver (b. 1955) is best known as the author of the novels: The Poisonwood Bible *(1999), which was nominated for the PEN/Faulkner Award,* Animal Dreams *(1991),* The Bean Trees *(1998), and* Prodigal Summer *(2001). She has recently collaborated with photographer Annie Griffiths Belt on* Last Stand: America's Virgin Lands *(2002). "Stone Soup" is taken from* High Tide in Tucson: Essays for Now or Never *(1995).*

In the catalog of family values, where do we rank an occasion like this? A curly-haired boy who wanted to run before he walked, age seven now, a soccer player scoring a winning goal. He turns to the bleachers with his fists in the air and a smile wide as a gap-toothed galaxy. His own cheering section of grown-ups and kids all leap to their feet and hug each other, delirious with love for this boy. He's Andy, my best friend's son. The cheering section includes his mother and her friends, his brother, his father and stepmother, a stepbrother and stepsister, and a grandparent. Lucky is the child with this many relatives on hand to hail a proud accomplishment. I'm there too, witnessing a family fortune. But in spite of myself, defensive words take shape in my head. I am thinking: I dare *anybody* to call this a broken home.

Families change, and remain the same. Why are our names for home so slow to catch up to the truth of where we live?

When I was a child, I had two parents who loved me without cease. One of them attended every excuse for attention I ever contrived, and the other made it to the ones with higher production values, like piano recitals and appendicitis. So I was a lucky child too, I played with a set of paper dolls called "The Family of Dolls," four in number, who came with the factory-assigned names of Dad, Mom, Sis, and Junior. I think you know what they looked like, at least before I loved them to death and their heads fell off.

Now I've replaced the dolls with a life. I knit my days around my daughter's survival and happiness, and am proud to say her head is still on. But we aren't the Family of Dolls. Maybe you're not, either. And if not, even though you are statistically no oddity, it's probably been suggested to you in a hundred ways that yours isn't exactly a real family, but an impostor family, a harbinger of cultural ruin, a slapdash substitute—something like counterfeit

money. Here at the tail end of our century, most of us are up to our ears in
the noisy business of trying to support and love a thing called family. But
there's a current in the air with ferocious moral force that finds its way even
into political campaigns, claiming there is only one right way to do it, the
Way It Has Always Been.

In the face of a thriving, particolored world, this narrow view is so 5
pickled and absurd I'm astonished that it gets airplay. And I'm astonished that
it still stings.

Every parent has endured the arrogance of a child-unfriendly grump sitting in judgment, explaining what those kids of ours really need (for example,
"a good licking"). If we're polite, we move our crew to another bench in the
park. If we're forthright (as I am in my mind, only, for the rest of the day),
we fix them with a sweet imperious stare and say, "Come back and let's talk
about it after you've changed a thousand diapers."

But it's harder somehow to shrug off the Family-of-Dolls Family Values crew when they judge (from their safe distance) that divorced people,
blended families, gay families, and single parents are failures. That our children are at risk, and the whole arrangement is messy and embarrassing. A marriage that ends is not called "finished," it's called *failed*. The children of this
family may have been born to a happy union, but now they are called *the
children of divorce*.

I had no idea how thoroughly these assumptions overlaid my culture
until I went through divorce myself. I wrote to a friend: "This might be worse
than being widowed. Overnight I've suffered the same losses — companionship,
financial and practical support, my identity as a wife and partner, the future
I'd taken for granted. I am lonely, grieving, and hard-pressed to take care of
my household alone. But instead of bringing casseroles, people are acting like
I had a fit and broke up the family china."

Once upon a time I held these beliefs about divorce: that everyone who
does it could have chosen not to do it. That it's a lazy way out of marital problems. That it selfishly puts personal happiness ahead of family integrity. Now I
tremble for my ignorance. It's easy, in fortunate times, to forget about the ambush that could leave your head reeling: serious mental or physical illness, death
in the family, abandonment, financial calamity, humiliation, violence, despair.

I started out like any child, intent on being the Family of Dolls. I set 10
upon young womanhood believing in most of the doctrines of my generation: I wore my skirts four inches above the knee. I had that Barbie with her
zebra-striped swimsuit and a figure unlike anything found in nature. And I
understood the Prince Charming Theory of Marriage, a quest for Mr. Right
that ends smack dab where you find him. I did not completely understand
that another whole story *begins* there, and no fairy tale prepared me for the
combination of bad luck and persistent hope that would interrupt my dream
and lead me to other arrangements. Like a cancer diagnosis, a dying marriage
is a thing to fight, to deny, and finally, when there's no choice left, to dig in

and survive. Casseroles would help. Likewise, I imagine it must be a painful reckoning in adolescence (or later on) to realize one's own true love will never look like the soft-focus fragrance ads because Prince Charming (surprise!) is a princess. Or vice versa. Or has skin the color your parents didn't want you messing with, except in the Crayola box.

It's awfully easy to hold in contempt the straw broken home, and that mythical category of persons who toss away nuclear family for the sheer fun of it. Even the legal terms we use have a suggestion of caprice. I resent the phrase "irreconcilable differences," which suggest a stubborn refusal to accept a spouse's little quirks. This is specious. Every happily married couple I know has loads of irreconcilable differences. Negotiating where to set the thermostat is not the point. A nonfunctioning marriage is a slow asphyxiation. It is waking up despised each morning, listening to the pulse of your own loneliness before the radio begins to blare its raucous gospel that you're nothing if you aren't loved. It is sharing your airless house with the threat of suicide or other kinds of violence, while the ghost that whispers, "Leave here and destroy your children," has passed over every door and nailed it shut. Disassembling a marriage in these circumstances is as much *fun* as amputating your own gangrenous leg. You do it, if you can, to save a life — or two, or more.

I know of no one who really went looking to hoe the harder row, especially the daunting one of single parenthood. Yet it seems to be the most American of customs to blame the burdened for their destiny. We'd like so desperately to believe in freedom and justice for all, we can hardly name that rogue bad luck, even when he's a close enough snake to bite us. In the wake of my divorce, some friends (even a few close ones) chose to vanish, rather than linger within striking distance of misfortune.

But most stuck around, bless their hearts, and if I'm any the wiser for my trials, it's from having learned the worth of steadfast friendship. And also, what not to say. The least helpful question is: "Did you want the divorce, or didn't you?" Did I want to keep that gangrenous leg, or not? How to explain, in a culture that venerates choice: two terrifying options are much worse than none at all. Give me any day the quick hand of cruel fate that will leave me scarred but blameless. As it was, I kept thinking of that wicked third-grade joke in which some boy comes up behind you and grabs your ear, starts in with a prolonged tug, and asks, "Do you want this ear any longer?"

Still, the friend who holds your hand and says the wrong thing is made of dearer stuff than the one who stays away. And generally, through all of it, you live. My favorite fictional character, Kate Vaiden (in the novel by Reynolds Price), advises: "Strength just comes in one brand — you stand up at sunrise and meet what they send you and keep your hair combed."

Once you've weathered the straits, you get to cross the tricky juncture from casualty to survivor. If you're on your feet at the end of a year or two, and have begun putting together a happy new existence, those friends who were kind enough to feel sorry for you when you needed it must now

15

accept you back to the ranks of the living. If you're truly blessed, they will dance at your second wedding. Everybody else, for heaven's sake, should stop throwing stones.

Arguing about whether nontraditional families deserve pity or tolerance is a little like the medieval debate about left-handedness as a mark of the devil. Divorce, remarriage, single parenthood, gay parents, and blended families simply are. They're facts of our time. Some of the reasons listed by sociologists for these family reconstructions are: the idea of marriage as a romantic partnership rather than a pragmatic one; a shift in women's expectations, from servility to self-respect and independence; and longevity (prior to antibiotics no marriage was expected to last many decades—in colonial days the average couple lived to be married less than twelve years). Add to all this, our growing sense of entitlement to happiness and safety from abuse. Most would agree these are all good things. Yet their result—a culture in which serial monogamy and the consequent reshaping of families are the norm—gets diagnosed as "failing."

For many of us, once we have put ourselves Humpty-Dumpty-wise back together again, the main problem with our reorganized family is that other people think we have a problem. My daughter tells me the only time she's uncomfortable about being the child of divorced parents is when her friends say they feel sorry for her. It's a bizarre sympathy, given that half the kids in her school and nation are in the same boat, pursuing childish happiness with the same energy as their married-parent peers. When anyone asks how *she* feels about it, she spontaneously lists the benefits: our house is in the country and we have a dog, but she can go to her dad's neighborhood for the urban thrills of a pool and sidewalks for roller-skating. What's more, she has three sets of grandparents!

Why is it surprising that a child would revel in a widened family and the right to feel at home in more than one house? Isn't it the opposite that should worry us—a child with no home at all, or too few resources to feel safe? The child at risk is the one whose parents are too immature themselves to guide wisely; too diminished by poverty to nurture; too far from opportunity to offer hope. The number of children in the United States living in poverty at this moment is almost unfathomably large: 20 percent. There are families among us that need help all right, and by no means are they new on the landscape. The rate at which teenage girls had babies in 1957 (ninety-six per thousand) was twice what it is now. That remarkable statistic is ignored by the religious right— probably because the teen birthrate was cut in half mainly by legalized abortion. In fact, the policy gatekeepers who coined the phrase "family values" have steadfastly ignored the desperation of too-small families, and since 1979 have steadily reduced the amount of financial support available to a single parent. But, this camp's most outspoken attacks seem aimed at the notion of families getting too complex, with add-ons and extras such as a gay parent's partner, or a remarried mother's new husband and his children.

To judge a family's value by its tidy symmetry is to purchase a book for its cover. There's no moral authority there. The famous family comprised of Dad, Mom, Sis, and Junior living as an isolated economic unit is not built on historical bedrock. In *The Way We Never Were*, Stephanie Coontz writes, "Whenever people propose that we go back to the traditional family, I always suggest that they pick a ballpark date for the family they have in mind." Colonial families were tidily disciplined, but their members (meaning everyone but infants) labored incessantly and died young. Then the Victorian family adopted a new division of labor, in which women's role was domestic and children were allowed time for study and play, but this was an upper-class construct supported by myriad slaves. Coontz writes, "For every nineteenth-century middle-class family that protected its wife and child within the family circle, there was an Irish or German girl scrubbing floors...a Welsh boy mining coal to keep the home-baked goodies warm, a black girl doing the family laundry, a black mother and child picking cotton to be made into clothes for the family, and a Jewish or an Italian daughter in a sweatshop making 'ladies' dresses or artificial flowers for the family to purchase."

The abolition of slavery brought slightly more democratic arrangements, 20 in which extended families were harnessed together in cottage industries; at the turn of the century came a steep rise in child labor in mines and sweatshops. Twenty percent of American children lived in orphanages at the time; their parents were not necessarily dead, but couldn't afford to keep them.

During the Depression and up to the end of World War II, many millions of U.S. households were more multigenerational than nuclear. Women my grandmother's age were likely to live with a fluid assortment of elderly relatives, in-laws, siblings, and children. In many cases they spent virtually every waking hour working in the company of other women—a companionable scenario in which it would be easier, I imagine, to tolerate an estranged or difficult spouse. I'm reluctant to idealize a life of so much hard work and so little spousal intimacy, but its advantage may have been resilience. A family so large and varied would not easily be brought down by a single blow: it could absorb a death, long illness, an abandonment here or there, and any number of irreconcilable differences.

The Family of Dolls came along midcentury as a great American experiment. A booming economy required a mobile labor force and demanded that women surrender jobs to returning soldiers. Families came to be defined by a single breadwinner. They struck out for single-family homes at an earlier age than ever before, and in unprecedented numbers they raised children in suburban isolation. The nuclear family was launched to sink or swim.

More than a few sank. Social historians corroborate that the suburban family of the postwar economic boom, which we have recently selected as our definition of "traditional," was no panacea. Twenty-five percent of Americans were poor in the mid-1950s, and as yet there were no food stamps.

Sixty percent of the elderly lived on less than $1,000 a year, and most had no medical insurance. In the sequestered suburbs, alcoholism and sexual abuse of children were far more widespread than anyone imagined.

Expectations soared, and the economy sagged. It's hard to depend on one other adult for everything, come what may. In the last three decades, that amorphous, adaptable structure we call "family" has been reshaped once more by economic tides. Compared with fifties families, mothers are far more likely now to be employed. We are statistically more likely to divorce, and to live in blended families or other extra-nuclear arrangements. We are also more likely to plan and space our children, and to rate our marriages as "happy." We are less likely to suffer abuse without recourse, or to stare out at our lives through a glaze of prescription tranquilizers. Our aged parents are less likely to become destitute, and we're half as likely to have a teenage daughter turn up a mother herself. All in all, I would say that if "intact" in modern family-values jargon means living quietly desperate in the bell jar, then hip-hip-hooray for "broken." A neat family model constructed to service the baby boom economy seems to be returning gradually to a grand, lumpy shape that human families apparently have tended toward since they first took root in the Olduvai Gorge. We're social animals, deeply fond of companionship, and children love best to run in packs. If there is a *normal* for humans, at all, I expect it looks like two or three Families of Dolls, connected variously by kinship and passion, shuffled like cards and strewn over several shoeboxes.

The sooner we can let go the fairy tale of families functioning perfectly 25 in isolation, the better we might embrace the relief of community. Even the admirable parents who've stayed married through thick and thin are very likely, at present, to incorporate other adults into their families—household help and babysitters if they can afford them, or neighbors and grandparents if they can't. For single parents, this support is the rock-bottom definition of family. And most parents who have split apart, however painfully, still manage to maintain family continuity for their children, creating in many cases a boisterous phenomenon that Constance Ahrons in her book *The Good Divorce* calls the "binuclear family." Call it what you will—when ex-spouses beat swords into plowshares and jump up and down at a soccer game together, it makes for happy kids.

Cinderella, look, who needs her? All those evil stepsisters? That story always seemed like too much cotton-picking fuss over clothes. A childhood tale that fascinated me more was the one called "Stone Soup," and the gist of it is this: once upon a time, a pair of beleaguered soldiers straggled home to a village empty-handed, in a land ruined by war. They were famished, but the villagers had so little they shouted evil words and slammed their doors. So the soldiers dragged out a big kettle, filled it with water, and put it on a fire to boil. They rolled a clean round stone into the pot, while the villagers peered through their curtains in amazement.

"What kind of soup is that?" they hooted.

"Stone soup," the soldiers replied. "Everybody can have some when it's done."

"Well, thanks," one matron grumbled, coming out with a shriveled carrot. "But it'd be better if you threw this in."

And so on, of course, a vegetable at a time, until the whole suspicious   30 village managed to feed itself grandly.

Any family is a big empty pot, save for what gets thrown in. Each stew turns out different. Generosity, a resolve to turn bad luck into good, and respect for variety—these things will nourish a nation of children. Name-calling and suspicion will not. My soup contains a rock or two of hard times, and maybe yours does too. I expect it's a heck of a bouillabaisse.

WHAT DOES SHE SAY?

1. Before you begin reading this essay, write at least five sentences that occur to you as you think of these two phrases: "broken home" and "children of divorce."

2. Kingsolver's essay was written in the mid-1990s. Does it still seem accurate that if you're in a blended family or living with a divorced parent, "it's probably been suggested to you in a hundred ways that yours isn't exactly a real family"? Do you think parents who divorce are selfishly putting "personal happiness ahead of family integrity"? Whatever your family situation, do you think our views have shifted much in ten years? Write a paragraph about this.

3. Part of this essay details some of the historic conceptions of family. What surprises you about this information? Does any of it help you understand your own family experience?

WHAT DO YOU THINK?

4. Kingsolver quotes Constance Ahrons's book *The Good Divorce*. Locate and look through at least two other authoritative sources that discuss what happens to children whose parents divorce. What do you learn as a result of this additional reading, and how does it help you understand what has happened in your own family? (Side question: what would constitute "authoritative sources" given this subject?)

5. Many children are now raised in settings that do not resemble what Kingsolver calls "The Family of Dolls." And Kingsolver says toward the end of her essay, "The sooner we can let go the fairy tale of families functioning perfectly in isolation, the better we might embrace the relief of community." That suggests that communities have some role in raising children. What's your sense of the ideal

way that children might be raised? Who would be involved? What would be essential?

WHAT WOULD THEY SAY?

6. Assume that Robert Coles, author of "I Listen to My Parents and I Wonder What They Believe" (p. 58), has read Barbara Kingsolver's essay and that she has read his. Then assume that Coles asks Kingsolver if she has thought about the message that her divorce has sent to her daughter. Based on what you understand from her essay, what would Kingsolver say in response?

7. Both Kingsolver's essay and Maxine Hong Kingston's "No Name Woman" (p. 45) deal with the notion of marriage as an institution designed to offer the best setting in which to raise children. Yet both essays seem to challenge this assumption. Based on their essays, on what points would Kingsolver and Kingston agree? Would they also disagree? If so, about what?

WINONA LaDUKE
Voices from White Earth

Winona LaDuke (b. 1959) knows her place in the world: the White Earth Reservation. In reaffirming a flourishing indigenous culture, this essay blends questions of location, history, ethnicity, and heritage in contrast to any "settler culture."

Author of Last Standing Woman *(1997), former board member of Greenpeace USA, and cochair of the Indigenous Women's Network, Winona LaDuke ran as the Green Party's vice presidential nominee in 1996 and 2000. She is currently program director of Honor the Earth. "Voices from White Earth" was originally published in* People, Land, and Community: Collected E. F. Schumacher Society Lectures *(1997).*

Thank you for inviting me to come here and talk about some of the things that are important to the Anishinabeg and to the wider community of native peoples. Today I would like to talk about *keewaydahn*, which means "going home" in the Anishinabeg language. It's something like what Wes Jackson said in his lecture earlier in today's program about the process of going home and finding home. I think that is essentially what we need to be talking about. It is a challenge that people of this society face in belonging to a settler culture. They have been raised in this land, but they do not know its ceremony, its song, or its naming. Early settlers reused names from other places, calling their settlements "New England," "New Haven," and "New York." But at the same time there are many indigenous names that coexist with them. I think naming, as well as knowing *why* names are, is very important in restoring your relationship with the earth and finding your place. Restoring this relationship is our challenge.

To introduce myself, I'll tell you a little bit about my work and about where I come from. I'm basically a community organizer, like a lot of you. I returned to the White Earth Reservation about ten years ago after being raised off-reservation, which is a common circumstance for our people. I then began to work on the land issue, trying to win back or buy back our reservation lands. In our community I am identified as Muckwuck or Bear clan, Mississippi band, Anishinabeg. That's my place in the universe. The headwaters of the Mississippi are on our reservation; where the river starts is where we are in the world.

Anishinabeg is our name for ourselves in our own language; it means "people." We are called Ojibways in Canada and Chippewas in the United States. Our aboriginal territory, and where we live today, is in the northern part of five American states and the southern part of four Canadian provinces.

It's in the center of the continent and is called the Wild Rice Bowl or the Great Lakes region. Today we are probably the single largest native population in North America: there are at least two hundred and fifty thousand of us. We're on both sides of the border, and most people don't know who we are or know much about us. That ignorance stems in part from the way Americans are taught about native people.

There are about seven hundred different native communities in North America. Roughly one hundred are Ojibway or Anishinabeg communities, but we're different bands. In Alaska there are two hundred native communities; in California there are eighty. In Washington State there are fourteen different kinds of Indian people living on the Yakima Reservation alone. All different kinds of indigenous people live in North America—all culturally and historically diverse. The same situation is found on a larger scale when you look at the entire continent, the Western Hemisphere, and the world. I want you to rethink the geography of North America in terms of cultural geography, in terms of land occupancy.

Now, if you look at the United States, about 4 percent of the land is held by Indian people. That is the extent of today's Indian reservations. The Southwest has the largest native population, and there's a significant population on the Great Plains. In northern Minnesota there are seven big reservations, all Ojibway or Anishinabeg. But if you go to Canada, about 85 percent of the population north of the fiftieth parallel is native. So if you look at it in terms of land occupancy and geography, in about two-thirds of Canada the majority of the population is native. I'm not even including Nunevat, which is an Inuit-controlled area the size of India in what used to be called the Northwest Territories.

If you look at the whole of North America, you find that the majority of the population is native in about a third of the continent. Within this larger area, indigenous people maintain their own ways of living and their cultural practices. This is our view of the continent, and it is different from the view of most other North Americans. When *we* look at the United States and Canada, we see our reservations and reserves as islands in the continent. When Indian people talk about their travels, they often mention reservations rather than cities: "I went to Rosebud, and then I went over to North Cheyenne." This is the indigenous view of North America.

Going beyond North America, I want to talk about the Western Hemisphere and the world from an indigenous perspective. My intent is to present you with an indigenous worldview and our perception of the world. There are a number of countries in the Western Hemisphere in which native peoples are the majority of the population: in Guatemala, Ecuador, Peru, Bolivia. In some South American countries we control as much as 22 to 40 percent of the land. Overall, the Western Hemisphere is not predominantly white. Indigenous people continue their ways of living based on generations and generations of knowledge and practice on the land.

On a worldwide scale there are about five thousand nations and a hundred and seventy states. Nations are groups of indigenous peoples who share common language, culture, history, territory, and government institutions. That is how international law defines a nation. And that is who *we* are: nations of people who have existed for thousands of years. There are about a hundred and seventy—maybe more now, about a hundred and eighty-five—states that are recognized by the United Nations. For the most part, these states are the result of colonial empires or colonial demarcations. And whereas indigenous nations have existed for thousands of years, many of the states in existence at the end of the twentieth century have been around only since World War II. That is a big difference. Yet the dominant worldview of industrial society is determined by these young states, not by the five thousand ancient nations.

The estimated number of indigenous people in the world depends on how you define indigenous people. It is said that there are currently about five hundred million of us in the world today, including such peoples as the Tibetans, the Masai, the Wara Wara, and the Quechua. I define indigenous peoples as those who have continued their way of living for thousands of years according to their original instructions.

That is a quick background on indigenous people. It should help you 10 understand that my perspective, the perspective of indigenous peoples, is entirely different from that of the dominant society in this country.

Indigenous peoples believe fundamentally in natural law and a state of balance. We believe that all societies and cultural practices must exist in accordance with natural law in order to be sustainable. We also believe that cultural diversity is as essential as biological diversity to maintaining sustainable societies. Indigenous peoples have lived on earth sustainably for thousands of years, and I suggest to you that indigenous ways of living are the only sustainable ways of living. Because of that, I believe there is something to be learned from indigenous thinking and indigenous ways. I don't think many of you would argue that industrial society is sustainable. I think that in two or three hundred years this society will be extinct because a society based on conquest cannot survive when there's nothing left to conquer.

Indigenous people have taken great care to fashion their societies in accordance with natural law, which is the highest law. It is superior to the laws made by nations, states, and municipalities. It is the law to which we are all accountable. There are no Twelve Commandments of natural law, but there are some things that I believe to be true about natural law. And this is my experience from listening to a lot of our older people. What I am telling you is not really my opinion; it's based on what has happened in our community, on what I've heard people say, and on their knowledge. We have noticed that much in nature is cyclical: the movements of moons, the tides, the seasons, our bodies. Time itself, in most indigenous worldviews, is cyclical. We also have experienced and believe that it is our essential nature and our need always to keep a balance in nature. Most indigenous ceremonies, if you look to their essence, are about the restoration of balance. That is our intent: to restore, and then to retain, balance. Nature itself continually tries to balance, to equalize.

According to our way of living and our way of looking at the world, most of the world is animate. This is reflected in our language, Anishinabemowin, in which most nouns are animate. *Mandamin*, the word for corn, is animate; *mitig*, the word for tree, is animate; so is the word for rice, *manomin*, and the word for rock or stone, *asin*. Looking at the world and seeing that most things are alive, we have come to believe, based on this perception, that they have spirit. They have standing on their own. Therefore, when I harvest wild rice on our reservation up north, I always offer *asemah*, tobacco, because when you take something, you must always give thanks to its spirit for giving itself to you, for it has a choice whether to give itself to you or not. In our cultural practice, for instance, it is not because of skill that a hunter can harvest a deer or a caribou; it is because he or she has been honorable and has given *asemah*. That is how you are able to harvest, not because you are a good hunter but because the animal gives itself to you. That is our perception.

And so we are always very careful when we harvest. Anthropologists call this reciprocity, which means something anthropological, I guess. But from our perspective it means that when you take, you always give. This is about balance and equalness. We also say that when you take, you must take only what you need and leave the rest. Because if you take more than you need, that means you are greedy. You have brought about imbalance, you have been selfish. To do this in our community is a very big disgrace. It is a violation of natural law, and it leaves you with no guarantee that you will be able to continue harvesting.

We have a word in our language that describes the practice of living in 15 harmony with natural law: *minobimaatisiiwin*. This word describes how you live your life according to natural law, how you behave as an individual in relationship with other individuals and in relationship with the land and all the things that are animate on the land. *Minobimaatisiiwin* is our cultural practice; it is what you strive towards as an individual as well as collectively as a society.

We have tried to retain this way of living and of thinking in spite of all that has happened to us over the centuries. I believe we do retain most of these practices to a great extent in many of our societies. In our community they are overshadowed at times by industrialism, but they still exist.

I would like to contrast what I've told you about indigenous thinking with what I call "industrial thinking." I think the Lakota have the best term to describe it. It actually refers to white people, although they are not the only ones who think this way. Indigenous peoples have interesting terms for white people: they are usually not just words, they are descriptions encapsulated in a word. I will tell you about one: the Lakota word for a white person is *wasichu*. It derives from the first time the Lakota ever saw a white person. There was a white man out on the prairie in the Black Hills, and he was starving. He came into a Lakota camp in the middle of the night, and the Lakota of course were astonished to see him. They began to watch him to see what he was doing. He went over to the food, took something, and ran away. A little while later, the Lakota looked to see what he had taken: he had stolen a large amount of fat. So the Lakota word for a white person, *wasichu*, means "he who steals the fat." Now, that is a description that doesn't necessarily have to do with white people, but taking more than you need has to do with industrial society. He who steals the fat. That's what I'm talking about when I refer to the industrial worldview.

Industrial thinking is characterized by several ideas that run counter to indigenous ideas. First, instead of believing that natural law is preeminent, industrial society believes that humans are entitled to full dominion over nature. It believes that man—and it *is* usually man of course—has some God-given right to all that is around him, that he has been created superior to the rest.

Second, instead of modeling itself on the cyclical structure of nature, this society is patterned on linear thinking. I went all the way through its school system, and I remember how time, for example, is taught in this society. It's taught on a timeline, usually one that begins around 1492. It has some dates on it that were important to someone, although I could never figure out to whom. The timeline is a clear representation of this society's linear way of thinking. And certain values permeate this way of thinking, such as the concept of progress. Industrial society wants to keep making progress as it moves down the timeline, progress defined by things like technological advancement and economic growth. This value accompanies linear thinking.

Third, there is the attitude toward what is wild as opposed to what is cul-   20 tivated or "tame." This society believes it must tame the wilderness. It also believes in the superiority of civilized over primitive peoples, a belief that also follows a linear model: that somehow, over time, people will become more civilized. Also related of course is the idea behind colonialism: that some people have the *right* to civilize other people. My experience is that people who are viewed as "primitive" are generally people of color, and people who are viewed as "civilized" are those of European descent. This prejudice still permeates industrial society and in fact even permeates "progressive" thinking. It holds that somehow people of European descent are smarter—they have some better knowledge of the world than the rest of us. I suggest that this is perhaps a racist worldview and that it has racist implications. That is, in fact, our experience.

Fourth, industrial society speaks a language of inanimate nouns. Even words for the land are becoming inanimate. Jerry Mander discusses this idea when he talks about the "commodification of the sacred." Industrial language has changed things from being animate, alive, and having spirit to being inanimate, mere objects and commodities of society. When things are inanimate, "man" can view them as his God-given right. He can take them, commodify them, and manipulate them in society. This behavior is also related to the linear way of thinking.

Fifth, the last aspect of industrial thinking I'm going to talk about (although it's always unpopular to question it in America) is the idea of capitalism itself. In this country we are taught that capitalism is a system that combines labor, capital, and resources for the purpose of accumulation. The capitalist goal is to use the least labor, capital, and resources to accumulate the most profit. The intent of capitalism is accumulation. So the capitalist's method is always to take more than is needed. Therefore, from an indigenous point of view capitalism is inherently out of harmony with natural law.

Based on this goal of accumulation, industrial society practices conspicuous consumption. Indigenous societies, on the other hand, practice what I would call "conspicuous distribution." We focus on the potlatch, the giveaway, an event that carries much more honor than accumulation does. In fact, the more you give away, the greater your honor. We make a great deal of these giveaways, and industrial society has something to learn from them.

Over the past five hundred years the indigenous experience has been one of conflict between the indigenous and the industrial worldviews. This conflict has manifested itself as holocaust. That is our experience. Indigenous people understand clearly that this society, which has caused the extinction of more species in the past hundred and fifty years than the total species extinction from the Ice Age to the mid-nineteenth century, is the same society that has caused the extinction of about two thousand different indigenous peoples in the Western Hemisphere alone. We understand intimately the relationship between extinction of species and extinction of peoples, because we experience both. And the extinction continues. Last year alone the Bureau of Indian Affairs, which has legal responsibility for people like myself—legally, I'm a ward of the federal government—declared nineteen different indigenous nations in North America extinct. The rate of extinction in the Amazon rainforest, for example, has been one indigenous people per year since 1900. And if you look at world maps showing cultural and biological distribution, you find that where there is the most cultural diversity, there is also the most biological diversity. A direct relationship exists between the two. That is why we argue that cultural diversity is as important to a sustainable global society as biological diversity.

Our greatest problem with all of this in America is that there has been no 25 recognition of the cultural extinction, no owning up to it, no atonement for what happened, and no education about it. When I ask people how many different kinds of Indians they can identify, they can name scarcely any. America's mythology is based on the denial of the native—of native humanity, even of native existence. Nobody admits that the holocaust took place. This is because the white settlers believed they had a God-given right to the continent, and anyone with this right wouldn't recognize what happened as holocaust. Yet it was a holocaust of unparalleled proportions: Bartholomew de Las Casas and other contemporaries of Columbus estimated that fifty million indigenous people in the Western Hemisphere perished in a sixty-year period. In terms of millions of people, this was probably the largest holocaust in world history.

Now, it is not appropriate for me to say that my holocaust was worse than someone else's. But it is absolutely correct for me to demand that my holocaust be recognized. And that has not happened in America. Instead, nobody knows anything about us, not even educated people. Why? Because this system is based on a denial of our existence. We are erased from the public consciousness because if you have no victim, you have no crime. As I said, most Americans can hardly name a single Indian nation. Those who can are only able to name those that have been featured in television Westerns: Comanche, Cheyenne, Navajo, Sioux, Crow. The only image of a native that is widely recognized in this society is the one shown in Westerns, which is a caricature. It is a portrayal created in Hollywood or in cartoons or more recently to a minimal degree in "New Age" paraphernalia. In this society we do not exist as full human beings with human rights, with the same rights to self-determination, to dignity, and to land—to territorial integrity—that other people have.

The challenge that people of conscience in this country face is to undo and debunk the mythology, to come clean, become honest, understand the validity of our demands, and recognize our demands. People must see the interlocking interests between their own ability to survive and indigenous peoples' continuing cultural sustainability. Indigenous peoples have lived sustainably in this land for thousands of years. I am absolutely sure that our societies could live without yours, but I'm not so sure that your society can continue to live without ours. This is why indigenous people need to be recognized now and included in the discussion of the issues affecting this country's future.

I'd like to tell you now about indigenous peoples' efforts to protect our land and restore our communities. All across this continent there are native peoples—in small communities with populations of one hundred, five hundred, even five thousand—who are trying to regain control of their community and their territory. I could tell you many stories of these different struggles, but I'll use my own community as an example. Here is our story.

The White Earth Reservation, located at the headwaters of the Mississippi, is thirty-six by thirty-six miles square, which is about 837,000 acres. It is very good land. A treaty reserved it for our people in 1867 in return for relinquishing a much larger area of northern Minnesota. Of all our territory, we chose this land for its richness and diversity. There are forty-seven lakes on the reservation. There's maple sugar; there are hardwoods and all the different medicine plants my people use—our reservation is called "the medicine chest of the Ojibways." We have wild rice; we have deer; we have beaver; we have fish—every food we need. On the eastern part of the reservation there are stands of white pine. On the part farthest west there used to be buffalo, but this area is now farmland, situated in the Red River Valley. That is our area, the land reserved to us under treaty.

Our traditional forms of land use and ownership are similar to those of a 30 community land trust. The land is owned collectively, and we have individual or, more often, family-based usufruct rights: each family has traditional areas where it fishes and hunts. In our language the words *Anishinabeg akiing* describe the concept of land ownership. They translate as "the land of the people," which doesn't infer that we own our land but that we belong on it. Our definition doesn't stand up well in court, unfortunately, because this country's legal system upholds the concept of private property.

Our community enforces its traditional practices by adhering to *minobimaatisiiwin*. Historically, this involved punishing people who transgressed these rules. For instance, in our community the worst punishment historically—we didn't have jails—was banishment. That still exists in our community to a certain extent. Just imagine if the worst punishment in industrial society were banishment! With us, each person wants to be part of the community.

We have also maintained our practices by means of careful management and observation. For example, we have "hunting bosses" and "rice chiefs," who make sure that resources are used sustainably in each region. Hunting bosses oversee trap-line rotation, a system by which people trap in an area for two years and then move to a different area to let the land rest. Rice chiefs coordinate wild rice harvesting. The rice on each lake is unique: each has its own taste and ripens at its own time. We also have a "tally man," who makes sure there are enough animals for each family in a given area. If a family can't sustain itself, the tally man moves them to a new place where animals are more plentiful. These practices are sustainable.

My children's grandfather, who is a trapper, lives on wild animals in the wintertime. When he intends to trap beavers, he reaches his hand into a beaver house and counts how many beavers are in there. (Beavers are not carnivorous; they won't bite.) By counting, he knows how many beavers he can take. Of course, he has to count only if he hasn't already been observing that beaver house for a long time. This is a very sustainable way to trap, one based on a kind of thorough observation that can come only with residency. Further, I suggest that this man knows more about his ecosystem than any PhD scholar who studies it from the university.

As I have indicated, the White Earth Reservation is a rich place. And it is our experience that industrial society is not content to leave other peoples' riches alone. Wealth attracts colonialism: the more a native people has, the more colonizers are apt to covet that wealth and take it away—whether it is gold or, as in our case, pine stands and Red River Valley farmland. A Latin American scholar named Eduardo Galeano has written about colonialism in communities like mine. He says: "In the colonial to neo-colonial alchemy, gold changes to scrap metal and food to poison. We have become painfully aware of the mortality of wealth, which nature bestows and imperialism appropriates." For us, our wealth was the source of our poverty: industrial society could not leave us be.

Our reservation was created by treaty in 1867; in 1887 the General 35 Allotment Act was passed on the national level, not only to teach Indians the concept of private property but also to facilitate the removal of more land from Indian Nations. The federal government divided our reservation into eighty-acre parcels of land and allotted each parcel to an individual Indian, hoping that through this change we would somehow become yeoman farmers, adopt the notion of progress, and become civilized. But the allotment system had no connection to our traditional land tenure patterns. In our society a person harvested rice in one place, trapped in another place, got medicines in a third place, and picked berries in a fourth. These locations depended on the ecosystem; they were not necessarily contiguous. But the government said to each Indian, "Here are your eighty acres; this is where you'll live." Then, after each Indian had received an allotment, the rest of the land was declared "surplus" and given to white people to homestead. On our reservation almost the entire land base was allotted except for some pinelands that were annexed by the state of Minnesota and sold to timber companies. What happened to my reservation happened to reservations all across the country.

The federal government was legally responsible for this; they turned our land into individual eighty-acre parcels, and then they looked the other way and let the state of Minnesota take some of our land and tax what was left. When the Indians couldn't pay the taxes, the state confiscated the land. How could these people pay taxes? In 1900 or 1910 they could not read or write English.

I'll tell you a story about how my great-grandma was cheated by a loan shark. She lived on Many Point Lake, where her allotment was. She had a bill at the local store, the Fairbanks grocery store, and she had run it up because she was waiting until fall when she could get some money from trapping or from a treaty annuity. So she went to a land speculator named Lucky Waller, and she said, "I need to pay this bill." She asked to borrow fifty bucks from him until treaty payment time, and he said: "Okay, you can do that. Just sign here and I'll loan you that fifty bucks." So she signed with her thumbprint and went back to her house on Many Point Lake. About three months later she came in to repay him the fifty bucks, and the loan shark said: "No, you keep that money; I bought land from you instead." He had purchased her eighty acres on Many Point Lake for fifty bucks. Today that location is a Boy Scout camp.

This story could be retold again and again in our communities. It is a story of land speculation, greed, and unconscionable contracts, and it exemplifies the process by which native peoples were dispossessed of their land. The White Earth Reservation lost two hundred and fifty thousand acres to the state of Minnesota because of unpaid taxes. And this was done to native peoples across the country: on a national average reservations lost a full two-thirds of their land this way.

By 1920, 99 percent of original White Earth Reservation lands were in non-Indian hands. By 1930 many of our people had died from tuberculosis and other diseases, and half of our remaining population lived off-reservation. Three generations of our people were forced into poverty, chased off our land, and made refugees in this society. Now a lot of our people live in Minneapolis. Of twenty thousand tribal members only four or five thousand live on reservation. That's because we're refugees, not unlike other people in this society.

Our struggle is to get our land back. That's what we've been trying to 40
do for a hundred years. By 1980, 93 percent of our reservation was still held by
non-Indians. That's the circumstance we are in at the end of the twentieth
century. We have exhausted all legal recourse for getting back our land. If you
look at the legal system in this country, you will find that it is based on the idea
that Christians have a God-given right to dispossess heathens of their land.
This attitude goes back to a papal bull of the fifteenth or sixteenth century declaring that Christians have a superior right to land over heathens. The implication for native people is that we have no legal right to our land in the United
States or in Canada. The only legal recourse we have in the United States is
the Indian Claims Commission, which pays you for land; it doesn't return land
to you. It compensates you at the 1910 market value for land that was seized.
The Black Hills Settlement is one example. It's lauded as a big settlement—
one that gives all this money to the Indians—but it's only a hundred and six
million dollars for five states. That's the full legal recourse for Indian people.

In the case of our own reservation, we had the same problem. The
Supreme Court ruled that to regain their land Indian people had to have filed
a lawsuit within seven years of the original time of taking. Now, legally we
are all people who are wards of the federal government. I have a federal enrollment number. Anything to do with the internal matters of Indian governments is subject to the approval of the Secretary of the Interior. So the federal
government, which is legally responsible for our land, watched its misman-
agement and did not file any lawsuits on our behalf. The courts are now declaring that the statute of limitations has expired for the Indian people, who,
when their land was taken, could not read or write English, had no money or
access to attorneys to file suit, and were the legal wards of the state. We have
therefore, the courts claim, exhausted our legal recourse and have no legal
standing in the court system. That is what has happened in this country with
regard to Indian land issues.

We have fought federal legislation for a decade without success. Yet we
look at the situation on reservation and realize that we must get our land
back. We do not really have any other place to go. That's why we started the
White Earth Land Recovery Project.

The federal, state, and county governments are the largest landholders
on the reservation. It is good land still, rich in many things; however, when
you do not control your land, you do not control your destiny. That's our
experience. What has happened is that two-thirds of the deer taken on our
reservation are taken by non-Indians, mostly by sports hunters from Minneapolis. In the Tamarac National Wildlife Refuge nine times as many deer
are taken by non-Indians as by Indians, because that's where sports hunters
from Minneapolis come to hunt. Ninety percent of the fish taken on our
reservation is taken by white people, and most of them are taken by people
from Minneapolis who come to their summer cabins and fish on our reservation. Each year in our region, about ten thousand acres are being clear cut for

paper and pulp in one county alone, mostly by the Potlatch Timber Company. We are watching the destruction of our ecosystem and the theft of our resources; in not controlling our land we are unable to control what is happening to our ecosystem. So we are struggling to regain control through the White Earth Land Recovery Project.

Our project is like several others in Indian communities. We are not trying to displace people who have settled there. A third of our land is held by the federal, state, and county governments. That land should just be returned to us. It certainly would not displace anyone. And then we have to ask the question about absentee land ownership. It is an ethical question that should be asked in this country. A third of the *privately* held land on our reservation is held by absentee landholders: they do not see that land, do not know it, and do not even know where it is. We ask these people how they feel about owning land on a reservation, hoping we can persuade them to return it.

Approximately sixty years ago in India the Gramdan movement dealt 45 with similar issues. Some million acres were placed in village trust as a result of the moral influence of Vinoba Bhave. The whole issue of absentee land ownership needs to be addressed—particularly in America, where the idea of private property is so sacred, where somehow it is ethical to hold land that you never see. As Vinoba said, "It is highly inconsistent that those who possess land should not till it themselves, and those who cultivate should possess no land to do so."

Our project also acquires land. It owns about nine hundred acres right now. We bought some land as a site for a roundhouse, a building that holds one of our ceremonial drums. We bought back our burial grounds, which were on private land, because we believe that we should hold the land our ancestors lived on. These are all small parcels of land. We also just bought a farm, a fifty-eight-acre organic raspberry farm. In a couple of years we hope to get past the "You Pick" stage into jam production. It is a very slow process, but our strategy is based on this recovery of the land and of our cultural and economic practices.

We are a poor community. People look at our reservation and comment on the 85 percent unemployment—they do not realize what we do with our time. They have no way of valuing our cultural practices. For instance, 85 percent of our people hunt, taking at least one or two deer annually, probably in violation of federal game laws; 75 percent of our people hunt for small game and geese; 50 percent of our people fish by net; 50 percent of our people sugarbush and garden on our reservation. About the same percentage harvest wild rice, not just for themselves; they harvest it to sell. About half of our people produce handcrafts. There is no way to quantify this in America. It is called the "invisible economy" or the "domestic economy." Society views us as unemployed Indians who need wage-earning jobs. That is not how we view ourselves. Our work is about strengthening and restoring our traditional economy. I have seen our people trained and retrained for off-reservation jobs that do not exist. I don't know how many Indians have gone through three or four carpenter and plumber training programs. It doesn't do any good if, after the third or fourth time, you still don't have a job.

Our strategy is to strengthen our own traditional economy (thereby strengthening our traditional culture as well) so that we can produce 50 percent or more of our own food, which we then won't need to buy elsewhere, and can eventually produce enough surplus to sell. In our case most of our surplus is in wild rice. We are rich in terms of wild rice. The Creator, Gitchi Manitu, gave us wild rice — said we should eat it and should share it; we have traded it for thousands of years. A lot of our political struggle is, I am absolutely sure, due to the fact that Gitchi Manitu did not give wild rice to Uncle Ben to grow in California. Commercial wild rice is totally different from the rice we harvest, and it decreases the value of our rice when marketed as authentic wild rice.

We've been working for several years now to increase the price of the rice we gather from fifty cents per pound to a dollar per pound, green. We are trying to market our rice ourselves. We try to capture the "value added" in our community by selling it ourselves. We went from about five thousand pounds of production on our reservation to about fifty thousand pounds last year. This is our strategy for economic recovery.

Other parts of our strategy include language immersion programs to re- 50 store our language and revival of drum ceremonies to restore our cultural practices. These are part of an integrated restoration process that is focused on the full human being.

In the larger picture, in Wisconsin and Minnesota our community is working hard to exercise specific treaty rights. Under the 1847 treaty, we have reserved-use rights to a much larger area than just our reservations. These are called extraterritorial treaty rights. We didn't say we were going to live there, we just said we wanted to keep the right to use that land in our usual and accustomed ways. This has led us to a larger political strategy, for although our harvesting practices are sustainable, they require an almost pristine ecosystem in order to take as much fish and grow as much rice as we need. To achieve this condition the tribes are entering into a comanagement agreement in northern Wisconsin and northern Minnesota to prevent further environmental degradation as a first step toward preserving an extraterritorial area in accordance with treaty rights.

There are many similar stories all across North America. A lot can be learned from these stories, and we can share a great deal in terms of your strategies and what you're trying to do in your own communities. I see this as a relationship among people who share common issues, common ground, and common agendas. It is absolutely crucial, however, that our struggle for territorial integrity and economic and political control of our lands not be regarded as a threat by this society. Deep-set in settler minds I know there's fear of the Indian having control. I've seen it on my own reservation: white people who live there are deathly afraid of our gaining control over half our land base, which is all we're trying to do. I'm sure they are afraid we will treat them as badly as they have treated us. I ask you to shake off your fear.

There's something valuable to be learned from our experiences, from the James Bay hydroelectric project in Quebec, for example, and from the Shoshone sisters in Nevada fighting the missile siting. Our stories are about people with a great deal of tenacity and courage, people who have been resisting for centuries. We are sure that if we do not resist, we will not survive. Our resistance will guarantee our children a future. In our society we think ahead to the seventh generation; however, we know that the ability of the seventh generation to sustain itself will be dependent on our ability to resist now.

Another important consideration is that traditional ecological knowledge is unheard knowledge in this country's institutions. Nor is it something an anthropologist can extract by mere research. Traditional ecological knowledge is passed from generation to generation; it is not an appropriate subject for a PhD dissertation. We who live by this knowledge have the intellectual property rights to it, and we have the right to tell our stories ourselves. There is a lot to be learned from our knowledge, but you need us in order to learn it, whether it is the story of my children's grandfather reaching his hand into that beaver house or of the Haida up on the Northwest coast, who make totem poles and plank houses. The Haida say they can take a plank off a tree and still leave the tree standing. If Weyerhaeuser could do that, I might listen to them, but they cannot.

Traditional ecological knowledge is absolutely essential for the future. 55 Crafting a relationship between us is absolutely essential. Native people are not quite at the table in the environmental movement—for example, in the management of the Great Plains. Environmental groups and state governors sat down and talked about how to manage the Great Plains, and nobody asked the Indians to come to the table. Nobody even noticed that there are about fifty million acres of Indian land out there in the middle of the Great Plains, land that according to history and law has never yet had a drink of water—that is, reservations have been denied water all these years because of water diversion projects. When water allocations are being discussed, someone needs to talk about how the tribes need a drink.

One proposal for the Great Plains is a Buffalo Commons, which would include one hundred and ten prairie counties that are now financially bankrupt and are continuing to lose people. The intent is to restore these lands ecologically, bringing back the buffalo, the perennial crops, and indigenous prairie grasses that Wes Jackson is experimenting with. I think we need to broaden the idea, though, because I don't think it should be just a Buffalo Commons; I think it should be an Indigenous Commons. If you look at the 1993 population in the area, you'll find that the majority are indigenous peoples who already hold at least fifty million acres of the land. We know this land of our ancestors, and we should rightly be part of a sustainable future for it.

Another thing I want to touch on is the necessity of shifting our perception. There is no such thing as sustainable development. Community is the only thing in my experience that is sustainable. We all need to be involved in building sustainable communities. We can each do that in our own way—whether it is European American communities or Dené communities or Anishinabeg communities—returning to and restoring the way of life that is based on the land. To achieve this restoration we need to reintegrate with cultural traditions informed by the land. That is something I don't know how to tell you to do, but it is something you're going to need to do. Garrett Hardin and others are saying that the only way you can manage a commons is if you share enough cultural experiences and cultural values so that you can keep your practices in order and in check: *minobimaatisiiwin*. The reason we have remained sustainable for all these centuries is that we are cohesive communities. A common set of values is needed to live together sustainably on the land.

Finally, I believe the issues deep in this society that need to be addressed are structural. This is a society that continues to consume too much of the world's resources. You know, when you consume this much in resources, it means constant intervention in other peoples' land and countries, whether it is mine or whether it is the Crees' up in James Bay or someone else's. It is meaningless to talk about human rights unless you talk about consumption. And that's a structural change we all need to address. It is clear that in order for native communities to live, the dominant society must change, because if this society continues in the direction it is going, our reservations and our way of life will continue to bear the consequences. This society has to be changed! We have to be able to put aside its cultural baggage, which is industrial baggage. It's not sustainable. Do not be afraid of discarding it. That's the only way we're going to make peace between the settler and the native.

Miigwech. I want to thank you for your time. *Keewaydahn.* It's our way home.

WHAT DOES SHE SAY?

1. Before you begin this essay, write a paragraph that talks about what it would mean to "find your place."

2. Read the second paragraph. You'll see near its end the sentence, "That's my place in the universe." Write a paragraph about your place in the universe—or write about how you're not yet sure of your place in the universe. Once you've written this paragraph, write another comparing yourself to LaDuke. Do you find describing your place in the universe a relatively straightforward effort?

3. Find two places in the essay where you can see that LaDuke's outlook contrasts significantly with the America that you see represented in television or magazine advertisements.

4. What does LaDuke mean when she speaks of "home"? Find two passages that help you answer this question.

WHAT DO YOU THINK?

5. Americans are often of two minds about their identification with their ethnic and cultural heritage. What do you think of LaDuke's connection to her community? Is it similar to yours?

6. What native peoples live (or once lived) near where you live now? What do you know of their history? What does research about them help you understand about LaDuke's essay?

7. "Voices from White Earth" announces itself as being about *keewaydahn,* or "going home." Is your sense of "home" similar to LaDuke's? What essay would you write about "going home," and how would it compare with LaDuke's?

WHAT WOULD THEY SAY?

8. Both Winona LaDuke and Barbara Kingsolver, in "Stone Soup" (p. 64), speak of "community." Look at each essay and make note of how each defines this idea. Do the definitions overlap? Contrast? Presuming that they are not precisely identical, how would you account for the differences?

9. What assumptions and claims about community does LaDuke make? How would they agree or disagree with those made by Garrett Hardin in "Lifeboat Ethics: The Case against Helping the Poor" (p. 130)? Write an essay that tries to make that comparison fairly and fully. Then end by coming to your own conclusions.

JOHN DANIELS
The Authentic Trail

WHAT HAPPENS when we feel unconnected to home, ethnicity, or family? For John Daniels (b. 1948), it means feeling as if nothing in his life has direction. He is someone at once free and adrift. Thus, all the questions already at work in this chapter seem not to apply to him. Only via the intense physical and mental challenge of a rock-climbing experience is this narrator able to break through to what he calls "the authentic trail."

A former Stegner Fellow at Stanford University, John Daniels has twice won the Oregon Book Award for nonfiction. His works include The Trail Home *(1992),* Looking After: A Son's Memoir *(1996), and* Winter Creek: One Writer's Natural History *(2002), from which "The Authentic Trail" is excerpted.*

A young man is a dangerous thing, says a friend of mine who once was one. Being a young man of good breeding and some manners, I directed against myself most of the danger I generated. I rode a motorcycle, a BSA Lightning, despite ditching it in a Portlander's begonia bed the first time I mounted it and ditching it several times thereafter. I liked the power, the rush of air, just as I liked the powerful rush of methamphetamine when it hit my system. No longer was I taking drugs for anything as nuanced as personal insight or spiritual vision. I wanted euphoria. I wanted to feel *right*. I was out in the world, but the world was not confirming me. I lived with friends in San Francisco, worked at various jobs, dabbled in Zen meditation, protested the draft and the Vietnam War, joined encounter groups, took sporadic college courses and more drugs. Nothing I did seemed to lead anywhere or to fit with anything else — a ramshackle life, and it was not at all clear who was living it.

The recurrent thread, the authentic trail I kept losing and finding again, was climbing. I bought a rack of pitons and rode my motorcycle to Yosemite, where I hung around Camp Four, the climbers' camp, long enough to work up my courage and ask a veteran if he needed a partner that morning. It happened that he did, and so he and eventually others led me onto the bright granite faces. I reveled in the rock's speckled polish, its tiny fingerholds and clean jam cracks, its rich flinty smell in sun warmth, its arched and pinnacled music always rising. I learned technique, pushed myself, began to lead some pitches and scrape up against my limits as a rock climber. I watched others making moves I couldn't do and envied them, but more than their climbing prowess I envied how they were with themselves, how some of them, only a few years older than me, had an ease about them, a fluid and deliberate way, a habit of being in no hurry and sure in every move.

I met a guy of about my own ability, a chemistry grad student at Cal, and we put ourselves to work on weekends practicing for a big wall. We chose the Chouinard-Herbert route on Sentinel Rock, a 1,700-foot line that climbers now scamper up in a few hours. In our primitive era, it was usually done in two days. Early one July morning in 1972, Ted and I scrambled up the brushy scree slope and easy fourth-class pitches, then hit the first roped pitch on the wall itself just as the sun hit us. We weren't bad, we discovered, but we were slow. Wall climbing, as then practiced, was cumbersome. One man led, climbing free where he could, standing in slings where he couldn't, pounding pitons into cracks up the hot vertical granite to a ledge or maybe just a place to hang. He secured himself, drank a quart of water wishing it were a gallon, and went to work raising the haul bag—the climber's equivalent of a steamer trunk—as his partner followed the pitch on a fixed rope, recovering the hardware. Then the partner leapfrogged ahead, at the same plodding pace, up the next pitch. It was an exercise in vertical freight hauling, a laborious raising of bodily mass and the mass of stuff that bodies must have to sustain themselves through two scorching days of hauling mass.

All day we'd been hearing snatches of speech and laughter floating down from a climbing party somewhere on the upper wall. Now came a shout. Something dark was dropping fast out of the brilliance of stone and sky, ripping the air with the sound of an erratic helicopter prop as I crammed myself against the face. The thing had hit the slope five hundred feet down and burst into pieces before I registered what it had been—a pack or a haul bag, crammed full.

"I thought it was a body," said Ted when he reached my belay ledge.   5

"I did too," I said.

Climbing is a spell, strenuously cast. Rope and hardware, hands and feet, simple will. If the spell breaks, there's only gravity.

It was dusk when we finished the last pitch to the bivouac ledge, which was big enough for two to semistretch out and smelled of human shit. Not that we cared. We spent the evening each drinking water and watching the other drink water. Watching like hawks.

"Better save the rest for tomorrow," Ted observed, finishing a long glug.

"Right," I agreed. "We'll need it." I reached for one of the last few   10 quarts and drank half of it. Ted drank the rest of his bottle. We might as well have been discussing foreign policy.

We ate everything in the haul bag that contained a drop of moisture— oranges, a can of corn, a memorable warm cucumber that we snatched from each other's grasp and devoured in big chomps. A thousand feet below, a few lights of sanity moved on the valley floor.

We awoke to pale dawn, the smell of sewage, and the need to move on. Our last swig of water was gone by midmorning. The climbing wasn't especially tough, but the afternoon was a cauldron. We knew it was dumb time, mistake time. We reminded each other to concentrate, to tie the knots right, to place plenty of protection. The last hard pitch was a bulging overhang of semidetached slabs dubbed the Afro-Cuban Flakes by Chouinard and Herbert, far better climbers than we, who had evidently had the time and good humor—and the water—to pause during their first ascent to draw music from the slabs with their hammers. The pitch seemed to take us hours and probably did. As Ted made the lead I watched inner-tubers float the Merced River in the green valley a quarter of a mile beneath me. When he reached the belay point I followed on the fixed rope, swinging wildly over the void as I carelessly unclipped the rope from one after another of the expansion bolts the first ascenders had pounded in to surmount the overhang.

Ted was belaying from a huge ledge. Above, it looked like easy ledge scrambling to the top. The sun was down. We decided to rest briefly, then climb up and over the top and down the easy gully behind Sentinel until we came to water. It would be dark, but we had a flashlight.

An hour later we were still sitting. Moving had turned out to be unlikely. We ate what we could get down without water and fell asleep where we were. My tongue felt huge, my mouth dry as the granite I lay on. Slow, fluent colors, vivid reds and purples, moved through me all night, not dreams exactly but a kind of hallucinatory tide. I felt empty, weightless. Ted's voice called me to daylight. We packed quickly and clambered up the easy ledges. At the top of Sentinel stood a solitary ponderosa pine, its bark a vibrant orange with black furrows, tigerish, its crown of boughs shot with sun. The tree glowed, seethed in my vision, as if it could not contain its own bright being. As Ted went ahead I stumbled to the pine and pressed my forehead to its trunk, breathing its hot vanillic aura. I took a flake of bark shaped like a puzzle piece.

We slid and scrambled down the dry gully, telling each other to slow 15 down and be careful as we both slid faster, slipping and scraping ourselves, breathing mouthfuls of dust. Where the gully opened onto the scree slope, a little stream flowed through grass and shrubs and horsetails so green they hurt my eyes. We dumped our packs and knelt in the stream and lifted spilling handfuls to our mouths. It burned like cold fire inside me. My heart skittered, beat double a few times, settled to a steady boom. We wet our hair, rubbed the grime from our hands and faces, laughed, chattered like children. The stream flowed from its high hidden springs, lively, clear, unmeasured, and free.

WHAT DOES HE SAY?

1. Assume that the first paragraph sets up a problem and that the second one begins to offer a solution to the problem. What's the problem? How would you phrase it in your own words?

2. As you read, make a running list of terms that pertain specifically to rock climbing. After each one, write a quick definition. If you're not sure what something means, take a guess at it.

3. Why does the narrator endure all of the trouble that rock climbing entails?

4. What portion of this piece stands out as particularly clear writing? Find a paragraph or cluster of sentences that fits this characterization and write a paragraph that explains what makes this writing so successful.

5. Write a paragraph about a time when you knew some joy or happiness similar to that which Daniels and his climbing partner feel at the end of this essay.

WHAT DO YOU THINK?

6. The earlier selections in this chapter have addressed the question "Where Are You Coming From?" on the basis of family, cultural and ethnic heritage, and sense of community. Do those factors play any role here? Or is this narrator finding his identity in commitment to an ambition and a set of physical actions? Or is it all of the above? Reread the piece and provide evidence for your answer.

7. What interest have you so committed yourself to that it defines you, at least in part? Is this a good thing? What about people who heavily commit themselves to work? Should work define them?

WHAT WOULD THEY SAY?

8. Read "The Authentic Trail" together with Cornel West's "The Moral Obligations of Living in a Democratic Society" (p. 123). What would Daniels and West have to say to each other? What do our essentially private pursuits have to do with living in larger communities?

9. Consider the various meanings of the term *education*. Would you agree that Daniels seeks and finds some form of education? Compare this to Adrienne Rich's "Claiming an Education" (p. 608). Explain how or to what extent these two essays might inform each other.

For Community Learning and Research

1. Think of your city or town in terms of its borders—both formal ones (for example, the boundaries between cities or between cities and unincorporated areas) and informal ones (such as neighborhoods). Sometimes these individual communities or areas will be reflected in real-estate classified ads. Identify at least three such neighborhoods or communities. Explain their boundaries (legal or not), and discuss the stereotypes that have been used to describe each of these places and to distinguish one from another. If possible, gather data—percentage of single-family housing and multifamily housing, average income, crime rate—to add to your descriptions. Once you understand these three neighborhoods or communities, what conclusions now seem evident to you?

2. Investigate the data that government agencies and various other entities might use to describe an area you know well because you have lived there. This data could include tax information, crime statistics, census data, business listings, real-estate information, ranking of school performance, and the like. In an essay, report on this data. Discuss what it implies (or seems to imply) and conclude with the ways that such data reflects, or does not reflect, your experience living in that area.

3. Identify the various schools in your area that seek to preserve and teach specific religious or ethnic traditions. Gather and read some of the brochures that these institutions use to describe and advertise themselves. See if you can determine where the students attending these schools live. Based on your information, how would you describe the religious and ethnic diversity in your area? That is, what religious, cultural, or ethnic traditions flourish where you live?

4. Pay attention to your local newspaper's reporting of local crimes. Who gets arrested? Who gets convicted? What can you discover about their family backgrounds, education, or economic status? Based on this reporting and on any other reasonable sources of information, write an essay that discusses the tensions at play in your community. What are their sources?

5. What social-service agencies exist in your community? What groups and needs do they serve? Visit at least three of these agencies and gather information about their services. Also pay attention to where they're located, how well funded they seem to be, and who seems to be seeking such services. Write an essay that discusses the experience of visiting these agencies and how or why you have been in need of similar services. If you haven't needed such services, explain why. Do you anticipate ever needing the help offered by a social-service agency? Explain.

6. What cultural celebrations are held throughout the calendar year in your community? What are their origins, and what do they celebrate? What local groups support these celebrations? Write an essay that charts one year according to these celebrations. Then discuss to what extent, or not, such celebrations answer the question, "Where are you coming from?"

7. Interview a long-time resident of your community. Ask this person for descriptions of how the community has changed. Ask how this person judges those changes. Has the community been improved? You're trying to find out two kinds of information in your interview: one kind has to do with the community and its changes

over time; the second kind has to do with the criteria your interviewee uses to assess whether or not the community's changes have been positive. Write a summary of your interview—quoting your interviewee often—and end by discussing how it has affected your understanding of what constitutes a healthy or vibrant community.

8. What individuals or groups are likely to feel lonely, unsupported, or even afraid in your community? Ask this question of at least five people in your community, and choose each of these people carefully so that they represent different ages, backgrounds, occupations, and so on. Report on each of the respondents and on what they said in answer to your question. What is clearer to you now about your community?

9. The weekly news magazine *Newsweek* carries a feature called "My Turn"—a short essay in which its author speaks both personally and as a member of a larger group on some issue or concern. Consider the various groups to which you belong (a member of the lacrosse team, a member of the nontraditional students association, a choir member, a person in a blended family, etc.). Write a "My Turn" essay that identifies an issue of concern and explains your viewpoint. Understand that you're writing as yourself and also as a representative of your group. So part of your effort should be to fairly represent your own views as well as the diversity (or unanimity, whatever the case may be) of the larger group.

2

*Are We Responsible
for Others?*

WHAT WOULD YOU DO? CONSIDERING AN INTERVENTION

Two of your friends are roommates living down the hall. Justin has developed a drinking problem since school started, bingeing two or three times a week, and when he's drunk he gets loud and obnoxious. He's skipping more and more classes. His grades are falling. Clearly Justin is in trouble, and his roommate, Kevin, is in trouble, too, struggling with lack of sleep and time to study.

Would you intervene in this situation? Would you talk to Justin or Kevin or both of them?

What would you say? Would you talk to someone else? If so, who?

Wherever you're from, when you come to the university you come together with other people, from other ways of life. Worlds converge, or collide, and that immediately raises ethical questions. Ethics has to do with how we get along, how we meet our own needs while respecting the needs of others. Ethics has to do with how we treat each other, particularly those who act in ways we don't approve of or understand. This is the focus of the essays that follow: community and the challenges it brings, from issues of race (Stephen L. Carter's "Welcoming the Stranger," p. 111) to issues of rights (Cornel West's "The Moral Obligations of Living in a Democratic Society," p. 123) to issues of environmental loss (Joy Williams, "Save the Whales, Screw the Shrimp," p. 146), from the local to the national to the global. What are our responsibilities? What is right, and what is possible? What do we do when the right and the possible conflict, when the good seems impossible to achieve? Who decides what and for whom? Whose business is my life or the life of someone else?

Opening the Question

*After reading and discussing several of the selections in this chapter, return to the situation above. **Now** what would you do? Write an essay answering this question, drawing on at least two of the selections. You don't need to have changed your mind, but you do need to demonstrate how the reading has complicated your thinking.*

HENRY WECHSLER, CHARLES DEUTSCH, AND GEORGE DOWDALL

Too Many Colleges Are Still in Denial about Alcohol Abuse

Not only do college students have an alcohol-abuse problem, the authors of this article claim, but many colleges also deny such a problem exists. Because it identifies such high levels of "binge drinking" on campuses, this article received a great deal of media attention when it was first published in 1995 in the Chronicle of Higher Education.

    Henry Wechsler (b. 1932) is the director of the College Alcohol Studies Program, and Charles Deutsch (b. 1947) is a senior research scientist and instructor in health and social policy, both at the Harvard School of Public Health. George Dowdall is a professor of sociology and assistant dean at St. Joseph's University. All three were members of a Harvard University research team investigating alcohol abuse on college campuses.

Colleges have a serious problem with alcohol abuse among students, and it's not getting any better. In 1989, a survey by the Carnegie Foundation for the Advancement of Teaching found that college presidents viewed alcohol abuse as their top campus-life problem. The recent national surveys of college students' drinking that we conducted for Harvard University's School of Public Health documented that alcohol abuse is still rife. Perhaps the second-largest problem in campus life is that many colleges are still in denial, just as many family members who live with alcohol abusers are.

    To be sure, on some campuses officials are making great efforts to reduce alcohol abuse. At others, however, they seem oblivious to the magnitude and effects of the abuse. Those in denial act as if they believe that this deep-seated American problem can be changed by someone, able and dedicated, working part time in a basement office at the student-health service.

    Alcohol abuse is a common, not a marginal, activity at most colleges, and we only fool ourselves if we expect marginal efforts to reduce it. If we really want to deal with the problem, administrators, faculty members, students, and parents must first gain a better understanding of how excessive drinking is affecting the academic and social climate of their institutions. Second, they must believe there are promising, practical strategies they can adopt that will improve the situation. Finally, they must be prepared to contend with the skepticism and resistance bound to be aroused by actions designed to curb the abuse.

    We should stress that our concern is with students' alcohol *abuse*—the drinking of amounts large enough to create problems for the drinker or for others around him or her. The crux of the problem is the *behavior* of the drinker, not the quantity of alcohol consumed. When people do dangerous or obnoxious things when they drink, that's alcohol abuse. Unfortunately, behavior that anywhere else would be classified as alcohol abuse now is not only acceptable but actually the norm on many campuses, in spite of excessive drinking's documented role in automobile crashes, violence, suicide, and high-risk sexual behavior.

Certainly, excessive drinking is not a new problem, on campus or in the society the campus reflects. A local sheriff still leads Harvard University's graduation procession, a tradition that began in colonial days, not for a ceremonial purpose but to control drunk and rowdy celebrants. Generations of college alumni have wistfully recalled the boozy high jinks of their student days, filtering out memories of illness, insane risk, unwanted consequences, and friends who never made it out of the hole they had dug for themselves.

Some alumni no doubt think their children and grandchildren deserve the same "good times." The problem is that, because of lethal sexually transmitted diseases, the easy availability of weapons, and roads filled with high-speed automobiles, the consequences of alcohol abuse are much more deadly today.

Binge drinking—defined as the heavy, episodic use of alcohol—has persisted on campuses despite both a general decrease in alcohol consumption among Americans and an increase in the number of abstainers. Some people (including the author of a recent front-page article in the *New York Times*) have assumed that the latter two trends have translated into more-moderate drinking on the campuses. Nothing could be further from the truth.

Our recent research, which received support from the Robert Wood Johnson Foundation, was the only large-scale study to date of the extent and consequences of binge drinking at a representative sample of American colleges and universities. Our detailed findings from surveys of 17,592 students at 140 randomly selected four-year colleges were published in the December 7, 1994, issue of the *Journal of the American Medical Association*.

For men, our study used the generally accepted criterion for binge drinking: the consumption of five or more drinks in a row at least once in the previous two weeks. We reduced the number of drinks to four in a row for women, to take into account our findings that for the average college woman four drinks produce the same level of alcohol-related problems as do five drinks for the average college man.

Our study found that 44 percent of all students in the sample were binge drinkers—50 percent of the men and 39 percent of the women. Although our 1993 study was the only one to survey a representative sample of colleges, the findings were very similar to those of two other national surveys conducted at about the same time. A study done in 1993 by the Institute for Social Research of the University of Michigan found that 40 percent of the college students surveyed were binge drinkers. And a similar study, conducted from 1990 to 1992 by the Core Institute at Southern Illinois University, also put the figure at 40 percent. Had our study used a five-drink standard for women, as the other two studies did, 41 percent of the students surveyed would have been classified as binge drinkers. The agreement among these three independent national studies is remarkable.

Certainly, not all students who have ever binged have an alcohol problem, but colleges with large numbers of binge drinkers *do*. The proportion of binge drinkers among students varied considerably among the 140 colleges in our study—from as low as 1 percent to as high as 70 percent. At 44 colleges, more than half of the students responding to the survey were binge drinkers. This variation contradicts the belief that among college students we will find a fairly constant and intractable proportion who will drink to excess. It suggests, instead, that colleges create or perpetuate their own drinking cultures through their selection of students, traditions, policies, and other practices.

Not surprisingly, our study shows a strong relationship between the frequency of binge drinking and alcohol-related problems. Nineteen percent of all students qualify as frequent binge drinkers—those who binge more than once a week. They were found to be from seven to ten times as likely as nonbinge drinkers to fail to use protection when having sex, to engage in unplanned sexual activity, to get into trouble with campus police, to damage property, or to suffer an injury. Half of the frequent binge drinkers reported experiencing five or more *different* alcohol-related problems. Yet very few of those students considered themselves to have an alcohol problem or even to be heavy drinkers.

On campuses where more than half of the students were binge drinkers, the vast majority of the nonbinge drinkers who lived on campus—fully 87 percent— reported experiencing one or more problems as a result of others' binge drinking. They were the victims of what we call "secondhand binge effects." Such students were up to three times as likely as students on campuses where 35 percent or fewer of students binge to report being pushed, hit, or assaulted, experiencing an unwanted sexual advance, or otherwise being bothered by the alcohol-related behavior of other students.

Colleges cannot claim to create a supportive learning environment when they tolerate such behavior. To fulfill their missions, colleges will have to reduce alcohol abuse markedly. How can this be done? Each college has its own level of binge drinking, traditions, and circumstances and thus must craft its own response to the problem. Still, our findings suggest strategies that could be effective.

Administrators must first decide where to focus their energies. They 15 should realize that about 85 percent of all college students drink (although they do not all binge) and that alcohol is easily available to students regardless of age. Thus programs at many colleges that seek to reduce drinking among all students are doomed to failure. Other programs try to inform binge drinkers about ways to avoid harmful consequences—for example, by designating a nondrinking friend to drive. But in a social system rife with alcohol abuse, whether a family or a campus, the least effective intervention point is the abuser.

Prevention cannot depend solely on the individual alcohol abuser's recognition of the problem and his or her willingness to accept help, nor can it depend on the cooperation of student organizations that are heavily involved in alcohol abuse. In fact, our study found that more than 80 percent of the students residing in fraternities or sororities were binge drinkers. If a college or university really aspires to be a community of civility and respect, the principal goal of its prevention efforts must be to help students who are adversely affected by the binge drinking of others to assert their rights. These students deserve to learn that college life need not include cleaning up after a vomiting roommate; being awakened at 3 AM several nights a week by revelers; or being physically, verbally, or sexually assaulted.

Students, faculty and staff members, administrators, and trustees should establish and enforce explicit rules about what kinds of behavior will not be tolerated. And since binge drinking is a highly social activity, colleges must offer better ways to help students make friends, find romance, and keep busy. We found that the students who spent the most time studying, performing community service, or working were the least likely to be binge drinkers.

Furthermore, because half of the students who binge in college were binge drinkers in high school, colleges should use the admission process to influence the drinking culture on campus. They can do this by making clear in their promotional material and through the information that recruiters provide to high-school teachers and counselors that they will protect the right of all students to an educational environment free from alcohol abuse and abusive behavior.

College officials also need to work more closely with city officials and with local businesses that sell alcohol to eliminate the sales to minors and to discourage "half-price beer nights" and other practices that encourage drunkenness. For their part, athletics directors can have enormous influence on the drinking culture of a campus if they can be pressed to use it constructively with their athletes. Finally, residence-hall advisers and academic counselors can play a key role in preventing alcohol abuse by intervening quickly in incidents of public drunkenness that violate codes of conduct. But they need much better training and support from the administration than most of them now receive.

Before these or other constructive steps can be taken, campus authori- 20 ties must stop denying the extent of the problem. Denial includes failing to recognize the impact and extensiveness of campus alcohol abuse and acting as if easy stratagems will produce change.

We recommend a weekend tour, beginning on Thursday night. As the night progresses, observe the campus and the clubs on its outskirts. Drop in on the health services, the fraternity houses, and the dorms in the early morning hours. Take a late-night ride with a security guard. Check out class attendance on Friday.

On Saturday, repeat the process. And later station yourself outside sorority houses and residence halls on Sunday morning and witness "the walk of shame"—a phrase students use to describe women's returning from a night's unplanned, and often unprotected, sex. Ask students to describe drinking behavior. Above all, fight the temptation to think of the alcohol abuse you see as merely the problem of "troubled" individuals. When the faces change but the numbers don't, something much more powerful and institutional is happening.

Don't expect change to be easy. Opponents of significant change will cite longstanding traditions, the need not to scare students away in a highly competitive marketplace, the damage to the institution's image of publicly acknowledging an alcohol problem, the real or imagined vulnerability of the institution to legal action, the displeasure of local merchants who depend on student drinking, and opposition from campus newspapers that depend on advertisements from those businesses.

But if you want change, acknowledge the existence of alcohol abuse and the challenge it poses to the college's mission. Commit resources from all parts of the institution, with visible support from the president, to coordinated, long-term actions. Make your intentions clear, not just in speeches but also in the budget. And expect change to be gradual. Remember, not so long ago we resigned ourselves to smoke-filled offices and thought little could be done to stop drunk driving.

WHAT DID THEY SAY?

1. Before reading this article, write a paragraph describing your sense of the drinking situation on your campus. What are the causes for this situation, whatever it is? If there is a problem, should your college or university try to do something about it?

2. Now read the article all the way through and write another paragraph describing your sense of the drinking problem on campus. Has reading this essay changed your mind? Why or why not? If yes, what in the article persuaded you? If not, why didn't the article persuade you?

3. "Too Many Colleges Are Still in Denial about Alcohol Abuse" is a good example of academic, argumentative writing. It couldn't be clearer. Go back through the article and chart this. Underline every sentence that makes a claim and put a C beside it in the margin. Draw a square around every passage that supports an argument with details, statistics, and examples, putting an E, for evidence, beside it in the margin.

4. Discuss your own experience with drinking on campus. Does it support the authors' assertions?

5. This article was first published in the *Chronicle of Higher Education*, a publication addressed to university teachers and administrators. How would the article have to be revised if it were to be published in a journal or magazine addressed to students? What would have to be deleted? What added?

WHAT DO YOU THINK?

6. Write a personal essay exploring your own experience with alcohol on campus. We realize this is risky. If you would prefer not to share such experience, by all means choose another topic. But the point of sharing your experience in this essay is to begin thinking critically about the ideas raised in "Too Many Colleges Are Still in Denial about Alcohol Abuse." What does your own experience help you understand about this article? What does this article help you understand about your own experience?

7. At the end of the article, the authors make a series of practical recommendations. Write an essay in the form of a long letter to the president of your university endorsing these recommendations (or adding your own). The essay will require you to summarize these recommendations in your own words and then to make a case for why they would be effective. If your university has already adopted some of these recommendations, write an essay supporting their continued use. Option: Write an essay, addressed to the university president, arguing *against* such recommendations. In either option, imitate the clear and well-documented style of the essay authors.

WHAT WOULD THEY SAY?

8. Read Garrett Hardin's "Lifeboat Ethics: The Case against Helping the Poor" (p. 130) and Joan Didion's "On Morality" (p. 167). On the basis of both of these selections, write an essay explaining how Hardin and Didion would respond to the authors of "Too Many Colleges Are Still in Denial about Alcohol Abuse." Hardin says that, in general, we shouldn't make ourselves responsible for others. Would he say the same thing in this situation? Didion argues in a more subtle way that ethical abstractions are not to be trusted. How would that argument apply here? End by asserting your own conclusions. Be sure to quote from all three of these essays.

9. Write an essay responding to the ethical situation in the introduction to this chapter—the struggle with the binge drinker down the hall—in light of the data and ideas presented in this article. Apply the authors' arguments to this particular situation and to your own behavior.

10. The authors claim that their findings "break new ground in exploring the extent to which alcohol-related behavior obstructs the possibility of 'building communities of civility and respect on campuses.'" Relate this idea of "communities of civility and respect" to at least two other selections in this chapter. What is required of such a community in a workplace, in a neighborhood, in a country, in an ecosystem? What other kinds of behavior, in addition to "alcohol-related behaviors," obstruct such communities?

BOWEN H. McCOY
The Parable of the Sadhu

T<small>HOUGH THE SPECIFICS</small> *of this piece may seem distant (it is set in Nepal and concerns a Himalayan trek), the issues it raises focus centrally on questions of individual and group responsibility. Bowen H. McCoy (b. 1937) ends the essay with its narrator, an investment banker, asking questions about his relationship to the "derelict on the street."*

McCoy retired in 1990 from Morgan Stanley, where he worked as an investment banker for thirty years. He has taught finance and ethics at Stanford, UCLA, and a number of other universities and is former chair of Standford's Center for Economic Policy. "The Parable of the Sadhu" was first published in the September/October 1983 issue of the Harvard Business Review.

Last year, as the first participant in the new six-month sabbatical program that Morgan Stanley has adopted, I enjoyed a rare opportunity to collect my thoughts as well as do some traveling. I spent the first three months in Nepal, walking six hundred miles through two hundred villages in the Himalayas and climbing some 120,000 vertical feet. On the trip my sole Western companion was an anthropologist who shed light on the cultural patterns of the villages we passed through.

During the Nepal hike, something occurred that has had a powerful impact on my thinking about corporate ethics. Although some might argue that the experience has no relevance to business, it was a situation in which a basic ethical dilemma suddenly intruded into the lives of a group of individuals. How the group responded I think holds a lesson for all organizations no matter how defined.

THE SADHU

The Nepal experience was more rugged and adventuresome than I had anticipated. Most commercial treks last two or three weeks and cover a quarter of the distance we traveled.

My friend Stephen, the anthropologist, and I were halfway through the 60-day Himalayan part of the trip when we reached the high point, an 18,000-foot pass over a crest that we'd have to traverse to reach the village of Muklinath, an ancient holy place for pilgrims.

Six years earlier I had suffered pulmonary edema, an acute form of altitude sickness, at 16,500 feet in the vicinity of Everest base camp, so we were understandably concerned about what would happen at 18,000 feet.

5

Moreover, the Himalayas were having their wettest spring in twenty years; hip-deep powder and ice had already driven us off one ridge. If we failed to cross the pass, I feared that the last half of our "once in a lifetime" trip would be ruined.

The night before we would try the pass, we camped at a hut at 14,500 feet. In the photos taken at that camp, my face appears wan. The last village we'd passed through was a sturdy two-day walk below us, and I was tired.

During the late afternoon, four backpackers from New Zealand joined us, and we spent most of the night awake, anticipating the climb. Below we could see the fires of two other parties, which turned out to be two Swiss couples and a Japanese hiking club.

To get over the steep part of the climb before the sun melted the steps cut in the ice, we departed at 3:30 AM. The New Zealanders left first, followed by Stephen and myself, our porters and Sherpas, and then the Swiss. The Japanese lingered in their camp. The sky was clear, and we were confident that no spring storm would erupt that day to close the pass.

At 15,500 feet, it looked to me as if Stephen were shuffling and staggering a bit, which are symptoms of altitude sickness. (The initial stage of altitude sickness brings a headache and nausea. As the condition worsens, a climber may encounter difficult breathing, disorientation, aphasia, and paralysis.) I felt strong, my adrenaline was flowing, but I was very concerned about my ultimate ability to get across. A couple of our porters were also suffering from the height, and Pasang, our Sherpa sirdar (leader), was worried.

Just after daybreak, while we rested at 15,500 feet, one of the New 10 Zealanders, who had gone ahead, came staggering down toward us with a body slung across his shoulders. He dumped the almost naked, barefoot body of an Indian holy man—a sadhu—at my feet. He had found the pilgrim lying on the ice, shivering and suffering from hypothermia. I cradled the sadhu's head and laid him out on the rocks. The New Zealander was angry. He wanted to get across the pass before the bright sun melted the snow. He said, "Look, I've done what I can. You have porters and Sherpa guides. You care for him. We're going on!" He turned and went back up the mountain to join his friends.

I took a carotid pulse and found that the sadhu was still alive. We figured he had probably visited the holy shrines at Muklinath and was on his way home. It was fruitless to question why he had chosen this desperately high route instead of the safe, heavily traveled caravan route through the Kali Gandaki gorge. Or why he was almost naked and with no shoes, or how long he had been lying in the pass. The answers weren't going to solve our problem.

Stephen and the four Swiss began stripping off outer clothing and opening their packs. The sadhu was soon clothed from head to foot. He was not able to walk, but he was very much alive. I looked down the mountain and spotted below the Japanese climbers marching up with a horse.

Without a great deal of thought, I told Stephen and Pasang that I was concerned about withstanding the heights to come and wanted to get over the pass. I took off after several of our porters who had gone ahead.

On the steep part of the ascent where, if the ice steps had given way, I would have slid down about 3,000 feet, I felt vertigo. I stopped for a breather, allowing the Swiss to catch up with me. I inquired about the sadhu and Stephen. They said that the sadhu was fine and that Stephen was just behind. I set off again for the summit.

Stephen arrived at the summit an hour after I did. Still exhilarated by 15 victory, I ran down the snow slope to congratulate him. He was suffering from altitude sickness, walking fifteen steps, then stopping, walking fifteen steps, then stopping. Pasang accompanied him all the way up. When I reached them, Stephen glared at me and said: "How do you feel about contributing to the death of a fellow man?"

I did not fully comprehend what he meant.

"Is the sadhu dead?" I inquired.

"No," replied Stephen, "but he surely will be!"

After I had gone, and the Swiss had departed not long after, Stephen had remained with the sadhu. When the Japanese had arrived, Stephen had asked to use their horse to transport the sadhu down to the hut. They had refused. He had then asked Pasang to have a group of our porters carry the sadhu. Pasang had resisted the idea, saying that the porters would have to exert all their energy to get themselves over the pass. He had thought they could not carry a man down 1,000 feet to the hut, reclimb the slope, and get across safely before the snow melted. Pasang had pressed Stephen not to delay any longer.

The Sherpas had carried the sadhu down to a rock in the sun at about 20 15,000 feet and had pointed out the hut another five hundred feet below. The Japanese had given him food and drink. When they had last seen him he was listlessly throwing rocks at the Japanese party's dog, which had frightened him.

We do not know if the sadhu lived or died.

For many of the following days and evenings Stephen and I discussed and debated our behavior toward the sadhu. Stephen is a committed Quaker with deep moral vision. He said, "I feel that what happened with the sadhu is a good example of the breakdown between the individual ethic and the corporate ethic. No one person was willing to assume ultimate responsibility for the sadhu. Each was willing to do his bit just so long as it was not too inconvenient. When it got to be a bother, everyone just passed the buck to someone else and took off. Jesus was relevant to a more individualistic stage of society, but how do we interpret his teaching today in a world filled with large, impersonal organizations and groups?"

I defended the larger group, saying, "Look, we all cared. We all stopped and gave aid and comfort. Everyone did his bit. The New Zealander carried him down below the snow line. I took his pulse and suggested we treat him for hypothermia. You and the Swiss gave him clothing and got him warmed up. The Japanese gave him food and water. The Sherpas carried him down to the sun and pointed out the easy trail toward the hut. He was well enough to throw rocks at a dog. What more could we do?"

"You have just described the typical affluent Westerner's response to a problem. Throwing money—in this case food and sweaters—at it, but not solving the fundamentals!" Stephen retorted.

"What would satisfy you?" I said. "Here we are, a group of New Zealan- 25 ders, Swiss, Americans, and Japanese who have never met before and who are at the apex of one of the most powerful experiences of our lives. Some years the pass is so bad no one gets over it. What right does an almost naked pilgrim who chooses the wrong trail have to disrupt our lives? Even the Sherpas had no interest in risking the trip to help him beyond a certain point."

Stephen calmly rebutted, "I wonder what the Sherpas would have done if the sadhu had been a well-dressed Nepali, or what the Japanese would have done if the sadhu had been a well-dressed Asian, or what you would have done, Buzz, if the sadhu had been a well-dressed Western woman?"

"Where, in your opinion," I asked instead, "is the limit of our responsibility in a situation like this? We had our own well-being to worry about. Our Sherpa guides were unwilling to jeopardize us or the porters for the sadhu. No one else on the mountain was willing to commit himself beyond certain self-imposed limits."

Stephen said, "As individual Christians or people with a Western ethical tradition, we can fulfill our obligations in such a situation only if (1) the sadhu dies in our care, (2) the sadhu demonstrates to us that he could undertake the two-day walk down to the village, or (3) we carry the sadhu for two days down to the village and convince someone there to care for him."

"Leaving the sadhu in the sun with food and clothing, while he demonstrated hand-eye coordination by throwing a rock at a dog, comes close to fulfilling items one and two," I answered. "And it wouldn't have made sense to take him to the village where the people appeared to be far less caring than the Sherpas, so the third condition is impractical. Are you really saying that, no matter what the implications, we should, at the drop of a hat, have changed our entire plan?"

THE INDIVIDUAL VERSUS THE GROUP ETHIC

Despite my arguments, I felt and continue to feel guilt about the sadhu. I had 30 literally walked through a classic moral dilemma without fully thinking through the consequences. My excuses for my actions include a high adrenaline flow, a superordinate goal, and a once-in-a-lifetime opportunity—factors in the usual corporate situation, especially when one is under stress.

Real moral dilemmas are ambiguous, and many of us hike right through them, unaware that they exist. When, usually after the fact, someone makes an issue of them, we tend to resent his or her bringing it up. Often, when the full import of what we have done (or not done) falls on us, we dig into a defensive position from which it is very difficult to emerge. In rare circumstances we may contemplate what we have done from inside a prison.

Had we mountaineers been free of physical and mental stress caused by the effort and the high altitude, we might have treated the sadhu differently. Yet isn't stress the real test of personal and corporate values? The instant decisions executives make under pressure reveal the most about personal and corporate character.

Among the many questions that occur to me when pondering my experience are: What are the practical limits of moral imagination and vision? Is there a collective or institutional ethic beyond the ethics of the individual? At what level of effort or commitment can one discharge one's ethical responsibilities? Not every ethical dilemma has a right solution. Reasonable people often disagree; otherwise there would be no dilemma. In a business context, however, it is essential that managers agree on a process for dealing with dilemmas.

The sadhu experience offers an interesting parallel to business situations. An immediate response was mandatory. Failure to act was a decision in itself. Up on the mountain we could not resign and submit our résumés to a headhunter. In contrast to philosophy, business involves action and implementation—getting things done. Managers must come up with answers to problems based on what they see and what they allow to influence their decision-making processes. On the mountain, none of us but Stephen realized the true dimensions of the situation we were facing.

One of our problems was that as a group we had no process for develop- 35 ing a consensus. We had no sense of purpose or plan. The difficulties of dealing with the sadhu were so complex that no one person could handle it. Because it did not have a set of preconditions that could guide its action to an acceptable resolution, the group reacted instinctively as individuals. The cross-cultural nature of the group added a further layer of complexity. We had no leader with whom we could all identify and in whose purpose we believed. Only Stephen was willing to take charge, but he could not gain adequate support to care for the sadhu.

Some organizations do have a value system that transcends the personal values of the managers. Such values, which go beyond profitability, are usually revealed when the organization is under stress. People throughout the organization generally accept its values, which, because they are not presented as a rigid list of commandments, may be somewhat ambiguous. The stories people tell, rather than printed materials, transmit these conceptions of what is proper behavior.

For twenty years I have been exposed at senior levels to a variety of corporations and organizations. It is amazing how quickly an outsider can sense the tone and style of an organization and the degree of tolerated openness and freedom to challenge management.

Organizations that do not have a heritage of mutually accepted, shared values tend to become unhinged during stress, with each individual bailing out for himself. In the great takeover battles we have witnessed during past years, companies that had strong cultures drew the wagons around them and fought it out, while other companies saw executives, supported by their golden parachutes, bail out of the struggles.

Because corporations and their members are interdependent, for the corporation to be strong the members need to share a preconceived notion of what is correct behavior, a "business ethic," and think of it as a positive force, not a constraint.

As an investment banker I am continually warned by well-meaning 40 lawyers, clients, and associates to be wary of conflicts of interest. Yet if I were to run away from every difficult situation, I wouldn't be an effective investment banker. I have to feel my way through conflicts. An effective manager can't run from risk either; he or she has to confront and deal with risk. To feel "safe" in doing this, managers need the guidelines of an agreed-on process and set of values within the organization.

After my three months in Nepal, I spent three months as an executive-in-residence at both Stanford Business School and the Center for Ethics and Social Policy at the Graduate Theological Union at Berkeley. These six months away from my job gave me time to assimilate twenty years of business experience. My thoughts turned often to the meaning of the leadership role in any large organization. Students at the seminary thought of themselves as antibusiness. But when I questioned them they agreed that they distrusted all large organizations, including the church. They perceived all large organizations as impersonal and opposed to individual values and needs. Yet we all know of organizations where peoples' values and beliefs are respected and their expressions encouraged. What makes the difference? Can we identify the difference and, as a result, manage more effectively?

The word *ethics* turns off many and confuses more. Yet the notions of shared values and an agreed-on process for dealing with adversity and change—what many people mean when they talk about corporate culture—seem to be at the heart of the ethical issue. People who are in touch with their own core beliefs and the beliefs of others and are sustained by them can be more comfortable living on the cutting edge. At times, taking a tough line or a decisive stand in a muddle of ambiguity is the only ethical thing to do. If a manager is indecisive and spends time trying to figure out the "good" thing to do, the enterprise may be lost.

Business ethics, then, has to do with the authenticity and integrity of the enterprise. To be ethical is to follow the business as well as the cultural goals of the corporation, its owners, its employees, and its customers. Those who cannot serve the corporate vision are not authentic business people and, therefore, are not ethical in the business sense.

At this stage of my own business experience I have a strong interest in organizational behavior. Sociologists are keenly studying what they call corporate stories, legends, and heroes as a way organizations have of transmitting the value system. Corporations such as Arco have even hired consultants to perform an audit of their corporate culture. In a company, the leader is the person who understands, interprets, and manages the corporate value system. Effective managers are then action-oriented people who resolve conflict, are tolerant of ambiguity, stress, and change, and have a strong sense of purpose for themselves and their organizations.

If all this is true, I wonder about the role of the professional manager 45 who moves from company to company. How can he or she quickly absorb the values and culture of different organizations? Or is there, indeed, an art of management that is totally transportable? Assuming such fungible managers do exist, is it proper for them to manipulate the values of others?

What would have happened had Stephen and I carried the sadhu for two days back to the village and become involved with the villagers in his care? In four trips to Nepal my most interesting experiences occurred in 1975 when I lived in a Sherpa home in the Khumbu for five days recovering from altitude sickness. The high point of Stephen's trip was an invitation to participate in a family funeral ceremony in Manang. Neither experience had to do with climbing the high passes of the Himalayas. Why were we so reluctant to try the lower path, the ambiguous trail? Perhaps because we did not have a leader who could reveal the greater purpose of the trip to us.

Why didn't Stephen with his moral vision opt to take the sadhu under his personal care? The answer is because, in part, Stephen was hard-stressed physically himself, and because, in part, without some support system that involved our involuntary and episodic community on the mountain, it was beyond his individual capacity to do so.

I see the current interest in corporate culture and corporate value systems as a positive response to Stephen's pessimism about the decline of the role of the individual in large organizations. Individuals who operate from a thoughtful set of personal values provide the foundation for a corporate culture. A corporate tradition that encourages freedom of inquiry, supports personal values, and reinforces a focused sense of direction can fulfill the need for individuality along with the prosperity and success of the group. Without such corporate support, the individual is lost.

That is the lesson of the sadhu. In a complex corporate situation, the individual requires and deserves the support of the group. If people cannot find such support from their organization, they don't know how to act. If such support is forthcoming, a person has a stake in the success of the group, and can add much to the process of establishing and maintaining a corporate culture. It is management's challenge to be sensitive to individual needs, to shape them, and to direct and focus them for the benefit of the group as a whole.

For each of us the sadhu lives. Should we stop what we are doing and 50 comfort him; or should we keep trudging up toward the high pass? Should I pause to help the derelict I pass on the street each night as I walk by the Yale Club en route to Grand Central Station? Am I his brother? What is the nature of our responsibility if we consider ourselves to be ethical persons? Perhaps it is to change the values of the group so that it can, with all its resources, take the other road.

WHAT DOES HE SAY?

1. The first half of this essay is a personal story, the second half an application of the story to the question of business ethics. Think of the story. If you didn't know that the author was an investment banker, what would you assume his occupation to be? Would you be surprised to find out that he's an investment banker? Why or why not?

2. McCoy's Quaker friend claims that the people involved in this incident would have reacted differently if the sadhu had been, for example, "a well-dressed Western woman." Do you agree? Why or why not? What is the role of ethnicity, culture, and economic class in our response to the suffering of others?

3. How would you have responded to the sadhu's situation that McCoy describes? Explain.

4. This essay asks a lot of questions. Make a list of them and circle two that seem particularly hard to answer.

5. Though this essay asks a lot of questions, it also comes to several specific conclusions. What are they? Explain them in your own words. Mark the paragraph where McCoy states these conclusions in the clearest and most definitive way. Why put the paragraph where he does rather than somewhere else in the essay?

WHAT DO YOU THINK?

6. If you could take a six-month sabbatical, where would you go and what would you do? Write an essay explaining your plans. Option: Write a grant proposal to a funding agency trying to persuade it to give you the money to make this trip. What value would the sabbatical have for you—say, in completing your major and getting a job?

7. "Real moral dilemmas are ambiguous, and many of us hike right through them, unaware that they exist." Write an essay exploring this idea through your own experiences.

8. "At times, taking a tough line or a decisive stand in a muddle of ambiguity is the only ethical thing to do." Write an essay exploring this idea through your reading and your experience.

WHAT WOULD THEY SAY?

9. McCoy "ponders" the meaning of a personal experience and then applies what he's learned to his profession. Identify and explain some experience that troubles you because it's ethically ambiguous. Reflect on its significance, bringing in at least one other essay in this chapter and quoting from it as a way to help you with that reflection.

10. Read Joy Williams's "Save the Whales, Screw the Shrimp" (p. 146). In light of that essay, what do you think she would say in response to McCoy? Williams's tone is clearly different from McCoy's, and she *seems* to be arguing against involvement in the affairs of others. What would she write in the margins and at the end of McCoy's essay?

STEPHEN L. CARTER
Welcoming the Stranger

THIS ESSAY, by Stephen L. Carter (b. 1954), one of the country's most important public intellectuals and ethicists, questions what we owe to a stranger. Carter argues that civility entails sacrifice and is "a moral imperative." In support, he offers two autobiographical narratives.

Carter, who is African American, earned his law degree from Yale, served as a law clerk for Supreme Court justice Thurgood Marshall, and is now the William Cromwell Professor of Law at Yale University. He has written many important works on legal and social issues, including The Culture of Disbelief: How American Law and Politics Trivialize Religious Devotion *(1993) and* Civility: Manners, Morals, and the Etiquette of Democracy *(1998), from which this selection is taken.*

There is—or recently was—a shameful bit of software floating around the Internet. Known as *AOL4FREE*, the program evidently helped users to break the law by setting up America OnLine accounts without the inconvenience of paying for them. Then, in the late spring of 1997, the United States Department of Energy distributed an alert about a fake version of *AOL4FREE*. This fake theft program looked like the real theft program but was actually a deadly computer virus. Any user who tried to run it received a surprise. Rather than establishing an illegal America OnLine account, the program would erase the entire contents of the user's hard drive.

There is a certain existential irony in the image of a federal agency issuing a warning that a program somebody uses because he thinks it is designed to abet fraud may actually be a fraudulent copy of a program designed to abet fraud and may do harm to the would-be defrauder. But I suppose this is less unusual than it seems. After all, government agencies publish studies all the time on the harm that is caused by illegal drugs, in what is presumably an effort at deterrence. And the attorney general of one of our largest states, it is said, once pursued a consumer fraud action against an individual who offered "grass by mail" at low prices—grass that turned out to be the kind mowed from the lawn, not the kind hidden under the mattress. So perhaps the warning was not as bizarre as it first appeared.

Nevertheless, my own initial reaction to the warning was, "Serves them right!" That is, I quickly decided that anybody who would try to steal computer time deserved to lose a hard drive or two. And although I soon recognized that this rather uncivil and certainly un-Christian response was a little bit like saying that people who decline to feed parking meters deserve to have their cars vandalized, a part of me clings to it still. My dislike for theft is, I confess, visceral.

My more sober reaction, the same reaction I have to the problem of computer viruses generally, was, "Why would anybody do such a thing?" Because lots of people undeniably do. From the creation of the first computer virus, apparently in 1983, to the present day, more than seven thousand different types of viruses have been created—recently at the rate of two or three new ones per day.[1] Although some viruses are relatively benign, others can cause losses ranging into the millions of dollars. Viruses are metaphorically violent—a typical name of one of the many virus-making kits easily available on the Internet is Nightmare Joker—and, in what cannot be an accident, many of the most vicious target only the products of Microsoft. (I also find it rather interesting that *every* identified virus writer has turned out to be male.)[2]

Nobody seems to know exactly why people create viruses, although experts talk confidently about pathological levels of loneliness, alienation, rejection, anger, and frustration, all the usual causes of vandalism, as well as, for that matter, suicide. "I don't have any real-life friends," moans one nineteen-year-old virus creator.[3] And, for the student of civility, that is the moral of the story. The virus writer never seeks recognition. Viruses are sent out to attack people the writer does not know. The virus writer who thinks the activity a big joke (as some evidently do) is able to play it with aplomb in part because the victims are strangers.

And here, indeed, is a point on which most students of civility seem to agree. A big part of our incivility crisis stems from the sad fact that we do not know each other or even want to try; and, not knowing each other, we seem to think that how we treat each other does not matter. For the virus writer, whose alienation from others may be extreme, this is particularly true: the same anonymity behind which the virus's creator hides also cloaks the virus's victims. To the virus writer, whether motivated by anger, perverse pleasure, or ideology, the infection of other people's computers is an end in itself. The people who pay the costs may not seem real...assuming he thinks of them at all.

The creation of a virus to harm a complete stranger perfectly exemplifies much that is uncivil in our turbulent age. An important part of civility, as we have already seen, is simple good manners as a signal of respect for others and for the community. Another important part, which has lately occasioned a substantial literature, is about reconstruction of our social institutions. But civility is, fundamentally, an ethic for relating to the stranger. Indeed, much of civility is premised on the notion that the concept of stranger actually exists—that everybody will not in fact come to know, still less grow close to, everybody else. Yet we live in a society in which each of us encounters strangers every day, by the dozens, the hundreds, even the thousands. Civility is about how we treat each and every one of them. So civility is not the same as affection, and when we try to treat the two of them as the same, we end up making matters worse.

I am annoyed when I go into a store and introduce myself, by my full name, to a sales clerk, only to be immediately called by my first name alone.

First names are commonly used among close friends, but it is only recently that they have trickled down into ordinary encounters. It may be that I am especially sensitive on this issue. Black Americans fought hard and long for the right to be called by *Mr.* and *Mrs.* (and, lately, *Ms.*) rather than by first names—only to discover, just as the battle is won, that an increasing number of white Americans think these politely formal sobriquets should be discarded.

I was raised to think—and I still think—that the use of a stranger's first name requires an invitation. It is a form of social intimacy, not an entitlement. Using a more formal manner in addressing those we have just met is more than common courtesy—it is a signal of respect. But, of course, respect for our fellow passengers is fast disintegrating. So I suppose I should not be surprised when I see a receptionist at a doctor's office, a young woman scarcely out of high school, call patients three times her age, whom she evidently has never met before, by their first names. No doubt the receptionist imagines that she is being politely informal, but what she is really doing is forcing on strangers an intimacy they should not be required to share. I suspect that the receptionist's thoughtless effort at familiarity offends some of the patients, actually making them less, not more, comfortable. We can be civil without being familiar, and recovering the skill of doing so is vital if we are to relate to strangers; otherwise, we run the risk of disappointment and even anger when these strangers do not reciprocate, a bitter sensation of rejection.

The social scientists agree. The psychologist Richard Sennett has argued 10 that the desire for some form of intimacy in all our relationships is the enemy of civility, that we cannot relate to each other as a polity unless we rediscover the value of "bonds of association and mutual commitment...between people who are not joined by ties of family or intimate association."[4] Similarly, the sociologist Benton Johnson, following the work of John Murray Cuddihy, has pointed to the ways that civility and "niceness" ease our relationships with strangers: "They make it possible to jostle someone by mistake in the elevator and avoid a flare-up. They enable customers and clerks, diners and waiters, clients and attorneys to conclude transactions with each other quickly and with a minimum of friction."[5]

Johnson's point is that none of these busily jostling and transacting people know each other. He goes on to quote Cuddihy's argument that civility allows us "to live with unknown others without transforming them into either brothers or enemies"[6]—that is, we need neither love them nor hate them in order to be civil toward them. Civility, in short, is a virtue that equips us for everyday life with strangers, our daily democratic train ride with people we do not like or do not even know. Thus, we see the second rule of civility:°

---

second rule of civility: In an earlier chapter of *Civility,* the book from which this piece is excerpted, Carter gives the first rule of civility: "Our duty to others does not depend on whether we like them or not" (35). In all, Carter's book presents fifteen rules for civility. [Unless otherwise noted, all notes are the Editors'.]

Civility requires that we sacrifice for strangers, not just for people we happen to know.

This is, in its way, rather a radical notion. Many of us have trouble being as civil as we should even toward those we love or with whom we are otherwise close: our family members, coworkers, neighbors, or friends. . . . But at least we believe that we *should* treat them well, however short of our aspirations we may fall. Dealing with strangers is harder, and we seem to be losing many of the tools that once enabled us to relate to them. The clerk in the convenience store, the beggar in the street, the passenger in the next seat: How are we to relate to these strangers? Certainly simple politeness—*Please, Thank you, Sir (Ma'am), Excuse me*—would be a good start.

When I was growing up, a frequent admonition, at home and school alike, was, "Say the magic word!" This phrase, always spoken with enormous gentleness, was a reminder to preface a request with *Please* and to acknowledge a kindness with *Thank you*. If we failed to say the magic words, we did not receive whatever we were asking for, a discipline that helps a child learn quite quickly. There is no simpler piece of the civility puzzle, not only because the magic words are a part of our letter of introduction to the rest of the world, but also because using them is a symbol of respect for others. Yet the magic words have become rarer to the ear because, it seems, they have become harder to pronounce.

The psychiatrist Robert Coles,° in his thoughtful book *The Moral Intelligence of Children*, argues that we should be quite proud of the many five- and six-year-olds who arrive at school already understanding and using the magic words. In these young people, writes Coles, "[c]ivilization has taken root."[7] Coles is right that we should recognize how considerable an accomplishment this degree of civility is in these tiny human beings so newly arrived on the earth. The troubling aspect is how many of these polite little children grow into sullen adolescents and mean-spirited adults, the magic words, like the rest of the magic of childhood, forgotten. Because nowadays the magic words are in a decline. Cashiers, cab drivers, the people for whom we hold open doors—all of them seem to have lost the art. We may smile and greet those we know well, but (in our cities at least) a sunny greeting offered to a stranger in the street may invite in response an angry glare or averted eyes.

So how are we to relate to these strangers? The simple answer is that we 15 are to be civil toward them, which means that we should accord them respect and even (although it may seem unfashionable) that we should be polite. We may certainly, in our civility, make *offers* of friendship. But we must not insist on friendship as the price of civility. If it turns out that the many strangers we meet each day do not, after all, desire close relationships with us, we should

---

Robert Coles (b. 1929): Coles's essay, "I Listen to My Parents and I Wonder What They Believe," appears on p. 58.

not repay them with incivility. The respect that we owe them does not diminish. Indeed, as we shall see, an important component of civility involves respecting the privacy of others, what used to be called the right to be left alone, accepting that parts of their lives are no part of our business. Another component, however, involves not insisting on our own right to be left alone when, by connecting with others, we can improve the community...and therein lies a story. In fact, therein lie two stories. By considering them, we can better understand what the relentless focus on the functionality of civility tends to miss—that treating each other with civility is a moral imperative.

STORY #1: A DARK, SKINNY STRANGER IN CLEVELAND PARK

In the summer of 1966, my parents moved with their five children to a large house near the corner of 35th and Macomb Streets in Cleveland Park, a neighborhood in the middle of Northwest Washington, D.C., and, in those days, a lily-white enclave. My father, trained as a lawyer, was working for the federal government, and this was an area of the city where many lawyers and government officials lived. There were senators, there were lobbyists, there were undersecretaries of this and that. My first impression was of block upon block of grim, forbidding old homes, each of which seemed to feature a massive dog and spoiled children in the uniforms of various private schools. My two brothers and two sisters and I sat on the front steps, missing our playmates, as the movers carried in our furniture. Cars passed what was now our house, slowing for a look, as did people on foot. We waited for somebody to say hello, to welcome us. Nobody did.

We children had no previous experience of white neighborhoods. But we had heard unpleasant rumors. The gang of boys I used to hang out with in Southwest Washington traded tall tales of places where white people did evil things to us, mostly in the South, where none of us had ever lived, nor wanted to. Now and then, perhaps on a Saturday afternoon, we would take a walk to see the evil empire. We would walk up Fourth Street, beneath the highway and the railroad tracks that separated our neighborhood from the federal areas of the city, past the red-brick police station, a half-mile or so up to the Mall. Then, nudging each other with nervous excitement, we would turn west and continue our march. We wanted to see. We would pass with barely a glance the museums that on any other day would keep us occupied for hours. We would circle around the Washington Monument, whose pointed top with twin windows on each side, some of the older boys said, reminded them of a Ku Klux Klan hood, an image that scared me a little, although at eleven years old, raised in the North by protective parents, I was none too sure what the Ku Klux Klan was. We would walk along the Reflecting Pool and continue past the Lincoln Memorial, which, then as now, seemed under constant repair.

At last we would reach the shores of the Potomac River which, in those days, exuded the fetid odors of sewage and industrial waste. And we would stand on the bank, a tiny band of dark skinny children, still growing into full awareness of our race; we would stand there and gaze across the river at the shores of the forbidden land. Mostly what we saw was trees. Sometimes we could pick out a house, perhaps a mansion, including one named for Robert E. Lee. We knew nothing of General Lee except that he had something to do with slavery. On the wrong side. That was enough. We looked, but from our safe distance. There were bridges, but we never crossed them. We had somehow picked up the idea that to go there for more than a short time meant death. Or maybe worse. Emboldened by the river running before us like a moat, we stood our ground and kept looking. A few of the boys claimed to have visited the evil empire, but the rest of us laughed uneasily to show our doubts. We stood, we gazed, we told bad jokes. We poked each other and pointed.

"That's Virginia," we would say, shuddering.

Times have changed. Virginia has changed. I have changed. Today I love the state, its beauty, its people, even its complicated sense of history. But in 1966, sitting on the front step of our grand new house in our grand new lonely white neighborhood of Washington, I felt as if we had moved to the fearsome Virginia of the sixties, which, in my child's mind, captured all the horror of what I knew of how white people treated black people. I watched the strange new people passing us and wordlessly watching back, and I knew we were not welcome here. I knew we would not be liked here. I knew we would have no friends here. I knew we should not have moved here. I knew...

And all at once, a white woman arriving home from work at the house 20 across the street from ours turned and smiled with obvious delight and waved and called out, "Welcome!" in a booming, confident voice I would come to love. She bustled into her house, only to emerge, minutes later, with a huge tray of cream cheese and jelly sandwiches, which she carried to our porch and offered around with her ready smile, simultaneously feeding and greeting the children of a family she had never met—and a black family at that—with nothing to gain for herself except perhaps the knowledge that she had done the right thing. We were strangers, black strangers, and she went out of her way to make us feel welcome. This woman's name was Sara Kestenbaum, and she died much too soon, but she remains, in my experience, one of the great exemplars of all that is best about civility.

Sara Kestenbaum's special contribution to civility back in 1966 was to create for us a sense of belonging where none had existed before. And she did so even though she had never seen any of us in her life. She managed, in the course of a single day, to turn us from strangers into friends, a remarkable gift that few share. (My wife is one of the few.) But we must never require friendship as the price of civility, and the great majority of us who lack that gift nevertheless hold the same obligation of civility.

This story illustrates what I mean when I say that civility is the set of sacrifices we make for the sake of our fellow passengers. Sara Kestenbaum was generous to us, giving of herself with no benefit to herself, and she demonstrated not merely a welcome that nobody else offered, but a faith in us, a trust that we were people to whom one could and should be generous. And so we have the beginning of a definition of the sacrificial civility we have been discussing:

> Civility has two parts: generosity, even when it is costly, and trust, even when there is risk.

Saying hello to a stranger on the street or driving with a bit more care are acts of generosity. Conceding the basic goodwill of my fellow citizens, even when I disagree with them, is an act of trust. By greeting us as she did, in the midst of a white neighborhood and a racially charged era, Sara was generous when nobody forced her to be, and trusting when there was no reason to be. Of such risks is true civility constructed.

...Our community, after all, is not limited to those to whom we are closest. Nowadays, whether we speak of our neighborhood, our town, our state, or our nation, our fellow passengers are mostly strangers. But our duty to be both respectful and kind does not disappear simply because they are people we do not know. Thus, we can see another rule of civility — one of the simplest and most straightforward — a simple duty of kindness:

> Civility creates not merely a negative duty not to do harm, but an affirmative duty to do good.

In the Jewish tradition, this duty is captured in the requirement of *chesed* — the doing of acts of kindness — which is in turn derived from the understanding that human beings are made in the image of God. This understanding imposes a duty to do as God would do.[8] Perhaps this teaching is part of what motivated Sara Kestenbaum, our welcoming neighbor back in 1966, whose family was deeply religious. Civility itself may be seen as a part of *chesed*: it does indeed require kindnesses toward our fellow citizens, including the ones who are strangers, and even when it is hard. When we are polite rather than rude, warm rather than cold, when we try to see God in others, we are doing acts of kindness. In all of these acts, we welcome the stranger, not because of any benefit we think will come to us, but because we come to believe that welcoming the stranger is right.

Remember what we have observed about desire: civility often demands its discipline. No matter what civility might counsel, we are always free not to be kind to each other, but it is almost always morally wrong to exercise that freedom. (I speak, of course, of self-restraint, not restraint through law.) We are free to remain impolite, and efforts to legislate otherwise have ended up looking a bit silly. The state of Washington has tried to forbid untruthful political

25

advertisements, to no noticeable effect. A town in New Jersey has tried to ban cursing, to the predictable and unfortunate fury of civil libertarians...and to no noticeable effect. Even antinoise ordinances, once the glory of many a small town, have fallen into desuetude. If we are to reconstruct civility, especially in a nation that prides itself on being free, we will have to do it through better habits, not better laws.

This raises some rather basic questions. It is one thing to carry sandwiches to new neighbors; that is, after all, an old and honored American tradition, even if it is still too often ignored when the new neighbors are the wrong color. But what does it mean, for example, to say we must be civil in this strong sense toward a homeless beggar who confronts us on the street? Are we to give him the money he seeks? Buy him a hot meal? Perhaps turn over to him all that we have? The admittedly unsatisfying answer is that civility by itself cannot provide the proper standard of charitable giving. Each of us must decide that for ourselves—in accordance, however, with strong norms of sacrifice for others. But civility, as we have used the term, does suggest that the one thing we cannot do about the beggar is ignore him. If we owe to our fellow passengers an obligation of respect, then to pass by the beggar as though he does not exist is to pretend that he is not a passenger at all—indeed, that he is other than human. We owe the beggar the same boon of greeting or conversation that we would bestow on anybody else we happen to meet.

At the same time, we must not force others to be our friends. We owe to everyone we meet the simple life space in which to carry on an intimate existence of which we know nothing. We owe to every stranger the chance to remain a stranger, whether the stranger is a seatmate on an airplane who is more interested in that book in her lap than in conversation, or a coworker who has no desire to share with us the slightest details of his love life. So civility requires respect for the privacy of others.

And then there is the matter of politics. The reader may well wonder how campaigning for office might be different if opposing candidates treated each other with the respect that comes of knowing they share equally in God's creation. Politics would not be less partisan—there are genuine differences to be aired—but it would undoubtedly be more polite. Opponents might decide that they could do business together. They would not sling mud (even though, as we have already seen, it seems to work). They would not lie about themselves or each other.

And if this all sounds like a pipe dream, that is but further evidence, if 30 any is needed, of how far our politics and our day-to-day lives diverge from any civil ideal. It might seem to require an awesome feat of imagination to persuade ourselves that we should try to feel this sense of awe, this need to give thanks, each time we meet another human being. But nothing less—and certainly no merely instrumental conception of civility—is likely to get us back to where Isaac Peebles° suggested we should be. Peebles calls upon us to respect the comfort of our companions along the way, even when it means less comfort for ourselves. The idea of civility as sacrifice is one that he would readily have understood, and one that we, even in this postmodern age when so much seems up for grabs, should understand and applaud. If it is a dream, I think it is an achievable one. But we have already gone as far as secular morality by itself can take us. I doubt that we can reconstruct civility in America without a revival of religion as a force in both our public and our private lives, because religion can give believers the power to resist the dangerous, self-seeking moral understandings that are coming to dominate our social life. Believers, in turn, can show by the power of their example the better way to live.

The creation of computer viruses—the subject that opened this... [essay]—is, in a peculiar way, an exercise in secular morality run rampant: it requires thinking of oneself to the exclusion of others, and somehow persuading oneself that a course of action is not a whim but a right. As to the claim that virus-making is harmful (all that data lost, all those hard drives damaged), many a virus writer will say, with evidently straight face, that this virtual information is not property, that it should be free for anybody to borrow, manipulate, or destroy. Or that the act is a protest against the domination of the human spirit by technology. Or a helpful means of indicating where computer security is weak—the defense offered by Fred Cohen, creator of the first computer virus.

Listening to these arguments, one is put in mind of the basketball player Dennis Rodman's justification for intentionally bumping his head into that of a referee (an act that led to a hefty fine and suspension): "I was making a statement that I was free and independent and not like everybody else."⁹ Like the virus maker's protest against intellectual property, it sounds vaguely like a liberal principle but is really nothing but an incoherent justification for the uncivilized self-indulgence that the student of civility abhors.°

Our secular moral conversation—sometimes, not accurately, referred to as liberalism—tends to answer such protests as these by stating the conclusion as a premise, suggesting, for example, that computer viruses do real harm because the damage they cause is measurable in dollars. This form of argument, often clothed as the "harm principle," is actually a surrender to the ideology of the market. It calls upon nothing admirable in the human spirit and, indeed, proposes that until we know how much money an action has cost, we

---

Isaac Peebles: Author of *Politeness on Railroads*, a book of etiquette for rail passengers published in the 1880s.

One can hardly answer by saying that digital information is property just because most people think it is. A purely majoritarian theory of property rights (or rights of any other kind) would play havoc with the ideal of constitutional law. [Carter's note.]

cannot know if it is immoral or not. It is reminiscent of the argument that chattel slavery is bad only if human beings who are enslaved turn out to be less efficient workers than human beings able to sell their labor freely.[10] Unfortunately, there is little in secular ethics to refute such claims.

But civility—civility as a moral proposition—begins with the assumption that humans matter, that we owe each other respect, and that treating each other well is a moral duty. As we have seen, civility so understood often requires us to put aside our own interests and desires for the benefit of others—which, as Erasmus understood, is what civilization is all about. Nothing in contemporary secular conversation calls us to give up anything truly valuable for anybody else. No politician would dare run for office asking us to sacrifice for others. Only religion offers a sacred language of sacrifice-selflessness-awe that enables believers to treat their fellow citizens as...fellow passengers. But even if religion is the engine of civility, it has too few serious practitioners, which is why those who are truly moved by it to love their fellow human beings are so special. I learned that truth in 1966, and, to this day, I can close my eyes and feel on my tongue the smooth, slick sweetness of the cream cheese and jelly sandwiches that I gobbled on that summer afternoon when I discovered how a single act of genuine and unassuming civility can change a life forever.

Notes

1. Michael Alexander, "Computer Security: How Much Backup Is Needed?" (book excerpt), *Computer Reseller News*, August 19, 1996, p. 164.

2. See Adrian Mars, "Keys to the Plague," *Guardian Online* (May 1, 1997), URL: http://go2 .guardian.co.uk/computing/archive/863011510virus.html.

3. Quoted in ibid.

4. Richard Sennett, *The Fall of Public Man: On the Social Psychology of Capitalism* (New York: Vintage, 1978), p. 3.

5. Benton Johnson, "Modernity and Pluralism," in Martin E. Marty and Frederick E. Greenspahn, eds., *Pushing the Faith: Proselytism and Civility in a Pluralistic World* (New York: Crossroad, 1988), pp. 10, 17.

6. John Murray Cuddihy, *The Ordeal of Civility: Freud, Marx, Lévi-Strauss, and the Jewish Struggle with Modernity* (New York: Basic Books, 1974), p. 12.

7. Robert Coles, *The Moral Intelligence of Children* (New York: Random House, 1997), p. 96.

8. See the discussion in Rabbi Zelig Pliskin, *Love Your Neighbor: You and Your Fellow Man in the Light of the Torah* (Brooklyn: Aish HaTorah, 1977).

9. Dennis Rodman, with Michael Silver, *Walk on the Wild Side* (New York: Delacorte Press, 1997).

10. For an analysis of this proposition, see Richard A. Posner, *The Economics of Justice* (Cambridge, Mass.: Harvard University Press, 1981), pp. 102–10. Posner once argued that we should be allowed to sell ourselves into slavery; see ibid., p. 86. I might add that I have always suspected that Professor (now Judge) Posner, a great believer in economic efficiency, was playing a role more than offering a serious argument when he wrote this.

WHAT DOES HE SAY?

1. When Stephen L. Carter finds out that one version of *AOL4FREE* doesn't connect would-be users to AOL but rather erases the user's hard drive, his first reaction is "Serves them right!" He initially sees that result as a just penalty for trying to steal AOL service. But Carter thinks again and decides his judgment is rather like "saying that people who decline to feed parking meters deserve to have their cars vandalized." What do you think? Did you find yourself agreeing or disagreeing with Carter? Write about this in a paragraph.

2. Make a list of the strangers you saw (or, perhaps didn't really see or pay much attention to) yesterday and today. Obviously you can't name them. But you can list where you saw these people, what they looked like (some of them, anyhow), and what they were doing (or what you guess they were doing). Do this for five individuals or small groups of people you saw. For each of these five instances, make notes as to whether or not you said anything to these people, made any kind of eye contact, or otherwise offered any acknowledgment that they existed. Don't interpret or explain yet.

3. In class, discuss with others how your collective examples illustrate "an ethic for relating to the stranger." What do you think of this ethic (or of the various ethics, if you identify more than one)?

4. Discuss occasions when you have clearly seen that you have been left out or ignored by others. What, if anything, did you do in response?

5. Carter advocates what he calls being civil toward others, "which means that we should accord them respect and even (although it may seem unfashionable) that we should be polite." Is this view foolish and naive?

WHAT DO YOU THINK?

6. Write an essay reflecting on a time when you welcomed a new neighbor or were welcomed by someone. Why did you extend such a welcome? Can you think of a time when you would probably not welcome a stranger? What were the results of those times when you were welcomed by someone else?

7. Identify two of Carter's notions of civility (for example, civility as sacrifice, civility as offering others welcome; he includes others). Explain each as Carter would view it. Then use examples from your own experience to show to what extent, if at all, you and Carter agree.

8. Based on this essay, what do you think Carter's response would be to the binge-drinking scenario we used to introduce this chapter?

WHAT WOULD THEY SAY?

9. Write about the ways that civility matters in educational settings and educational efforts. If you can, include an example of an instance when incivility hurt the learning

process and a time when civility made a large, important contribution. Relate your argument to Adrienne Rich's "Claiming an Education" (p. 608) and Parker Palmer's "The Community of Truth" (p. 627) or to Donald McCabe and Linda Klebe Trevino's "Honesty and Honor Codes" (p. 405) and Lawrence Hinman's "Virtual Virtues: Reflections on Academic Integrity in the Age of the Internet" (p. 415).

10. Chapter 5, "Is Honesty the Best Policy?", also contains a selection by Stephen L. Carter: "The Best Student Ever" (p. 391), from his book *Integrity*. Based just on these two pieces, how would you define Carter's notion of ethics? Write an essay explaining its three or four key points.

CORNEL WEST

The Moral Obligations of Living in a Democratic Society

*C*ORNEL *W*EST *(b. 1953) believes that what he calls "the market culture" is at odds with true democracy. West argues that democracy itself is threatened when we do not feel an obligation to others and do not feel ourselves to be "a citizen among citizens." Thus the opening question of this chapter takes on decidedly economic and political implications in light of his essay.*

An influential African American social critic and one of the most important public intellectuals in America, Cornel West taught for many years in the Afro-American Studies Department at Harvard University and is now on the faculty at Princeton. A popular speaker, he is also the author of more than a dozen books, including Race Matters *(1993) and* Keeping Faith: Philosophy and Race in America *(1993). This essay was first published in* The Good Citizen *(1999). His hip-hop album,* Sketches of My Culture, *was released in 2001.*

One of the fundamental questions of our day is whether the tradition of struggle can be preserved and expanded. I refer to the struggle for decency and dignity, the struggle for freedom and democracy.

In *Tradition and Individual Talent* (1919) T. S. Eliot claims that tradition is not something you inherit—if you want it, you must sacrifice for it. In other words, tradition must be fought for. . . .

In any discussion about race matters it is vital to situate yourself in a tradition, in a larger narrative that links the past to the present. When we think of Sojourner Truth, Harriet Tubman, Ida Buelle Wells-Barnett, A. Philip Randolph, Marcus Garvey, Ella Baker, James Baldwin, and so many nameless and anonymous ones, we cannot but be moved by their standards of vision and courage. They are wind at one's back.

The recovery of a tradition always begins at the existential level, with the experience of what it is to be human under a specific set of circumstances and conditions. It is very difficult to engage in a candid and frank critical discussion about race by assuming it is going to be a rational exchange. Race must be addressed in a form that can deal with its complexity and irrationality.

Perhaps no one understood the existential dimension of being human 5 and African in America better than W. E. B. Du Bois. He recognized the absurd in American society and realized that being Black in America is to be a problem. Du Bois asserted that race in this country is the fetishization of a problem, black bodies in white space. He understood what it meant to be cast as part of a problem people rather than people with problems. Once the humanity of a people is problematized, they are called into question perennially. Their beauty is attacked: wrong hips, lips, noses, skin texture, skin pigmentation, and hair texture. Black intelligence is always guilty before proven innocent in the court of the life of the mind: *The Bell Curve* is just a manifestation of the cycle. Perhaps the gravest injustice is the image of the welfare queen. Looking at the history of black women in America, on the plantation taking care of white children in white households, how is it possible that they could become the symbol of laziness? All of the foregoing are signs of a humanity that has been problematized.

Du Bois also underscored that to be part of a problem people is to be viewed as part of an undifferentiated blob, a monolithic block. Problem people become indistinguishable and interchangeable, which means that only one of them has to be asked to find out what all the rest of them think.

It is rare in human history, of course, that the notion of individuality and the civic are coupled so that a democratic project is generated. For most of history ordinary people have been viewed as "weeds and rain drops," as part of a mob, a rabble, all of which are ways of constituting them as an undifferentiated mob. Even the Greeks, despite their glorious yet truncated democratic experiment, would only apply the tragic to the elite. Ordinary people were limited to the idyllic and the comic, the assumption being that their lives were less complex and one-dimensional.

A democratic sensibility undeniably cuts against the grain of history. Most of human history is the history of elites, of kings, queens, princes, prelates, magistrates, potentates, knights, earls, and squires, all of whom subordinated and exploited everyday people.

This is why it becomes vital to talk about prevailing forms of oligarchy and plutocracy, and to some degree "pigmentocracy," in America. One percent of the population owns 48 percent of the total net financial wealth. The top 10 percent owns 86 percent of the wealth, while the top 20 percent owns 94 percent of the wealth. Meanwhile, 80 percent of the population is experiencing stagnating and declining wages.

Corporations speak glibly about downsizing—bureaucratic language 10 that simply means you do not have a job even though we have the highest profits we have had since 1948. And yet 25 percent of all of America's children live in poverty, and 42 percent of young brown brothers and sisters live in poverty, and 51 percent of young black brothers and sisters live in poverty in the richest nation in the history of the world. These sets of conditions are immoral.

When I examine the present state of American democracy, I believe we are living in one of the most terrifying moments in the history of this nation. We are experiencing a lethal and unprecedented linkage of relative economic decline (i.e., working-class wage stagnation), cultural decay, and political lethargy. No democracy can survive with a middle class so insecure that it is willing to accept any authoritarian option in order to provide some sense of normalcy and security in their lives. It also opens the door for significant segments of that middle class to scapegoat those who are most vulnerable.

It is past time that we consider in our public discourse the civic responsibilities of corporations. There must be prescribed forms of public accountability for institutions that have a disproportionate amount of wealth, power, and influence. This is not a matter of demonizing corporations, but an issue of democratic survival.

We are all in the same boat, on the same turbulent sea. The boat has a huge leak in it and in the end, we go up and down together. A corporate executive recently said to me, "We are not in the same boat. We're global." His response suggests why it is vital to inquire when corporate commercial interests must be subordinate to the public interest.

Democracy always raises the fundamental question: what is the role of the most disadvantaged in relation to the public interest? It is similar in some ways to the biblical question: what are you to do with the least of these? If we do not want to live in a democracy, we are not obliged to raise that question. In fact, the aristocracy does not address that question at all. Chekhov wrote in a play, "The Czar's police, they don't give a damn about raising that question. That's not the kind of society they are." But within a democratic society that question must be continually raised and pushed.

The conversation matters because the preservation of democracy is 15 threatened by real economic decline. While it is not identical to moral and cultural decay, it is inseparable from it. Even though the pocketbook is important, many Americans are concerned more about the low quality of their lives, the constant fear of violent assault and cruel insult, the mean-spiritedness and coldheartedness of social life, and the inability to experience deep levels of intimacy. These are the signs of a culturally decadent civilization.

By *decadent* I mean the relative erosion of systems of nurturing and caring, which affects each of us, but which has an especially devastating impact on young people. Any civilization that is unable to sustain its networks of caring and nurturing will generate enough anger and aggression to make communication near impossible. The result is a society in which we do not even respect each other enough to listen to each other. Dialogue is the lifeblood of democracy and is predicated on certain bonds of trust and respect. At this moment of cultural decay, it is difficult to find places where those ties of sympathy may be nurtured.

The roots of democracy are fundamentally grounded in mutual respect, personal responsibility, and social accountability. Yet democracy is also about giving each person a dignified voice in the decision-making processes in those institutions that guide and regulate their lives. These deeply moral suppositions have a certain spiritual dimension. John Dewey and Josiah Royce,° among others, identified a spirituality of genuine questioning and dialogical exchange that allows us to transcend our egocentric predicaments. Spirituality requires an experience of something bigger than our individual selves that binds us to a community. It could be in an authoritarian bind, of course, which is why the kind of spiritual and moral awakening that is necessary for a democracy to function is based on a sense of the public—a sense of what it is to be a citizen among citizens.

Nurturing spirituality is so difficult today because we are bombarded by a market culture that evolves around buying and selling, promoting and advertising. The market tries to convince us that we are really alive only when we are addicted to stimulation and titillation. Given the fact that so much of American culture revolves around sexual foreplay and orgiastic intensity, for many people the good life might mean being hooked up to an orgasm machine and being perennially titillated.

The ultimate logic of a market culture is the gangsterization of culture: I want power now. I want pleasure now. I want property now. Your property. Give it to me.

Young black people call their block a "hood" now. I grew up in a neigh-   20 borhood; it is a big difference. A neighborhood was a place not only for the nuclear family, but also included aunts and uncles, friends and neighbors, rabbis and priests, deacons and pastors, Little League coaches and dance teachers—all of whom served as a backdrop for socializing young people. This backdrop provided children with a sense of what it is to be human, with all its decency, integrity, and compassion. When those values are practiced, a neighborhood emerges.

Unfortunately, neighborhoods often took shape in my boyhood under patriarchal and homophobic conditions, and that history must be called into question. Still, we must recover its flow of nonmarket values and nonmarket activity.

These days we cannot even talk about love the way James Baldwin and Martin Luther King Jr. did. Nobody wants to hear that syrupy, mushy stuff. James Baldwin, however, said love is the most dangerous discourse in the world. It is daring and difficult because it makes you vulnerable, but if you experience it, it is the peak of human existence.

In our own time it is becoming extremely difficult for nonmarket values to gain a foothold. Parenting is a nonmarket activity; so much sacrifice and service goes into it without any assurance that the providers will get anything back. Mercy, justice; they are nonmarket. Care, service; nonmarket.

John Dewey and Josiah Royce: John Dewey (1859–1952), an influential American philosopher and education theorist; Josiah Royce (1855–1916), American philosopher. [Eds.]

Solidarity, fidelity; nonmarket. Sweetness and kindness and gentleness. All nonmarket.

Tragically, nonmarket values are relatively scarce, which is one of the reasons why it is so tough to mobilize and organize people in our society around just about any cause. It is hard to convince people that there are alternative options for which they ought to sacrifice. Ultimately, there can be no democratic tradition without nonmarket values.

In the last decade we have witnessed within popular culture wonderful innovation in forms of hip hop and rap. Compare that phenomenon to the 1960s when the Black Panther Party emerged and note the big difference between the two movements. One has to do with sacrifice, paying the price, dealing with the consequences as you bring power and pressure to bear on the prevailing status quo. The other has to do with marketing black rage. One movement had forty-seven local branches across the nation, the other sells millions of albums and CDs. The comparison is not a matter of patronizing this generation. Frankly, it is a critique of each of us who has to deal with this market culture and through market mechanisms try to preserve some nonmarket values.

What then are we to do? There is no overnight solution or panacea, of course. We need to begin with something profoundly un-American, namely, recalling a sense of history, a very deep, tragic, and comic sense of history, a historical sensibility linked to empathy. Empathy is not simply a matter of trying to imagine what others are going through, but having the will to muster enough courage to do something about it. In a way, empathy is predicated upon hope.

Hope has nothing to do with optimism. I am in no way optimistic about America, nor am I optimistic about the plight of the human species on this globe. There is simply not enough evidence that allows me to infer that things are going to get better. That has been the perennial state and condition of not simply black people in America, but all self-conscious human beings who are sensitive to the forms of evil around them. We can be prisoners of hope even as we call optimism into question.

To be part of the democratic tradition is to be a prisoner of hope. And you cannot be a prisoner of hope without engaging in a form of struggle in the present moment that keeps the best of the past alive. To engage in that struggle means that one is always willing to acknowledge that there is no triumph around the corner, but that you persist because you believe it is right and just and moral. As T. S. Eliot said, "Ours is in the trying. The rest is not our business."

We are not going to save each other, ourselves, America, or the world. But we certainly can leave it a little bit better. As my grandmother used to say, "If the Kingdom of God is within you, then everywhere you go, you ought to leave a little Heaven behind."

WHAT DOES HE SAY?

1. Cornel West is African American, and he grounds his essay in a discussion of the African American "struggle" in this country. What is the relevance of this discussion for readers who are not African American? In what paragraph or section of the essay does this relevance become clear?

2. West invents a word, *pigmentocracy,* and aligns it with two existing words, *oligarchy* and *plutocracy.* Look up the definitions of these two words and use them to explain the meaning of West's invented word. The statistics in the remainder of this paragraph and in the next paragraph also help you figure out the meaning of West's new word. Use these statistics to help you explain your definition.

3. Though West is not explicit about his own religious values, religious ideas do seem to be implied in several of his statements. Mark these statements and discuss the values they seem to suggest. What assumptions might West be making about himself and about his readers? Do you find these implicit references to religion persuasive? Why or why not?

4. As in Bowen H. McCoy's essay "The Parable of the Sadhu" (p. 102), West's essay depends on the strategy of explicitly asking questions. As you read, mark these questions. What is their function in the essay—how do they work stylistically and rhetorically? How does West answer these questions?

WHAT DO YOU THINK?

5. Write an essay explaining West's distinction between "optimism" and "hope," applying it to any complicated problem in your own life or in the community around you, on campus or beyond.

6. Write an essay profiling an organization, a business, or an individual who seems to be acting out West's call for civic responsibility in your local community or beyond. Consider volunteering your time for this group; if you do, include your experience in the conclusion of the essay.

7. Research, update, and expand the statistics that West uses to explain the idea of "oligarchy" in this country, then write an essay presenting your findings. Option: Write an essay denying that an oligarchy exists.

WHAT WOULD THEY SAY?

8. What would Cornel West write in the margins and at the end of Bowen H. McCoy's essay "The Parable of the Sadhu" (p. 102), and what would McCoy write in the margins and at the end of West's? Based on your reading of "The Parable of the Sadhu," explain why McCoy would clearly agree with West's call for "civic responsibility" in corporations.

9. Consider Cornel West's essay together with Stephen L. Carter's "Welcoming the Stranger" (p. 111). Explain what you think they'd agree about in terms of community and democracy.

10. Get these three intellectuals into a debate: Garrett Hardin in "Lifeboat Ethics: The Case against Helping the Poor" (p. 130), Esther Dyson in "Cyberspace: If You Don't Love It, Leave It" (p. 141), and West in this essay. Call this discussion, "Are We Responsible for Others?" What are the nuances and points of agreement and disagreement?

GARRETT HARDIN

Lifeboat Ethics:
The Case against Helping the Poor

IN THIS FAMOUS ESSAY, Garrett Hardin (1915–2003) asks a clear question—a version of the question we ask in the title of this chapter—then gives an unambiguous, unequivocal answer, using the metaphor of the lifeboat, a finite space with an inherently limited capacity. Only responsible systems of control—limits on aid, on immigration, and on the use of natural resources—can keep the boat afloat, Hardin argues.

Hardin, an ecologist and microbiologist, was professor of human ecology for the University of California for more than thirty years, retiring in 1978. He published more than three hundred articles and twenty-seven books, including Living Within Limits: Ecology, Economics, and Population Taboos *(1993) and* The Ostrich Factor: Our Population Myopia *(1999). "Lifeboat Ethics: The Case against Helping the Poor" was first published in the September 1974 issue of* Psychology Today.

Environmentalists use the metaphor of the earth as a "spaceship" in trying to persuade countries, industries, and people to stop wasting and polluting our natural resources. Since we all share life on this planet, they argue, no single person or institution has the right to destroy, waste, or use more than a fair share of its resources.

But does everyone on Earth have an equal right to an equal share of its resources? The spaceship metaphor can be dangerous when used by misguided idealists to justify suicidal policies for sharing our resources through uncontrolled immigration and foreign aid. In their enthusiastic but unrealistic generosity, they confuse the ethics of a spaceship with those of a lifeboat.

A true spaceship would have to be under the control of a captain, since no ship could possibly survive if its course were determined by committee. Spaceship Earth certainly has no captain; the United Nations is merely a toothless tiger, with little power to enforce any policy upon its bickering members.

If we divide the world crudely into rich nations and poor nations, two-thirds of them are desperately poor, and only one-third comparatively rich, with the United States the wealthiest of all. Metaphorically each rich nation can be seen as a lifeboat full of comparatively rich people. In the ocean outside each lifeboat swim the poor of the world, who would like to get in or at least to share some of the wealth. What should the lifeboat passengers do?

First, we must recognize the limited capacity of any lifeboat. For example, a nation's land has a limited capacity to support a population and as the

5

current energy crisis has shown us, in some ways we have already exceeded the carrying capacity of our land.

ADRIFT IN A MORAL SEA

So here we sit, say fifty people in our lifeboat. To be generous, let us assume it has room for ten more, making a total capacity of sixty. Suppose the fifty of us in the lifeboat see one hundred others swimming in the water outside, begging for admission to our boat or for handouts. We have several options: we may be tempted to try to live by the Christian ideal of being "our brother's keeper" or by the Marxist ideal of "to each according to his needs." Since the needs of all in the water are the same, and since they can all be seen as "our brothers," we could take them all into our boat, making a total of one hundred fifty in a boat designed for sixty. The boat swamps, everyone drowns. Complete justice, complete catastrophe.

Since the boat has an unused excess capacity of ten more passengers, we could admit just ten more to it. But which ten do we let in? How do we choose? Do we pick the best ten, "first come, first served"? And what do we say to the ninety we exclude? If we do let an extra ten into our lifeboat, we will have lost our "safety factor," an engineering principle of critical importance. For example, if we don't leave room for excess capacity as a safety factor in our country's agriculture, a new plant disease or a bad change in the weather could have disastrous consequences.

Suppose we decide to preserve our small safety factor and admit no more to the lifeboat. Our survival is then possible although we shall have to be constantly on guard against boarding parties.

While this last solution clearly offers the only means of our survival, it is morally abhorrent to many people. Some say they feel guilty about their good luck. My reply is simple: "Get out and yield your place to others." This may solve the problem of the guilt-ridden person's conscience, but it does not change the ethics of the lifeboat. The needy person to whom the guilt-ridden person yields his place will not himself feel guilty about his good luck. If he did, he would not climb aboard. The net result of conscience-stricken people giving up their unjustly held seats is the elimination of that sort of conscience from the lifeboat.

This is the basic metaphor within which we must work out our solu- 10 tions. Let us now enrich the image, step by step, with substantive additions from the real world, a world that must solve real and pressing problems of overpopulation and hunger.

The harsh ethics of the lifeboat become even harsher when we consider the reproductive differences between the rich nations and the poor nations. The people inside the lifeboats are doubling in numbers every eighty-seven years; those swimming around outside are doubling, on the average, every thirty-five years, more than twice as fast as the rich. And since the world's re-sources are dwindling, the difference in prosperity between the rich and the poor can only increase.

As of 1973, the United States had a population of 210 million people, who were increasing by 0.8 percent per year. Outside our lifeboat, let us imag-ine another 210 million people (say the combined populations of Colombia, Ecuador, Venezuela, Morocco, Pakistan, Thailand, and the Philippines) who are increasing at a rate of 3.3 percent per year. Put differently, the doubling time for this aggregate population is twenty-one years, compared to eighty-seven years for the United States.

The harsh ethics of the lifeboat become harsher when we consider the reproductive differences between rich and poor.

MULTIPLYING THE RICH AND THE POOR

Now suppose the United States agreed to pool its resources with those seven countries, with everyone receiving an equal share. Initially the ratio of Ameri-cans to non-Americans in this model would be one-to-one. But consider what the ratio would be after eighty-seven years, by which time the Americans would have doubled to a population of 420 million. By then, doubling every twenty-one years, the other group would have swollen to 354 billion. Each American would have to share the available resources with more than eight people.

But, one could argue, this discussion assumes that current population 15 trends will continue, and they may not. Quite so. Most likely the rate of pop-ulation increase will decline much faster in the United States than it will in the other countries, and there does not seem to be much we can do about it. In sharing with "each according to his needs," we must recognize that needs are determined by population size, which is determined by the rate of repro-duction, which at present is regarded as a sovereign right of every nation, poor or not. This being so, the philanthropic load created by the sharing ethic of the spaceship can only increase.

THE TRAGEDY OF THE COMMONS

The fundamental error of spaceship ethics, and the sharing it requires, is that it leads to what I call "the tragedy of the commons." Under a system of private property, the men who own property recognize their responsibility to care for it, for if they don't they will eventually suffer. A farmer, for instance, will allow no more cattle in a pasture than its carrying capacity justifies. If he overloads it, erosion sets in, weeds take over, and he loses the use of the pasture.

If a pasture becomes a commons open to all, the right of each to use it may not be matched by a corresponding responsibility to protect it. Asking everyone to use it with discretion will hardly do, for the considerate herdsman who refrains from overloading the commons suffers more than a selfish one who says his needs are greater. If everyone would restrain himself, all would be well; but it takes only one less than everyone to ruin a system of voluntary restraint. In a crowded world of less than perfect human beings, mutual ruin is inevitable if there are no controls. This is the tragedy of the commons.

One of the major tasks of education today should be the creation of such an acute awareness of the dangers of the commons that people will recognize its many varieties. For example, the air and water have become polluted because they are treated as commons. Further growth in the population or per capita conversion of natural resources into pollutants will only make the problem worse. The same holds true for the fish of the oceans. Fishing fleets have nearly disappeared in many parts of the world, technological improvements in the art of fishing are hastening the day of complete ruin. Only the replacement of the system of the commons with a responsible system of control will save the land, air, water, and oceanic fisheries.

THE WORLD FOOD BANK

In recent years there has been a push to create a new commons called a world food bank, an international depository of food reserves to which nations would contribute according to their abilities and from which they would draw according to their needs. This humanitarian proposal has received support from many liberal international groups and from such prominent citizens as Margaret Mead, UN secretary general Kurt Waldheim, and Senators Edward Kennedy and George McGovern.

A world food bank appeals powerfully to our humanitarian impulses. 20 But before we rush ahead with such a plan, let us recognize where the greatest political push comes from, lest we be disillusioned later. Our experience with the "Food for Peace program," or Public Law 480, gives us the answer. This program moved billions of dollars worth of U.S. surplus grain to food-short, population-long countries during the past two decades. But when PL 480 first became law, a headline in the business magazine *Forbes* revealed the real power behind it: "Feeding the World's Hungry Millions: How It Will Mean Billions for U.S. Business."

And indeed it did. In the years 1960 to 1970, U.S. taxpayers spent a total of $7.9 billion on the Food for Peace program. Between 1948 and 1970, they also paid an additional $50 billion for other economic-aid programs, some of which went for food and food-producing machinery and technology. Though all U.S. taxpayers were forced to contribute to the cost of PL 480 certain special-interest groups gained handsomely under the program. Farmers did not have to contribute the grain; the government, or rather the taxpayers, bought it from them at full market prices. The increased demand raised prices of farm products generally. The manufacturers of farm machinery, fertilizers, and pesticides benefited by the farmers' extra efforts to grow more food. Grain elevators profited from storing the surplus until it could be shipped. Railroads made money hauling it to ports, and shipping lines profited from carrying it overseas. The implementation of PL 480 required the creation of a vast government bureaucracy, which then acquired its own vested interest in continuing the program regardless of its merits.

Extracting Dollars

Those who proposed and defended the Food for Peace program in public rarely mentioned its importance to any of these special interests. The public emphasis was always on its humanitarian effects. The combination of silent selfish interests and highly vocal humanitarian apologists made a powerful and successful lobby for extracting money from taxpayers. We can expect the same lobby to push now for the creation of a World Food Bank.

However great the potential benefit to selfish interests, it should not be a decisive argument against a truly humanitarian program. We must ask if such a program would actually do more good than harm, not only momentarily but also in the long run. Those who propose the food bank usually refer to a current "emergency" or "crisis" in terms of world food supply. But what is an emergency? Although they may be infrequent and sudden, everyone knows that emergencies will occur from time to time. A well-run family, company, organization, or country prepares for the likelihood of accidents and emergencies. It expects them, it budgets for them, it saves for them.

Learning the Hard Way

What happens if some organizations or countries budget for accidents and others do not? If each country is solely responsible for its own well-being, poorly managed ones will suffer. But they can learn from experience. They may mend their ways, and learn to budget for infrequent but certain emergencies. For example, the weather varies from year to year, and periodic crop failures are certain. A wise and competent government saves out of the production of the good years in anticipation of bad years to come. Joseph taught this policy to pharaoh in Egypt more than two thousand years ago. Yet the great majority of the governments in the world today do not follow such a policy. They lack either the wisdom or the competence, or both. Should those nations that do manage to put something aside be forced to come to the rescue each time an emergency occurs among the poor nations?

"But it isn't their fault!" some kind-hearted liberals argue. "How can 25 we blame the poor people who are caught in an emergency? Why must they suffer for the sins of their governments?" The concept of blame is simply not relevant here. The real question is What are the operational consequences of establishing a world food bank? If it is open to every country every time a need develops, slovenly rulers will not be motivated to take Joseph's advice. Someone will always come to their aid. Some countries will deposit food in the world food bank, and others will withdraw it. There will be almost no overlap. As a result of such solutions to food shortage emergencies, the poor countries will not learn to mend their ways and will suffer progressively greater emergencies as their populations grow.

POPULATION CONTROL THE CRUDE WAY

On the average poor countries undergo a 2.5 percent increase in population each year; rich countries, about 0.8 percent. Only rich countries have anything in the way of food reserves set aside, and even they do not have as much as they should. Poor countries have none. If poor countries received no food from the outside, the rate of their population growth would be periodically checked by crop failures and famines. But if they can always draw on a world food bank in time of need, their population can continue to grow unchecked, and so will their "need" for aid. In the short run, a world food bank may diminish that need, but in the long run it actually increases the need without limit.

Without some system of worldwide food sharing, the proportion of people in the rich and poor nations might eventually stabilize. The overpopulated poor countries would decrease in numbers, while the rich countries that had room for more people would increase. But with a well-meaning system of sharing, such as a world food bank, the growth differential between the rich and the poor countries will not only persist, it will increase. Because of the higher rate of population growth in the poor countries of the world, 88 percent of today's children are born poor and only 12 percent rich. Year by year the ratio becomes worse, as the fast-reproducing poor outnumber the slow-reproducing rich.

A world food bank is thus a commons in disguise. People will have more motivation to draw from it than to add to any common store. The less provident and less able will multiply at the expense of the abler and more provident, bringing eventual ruin upon all who share in the commons. Besides, any system of "sharing" that amounts to foreign aid from the rich nations to the poor nations will carry the taint of charity, which will contribute little to the world peace so devoutly desired by those who support the idea of a world food bank.

As past U.S. foreign-aid programs have amply and depressingly demonstrated, international charity frequently inspires mistrust and antagonism rather than gratitude on the part of the recipient nation.

CHINESE FISH AND MIRACLE RICE

The modern approach to foreign aid stresses the export of technology and ad- 30
vice, rather than money and food. As an ancient Chinese proverb goes, "Give
a man a fish and he will eat for a day; teach him how to fish and he will eat
for the rest of his days." Acting on this advice, the Rockefeller and Ford
Foundations have financed a number of programs for improving agriculture
in the hungry nations. Known as the "green revolution," these programs have
led to the development of "miracle rice" and "miracle wheat," new strains that
offer bigger harvests and greater resistance to crop damage. Norman Borlaug,
the Nobel Prize–winning agronomist who, supported by the Rockefeller
Foundation, developed "miracle wheat," is one of the most prominent advocates of a world food bank.

Whether or not the green revolution can increase food production as
much as its champions claim is a debatable but possibly irrelevant point. Those
who support this well-intended humanitarian effort should first consider some
of the fundamentals of human ecology. Ironically, one man who did was
the late Alan Gregg, a vice president of the Rockefeller Foundation. Two decades ago he expressed strong doubts about the wisdom of such attempts to
increase food production. He likened the growth and spread of humanity
over the surface of the earth to the spread of cancer in the human body, re-
marking that "cancerous growths demand food; but, as far as I know, they have
never been cured by getting it."

OVERLOADING THE ENVIRONMENT

Every human born constitutes a draft on all aspects of the environment: food,
air, water, forests, beaches, wildlife, scenery, and solitude. Food can, perhaps,
be significantly increased to meet a growing demand. But what about clean
beaches, unspoiled forests, and solitude? If we satisfy a growing population's
need for food, we necessarily decrease its per capita supply of the other resources needed by men.

India, for example, now has a population of 600 million, which increases by 15 million each year. This population already puts a huge load on a
relatively impoverished environment. The country's forests are now only
a small fraction of what they were three centuries ago and floods and erosion
continually destroy the insufficient farmland that remains. Every one of the 15
million new lives added to India's population puts an additional burden on
the environment and increases the economic and social costs of crowding.
However humanitarian our intent, every Indian life saved through medical
or nutritional assistance from abroad diminishes the quality of life for those
who remain, and for subsequent generations. If rich countries make it possible,

through foreign aid, for 600 million Indians to swell to 1.2 billion in a mere twenty-eight years, as their current growth rate threatens, will future generations of Indians thank us for hastening the destruction of their environment? Will our good intentions be sufficient excuse for the consequences of our actions?

My final example of a commons in action is one for which the public has the least desire for rational discussion—immigration. Anyone who publicly questions the wisdom of current U.S. immigration policy is promptly charged with bigotry, prejudice, ethnocentrism, chauvinism, isolationism, or selfishness. Rather than encounter such accusations, one would rather talk about other matters leaving immigration policy to wallow in the crosscurrents of special interests that take no account of the good of the whole or the interests of posterity.

Perhaps we still feel guilty about things we said in the past. Two genera- 35 tions ago the popular press frequently referred to Dagos, Wops, Polacks, Chinks, and Krauts in articles about how America was being "overrun" by foreigners of supposedly inferior genetic stock. But because the implied inferiority of foreigners was used then as justification for keeping them out, people now assume that restrictive policies could only be based on such misguided notions. There are other grounds.

A Nation of Immigrants

Just consider the numbers involved. Our government acknowledges a net inflow of 400,000 immigrants a year. While we have no hard data on the extent of illegal entries, educated guesses put the figure at about 600,000 a year. Since the natural increase (excess of births over deaths) of the resident population now runs about 1.7 million per year, the yearly gain from immigration amounts to at least 19 percent of the total annual increase, and may be as much as 37 percent if we include the estimate for illegal immigrants. Considering the growing use of birth-control devices, the potential effect of education campaigns by such organizations as Planned Parenthood Federation of America and Zero Population Growth, and the influence of inflation and the housing shortage, the fertility rate of American women may decline so much that immigration could account for all the yearly increase in population. Should we not at least ask if that is what we want?

For the sake of those who worry about whether the "quality" of the average immigrant compares favorably with the quality of the average resident, let us assume that immigrants and native-born citizens are of exactly equal quality, however one defines that term. We will focus here only on quantity; and since our conclusions will depend on nothing else, all charges of bigotry and chauvinism become irrelevant.

IMMIGRATION VERSUS FOOD SUPPLY

World food banks move food to the people, hastening the exhaustion of the environment of the poor countries. Unrestricted immigration, on the other hand, moves people to the food, thus speeding up the destruction of the environment of the rich countries. We can easily understand why poor people should want to make this latter transfer, but why should rich hosts encourage it?

As in the case of foreign-aid programs, immigration receives support from selfish interests and humanitarian impulses. The primary selfish interest in unimpeded immigration is the desire of employers for cheap labor, particularly in industries and trades that offer degrading work. In the past, one wave of foreigners after another was brought into the United States to work at wretched jobs for wretched wages. In recent years the Cubans, Puerto Ricans, and Mexicans have had this dubious honor. The interests of the employers of cheap labor mesh well with the guilty silence of the country's liberal intelligentsia. White Anglo-Saxon Protestants are particularly reluctant to call for a closing of the doors to immigration for fear of being called bigots.

But not all countries have such reluctant leadership. Most educated 40 Hawaiians, for example, are keenly aware of the limits of their environment, particularly in terms of population growth. There is only so much room on the islands, and the islanders know it. To Hawaiians, immigrants from the other forty-nine states present as great a threat as those from other nations. At a recent meeting of Hawaiian government officials in Honolulu, I had the ironic delight of hearing a speaker who like most of his audience was of Japanese ancestry, ask how the country might practically and constitutionally close its doors to further immigration. One member of the audience countered: "How can we shut the doors now? We have many friends and relatives in Japan that we'd like to bring here some day so that they can enjoy Hawaii too." The Japanese American speaker smiled sympathetically and answered: "Yes, but we have children now, and someday we'll have grandchildren too. We can bring more people here from Japan only by giving away some of the land that we hope to pass on to our grandchildren some day. What right do we have to do that?"

At this point, I can hear U.S. liberals asking: "How can you justify slamming the door once you're inside? You say that immigrants should be kept out. But aren't we all immigrants, or the descendants of immigrants? If we insist on staying, must we not admit all others?" Our craving for intellectual order leads us to seek and prefer symmetrical rules and morals: a single rule for me and everybody else; the same rule yesterday, today, and tomorrow. Justice, we feel, should not change with time and place.

We Americans of non-Indian ancestry can look upon ourselves as the descendants of thieves who are guilty morally, if not legally, of stealing this land from its Indian owners. Should we then give back the land to the now living American descendants of those Indians? However morally or logically sound this proposal may be, I, for one, am unwilling to live by it and I know no one else who is. Besides, the logical consequence would be absurd. Suppose that, intoxicated with a sense of pure justice, we should decide to turn our land over to the Indians. Since all our other wealth has also been derived from the land, wouldn't we be morally obliged to give that back to the Indians too?

PURE JUSTICE VERSUS REALITY

Clearly, the concept of pure justice produces an infinite regression to absurdity. Centuries ago, wise men invented statutes of limitations to justify the rejection of such pure justice, in the interest of preventing continual disorder. The law zealously defends property rights, but only relatively recent property rights. Drawing a line after an arbitrary time has elapsed may be unjust, but the alternatives are worse.

We are all the descendants of thieves, and the world's resources are inequitably distributed. But we must begin the journey to tomorrow from the point where we are today. We cannot remake the past. We cannot safely divide the wealth equitably among all peoples so long as people reproduce at different rates. To do so would guarantee that our grandchildren and everyone else's grandchildren, would have only a ruined world to inhabit.

To be generous with one's own possessions is quite different from being 45 generous with those of posterity. We should call this point to the attention of those who from a commendable love of justice and equality, would institute a system of the commons, either in the form of a world food bank, or of unrestricted immigration. We must convince them if we wish to save at least some parts of the world from environmental ruin.

Without a true world government to control reproduction and the use of available resources, the sharing ethic of the spaceship is impossible. For the foreseeable future, our survival demands that we govern our actions by the ethics of a lifeboat, harsh though they may be. Posterity will be satisfied with nothing less.

WHAT DOES HE SAY?

1. Read through this essay once, then write a paragraph recording your first, quick response. Do you resist this essay? Does it offend you? If so, why? Or do you find Hardin's arguments intuitively reasonable?

2. Now reread the essay, carefully charting its argument. Mark each of the key questions he asks and the answers he gives with a *Q* and an *A*. Then draw a square around the examples or statistics he uses to support his claims and mark each of these with an *E* for evidence.

3. Describe the tone of this essay—harsh or gentle, loud or soft? To put this another way, describe the image of the writer that the words imply. Is he reasonable? sympathetic? logical?

4. "Without a true world government to control reproduction and the use of available resources," Hardin concludes, "the sharing ethic of the spaceship is impossible." Is Hardin actually arguing for such a world government? Would you?

5. How would Hardin respond to the binge-drinking scenario in the introduction to this chapter?

WHAT DO YOU THINK?

6. Hardin's essay was written in 1974. Do research to update the facts and statistics that he uses, and write a paper presenting your findings. Has the situation changed for the better or worse in the last thirty years? Do your findings alter your own responses to Hardin's arguments?

7. Apply Hardin's principles to a personal problem. Write an essay imagining how someone you know would respond if you acted in your personal life the way Hardin suggests that we act as a nation.

WHAT WOULD THEY SAY?

8. Cornel West says that we are all in the "same boat, on the same turbulent sea" ("The Moral Obligation of Living in a Democratic Society," p. 123). Hardin uses the same metaphor but takes a different position, expanding it to include the metaphor of the "spaceship" as well. Write an essay exploring other ways of using this metaphor of the lifeboat: What other variations or details might you provide? What are some other implications of lifeboats? Or write an essay changing the metaphor: for example, we're all wandering around in a forest, lost; we're all cooking in the same kitchen. Decide on the best metaphor and reflect on what that metaphor assumes or reveals.

9. Write an essay that compares and contrasts Bowen H. McCoy's "The Parable of the Sadhu" (p. 102) with Hardin's "Lifeboat Ethics." Is the plight of the Sadhu the same as the plight of the people in the lifeboat? Is it different? How? Which metaphor or analogy do you think best fits reality?

10. Much of Hardin's argument depends on environmental concerns—the limits of our natural resources and the pressing demands of increasing population. These are also the concerns of "The Earth Charter" (p. 158). Compare and contrast Hardin's approach to the use of resources and the approach of "The Earth Charter." Which do you find most practical and why?

11. Hardin's argument is diametrically opposed to the argument of Peter Singer in "The Singer Solution to World Poverty" (p. 661) in chapter 8. In an essay, explain why, summarizing these two opposing views and arguing for the one you think is the most persuasive.

12. Hardin would obviously disagree with Stephen L. Carter in "Welcoming the Stranger" (p. 111). Or would he? Explain your viewpoint in an essay.

ESTHER DYSON

Cyberspace: If You Don't Love It, Leave It

ESTHER DYSON *(b. 1951) claims that cyberspace is a place you can go to be yourself without worrying about what others think. Chair of an information technology company, Dyson makes Garrett Hardin's argument from the perspective of the Internet. In this new and virtual world, she suggests, the plea for empathy and social responsibility no longer has the same moral force.*

Esther Dyson graduated from Harvard University with a degree in economics, worked as a reporter for Forbes, *and is now chair of EDventure Holdings, a company focused on global information technology and computer markets.* Fortune *magazine named her one of the most powerful women in American business. "Cyberspace: If You Don't Love It, Leave It" first appeared in the July 6, 1995, issue of the* New York Times Magazine.

Something in the American psyche loves new frontiers. We hanker after wide open spaces; we like to explore; we like to make rules instead of follow them. But in this age of political correctness and other intrusions on our national cult of independence, it's hard to find a place where you can go and be yourself without worrying about the neighbors.

There is such a place: cyberspace. Lost in the furor over porn on the Net is the exhilarating sense of freedom that this new frontier once promised—and still does in some quarters. Formerly a playground for computer nerds and techies, cyberspace now embraces every conceivable constituency: schoolchildren, flirtatious singles, Hungarian Americans, accountants—along with pederasts and porn fans. Can they all get along? Or will our fear of kids surfing for cyberporn behind their bedroom doors provoke a crackdown?

The first order of business is to grasp what cyberspace *is*. It might help to leave behind metaphors of highways and frontiers and to think instead of real estate. Real estate, remember, is an intellectual, legal, artificial environment constructed *on top of* land. Real estate recognizes the difference between parkland and shopping mall, between red-light zone and school district, between church, state, and drugstore.

In the same way, you could think of cyberspace as a giant and unbounded world of virtual real estate. Some property is privately owned and rented out; other property is common land; some places are suitable for children, and others are best avoided by all but the kinkiest citizens. Unfortunately, it's those places that are now capturing the popular imagination: places that offer bomb-making instructions, pornography, advice on how to procure **141** stolen credit cards. They make cyberspace sound like a nasty place. Good citizens jump to a conclusion: better regulate it. . . .

Regardless of how many laws or lawsuits are launched, regulation won't   5
work.

Aside from being unconstitutional, using censorship to counter indecency and other troubling "speech" fundamentally misinterprets the nature of cyberspace. Cyberspace isn't a frontier where wicked people can grab unsuspecting children, nor is it a giant television system that can beam offensive messages at unwilling viewers. In this kind of real estate, users have to *choose* where they visit, what they see, what they do. It's optional, and it's much easier to bypass a place on the Net than it is to avoid walking past an unsavory block of stores on the way to your local 7-Eleven.

Put plainly, cyberspace is a voluntary destination—in reality, many destinations. You don't just get "onto the Net"; you have to go someplace in particular. That means that people can choose where to go and what to see. Yes, community standards should be enforced, but those standards should be set by cyberspace communities themselves, not by the courts or by politicians in Washington. What we need isn't government control over all these electronic communities: we need self-rule.

What makes cyberspace so alluring is precisely the way in which it's *different* from shopping malls, television, highways, and other terrestrial jurisdictions. But let's define the territory:

First, there are private e-mail conversations, akin to the conversations you have over the telephone or voice mail. These are private and consensual and require no regulation at all.

Second, there are information and entertainment services, where people   10
can download anything from legal texts and lists of "great new restaurants" to game software or dirty pictures. These places are like bookstores, malls, and movie houses—places where you go to buy something. The customer needs to request an item or sign up for a subscription; stuff (especially pornography) is not sent out to people who don't ask for it. Some of these services are free or included as part of a broad service like CompuServe or American Online; others charge and may bill their customers directly.

Third, there are "real" communities—groups of people who communicate among themselves. In real-estate terms, they're like bars or restaurants or bathhouses. Each active participant contributes to a general conversation, generally through posted messages. Other participants may simply listen or watch. Some are supervised by a moderator; others are more like bulletin boards—anyone is free to post anything. Many of these services started out unmoderated but are now imposing rules to keep out unwanted advertising, extraneous discussions, or increasingly rude participants. Without a moderator, the decibel level often gets too high.

Ultimately, it's the rules that determine the success of such places. Some of the rules are determined by the supplier of content; some of the rules concern prices and membership fees. The rules may be simple: "Only high-quality content about oil-industry liability and pollution legislation: $120 an hour." Or: "This forum is unmoderated, and restricted to information about copyright issues. People who insist on posting advertising or unrelated material will be asked to desist (and may eventually be barred)." Or: "Only children 8 to 12, on school-related topics and only clean words. The moderator will decide what's acceptable."

Cyberspace communities evolve just the way terrestrial communities do: people with like-minded interests band together. Every cyberspace community has its own character. Overall, the communities on CompuServe tend to be more techy or professional; those on America Online, affluent young singles; Prodigy, family oriented. Then there are independents like Echo, a hip, downtown New York service, or Women's Wire, targeted to women who want to avoid the male culture prevalent elsewhere on the Net. There's SurfWatch, a new program allowing access only to locations deemed suitable for children. On the Internet itself, there are lots of passionate noncommercial discussion groups on topics ranging from Hungarian politics (Hungary-Online) to copyright law.

And yes, there are also porn-oriented services, where people share dirty pictures and communicate with one another about all kinds of practices, often anonymously. Whether these services encourage the fantasies they depict is subject to debate—the same debate that has raged about pornography in other media. But the point is that no one is forcing this stuff on anybody.

What's unique about cyberspace is that it liberates us from the tyranny of 15 government, where everyone lives by the rule of the majority. In a democracy, minority groups and minority preferences tend to get squeezed out, whether they are minorities of race and culture or minorities of individual taste. Cyberspace allows communities of any size and kind to flourish; in cyberspace, communities are chosen by the users, not forced on them by accidents of geography. This freedom gives the rules that preside in cyberspace a moral authority that rules in terrestrial environments don't have. Most people are stuck in the country of their birth, but if you don't like the rules of a cyberspace community, you can just sign off. Love it or leave it. Likewise, if parents don't like the rules of a given cyberspace community, they can restrict their children's access to it.

What's likely to happen in cyberspace is the formation of new communities, free of the constraints that cause conflict on earth. Instead of a global village, which is a nice dream but impossible to manage, we'll have invented another world of self-contained communities that cater to their own members' inclinations without interfering with anyone else's. The possibility of a real market-style evolution of governance is at hand. In cyberspace, we'll be able to test and evolve rules governing what needs to be governed—intellectual property, content and access control, rules about privacy and free speech.

Some communities will allow anyone in; others will restrict access to members who qualify on one basis or another. Those communities that prove self-sustaining will prosper (and perhaps grow and split into subsets with ever more particular interests and identities). Those that can't survive—either because people lose interest or get scared off—will simply wither away.

In the near future, explorers in cyberspace will need to get better at defining and identifying their communities. They will need to put in place—and accept—their own local governments, just as the owners of expensive real estate often prefer to have their own security guards rather than call in the police. But they will rarely need help from any terrestrial government.

Of course, terrestrial governments may not agree. What to do, for instance, about pornography? The answer is labeling—not banning—questionable material. In order to avoid censorship and lower the political temperature, it makes sense for cyberspace participants themselves to agree on a scheme for questionable items, so that people or automatic filters can avoid them. In other words, posting pornography in "alt.sex.bestiality" would be OK; it's easy enough for software manufacturers to build an automatic filter that would prevent you—or your child—from ever seeing that item on a menu. (It's as if all the items were wrapped, with labels on the wrapper.) Someone who posted the same material under the title "Kid-Fun" could be sued for mislabeling.

Without a lot of fanfare, private enterprises and local groups are already producing a variety of labeling and ranking services, along with kid-oriented sites like Kidlink, EdWeb, and Kid's Space. People differ in their tastes and values and can find services or reviewers on the Net that suit them in the same way they select books and magazines. Or they can wander freely if they prefer, making up their own itinerary.

In the end, our society needs to grow up. Growing up means understand- 20 ing that there are no perfect answers, no all-purpose solutions, no government-sanctioned safe havens. We haven't created a perfect society on earth and we won't have one in cyberspace either. But at least we can have individual choice—and individual responsibility.

WHAT DOES SHE SAY?

1. Esther Dyson makes a distinction throughout this essay between the kinds of communities that are possible in our physical world and the kinds that are possible in cyberspace. As you read, make two lists: characteristics of "real world" communities and characteristics of cyberspace communities.

2. In the margins as you read, indicate your level of attraction or resistance. When Dyson says something that you find interesting and right, make a straight line. When she says something that doesn't quite make sense to you or that you disagree with, make a squiggly line. Discuss these instances with other students in your class.

3. In two places, this essay makes use of extra space to separate text; thus the discourse falls into three major parts. Write subheadings or subtitles that describe the emphasis and function of each of these pieces. What are the advantages to using such subheadings? What are the advantages to leaving them out? Could you follow this essay if the blank spaces were eliminated and the three sections ran together? Why or why not?

4. Write a paragraph about your own experience in cyberspace. Does it support the claims that Dyson is making?

WHAT DO YOU THINK?

5. Write an essay comparing your own personal experience with cyberspace to the claims that Dyson makes. Do you agree or disagree?

6. Dyson states that "it's hard to find a place where you can go and be yourself without worrying about the neighbors." Write an essay exploring this statement. Do you ever want to go and be yourself without worrying about the neighbors? Is it possible? Are there other places to do that besides cyberspace? Is cyberspace really such a place?

WHAT WOULD THEY SAY?

7. In the first part of his essay "Welcoming the Stranger" (p. 111), Stephen L. Carter talks about the problem of virus writers on the Internet. Dyson, too, mentions this issue. Write an essay exploring the predicament of policing the Internet, comparing and contrasting the essays of Carter and Dyson and arguing your own position.

8. Of the other writers you have read in this section, with whom would Dyson agree and with whom would she argue? Write an essay explaining these agreements and disagreements, and close by explaining your own responses to Dyson's essay.

JOY WILLIAMS

Save the Whales, Screw the Shrimp

The tone of this essay is complex. Williams's essay at first glance seems to be another "no" answer to the chapter's question—a question she extends not just to our obligations toward people but also toward nature. Yet the essay ends by affirming the need for a deep change in our consciousness.

The author of four novels and two short-story collections, Joy Williams (b. 1944) is best known as a fiction writer, though she has also recently published a collection of essays on environmental themes, Ill Nature *(2002). She is the recipient of fellowships from both the National Endowment for the Arts and the Guggenheim Foundation. "Save the Whales, Screw the Shrimp" first appeared in* Esquire.

I don't want to talk about *me*, of course, but it seems as though far too much attention has been lavished on *you* lately—that your greed and vanities and quest for self-fulfillment have been catered to far too much. You just want and want and want. You haven't had a mandala dream since the eighties began. To have a mandala dream you'd have to instinctively know that it was an attempt at self-healing on the part of Nature, and you don't believe in Nature anymore. It's too isolated from you. You've abstracted it. It's so messy and damaged and sad. Your eyes glaze as you travel life's highway past all the crushed animals and the Big Gulp cups. You don't even take pleasure in looking at nature photographs these days. Oh, they can be just as pretty, as always, but don't they make you feel increasingly...anxious? Filled with more trepidation than peace? So what's the point? You see the picture of the baby condor or the panda munching on a bamboo shoot, and your heart just sinks, doesn't it? A picture of a poor old sea turtle with barnacles on her back, all ancient and exhausted, depositing her five gallons of doomed eggs in the sand hardly fills you with joy, because you realize, quite rightly, that just outside the frame falls the shadow of the condo. What's cropped from the shot of ocean waves crashing on a pristine shore is the plastics plant, and just beyond the dunes lies a parking lot. Hidden from immediate view in the butterfly-bright meadow, in the dusky thicket, in the oak and holly wood, are the surveyor's stakes, for someone wants to build a mall exactly there—some gas stations and supermarkets, some pizza and video shops, a health club, maybe a bulimia treatment center. Those lovely pictures of leopards and herons and wild rivers, well, you just know they're going to be accompanied by a text that will serve only to bring you down. You don't want to think about it! It's all so uncool. And you don't want to feel guilty either. Guilt is uncool.

146

Regret maybe you'll consider. *Maybe*. Regret is a possibility, but don't push me, you say. Nature photographs have become something of a problem, along with almost everything else. Even though they leave the bad stuff out— maybe because you *know* they're leaving all the bad stuff out—such pictures are making you increasingly aware that you're a little too late for Nature. Do you feel that? Twenty years too late, maybe only ten? Not *way* too late, just a little too late? Well, it appears that you are. And since you are, you've decided you're just not going to attend this particular party.

Pascal said that it is easier to endure death without thinking about it than to endure the thought of death without dying. This is how you manage to dance the strange dance with that grim partner, nuclear annihilation. When the U.S. Army notified Winston Churchill that the first atom bomb had been detonated in New Mexico, it chose the code phrase BABIES SATISFACTORILY BORN. So you entered the age of irony, and the strange double life you've been leading with the world ever since. Joyce Carol Oates° suggests that the reason writers—*real* writers, one assumes—don't write about Nature is that it lacks a sense of humor and registers no irony. It just doesn't seem to be of the times—these slick, sleek, knowing, objective, indulgent times. And the word *Environment*. Such a bloodless word. A flat-footed word with a shrunken heart. A word increasingly disengaged from its association with the natural world. Urban planners, industrialists, economists, and developers use it. It's a lost word, really. A cold word, mechanistic, suited strangely to the coldness generally felt toward Nature. It's their word now. You don't mind giving it up. As for *Environmentalist*, that's one that can really bring on the yawns, for you've tamed and tidied it, neutered it quite nicely. An environmentalist must be calm, rational, reasonable, and willing to compromise, otherwise you won't listen to him. Still, his beliefs are *opinions* only, for this is the age of radical subjectivism. Not long ago, Barry Commoner° spoke to the Environmental Protection Agency. He scolded them. They loved it. The way they protect the environment these days is apparently to find an "acceptable level of harm from a pollutant and then issue rules allowing industry to pollute to that level." Commoner suggested that this was inappropriate. An EPA employee suggested that any other approach would place limits on economic growth and implied that Commoner was advocating this. Limits on economic growth! Commoner vigorously denied this. Oh, it was a healthy exchange of ideas, healthier certainly than our air and water. We needed that little spanking, the EPA felt. It was refreshing. The agency has recently lumbered into action in its campaign to ban dinoseb. You seem to have liked your dinoseb. It's been a popular weed killer, even though it has been directly linked with birth defects. You must hate weeds a lot. Although the EPA appears successful in banning the poison, it will

---

Joyce Carol Oates (b. 1938): Contemporary novelist and critic. [All notes are the Editors'.]
Barry Commoner (b. 1917): Environmental scientist.

still have to pay the disposal costs and compensate the manufacturers for the market value of the chemicals they still have in stock.

That's ironic, you say, but farmers will suffer losses, too, oh dreadful financial losses, if herbicide and pesticide use is restricted.

Farmers grow way too much stuff anyway. They grow surplus crops with subsidized water created by turning rivers great and small into a plumbing system of dams and canals. Rivers have become *systems*. Wetlands are increasingly being referred to as *filtering systems*—things deigned *useful* because of their ability to absorb urban run-off, oil from roads, et cetera.

We know that. We've known that for years about farmers. We know a   5
lot these days. We're very well-informed. If farmers aren't allowed to make a profit by growing surplus crops, they'll have to sell their land to developers, who'll turn all that *arable land* into office parks. Arable land isn't Nature anyway, and besides, we like those office parks and shopping plazas, with their monster supermarkets open twenty-four hours a day with aisle after aisle after aisle of *products*. It's fun. Products are fun.

Farmers like their poisons, but ranchers like them even more. There are well-funded predominantly federal and cooperative programs like the Agriculture Department's Animal Damage Control Unit that poison, shoot, and trap several thousand animals each year. This unit loves to kill things. It was created to kill things—bobcats, foxes, black bears, mountain lions, rabbits, badgers, countless birds—all to make this great land safe for the string bean and the corn, the sheep and the cow, even though you're not consuming as much cow these days. A burger now and then, but burgers are hardly cows at all, you feel. They're not all *our* cows in any case, for some burger matter is imported. There's a bit of Central American burger matter in your bun. Which is contributing to the conversion of tropical rain forest into cow pasture. Even so, you're getting away from meat these days. You're eschewing cow. It's seafood you love, shrimp most of all. And when you love something, it had better watch out, because you have a tendency to love it to death. Shrimp, shrimp, shrimp. It's more common on menus than chicken. In the wilds of Ohio, far, far from watery shores, four out of the six entrées on a menu will be shrimp, for some modest sum. Everywhere, it's all the shrimp you can eat or all you *care* to eat, for sometimes you just don't feel like eating all you *can*. You are intensively *harvesting* shrimp. Soon there won't be any left and then you can stop. It takes that, often, to make you stop. Shrimpers shrimp, of course. That's their *business*. They put out these big nets and in these nets, for each pound of shrimp, they catch more than ten times that amount of fish, turtles, and dolphins. These, quite the worse for wear, they dump back in. There is an object called TED (Turtle Excluder Device), which would save thousands of turtles and some dolphins from dying in the nets, but the shrimpers are loath to use TEDs, as they say it would cut the size of their shrimp catch.

We've heard about TED, you say.

They want you, all of you, to have all the shrimp you can eat and more. At Kiawah Island, off the coast of South Carolina, visitors go out on Jeep "safaris" through the part of the island that hasn't been developed yet. ("Wherever you see trees," the guide says, "really, that's a lot.") The safari comprises six Jeeps, and these days they go out at least four times a day, with more trips promised soon. The tourists drive their own Jeeps and the guide talks to them by radio. Kiawah has nice beaches, and the guide talks about turtles. When he mentions the shrimpers' role in the decline of the turtle, the shrimpers, who share the same frequency, scream at him. Shrimpers and most commercial fishermen (many of them working with drift and gill nets any-where from six to thirty miles long) think of themselves as an *endangered species.* A recent newspaper headline said, "Shrimpers Spared Anti-Turtle Devices." Even so, with the continuing wanton depletion of shrimp beds, they will un-doubtedly have to find some other means of employment soon. They might, for instance, become part of that vast throng laboring in the *tourist industry.*

Tourism has become an industry as destructive as any other. You are no longer benign in your traveling somewhere to look at the scenery. You never thought there was much gain in just looking anyway, you've always preferred to *use* the scenery in some manner. In your desire to get away from what you've got, you've caused there to be no place to get away *to.* You're just all bumpered up out there. Sewage and dumps have become prime indicators of America's lifestyle. In resort towns in New England and the Adirondacks, mea-suring the flow into the sewage plant serves as a business barometer. Tourism is a growth industry. You believe in growth. *Controlled* growth, of course. Con-trolled exponential growth is what you'd really like to see. You certainly don't want to put a moratorium or a cap on anything. That's illegal, isn't it? Retro you're not. You don't want to go back or anything. Forward. Maybe ask directions later. Growth is *desirable* as well as being *inevitable.* Growth is the one thing you seem to be powerless before, so you try to be realistic about it. Growth is—it's weird—it's like cancer or something.

Recently you, as tourist, have discovered your national parks and are 10 quickly *overburdening* them. Spare land and it belongs to you! It's exotic land too, not looking like all the stuff around it that looks like everything else. You want to take advantage of this land, of course, and use it in every way you can. Thus the managers—or *stewards,* as they like to be called—have de-veloped *wise* and *multiple-use* plans, keeping in mind exploiters' interests (for they have their needs, too) as well as the desires of the backpackers. Thus mining, timbering, and ranching activities take place in the national forests, where the Forest Service maintains a system of logging roads eight times larger than the interstate highway system. The national parks are more of a public playground and are becoming increasingly Europeanized in their look and management. Lots of concessions and motels. You deserve a clean bed and a hot meal when you go into the wilderness. At least your stewards think that you do. You keep your stewards busy. Not only must they cater to your multiple and conflicting desires, they have to manage your wildlife *resources*. They have managed wildfowl to such an extent that the reasoning has become, If it weren't for hunters, ducks would disappear. Duck stamps and licensing fees support the whole rickety duck-management system. Yes! If it weren't for the people who killed them, wild ducks wouldn't exist! Managers are managing all wild creatures, not just those that fly. They track and tape and tag and band. They relocate, restock, and reintroduce. They cull and control. It's hard to keep it all straight. Protect or poison? Extirpate or just mostly eliminate? Sometimes even the stewards get mixed up.

This is the time of machines and models, hands-on management and master plans. Don't you ever wonder as you pass that billboard advertising another MASTER-PLANNED COMMUNITY just what master they are actually talking about? Not the Big Master, certainly. Something brought to you by one of the tiny masters, of which there are many. But you like these tiny masters and have even come to expect and require them. In Florida they've just started a ten-thousand-acre city in the Everglades. It's a *megaproject*, one of the largest ever in the state. Yes, they must have thought you wanted it. No, what you thought of as the Everglades, the Park, is only a little bitty part of the Everglades. Developers have been gnawing at this irreplaceable, strange land for years. It's like they just *hate* this ancient sea of grass. Maybe you could ask them about this sometime. Roy Rogers is the senior vice president of strategic planning, and the old cowboy says that every tree and bush and inch of sidewalk in the project has been planned. Nevertheless, because the whole thing will take twenty-five years to complete, the plan is going to be constantly changed. You can understand this. The important thing is that there be a blueprint. You trust a blueprint. The tiny masters know what you like. You like *a secure landscape* and *access to services*. You like grass—that is, lawns. The ultimate lawn is the golf course, which you've been told has "some ecological value." You believe this! Not that it really matters, you just like to play golf. These golf courses require a lot of watering. So much that the more inspired of the masters have taken to watering them with effluent, *treated* effluent, but yours, from all the condos and villas built around the stocked artificial lakes you fancy.

I really don't want to think about sewage, you say, but it sounds like progress.

It is true that the masters are struggling with the problems of your incessant flushing. Cuisine is also one of their concerns. Advances in sorbets—sorbet intermezzos—in their clubs and fine restaurants. They know what you want. You want A HAVEN FROM THE ORDINARY WORLD. If you're A NATURE LOVER in the West you want to live in a $200,000 home in A WILD ANIMAL HABITAT. If you're eastern and consider yourself more hip, you want to live in new towns—brand-new reconstructed-from-scratch towns—in a house of

NINETEENTH-CENTURY DESIGN. But in these new towns the masters are build-ing, getting around can be confusing. There is an abundance of curves and an infrequency of through streets. It's the new wilderness without any trees. You can get lost, even with all the "mental bread crumbs" the masters scatter about as visual landmarks—the windmill, the water views, the various groupings of landscape "material." You *are* lost, you know. But you trust a Realtor will show you the way. There are many more Realtors than tiny masters, and many of them have to make do with less than a loaf—that is, trying to sell stuff that's already been built in an environment already "enhanced" rather than something being planned—but they're everywhere, willing to show you the path. If Dante returned to Hell today, he'd probably be escorted down by a Realtor, talking all the while about how it was just another level of Paradise.

When have you last watched a sunset? Do you remember where you were? With whom? At Loews Ventana Canyon Resort, the Grand Foyer will provide you with that opportunity through lighting which is computerized to diminish with the approach-ing sunset!

The tiny masters are willing to arrange Nature for you. They will compose it 15 into a picture that you can look at at your leisure, when you're not doing work or something like that. Nature becomes scenery, a prop. At some golf courses in the Southwest, the saguaro cacti are reported to be repaired with green paste when balls blast into their skin. The saguaro can attempt to heal themselves by growing over the balls, but this takes time, and the effect can be somewhat...baroque. It's better to get out the pastepot. Nature has be-come simply a visual form of entertainment, and it had better look snappy.

   Listen, you say, we've been at Ventana Canyon. It's in the desert, right? It's very, very nice, a world-class resort. A totally self-contained environment with everything that a person could possibly want, on more than a thousand acres in the middle of zip. It sprawls but nestles, like. And they've maintained the integrity of as much of the desert ecosystem as possible. Give them credit for that. *Great* restaurant, too. We had baby bay scallops there. Coming into the lobby there are these two big hand-carved coyotes, mutely howling. And that's the way we like them, *mute*. God, why do those things howl like that?

Wildlife is a personal matter, you think. The attitude is up to you. You can prefer to see it dead or not dead. You might want to let it mosey about its business or blow it away. Wild things exist only if you have the graciousness to allow them to. Just outside Tucson, Arizona, there is a brand-new structure modeled after a French foreign legion outpost. It's the *International Wildlife Museum*, and it's full of dead animals. Three hundred species are there, at least a third of them—the rarest ones—killed and collected by one C. J. McElroy, who enjoyed doing it and now shares what's left with you. The museum claims to be educational because you can watch a taxidermist at work or touch a lion's tooth. You can get real close to these dead animals, closer than you can in a zoo. Some of you prefer zoos, however, which are becoming bigger, better, and bioclimatic. New-age zoo designers want the animals to *flow right out into your space*. In Dallas there will soon be a Wilds of Africa exhibit; in San Diego there's a simulated rain forest, where you can thread your way "down the side of a lush canyon, the air filled with a fine mist from three hundred high-pressure nozzles"; in New Orleans you've constructed a swamp, the real swamp not far away on the verge of disappearing. Animals in these places are abstractions — wandering relics of their true selves, but that doesn't matter. Animal behavior in a zoo is nothing like natural behavior, but that doesn't really matter, either. Zoos are pretty, contained, and accessible. These new habitats can contain one hundred different species — not more than one or two of each thing, of course — on seven acres, three, one. You don't want to see *too much* of anything, certainly. An *example* will suffice. Sort of like a biological Crabtree & Evelyn basket selected with *you* in mind. You like things reduced, simplified. It's easier to take it all in, park it in your mind. You like things inside better than outside anyway. You are increasingly looking at and living in proxy environments created by substitution and simulation. *Resource economists* are a wee branch in the tree of tiny masters, and one, Martin Krieger,° wrote, "Artificial prairies and wildernesses have been created, and there is no reason to believe that these artificial environments need be unsatisfactory for those who experience them.... We will have to realize that the way in which we experience nature is conditioned by our society — which more and more is seen to be receptive to responsible intervention."

Nature has become a world of appearances, a mere source of materials. You've been editing it for quite some time; now you're in the process of deleting it. Earth is beginning to look like not much more than a launching pad. Back near Tucson, on the opposite side of the mountain from the dead-animal habitat, you're building Biosphere II (as compared with or opposed to Biosphere I, more commonly known as Earth) — a $2\frac{1}{2}$-acre terrarium, an artificial ecosystem that will include a rain forest, a desert, a thirty-five-foot ocean, and several thousand species of life (lots of microbes), including eight human beings, who will cultivate a bit of farmland. You think it would be nice to colonize other worlds after you've made it necessary to leave this one.

Hey, that's pretty good, you say, all that stuff packed into just $2\frac{1}{2}$ acres. That's only about three times bigger than my entire *house*.

It's small all right, but still not small enough to be, apparently, useful. For 20 the purposes of NASA, say, it would have to be smaller, oh much smaller, and energy-efficient too. Fiddle, fiddle, fiddle. You support fiddling, as well as meddling. This is how you learn. Though it's quite apparent the environment has been grossly polluted and the natural world abused and defiled, you seem

---

Dr. Martin Krieger: Contemporary mathematician, physicist, and social scientist.

to prefer to continue pondering effects rather than preventing causes. You want proof, you insist on proof. A Dr. Lave° from Carnegie-Mellon—and he's an expert, an economist, and an environmental *expert*—says that scientists will have to prove to you that you will suffer if you don't become less of a "throwaway society." *If you really want me to give up my car or my air conditioner, you'd better prove to me first that the earth would otherwise be uninhabitable,* Dr. Lave says. *Me* is *you,* I presume, whereas *you* refers to them. You as in me—that is, *me, me, me*—certainly strike a hard bargain. Uninhabitable the world has to get before you rein in your requirements. You're a consumer after all, *the* consumer upon whom so much attention is lavished, the ultimate user of a commodity that has become, these days, everything. To try to appease your appetite for proof, for example, scientists have been leasing for experimentation forty-six pristine lakes in Canada.

They don't want to *keep* them, they just want to *borrow* them.

They've been intentionally contaminating many of the lakes with a variety of pollutants dribbled into the propeller wash of research boats. *It's one of the boldest experiments in lake ecology ever conducted.* They've turned these remote lakes into huge *real-world test tubes.* They've been doing this since 1976! And what they've found so far in these *preliminary* studies is that pollutants are really destructive. The lakes get gross. Life in them ceases. It took about eight years to make this happen in one of them, everything carefully measured and controlled all the while. Now the scientists are slowly reversing the process. But it will take hundreds of years for the lakes to recover. They think.

Remember when you used to like rain, the sound of it, the feel of it, the way it made the plants and trees all glisten. We needed that rain, you would say. It looked pretty too, you thought, particularly in the movies. Now it rains and you go, Oh-oh. A nice walloping rain these days means *overtaxing our sewage treatment plants.* It means *untreated waste discharged directly into our waterways.* It means...

Okay. Okay.

Acid rain! And we all know what this is. Or most of us do. People of 25 power in government and industry still don't seem to know what it is. Whatever it is, they say, they don't want to curb it, but they're willing to study it some more. Economists call air and water pollution "externalities" anyway. Oh, acid rain. You do get so sick of hearing about it. The words have already become a white-noise kind of thing. But you think in terms of *mitigating* it maybe. As for *the greenhouse effect,* you think in terms of *countering* that. One way that's been discussed recently is the planting of new forests, not for the sake of the forests alone, oh my heavens, no. Not for the sake of majesty and mystery or of Thumper and Bambi, are you kidding me, but because, as every

---

Dr. Jean Lave: Contemporary social anthropologist and learning theorist.

schoolchild knows, trees absorb carbon dioxide. They just soak it up and store it. They just love it. So this is the plan: you plant millions of acres of trees, and you can go on doing pretty much whatever you're doing—driving around, using staggering amounts of energy, keeping those power plants fired to the max. Isn't Nature remarkable? So willing to serve? You wouldn't think it had anything more to offer, but it seems it does. Of course these "forests" wouldn't exactly be forests. They would be more like trees. *Managed* trees. The Forest Service, which now manages our forests by cutting them down, might be called upon to evolve in their thinking and allow these trees to grow. They would probably be patented trees after a time. Fast-growing, uniform, genetically-created-to-be-toxin-eating *machines*. They would be *new-age* trees, because the problem with planting the old-fashioned variety to *combat* the greenhouse effect, which is caused by pollution, is that they're already dying from it. All along the crest of the Appalachians from Maine to Georgia, forests struggle to survive in a toxic soup of poisons. They can't *help* us if we've killed them, now can they?

All right, you say, wow, lighten up will you? Relax. Tell me about yourself.

Well, I say, I live in Florida...

Oh my God, you say. Florida! Florida is a joke! How do you expect us to take you seriously if you still live there! Florida is crazy, it's pink concrete. It's paved, it's over. And a little girl just got eaten by an alligator down there. It came out of some swamp next to a subdivision and just carried her off. That set your Endangered Species Act back fifty years, you can bet.

I...

Listen, we don't want to hear any more about Florida. We don't want to hear about Phoenix or Hilton Head or California's Central Valley. If our wetlands—our *vanishing* wetlands—are mentioned one more time, we'll scream. And the talk about condors and grizzlies and wolves is becoming too de trop. We had just managed to get whales out of our minds when those three showed up under the ice in Alaska. They even had *names*. Bone is the dead one, right? It's almost the twenty-first century! Those last condors are *pathetic*. Can't we just get this over with?

Aristotle said that all living things are ensouled and striving to participate in eternity.

Oh, I just bet he said that, you say. That doesn't sound like Aristotle. He was a humanist. We're all humanists here. This is the age of humanism. And it has been for a long time.

You are driving with a stranger in the car, and it is the stranger behind the wheel. In the back seat are your pals for many years now—DO WHAT YOU LIKE and his swilling sidekick, WHY NOT. A deer, or some emblematic animal, something from that myriad natural world you've come from that you now treat with such indifference and scorn—steps from the dimming woods and tentatively upon the highway. The stranger does not decelerate or brake, not yet, maybe not at all. The feeling is that whatever it is *will get out of the way*. Oh, it's a fine car you've got, a fine machine, and oddly you don't mind the stranger driving it, because in a way, everything has gotten too complicated, way, way out of your control. You've given the wheel to the masters, the managers, the comptrollers. Something is wrong, *maybe*, you feel a little sick, *actually*, but the car is luxurious and fast and you're *moving*, which is the most important thing by far.

Why make a fuss when you're so comfortable? Don't make a fuss, make a baby. Go out and get something to eat, build something. Make *another* baby. Babies are cute. Babies show you have faith in the future. Although faith is perhaps too strong a word. They're everywhere these days, in all the crowds and traffic jams, there are the babies too. You don't seem to associate them with the problems of population increase. They're just babies! And you've come to believe in them again. They're a lot more tangible than the afterlife, which, of course, you haven't believed in in ages. At least not for yourself. The afterlife now belongs to plastics and poisons. Yes, plastics and poisons will have a far more extensive afterlife than you, that's known. A disposable diaper, for example, which is all plastic and wood pulp—you like them for all those babies, so easy to use and toss—will take around four centuries to degrade. Almost all plastics do, centuries and centuries. In the sea, many marine animals die from ingesting or being entangled in discarded plastic. In the dumps, plastic squats on more than 25 percent of dump space. But your heart is disposed toward plastic. Someone, no doubt the plastics industry, told you it was convenient. This same industry is now looking into recycling in an attempt to get the critics of their nefarious, multifarious products off their backs. That should make you feel better, because *recycling* has become an honorable word, no longer merely the hobby of Volvo owners. The fact is that people in plastics are born obscurants. Recycling (practically impossible) won't solve the plastic glut, only reduction of production will, and the plastics industry isn't looking into that, you can be sure. Waste is not just the stuff you throw away, of course, it's the stuff you use to excess. With the exception of *hazardous waste*, which you do worry about from time to time, it's even thought you have a declining sense of emergency about the problem. Builders are building bigger houses because you want bigger. You're trading up. Utility companies are beginning to worry about your constantly rising consumption. Utility companies! You haven't entered a new age at all but one of upscale nihilism, deluxe nihilism.

In the summer, particularly in *the industrial Northeast,* you did get a little excited. 35 The filth cut into your fun time. Dead stuff floating around. Sludge and bloody vials. Hygienic devices—appearing not quite so hygienic out of context—all coming in on the tide. The air smelled funny, too. You tolerate a great deal, but the summer of '88 was truly creepy. It was even thought for a moment that the environment would become a political issue. But it didn't. You didn't want it to be, preferring instead to continue in your politics of subsidizing and advancing avarice. The issues were the same as always—jobs, defense, the economy, maintaining and improving the standard of living in this greedy, selfish, expansionistic, industrialized society.

You're getting a little shrill here, you say.

You're pretty well off. You expect to be better off soon. You do. What does this mean? More software, more scampi, more square footage? You have created an ecological crisis. The earth is infinitely variable and alive, and you are killing it. It seems safer this way. But you are not safe. You want to find wholeness and happiness in a land increasingly damaged and betrayed, and you never will. More than material matters. You must change your ways.

What is this? *Sinners in the Hands of an Angry God?*

The ecological crisis cannot be resolved by politics. It cannot be solved by science or technology. It is a crisis caused by culture and character, and a deep change in personal consciousness is needed. Your fundamental attitudes toward the earth have become twisted. You have made only brutal contact with Nature, you cannot comprehend its grace. You must change. Have few desires and simple pleasures. Honor nonhuman life. Control yourself, become more authentic. Live lightly upon the earth and treat it with respect. Redefine the word *progress* and dismiss the managers and masters. Grow inwardly and with knowledge become truly wiser. Make connections. Think differently, behave differently. For this is essentially a moral issue we face and moral decisions must be made.

A *moral issue!* Okay, this discussion is now toast. A *moral* issue...And 40 who's this *we* now? Who are *you* is what I'd like to know. You're not me, anyway. I admit, someone's to blame and something should be done. But I've got to go. It's getting late. That's dusk out there. That is dusk, isn't it? It certainly doesn't look like any dawn I've ever seen. Well, take care.

WHAT DOES SHE SAY?

1. The key to comprehending this essay is understanding Joy Williams's tone. Be alert to this issue as you read. After reading the first paragraph, write a phrase in the margin that describes how you hear her voice. Is it angry? sad? sarcastic? serious? Underline the phrases that help you decide. Then read several more paragraphs, pause, and do the same. Repeat this process several times. When does the tone become obvious to you? How does that influence your understanding of the essay?

2. One of Williams's strategies is to use the second-person point of view, or "you" throughout this essay. What is your reaction to this strategy? When Williams summarizes what "you" think, is she summarizing what *you*, the reader, think? Explain.

3. Discuss the last few paragraphs of this essay, beginning with "In the summer" (para. 35, p. 155). Who is talking here? Do these paragraphs express Williams's real point? How do you know? If they do, why does she put her real argument here and frame it the way she does? What's the purpose of the last paragraph in particular? How does it relate to the rest of this final, short section?

WHAT DO YOU THINK?

4. This is an essay about environmental issues. Write a paragraph explaining what you think it's doing in a chapter called, "Are We Responsible for Others?"

5. "You want proof, you insist on proof," Williams says, speaking of our skepticism about the environmental crisis. Write an essay reflecting on this skepticism. Much scientific evidence exists to support the claim that our environment is in danger of collapsing through overuse. Why do so many people resist such evidence or seem not to know about it? What is it about human beings and the environmental crisis that makes issues of proof so difficult? What proof would you need personally? Is proof enough to change people's habits?

WHAT WOULD THEY SAY?

6. Compare the tone or voice of this essay with the tone of Cornel West's "The Moral Obligation of Living in a Democratic Society" (p. 123) or the tone of the authors in "Too Many Colleges Are Still in Denial about Alcohol Abuse" (p. 96). What would you have to do to rewrite the piece in the voice of Joy Williams in "Save the Whales, Screw the Shrimp"? What would the effect of these changes be on the audience and purpose of the selection?

7. Write an essay on any other topic we've suggested in this book but in the voice of Joy Williams in "Save the Whales, Screw the Shrimp." Use "you" as the point of view. Call it, "Save the ——, Screw the ——."

8. Write an essay relating Williams's points to "The Earth Charter" (p. 158) in this chapter and Aldo Leopold's "The Land Ethic" (p. 531) in chapter 6. In your reflections, explain why environmental issues might fit under the heading, "Are We Responsible for Others?"

9. Write an essay comparing and contrasting the views of Joy Williams and the views of Esther Dyson (p. 141). They're clearly writing on different themes, but can you discern any underlying similarities or differences in their ethical philosophies? What would Williams say about cyberspace? What would Dyson say about the environment? Or are these two issues unrelated?

The Earth Charter

*T*HE ESSENCE OF ETHICS *is choice, and in "The Earth Charter" those choices are presented in their largest context, that of the planet itself. We survive only in community, so affirms this piece. Thus the chapter's opening question has now been raised in its largest possible sense.*

The idea for "The Earth Charter" was first proposed at the United Nations Rio Earth Summit in 1992. In 1994, Maurice Strong, the secretary general of that summit, and Mikhail Gorbachev, president of Green Cross International, began work to draft this document, a process that in 1997 was taken over by The Earth Charter Commission. The final version was approved by the commission in 2000.

PREAMBLE

We stand at a critical moment in Earth's history, a time when humanity must choose its future. As the world becomes increasingly interdependent and fragile, the future at once holds great peril and great promise. To move forward we must recognize that in the midst of a magnificent diversity of cultures and life forms we are one human family and one Earth community with a common destiny. We must join together to bring forth a sustainable global society founded on respect for nature, universal human rights, economic justice, and a culture of peace. Towards this end, it is imperative that we, the peoples of Earth, declare our responsibility to one another, to the greater community of life, and to future generations.

Earth, Our Home

Humanity is part of a vast evolving universe. Earth, our home, is alive with a unique community of life. The forces of nature make existence a demanding and uncertain adventure, but Earth has provided the conditions essential to life's evolution. The resilience of the community of life and the well-being of humanity depend upon preserving a healthy biosphere with all its ecological systems, a rich variety of plants and animals, fertile soils, pure waters, and clean air. The global environment with its finite resources is a common concern of all peoples. The protection of Earth's vitality, diversity, and beauty is a sacred trust.

The Global Situation

The dominant patterns of production and consumption are causing environmental devastation, the depletion of resources, and a massive extinction of species. Communities are being undermined. The benefits of development are not shared equitably and the gap between rich and poor is widening. In-justice, poverty, ignorance, and violent conflict are widespread and the cause of great suffering. An unprecedented rise in human population has overburdened ecological and social systems. The foundations of global security are threatened. These trends are perilous—but not inevitable.

The Challenges Ahead

The choice is ours: form a global partnership to care for Earth and one another or risk the destruction of ourselves and the diversity of life. Fundamental changes are needed in our values, institutions, and ways of living. We must realize that when basic needs have been met, human development is primarily about being more, not having more. We have the knowledge and technology to provide for all and to reduce our impacts on the environment. The emergence of a global civil society is creating new opportunities to build a democratic and humane world. Our environmental, economic, political, social, and spiritual challenges are interconnected, and together we can forge inclusive solutions.

Universal Responsibility

To realize these aspirations, we must decide to live with a sense of universal responsibility, identifying ourselves with the whole Earth community as well as our local communities. We are at once citizens of different nations and of one world in which the local and global are linked. Everyone shares responsibility for the present and future well-being of the human family and the larger living world. The spirit of human solidarity and kinship with all life is strengthened when we live with reverence for the mystery of being, gratitude for the gift of life, and humility regarding the human place in nature.

We urgently need a shared vision of basic values to provide an ethical foundation for the emerging world community. Therefore, together in hope we affirm the following interdependent principles for a sustainable way of life as a common standard by which the conduct of all individuals, organizations, businesses, governments, and transnational institutions is to be guided and assessed.

PRINCIPLES

I. Respect and Care for
the Community of Life

1. Respect Earth and life in all its diversity.
    a. Recognize that all beings are interdependent and every form of life has value regardless of its worth to human beings.

    b. Affirm faith in the inherent dignity of all human beings and in the intellectual, artistic, ethical, and spiritual potential of humanity.

2. Care for the community of life with understanding, compassion, and love.
    a. Accept that with the right to own, manage, and use natural resources comes the duty to prevent environmental harm and to protect the rights of people.
    b. Affirm that with increased freedom, knowledge, and power comes increased responsibility to promote the common good.

3. Build democratic societies that are just, participatory, sustainable, and peaceful.
    a. Ensure that communities at all levels guarantee human rights and fundamental freedoms and provide everyone an opportunity to realize his or her full potential.
    b. Promote social and economic justice, enabling all to achieve a secure and meaningful livelihood that is ecologically responsible.

4. Secure Earth's bounty and beauty for present and future generations.
    a. Recognize that the freedom of action of each generation is qualified by the needs of future generations.
    b. Transmit to future generations values, traditions, and institutions that support the long-term flourishing of Earth's human and ecological communities.

In order to fulfill these four broad commitments, it is necessary to:

II. Ecological Integrity

5. Protect and restore the integrity of Earth's ecological systems, with special concern for biological diversity and the natural processes that sustain life.
    a. Adopt at all levels sustainable development plans and regulations that make environmental conservation and rehabilitation integral to all development initiatives.
    b. Establish and safeguard viable nature and biosphere reserves, including wild lands and marine areas, to protect Earth's life-support systems, maintain biodiversity, and preserve our natural heritage.
    c. Promote the recovery of endangered species and ecosystems.
    d. Control and eradicate nonnative or genetically modified organisms harmful to native species and the environment, and prevent introduction of such harmful organisms.

e. Manage the use of renewable resources such as water, soil, forest products, and marine life in ways that do not exceed rates of regeneration and that protect the health of ecosystems.

f. Manage the extraction and use of nonrenewable resources such as minerals and fossil fuels in ways that minimize depletion and cause no serious environmental damage.

6. Prevent harm as the best method of environmental protection and, when knowledge is limited, apply a precautionary approach.

a. Take action to avoid the possibility of serious or irreversible environmental harm even when scientific knowledge is incomplete or inconclusive.

b. Place the burden of proof on those who argue that a proposed activity will not cause significant harm, and make the responsible parties liable for environmental harm.

c. Ensure that decision making addresses the cumulative, long-term, indirect, long distance, and global consequences of human activities.

d. Prevent pollution of any part of the environment and allow no buildup of radioactive, toxic, or other hazardous substances.

e. Avoid military activities damaging to the environment.

7. Adopt patterns of production, consumption, and reproduction that safeguard Earth's regenerative capacities, human rights, and community well-being.

a. Reduce, reuse, and recycle the materials used in production and consumption systems, and ensure that residual waste can be assimilated by ecological systems.

b. Act with restraint and efficiency when using energy, and rely increasingly on renewable energy sources such as solar and wind.

c. Promote the development, adoption, and equitable transfer of environmentally sound technologies.

d. Internalize the full environmental and social costs of goods and services in the selling price, and enable consumers to identify products that meet the highest social and environmental standards.

e. Ensure universal access to health care that fosters reproductive health and responsible reproduction.

f. Adopt lifestyles that emphasize the quality of life and material sufficiency in a finite world.

8. Advance the study of ecological sustainability and promote the open exchange and wide application of the knowledge acquired.

a. Support international scientific and technical cooperation on sustainability, with special attention to the needs of developing nations.

b. Recognize and preserve the traditional knowledge and spiritual wisdom in all cultures that contribute to environmental protection and human well-being.

c. Ensure that information of vital importance to human health and environmental protection, including genetic information, remains available in the public domain.

III. Social and Economical Justice

9. Eradicate poverty as an ethical, social, and environmental imperative.
   a. Guarantee the right to potable water, clean air, food security, uncontaminated soil, shelter, and safe sanitation, allocating the national and international resources required.
   b. Empower every human being with the education and resources to secure a sustainable livelihood, and provide social security and safety nets for those who are unable to support themselves.
   c. Recognize the ignored, protect the vulnerable, serve those who suffer, and enable them to develop their capacities and to pursue their aspirations.

10. Ensure that economic activities and institutions at all levels promote human development in an equitable and sustainable manner.
    a. Promote the equitable distribution of wealth within nations and among nations.
    b. Enhance the intellectual, financial, technical, and social resources of developing nations, and relieve them of onerous international debt.
    c. Ensure that all trade supports sustainable resource use, environmental protection, and progressive labor standards.
    d. Require multinational corporations and international financial organizations to act transparently in the public good, and hold them accountable for the consequences of their activities.

11. Affirm gender equality and equity as prerequisites to sustainable development and ensure universal access to education, health care, and economic opportunity.
    a. Secure the human rights of women and girls and end all violence against them.
    b. Promote the active participation of women in all aspects of economic, political, civil, social, and cultural life as full and equal partners, decision makers, leaders, and beneficiaries.

    c. Strengthen families and ensure the safety and loving nurture of all family members.

12. Uphold the right of all, without discrimination, to a natural and social environment supportive of human dignity, bodily health, and spiritual well-being, with special attention to the rights of indigenous peoples and minorities.

    a. Eliminate discrimination in all its forms, such as that based on race, color, sex, sexual orientation, religion, language, and national, ethnic, or social origin.

    b. Affirm the right of indigenous peoples to their spirituality, knowledge, lands, and resources and to their related practice of sustainable livelihoods.

    c. Honor and support the young people of our communities, enabling them to fulfill their essential role in creating sustainable societies.

    d. Protect and restore outstanding places of cultural and spiritual significance.

IV. Democracy, Nonviolence, and Peace

13. Strengthen democratic institutions at all levels, and provide transparency and accountability in governance, inclusive participation in decision making, and access to justice.

    a. Uphold the right of everyone to receive clear and timely information on environmental matters and all development plans and activities which are likely to affect them or in which they have an interest.

    b. Support local, regional, and global civil society, and promote the meaningful participation of all interested individuals and organizations in decision making.

    c. Protect the rights to freedom of opinion, expression, peaceful assembly, association, and dissent.

    d. Institute effective and efficient access to administrative and independent judicial procedures, including remedies and redress for environmental harm and the threat of such harm.

    e. Eliminate corruption in all public and private institutions.

    f. Strengthen local communities, enabling them to care for their environments, and assign environmental responsibilities to the levels of government where they can be carried out most effectively.

14. Integrate into formal education and life-long learning the knowledge, values, and skills needed for a sustainable way of life.

    a. Provide all, especially children and youth, with educational opportunities that empower them to contribute actively to sustainable development.

    b. Promote the contribution of the arts and humanities as well as the sciences in sustainability education.

    c. Enhance the role of the mass media in raising awareness of ecological and social challenges.

    d. Recognize the importance of moral and spiritual education for sustainable living.

15. Treat all living beings with respect and consideration.
    a. Prevent cruelty to animals kept in human societies and protect them from suffering.

    b. Protect wild animals from methods of hunting, trapping, and fishing that cause extreme, prolonged, or avoidable suffering.

    c. Avoid or eliminate to the full extent possible the taking or destruction of nontargeted species.

16. Promote a culture of tolerance, nonviolence, and peace.
    a. Encourage and support mutual understanding, solidarity, and cooperation among all peoples and within and among nations.

    b. Implement comprehensive strategies to prevent violent conflict and use collaborative problem solving to manage and resolve environmental conflicts and other disputes.

    c. Demilitarize national security systems to the level of a nonprovocative defense posture, and convert military resources to peaceful purposes, including ecological restoration.

    d. Eliminate nuclear, biological, and toxic weapons and other weapons of mass destruction.

    e. Ensure that the use of orbital and outer space supports environmental protection and peace.

    f. Recognize that peace is the wholeness created by right relationships with oneself, other persons, other cultures, other life, Earth, and the larger whole of which all are a part.

THE WAY FORWARD

As never before in history, common destiny beckons us to seek a new beginning. Such renewal is the promise of these Earth Charter principles. To fulfill this promise, we must commit ourselves to adopt and promote the values and objectives of the Charter.

This requires a change of mind and heart. It requires a new sense of global interdependence and universal responsibility. We must imaginatively develop and apply the vision of a sustainable way of life locally, nationally, regionally, and globally. Our cultural diversity is a precious heritage and different cultures will find their own distinctive ways to realize the vision. We must deepen and expand the global dialogue that generated the Earth Charter, for we have much to learn from the ongoing collaborative search for truth and wisdom.

Life often involves tensions between important values. This can mean difficult choices. However, we must find ways to harmonize diversity with unity, the exercise of freedom with the common good, short-term objectives with long-term goals. Every individual, family, organization, and community has a vital role to play. The arts, sciences, religions, educational institutions, media, businesses, nongovernmental organizations, and governments are all called to offer creative leadership. The partnership of government, civil society, and business is essential for effective governance.

In order to build a sustainable global community, the nations of the world must renew their commitment to the United Nations, fulfill their obligations under existing international agreements, and support the implementation of Earth Charter principles with an international legally binding instrument on environment and development.

Let ours be a time remembered for the awakening of a new reverence for life, the firm resolve to achieve sustainability, the quickening of the struggle for justice and peace, and the joyful celebration of life.

WHAT DOES IT SAY?

1. "The Earth Charter" is not an essay but a list of declarations and intentions. As a form, the charter—or the declaration or the mission statement—isn't required to support its generalizations or spell out all its underlying assumptions. Read between the lines. What assumptions are behind these declarations and generalizations? What are the values implied in this document? Make a list of at least three of these values or assumptions, and for each write a sentence identifying the data or evidence or support that would convince you these assumptions are true.

2. "The Earth Charter" assumes that a connection exists between the rights of human beings and the respect that we should all have for the earth—a connection, in other words, between human and environmental ethics. How does respect for other people relate to respect for a landscape or a watershed? How does respect for a landscape or watershed relate to respect for people?

3. Working in groups, write a charter containing at least five points declaring the goals and intentions of the class you are taking. Call it "The Class Charter." As in "The Earth Charter," use a verb to begin each statement of purpose.

WHAT DO YOU THINK?

4. Write a charter of your own, imitating the form used in "The Earth Charter." Include at least ten statements or declarations, each centered on a verb: respect, listen, investigate, and so on. The subject can be anything: the rules for your family, dorm, living situation, job, relationship. For example, "The Family Charter," "John's Automotive Charter." When thinking of *charter*, think of *mission statement* too.

5. Do Internet research on the origin of "The Earth Charter" and the history of its development. Present your findings in the form of an informative essay.

6. Write an essay agreeing with "The Earth Charter" that human and environmental ethics are necessarily related. Explain.

WHAT WOULD THEY SAY?

7. Relate "The Earth Charter" to Aldo Leopold's "The Land Ethic" (p. 531) in chapter 6, "What Is This Worth?" How does Leopold's argument help you understand the assumptions and values of the "The Earth Charter"?

8. Relate this selection to "Too Many Colleges Are Still in Denial about Alcohol Abuse" (p. 96) by writing a charter on drinking. Think of this charter as suggesting a comparable charter for your dorm or living situation. Attach an analysis of several pages in which you quote both "Too Many Colleges" and at least one other essay in this section.

9. Garrett Hardin's "Lifeboat Ethics: The Case against Helping the Poor" (p. 130) alludes to environmental concerns as support for its claim that we should not take care of the poor and outcast. How would the authors of "The Earth Charter" respond? How would Hardin respond to "The Earth Charter"?

10. Write an earth charter (ten statements) but do so in the tone employed by Joy Williams in "Save the Whales, Screw the Shrimp" (p. 146). In other words, make it a kind of anti-earth charter that readers will realize actually articulates the opposite of what it advocates.

JOAN DIDION
On Morality

*D*ɪᴅɪᴏɴ'ꜱ ᴇꜱꜱᴀʏ *brings the chapter back from global concerns to what one should do in particular cases. Didion, in fact, is greatly wary of large formulations and of the permission that phrases like "moral imperative" might confer.*

One of the most important essayists of the twentieth century, Joan Didion (b. 1934) is the author of several pivotal collections, including Slouching Towards Bethlehem *(1968), from which "On Morality" is taken, and* The White Album *(1979). She is also the author of several novels. Her more recent nonfiction includes* Political Fictions *(2001) and* Where I Was From *(2003).*

As it happens I am in Death Valley, in a room at the Enterprise Motel and Trailer Park, and it is July, and it is hot. In fact it is 119°. I cannot seem to make the air conditioner work, but there is a small refrigerator, and I can wrap ice cubes in a towel and hold them against the small of my back. With the help of the ice cubes I have been trying to think, because *The American Scholar* asked me to, in some abstract way about *morality*, a word I distrust more every day, but my mind veers inflexibly toward the particular.

Here are some particulars. At midnight last night, on the road in from Las Vegas to Death Valley Junction, a car hit a shoulder and turned over. The driver, very young and apparently drunk, was killed instantly. His girl was found alive but bleeding internally, deep in shock. I talked this afternoon to the nurse who had driven the girl to the nearest doctor, 185 miles across the floor of the Valley and three ranges of lethal mountain road. The nurse explained that her husband, a talc miner, had stayed on the highway with the boy's body until the coroner could get over the mountains from Bishop, at dawn today. "You can't just leave a body on the highway," she said. "It's immoral."

It was one instance in which I did not distrust the word, because she meant something quite specific. She meant that if a body is left alone for even a few minutes on the desert, the coyotes close in and eat the flesh. Whether or not a corpse is torn apart by coyotes may seem only a sentimental consideration, but of course it is more: one of the promises we make to one another is that we will try to retrieve our casualties, try not to abandon our dead to the coyotes. If we have been taught to keep our promises—if, in the simplest terms, our upbringing is good enough—we stay with the body, or have bad dreams.

I am talking, of course, about the kind of social code that is sometimes called, usually pejoratively, "wagon-train morality." In fact that is precisely what it is. For better or worse, we are what we learned as children: my own

167

childhood was illuminated by graphic litanies of the grief awaiting those who failed in their loyalties to each other. The Donner-Reed Party°, starving in the Sierra snows, all the ephemera of civilization gone save that one vestigial taboo, the provision that no one should eat his own blood kin. The Jayhawkers°, who quarreled and separated not far from where I am tonight. Some of them died in the Funerals and some of them died down near Badwater and most of the rest of them died in the Panamints°. A woman who got through gave the Valley its name. Some might say that the Jayhawkers were killed by the desert summer, and the Donner Party by the mountain winter, by circumstances beyond control; we were taught instead that they had somewhere abdicated their responsibilities, somehow breached their primary loyalties, or they would not have found themselves helpless in the mountain winter or the desert summer, would not have given way to acrimony, would not have deserted one another, would not have *failed*. In brief, we heard such stories as cautionary tales, and they still suggest the only kind of "morality" that seems to me to have any but the most potentially mendacious meaning.

You are quite possibly impatient with me by now; I am talking, you want to   5
say, about a "morality" so primitive that it scarcely deserves the name, a code that has as its point only survival, not the attainment of the ideal good. Exactly. Particularly out here tonight, in this country so ominous and terrible that to live in it is to live with antimatter, it is difficult to believe that "the good" is a knowable quantity. Let me tell you what it is like out here tonight. Stories travel at night on the desert. Someone gets in his pickup and drives a couple of hundred miles for a beer, and he carries news of what is happening, back wherever he came from. Then he drives another hundred miles for another beer, and passes along stories from the last place as well as from the one before; it is a network kept alive by people whose instincts tell them that if they do not keep moving at night on the desert they will lose all reason. Here is a story that is going around the desert tonight: over across the Nevada line, sheriff's deputies are diving in some underground pools, trying to retrieve a couple of bodies known to be in the hole. The widow of one of the drowned boys is over there; she is eighteen, and pregnant, and is said not to leave the hole. The divers go down and come up, and she just stands there and stares into the water. They have been diving for ten days but have found no bottom to the caves, no bodies and no trace of them, only the black 90° water going

---

Donner-Reed Party: Stranded by cold and snow in the Sierra Mountains of California, members of the Donner-Reed Party resorted to cannibalism before being rescued in March 1847. [All notes are the Editors'.]

Jayhawkers: A group of gold seekers, originally from Illinois, some of whom died traversing Death Valley in December 1849.

Funerals . . . Badwater . . . Panamints: Mountain ranges surrounding Death Valley, California; Badwater is the Valley's lowest point.

down and down and down, and a single translucent fish, not classified. The story tonight is that one of the divers has been hauled up incoherent, out of his head, shouting—until they got him out of there so that the widow could not hear—about water that got hotter instead of cooler as he went down, about light flickering through the water, about magma, about underground nuclear testing.

That is the tone stories take out here, and there are quite a few of them tonight. And it is more than the stories alone. Across the road at the Faith Community Church a couple of dozen old people, come here to live in trailers and die in the sun, are holding a prayer sing. I cannot hear them and do not want to. What I can hear are occasional coyotes and a constant chorus of "Baby the Rain Must Fall" from the jukebox in the Snake Room next door, and if I were also to hear those dying voices, those Midwestern voices drawn to this lunar country for some unimaginable atavistic rites, *rock of ages cleft for me*, I think I would lose my own reason. Every now and then I imagine I hear a rattlesnake, but my husband says that it is a faucet, a paper rustling, the wind. Then he stands by a window, and plays a flashlight over the dry wash outside.

What does it mean? It means nothing manageable. There is some sinister hysteria in the air out here tonight, some hint of the monstrous perversion to which any human idea can come. "I followed my own conscience." "I did what I thought was right." How many madmen have said it and meant it? How many murderers? Klaus Fuchs° said it, and the men who committed the Mountain Meadows Massacre° said it, and Alfred Rosenberg° said it. And, as we are rotely and rather presumptuously reminded by those who would say it now, Jesus said it. Maybe we have all said it, and maybe we have been wrong. Except on that most primitive level—our loyalties to those we love—what could be more arrogant than to claim the primacy of personal conscience? ("Tell me," a rabbi asked Daniel Bell° when he said, as a child, that he did not believe in God. "Do you think God cares?") At least some of the time, the world appears to me as a painting by Hieronymous Bosch; were I to follow my conscience then, it would lead me out onto the desert with Marion Faye,° out to where he stood in *The Deer Park* looking east to Los Alamos° and

---

Klaus Fuchs (1911–1988): German-born nuclear scientist who disclosed secrets to the Soviet Union, was convicted of espionage in 1950, and served nine years in prison.

Mountain Meadows Massacre: Refers to the deaths of 127 individuals at the hands of a combined force of Paiutes and Mormon militia in southern Utah in 1857.

Alfred Rosenberg (1893–1946): A high-ranking Nazi official found guilty of war crimes and executed in 1946.

Daniel Bell (b. 1919): Henry Ford II professor emeritus of the social sciences at Harvard University.

Marion Faye: A character in the movie *The Deer Park*, based on the Norman Mailer novel of the same name.

Los Alamos: Site in New Mexico where the first U.S. atomic bombs were designed and tested.

praying, as if for rain, that it would happen: *". . . let it come and clear the rot and the stench and the stink, let it come for all of everywhere, just so it comes and the world stands clear in the white dead dawn."*

Of course you will say that I do not have the right, even if I had the power, to inflict that unreasonable conscience upon you; nor do I want you to inflict your conscience, however reasonable, however enlightened, upon me. ("We must be aware of the dangers which lie in our most generous wishes," Lionel Trilling° once wrote. "Some paradox of our nature leads us, when once we have made our fellow men the objects of our enlightened interest, to go on to make them the objects of our pity, then of our wisdom, ultimately of our coercion.") That the ethic of conscience is intrinsically insidious seems scarcely a revelatory point, but it is one raised with increasing infrequency; even those who do raise it tend to segue with troubling readiness into the quite contradictory position that the ethic of conscience is dangerous when it is "wrong," and admirable when it is "right."

You see I want to be quite obstinate about insisting that we have no way of knowing—beyond that fundamental loyalty to the social code—what is "right" and what is "wrong," what is "good" and what "evil." I dwell so upon this because the most disturbing aspect of "morality" seems to me to be the frequency with which the word now appears; in the press, on television, in the most perfunctory kinds of conversation. Questions of straightforward power (or survival) politics, questions of quite indifferent public policy, questions of almost anything: they are all assigned these factitious moral burdens. There is something facile going on, some self-indulgence at work. Of course we would all like to "believe" in something, like to assuage our private guilts in public causes, like to lose our tiresome selves; like, perhaps, to transform the white flag of defeat at home into the brave white banner of battle away from home. And of course it is all right to do that; that is how, immemorially, things have gotten done. But I think it is all right only so long as we do not delude ourselves about what we are doing, and why. It is all right only so long as we remember that all the ad hoc committees, all the picket lines, all the brave signatures in the *New York Times*, all the tools of agitprop straight across the spectrum, do not confer upon anyone any ipso facto virtue. It is all right only so long as we recognize that the end may or may not be expedient, may or may not be a good idea, but in any case has nothing to do with "morality." Because when we start deceiving ourselves into thinking not that we want something or need something, not that it is a pragmatic necessity for us to have it, but that it is a *moral imperative* that we have it, then is when we join the fashionable madmen, and then is when the thin whine of hysteria is heard in the land, and then is when we are in bad trouble. And I suspect we are already there.

Lionel Trilling (1905–1975): American literary and social critic.

WHAT DOES SHE SAY?

1. Joan Didion doesn't spend much time in this essay talking in the abstract. She says that she distrusts abstractions like the word *morality*. Why this distrust? What does Didion spend her time on in this essay? If not generalizing, what *does* she do? Find a paragraph that you think clearly shows this.

2. Explain what Didion means by "wagon-train morality" and how this idea fits into the essay.

3. In paragraph 5, Didion stops and says, addressing the reader directly, "You are quite possibly impatient with me by now." Are you? If so, why? If not, why not? Why would Didion adopt this strategy of direct address?

4. In the middle of this essay, Didion tells the story of divers looking for drowned bodies in underground desert pools. What is the significance of this story? Why does she tell it?

WHAT DO YOU THINK?

5. Didion says that "we have no way of knowing...what is 'right' and what is 'wrong'...." Write an essay agreeing or disagreeing.

6. Write an essay that contains the sentence, "You see I want to be quite obstinate about insisting that we have no way of knowing———." Fill in the blank.

7. Write an essay beginning with a sustained narrative about an ethical problem. Conclude with one or more paragraphs beginning with this question and answer: "What does this story mean? It means nothing manageable."

8. Didion says that we tell certain stories as "cautionary tales," stories to warn us against certain actions. Write an essay telling your own cautionary tale, drawn from your own experience, from your reading, or from current events.

WHAT WOULD THEY SAY?

9. Consider Cornel West's "The Moral Obligations of Living in a Democratic Society" (p. 123), Garrett Hardin's "Lifeboat Ethics: The Case against Helping the Poor" (p. 130), or Stephen L. Carter's "Welcoming the Stranger" (p. 111). Choose one of these essays and write about how you believe Didion would respond to it. What would she find agreeable, problematic, or objectionable?

10. Of the writers listed above (West, Hardin, Carter, or Didion), which would you want to have lunch with, and why? Write an essay explaining your choice and quoting at least two of that essayist's works.

WILLIAM STAFFORD

Traveling through the Dark

*I*N THIS SHORT POEM, *William Stafford (1914–1993) thinks "hard for us all." The poem suggests that given circumstances dictate available choices and that none of these might be what we'd wish.*

Stafford is the author of more than sixty-seven books, including Traveling through the Dark, *which won the 1962 National Book Award for poetry. He taught at Lewis and Clark College in Portland, Oregon, and was a much beloved mentor and member of the writing community in the Northwest and in the nation. He wrote before dawn each day of his adult life and died in 1993—after getting up early and writing a draft of his final poem.*

Traveling through the dark I found a deer
dead on the edge of the Wilson River road.
It is usually best to roll them into the canyon:
that road is narrow; to swerve might make more dead.

By glow of the tail-light I stumbled back of the car   5
and stood by the heap, a doe, a recent killing;
she had stiffened already, almost cold.
I dragged her off; she was large in the belly.

My fingers touching her side brought me the reason—
her side was warm; her fawn lay there waiting,   10
alive, still, never to be born.
Beside that mountain road I hesitated.

The car aimed ahead its lowered parking lights;
under the hood purred the steady engine.
I stood in the glare of the warm exhaust turning red;   15
around our group I could hear the wilderness listen.

I thought hard for us all—my only swerving—
then pushed her over the edge into the river.

WHAT DOES HE SAY?

1. Write a paragraph describing your first reaction when you've been assigned to read a poem. Attraction? Resistance? Why? How does a poem invite you to read? What have been your past experiences reading poetry?

2. Read this poem aloud and underline three or four words or phrases that stand out—words that seem to have special energy, power, or resonance. Discuss these words with other students in class. Have you underlined the same words? What do these words have in common? What possible meanings do the words imply?

3. Stafford says that "around our group I could hear the wilderness listen." What do you think he means by the phrase "our group"?

4. Stafford says that he "thought hard for us all—my only swerving." What does *swerving* mean here? Why is Stafford thinking hard for us all? What is he thinking about? How does this event involve "us"?

WHAT DO YOU THINK?

5. This poem doesn't explain its meaning. Stafford gives us details, a situation, a moment, and lets us draw our own conclusions—though there are hints of his theme in the position and subtleties of certain otherwise simple words. Write an essay arguing for what you think the poem means, supporting your argument with details from the poem.

6. Based on this poem, what would Stafford say in response to the binge-drinking scenario described in the introduction to this chapter? Would he intervene in the affairs of his friends? If so, why? If not, why not? Or are these two situations—the binge drinking and the traveling through the dark—too different to be compared?

7. Based on this poem, do you think that Stafford believes we are responsible for others? Which others?

WHAT WOULD THEY SAY?

8. Write an essay arguing that Stafford's implied position in "Traveling through the Dark" is very similar to the position that Joan Didion takes in "On Morality" (p. 167). In your essay, comment on the similarities in Stafford's and Didion's imagery and examples, as well as their emphasis on concrete details over abstract speculation.

9. Write an essay arguing that Stafford disagrees with Garrett Hardin's "Lifeboat Ethics: The Case against Helping the Poor" (p. 130). Would Hardin "swerve" or "hesitate"?

For Community Learning and Research

1. Research the history and philosophy of Alcoholics Anonymous and other 12-step programs—for example, Overeaters Anonymous—then investigate the number of 12-step programs that exist on your campus or in your community. Collect as many brochures and copy as many Web sites as you need to represent these programs. Anonymity is an important part of the process for 12-step groups, and it's important that you respect this anonymity, but if possible try to find out the number of people who attend such meetings on a regular basis in your area. Write a paper that presents this information. Imagine as your audience a reader who wants to understand both the extent of alcohol and other addiction problems in your community and the availability of this kind of treatment program. The paper should include a brief discussion of the history and philosophy of this movement, as well as cite at least one passage from Wechsler, Deutsch, and Dowdall's "Too Many Colleges Are Still in Denial about Alcohol Abuse" (p. 96).

2. Write a paper analyzing the effectiveness of the brochures and other material that you gathered for the assignment above. Make sure to comment on the rhetorical "moves" and style of the documents.

3. Design a brochure that represents the information you gathered for topic one, a brochure that would make this information easily available for students in your dorm or apartment or neighborhood.

4. Research either the Democratic or Republican Party in your area, gathering brochures and looking at Web pages. Interview several leaders about the nature and extent of the political party's activities in your community. Based on this research, write a profile of either group.

5. Based on the information you gathered above, write a letter to the editor of your local or school newspaper urging people to join a political party. Quote Cornel West's "The Moral Obligation of Living in a Democratic Society" (p. 123).

6. Write a letter to your local paper arguing for or against a local initiative. Cite at least one of the essays in this chapter.

7. Interview the person in charge of recycling on your campus or in your community, paying particular attention to statistics: the number of pounds of recyclable material generated versus the number of pounds actually recycled, the cost of the program versus the cost of material, and so on. Present your findings as an informative research paper.

8. Drawing on the information you gathered in the topic above, design a poster or a half-page advertisement encouraging people to recycle. Use a short statement from one of the selections in this chapter as a caption or slogan.

9. Interview the person in charge of your local homeless shelter and convert that dialogue into a profile for your campus newspaper. Or spend a night in your local homeless shelter and write a personal essay describing your experience. Or interview the person in charge of a local residential program for adults with developmental disabilities or spend an evening at such a program; then write a personal

essay describing your experience. Quote at least one of the selections in this chapter.

10. Research your school's program for students with disabilities. Who qualifies as "disabled"? What is the range of disabilities recognized by the school? What programs and resources are available for such students? How many such students attend your school? Present this material in the form of a brochure for individuals with disabilities who might be considering attending your college or university.

11. Consult your university's Web page. How welcoming is its content or design, and for whom? If you were, or are, a person of color, would you feel welcome? If you had a disability, would you feel welcome? Write an essay exploring your responses, quoting from both Bowen H. McCoy's "The Parable of the Sadhu" (p. 102) and Stephen L. Carter's "Welcoming the Stranger" (p. 111).

12. Do a Google search under any controversial heading: making bombs at home, for example, or an anti-Muslim, anti-Jewish, antiwoman, anti-person-of-color site—any anti-site. Consult a number of these sites. In light of this research, write an essay addressed to parents advising them on the use of the Internet by their children. Quote a passage from Esther Dyson's "Cyberspace: If You Don't Love It, Leave It" (p. 141) and explain why you agree or disagree with her.

13. Research the statistics on hunger in your town or county. Consult local government Web sites and government documents at your library. Consult, too, the archives for your local paper. Also investigate various church and nonprofit organizations in your community that try to serve the poor—for example, soup kitchens and homeless shelters. On the basis of this research, write an informative paper on the hunger problem in your area, addressed to a general reader and quoting at least one of the selections in this chapter.

14. On the basis of the research above, write an editorial arguing that some particular action should be taken to alleviate hunger in your area. Quote one of the essays in this chapter.

15. Survey your friends and classmates on the amount of money they spend each week or month on alcohol, lattes, compact discs, or other forms of entertainment. Calculate how much this "entertainment" or "luxury" expense costs the average student each day. Drawing again on the research you did for topic 13, calculate the amount of money each citizen in your community spends in taxes or for charity on helping the poor or the hungry. (We realize that these statistics may be hard to find. Narrow your search as you discover what information is available). Present your findings in the form of a one-page table, graph, or advertisement. If possible, include a quote or statistic from one of the essays in this chapter. Your purpose is to convince people to devote some of their entertainment budget to helping others.

16. Write a letter to the editor of a local publication arguing against the assumptions and purpose of the topic above, drawing on Garrett Hardin's arguments in "Lifeboat Ethics: The Case against Helping the Poor" (p. 130).

3.

Is Violence Necessary?

WHAT WOULD YOU DO?
MEDIATING A CONFRONTATION

You have just arrived at a large party where a lot of drinking is taking place. Within minutes you walk past a room where Tyler (whom you recognize but do not know well) is shouting at his girlfriend, Jessica (whom you also know, though vaguely). He's very angry, he's using a lot of profanity, and something in the way he's standing over Jessica and waving his arms suddenly seems alarming. Without really thinking, you walk in and stand between the two of them, Tyler standing on one side, Jessica sitting on the other.

Tyler turns his attention to you. "Who do you think you are?" he says. "Why is this your business?" And as he's shouting and swearing, he's moving closer and closer to you. You're almost touching now, standing face to face. He's balling up his fists.

What would you do?

Let's say that you're female. How would you respond, and why? Let's say you're male. Would you respond differently than a woman would? Why or why not? In either case, would you resort to some sort of violence as Tyler comes toward you? Would you push him or hit him? What would you do? What elements of this scenario would make a difference to you if they were changed? Suppose, for example, that Tyler and Jessica were complete strangers to you, would that change your reaction? What if it was Jessica who was threatening Tyler? (Women abusing men is rampant, but not well-publicized.)

What about the aftermath? What happens the next day, and the next? Should you have gotten involved at all? Would you have? Should you have walked on by?

Violence is the great mystery of our coming together, for there is always the potential for tension and conflict. We seek happiness, but disagree about the definition. Our circumstances, abilities, and experiences differ. Space is limited, resources are limited, and yet there are so many people, so many competing demands. Nearly all of us have consciences, nearly all of us have good intentions, but we're all flawed human beings, too, capable of blindness and selfishness. Sometimes we crack. Sometimes words don't seem to work, reason seems to fail, and then our physicality comes into play. Then we come to blows. Whether in our private relationships (Andre Dubus, "Giving Up the Gun," p. 180) or in the relationships among countries (Terry Tempest Williams, "Two Words," p. 214, or Andrew Sullivan, "The Pursuit of Happiness: Four Revolutionary Words" p. 217), violence or the threat of violence is a sad and complex reality. The question is, Does it have to be that way? Is it possible for people to address problems without recourse to violence? Or is such a desire foolish and naive? Are there situations in which violence is the only alternative? The Dalai Lama says no ("The Need for Discernment," p. 205), we must always seek to avoid harm. Chris Hedges, in "Eros and Thanatos" (p. 247), says that because there is a dark instinct within all of us violence may be unavoidable. Other writers in this chapter, while accepting the reality of conflict, look for ways to mediate disputes when injustice has been done.

Opening the Question

*After reading and discussing several of the selections in this chapter, return to the situation above. **Now** what would you do? Write an essay answering this question, drawing on at least two of the selections. You don't need to have changed your mind, but you do need to demonstrate how the reading has complicated your thinking.*

Do the readings suggest that violence is unavoidable? Do the readings suggest ways of interpreting violence, seeking its hidden causes? Do the readings suggest practical strategies for mediating disputes?

ANDRE DUBUS
Giving Up the Gun

IN THIS ESSAY, Andre Dubus (1936–1999) confronts questions of fear of bodily harm—to himself and his loved ones—and of the choices available in confronting that fear.

The author of nine works of fiction, including the short-story collection Dancing after Hours *(1996), Dubus taught at Bradford College in Massachusetts from 1966 to 1984. His books won several awards, including the PEN/Malamud Award and the REA Award. In 1986, while stopped along Interstate I-93 to help a stranded motorist, he was struck by a passing car and left paralyzed from the waist down, an event which gave rise to the essays in* Meditations from a Moveable Chair *(1998), from which "Giving Up the Gun" is taken.*

In the winter of 1990, sitting in my wheelchair in a sleeping compartment on a train from Portland, Oregon, to Chicago, I gave up my guns and the protection I believed they gave people I loved, and strangers whose peril I might witness, and me. At home in Massachusetts, I had a metal gun box with two locks, and in it were eight handguns, one a small twenty-two-caliber revolver that is four and a half inches long. In my wallet on the train, I had a Massachusetts license to carry firearms. In the space on the card for occupation, a police officer had typed *Author*; in the space under *Reason for Issuing License*, he had typed *Protection*.

For thirteen years, I had a license, renewing it every five years. I still have the one that was with me on the train, but it expired four years ago, in 1991, and the guns have been locked in their box since I returned from Oregon. Thirteen years before I rode that train, someone I love was raped in Boston by a man who held a knife at her throat. I went to my local police chief and told him I wanted a license, and that my father had taught me to shoot, and the Marine Corps had, and I would safely own a gun, and no woman would ever be raped if I were with her. I cursed and wept and he was sympathetic and said he would immediately start the background investigation by the state. A detective made a rolled impression of my right index finger, and I went to a photographer for a picture.

In about three weeks, I had my license and I went to a sporting-goods store to choose and buy a gun: a Charter Arms thirty-eight-caliber snubnosed revolver, because it cost less than a Smith & Wesson or a Colt. I did not own a suit and rarely wore a sport coat, so a shoulder holster would not do. The store owner made me a shadow holster: a leather one whose belt slot was low, so that most of the holster and the gun were above my waist. I could wear a pullover shirt, or sweater, or even a loose-fitting T-shirt, and you could not see the gun. So my thirteen years as an armed man began.

For a long time, I put the gun on my belt only when I went to Boston with a woman. Then I was certain that she was safe, and I was also certain that I would never have to use the gun; that simply being prepared for rapists or other violent men would keep them from my path. And if that failed, I was certain that I would not have to shoot anyone; I would only have to hold the gun in my hand and point it at a man while the woman with me called the police. Maybe I would have to fire a shot straight up in the air, if this man I did not believe would be part of my life appeared anyway, intent on removing me with his fists or a weapon, and taking the woman. If a shot in the air did not change his dark direction and send him running, if instead he attacked, I would shoot his leg or shoulder. This was all very tidy, and I believed it.

After a few years, and a lot of newspaper stories, I began asking myself   5 questions whose answers were not in my brain, my body, my gun, but in my soul, though I did not know that. What if I went with a man to watch the Red Sox or a movie, and we saw several men or one big one attacking a woman or a man, not to steal, but to harm or rape or kill? I was no hand-to-hand fighter, and did not intend to be. I also did not intend to watch a crucifixion in any form. I started bringing a gun every time I went to Boston: to Fenway Park, to jazz clubs, to dinner in restaurants, to movies.

When I fired the Charter Arms thirty-eight at a target, it often spit tiny fragments of lead toward my face. I sold it at a gun store and bought a used three-eighty semiautomatic, which looks like a very small forty-five, and I put it in the pocket of my jeans, with my keys and coins, and it was flat enough to be concealed. Through the years, when I had the money, I bought other guns. One was a Smith & Wesson snub-nosed thirty-eight that fit in the shadow holster. By now, I had begun loading guns with hollow-point bullets, so if I had to shoot a human being in the shoulder or leg, the bullet would not go through him and hit someone else; it would shatter into pieces inside his body. The guns were to protect other people. No one would rape me. If someone wanted my money, he could have it. If someone felt like beating me, I could run. But I had the gun, and I believed that nothing would happen, simply because I was prepared for it; and that if something did happen, it would be as I had imagined it. My confidence in this was foolish, and the foolishness was as concealed from my soul as the gun in my pocket or holster was concealed from the eyes of other people.

Alabama has stricter handgun laws than Massachusetts, or it did in 1985, when I went by train with my wife and our three-year-old daughter, and brought guns for hunting, target shooting, and to put in my pocket or in a holster under my coat, if I felt I needed it in Tuscaloosa. I went there to earn money, to hold the writing chair for a semester at the University of Alabama. Because I grew up in Louisiana, where guns in homes were ordinary, where an adult could carry a gun if it was not concealed, and men who worked in woods or swamps often wore holstered handguns so they could shoot snakes, I assumed that Alabama in 1985 would be like Louisiana in the forties and fifties. A few days after we moved into the large and free house that came with the job in Tuscaloosa, I went to the sheriff's office and showed a deputy my Massachusetts permit, and asked him if I could carry a handgun. He said that no one could carry a handgun in Alabama; that a resident, after a background investigation, could buy one and take it home but could not take it out of the home. The deputy was a friendly man, and after we talked for a while, he told me to get a letter from the English department, showing that I was employed in Alabama. He said the letter and my Massachusetts license would make everything all right.

"If it went to court," he said, "the judge would throw it out."

"What if there's trouble, and I have to use it?"

"Then it's never a problem."   10

Tuscaloosa did not feel like a place where I needed a gun. Of course if you feel the need to carry a gun, you need one everywhere. But the territory of violence was in my imagination: cities were places where predators lived; towns and small cities were not. Unarmed, I drove and walked in Tuscaloosa, until I bought the four-and-a-half-inch-long twenty-two revolver, stainless steel, with brown plastic handgrips. It holds five rounds, and you load and unload it by removing the cylinder, which means the gun is as safe as a handgun can be: the cylinder is either in place or it is not; and if it is, you handle the gun as though it is loaded, even when you know it is not. Because of the training given me by my father and the Marine Corps, I always assume a gun is loaded. I also attribute to a gun the ability to load itself, even fire itself, without being touched by a human hand.

I love guns, especially well-made pistols and revolvers. Many of them are beautiful, and their shape and balanced weight are pleasing to hold. I love the relaxed concentration of aiming a gun and squeezing its trigger, the thrill of hitting a bull's-eye or a can. When I hold a gun, I do not imagine the death of a human being, which is the purpose of most handguns. I know people who are frightened or appalled by guns and do not want to hold one, spin its cylinder or pull its slide to the rear and watch and hear it move forward, hear that perfect and final click as the slide pushes a bullet into the chamber. These people are right: they see a bullet entering a human body. In the gun store in Alabama, I held the tiny twenty-two as another person might hold a pocket watch or a ring, a hammer or a golf club. To me, that gun, like all my guns, was somehow alive, with a history and a future; with a soul. I loved it, and bought it.

Before I could take it home, I had to wait about a week for permission from the state of Alabama. At home, I took out the cylinder, loaded it with four rounds of hollow-points, leaving an empty chamber under the hammer, and put the gun in the right pocket of my jeans, with my coins, keys, and lighter, and it was always there, when I left the house for Mass or work, errands or shopping, or pleasure. I had not fired it, and did not expect to until I went home to Massachusetts, where in my basement I had a target for twenty-two-caliber weapons. The little gun in my pocket amused me. It was, I said, for gentle places, where there would be no trouble. I called it "Misty."

If it had not been in my pocket the night I aimed it at a man's stomach, I do not know what would have happened on that crowded sidewalk across the street from the university. The night was a Friday, my wife and daughter were out of town, visiting relatives in the North, the evening was warm, and I began it with happy hour on the patio of a restaurant we writers liked. Most of the writers I knew were graduate students, and we liked this place because we could drink cheaply and afford Mexican appetizers until six o'clock. One of the women that evening on the patio was a graduate student who was separated from her husband, and had a young daughter she was afraid would live with the father. Later, she and her husband lived together and remained married, but that night it did not seem possible, and she was in pain.

   She had driven me to the bar, and at six o'clock, when the prices of 15 drinks changed and the writers dispersed and went to other cheap bars or home for dinner, the woman and I drove to a video store. We had decided while drinking that we wanted to watch *Rebel Without a Cause*. We rented it to watch at my house, but we wanted first to sit in a quiet air-conditioned bar and drink club sodas and talk about divorce, and she drove there; it was twilight now and the streetlamps were on. She parked around the corner from a block of bars and restaurants facing the campus. We walked to the corner. Then a man with no hands came around it and stopped in front of me. He was stocky and short, and I looked down at his face. I was taking a cigarette from a pack when he asked me for money. I offered him a cigarette; I did not know how he would smoke it, but I felt that he did not want my help. Somehow, with his stumps or an elbow, he got it to his lips. I was not watching; I was taking money from my wallet and slipping it into the left pocket of his pants. Then I gave him a light. He said: "I saw that."

   I do not remember what he did with the cigarette. I said: "You can buy me a drink."

   "Where?"

   I nodded at the bar beside us. He said: "I can't go in there."

   "Why?"

   "I'm eighty-sixed."   20

   "Let's go anyway."

   The three of us went inside; it was crowded with students, and dark, with loud talk and laughter and music from the jukebox, and I went to the bar. The bartender was a young man. He said: "Sir, that man can't come in here."

   "Why?"

   "He makes trouble."

I wondered what kind of trouble a man with no hands could make. We 25
went outside. The man without hands said: "Let's go to my place."

"No thanks; we're going down the street."

He crossed the street to a liquor store on the opposite corner, and the
woman and I watched. He came out with a case of beer on his right shoulder,
his stump holding it in place. He lifted the other to wave, and we waved at
him. Then a young blond man was standing with us; he had come out of the
bar. He looked like an undergraduate. He said: "Mister, that man is trouble."

"What can he do, without hands?"

"Believe me, he's trouble."

He was an affable young man, and the three of us chatted for a while. 30
He invited us to have a drink, but we thanked him and walked down the
block to a well-lighted bar where you could nearly always sit among quiet
strangers. We did that, and drank club sodas with wedges of lime and dashes
of bitters, and talked about divorce. We assumed her daughter would not live
with her. I had never known a woman who had lost custody of her child, but
I knew her pain. We talked about it and drank club sodas for two hours or
more, and I no longer felt the happy-hour margaritas. While we were becoming sober, the young blond man, in the bar at the corner, was probably
drinking too much. It is easy to conclude that someone dangerous at night,
outside of a bar, is drunk; but I shall never know whether that man was drunk
and was doing something he would not want to do in his normal state, or was
a violent man whose trajectory met mine on a sidewalk in Alabama.

When the woman and I left our seats at the bar, I was tired because of
what we had talked about, and neither of us was certain we still wanted to
watch the movie. Deciding to see it had been delightful when the sun was
shining and we were drinking in its light on the patio. Now it was nearly ten
o'clock. We stepped out of the air-conditioned bar, into the warm air and
streetlights, and I held her elbow, guiding her through a group of large black
men who had come down a stairway from an upstairs bar. I felt her body
tense, and I looked at her face. She looked afraid. I do not know why. In Alabama, except for that Friday night, I saw no trouble between white and black
people, and I did not hear any bigotry. This was one of many reasons I loved my
time there.

When I left Louisiana in the spring of 1958, integration was inchoate.
In my sophomore year of college, black students had enrolled. In the student
union, they sat with one another; I do not remember any black men playing
on a varsity team. I grew up feeling compassion for black people; you could
not live in a segregated town, even as a young boy, and not see injustice. I
also felt involved in this injustice, and stained by it; I still do. I did not want
black people to drink at different public water fountains, go into different public bathrooms, sit in the balcony of one movie theater (they could not go into
our other two theaters); I did not want them to ride on the back of the bus,
but they did, and there I was at the front of the bus, even if black people had

to stand in its crowded rear. And my parents had taught me, their only son, always to offer my seat to a woman. I did not want black people to live in their part of town, with its dirt roads and hovels. I did not want them to be subservient, and their work to be menial, but they were and it was; and I grew and learned and played in the sun.

This was in Lafayette, Louisiana, a small city then, and I do not remember any violence engendered by black boys or men. Nor do I remember white boys or men assaulting black people. As I write this in 1995, black people in America are still beyond the pale; white people have created and maintained ghettos where understandable hopelessness and rage keep true freedom of the body and spirit at bay. It is a world I was born to skirt, for I am white, and it is a world I can avoid by simply having enough money to buy a house on an acre and a quarter of land in Massachusetts. I would not wheel about in my chair in a ghetto, because I am afraid; and I am afraid because I believe that only God's grace can keep many black people from feeling anger about anyone who is white; and we often turn away from God's grace; or His voice is lost in the clamor of simply being alive.

In Lafayette in the forties and fifties, we were not afraid of black people. Some of us—I think most of us—were respectful, some were scornful, some were hateful. I doubt that any of us, boys and girls, men and women, felt that we and black people were equal, despite what our priests told us. How can you feel equal, save in the heart of God, with someone who is always excluded? I believe I saw no violence between white and black boys because we were never with one another in schools, or on playgrounds, or in swimming pools, or even in groups on the street or, as we grew older, in bars and nightclubs; and I believe also that black people were afraid of us. Many of them moved among us with the caution of wild birds. In my boyhood, there were no lynchings in Louisiana; or I do not remember any. But how could any black person in the segregated South not be aware of this horror?

In Tuscaloosa in 1985, black people were everywhere, in the stores, on the 35 sidewalks, on the campus and in classrooms, in bars and theaters and churches. I do not know why the woman seemed afraid as we strolled through the group of black men, standing happily at ease on a hot night. She and I walked nearly the length of the block, were at the corner where we had talked with the man without hands and the young blond man, when I heard a man's voice say: "Nigger."

I stopped and turned. The young blond man stood about twenty-five feet from me, in front of the plate-glass window of a restaurant; in his right hand was an open pocketknife with a long and wide blade, and he was looking at a small black man. Behind the black man was a wall, and his back touched it. The blond man slowly moved toward him. I put my right hand in the pocket of my jeans, gripped the revolver and pulled it out and cocked it and aimed it at the blond man's stomach. I knew nothing about the accuracy of this little gun; if I fired at his shoulder or leg, I might not hit him at all.

I saw the gun sight at the front of the barrel, his stomach, the silver blade of his knife, and his face. To his right, some young white men were telling him not to do this; but to me, they were as distant as campus buildings hundreds of yards away. I still do not know how many of them stood there. My hand aiming the gun was steady and I said loudly: "Put away the knife."

He looked at me, recognized me, and said: "Fuck you."

I had no images of my history or my future, not even of pulling the trigger or not pulling the trigger. The voices of his friends, indeed all sounds on the sidewalk and street and coming from the bar on the corner, only a few feet to my right, were like wind you have been hearing for hours. All of me focused on the knife; it had to disappear; and I was mysteriously calm. I said: "Put it back in your pocket, or I'll shoot."

"Fuck you." He was not moving. I glanced at the black man, standing against the wall. The woman stood to my left; either she was silent or I did not hear her; she too was as distant from me as everyone else on the sidewalk, save the blond man and the black man at the wall. I remember only one instant of one wish: that the black man would run away. I said: "I mean it."

He spread his arms from his body, and said: "Fuck you. Shoot. Go 40 ahead. Shoot."

The voices of his friends rose, I could see their hands and faces to his right, and they were pleading with him; but they did not touch him. By now, probably the group of black men the woman and I had walked through had gathered, watching us; I did not see them; but when it ended, they were standing near us. The young man's arms were still spread, and he said: "Shoot me. Go ahead. Shoot me."

Over the barrel of the gun, I looked at his stomach; my arm was extended; the gun was steady. I said: "It's a twenty-two hollow-point, son. It'll spread your guts all over that window."

"All right." He started walking toward me, his friends on his right moving with him, talking to him. Then he was close to me, and everything had changed. I pointed the gun in the air, held its hammer with my thumb, gently squeezed the trigger, and lowered the hammer into place. Then I held the gun at my side. He still held the knife; when he was two feet from me, he stopped and said: "Tell you what. I'll give my buddy the knife, and you give her the gun, and you and me'll fight it out."

I imagined the back of my head hitting the sidewalk. He was young and he looked strong and he would knock me down and the concrete would fracture my skull and I would die here. I said: "I don't want to fight."

I do not remember the sentence he spoke then, only the word *nigger*; 45 then all I felt was resignation. I would have to fight him, receive whatever pain and injury he dealt, until someone stopped him, or he was done with me. I was not angry; I felt nothing about him.

"That's it," I said, and I dropped the revolver into the woman's large purse. Then one of his friends stood between us, his face close to mine, and said: "Mister, I know you can whip his ass. But please leave. I've got to get him out of here before the cops come."

"Okay," I said, and held the woman's elbow and walked away, around the corner. We stopped, and I took the gun from her purse. Then a cruiser came onto the street of bars, quietly, but with flashing lights, and I looked around the corner and watched it stop; two police officers got out and walked to the young blond man. The woman and I went to her car and, as she started it, I said: "Men are funny. If that guy had said: 'I know he can whip *your* ass,' I would have had to fight him. But he said: 'You can whip his ass.' So he let me off the hook."

Then she was trembling.

"Violence scares me," she said. "I have to go home."

"Me too." 50

She drove me there, and I took the video, to return it to the store, and went inside and filled a glass with ice and took it and a Coke to the front porch. I sat on the steps in the warm night and looked at trees and the sky. I needed the company of women and children; I wanted my wife and daughter to be upstairs, sleeping. I sat for a long time. Saturday morning, I phoned my wife, then a man who was a poet, a hunter, a fisherman, and who lived in the country near Tuscaloosa, and I told him about Friday night, and said I wanted to go out and hunt squirrels with him, to be in the beautiful woods and use a gun the way it ought to be used.

Monday, my wife and daughter were home, and I went to Mass at noon. After Mass, I talked to the young chaplain and a young nun. We stood in front of the chapel, in warm sunlight. The nun was pretty and wore jeans; I always liked seeing her and talking to her; being attracted to a woman and knowing that what we shared was God and my attraction could not become carnal was lovely. I told them about the man and the knife and my gun. I said: "I understand turning the other cheek. But what about turning somebody else's cheek? Christ doesn't say anything about that. What about the woman they were going to stone for adultery? What would He have done if they had picked up rocks and started throwing them at her? It wasn't His time yet. He couldn't stand in front of her and get killed. He had to wait to be crucified. Would He throw rocks at them?" I looked at the priest's eyes, and nodded toward the nun. "What would you do if some guys tried to rape her?"

"I'd fight them."

Still I had no peace. A young man could be dead because of one moment on a Friday night. I did not know what else I could have done but aim my gun at him until either the knife or the black man was gone. I still do not know. I could have kept the gun in my pocket and tried to disarm him. When I was a Marine officer candidate, the sergeant who taught hand-to-hand fighting said: "If someone pulls a knife on you in a bar, run; if you can't run, throw an ashtray or bottle at his face and charge him." Then the sergeant showed us one way to grab the man's wrist, move behind him, and push his arm into a hammerlock. It was a move you would have to practice. I thought about this, during those days and nights in Tuscaloosa, while I kept hoping to know what I should have done. Sometimes, seeing the young man's face, I saw myself trying to grab his wrist, saw his knife piercing my flesh, my aorta. But none of this applied: that night on the sidewalk, my only instinct had been to aim a gun. I had no conflict, because I had only one choice. Now I wanted more choices, and I wanted to know what they were.

At Thanksgiving, my wife and daughter and I rode on the train to Baton Rouge to visit my oldest sister, Kathryn. In the evening, after dinner, people came to Kathryn's house. One was a priest, and one was a nun in her fifties. I imagined the eyes of Christ were like her eyes: in them were strength and depth, and she was cheerful and wise. The priest was in his thirties, short and graceful and athletically built. He lifted weights and had a black belt in karate, and he engaged in contact karate matches. His eyes were like John the Baptist's, or the way I imagined his to be: they were dark and bright with embers that could become rage. He and the nun and I stood with drinks; I felt he would have an answer for me, and I told him my story. He said: "Within the realm of human possibility, you did what you could. You wanted no one to be harmed. And no one was. I beat up a man on Christmas Eve, then said the midnight Mass."

"You did?"

"I was delivering food to the poor. When I got to his house, he was beating his wife. I took her and the children to another house, then went back to talk to him. Then he tried to beat me."

So I had my answer, and the comfort of it. Within the realm of human possibility, I had done what I could.

I have written all of this to try to discover why, sitting in my wheelchair on a train, I gave up my guns. But I do not know. Eight months after that Thanksgiving in Baton Rouge, I was driving home from Boston, armed with a pistol, and I stopped on the highway and got out of my car to help two people who had driven over an abandoned motorcycle. Then a car hit me, and I have been in a wheelchair for over nine years. My body can no longer do what I want to do, and it cannot protect my two young daughters, and my grandchildren, from perils I used to believe I could save people from. I have not learned the virtue of surrender—which I want—but I have learned the impossibility of avoiding surrender. I am also more afraid now. For the first three years and eight months after my injury, until those moments on the train, I believed I needed a gun more than I ever had. Alone in my house, I kept a small twenty-two Beretta semiautomatic in my shoulder bag, its loaded magazine in one of the bag's pockets, and for the first time in my life, the gun was to protect myself.

I only know this: on the train, images came to me: I was alone in my 60
house, on the couch, watching a movie on video, and a man kicked my door
open and came in, to steal, beat, kill; and I shoved the magazine into the pistol and worked its slide and aimed the gun, but he kept coming at me, and I
shot his leg, but he kept coming, and I shot his chest, again and again, till he
stopped coming. Then, as I looked out the train window at snow on the
ground, one sentence came to me: With my luck, I'll kill someone.

That was all. *Luck* was not the accurate word, and I do not know what
the accurate word is. But with that sentence, I felt the fence and gate, not
even the lawn and porch and door to the house of sorrow I would live in if I
killed someone. Then I felt something detach itself from my soul, departing,
rising, vanishing; and I said to God: *It's up to You now.* This is not the humble
and pure and absolutely spiritual love of turning the other cheek. It is not an
answer to turn someone else's cheek. On the train, I gave up answers that are
made of steel that fire lead, and I decided to sit in a wheelchair on the fright-
eningly invisible palm of God.

WHAT DOES HE SAY?

1. Why did the narrator begin to buy and use guns?

2. "My confidence in this," the narrator says, "was foolish." What is "this"? Why
   was his confidence in it foolish?

3. The narrator says that he loves guns. Why does he love them?

4. Assume that you were a witness to all the events described in the pivotal scene in
   this story: you were with the narrator and his friend all evening and you witnessed
   the encounter with the man holding the knife. Narrate everything that happened
   exactly as you would to a police officer investigating the incident: flatly, detail by
   detail, in chronological order.

5. Describe the tone of this essay. Is it loud? soft? angry? sad? Describe the image of
   the writer that the words suggest. Is this someone you would trust? Someone you
   would want to meet? Would you go out for a drink with this narrator? Take a class
   from him? Why or why not?

WHAT DO YOU THINK?

6. Gender, race, and religion each play significant roles in this story. Select one of
   these factors and explain that role.

7. Near the end of this story the narrator asks a series of questions of a priest: "I understand turning the other cheek. But what about turning somebody else's cheek?
   Christ doesn't say anything about that. What about the woman they were going
   to stone for adultery? What would He have done if they had picked up rocks and

started throwing them at her?" What do you think about this biblical idea of "turning the other cheek"—of letting someone hurt you? What do you think about the idea of letting someone hurt someone else? Is turning the other cheek a practical solution to the problem of violence? In the end, what is the narrator's answer to this question?

8. This essay tells the story of someone who changed his mind about a particular issue. In the beginning, he owns and carries guns. In the end, he has given up his guns. What factors have caused this change of mind? In the same circumstances, would you have changed your mind, too? Does the essay change your mind?

9. "[T]he territory of violence was my imagination," the narrator says. Explain what he means, and write an essay exploring this idea, using your own experience.

10. The narrator talks about the "virtue of surrender." Explain what he means, and write an essay exploring this idea, using your own experience.

WHAT WOULD THEY SAY?

11. Compare and contrast the figure of C. P. Ellis in Studs Terkel's profile (p. 568), in chapter 7, "Why Change your Mind?", with the narrator in "Giving Up the Gun." Both change their minds. Why do they? For different reasons? Is their experience similar or dissimilar? On the basis of these two essays, what is required to change another person's mind? *Can* one person change another person's mind?

12. In "The Case for Torture" (p. 201), Michael Levin argues that sometimes torture is necessary to achieve the higher end of security and protection. Based on "Giving Up the Gun," what would Dubus say?

13. Put Dubus and the Dalai Lama ("The Need for Discernment," p. 205) in conversation. What would the Dalai Lama say after reading Dubus's essay? What would Dubus say in response to the Dalai Lama's essay? Write a paper arguing that they agree more than they disagree.

MERRILL JOAN GERBER
"I Don't Believe This"

*I*ɴ ᴛʜɪs sʜᴏʀᴛ sᴛᴏʀʏ, *Merrill Joan Gerber (b. 1938) addresses the issue of domestic violence and its lasting aftereffects. Gerber is the author of seven novels, including* King of the World, *which won a Pushcart Press Editor's Book Award, and several collections of short stories.*

She earned her MA from Brandeis University and received a Wallace Stegner Fiction Fellowship at Stanford University. Currently, Gerber teaches fiction writing at the California Institute of Technology. "I Don't Believe This" was first published in the Atlantic Monthly *in October 1984 and was included in the 1986 O. Henry Award anthology.*

After it was all over, a final detail emerged, one so bizarre that my sister laughed crazily, holding both hands over her ears as she read the long article in the newspaper. I had brought it across the street to show to her; now that she was my neighbor, I came to see her and the boys several times a day. The article said that the crematorium to which her husband's body had been entrusted for cremation had been burning six bodies at a time and dumping most of the bone and ash into plastic garbage bags, which went directly into their dumpsters. A disgruntled employee had tattled.

"Can you imagine?" Carol said, laughing. "Even that! Oh, his poor mother! His poor *father!*" She began to cry. "I don't believe this," she said. That was what she had said on the day of the cremation, when she had sat in my back yard in a beach chair at the far end of the garden, holding on to a washcloth. I think she was prepared to cry so hard that an ordinary handkerchief would never have done. But she remained dry-eyed. When I came outside after a while, she said, "I think of his beautiful face burning, of his eyes burning." She looked up at the blank blue sky and said, "I just don't believe this. I try to think of what he was feeling when he gulped in that stinking exhaust. What could he have been thinking? I know he was blaming me."

She rattled the newspaper. "A dumpster! Oh, Bard would have loved that. Even at the end he couldn't get it right. Nothing ever went right for him, did it? And all along I've been thinking that I won't ever be able to go in the ocean again, because his ashes are floating in it! Can you believe it? How that woman at the mortuary promised they would play Pachelbel's Canon on the little boat, how the remains would be scattered with 'dignity and taste'? His mother even came all the way down with that jar of his father's ashes that she had saved for thirty years, so father and son could be mixed together for all eternity. Plastic garbage baggies! You know," she said, looking at me, "life is just a joke, a bad joke, isn't it?"

Bard had not believed me when I'd told him that my sister was in a shelter for battered women. Afraid of *him*? Running away from *him*? The world was full of dangers from which only *he* could protect her! He had accused me of hiding her in my house. "Would I be so foolish?" I had said. "She knows it's the first place you'd look."

"You better put me in touch with her," he had said, menacingly. "You   5
both know I can't handle this for long."

It had gone on for weeks. On the last day, he called me three times, demanding to be put in touch with her. "Do you understand me?" he shouted. "If she doesn't call here in ten minutes, I'm checking out. Do you believe me?"

"I believe you," I said. "But you know she can't call you. She can't be reached in the shelter. They don't want the women there to be manipulated by their men. They want them to have space and time to think."

"Manipulated?" He was incredulous. "I'm checking *out*, this is *IT*. Good-bye forever!"

He hung up. It wasn't true that Carol couldn't be reached. I had the number. Not only had I been calling her but I had also been playing tapes for her of his conversations over the phone during the past weeks. This one I hadn't taped. The tape recorder was in a different room.

"Should I call her and tell her?" I asked my husband.   10

"Why bother?" he said. He and the children were eating dinner; he was becoming annoyed by this continual disruption of our lives. "He calls every day and says he's killing himself and he never does. Why should this call be any different?"

Then the phone rang. It was my sister. She had a fever and bronchitis. I could barely recognize her voice.

"Could you bring me some cough syrup with codeine tomorrow?" she asked.

"Is your cough very bad?"

"No, it's not too bad, but maybe the codeine will help me get to sleep.   15
I can't sleep here at all. I just can't sleep."

"He just called."

"Really," she said. "What a surprise!" But the sarcasm didn't hide her fear. "What this time?"

"He's going to kill himself in ten minutes unless you call him."

"So what else is new?" She made a funny sound. I was frightened of her these days. I couldn't read her thoughts. I didn't know if the sound was a cough or a sob.

"Do you want to call him?" I suggested. I was afraid to be responsible.   20
"I know you're not supposed to."

"I don't know," she said. "I'm breaking all the rules anyway."

The rules were very strict. No contact with the batterer, no news of him, no worrying about him. Forget him. Only female relatives could call, and they were not to relay any news of him—not how sorry he was, not how desperate he was, not how he had promised to reform and never do it again, not how he was going to kill himself if she didn't come home. Once, I had called the shelter for advice, saying that I thought he was serious this time, that he was going to do it. The counselor there—a deep-voiced woman named Katherine—had said to me, very calmly, "It might just be the best thing; it might be a blessing in disguise."

My sister blew her nose. "I'll call him," she said. "I'll tell him I'm sick and to leave you alone and to leave me alone."

I hung up and sat down to try to eat my dinner. My children's faces were full of fear. I could not possibly reassure them about any of this. Then the phone rang again. It was my sister.

"Oh, God," she said. "I called him. I told him to stop bothering you, 25 and he said, *I have to ask you one thing, just one thing. I have to know this. Do you love me?*" My sister gasped for breath. "I shouted *No*—what else could I say? That's how I *felt*. I'm so sick, this is such a nightmare; and then he just hung up. A minute later I tried to call him back to tell him that I didn't mean it, that I did love him, that I *do*, but he was gone." She began to cry. "He was gone."

"There's nothing you can do," I said. My teeth were chattering as I spoke. "He's done this before. He'll call me tomorrow morning, full of remorse for worrying you."

"I can hardly breathe," she said. "I have a high fever and the boys are going mad cooped up here." She paused to blow her nose. "I don't believe any of this. I really don't."

Afterward she moved right across the street from me. At first she rented the little house, but then it was put up for sale, and my mother and aunt found enough money to make a down payment so that she could be near me and I could take care of her till she got her strength back. I could see her bedroom window from my bedroom window—we were that close. I often thought of her trying to sleep in that house, alone there with her sons and the new, big watchdog. She told me that the dog barked at every tiny sound and frightened her when there was nothing to be frightened of. She was sorry she had got him. I could hear his barking from my house, at strange hours, often in the middle of the night.

I remembered when she and I had shared a bedroom as children. We giggled every night in our beds and made our father furious. He would come in and threaten to smack us. How could he sleep, how could he go to work in the morning, if we were going to giggle all night? That made us laugh even harder. Each time he went back to his room, we would throw the quilts over our heads and laugh till we nearly suffocated. One night our father came to quiet us four times. I remember the angry hunch of his back as he walked, barefoot, back to his bedroom. When he returned for the last time, stomping like a giant, he smacked us, each once, very hard, on our upper thighs. That made us quiet. We were stunned. When he was gone, Carol turned on the light and pulled down her pajama bottoms to show me the marks of his violence. I showed her mine. Each of us had our father's handprint, five red fingers, on the white skin of her thigh. She crept into my bed, where we clung to each other till the burning, stinging shock subsided and we could sleep.

Carol's sons, living on our quiet, adult street, complained to her that they 30 missed the shelter. They rarely asked about their father and only occasionally said that they wished they could see their old friends and their old school. For a few weeks they had gone to a school near the shelter; all the children had had to go to school. But one day Bard had called me and told me he was trying to find the children. He said he wanted to take them out to lunch. He knew they had to be at some school. He was going to go to every school in the district and look in every classroom, ask everyone he saw if any of the children there looked like his children. He would find them. "You can't keep them from me," he said, his voice breaking. "They belong to me. They love me."

 Carol had taken them out of school at once. An art therapist at the shelter held a workshop with the children every day. He was a gentle, soft-spoken man named Ned, who had the children draw domestic scenes and was never once surprised at the knives, bloody wounds, or broken windows that they drew. He gave each of them a special present, a necklace with a silver running-shoe charm, which only children at the shelter were entitled to wear. It made them special, he said. It made them part of a club to which no one else could belong.

 While the children played with crayons, their mothers were indoctrinated by women who had survived, who taught the arts of survival. The essential rule was *Forget him, he's on his own, the only person you have to worry about is yourself.* A woman who was in the shelter at the same time Carol was had had her throat slashed. Her husband had cut her vocal cords. She could speak only in a grating whisper. Her husband had done it in the bathroom, with her son watching. Yet each night she sneaked out and called her husband from a nearby shopping center. She was discovered and disciplined by the administration; they threatened to put her out of the shelter if she called him again. Each woman was allowed space at the shelter for a month, while she got legal help and made new living arrangements. Hard cases were allowed to stay a little longer. She said that she was sorry, but that he was the sweetest man, and when he loved her up, it was the only time she knew heaven.

Carol felt humiliated. Once each week the women lined up and were given their food: three very small whole frozen chickens, a package of pork hot dogs, some plain-wrapped cans of baked beans, eggs, milk, margarine, white bread. The children were happy with the food. Carol's sons played in the courtyard with the other children. Carol had difficulty relating to the other mothers. One had ten children. Two had black eyes. Several were pregnant. She began to have doubts that what Bard had done had been violent enough to cause her to run away. Did mental violence or violence done to furniture really count as battering? She wondered if she had been too hard on her husband. She wondered if she had been wrong to come here. All he had done — he said so himself, in the taped conversations, dozens of times — was to break a lousy hundred-dollar table. He had broken it before, he had fixed it before. Why was this time different from any of the others? She had pushed all his buttons, that's all, and he had gotten mad, and he had pulled the table away from the wall and smashed off its legs and thrown the whole thing out into the yard. Then he had put his head through the wall, using the top of his head as a battering ram. He had knocked open a hole to the other side. Then he had bitten his youngest son on the scalp. What was so terrible about that? It was just a momentary thing. He didn't mean anything by it. When his son had begun to cry in fear and pain, hadn't he picked the child up and told him it was nothing? If she would just come home, he would never get angry again. They'd have their sweet life. They'd go to a picnic, a movie, the beach. They'd have it better than ever before. He had just started going to a new church that was helping him to become a kinder and more sensitive man. He was a better person than he had ever been; he now knew the true meaning of love. Wouldn't she come back?

One day Bard called me and said, "Hey, the cops are here. You didn't send them, did you?"

"*Me?*" I said. I turned on the tape recorder. "What did you do?"   35

"Nothing. I busted up some public property. Can you come down and bail me out?"

"How can I?" I said. "My children..."

"How can you *not?*"

I hung up and called Carol at the shelter. I said, "I think he's being arrested."

"Pick me up," she said, "and take me to the house. I have to get some   40 things. I'm sure they'll let me out of the shelter if they know he's in jail. I'll check to make sure he's really there. I have to get us some clean clothes, and some toys for the boys. I want to get my picture albums. He threatened to burn them."

"You want to go to the house?"

"Why not? At least we know he's not going to be there. At least we know we won't find him hanging from a beam in the living room."

We stopped at a drugstore a few blocks away and called the house. No one was there. We called the jail. They said their records showed that he had been booked, but they didn't know for sure whether he'd been bailed out. "Is there any way he can bail out this fast?" Carol asked.

"Only if he uses his own credit card," the man answered.

"I *have* his credit card," Carol said to me, after she had hung up. "We're 45
so much in debt that I had to take it away from him. Let's just hurry. I hate
this! I hate sneaking into my own house this way."

I drove to the house and we held hands going up the walk. "I feel his
presence here, that he's right here seeing me do this," she said, in the dusty,
eerie silence of the living room. "Why do I give him so much power? It's as if
he knows whatever I'm thinking, whatever I'm doing. When he was trying to
find the children, I thought that he had eyes like God, that he would go directly
to the school where they were and kidnap them. I had to warn them, 'If you
see your father anywhere, run and hide. Don't let him get near you!' Can you
imagine telling your children that about their father? Oh, God, let's hurry."

She ran from room to room, pulling open drawers, stuffing clothes in
paper bags. I stood in the doorway of their bedroom, my heart pounding as I
looked at their bed with its tossed covers, at the phone he used to call me.
Books were everywhere on the bed—books about how to love better, how
to live better; books on the occult, on meditation; books on self-hypnosis for
peace of mind. Carol picked up an open book and looked at some words underlined in red. *"You can always create your own experience of life in a beautiful and
enjoyable way if you keep your love turned on within you—regardless of what other
people say or do,"* she read aloud. She tossed it down in disgust. "He's paying
good money for these," she said. She kept blowing her nose.

"Are you crying?"

"No!" she said. "I'm allergic to all this dust."

I walked to the front door, checked the street for his car, and went into 50
the kitchen.

"Look at this," I called to her. On the counter was a row of packages,
gift-wrapped. A card was slipped under one of them. Carol opened it and
read it aloud: "I have been a brute and I don't deserve you. But I can't live
without you and the boys. Don't take that away from me. Try to forgive me."
She picked up one of the boxes and then set it down. "I don't believe this,"
she said. "God, where are the children's picture albums! I can't *find* them." She
went running down the hall.

In the bathroom I saw the fishbowl, with the boys' two goldfish swimming in it. The water was clear. Beside it was a piece of notebook paper.
Written on it in his hand were the words *Don't give up, hang on, you have the
spirit within you to prevail.*

Two days later he came to my house, bailed out of jail with money his mother
had wired. He banged on my front door. He had discovered that Carol had
been to the house. "Did *you* take her there?" he demanded. "*You* wouldn't do
that to me, would you?" He stood on the doorstep, gaunt, hands shaking.

"Was she at the house?" I asked. "I haven't been in touch with her lately."

"Please," he said, his words slurred, his hands out for help. "Look at this." 55
He showed me his arms; the veins in his forearms were black and blue. "When I

saw that Carol had been home, I took the money my mother sent me for food and bought three packets of heroin. I wanted to OD. But it was lousy stuff; it didn't kill me. It's not so easy to die, even if you want to. I'm a tough bird. But please, can't you treat me like regular old me? Can't you ask me to come in and have dinner with you? I'm not a monster. Can't anyone, *anyone*, be nice to me?"

My children were hiding at the far end of the hall, listening. "Wait here," I said. I went and got him a whole ham I had. I handed it to him where he stood on the doorstep and stepped back with distaste. Ask him in? Let my children see *this*? Who knew what a crazy man would do? He must have suspected that I knew Carol's whereabouts. Whenever I went to visit her at the shelter, I took a circuitous route, always watching in my rearview mirror for his blue car. Now I had my tear gas in my pocket; I carried it with me all the time, kept it beside my bed when I slept. I thought of the things in my kitchen: knives, electric cords, mixers, graters, elements that could become white-hot and sear off a person's flesh.

He stood there like a supplicant, palms up, eyebrows raised in hope, waiting for a sign of humanity from me. I gave him what I could—a ham, and a weak, pathetic little smile. I said, dishonestly, "Go home. Maybe I can reach her today; maybe she will call you once you get home." He ran to his car, jumped in it, sped off. I thought, coldly, *Good, I'm rid of him. For now we're safe.* I locked the door with three locks.

Later Carol found among his many notes to her one that said, "At least your sister smiled at me, the only human thing that happened in this terrible time. I always knew she loved me and was my friend."

He became more persistent. He staked out my house, not believing I wasn't hiding her. "How could I possibly hide her?" I said to him on the phone. "You know I wouldn't lie to you."

"I know you wouldn't," he said. "I trust you." But on certain days I saw ₆₀ his blue car parked behind a hedge a block away, saw him hunched down like a private eye, watching my front door. One day my husband drove away with my daughter beside him, and an instant later the blue car tore by. I got a look at him then, curved over the wheel, a madman, everything at stake, nothing to lose, and I felt he would kill, kidnap, hold my husband and child as hostages till he got my sister back. I cried out. As long as he lived he would search for her, and if she hid, he would plague me. He had once said to her (she told me this), "You love your family? You want them alive? Then you'd better do as I say."

On the day he broke the table, after his son's face crumpled in terror, Carol told him to leave. He ran from the house. Ten minutes later he called her and said, in the voice of a wild creature, "I'm watching some men building a house, Carol. I'm never going to build a house for you now. Do you know that?" He was panting like an animal. "And I'm coming back for you. You're going to be with me one way or the other. You know I can't go on without you."

She hung up and called me. "I think he's coming back to hurt us."

"Then get out of there," I cried, miles away and helpless. "Run!"

By the time she called me again, I had the number of the shelter for her. She was at a gas station with her children. Outside the station were two phone booths. She hid her children in one; she called the shelter from the other. I called the boys in their booth and I read to them from a book called *Silly Riddles* while she made arrangements to be taken in. She talked for almost an hour to a counselor at the shelter. All the time I was sweating and reading riddles. When it was settled, she came into her children's phone booth and we made a date to meet in forty-five minutes at Sears, so that she could buy herself some underwear and her children some blue jeans. They were still in their pajamas.

Under the bright fluorescent lights in the department store we looked at price tags, considered quality and style, while her teeth chattered. Our eyes met over the racks, and she asked me, "What do you think he's planning now?" 65

My husband got a restraining order to keep him from our doorstep, to keep him from dialing our number. Yet he dialed it, and I answered the phone, almost passionately, each time I heard it ringing, having run to the room where I had the tape recorder hooked up. "Why is she so afraid of me? Let her come to see me without bodyguards! What can happen? The worst I could do is kill her, and how bad could that be, compared with what we're going through now?"

I played her that tape. "You must never go back," I said. She agreed; she had to. I took clean nightgowns to her at the shelter; I took her fresh vegetables, and bread that had substance.

Bard had hired a psychic that last week, and had gone to Las Vegas to confer with him, taking along a $500 money order. When Bard got home, he sent a parcel to Las Vegas containing clothing of Carol's and a small gold ring that she often wore. A circular that Carol found later under the bed promised immediate results: *Gold has the strongest psychic power — you can work a love spell by burning a red candle and reciting "In this ring I place my spell of love to make you return to me." This will also prevent your loved one from being unfaithful.*

Carol moved in across the street from my house just before Halloween. We devised a signal so that she could call me for help if some maniac cut her phone lines. She would use the antique gas alarm our father had given to me. It was a loud wooden clacker that had been used in the war. She would open her window and spin it. I could hear it easily. I promised her that I would look out my window often and watch for suspicious shadows near the bushes under her windows. Somehow neither of us believed he was really gone. Even though she had picked up his wallet at the morgue, the wallet he'd had with him while he breathed his car's exhaust through a vacuum-cleaner hose and thought his thoughts, told himself she didn't love him and so he had to do this and do it now; even though his ashes were in the dumpster; we felt that he was still out there, still looking for her.

Her sons built a six-foot-high spider web out of heavy white yarn for a decoration and nailed it to the tree in her front yard. They built a graveyard 70 around the tree, with wooden crosses. At their front door they rigged a noose and hung a dummy from it. The dummy, in their father's old blue sweat shirt with a hood, swung from the rope. It was still there long after Halloween, swaying in the wind.

Carol said to me, "I don't like it, but I don't want to say anything to them. I don't think they're thinking about him. I think they just made it for Halloween, and they still like to look at it."

WHAT DOES SHE SAY?

1. Merrill Joan Gerber's short story doesn't make points or present an argument like an essay might; instead, it throws the reader into a situation. In your journal or on a separate piece of paper, keep track of the characters by noting each time a new name is given. Beside each name, make a short note of who this person seems to be. Consider the narrator a character too, even though we don't immediately know her name.

2. The story begins late in the sequence of events that we eventually learn. As you're reading, construct a timeline of these events. Don't be surprised if you need to revise it as you continue to read.

3. Several of the characters in this story mention that they are fearful. Pay attention to these moments. In each case, what or who is the source of the fear?

4. Make a list of adjectives that describe Carol's husband. At what point do you see him most clearly in this story? Identify this place and then write a paragraph in response to what you see.

WHAT DO YOU THINK?

5. Recall the various things that Carol does and says in this story. Based on all that you see her do and hear her say, explain how you think readers ought to understand and then judge her actions.

6. Consider the various things that Bard does and says in this story. Based on all that you see him do and hear him say (including his various notes and so on), explain how you think readers ought to understand and then judge his actions.

7. What kinds of power do you see exercised by Carol and by Bard? Which kinds of power ultimately prevail in the story?

8. Investigate the frequency of spouse abuse (sometimes called "intimate partner abuse") in your area or your state and compare it to other health threats to women. For example, is such abuse more common or less common than breast cancer? Beyond the frequency of this problem, what are its long-term effects on women? What about the effects on their children? Write a research report that presents your findings and that ends by detailing your reactions to what you've learned.

WHAT WOULD THEY SAY?

9. Read Andre Dubus's "Giving Up the Gun" (p. 180) together with Gerber's story. What do these stories suggest are the causes of violence? What are the answers to it?

10. Read Gerber's story together with Chris Hedges's "Eros and Thanatos" (p. 247). To what extent do each of these pieces help you understand the other? Write an essay that explores this question and explains how or why you think the two essays, read together, clarify or confuse the question of where violence originates.

11. Read Gerber's story together with Sarah Vowell's "Shooting Dad" (p. 29). Then write an essay explaining how Vowell's recollection of her childhood would, or would not, be similar to a recollection made by one of the children in Gerber's story.

MICHAEL LEVIN
The Case for Torture

I~N~ THIS BRIEF and surprising article, Michael Levin argues that torture is a mortal necessity in some situations, that torturing a terrorist is the moral thing to do if it prevents "future evils." Levin is a professor of philosophy at City College of City University of New York. He has written many papers for professional journals and several books, including Metaphysics and the Mind–Body Problem *(1979) and the controversial* Why Race Matters *(1997). "The Case for Torture" was first published in* Newsweek *in 1982.*

It is generally assumed that torture is impermissible, a throwback to a more brutal age. Enlightened societies reject it outright, and regimes suspected of using it risk the wrath of the United States.

I believe this attitude is unwise. There are situations in which torture is not merely permissible but morally mandatory. Moreover, these situations are moving from the realm of imagination to fact.

Death: Suppose a terrorist has hidden an atomic bomb on Manhattan Island which will detonate at noon on July 4 unless...(here follow the usual demands for money and release of his friends from jail). Suppose, further, that he is caught at 10 AM of the fateful day, but—preferring death to failure— won't disclose where the bomb is. What do we do? If we follow due process— wait for his lawyer, arraign him—millions of people will die. If the only way to save those lives is to subject the terrorist to the most excruciating possible pain, what grounds can there be for not doing so? I suggest there are none. In any case, I ask you to face the question with an open mind.

Torturing the terrorist is unconstitutional? Probably. But millions of lives surely outweigh constitutionality. Torture is barbaric? Mass murder is far more barbaric. Indeed, letting millions of innocents die in deference to one who flaunts his guilt is moral cowardice, an unwillingness to dirty one's hands. If *you* caught the terrorist, could you sleep nights knowing that millions died because you couldn't bring yourself to apply the electrodes?

Once you concede that torture is justified in extreme cases, you have ad- 5
mitted that the decision to use torture is a matter of balancing innocent lives against the means needed to save them. You must now face more realistic cases involving more modest numbers. Someone plants a bomb on a jumbo jet. He alone can disarm it, and his demands cannot be met (or if they can, we refuse to set a precedent by yielding to his threats). Surely we can, we must, do anything to the extortionist to save the passengers. How can we tell three hundred, or one hundred, or ten people who never asked to be put in danger, "I'm sorry, you'll have to die in agony, we just couldn't bring ourselves to..."

Here are the results of an informal poll about a third, hypothetical, case. Suppose a terrorist group kidnapped a newborn baby from a hospital. I asked four mothers if they would approve of torturing kidnappers if that were necessary to get their own newborns back. All said yes, the most "liberal" adding that she would like to administer it herself.

I am not advocating torture as punishment. Punishment is addressed to deeds irrevocably past. Rather, I am advocating torture as an acceptable measure for preventing future evils. So understood, it is far less objectionable than many extant punishments. Opponents of the death penalty, for example, are forever insisting that executing a murderer will not bring back his victim (as if the purpose of capital punishment were supposed to be resurrection, not deterrence or retribution). But torture, in the cases described, is intended not to bring anyone back but to keep innocents from being dispatched. The most powerful argument against using torture as a punishment or to secure confessions is that such practices disregard the rights of the individual. Well, if the individual is all that important—and he is—it is correspondingly important to protect the rights of individuals threatened by terrorists. If life is so valuable that it must never be taken, the lives of the innocents must be saved even at the price of hurting the one who endangers them.

Better precedents for torture are assassination and preemptive attack. No Allied leader would have flinched at assassinating Hitler, had that been possible. (The Allies did assassinate Heydrich.°) Americans would be angered to learn that Roosevelt could have had Hitler killed in 1943—thereby shortening the war and saving millions of lives—but refused on moral grounds. Similarly, if nation *A* learns that nation *B* is about to launch an unprovoked attack, *A* has a right to save itself by destroying *B*'s military capability first. In the same way, if the police can by torture save those who would otherwise die at the hands of kidnappers or terrorists, they must.

Idealism: There is an important difference between terrorists and their victims that should mute talk of the terrorists' "rights." The terrorist's victims are at risk unintentionally, not having asked to be endangered. But the terrorist knowingly initiated his actions. Unlike his victims, he volunteered for the risks of his deed. By threatening to kill for profit or idealism, he renounces civilized standards, and he can have no complaint if civilization tries to thwart him by whatever means necessary.

Just as torture is justified only to save lives (not extort confessions or re- 10 cantations) it is justifiably administered only to those *known* to hold innocent lives in their hands. Ah, but how can the authorities ever be sure they have the right malefactor? Isn't there a danger of error and abuse? Won't We turn into Them?

Heydrich: Reinhard Heydrich (1904–1942), one of the central planners of the Holocaust, was shot and killed by Czech resistance fighters. [EDS.]

Questions like these are disingenuous in a world in which terrorists proclaim themselves and perform for television. The name of their game is public recognition. After all, you can't very well intimidate a government into releasing your freedom fighters unless you announce that it is your group that has seized its embassy. "Clear guilt" is difficult to define, but when forty million people see a group of masked gunmen seize an airplane on the evening news, there is not much question about who the perpetrators are. There will be hard cases where the situation is murkier. Nonetheless, a line demarcating the legitimate use of torture can be drawn. Torture only the obviously guilty, and only for the sake of saving innocents, and the line between Us and Them will remain clear.

There is little danger that the Western democracies will lose their way if they choose to inflict pain as one way of preserving order. Paralysis in the face of evil is the greater danger. Some day soon a terrorist will threaten tens of thousands of lives, and torture will be the only way to save them. We had better start thinking about this.

WHAT DOES HE SAY?

1. Levin uses three hypothetical examples to develop his argument. Take one of these and quickly write down your first, unconsidered response—not necessarily how you would solve the problem that the scenario poses but your visceral, emotional reaction to it.

2. Levin makes a distinction between torture and punishment. Explain it as you understand it.

3. Levin makes a distinction between terrorists and their victims. Explain your understanding of what he means.

4. In light of recent history, the last paragraph of this essay has an eerie, prophetic quality: "Some day soon a terrorist will threaten tens of thousands of lives...." Is your response to Levin's argument different now than it would have been before September 11, 2001? How have current events shaped your response?

5. Summarize Levin's argument in a single sentence. Don't worry about how smooth or persuasive it sounds. Just summarize the idea as directly and clearly as you can: "Levin believes that torture is justified because..."

WHAT DO YOU THINK?

6. Take one of Levin's three scenarios and assume that there is at least one alternative solution that Levin doesn't consider, something besides letting the bomb go off, for example, or torturing the prisoner to find out where the bomb is. Work together in groups. Brainstorm as many other possibilities as you can.

7. Do research on the effectiveness of torture in the kinds of hypothetical situations that Levin proposes. Levin assumes that torture actually works, producing information that can prevent further violence. Does it? Has it in the past?

8. Levin acknowledges that the use of torture raises the question: "Won't We turn into Them?" Explain what this question means in your own words, and explain Levin's answer. Then explain why you're persuaded, or not, by what Levin says.

WHAT WOULD THEY SAY?

9. The Dalai Lama (p. 205) argues strongly that ethical thinking depends on nonviolence. We should do all we can, he says, to avoid doing violence to others. How would the Dalai Lama respond to any of the three scenarios that Levin describes? Write an essay explaining your answer. Make sure you quote Levin and the Dalai Lama at least once.

10. How would Levin respond to the ethical scenario that we describe in the introduction to this chapter? If Levin witnessed that event, what would he say and what would he do?

THE DALAI LAMA
The Need for Discernment

In this essay, the Dalai Lama (b. 1934) suggests that ethical action is based in our desire to achieve happiness and avoid suffering. Thus, he argues, our experience matters in determining ethical conduct.

The exiled head of state and spiritual leader of the Tibetan people, the Dalai Lama received the Nobel Peace Prize in 1989, which he accepted on behalf of oppressed peoples everywhere. He has written more than thirty books, ranging from autobiography to essay to prayer instruction. "The Need for Discernment" is an excerpt from his work Ethics for the New Millennium *(2001).*

In our survey of ethics and spiritual development, we have spoken a great deal about the need for discipline. This may seem somewhat old-fashioned, even implausible, in an age and culture where so much emphasis is placed on the goal of self-fulfillment. But the reason for people's negative view of discipline is, I suggest, mainly due to what is generally understood by the term. People tend to associate discipline with something imposed against their will. It is worth repeating, therefore, that what we are talking about when we speak of ethical discipline is something that we adopt voluntarily on the basis of full recognition of its benefits. This is not an alien concept. We do not hesitate to accept discipline when it comes to our physical health. On doctors' advice, we avoid foods that are harmful even when we crave them. Instead, we eat those that benefit us. And while it is true that at the initial stage, self-discipline, even when voluntarily adopted, may involve hardship and even a degree of struggle, this lessens over time through habituation and diligent application. It is a bit like diverting the course of a stream. First we have to dig the channel and build up its banks. Then, when the water is released into it, we may have to make adjustments here and there. But when the course is fully established, water flows in the direction we desire.

Ethical discipline is indispensable because it is the means by which we mediate between the competing claims of my right to happiness and others' equal right. Naturally, there will always be those who suppose their own happiness to be of such importance that others' pain is of no consequence. But this is short-sighted. If the reader accepts my characterization of happiness, it follows that no one truly benefits from causing harm to others. Whatever immediate advantage is gained at the expense of someone else is necessarily only temporary. In the long run, causing others hurt and disturbing their peace and happiness causes us anxiety. Because our actions have an impact both on ourselves and others, when

205

we lack discipline, eventually anxiety arises in our mind, and deep in our heart we come to feel a sense of disquiet. Conversely, whatever hardship it entails, disciplining our response to negative thoughts and emotions will cause us fewer problems in the long run than indulging in acts of selfishness.

Nevertheless, it is worth saying again that ethical discipline entails more than just restraint. It also entails the cultivation of virtue. Love and compassion, patience, tolerance, forgiveness, and so on are essential qualities. When they are present in our lives, everything we do becomes an instrument to benefit the whole human family. Even in terms of our daily occupation—whether this is looking after children in the home, working in a factory, or serving the community as a doctor, lawyer, businessperson, or teacher—our actions contribute toward the well-being of all. And because ethical discipline is what facilitates the very qualities which give meaning and value to our existence, it is clearly something to be embraced with enthusiasm and conscious effort.

Before looking at how we apply this inner discipline to our interactions with others, it may be worth reviewing the grounds for defining ethical conduct in terms of non-harming. As we have seen, given the complex nature of reality, it is very difficult to say that a particular act or type of act is right or wrong in itself. Ethical conduct is thus not something we engage in because it is somehow right in itself. We do so because we recognize that just as I desire to be happy and to avoid suffering, so do all others. For this reason, a meaningful ethical system divorced from the question of our experience of suffering and happiness is hard to envisage.

Of course, if we want to ask all sorts of difficult questions based on metaphysics, ethical discourse can become exceedingly complicated. Yet while it is true that ethical practice cannot be reduced to a mere exercise in logic, or to simple rule-following, whichever way we look at it, in the end we are brought back to the fundamental questions of happiness and suffering. Why is happiness good and suffering bad for us? Perhaps there is no conclusive answer. But we can observe that it is in our nature to prefer the one to the other, just as it is to prefer the better over what is merely good. We simply aspire to happiness and not to suffering. If we were to go further and ask why this is so, surely the answer would have to be something like, "That's the way it is," or, for theists, "God made us that way."

So far as the ethical character of a given action is concerned, we have seen how this is dependent on a great many factors. Time and circumstance have an important bearing on the matter. But so, too, does an individual's freedom or lack of it. A negative act can be considered more serious when the perpetrator commits the deed with full freedom as opposed to someone who is forced to act against his or her will. Similarly, given the lack of remorse this reflects, negative acts repeatedly indulged can be considered graver than an isolated act. But we must also consider the intention behind the action, as well as its content. The overriding question, however, concerns the individual's spiritual state, their overall state of heart and mind (*kun long*) in the moment of action. Because, generally speaking, this is the area over which we have the most control, it is the most significant element in determining the ethical character of our acts. As we have seen, when our intentions are polluted by selfishness, by hatred, by desire to deceive, however much our acts may have the appearance of being constructive, inevitably their impact will be negative, both for self and others.

How, though, are we to apply this principle of non-harming when confronted with an ethical dilemma? This is where our critical and imaginative powers come in. I have described these as two of our most precious resources, and suggested that possessing them is one of the things that distinguishes us from animals. We have seen how afflictive emotions destroys them. And we have seen how important they are in learning to deal with suffering. As far as ethical practice is concerned, these qualities are what enable us to discriminate between temporary and long-term benefit, to determine the degree of ethical fitness of the different courses of action open to us, and to assess the likely outcome of our actions and thereby to set aside lesser goals in order to achieve greater ones. In the case of a dilemma, we need in the first instance to consider the particularity of the situation in the light of what, in the Buddhist tradition, is called the "union of skillful means and insight." *Skillful means* can be understood in terms of the efforts we make to ensure that our deeds are motivated by compassion. *Insight* refers to our critical faculties and how, in response to the different factors involved, we adjust the ideal of non-harming to the context of the situation. We could call it the faculty of wise discernment.

Employing this faculty—which is especially important when there is no appeal to religious belief—involves constantly checking our outlook and asking ourselves whether we are being broad-minded or narrow-minded. Have we taken into account the overall situation or are we considering only specifics? Is our view short-term or long-term? Are we being shortsighted or clear-eyed? Is our motive genuinely compassionate when considered in relation to the totality of all beings? Or is our compassion limited just to our families, our friends, and those we identify with closely? Just as in the practice of discovering the true nature of our thoughts and emotions, we need to think, think, think.

Of course, it will not always be possible to devote time to careful discernment. Sometimes we have to act at once. This is why our spiritual development is of such critical importance in ensuring that our actions are ethically sound. The more spontaneous our actions, the more they will tend to reflect our habits and dispositions in that moment. If these are unwholesome, our acts are bound to be destructive. At the same time, I believe it is very useful to have a set of basic ethical precepts to guide us in our daily lives. These can help us to form good habits, although I should add my opinion that in adopting such precepts, it is perhaps best to think of them less in terms of moral legislation than as reminders always to keep others' interests at heart and in the forefront of our minds.

So far as the content of such precepts is concerned, it is doubtful whether 10 we could do better than turn to the basic ethical directives articulated not only by each of the world's great religions but also by the greater part of the humanist philosophical tradition. The consensus among them, despite differences of opinion concerning metaphysical grounding, is to my mind compelling. All agree on the negativity of killing, stealing, telling lies, and sexual misconduct. In addition, from the point of view of motivational factors, all agree on the need to avoid hatred, pride, malicious intent, covetousness, envy, greed, lust, harmful ideologies (such as racism), and so on.

Some people may wonder whether the injunctions against sexual misconduct are really necessary in these times of simple and effective contraception. However, as human beings, we are naturally attracted to external objects, whether it be through the eyes, when we are attracted by form, through the ears, when the attraction arises in relation to sound, or through any of the other senses. Each of them has the potential to be a source of difficulty for us. Yet sexual attraction involves all five senses. As a result, when extreme desire accompanies sexual attraction, it has the ability to cause us enormous problems. It is, I believe, this fact that is recognized in the ethical directives against sexual misconduct articulated by every major religion. And, at least in the Buddhist tradition, they remind us of the tendency for sexual desire to become obsessive. It can quickly reach the point where a person has almost no room left for constructive activity. In this connection, consider, for example, a case of infidelity. Given that wholesome ethical conduct entails considering the impact of our actions not only on ourselves but on others, too, there are the feelings of third parties to consider. In addition to our actions being violent toward our partner, given the trust that the relationship implies, there is the question of the lasting impact this kind of upset in the family can have on our children. It is now more or less universally accepted that they are the principal victims both of family breakup and of unhealthy relationships in the home. From our own perspective as the person who has committed the act, we must also acknowledge that it is likely to have the negative effect of gradually corroding our self-respect. Finally, there is the fact that in being unfaithful, other gravely negative acts may result as a direct consequence—lying and deception being perhaps the least of them. An unwanted pregnancy could easily be the cause of a desperate prospective parent to seeking an abortion.

When we think in this way, it becomes obvious that the momentary pleasures afforded by an adulterous liaison are far outweighed by the risk of the likely negative impact of our actions on both ourselves and others. So rather than seeing strictures against sexual misconduct as limiting to freedom, we do better to see them as commonsense reminders that such actions directly affect the well-being of both oneself and others.

Does this mean that merely following precepts takes precedence over wise discernment? No. Ethically sound conduct depends on us applying the principle of non-harming. However, there are bound to be situations when any course of action would appear to involve breaking a precept. Under such circumstances, we must use our intelligence to judge which course of action will be least harmful in the long run. Imagine, for example, a situation where we witness someone running away from a group of people armed with knives and clearly intent on doing him harm. We see the fugitive disappear into a doorway. Moments later, one of the pursuers comes up to us and asks which way he went. Now, on the one hand, we do not want to lie, to injure the other's trust. On the other, if we tell the truth, we realize that we may contribute to the injury or death of a fellow human being. Whatever we decide, the appropriate course of action would appear to involve a negative deed. Under such circumstances, because we are certain that in so doing we are serving a higher purpose—preserving someone from harm—it might well be appropriate to say, "Oh, I didn't see him," or vaguely, "I think he went the other way." We have to take into account the overall situation and weigh the benefits of telling a lie or telling the truth and do what we judge to be least harmful overall. In other words, the moral value of a given act is to be judged in relation both to time, place, and circumstance and to the interests of the totality of all others in the future as well as now. But while it is conceivable that a given act is ethically sound under one particular set of circumstances, the same act at another time and place and under a different set of circumstances may not be.

What, though, are we to do when it comes to others? What are we to do when they seem clearly to be engaging in actions which we consider wrong? The first thing is to remember that unless we know down to the last detail the full range of circumstances, both internal and external, we can never be sufficiently clear enough about individual situations to be able to judge with complete certainty the moral content of others' actions. Of course, there will be extreme situations when the negative character of others' acts will be self-evident. But mostly this is not the case. This is why it is far more useful to be aware of a single shortcoming in ourselves than it is to be aware of a thousand in somebody else. For when the fault is our own, we are in a position to correct it.

Nevertheless, remembering that there is an essential distinction to be 15 made between a person and their particular acts, we may come across circumstances when it is appropriate to take action. In everyday life, it is normal and fitting to adapt in some degree to one's friends and acquaintances and to respect their wishes. The ability to do so is considered a good quality. But when we mix with those who clearly indulge in negative behavior, seeking only their own benefit and ignoring others', we risk losing our own sense of direction. As a result, our ability to help others becomes endangered. There is a Tibetan proverb which says that when we lie on a mountain of gold, some of it rubs off on us; the same happens if we lie on a mountain of dirt. We are right to avoid such people, though we must be careful not to cut them off completely. Indeed, there are sure to be times when it is appropriate to try to stop them from acting in this way—provided, of course, that our motives in doing so are pure and our methods are non-harming. Again, the key principles are compassion and insight.

The same is true in respect to those ethical dilemmas we face at the level of society, especially the difficult and challenging questions posed by modern science and technology. For example, in the field of medicine, it has become possible to prolong life in cases which just a few years ago would have been hopeless. This can, of course, be a source of great joy. But quite often, there arise complicated and very delicate questions concerning the limits of care. I think that there can be no general rule in respect to this. Rather, there is likely to be a multiplicity of competing considerations, which we must assess in the light of reason and compassion. When it becomes necessary to make a difficult decision on behalf of a patient, we must take into account all the various different elements. These will, of course, be different in each case. For example, if we prolong the life of a person who is critically ill but whose mind remains lucid, we give that person the opportunity to think and feel in a way that only a human being can. On the other hand, we must consider whether in doing so they will experience great physical and mental suffering as a result of extreme measures taken to keep them alive. This in itself is not an overriding factor, however. As someone who believes in the continuation of consciousness after the death of the body, I would argue that it is much better to have pain with this human body. At least we can benefit from others' care whereas, if we choose to die, we may find that we have to endure suffering in some other form.

If the patient is not conscious and therefore unable to participate in the decision-making process, that is yet another problem. And on top of everything, there may be the wishes of the family to take into account, along with the immense problems that prolonged care can cause them and others. For example, it may be that in order to continue to support one life, valuable funds are kept from projects which would benefit many others. If there is a general principle, I think it is simply that we recognize the supreme preciousness of life and try to ensure that when the time comes, the dying person departs as serenely and peacefully as possible.

In the case of work in such fields as genetics and biotechnology, the principle of non-harming takes on special importance because lives may be at stake. When the motivation behind such research is merely profit, or fame, or even when research is carried out merely for its own sake, it is very much open to question where it will lead. I am thinking particularly of the development of techniques to manipulate physical attributes, such as gender or even hair and eye color, which can be used commercially to exploit the prejudices of parents. Indeed, let me say here that while it is difficult to be categorically against all forms of genetic experimentation, this is such a delicate area that it is essential that all those involved proceed with caution and deep humility. They must be especially aware of the potential for abuse. It is vital that they keep in mind the wider implications of what they are doing and, most important, ensure that their motives are genuinely compassionate. For if the general principle behind such work is simply utility, whereby those that are deemed useless can legitimately be used to benefit those judged to be useful, then there is nothing to stop us from subordinating the rights of those who fall into the former category to those who fall into the latter. Yet the attribute of utility can surely never justify the deprivation of an individual's rights. This is a highly dangerous and very slippery slope.

Recently I saw a BBC television documentary about cloning. Using computer-generated imagery, this film showed a creature scientists were working on, a sort of semihuman being with large eyes and several other recognizably human features lying down in a cage. Of course, at present this is just fantasy, but, they explained, it is possible to foresee a time when it will be possible to create beings like this. They could then be bred and their organs and other parts of their anatomy used in "spare parts" surgery for the benefit of human beings. I was utterly appalled at this. Oh, terrible. Surely this is taking scientific endeavor to an extreme? The idea that one day we might actually create sentient beings specifically for that purpose horrifies me. I felt the same at this prospect as I do at the idea of experiments involving human fetuses.

At the same time, it is difficult to see how this kind of thing can be pre- 20 vented in the absence of individuals' disciplining their own actions. Yes, we can promulgate laws. Yes, we can have international codes of conduct—as indeed we should have both. Yet if the individual scientists do not have any sense that what they are doing is grotesque, destructive, and negative in the extreme, then there is no real prospect of putting an end to such disturbing endeavors.

What about issues like vivisection, where animals are routinely caused terrible suffering before being killed as a means to furthering scientific knowledge? Here I only want to say that to a Buddhist, such practices are equally shocking. I can only hope that the rapid advances being made in computer technology will mean there is less and less call for animal experimentation in scientific research. One positive development within modern society is the way in which, together with a growing appreciation of the importance of human rights, people are coming to have greater concern for animals. For example, there is growing recognition of the inhumanity of factory farming. It seems, too, that more and more people are taking an interest in vegetarianism and cutting down on their consumption of meat. I welcome this. My hope is that in the future, this concern will be extended to consideration for even the smallest creatures of the sea.

Here, though, I should perhaps sound a word of warning. The campaigns to protect human and animal life are noble causes. But it is essential that we do not allow ourselves to be carried away by our sense of injustice so that we ignore others' rights. We need to ensure that we are wisely discerning in pursuit of our ideals.

Exercising our critical faculties in the ethical realm entails taking responsibility both for our acts and for their underlying motives. If we do not take responsibility for our motives, whether positive or negative, the potential for harm is much greater. As we have seen, negative emotions are the source of unethical behavior. Each act affects not only the people closest to us but also our colleagues, friends, community, and, ultimately, the world.

WHAT DOES HE SAY?

1. As you read, mark three short passages—in the beginning, the middle, and the end of the essay—that seem particularly interesting or powerful or important. Write them out on a separate sheet of paper, leaving a space between each. How are these statements connected? Are they versions of the same idea? Is one more general than the others?

2. "[N]o one truly benefits from causing harm to others," the Dalai Lama says. In your own words, explain what he means.

3. Write a paragraph explaining the connection that the Dalai Lama sees between "ethical discipline" and happiness. Does this make sense in your own life?

4. What does the Dalai Lama mean by the "faculty of wise discernment"?

WHAT DO YOU THINK?

5. What did you know or assume about the Dalai Lama before you read the essay? Were you positively or negatively predisposed toward him? Did the essay match your expectations or surprise you? Explain. (It's all right if you knew nothing about the Dalai Lama in advance. What is your impression of him now, after having read this essay?)

6. The Dalai Lama suggests that there are certain ethical principles common to all the major world religions. What are they, according to him, and do you agree? Are there certain universal values that cut across cultures, ethnicities, regions?

7. Explain how the Dalai Lama applies the principle of non-harming to the question of sexual misconduct. What is your reaction to this argument? Does it surprise you?

8. "[T]he moral value of a given act is to be judged in relation both to time, place, and circumstance and to the interests of the totality of all others in the future as well as now." Relate this statement to the idea of "wise discernment," then agree or disagree. Do you agree with the Dalai Lama that there can be no "general rule" in most ethical matters—that we can never "judge with complete certainty" the moral nature of a person or an act? Explain.

9. Write an essay exploring the Tibetan proverb that says, "when we lie on a mountain of gold, some of it rubs off on us; the same happens if we lie on a mountain of dirt." Apply this to your own experience or to contemporary events.

10. Write an essay applying the Dalai Lama's notion of "ethical discernment" (what he also calls the "union of skillful means and insight") to the idea of the university. Argue that ethical discernment is the principle of all genuine learning and so should be the goal of every class you take. For example, how would ethical discernment work in a chemistry course? a literature course? a writing course?

WHAT WOULD THEY SAY?

11. Take the essay topic above—the idea of ethical discernment as the principle of all education—and expand it to include a discussion of Adrienne Rich's "Claiming an Education" (p. 608) and Parker Palmer's "The Community of Truth" (p. 627). Use these three essays to develop a theory of education and a broad argument about the purpose of the university.

12. At one point in this essay the Dalai Lama applies his theory of doing no harm to the question of bioethics. Read Bill McKibben's "Designer Genes" (p. 360) in chapter 4. What would McKibben say about the Dalai Lama's analysis? How would he agree or disagree? How would the Dalai Lama respond to McKibben?

13. Based on this essay, how do you think the Dalai Lama would respond to the scenario in the introduction to this chapter? Would he have intervened in the argument between Tyler and Jessica? How would he have responded to Tyler's implied threat of violence?

TERRY TEMPEST WILLIAMS
Two Words

Terry Tempest Williams (b. 1955) begins her essay with a quote from Archbishop Desmond Tutu that rhetorically asks, When will we learn that we must live together? The brief essay goes on to relate Tutu's notion of "restorative justice" as opposed to "justice and retribution." Thus, the questions of communities torn by violence become also questions of individuals' willingness to forgive. This essay is a challenge in that it poses the question of whether or not forgiveness is possible or sufficient as a way to end a cycle of violence.

Williams has written several books, including Refuge: An Unnatural History of Family and Place *(1991) and* Red: Patience and Passion in the Desert *(2001). An active environmentalist, she serves on the advisory boards of the National Parks and Conservation Association and the Nature Conservancy. "Two Words" first appeared in the Winter 1999 issue of* Orion.

The voice of Archbishop Desmond Tutu° from South Africa is singing:

> When will we learn, when will the people of the world get up and say, Enough is enough.... We are not made for an exclusive self-sufficiency but for interdependence, and we break the law of our being at our peril.

At the end of this century, it is his voice that keeps whispering in my ear.

On a clear November day in Charlottesville, Virginia, Archbishop Tutu tells an audience of Americans that there is much conflict in the world and that most of it exists within the confines of individual countries in the form of a civil war. As he speaks these words in the state where 60 percent of the battles of the Civil War were fought, I couldn't help but think, this is the perfect place for the message of restoration to be received.

He asked the simple question, "How in fact do we live together?" He posed three scenarios: An eye for an eye? Forget the past and move toward the future, let bygones be bygones? Or do what South Africa is doing: granting amnesty in exchange for truth. This is the work of the Truth and Reconciliation Commission.

"We have found in the act of telling the story, people experience a healing," he said. "There was a terrible massacre that occurred outside of Johannesburg. A woman was hit by shrapnel. Before the commission, she said, 'I would

---

°*Archbishop Desmond Tutu:* Tutu (b. 1931) won the Nobel Peace Prize in 1984 for his promotion of equality in South Africa. He chaired that country's Truth and Reconciliation Commission in 1995. [EDS.]

like to meet my perpetrator in the spirit of forgiveness.' A silence followed. Four policeman came forward, three black, one white. The white policeman spoke, 'We are your perpetrators. Yes, we ordered the firing to occur during this massacre.' There was an uproar in the audience. The man continued to speak, 'Please forgive us. Please forgive these three men in particular and take them back into your community.' The woman and the audience stood up and broke into uncontrollable applause."

Bishop Tutu pauses. "I said to my people, 'Now let us feel the silence of this moment, for this is holy. Let us take off our shoes. This spot is now holy ground.'"

A man raised his hand, "But what about personal accountability?"

Archbishop Tutu looked at him and said, "To say you are guilty, that is accountability.... You see, lurking behind your question is your concept of justice and retribution. That is not the only kind. We believe in restorative justice. In South Africa, we are trying to find our way toward healing and the restoration of harmony within our communities. If retributive justice is all you seek through the letter of the law, you are history. You will never know stability. You need something beyond reprisal. You need forgiveness."

As I sat in this audience, I bowed my head. These two words: *forgiveness* and *restoration*. May we bring these two words into our communities through our own small and simple acts.

WHAT DOES SHE SAY?

1. This is a relatively short essay, and it celebrates the power of two simple words. As you read, consider ways that the essay could be expanded—ideas pursued, arguments made, examples given. Write a paragraph about that once you've finished reading.

2. Make a list of the questions raised in this essay and where they appear. How does Williams—or Archbishop Tutu—answer them?

3. As you read how Williams describes her reaction to a speech given by Archbishop Tutu, underline the words or phrases that suggest her emotional response. What kind of language does she use to convey what she thinks and feels and what others think and feel? How does this influence your own reaction, both to Tutu and to Williams?

4. In a sense, Williams answers the question "What Did He Say?" in response to the archbishop's speech. Based on her answer, summarize the main points of that speech.

WHAT DO YOU THINK?

5. Do research on Archbishop Desmond Tutu. Write a profile introducing him to those who know little or nothing about him.

6. Do research on the Truth and Reconciliation Commission in South Africa. Write a profile of the commission's work.

7. Williams says that it is Archbishop Desmond Tutu's voice that "keeps whispering" in her ear. In the spirit of Williams's essay, what voice keeps whispering in your ear? Write an essay explaining.

8. Write your own essay entitled "Two Words," but choose your own two words: for example, *grief* and *anger*, *competition* and *craziness*, *sleep* and *television*.

9. Williams asks that we bring the two words *forgiveness* and *restoration* "into our communities through our own small and simple acts." Write an essay about several ways you could bring forgiveness and restoration into your community through small and simple acts. Be specific. Option: Write an essay profiling another person or a community group that brings these words into action.

WHAT WOULD THEY SAY?

10. How would Jenefer Shute, in "Life-Size" (p. 279) in chapter 4, respond to Williams's essay? How would Williams respond to Shute? How would the words *forgiveness* and *restoration* apply to Shute's situation?

11. How would Joy Williams—in "Save the Whales, Screw the Shrimp" (p. 146) in chapter 2—respond to Terry Tempest Williams? If Joy Williams were sitting in the audience listening to Archbishop Tutu's speech, what would her reaction be?

12. Write an essay relating "The Earth Charter" (p. 158) to the words *forgiveness* and *restoration*. Would the authors of the charter embrace these words? Explain why or why not.

ANDREW SULLIVAN

The Pursuit of Happiness: Four Revolutionary Words

In this essay, Andrew Sullivan (b. 1963) analyzes "the pursuit of happiness and uses it as a lens by which we might understand the reasons that Islamic fundamentalists find America and American values threatening. Thus, questions of violence must now include contemporary acts of terrorism in the discussion. Maybe we will have to fight again for what we believe, the author suggests.

A contributing editor to the New York Times Magazine *and senior editor at the* New Republic, *Sullivan has published books and essays on various social and political issues, including a reader on the issue of homosexuality. "The Pursuit of Happiness: Four Revolutionary Words" first appeared in the November 2001 issue of* Forbes.

It's a small phrase when you think about it: "the pursuit of happiness." It's somewhat overshadowed in the Declaration of Independence by the weightier notions of "life" and "liberty." In today's mass culture, it even comes close to being banal. Who, after all, doesn't want to pursue happiness? But in its own day, the statement was perhaps the most radical political statement ever delivered. And when we try and fathom why it is that the United States still elicits such extreme hatred in some parts of the world, this phrase is as good a place to start as any.

Take the first part: pursuit. What America is based on is not the achievement of some goal, the capture of some trophy, or the triumph of success. It's about the process of seeking something. It's about incompletion, dissatisfaction, striving, imperfection. In the late eighteenth century, this was a statement in itself. In the Europe of the preceding centuries, armies had gone to war, human beings had been burned at stakes, monarchs had been dethroned, and countries torn apart because imperfection wasn't enough. From the Reformation to the Inquisition, religious fanatics had demanded that the state enforce holiness, truth, and virtue. Those who resisted were exterminated. Moreover, the power and status of rulers derived from their own perfection. Kings and queens had artists portray them as demigods. Dissenters were not merely troublemakers, they were direct threats to the perfect order of the modern state. This was a political order in which everything had to be perfectly arranged—even down to the internal thoughts of individual consciences.

Enter the Americans. Suddenly the eternal, stable order of divine right and church authority was replaced by something far more elusive, difficult, even intangible. Out of stability came the idea of pursuit. To an older way of thinking, the very idea is heretical. The pursuit of what? Where? By whom? Who authorized this? By whose permission are you off on some crazy venture of your own? Think of how contemporary Islamic fundamentalists must think of this. For them, the spiritual and intellectual life is not about pursuit; it's about submission. It's not about inquiry into the unknown. It's about struggle for the will of Allah. Since the result of this struggle is literally the difference between heaven and hell, there can be no doubt about what its content is, or the duty of everyone to engage in it. And since doubt can lead to error, and error can lead to damnation, it is also important that everyone within the community adhere to the same struggle — and extend the struggle in a fight against unbelievers.

Today, we find this religious extremism alien. But it was not alien to the American founders. The European Christians of the sixteenth and seventeenth centuries were not so different in their obsessiveness and intolerance from many Islamic fundamentalists today. And against that fundamentalist requirement for uniformity, the Founders of a completely new society countered with the notion of a random, chaotic, cacophonous pursuit of any number of different goals. No political authority would be able to lay down for all citizens what was necessary for salvation, or even for a good life. Citizens would have to figure out the meaning of their own lives, and search for that meaning until the day they died. There would be no certainty; no surety even of a destination. Pursuit was everything. And pursuit was understood as something close to adventure.

And then comes the even more radical part. The point of this pursuit was happiness! Again, this seems almost banal to modern ears. But it was far from banal in the eighteenth century and it is far from banal when interpreted by the radical mullahs of political Islam. Here's the difference. Before the triumph of American democracy, governments and states and most philosophers viewed happiness as incidental to something else. For Christians, happiness was only achieved if you were truly virtuous. Happiness was the spiritual calm that followed an act of charity; the satisfied exhaustion after a day caring for others. For Aristotle, happiness was simply impossible without virtue. Happiness was an incidental experience while pursuing what was good and true. The idea of pursuing happiness for its own sake would have struck Aristotle as simple hedonism. The happiness someone feels drinking a cold beer on a hot day or bungee-jumping off a bridge was not a happiness he recognized. And for almost every pre-American society, other goals clearly had precedence over the subjective sense of well-being. Remember Cromwell's England? Or Robespierre's France? Or Stalin's Russia? They weren't exactly pleasure-fests. Again, in radical Islam today, American notions of happiness — choice, indulgence, whimsy, humor, leisure, art — always have to be subjected to moral inspection. Do these activities conform to religious law? Do they encourage or discourage virtuous behavior, without which happiness is impossible and meaningless? These are the questions human beings have always historically asked of the phenomenon we call happiness.

Not so in America. Here, happiness is an end in itself. Its content is up to each of us. Some may believe, as American Muslims or Christians do, that happiness is still indeed only possible when allied to virtue. But just as importantly, others may not. And the important thing is that the government of the United States takes no profound interest in how any of these people define their own happiness. All that matters is that no one is coerced into a form of happiness he hasn't chosen for himself—by others or by the state. Think of this for a moment. What America means is that no one can forcibly impose a form of happiness on anyone else—even if it means that some people are going to hell in a handbasket. Yes, there have been many exceptions to this over the years—and America has often seen religious revivals, spasms of cultural puritanism, cultural censorship, and so on. But the government has been barred from the deepest form of censorship—the appropriation of any single religion under the auspices of the state. You can call this all sorts of things. In my book, it's as good a definition of freedom as any. But to others—countless others—it seems a callous indifference to the fate of others' souls, even blasphemy and degeneracy. This view is held by some Christian fundamentalists at home. And it is surely held by Islamic fundamentalists abroad. We ignore this view at our peril.

There are, of course, many reasons why America evokes hostility across the globe. There are foreign policies; there are historical failings. There is resentment of American wealth and power. There is fear of the social dislocation inherent in globalization. But there is also something far deeper. What we have forgotten is how anomalous America is in the history of the world. Most other countries have acquired identity and culture through ancient inheritance, tribal loyalty, or religious homogeneity. Even a country very like the United States, Britain, still has a monarchy and an established church. If you told the average Brit that his government was designed to help him pursue "happiness," he'd laugh. Other developed countries, like Germany, have succumbed to the notion of race as a purifying and unifying element. Many others, like Pakistan or India, cling to a common religious identity to generate a modicum of political unity. In none of these countries is "happiness" even a political concept. And in none of these places is the pursuit of something in and of itself an admirable goal, let alone at the center of the meaning of the state and constitution.

And when the society which has pioneered this corrosively exhilarating idea of happiness becomes the most powerful and wealthy country on earth, then the risks of backlash increase exponentially. In the late eighteenth century Europeans could scoff at banal American encomiums to happiness as an amusing experiment doomed to failure. At the beginning of the twenty-first century, with the products of such happiness—from McDonald's to Starbucks to MTV—saturating the globe, foreigners can afford no such condescension. Happiness is coming to them—and moral, theological certainty is departing. In response to this, they can go forward and nervously integrate—as countries like China, South Korea, and Russia are attempting. Or they can go back, far, far back to a world where such notions of happiness were as alien as visitors from outer space.

Far, far back is where some in the Middle East now want to go. The roots of Islamic fundamentalism go back centuries and bypass many more recent, and more open, strains of Islam. And we are foolish if we do not see the internal logic of this move. The fundamentalist Muslims are not crazy. They see that other cultures are slowly adapting to the meme of the pursuit of happiness — from Shanghai to Moscow, from Bombay to Buenos Aires. They see that they are next in line. But they also see that such a change would deeply alter their religion and its place in society. So they resist. They know that simply accommodating piecemeal to slow change will doom them. So they are pulling a radical move — a step far back into the past, allied with a militarist frenzy and rampant xenophobia to buttress it. This move is the belated response of an ancient religious impulse to the most radical statement of the Enlightenment, which is why it is indeed of such world-historical importance. As I write I have no idea as to the conclusion of this new drama in world history — except that it will have ramifications as large and as lasting as the end of the cold war.

What power four little words still have. And what carnage they must 10 still endure to survive.

WHAT DOES HE SAY?

1. Before you begin reading, consider your own pursuit of happiness: What is it that you're pursuing? What is happiness to you? Write a paragraph about this (and don't expect to exhaust the subject).

2. Sullivan points out that the declaration emphasizes not so much the attainment of happiness but its pursuit — "the process of seeking something." Do you normally think of happiness as actions or efforts? Do you think of it as the purchase of things (car, clothes, etc.)?

3. This essay contrasts Sullivan's sense of American "pursuit" with his sense of Islamic fundamentalism and its emphasis on "submission." As you're reading, make a list of all the observations or assertions that fall under "pursuit" and a separate list of those that fall under "submission." Don't try to judge this list, just try to make it accurate to Sullivan's presentation.

4. At one point, this essay says, "Think of this for a moment. What America means is that no one can forcibly impose a form of happiness on anyone else — even if it means that some people are going to hell in a handbasket." What's your reaction to this observation? Write a paragraph that does "Think of this for a moment."

WHAT DO YOU THINK?

5. If you were to summarize Sullivan's essay in three main points, what would they be? What specific parts of the essay would you quote in order to illustrate each of those three main points?

6. Go to the Internet and locate two Web sites that focus on Islam. In particular, find one site that seems to advocate the kind of fundamentalism that Sullivan discusses. Also locate a site that focuses on Islam in ways that do not advocate a fundamentalist position. Then do the same thing for Christianity: locate a site that seems to you fundamentalist in its advocacy and one that is not. Print at least one page from each of these four sites. Then write a paper that relates these sites to Sullivan's essay. Part of your paper should help readers see how you understand and interpret the sites themselves.

7. Sullivan's essay ends saying, "What power four little words still have. And what carnage they must still endure to survive." According to Sullivan, what is it that provokes "carnage"? That is, what provokes people to so violently disagree with these four words? What is the fight about? Write an essay explaining Sullivan's piece and then explaining your own thinking in response to it.

WHAT WOULD THEY SAY?

8. Read Sullivan's essay together with Stephen L. Carter's "Welcoming the Stranger" (p. 111). In what ways does Carter's essay echo and support what Sullivan says? Do they disagree? Based on your reading of these two essays, what do Sullivan and Carter identify as essentially American? Explain why you agree or disagree.

9. Consider Andrew Sullivan's essay together with Barbara Ehrenreich's "Serving in Florida" (p. 483). Does Ehrenreich's essay have anything to do with "the pursuit of happiness"? Carefully explain whether these essays are or are not related to each other.

10. Pair Sullivan's essay together with Jenefer Shute's fictional excerpt "Life-Size" (p. 279). Explain how Shute's essay makes a convincing (or unconvincing or partially convincing) argument for her own "pursuit of happiness." End by explaining why you believe it's just or unjust that she is confined and treated as her essay shows.

ALEX GREGORY

"If you still want to belong to an organization dedicated to killing Americans, there's always the tobacco lobby."

Sɪɴᴄᴇ ᴄᴏɴᴛʀɪʙᴜᴛɪɴɢ ʜɪs ғɪʀsᴛ ᴄᴀʀᴛᴏᴏɴ *to* The New Yorker *in 1999, Alex Gregory (b. 1971) has written more than 180 cartoons for the magazine. Gregory is also a TV writer and has written for such shows as* The Late Show with David Letterman, Frasier, *and* King of the Hill. *This cartoon first appeared in the February 4, 2002, issue of* The New Yorker.

"If you still want to belong to an organization dedicated to killing Americans, there's always the tobacco lobby."

WHAT DOES IT SAY?

1. This cartoon seems to present Taliban fighters (identifiable by their turbans and beards) who have been defeated in Afghanistan. They appear to be hiding in a cave. The consolation one offers the other is that he can always work for the tobacco lobby. What's the tobacco lobby? What's the job of the tobacco lobby, as you understand it?

2. What's your first response to this cartoon? Write a paragraph that tries to capture it, including any uncertainties or contradictions.

3. Clearly, the two figures in the cartoon are supposed to portray terrorists whose methods include violence (hence the rifle one of them holds). Aiming a rifle at someone is certainly an act of violence: guns can kill. According to the surgeon general's warning on cigarette packs, cigarettes can kill too. So, is selling cigarettes an act of violence? Sort of? Not at all? Make two lists. In one of them, put down three reasons why selling cigarettes or promoting their sale is an act of violence. In the other, list three reasons why such sale or promotion is not an act of violence.

WHAT DO YOU THINK?

4. Investigate the number of deaths in the United States attributed to terrorism since 2000. Then investigate the number of deaths attributed to cigarette smoking since 2000. Why is it fair or unfair to compare these statistics? Explain the rationale you disagree with. Present it as clearly and honestly as you can. Then explain the rationale you advocate.

5. Consider this set of assertions:

    To point a gun at someone and pull the trigger is to knowingly create a situation that might result in harm to or the death of someone hit by that bullet.

    Shooting someone is wrong except in self-defense.

    To manufacture and sell cigarettes is to knowingly create a situation that might result in harm to or the death of someone who smokes those cigarettes.

    Therefore, manufacturing and selling cigarettes is wrong.

    How would you ask others to understand this set of assertions?

6. Look through a back issue of *The New Yorker* and pay particular attention to its cartoons. Based on what you see there, what qualities make for a publishable cartoon? Write an essay that explains how and why you think the cartoon editors make their choices. *Or:* Pretend that you are the cartoon editor of *The New Yorker* and that this cartoon arrives on your desk. You have to decide whether or not to publish it. What would you do?

WHAT WOULD THEY SAY?

7. Read Naomi Shihab Nye's essay "Long Overdue" (p. 578). Based on that essay, how do you think she would respond to Gregory's cartoon? What two places in the Nye essay seem most crucial to your assertions and interpretations? Make sure you quote these and explain them in an essay.

8. Consider this cartoon together with Paul Hawken's "A Teasing Irony" (p. 547). Do you think Hawken would approve of the views the cartoon seems to advance?

KOFI ANNAN
Nobel Lecture

*T*HE SEVENTH SECRETARY-GENERAL *of the United Nations, Kofi Annan (b. 1938) grew up in Kumasi, Ghana, where he attended the University of Science and Technology. In 1962, he joined the United Nations as an administrative and budget officer with the World Health Organization (WHO) in Geneva and served in various capacities at the UN before becoming secretary-general in 1997. In December 2001, Annan and the United Nations received the Nobel Peace Prize; the following selection is his Nobel lecture, in which he suggests that each human deserves to live in peace and that we can achieve peace for each person by ending poverty, preventing violent conflict, and encouraging democracy.*

Your Majesties, Your Royal Highnesses, Excellencies, Members of the Norwegian Nobel Committee, Ladies and Gentlemen,

Today, in Afghanistan, a girl will be born. Her mother will hold her and feed her, comfort her and care for her—just as any mother would anywhere in the world. In these most basic acts of human nature, humanity knows no divisions. But to be born a girl in today's Afghanistan is to begin life centuries away from the prosperity that one small part of humanity has achieved. It is to live under conditions that many of us in this hall would consider inhuman.

I speak of a girl in Afghanistan, but I might equally well have mentioned a baby boy or girl in Sierra Leone. No one today is unaware of this divide between the world's rich and poor. No one today can claim ignorance of the cost that this divide imposes on the poor and dispossessed who are no less deserving of human dignity, fundamental freedoms, security, food and education than any of us. The cost, however, is not borne by them alone. Ultimately, it is borne by all of us—North and South, rich and poor, men and women of all races and religions.

Today's real borders are not between nations, but between powerful and powerless, free and fettered, privileged and humiliated. Today, no walls can separate humanitarian or human rights crises in one part of the world from national security crises in another.

Scientists tell us that the world of nature is so small and interdependent that a butterfly flapping its wings in the Amazon rainforest can generate a violent storm on the other side of the earth. This principle is known as the "butterfly effect." Today, we realize, perhaps more than ever, that the world of human activity also has its own butterfly effect—for better or for worse.

Ladies and Gentlemen, we have entered the third millennium through a gate of fire. If today, after the horror of 11 September, we see better, and we   5 see further—we will realize that humanity is indivisible. New threats make no distinction between races, nations, or regions. A new insecurity has entered every mind, regardless of wealth or status. A deeper awareness of the bonds that bind us all—in pain as in prosperity—has gripped young and old.

In the early beginnings of the twenty-first century—a century already violently disabused of any hopes that progress towards global peace and prosperity is inevitable—this new reality can no longer be ignored. It must be confronted.

The twentieth century was perhaps the deadliest in human history, devastated by innumerable conflicts, untold suffering, and unimaginable crimes. Time after time, a group or a nation inflicted extreme violence on another, often driven by irrational hatred and suspicion, or unbounded arrogance and thirst for power and resources. In response to these cataclysms, the leaders of the world came together at midcentury to unite the nations as never before.

A forum was created—the United Nations—where all nations could join forces to affirm the dignity and worth of every person, and to secure peace and development for all peoples. Here states could unite to strengthen the rule of law, recognize and address the needs of the poor, restrain man's brutality and greed, conserve the resources and beauty of nature, sustain the equal rights of men *and* women, and provide for the safety of future generations.

We thus inherit from the twentieth century the political, as well as the scientific and technological power, which—if only we have the will to use them—give us the chance to vanquish poverty, ignorance, and disease.

In the twenty-first century I believe the mission of the United Nations 10 will be defined by a new, more profound, awareness of the sanctity and dignity of every human life, regardless of race or religion. This will require us to look beyond the framework of states, and beneath the surface of nations or communities. We must focus, as never before, on improving the conditions of the individual men and women who give the state or nation its richness and character. We must begin with the young Afghan girl, recognizing that saving that one life is to save humanity itself.

Over the past five years, I have often recalled that the United Nations' Charter begins with the words: "We the peoples." What is not always recognized is that "we the peoples" are made up of individuals whose claims to the most fundamental rights have too often been sacrificed in the supposed interests of the state or the nation.

A genocide begins with the killing of one man—not for what he has done, but because of who he is. A campaign of "ethnic cleansing" begins with one neighbor turning on another. Poverty begins when even one child is denied his or her fundamental right to education. What begins with the failure to uphold the dignity of one life, all too often ends with a calamity for entire nations.

In this new century, we must start from the understanding that peace belongs not only to states or peoples, but to each and every member of those communities. The sovereignty of states must no longer be used as a shield for gross violations of human rights. Peace must be made real and tangible in the daily existence of every individual in need. Peace must be sought, above all, because it is the condition for every member of the human family to live a life of dignity and security.

The rights of the individual are of no less importance to immigrants and minorities in Europe and the Americas than to women in Afghanistan or children in Africa. They are as fundamental to the poor as to the rich; they are as necessary to the security of the developed world as to that of the developing world.

From this vision of the role of the United Nations in the next century 15 flow three key priorities for the future: eradicating poverty, preventing conflict, and promoting democracy. Only in a world that is rid of poverty can all men and women make the most of their abilities. Only where individual rights are respected can differences be channeled politically and resolved peacefully. Only in a democratic environment, based on respect for diversity and dialogue, can individual self-expression and self-government be secured, and freedom of association be upheld.

Throughout my term as secretary-general, I have sought to place human beings at the center of everything we do—from conflict prevention to development to human rights. Securing real and lasting improvement in the lives of individual men and women is the measure of all we do at the United Nations.

It is in this spirit that I humbly accept the Centennial Nobel Peace Prize. Forty years ago today, the prize for 1961 was awarded for the first time to a secretary-general of the United Nations—posthumously, because Dag Hammarskjöld had already given his life for peace in Central Africa. And on the same day, the prize for 1960 was awarded for the first time to an African— Albert Luthuli, one of the earliest leaders of the struggle against apartheid in South Africa. For me, as a young African beginning his career in the United Nations a few months later, those two men set a standard that I have sought to follow throughout my working life.

This award belongs not just to me. I do not stand here alone. On behalf of all my colleagues in every part of the United Nations, in every corner of the globe, who have devoted their lives—and in many instances risked or given their lives in the cause of peace—I thank the members of the Nobel committee for this high honor. My own path to service at the United Nations was made possible by the sacrifice and commitment of my family and many friends from all continents—some of whom have passed away—who taught me and guided me. To them, I offer my most profound gratitude.

In a world filled with weapons of war and all too often words of war, the Nobel committee has become a vital agent for peace. Sadly, a prize for peace is a rarity in this world. Most nations have monuments or memorials to war, bronze salutations to heroic battles, archways of triumph. But peace has no parade, no pantheon of victory.

What it does have is the Nobel Prize—a statement of hope and courage 20
with unique resonance and authority. Only by understanding and addressing
the needs of individuals for peace, for dignity, and for security can we at the
United Nations hope to live up to the honor conferred today, and fulfill the
vision of our founders. This is the broad mission of peace that United Nations
staff members carry out every day in every part of the world.

A few of them, women and men, are with us in this hall today. Among
them, for instance, are a military observer from Senegal who is helping to provide basic security in the Democratic Republic of the Congo; a civilian police
adviser from the United States who is helping to improve the rule of law in
Kosovo; a UNICEF child protection officer from Ecuador who is helping to
secure the rights of Colombia's most vulnerable citizens; and a World Food
Program Officer from China who is helping to feed the people of North Korea.

Distinguished guests, the idea that there is one people in possession of
the truth, one answer to the world's ills, or one solution to humanity's needs,
has done untold harm throughout history—especially in the last century.
Today, however, even amidst continuing ethnic conflict around the world,
there is a growing understanding that human diversity is both the reality that
makes dialogue necessary, and the very basis for that dialogue.

We understand, as never before, that each of us is fully worthy of the
respect and dignity essential to our common humanity. We recognize that we
are the products of many cultures, traditions, and memories; that mutual respect
allows us to study and learn from other cultures; and that we gain strength by
combining the foreign with the familiar.

In every great faith and tradition one can find the values of tolerance and
mutual understanding. The Qur'an, for example, tells us that "We created you
from a single pair of male and female and made you into nations and tribes, that
you may know each other." Confucius urged his followers: "when the good
way prevails in the state, speak boldly and act boldly. When the state has lost the
way, act boldly and speak softly." In the Jewish tradition, the injunction to "love
thy neighbor as thyself," is considered to be the very essence of the Torah.

This thought is reflected in the Christian Gospel, which also teaches us to 25
love our enemies and pray for those who wish to persecute us. Hindus are
taught that "truth is one, the sages give it various names." And in the Buddhist
tradition, individuals are urged to act with compassion in every facet of life.

Each of us has the right to take pride in our particular faith or heritage.
But the notion that what is ours is necessarily in conflict with what is theirs is
both false and dangerous. It has resulted in endless enmity and conflict, leading men to commit the greatest of crimes in the name of a higher power.

It need not be so. People of different religions and cultures live side by
side in almost every part of the world, and most of us have overlapping identities which unite us with very different groups. We *can* love what we are,
without hating what—and who—we are *not*. We can thrive in our own tradition, even as we learn from others, and come to respect their teachings.

This will not be possible, however, without freedom of religion, of expression, of assembly, and basic equality under the law. Indeed, the lesson of the past century has been that where the dignity of the individual has been trampled or threatened—where citizens have not enjoyed the basic right to choose their government, or the right to change it regularly—conflict has too often followed, with innocent civilians paying the price, in lives cut short and communities destroyed.

The obstacles to democracy have little to do with culture or religion, and much more to do with the desire of those in power to maintain their position at any cost. This is neither a new phenomenon nor one confined to any particular part of the world. People of all cultures value their freedom of choice, and feel the need to have a say in decisions affecting their lives.

The United Nations, whose membership comprises almost all the states 30 in the world, is founded on the principle of the equal worth of every human being. It is the nearest thing we have to a representative institution that can address the interests of all states, and all peoples. Through this universal, indispensable instrument of human progress, states can serve the interests of their citizens by recognizing common interests and pursuing them in unity. No doubt, that is why the Nobel committee says that it "wishes, in its centenary year, to proclaim that the only negotiable route to global peace and cooperation goes by way of the United Nations."

I believe the committee also recognized that this era of global challenges leaves no choice but cooperation at the global level. When states undermine the rule of law and violate the rights of their individual citizens, they become a menace not only to their own people, but also to their neighbors, and indeed the world. What we need today is better governance—legitimate, democratic governance that allows each individual to flourish, and each state to thrive.

Your Majesties,
Excellencies,
Ladies and Gentlemen,

You will recall that I began my address with a reference to the girl born in Afghanistan today. Even though her mother will do all in her power to protect and sustain her, there is a one-in-four risk that she will not live to see her fifth birthday. Whether she does is just one test of our common humanity—of our belief in our individual responsibility for our fellow men and women. But it is the only test that matters.

Remember this girl and then our larger aims—to fight poverty, prevent conflict, or cure disease—will not seem distant, or impossible. Indeed, those aims will seem very near, and very achievable—as they should. Because beneath the surface of states and nations, ideas and language, lies the fate of individual human beings in need. Answering their needs will be the mission of the United Nations in the century to come.

Thank you very much.

WHAT DOES HE SAY?

1. As you're reading, make a list of Kofi Annan's major assertions. You can copy out his sentences, if you wish, or you can summarize in your own words. Either way, make sure your list includes at least five major statements.

2. Annan's speech begins and ends by mentioning a girl born in Afghanistan. Why does he structure his discussion in this way? What would be lost if his speech simply dropped those references?

3. What is Annan's view of the mission and goals of the United Nations? Where in his speech do you see it most clearly?

4. As you read Annan's lecture, think about American culture. Write a paragraph discussing some of the aspects of American culture that are not included or mentioned in his Nobel speech.

WHAT DO YOU THINK?

5. Carefully and accurately summarize Kofi Annan's speech in five hundred words. Then skip extra lines and follow your summary with a five-hundred-word discussion of what you believe would be necessary in order to "fight poverty, prevent conflict, and cure disease."

6. Locate a copy of a national news magazine like *Newsweek* or *Time*. Page through its contents. Pay attention to any stories of conflict among nations. Where is this conflict? What are its reported causes? Also pay attention to the advertisements. What do they imply as criteria for a successful life? Based on your analysis, write an essay that uses Kofi Annan's "Nobel Lecture" as a tool for interrogating what you're seeing in this magazine. To what extent does his speech help explain the conflicts you see reported? To what extent—or not—do all the contents (the reporting and the advertising) reflect his assertion that "[w]e must focus, as never before, on improving the conditions of the individual men and women who give the state or nation its richness and character"? End by explaining how your analysis of the magazine deepens or changes your understanding and response to Annan's lecture.

WHAT WOULD THEY SAY?

7. Compare the assertions you see in Kofi Annan's "Nobel Lecture" with the argument made by Garrett Hardin in his essay "Lifeboat Ethics: The Case against Helping the Poor" (p. 130). What basic assumptions or basic principles do you see at work in each discussion? Explain to what extent you see these two essays to be in fundamental agreement or disagreement. If you see points of argument, don't try to resolve them. Rather, aim for accurate reporting of what you see.

8. Read Kofi Annan's "Nobel Lecture" together with Merrill Joan Gerber's short story "I Don't Believe This" (p. 191). Then write an essay explaining how reading one

can help make sense of reading the other. Variation: Use Andre Dubus's "Giving Up the Gun" (p. 180) instead of Gerber's story.

9. Think about Kofi Annan's "Nobel Lecture" in relationship to Ruth Benedict's "The Case for Moral Relativism" (p. 619). To what extent, or not, do their assertions and viewpoints overlap, inform, or contradict each other? How does reading one make the other clearer? Variation: Substitute Andrew Sullivan's "The Pursuit of Happiness: Four Revolutionary Words" (p. 217) for Benedict's essay.

DAN BAUM

The Casualty

*T*HIS PIECE *looks at how the violence of war can affect one soldier, detailing the injury and return of an American soldier wounded in Iraq. Published under Dan Baum's byline, "The Casualty" was actually written by both Baum and his collaborator and wife, Margaret L. Knox. Freelance writers, Baum and Knox have been collaborating since 1987, publishing many articles—most under Baum's byline—and two books:* Smoke and Mirrors: The War on Drugs and the Politics of Failure *(1996) and* Citizen Coors: An American Dynasty *(2000). They live in Boulder, Colorado. "The Casualty" was first published in the March 8, 2004, issue of* The New Yorker.

When people talk about the army being good for a certain kind of young man, it's boys like Michael Cain they have in mind. Tall and lean, with a sweet smile and doll's eyes, Michael spent his high-school years searching fitfully for the disciplined achiever within him. His home, a converted schoolhouse that his parents rented amid the dairy pastures and cornfields outside Berlin, Wisconsin, was a loving if unruly place, noisy with two little sisters and cluttered with the winter coats, boots, and other items it takes to keep a family going in the rural Midwest. Michael's mother, Charlene, a sturdy woman with a broad, pretty face, earned most of the family income as a clerk in a Winnebago County mental-health clinic, forty-five minutes away. His father, Kenneth, a heavyset former machinist disabled by back pain, kept llamas in the back yard as a hobby. Michael loafed through school in his early teens, playing sousaphone in the marching band and clowning around in class. He liked to watch professional wrestling on TV. In his junior year, though, he found himself thinking that Berlin, population fifty-three hundred, looked small. Envisioning a career in computers, he bore down on his schoolwork and got decent grades, but then he seemed to lose interest in the prospect of going to college.

Graduation, in 1999, marooned him. Having no clear idea what to do, Michael took a job stocking shelves at Wal-Mart. Within months, the thrill of adulthood had faded to a dreary routine of unpacking boxes under fluorescent lights and, after hours, gazing into the PlayStation 2 upstairs in his bedroom. In May of 2000, Michael drove forty minutes to an army recruiting station in the Oshkosh City Center shopping mall and got the paperwork to sign up for a four-year hitch. Charlene first heard of her son's plans when he came home that night and asked for his birth certificate.

Charlene thought the military would be too tough for her easygoing son. "You hate having people tell you what to do," she told him. Though

Michael was nineteen and parental consent wasn't required, the recruiter drove out to the Cains' house to sit at the kitchen table among the canned goods and wrestling magazines and show her on his laptop the range of army opportunities. "Are you sure you want to do this?" Charlene kept asking Michael as the recruiter, in crisp dress greens, sat stiffly between them. The laptop glowed with images of men flying helicopters and driving tanks. Less than a week later, Michael Cain was at the induction center in Milwaukee with a gym bag in his hand.

To Charlene's amazement, Michael thrived under military discipline. The unity of purpose, the clarity of authority, and the hard physical work all gave him hope of becoming the man he wanted to be—serious, competent, respected. His biggest gripe in calls home was that other soldiers were insufficiently respectful to the drill sergeant—a complaint that left his mother speechless. His score on the army entrance exam wasn't high enough to get him into electronics, but it qualified him to be an "eighty-eight mike"—a truck driver. For Private Cain, barreling along in a thirty-eight-thousand-pound transport at highway speeds was more fun than arranging displays of toaster ovens. He twice wrote to his recruiter, describing how he was getting his "ass kicked" so hard he'd lost twenty-eight pounds, but also to thank him for helping him "fulfill a life long dream, being AN AMERICAN SOLDIER!!!" After basic, he was sent to Vicenza, Italy, and spent two years driving trucks and taking parachute training in order to get his jump wings. The army worked its traditional alchemy. Michael rose smoothly to the rank of specialist and was sent to Fort Hood, Texas. He met an attractive woman named Leslie Lantz, who worked at a Denny's restaurant in the nearby town of Killeen, and they began seeing each other. On April 1st of last year, Cain departed for Kuwait, and left in her care his most precious possession—a new Dodge Ram pickup.

Two decorations hold particular fascination for soldiers who are shipping out. The Combat Infantryman Badge, or C.I.B., is awarded for spending at least sixty days under fire. The Purple Heart goes to soldiers wounded by enemy action. Together, they mean that a soldier has experienced the essence of warfare. What soldiers want when they envision the Purple Heart is to get shot, patched up, and returned to their platoons in one piece. When Cain left for Iraq, he knew he'd get his C.I.B. But he also boasted to his mother that he'd win a Purple Heart.

Assigned to the 299th Engineer Battalion in Tikrit, Cain took command of a Heavy Expanded Mobility Tactical Truck—or *hemmit*—a monstrous land schooner that rides on eight four-foot-tall tires and hauls everything from gasoline to tampons. The battalion was comfortably billeted in an unfinished palace that had belonged to one of Saddam Hussein's brothers-in-law, with rows of army cots spread out under soaring arches. Twice a day, Cain and Specialist Keisha Duff, a twenty-seven-year-old eighty-eight mike from Humboldt, Tennessee, drove rations and water to soldiers camped two miles south

5

on the four-lane road the army calls Highway One. Cain impressed his company commander, Captain James Blain, as a particularly enthusiastic soldier, always ready to grab an M249 machine gun and volunteer for dangerous missions. Cain, the captain wrote me, "was ready to rock and roll," and was in the process of being promoted to sergeant. The unit never had quite enough water. But for that—and for having to wear a sixteen-pound flak vest, web gear laden with ammunition, and a four-pound Kevlar helmet in the hundred-plus heat—Cain considered Tikrit easy duty, with plenty of time to watch movies and play video games. He liked hanging around the battalion aid station, a tent with a couple of gurneys, swapping CDs and DVDs with Private First Class George Blohm and Private First Class Jeremy Brown, a pair of "ninety-one whiskeys"—medics.

August 10th was a Sunday. At 9:40 AM, Duff took the wheel of the hemmit and Cain the shotgun seat. A Humvee mounted with an M249 led the hemmit out of the palace compound, and another fell in behind. The vehicles lumbered up the short gravel road to Highway One. A hemmit's cab extends several feet ahead of the front tires, and Cain recalls it swinging out over the blacktop of the highway as the truck made its turn. It is his last memory of Iraq.

Medics Brown and Blohm were sitting in the aid station when their master sergeant ran in to report a possible casualty out on the highway. Medics no longer wear big red crosses on their helmets; during the Second World War, they suffered high losses because they were easy to pick off. Nowadays they look and dress like other soldiers, down to the weaponry, and address each other as "soldier-medic," with the emphasis on "soldier." Their primary mission is that of any warrior, which, as the Soldier's Creed puts it, is to "engage and destroy the enemies of the United States of America in close combat." Often the first thing a medic will do for a wounded soldier is shoot back, in order to protect him. Brown grabbed a rifle and a thirty-pound aid bag, Blohm took a stretcher, and together they raced toward a greasy cloud of smoke rising up from the highway.

They could see at once that the hemmit had hit a mine; the enormous right front wheel was gone and the cab was crumpled. Blood, shiny oil, and bright-green engine coolant made a mess on the tarmac. Soldiers had ringed the scene and were pointing their rifles into the desert; mine strikes are frequently overtures to ambush. Keisha Duff had been thrown clear of the driver's seat and was being rolled onto a stretcher. Jagged chunks of the cab were embedded in her arm, and she had a bad burn under her flak jacket. Screams echoed from the hemmit's twisted cab; Blohm glanced inside. "Oh, shit," he remembers thinking. "It's my friend." In addition to having to duck and return fire while administering aid, combat medics, unlike their civilian counterparts, often find themselves wrist-deep in the hot ruined flesh of their best friends.

Cain's right leg was a mangled slab of splintered bone and stringy red 10 muscles; Blohm knew it couldn't be saved. Both knees were visibly dislocated.

The left thigh was twisted at a bad angle, indicating a broken femur, and the leg appeared both seared and flayed. Cain was shrieking in agony and panic. Brown, the senior medic on the scene, climbed up into the cab with him.

The clock was running fast on what medics call "the golden hour"—the first sixty minutes after injury, when timely treatment can determine whether a soldier lives or dies. As recently as the Persian Gulf War, in 1991, the most highly trained medics were held behind the front lines at battalion aid stations. Front-line combat medics had neither the training nor the equipment, for example, to insert an airway tube into a patient's throat. And, while they carried IV bags of plasma, they knew little of medication beyond morphine. Modern desert warfare involves such swift travel, though, that soldiers in a forty-mph Bradley fighting vehicle can quickly move beyond the reach of an aid station. And, in the kind of "asymmetric warfare" the army finds itself conducting in Iraq, there are no "lines" anymore. In the 1980s, the Army Medical Command decided that every soldier would carry his or her own wound dressing; today, it is a big cotton pad that can absorb about half a liter of blood. Each thirteen-soldier squad has at least one "combat lifesaver," a soldier with additional first-aid training who carries tourniquets, extra dressings, and maybe a few IV bags. Field soldier-medics like Brown and Blohm get the same level of training that used to be reserved for rear-echelon sergeant-medics—sixteen weeks of advanced first aid, drug mathematics, and training in invasive procedures like airway and nasal-gastric tubes and urinary catheters. One medic is usually assigned to every twenty-five-to-thirty-man combat platoon.

Brown resisted the impulse to move straight to the glaring red wounds, and instead snapped into protocols. Doing his best to ignore Cain's shrieking, he did an ABC check on his friend—airway, breathing, and circulation. Then he, Blohm, and two other medics lifted Cain out of the shattered cab and laid him on a litter. Cain wasn't in danger of bleeding to death; the bubbly, malodorous burns caused by the blast had cauterized his arteries. Though the pain was obviously horrible, Brown gave Cain no morphine, because he knew that he would be heading for immediate surgery and wanted him lucid enough to sign surgical-consent papers.

Soldiers speak to each other in a stream of acronyms and abbreviations that are incomprehensible to civilians but essential when shouting complex information over the din of battle. After the ABC check, Brown and Blohm ran through DCAP-BTLS—an inventory of deformities, contusions, abrasions, punctures/penetrations, burns, tenderness, lacerations, and swelling. Then they palpated Cain's body in a limb-by-limb TIC, or a search for tenderness, instability, and crepitation (bone grinding on bone). They did a CCT, checking for color, condition, and temperature of Cain's skin; and a PMS—pulse, motor, and sensory—check. They found no circulation in the right leg and a weak and inconsistent—"thready"—pulse in the left.

Cain was writhing and crying, and as Blohm and Brown worked they tried to calm him with stock assurances—"You'll be fine," "Everything's

OK"—and jokes about attractive women soldiers in the battalion. When they finished checking vital signs, they turned to Cain's obvious injuries, wrapping what Blohm called the "mush" of the right leg in bandages, splinting both legs. Supporting their friend's head, they rolled him on his side and discovered that his left buttock was half torn off, the flesh laced with rough bits of the truck cab.

An M113 personnel carrier-cum-ambulance—a steel box on tracks— 15
rumbled up. The medics loaded Cain aboard, and started an IV of lactated Ringer's, an electrolyte solution. An army chaplain slipped in beside Cain. With Blohm holding the IV bag and Brown driving, they sped for a landing zone where a Black Hawk helicopter was waiting to take Cain to the twenty-eighth Combat Support Hospital—the modern-day equivalent of a MASH unit—in Baghdad. Thirty-four minutes had elapsed since the mine blast. Blohm was twenty-three years old. Brown, the senior medic, was twenty-four. Cain was twenty-two.

When an American soldier dies in Iraq, newspapers publish the name. When a soldier is wounded, the incident, if reported at all, is usually an aside. Names are rarely given. The wounding of Michael Cain wasn't news-worthy; a search of wire-service and *Times* stories for August 11th and 12th turns up little mention of the attack; the Associated Press reported that "four American soldiers were wounded in guerrilla attacks, including two at the Baghdad University complex and two others in Saddam's hometown of Tikrit. One U.S. soldier died of heat stroke and another was found dead in his living quarters on Sunday, the military said." The day after Cain and Duff were injured, the *Times* reported that Americans were suffering Iraq-war "news burnout."

The Defense Department publishes an online tally of American servicemen killed and wounded in Iraq, updating it every few days. As of February 25th, 449 had been killed and 2,420 wounded by hostile fire. The ratio of wounded soldiers to killed is higher in this war (a little more than five to one) than in the Second World War and Vietnam, probably because of body armor and advances in battlefield medicine. (In the Second World War, the ratio was a little more than two to one; by the time of Korea, it had risen to three to one, where it remained until last spring.)

By most American soldiers' accounts, the Iraqis are lousy shots. In any case, they know that the Americans are wearing body armor. Rather than trying to pierce shielded torsos with bullets, the Iraqis increasingly rely on blowing off the Americans' unprotected arms and legs with explosives: car bombs, mines, rocket-propelled grenades, and "improvised explosive devices," which are often old artillery shells that have been buried and then detonated from a distance by some kind of cheap commercial electronic device—a garage-door opener, say, or the joystick of a ten-dollar radio-controlled toy car. As of January 9th, sixty-six service people—almost all of them army soldiers—had suffered amputation of a hand, a foot, an arm, or a leg. Of those, ten had lost more than one limb.

Cain was injured by an Italian plastic antivehicle mine about the size of a tin of butter cookies. (His friends found pieces of the mine afterward.) It would have been easy for someone to feign a flat tire and bury the device quickly in the soft sand at the point where Highway One and the packed-gravel road to the palace compound meet. Apparently, the hemmit did just what the saboteur was hoping. It cut the corner a hair too sharp and depressed the mine's detonator.

Kenneth Cain was at home when the call came from Fort Hood, two days after the blast. Kenneth is stout, with a big white beard that makes him look a little like Santa Claus. He called Charlene at work. The first thing she heard when she picked up the phone was her husband weeping. Then he told her that Michael had been seriously wounded.

Cain was lying in a coma at Landstuhl Regional Medical Center, in western Germany, where all Iraq-war casualties are taken. Doctors had amputated his right leg below the knee. The condition of the left leg was uncertain. Cain also had a smashed jaw, a broken thumb, a broken arm, and a wound on the back of his head. He'd lost a lot of blood. During the Second World War, families were lucky to get a telegram days or weeks after a son or a husband was hurt. In this war, the army kept the Cains informed hour by hour; a major at Fort Hood called them five times in two days. Charlene was even able to speak by telephone with the doctor who was treating her son; she learned that they were about to try turning off life support, leaving it in place in case Cain didn't respond. When she called a second time, a nurse told her they'd switched it off and he'd started breathing on his own. The Fort Hood major was working on getting the Cains plane tickets to Germany when they learned that their son was being flown to Walter Reed Army Medical Center, in Washington, D.C.

Cain remembers none of this; other soldiers say that the trip from Landstuhl to Walter Reed is grim. Litters are loaded into the fuselage of an air force transport, which is made of aluminum and tends to be chilly. The roar of the engines barely masks the moaning and crying of the wounded. When a soldier dies en route, his body is simply covered with a sheet.

Walter Reed is a vast campus of red brick buildings in north-central Washington; its centerpiece is the main hospital, a gigantic edifice, which opened in 1977. It's a surprisingly cheerful building, with wide, airy halls and a determinedly upbeat staff. On August 17th, Cain opened his eyes. Finding himself in a hospital bed, he believed that he must be dreaming. A nurse asked him if he wanted anything. "McDonald's," he told her. Then his eyes traveled over the machines and tubes, and he said, "My mom and dad." As it happened, they'd just arrived.

Kenneth and Charlene had been flown to Washington at the army's expense. They were shown to a room on Ward 57—the orthopedic ward, where amputees go—and found Michael with his head arched back in a high cervical collar. A tube full of "disgusting green fluid," as Charlene recalls it, ran from his nose. His thumb was in a cast, and a three-inch round scab covered the back of his head; a catheter snaked from under the covers, and an IV was attached to his arm. Charlene had to tell her son that his leg was gone. He glanced at the end of the bed, where only one foot tented the blanket, then stared at the ceiling for a long time. When they pulled back the covers, Kenneth and Charlene found that Michael's right leg ended in a bandaged stump. His left leg looked as though a dog had been chewing on it: long, crosshatched crimson scars ran up its sides and back. An instrument that Charlene called a "cheese grater" had been run over the skin graft, leaving a pattern of holes that allow the skin to expand and to cover the wounded area. A metal contraption that looked like a miniature offshore oil platform rose out of his left hip, and a big square of skin had been peeled from his upper thigh to provide a graft for the stump. Cain sent Kenneth and Charlene down to the gift shop for a disposable camera and had them take photographs of his gruesome injuries. He pasted them into a flowered "Special Memories" album that he has titled "My Accident in Iraq."

Outwardly, Michael was still Sergeant Cain, telling his parents he 25 wanted only to go back to the 299th in Iraq. (Keisha Duff did in fact return to active duty in Iraq.) He felt responsible for his men. "War's war," he told his mother. "This one was a good thing; it gave people their freedom." But when Charlene told him that his cousin was thinking of joining the army, he asked for the phone so he could talk him out of it. "He's crazy," Michael said. "I wouldn't let him go. He could end up like me."

A bomb injures in many ways. The shock wave can loosen organs and leave a victim to bleed to death internally, or rake him with shrapnel. Long after the initial wounds are treated, the effects of the bomb continue to plague the victim. In Cain's case, the blast pulverized dirt, truck metal, engine fluids, and his own clothing, and drove microscopic debris deep into his muscles, macerating the tissue. Each tiny fleck had to be dug out, the pulped flesh cut away, and the wounds cleaned and recleaned—a process that took twelve surgeries, over three months. (Had there been any people between him and the mine, their flesh might have been atomized and driven into his, which can cause particularly dangerous infections.)

Starting the day after he regained consciousness, Cain was in the care of Lieutenant Justin LaFerrier, an army physical therapist whose bulging muscles, under a tight white coat, make him a walking advertisement for the active life. LaFerrier is in charge of many of the Iraq-war amputees at Walter Reed. While Cain was still undergoing surgeries to clean his wounds, LaFerrier had him wheeled most days to the physical-therapy room on the third floor. It's the size of a gymnasium, filled with bars, racks, and machines that look like torture instruments from the Middle Ages. An amputee, particularly one who has lost a leg, has to reestablish his body's balance, and LaFerrier put Cain through hours of exercises to build up the muscles he'd need to operate crutches and a prosthesis. "Your core is your stable basis of support," LaFerrier, a Rhode Island native, explained to me. "When you take a step, you don't think about it. When an amputee does that, he has to first stabilize the residual limb in the socket. You have to train those muscles to do that." We watched a sweaty, gasping soldier who had lost both legs and one arm inch along the parallel bars in shiny, high-tech prosthetics. "I like to push them to the limit," LaFerrier said. "They're young. They're strong. I want to cause muscle soreness, but not the 'Ooh, I shouldn't have done that' pain. I take them as far as they can tolerate." The amputees call LaFerrier their "physical terrorist."

Although Charlene took all her sick days and vacation days and her coworkers donated a hundred hours of theirs, she and Kenneth eventually had to return to Wisconsin. After they left, Cain's warrior spirit drained away. One day, he refused to go to physical therapy, and when he was wheeled there against his will he was sullen and uncooperative. Frequent phone calls from his men in Tikrit—another amenity unknown to casualties of earlier wars—would cheer him up for a few minutes, but then he'd start to miss them, and sink lower in spirits. Captain Blain sent his father and wife, both of whom live in the Washington area, to visit. Celebrities passed through, too—Cain met the actor Gary Sinise, who played a Vietnam War amputee in *Forrest Gump*, and the country singer Shania Twain. One day, President Bush sat on the edge of his bed and asked him if he wanted anything. Cain told the president that his men needed water. When Cain spoke to them by phone two days later, they told him that they suddenly had more water than they could possibly use.

Still, Cain couldn't shake the feeling that he'd be stuck in a chair and useless the rest of his life. He was withdrawn, and continued to refuse physical therapy. The hospital finally asked Charlene to come back, figuring she could make him work for LaFerrier the way she'd once made him practice the sousaphone. She somehow found a way to take time off. Mothers are often asked to assist in the recovery process at Walter Reed, LaFerrier told me.

I met Cain in December at Mologne House, a hotel on the Walter Reed campus for visiting families and for soldiers undergoing outpatient treatment, including physical therapy. The Federal style of the two-story lobby, with a gigantic chandelier and a grand staircase, belies the building's age; Mologne House opened in 1997. It is adamantly a hotel, not a medical facility. Its rooms are indistinguishable from, say, rooms at a Hilton, except that the bathroom cabinets frequently resemble pharmacy shelves, with doxycycline, Ambien, and Percocet nestling among Old Spice and Mega-Men dietary supplements. The Mologne House staff are upbeat and pleasant amid a high percentage of guests who are adjusting to blindness, facial scars, and missing limbs. They differ from the staff of an ordinary hotel only in their mandatory daily inspections of every room, a practice instituted in July as a suicide-prevention measure.

Cain was sitting on the edge of his unmade bed wearing shorts and a Packers jersey and cap, his naked stump jutting out. Saddam Hussein had been captured the night before and President Bush happened to be speaking on television, but Cain was absorbed by a hockey simulation on his PlayStation 2. He looked terrible—sallow and sunken-eyed, with a two-day stubble. He'd dyed his hair a garish chrome yellow. He kept shifting uncomfortably on his hollowed buttock. Every surface in the room was covered with CDs, model airplanes, hockey magazines, Packers memorabilia, boxes of Frosted Mini-Wheats, and bags of Funyuns. Dirty laundry and candy wrappers were strewn on the floor. Cain's prosthesis, a white-and-magenta running shoe with a complicated steel-and-plastic ankle joint, rose like a tower from the rubble, a pattern of American flags decorating the calf-size plastic socket that fits his stump. He told me that he had no regrets, and that he would do it again if he could. Would he let his son join the army? "Fuck no," he said. "I'd tell him, 'I'll beat the shit out of you if you try it.'"

Cain's girlfriend, Leslie Lantz, a muscular, dark-eyed beauty, who had arrived from Texas the week before, was flipping through *Portraits of War*, a book of Iraq-war drawings published by *Detroit Free Press*. Charlene was making a halfhearted attempt to straighten the room. She had been there for three weeks, sleeping in the bed next to the one Cain shared with Leslie. "I knew Mom would come," Cain said sheepishly. "I quit doing everything, so they had to call her." I asked how it felt to have his mom in the bed next to his and Leslie's. He didn't answer directly. "It's nice having Mom here," he said. "But she cries a lot." He swiveled his gaze back to his hockey game.

"I'm on antidepressants," Charlene said. "After this happened with Michael, I couldn't deal."

At Walter Reed, an informal network of gruff Vietnam and Gulf War veterans minister to the blind and the bandaged with great tenderness. Jim Mayer, for example, fought with the twenty-fifth Infantry Division in Vietnam. Today, at fifty-eight, he runs an executive-training program in the Department of Veterans Affairs, but to the soldiers lying in Ward 57 he's the Milkshake Man. He arrives three days a week after work with a box of McDonald's milkshakes, which he offers from bed to bed. I had been at the hospital three days before I realized that his legs are carbon, graphite, and plastic below the knee; he had stepped on a mine near the Cambodian border. One afternoon, he cried "Watch this!" and went skipping down the hall. The amputees couldn't take their eyes off him.

"We want to make sure no veteran is ever again treated the way we were 35 when we came home," Mayer told me. The vets help organize trips to the Smithsonian and the White House and arrange free tickets for the young men to see the Wizards play basketball and the Capitals play hockey. Wounded soldiers who can make the trip are also invited every Friday night to Fran O'Brien's, a fancy steak house in downtown Washington, where they can load up on thirty-dollar steaks and all the beer they can drink, free of charge. Hal Koster, one of the restaurant's two owners, served three tours as a gunship crew chief in Vietnam. "It's an honor," he told me one Friday before Christmas as he watched more than two dozen young men consume a few thousand dollars' worth of beef, crab cakes, and tiramisu. "Nobody did this for us."

The amputees I met were all eager to talk about their wounds, and welcomed the chance to tell the story. War stories, like Holocaust stories, are all both alike and different, and all improbable; each turns on moments of horror, serendipity, and unimaginable bravery. Sitting next to me at Fran O'Brien's was Steve Reighard, of Bloomington, Indiana, who was hacking one-handed with a combination knife-fork at a steak the size of a dictionary. "They ambushed us," he said. "I'm standing there trying to realize what happened and my arm is laying there. I picked it up and fell in the dirt." Across the table, Robert Acosta, of Santa Ana, California, manipulated a steak knife with his stainless-steel hook. "They threw a hand grenade in my truck," he said. "I picked it up and, damn, dropped it down between my legs. When I grabbed it again, it blew up in my hand." At Walter Reed, Phil Bauer, a strapping cavalry scout from upstate New York, had described being on a Chinook helicopter that was shot down on November 2nd, killing fifteen soldiers on their way to a short leave. When he came to, he said, he was pinned atop the open-eyed corpse of a woman soldier to whom he'd just given a piece of gum. His leg was jammed beneath the burning roof of the Chinook, and he had to lie there, without morphine, for two hours while a "jaws of life" apparatus was flown in from Tikrit. "It was like cooking a steak with the cover down," he said. He lost his right leg below the knee. At the dinner, a soldier named Ed Platt, from Harrisburg, Pennsylvania, told me that the signature moment of his calamity was when the medics used the ribbons of his leg—shattered by a rocket-propelled grenade—as its own tourniquet. "They just folded it up," he said. "I looked down and I'm looking at the sole of my boot." He shuddered. "OK, cool, whatever, dude," he muttered to himself as he finished his story. Doctors amputated just below Platt's right hip.

Platt sat across from Michael Cain, who was playing keep-away with another soldier's cap. "He's a 'baloney,' " Platt said of Cain. The word was a play on "below knee" but perfectly evoked the unnatural pink cylinder that Cain's lower leg had become. Though the Purple Heart club is a band of brothers, there is a hierarchy of wounds. A whole leg trumps a half. A right hand trumps a left. And everybody was down on one soldier who was physically unmarked but said he had been mentally wounded by the war.

It was possible to forget how young some of the soldiers were as they told their stories of wounds and weapons, of campaigns and tactics, and of the time one of them, under orders to do nothing, watched a crowd of Iraqi men drop a woman who was said to be an adulteress from a high bridge ("We were, like, 'Fuck!' "). But then they started talking about their favorite movies. All of them liked *Elf*, while their hands-down favorite was *Finding Nemo*.

The conversation turned, as it often does among Iraq-war amputees, to the mysterious workings of the Med Board. Officially called the Physical Evaluation Board, it determines whether a wounded soldier may continue in his or her army job, is fit for some other army job, or should be medically retired. It also quantifies a soldier's disability, which determines what percentage of a soldier's base pay will be awarded in benefits. Soldiers talk about the Med Board the way people in the Old Testament talk about God—as an in-scrutable, mercurial, sometimes vengeful force. None of them understand how the board works, and all fear they will get "Burger-Kinged out," mean-ing medically retired with a meager benefit. A missing arm has to be worth 30 percent, right? they asked each other. And a missing leg 40?

Whatever their retirement prospects, all the amputees said they had no   40 regrets. Robert Acosta spoke of the need to fight terrorism and the choice a soldier makes to face death. "Shit happens," he said. Steve Reighard said, "I believed in what we were doing." If we hadn't gone to war, he said, "eventu-ally we'd see chemical arms and those kind of munitions on our streets." The other soldiers nodded. At one point, Reighard leaned over and said quietly, "You know, we kind of have to think that." He gestured at his missing arm. "Otherwise, this is in vain."

Michael Cain was pale and his voice raspy as he hobbled toward the door on his cane and prosthesis, which, being new, was painful to wear. But he kept up the hard, edgy banter that amputees use among themselves. "Hey, Acosta, give me a hand!" he yelled to the one who'd fumbled the grenade. "Platt, shake a leg." I walked two blocks for my car and pulled into the restau-rant's semicircular driveway. Cain got in front and, with the door still open, pulled off his prosthesis for relief. A line of well-dressed diners, standing on the curb waiting for valets to bring their cars, stared at him, aghast. When Cain noticed, he waved his prosthesis and yelled in a falsetto singsong, "Look! My leg comes off! Look!" The onlookers turned away. Cain was still laughing cruelly as we drove off.

Shortly after the holidays, I flew to Milwaukee and drove two hours north-west to Berlin. (The name is pronounced with the accent on the first syllable.) Downtown Berlin has a lot of quaint brick buildings, but, with the Wal-Mart on its outskirts and the chains in nearby Oshkosh, there are not many people on the streets.

Michael was home, though not yet out of the army; he was waiting for the Med Board to rule on his case. Following a final medical evaluation, it generally takes two to four months to get a decision. I found him in his par-ents' living room, watching the pro-wrestling show *Monday Night Raw* at top volume on a television screen the size of a bedsheet. Michael reached up to shake my hand without taking his eyes from the screen. His prosthesis sat amid a pile of wrestling magazines and empty bottles of Mountain Dew Code Red, and he rubbed his elevated stump as though it ached. Leslie was still around; she sat across the room, flipping through a magazine. One of Michael's younger sisters, Stephanie, sat at a computer in the corner of the living room, searching online for nursing-aide jobs, and his father was in the kitchen, cooking himself a late supper of fried ham and eggs on toast spread with peanut butter. He is a fatalist, and, when asked how he felt about Michael's decision to enlist or what he thinks of the army's policies on disability payments, he falls back constantly on the phrase "There's nothing you can do." Besides taking care of his llamas, he often feeds his neighbors' animals as well. He is the family cook, and always has dinner on the table when Charlene gets home from work.

Charlene, who arises around 4:30 in the morning to go to her job, is the family rock. She absorbs blow after blow without appearing to crack. Michael's injury is her project. She's in charge. On the phone to a friend, she uses phrases like "I brought him home on December 16th," "I want to catch that before it becomes a full-blown infection," and "I need to get him to Milwaukee because he has a torn medial meniscus and PCL." At the kitchen table, she is often immersed in the maze of forms required for every treatment, trying to insure that care will be adequate and costs will be covered— complexities that sometimes take her hours a day to manage.

Until last year, Charlene and Kenneth had raised their granddaughter Felicia, who is now six, because Michael's older sister, Yolanda, was unable to care for her. When Charlene was at Walter Reed with Michael, she got a call that Yolanda, who was seven months pregnant with her second child, was going into labor, and that the baby had hydroencephaly. The baby was born on September 29th, and has brain damage of indeterminate severity. "His brain is not developed totally," Charlene said. "We won't know for a while how damaged he is. So I'm dealing with all this stuff. Then I get a call to go back to Michael's room, because he needs me. Then my phone rings, and it's my youngest saying, 'Yolanda's back in the hospital with a kidney infection.'"

When I asked Charlene how she felt about the war, she said, "I don't like the fact that these young kids are joining up. I realize somebody has to do it. I still have my doubts about Saddam. I can't say I supported the war. Thinking about it now, maybe, I'm just kind of neutral about it. I'm angry Michael got hurt. I don't know who at. I'm just angry."

At Walter Reed, Michael's spirits had been buoyed by routine, army discipline, and the loving ministrations of the Vietnam vets, as well as of his mother. In Berlin, he was no longer Sergeant Cain, or a war hero in the nation's entertainment- and star-filled capital, but a one-legged guy in a Barcalounger with little to fill his days beyond PlayStation 2 and thrice-weekly physical-therapy appointments. Gone was the gung-ho warrior counting on a twenty-year career. Michael was even thinner and paler than he'd been a month earlier, and he was so withdrawn he spoke only in monosyllables. Charlene said that he hadn't been sleeping well. Michael wasn't working, though he told me he was thinking of taking an assistant manager's job at the local McDonald's. In the fall, he said, he was going to the University of Wisconsin at Madison "to study computers, computer programming, something like that." I asked if he'd applied and he said no. "But they've got to take me."

45

After the wrestling match, Leslie drove us to a dingy roadhouse called the Country Inn; the two of them hardly spoke, and seemed more like an old married couple than like sweethearts. Michael spent most of the evening at a video slot machine, his thin frame lost in a voluminous green-and-gold Packers coat, downing one Coors Light after another, dribbling away his money. Our destination the next day was the Fox River Mall, an hour away, in Appleton. Michael is still drawing nineteen hundred dollars a month in base pay; he spent a hundred and fifty on a pile of Green Bay Packers memorabilia—jersey, helmet, stickers, and flags for the car—to add to his already extensive collection. Leslie did the driving again, and again they hardly spoke. Every few minutes, he'd raise her fingertips to his lips and kiss them, and she'd smile.

On January 21st, Michael returned to Berlin High School to speak to an assembly. He limped to the podium wearing a Washington Capitals jersey, which the star right wing Jaromir Jagr had given him in the team's locker room during Michael's celebrity-wounded phase. After admitting he'd come unprepared, Michael bashfully delivered some uplifting bumper-sticker slogans about keeping a positive outlook on life (a phrase he used three times). He made no appeal to patriotism, though he told the students he had no regrets.

During questions, someone asked if they could see Michael's "new leg." 50 He rolled up his pant leg to show the prosthesis; the auditorium fell silent. Then he pulled it off, and a few kids squealed "Eeew!" The room exploded in applause. When he was asked about compensation, Michael seemed to get carried away by the attention he was receiving, saying that he would get "thousands of dollars" and "a hundred-percent disability," that the army had promised him a hundred thousand dollars for college. "And if I have children their college will be paid for," he said. "Their birthing process will be paid for.... I pretty much have everything paid for."

The truth is that Michael will need several more surgeries; the ankle of the left leg is fractured and may need to be reset; he suffers from hammertoe, a downward contraction of the toes; and many nerves are damaged. The army and the Veterans Administration will pay for the surgical procedures, but disability compensation is still a mystery to him and to most other soldiers. It is based on a complex formula that includes an estimate of lost-earnings potential. Now that most jobs don't involve much physical movement, the amputees are afraid they'll receive little.

At the end of February, Michael was back at Walter Reed because his prosthesis was still painful. He has "heterotopic ossification," or calcium deposits that caused the bone to protrude. He was being fitted for a new liner and socket. I found him and Leslie, now his fiancée, in their room at Mologne House, and though I expected him to be depressed by being in the hospital, his spirits seemed enormously lifted. He looked more filled out, with better color in his face, and he was back to making endless jokes. We took a taxi to a nearby Mexican restaurant. Michael went outside for a cigarette, and stood at the window pantomiming being a homeless old drunk. Leslie put her face in her hands. Then he came inside, draped a paper napkin over his arm, and, in a Pepé Le Pew accent, pretended to be a fancy waiter until Leslie pulled him into his seat.

Because he seemed so much happier being back in the military milieu, I asked him why he didn't consider trying to stay in the army and get a job suitable for a one-legged soldier. A career working with computers, after all, doesn't require two whole legs. He waved away the suggestion, saying only, "Nah. I don't want it." A little later, he said that sitting at a computer all day "isn't really being a soldier." I asked if he had applied to Madison yet. "No, we're putting that on hold because we have the baby coming," he said. Leslie grew very still, staring at her plate. Michael put his arm around her proudly, and she glanced up quickly through her falling brown hair. The baby is due in August.

WHAT DOES HE SAY?

1. Mark the margin of your book whenever you can see Michael Cain identifying what it means to be an American soldier.

2. Identify three places in this essay where the writing stands out as particularly powerful. Write a sentence indicating those three places and then write a paragraph on one of them. What provokes your strong response?

3. Once you've finished reading this essay, what do you understand more clearly than when you started reading? Write a few sentences to briefly explain this. What do you now wonder about that you previously had not thought about or considered? Write a few sentences briefly explaining this, too.

4. Does Dan Baum make an argument in this essay? Write a paragraph explaining your first response to this question.

WHAT DO YOU THINK?

5. At one point, Michael says, "War's war. This one was a good thing; it gave people their freedom." Read the rest of the essay carefully. What later parts of the essay lead you to conclude that Michael's thinking stays essentially the same or that it changes? Identify the evidence you find and carefully explain how you interpret it.

6. Dan Baum's essay on Michael Cain presents much evidence, but it does not end with any sort of clear conclusion. Rather, the story proceeds as far as it can go, then stops. Write a three-page conclusion to this piece. In it, make some argument for how we should understand and value the evidence that Baum presents.

WHAT WOULD THEY SAY?

7. Read Bowen H. McCoy's "The Parable of the Sadhu" (p. 102); then write an essay explaining what you think McCoy would say about Michael Cain and about America's responsibilities to him and others like him.

8. Read Garrett Hardin's "Lifeboat Ethics: The Case against Helping the Poor" (p. 130), and apply Hardin's argument to Michael Cain and to others like him. Assume that the U.S. budget is akin to a lifeboat: it cannot pay for everything. You don't have to agree with Hardin's analysis. But your essay here does need to discuss how you believe Hardin would allocate scarce resources, especially when it comes to those injured or disabled in the line of duty.

9. Consider Michael Cain's story in light of Chris Hedges's essay "Eros and Thanatos" (p. 247). To what extent, or not, can you see Michael Cain's story as one that illustrates both Eros ("the impulse within us that propels us to become close to others") and Thanatos ("the impulse that works towards the annihilation of all living things, including ourselves")? Where can you see Michael Cain influenced by Eros? by Thanatos? Write an essay that uses these distinctions, as Hedges explains them, to help us understand the shifting character of Michael Cain's experience and outlook.

CHRIS HEDGES
Eros and Thanatos

*I*N THIS PIECE, *Chris Hedges quotes Freud in order to suggest that war provides us with clarity and meaning and "fills our spiritual void." He also suggests that war might be a "false covenant." But this essay is more exploration than argument, engaging the struggle to comprehend war experience.*

In more than twenty years as a journalist, Chris Hedges has reported from some of the most war-torn regions of the world, including the Balkans and the Persian Gulf. In 2002, he was part of a New York Times *reporting team that won the Pulitzer Prize for Explanatory Reporting for their coverage of terrorism. "Eros and Thanatos" is an excerpt from his recent book,* War Is a Force That Gives Us Meaning *(2002). (The endnotes have been omitted.)*

> Beyond all this, the wish to be alone
> However the sky grows dark with invitation-cards
> However we follow the printed directions of sex
> However the family is photographed under the flagstaff—
> Beyond all this, the wish to be alone
>
> Beneath it all desire of oblivion runs
> Despite the artful tensions of the calendar,
> The life insurance, the tabled fertility rites,
> The costly aversion of the eyes from death—
> Beneath it all desire of oblivion runs.
>
> —PHILIP LARKIN

During the war in El Salvador I worked with a photographer who had a slew of close calls and then called it quits. He moved to Miami. He took pictures of tepid domestic stories for one of the newsweeklies. But life in Florida was flat, dull, uninteresting. He could not adjust and soon came back. From the moment he stepped off the plane it was clear he had returned to die. Just as there are some soldiers or war correspondents who seem to us immortal and whose loss comes as a sobering reminder that death has no favorites, there are also those in war who are locked in a grim embrace with death from which they cannot escape. He was frightening to behold, a walking corpse. He was shot a few months later through the back in a firefight. It took him less than a minute to die.

Sigmund Freud divided the forces in human nature between the Eros instinct, the impulse within us that propels us to become close to others, to

247

preserve and conserve, and the Thanatos, or death instinct, the impulse that works towards the annihilation of all living things, including ourselves. For Freud these forces were in eternal conflict. He was pessimistic about ever eradicating war. All human history, he argued, is a tug-of-war between these two instincts.

"The meaning of the evolution of civilization is no longer obscure to us," Freud wrote in *Civilization and Its Discontents*. "It must present the struggle between Eros and Death, between the instinct of life and the instinct of destruction, as it works itself out in the human species. This struggle is what all life essentially consists of."

We believe in the nobility and self-sacrifice demanded by war, especially when we are blinded by the narcotic of war. We discover in the communal struggle, the shared sense of meaning and purpose, a cause. War fills our spiritual void. I do not miss war, but I miss what it brought. I can never say I was happy in the midst of the fighting in El Salvador, or Bosnia, or Kosovo, but I had a sense of purpose, of calling. And this is a quality war shares with love, for we are, in love, also able to choose fealty and self-sacrifice over security.

Happiness is elusive and protean. And it is sterile when devoid of mean-   5
ing. But meaning, when it is set in the vast arena of war with its high stakes, its adrenaline-driven rushes, its bold sweeps and drama, is heartless and self-destructive. The initial selflessness of war mirrors that of love, the chief emotion war destroys. And this is what war often looks and feels like, at its inception: love. The ancient Greeks understood this strange relationship between love and death in wartime. When Achilles kills Penthesilea, the queen of the Amazons, in the Trojan War, he falls in love with her as she expires on the battlefield. Once she is dead, once love is dead, Achilles is doomed.

We are tempted to reduce life to a simple search for happiness. Happiness, however, withers if there is no meaning. The other temptation is to disavow the search for happiness in order to be faithful to that which provides meaning. But to live only for meaning—indifferent to all happiness—makes us fanatic, self-righteous, and cold. It leaves us cut off from our own humanity and the humanity of others. We must hope for grace, for our lives to be sustained by moments of meaning and happiness, both equally worthy of human communion.

During the first phases of the war in Kosovo I moved about the countryside in an armored jeep. I slept in wooden sheds and barns or on the floors of peasant homes. One bitterly cold winter morning I woke at first light in a hut. I watched the wind blow snow through the slates over my sleeping bag. I heard from local rebels about a Serb attack on a nearby village. The victims would be buried in a few hours. As so often happened, I had to leave my vehicle behind because of the extensive Serb roadblocks. I walked to the site on foot. It was, as usual, a perilous game of cat-and-mouse, one I had played for five years with the military in El Salvador. During the funeral Serb snipers opened fire on the crowd. We darted for cover. I filed my story, quickly typed out and sent over the satellite phone I carried in my backpack. Then I walked out. To record the atrocities, even as I knew the killings would continue, was my task. But by then it was destroying me. I felt profoundly alone.

In the wake of catastrophe, including the attacks of September 11, 2001, there is a desperate longing by all those affected to be in the physical presence of those they love. When a heavy shell landed in Sarajevo, or an assassination took place in the streets of San Salvador, or a suicide bomber blew himself up in Jerusalem, mothers, fathers, husbands, wives, and children pawed through the onlookers seeking physical reunification with those they loved. This love, like death, radiates outwards. It battles Thanatos at the very moment of death's sting. These two fundamental human impulses crash like breakers into each other. And however much beyond reason, there is always a feeling that love is not powerless or impotent as we had believed a few seconds before. Love alone fuses happiness and meaning. Love alone can fight the impulse that lures us toward self-destruction.

The question is whether America now courts death. We no longer seem chastened by war as we were in the years after the Vietnam War. The Bush administration has revised its "Nuclear Posture Review" to give us "more flexible nuclear strike capabilities." Washington wants "more options" with which to confront contingencies "immediate, potential, and unexpected," for smaller but more effective mega-tonnages to be deployed. This flirtation with weapons of mass destruction is a flirtation with our own obliteration, an embrace again of Thanatos.

There are few sanctuaries in war. But one is provided by couples in 10 love. They are not able to staunch the slaughter. They are often powerless and can themselves often become victims. But it was with them, seated around a wood stove, usually over a simple meal, that I found sanity and was reminded of what it means to be human. Love kept them grounded. It was to such couples that I retreated during the wars in Central America, the Middle East, and the Balkans. Love, when it is deep and sustained by two individuals, includes self-giving—often self-sacrifice—as well as desire. For the covenant of love is such that it recognizes both the fragility and the sanctity of the individual. It recognizes itself in the other. It alone can save us.

I did not sleep well in war. I could rarely recall my dreams, waking only to know that they had been harsh and violent. When I left the war zones, the nightmares descended on me like furies. I had horrible visions of war. I would dream of being in combat with my father or young son and unable to protect them. But I could sleep in the homes of such couples. Their love spread a protective blanket over us. It was able to blot out the war, although the lure of combat, the distant rattle of automatic weapons beckoned us back, and we always went.

Aristotle said that only two living entities are capable of complete solitude and complete separateness: God and beast. Because of this the most acute form of suffering for human beings is loneliness. The isolated individual can never be adequately human. And many of war's most fervent adherents are those atomized individuals who, before the war came, were profoundly alone and unloved. They found fulfillment in war, perhaps because it was the closest they came to love. If we do not acknowledge such an attraction, which is, in some ways, so akin to love, we can never combat it.

We are all tempted to honor false covenants of race, nationalism, class, and gender. They sometimes compete for our loyalty. War, of course, is often—maybe always—a false covenant. Sham covenants are based on exclusion rather than universality. All covenants that lack an adequate sense of humility and an acknowledgment of the sinfulness of our own cause are false covenants. The prophets warned us about them.

The cost of war is often measured in the physical destruction of a country's infrastructure, in the blasted buildings, factories, and bridges, in the number of dead. But probably worse is the psychological and spiritual toll. This cost takes generations to heal. It cripples and perverts whole societies, as Europe saw with the shattered veterans from World War I. But even for those who know the cost of war, it still holds out the promise of eradicating the thorny problems of life.

In the beginning war looks and feels like love. But unlike love it gives 15 nothing in return but an ever-deepening dependence, like all narcotics, on the road to self-destruction. It does not affirm but places upon us greater and greater demands. It destroys the outside world until it is hard to live outside war's grip. It takes a higher and higher dose to achieve any thrill. Finally, one ingests war only to remain numb. The world outside war becomes, as Freud wrote, "uncanny." The familiar becomes strangely unfamiliar—many who have been in war find this when they return home. The world we once understood and longed to return to stands before us as alien, strange, and beyond our grasp.

In 1999 the British journalist Anthony Loyd published *My War Gone By, I Miss It So*, a book about his twin addictions to heroin and to the war in Bosnia. His account illuminates the self-destruction impulse that is fed by war and drugs as well as the highs that propel many into combat. For Loyd, like Michael Herr,° war was the ultimate drug experience. It was the chance to taste extremes that would, he hoped, bring about a catharsis or obliteration. In times of peace, drugs are war's pale substitute. But drugs, in the end, cannot compare with the awful power and rush of battle. This was not why I went to war, but the twisted voyeurism and narcotic of war Loyd described attracted many to the battlefields and held them there.

Michael Herr (b. 1940): Vietnam war correspondent and the author of *Dispatches*; he collaborated on the screenplays for *Apocalypse Now* and *Full Metal Jacket*. [All notes are the Editors'.]

Deep down I was aware at the time that many of my motivations were fairly dark. On one level my sense of despair had been dispelled by therapy, yet on another it had not been replaced by either the desire for a future or the concept of one. I felt more aware of who I was, but that in itself—dominated as it was by sensations of fragmentation and isolation—filled me with no great hope, and in many ways only fueled an appetite for destruction.

There are those for whom violence is sexual. They carry their phallic weapons slung low at an angle toward the ground. Most of these fighters are militiamen, those who stay away from real combat, have little training or discipline, and primarily terrorize the weak and defenseless. And they look the part, often with tight black fatigues, wraparound sunglasses, and big ugly jeeps or cars with tinted windows. For them war is about empowerment. They have turned places like the Congo into Hobbesian° playgrounds.

These warlords rise to power with gangs who prey on minorities and the weak. When they are done, they turn on those they were fighting to protect. I was in the Bosnian Serb town of Banja Luka in the summer of 1995 not long after Serbian militias had driven out most of the ethnic Croats. Once the militias had finished looting the homes of the ethnic Croats and stealing their cars, they set up roadblocks to steal cars from the Serbs who lived in the city. The cars were then driven over the border into Serbia for sale.

When the mask of war slips away and the rot and corruption is exposed, when the addiction turns sour and rank, when the myth is exposed as a fraud, we feel soiled and spent. It is then that we sink into despair, a despair that can lead us to welcome death. This despair is more common than many expect.

In the 1973 Arab-Israeli war, almost a third of all Israeli casualties were 20 due to psychiatric causes, and the war lasted only a few weeks. A World War II study determined that after sixty days of continuous combat, 98 percent of all surviving soldiers will have become psychiatric casualties. They found that a common trait among the 2 percent who were able to endure sustained combat was a predisposition toward "aggressive psychopathic personalities."

During the war in El Salvador soldiers could serve in the army for three or four years or longer, virtually until they psychologically collapsed. In garrison towns commanders banned the sale of sedatives because of abuse by troops. In this war the emotionally maimed were common.

Edilberto Ayala, a nineteen-year-old Salvadoran army sergeant, spent five years fighting, and suddenly lost his vision after his unit walked into a rebel ambush. The rebels killed eleven soldiers in the firefight, including Ayala's closest friend. A couple dozen soldiers were wounded. He was unable to see again until he was placed in an army hospital.

Hobbesian: A reference to the philosophy of Thomas Hobbes (1588–1679), who viewed human beings as essentially self-interested and hence naturally prone to conflict with each other.

"I have these horrible headaches," he told me, sitting on the edge of his hospital bed. "There is shrapnel in my head. I keep telling the doctors to take it out."

But the doctors told me he had no head wounds.

J. Glenn Gray, a World War II combat veteran who taught philosophy 25 after the war, wrote: "Few of us can hold on to our real selves long enough to discover the real truths about ourselves and this whirling earth to which we cling. This is especially true of men in war. The great god Mars tries to blind us when we enter his realm, and when we leave he gives us a generous cup of the waters of Lethe° to drink."

This self-deception is powerful. It propels those in war forward. When it falls away, when we grasp war's reality, a universe collapses. Many of those who suddenly perceive the raw brutality and lie of war crumble into heaps.

Jon Steele, a cameraman who spent years in war zones, had a nervous breakdown in a crowded Heathrow Airport in 1994 after returning from Sarajevo, when for a moment he saw the cold reality of what he was doing, a reality that stripped away the self-righteous gloss and addiction to battle.

"I came back from Sarajevo," he said in an interview in the Israeli newspaper *Ha'aretz.* "We were in a place called Sniper's Alley, and I filmed a girl there who had been hit in the neck by a sniper's bullet. I filmed her dying in the ambulance and only after she was dead, I suddenly understood that the last thing she had seen was the reflection of the lens of the camera I was holding in front of her face. This wiped me out. I grabbed the camera and I started running down Snipers' Alley, filming at knee level the Bosnians running from place to place. I think that I broke down because I got things backward— I thought that because I was trying to be a hero and get exclusive pictures, people were dying."

War is necrophilia. And this necrophilia is central to soldiering, just as it is central to the makeup of suicide bombers and terrorists. The necrophilia is hidden under platitudes about duty or comradeship. It waits, especially in moments when we seem to have little to live for and no hope, or in moments when the intoxication of war is at its pitch, to be unleashed. When we spend long enough in war it comes to us as a kind of release, a fatal and seductive embrace that can consummate the long flirtation in war with our own destruction. The ancient Greeks had a word for such a drive. They called it *ekpyrosis*—to be consumed by a ball of fire. They used the word to describe heroes.

War throws us into a frenzy in which all human life, including our 30 own, seems secondary. The atavism of war creates us in war's image. In Chuck Sudetic's book *Blood and Vengeance* the former reporter for the *New York Times* writes of how he was eventually overpowered by the culture of death in wartime:

Lethe: A mythological river that the dead drink from in order to forget their life on earth.

I once walked through a town littered with the purple-and-yellow bodies of men and women and a few children, some shot to death, some with their heads torn off, and I felt nothing; I strolled around with a photographer, scratched notes, and lifted sheets covering the bodies of dead men to see if they had been castrated; I picked up a white flag from the ground near the twisted bodies of half a dozen men in civilian clothes who had been shot next to a wall, and then I carried the flag home and hung it above my desk. I once saw soldiers unload babies crushed to death in the back of a truck and immediately ran off to interview their mothers. I accidentally killed an eighteen-year-old man who raced in front of my car on a bike; his head was smashed; I held the door when they loaded him into the backseat of the automobile that carried him to the emergency room of Sarajevo's main hospital; I expressed my condolences to his father; then I got a tow back to my hotel, went to my room, and sent that day's story to New York.

In Milovan Djilas's memoir of the partisan war in Yugoslavia, he too wrote of the enticement death held for the combatants. He stood over the body of his comrade, the commander Sava Kovačević, and found that

> Dying did not seem terrible or unjust. This was the most extraordinary, the most exalted moment of my life: death did not seem strange or undesirable. That I restrained myself from charging blindly into the fray and death, was perhaps due to my sense of obligation to the troops, or to some comrade's reminder concerning the tasks at hand. In my memory I returned to those moments many times, with the same feeling of intimacy with death and desire for it, while I was in prison, particularly during my first incarceration.

War ascendant wipes out Eros. It wipes out all delicacy and tenderness. And this is why those in war swing from rank sentimentality to perversion, with little in between. Stray puppies, street kids, cats, anything that can be an object of affection for soldiers are adopted and pampered even in the midst of killing, the beating and torture of prisoners, and the razing of villages. If the pets die they are buried with elaborate rituals and little grave markers. But it is not only love, although the soldiers insist it feels like love. These animals, as well as the young waifs who collect around military units, are total dependents. They pay homage to the absolute power above them. Indeed, it may be that at times they please or they die.

In the midst of slaughter the only choice is often between hate and lust. Human beings become objects, objects to extinguish or to provide carnal gratification. The widespread casual and frenetic sex in wartime often crosses the line into perversion and violence. It exposes the vast moral void. When life becomes worth nothing, when one is not sure of survival, when a society is ruled by fear, there often seems only death or fleeting, carnal pleasure. This is why Lady Ann in Shakespeare's *Richard III* goes to Richard's bed. She sleeps with Richard because her moral universe has been destroyed. This kind of love is the product of the impersonal violence of war.

In war we may deform ourselves, our essence, by subverting passion, loyalty, and love to duty. Perhaps one could argue that this is why Virgil's Aeneas appears so woefully unhappy in *The Aeneid.* Despite his love for Dido he must leave her to found the empire in Italy: *hic amor, haec patria est*—there is my love, there my country. Yet in moments of extremity to make a moral choice, to defy war's enticement, to defend love, can be self-destructive. Shakespeare shows it in Antony in *Antony and Cleopatra*, as he does in the final defeat of Coriolanus. Antony embraces love and passion and loses empire. Like Dido, by giving himself to love, he dooms his empire and cuts his life short. He is no match for Octavius's bloodless thirst for power.

In the rise to power we become smaller, power absorbs us, and once 35 power is attained we are often its pawn. As in *Richard III*, the all-powerful prince can swiftly fall prey to the forces he thought he had harnessed. So too in war. Shakespeare's Lear and Richard III gain knowledge only as they are pushed down the ladder, as they are stripped of all illusions. Love may not always triumph, but it keeps us human. It offers the only chance to escape from the contagion of war. Perhaps it is the only antidote. And there are times when remaining human is the only victory possible.

Kurt Schork, a Reuters correspondent who spent a decade in war zones before being killed in an ambush in Sierra Leone, wrote a story out of Sarajevo about Bosko Brckić, a Serb, and Admira Ismić, a Muslim, both twenty-five. They had been sweethearts since high school. The lovers tried to flee the besieged city in May 1993, a year after the war started, but were gunned down by Serb snipers.

They died together on the banks of Sarajevo's Miljacka River. Bosko fell dead instantly. Admira was badly wounded. She crawled over and hugged him. She expired in his arms. Bosko lay face-down on the pavement, his right arm bent awkwardly behind him. Admira lay next to him, her left arm across his back. Another corpse, that of a man shot five months earlier, lay decomposing nearby.

Their bodies lay there for four days, sprawled near the Vrbana bridge, a pitted wasteland of shell-blasted rubble, downed tree branches, and dangling power lines, before they were recovered. .

They are buried together, under a heart-shaped headstone, in the Lion's Cemetery for the victims of the war. Kurt is buried next to them. Kurt, brilliant, courageous, and driven, had been unable to break free from the addiction of war. His entrapment, his long flirtation with Thanatos, was never mentioned at the memorial service staged for him in Washington by the Reuters bureaucrats he did not respect. Everyone tiptoed around it. But those of us who knew him understood that he had been consumed by his addiction. I had worked with Kurt for ten years, starting in northern Iraq. Literate, funny—it seems the brave are often funny—he and I passed books back and forth in our struggle to make sense of the madness around us. His loss was a hole that will never be filled.

I flew to Sarajevo and met the British filmmaker Dan Reed. It was an 40 overcast November day. We stood over the grave and downed a pint of whiskey. Dan lit a candle. I recited a poem the Roman lyric poet Catullus had written to honor his dead brother.

> By strangers' coasts and waters, many days at sea,
> I come here for the rites of your unworlding,
> Bringing for you, the dead, these last gifts of the living
> And my words — vain sounds for the man of dust.
> Alas, my brother,
> You have been taken from me. You have been taken from me,
> By cold chance turned a shadow, and my pain.
> Here are the foods of the old ceremony, appointed
> Long ago for the starvelings under the earth:
> Take them: your brother's tears have made them wet; and take
> Into eternity my hail and my farewell.

It was there, among a few thousand war dead, that Kurt belonged. He died because he could not free himself from war, from the death impulse. He was in Africa searching for new highs. He was trying to replicate what he had found in Sarajevo. But he could not. War could never be new again. I had tried for years after El Salvador to make it come back. It was never the same. Kurt had been in East Timor and Chechnya. Sierra Leone, I was sure, meant little to him. Miguel Gil Morano, a Spanish cameraman, who had also covered the wars in Bosnia and Kosovo, died with him. They were, like all who do not let go, consumed by a ball of fire. But they lit the fuse. And they would be the first to admit it.

Viktor Frankl, in *Man's Search for Meaning,* writes of the grim battle between love and Thanatos in Auschwitz. He recalls being on a work detail, freezing in the blast of the Polish winter, when he began to think about his wife, who had already been gassed, although he did not know this at the time.

> A thought transfixed me: for the first time in my life I saw the truth
> as it is set into song by so many poets, proclaimed as the final wisdom
> by so many thinkers. The truth — that love is the ultimate and the
> highest goal to which man can aspire. Then I grasped the meaning of
> the greatest secret that human poetry and human thought and belief
> have to impart: the salvation of man is through love and in love.

The Thanatos instinct is a drive toward suicide, individual and collective. War celebrates only power — and we come to believe in wartime that it is the only real form of power. It preys on our most primal and savage impulses. It allows us to do what peacetime society forbids or restrains us from doing. It allows us to kill. However much soldiers regret killing once it is finished, however much they spend their lives trying to cope with the experience, the act itself, fueled by fear, excitement, the pull of the crowd, and the godlike exhilaration of destroying, is often thrilling.

I have watched fighters in El Salvador, Nicaragua, Guatemala, the Sudan, the Punjab, Iraq, Bosnia, and Kosovo enter villages, tense, exhausted, wary of ambushes, with the fear and tension that comes from combat, and begin to shoot at random. Flames soon lick up from houses. Discipline, if there was any, disintegrates. Items are looted, civilians are battered with rifle butts, units fall apart, and the violence directed toward unarmed men, women, and children grows as it feeds on itself. The eyes of the soldiers who carry this orgy of death are crazed. They speak only in guttural shouts. They are high on the power to spare lives or take them, the divine power to destroy. And they are indeed, for a moment, gods swatting down powerless human beings like flies. The lust for violence, the freedom to eradicate the world around them, even human lives, is seductive. And the line that divides us, who would like to see ourselves as civilized and compassionate, from such communal barbarity is razor thin. In wartime it often seems to matter little where one came from or how well-schooled and moral one was before the war began. The frenzy of the crowd is overpowering.

Bob Kerrey, a former United States senator who won the Medal of 45 Honor for his military service in Vietnam, once led a combat mission that caused the deaths of thirteen to twenty unarmed civilians, most of them women and children. When this story was first revealed in the spring of 2001, there was, among an unknowing public, an expression of shock and an effort to explain such behavior. But the revelation was, rather than an anomaly, an example of how most wars are fought. It was a glimpse into the reality of war that many in the public, anxious not to see war's sordid nature, worked hard to shut. Kerrey, in a speech at the Virginia Military Institute soon after the incident was made public, said: "I have been haunted by it for thirty-two years."

The raid, which took place in 1969, saw Kerrey, then a twenty-five-year-old lieutenant who had arrived in Vietnam a month earlier, lead a group of six navy SEALS—the informal name for sea-air-land units—behind enemy lines. They hoped to capture a Vietcong leader who was reported to be holding a meeting that night. The unit was ferried to the spot by boat. They encountered a thatched hut and killed those inside. There were, those in the unit said, women inside. They ran into more huts. More women and children were killed, although Kerrey says he and his men came under fire. "The thing that I will remember until the day I die is walking in and finding, I don't know, fourteen or so, I don't even know what the number was, women and children who were dead," he told the *New York Times Magazine*.

In an interview with the *Wall Street Journal*, Kerrey said, "This is killing me. I'm tired of people describing me as a hero and holding this inside."

The military histories—which tell little of war's reality—crowd out the wrenching tales by the emotionally maimed. Each generation again responds to war as innocents. Each generation discovers its own disillusionment—often after a terrible price. The myth of war and the drug of war wait to be tasted. The mythical heroes of the past loom over us. Those who can tell us the truth are silenced or prefer to forget. The state needs the myth, as much as it needs its soldiers and its machines of war, to survive.

To say the least, killing is nearly always a sordid affair. Those who carry such memories do so with difficulty, even when the cause seems just. Moreover, those who are killed do not die the clean death we see on television or film. They die messy, disturbing deaths that often plague the killers. And the bodies of the newly slain retain a disquieting power. The rows of impersonal dead, stacked like firewood one next to the other, draped on roadsides, twisted into strange, often grimly humorous shapes, speak. I have looked into the open eyes of dead men and wished them shut, for they seemed to beckon me into the underworld. You will be me, the eyes call out, see what you will become. Even hardened soldiers drape cloth over such faces or reach out and push the eyelids shut. The eyes of the dead are windows into a world we fear.

Goodbye Darkness, William Manchester's memoir of the Pacific war in 50 World War II, has an unvarnished account of what it feels like to shoot another man. Nothing is more sickening in war than watching human lives get snuffed out. Nothing haunts you more. And it is never, as outsiders think, clean or easy or neat. Killing is a dirty business, more like butchering animals.

Manchester describes, in the opening pages of his memoir, the only time he shot a Japanese soldier he could see.

> Not only was he the first Japanese soldier I had ever shot at; he was the only one I had seen at close quarters. He was a robin-fat, moon-faced, roly-poly little man with his thick, stubby, trunk-like legs sheathed in faded khaki puttees and the rest of him squeezed into a uniform that was much too tight. Unlike me, he was wearing a tin hat, dressed to kill. But I was quite safe from him. His Arisaka rifle was strapped on in a sniper's harness, and though he had heard me, and was trying to turn toward me, the harness sling had him trapped. He couldn't disentangle himself from it. His eyes were rolling in panic. Realizing that he couldn't extricate his arms and defend himself, he was backing toward a corner with a curious, crablike motion.
>
> My first shot had missed him, embedding itself in the straw wall, but the second caught him dead-on in the femoral artery. His left thigh blossomed, swiftly turning to mush. A wave of blood gushed from the wound; then another boiled out, sheeting across his legs, pooling on the earthen floor. Mutely he looked down at it. He dipped a hand in it and listlessly smeared his cheek red. His shoulders gave a little spasmodic jerk, as though someone had whacked him on the back; then he emitted a tremendous, raspy fart, slumped down, and died. I kept firing, wasting government property. Already I thought I detected the dark brown effluvium of the freshly slain, a sour, pervasive emanation which is different from anything you have known. Yet seeing death at this range, like smelling it, requires no previous

experience. You instantly recognize it, the spastic convulsion and the rattle, which in his case was not loud, but deprecating and conciliatory, like the manners of the civilian Japanese. He continued to sink until he reached the earthen floor. His eyes glazed over. Almost immediately a fly landed on his left eyeball. It was joined by another. I don't know how long I stood there staring. I knew from previous combat what lay ahead for the corpse. It would swell, the bloat, bursting out of the uniform. Then the face would turn from yellow to red, to purple, to green, to black. My father's account of the Argonne had omitted certain vital facts. A feeling of disgust and self-hatred clotted darkly in my throat, gagging me.

Jerking my head to shake off the stupor, I slipped a new, fully loaded magazine into the butt of my .45. Then I began to tremble, and next to shake, all over. I sobbed, in a voice still grainy with fear: "I'm sorry." Then I threw up all over myself. I recognized the half-digested C-ration beans dribbling down my front, smelled the vomit above the cordite. At the same time I noticed another odor; I had urinated in my skivvies. I pondered fleetly why our excretions become so loathsome the instant they leave the body. Then Barney burst in on me, his carbine at the ready, his face gray, as though he, not I, had just become a partner in the firm of death. He ran over to the Nip's body, grabbed its stacking swivel—its neck—and let go, satisfied that it was a cadaver. I marveled at his courage; I couldn't have taken a step toward that corner. He approached me and then backed away in revulsion, from my foul stench. He said: "Slim, you stink." I said nothing. I knew I had become a thing of tears and twitchings and dirtied pants. I remember wondering dumbly: Is that what they mean by "conspicuous gallantry"?

There is among many who fight in war a sense of shame, one that is made worse by the patriotic drivel used to justify the act of killing in war. Those who seek meaning in patriotism do not want to hear the truth of war, wary of bursting the bubble. The tensions between those who were there and those who were not, those who refuse to let go of the myth and those who know it to be a lie feed into the dislocation and malaise after war. In the end, neither side cares to speak to the other. The shame and alienation of combat soldiers, coupled with the indifference to the truth of war by those who were not there, reduces many societies to silence. It seems better to forget.

"I, too, belong to this species," J. Glenn Gray wrote. "I am ashamed not only of my own deeds, not only of my nation's deeds, but of human deeds as well. I am ashamed to be a man."

When Ernie Pyle, the American war correspondent in World War II, was killed on the Pacific island of Ie Shima in 1945, a rough draft of a column was found on his body. He was preparing it for release upon the end of the war in Europe. He had done much to promote the myth of the warrior and the heroism of soldiering, but by the end he seemed to tire of it all.

But there are many of the living who have had burned into their brains forever the unnatural sight of cold dead men scattered over the hillsides and in the ditches along the high rows of hedge throughout the world.

Dead men by mass production—in one country after another—month after month and year after year. Dead men in winter and dead men in summer.

Dead men in such familiar promiscuity that they become monotonous.

Dead men in such monstrous infinity that you come almost to hate them. These are the things that you at home need not even try to understand. To you at home they are columns of figures, or he is a near one who went away and just didn't come back. You didn't see him lying so grotesque and pasty beside the gravel road in France.

We saw him, saw him by the multiple thousands. That's the difference.

Discarded veterans are never a pretty sight. They are troubled and some 55 physically maimed. They often feel betrayed, misunderstood and alone. It is hard to integrate again into peacetime society. Many are shunted aside, left to nuture their resentment and pain.

I found Kazem Ahangaron in Naushahr, on Iran's Caspian coast, not long after the end of the eight-year war with Iraq. He was once a disciple of war. But the violence he turned on Iraqi soldiers he had turned against himself.

"I tried to do it with pills, Valium and depressants, mostly," the gaunt twenty-eight-year-old veteran said, seated on a white pebble beach. "They pumped my stomach out at the hospital. But twelve of my friends have killed themselves this year."

The Caspian resort city, skirted by jagged mountains and towering fir trees, was once the summer capital of the shah. Its faded yet elegant white-washed villas belonged to the officials of the monarchy before the 1979 Islamic revolution.

When I visited the seedy remains of Naushahr it had one of the highest rates of suicides in Iran, most by unemployed and disillusioned veterans of the war with Iraq. Figures in Iran are hard to come by and often unreliable, but doctors in the city told me that there had been four hundred suicides of the town's eighty thousand people in the past year. The men, out of work and alienated from the puritanical rule of the clerics, were unable to find a home or marry. They looked back on the raw carnage of the war with bitterness and ahead with despair. Drugs took the place of battle. Suicide took the place of heroic death.

Many of the suicides in Naushahr were caused by Phostoxin, small 60 phosphate tablets known as "rice pills" that were used in granaries to kill insects. The tablets would paralyze the nervous system and send the young men into a coma. The city did not have a psychiatrist. Many rice merchants, in an effort to curb the suicides, had stopped selling the German-made tablets.

The Islamic clerics who took over Iran sought to reshape the country into a nation of devout Muslims. They spurned the decadence of the West, including what the clerics condemned as the West's loose sexual mores, drug use, and thirst for sensual gratification.

Naushahr's dance halls and bars had been turned over to shopkeepers or boarded over. The beaches were segregated by sex and patrolled by squads of morality police. At the crest of a hill, the lavish Chinese Horse casino, which once glittered through the night like a huge ocean liner, lay in rubble.

But rather than build a new generation of believers, the fundamentalist leaders created a generation of men who were alienated and infected with the hopeless despair of war and violence.

"Life has become a charade," Ahangaron said. "We carry out one life in public and another in private."

The war, once, captured their imaginations. But the years of slaughter 65 had left them listless and addicted to hashish and opium. Many were volunteers who believed that they were not only defending their nation but helping to create a new society in the war with Iraq. The disillusionment was total.

"Iran's best wrestlers come from Naushahr," said Ramazan Gharib, a thirty-five-year-old veteran, "and the army recruiters, very cleverly, used this. When the war started we were all exhorted to show our strength, our manliness, and we went down to enlist."

But the front lines, where Iranian units were butchered en masse as they tried to sweep in human waves across the mud flats, held little glory. And many who survived the war, which began in 1980 and ended in 1988, returned changed and unsettled by the senseless carnage.

The town's leading cleric, Mohammed Masha Yekhi, had called on young people to choose life rather than suicide. He said he would not allow those who committed suicide a Muslim burial.

I sat one morning with two war veterans on the porch of a dilapidated villa overlooking the Caspian. The men, who fished and used their boats to take people water skiing, were slumped in wicker chairs drinking cups of sweet tea.

The two men told me that they had easy access to the drugs, homemade 70 beer, and grain alcohol that was sold on the beach. They smuggled out tins of caviar from the state-run packaging plant and traded it with Russian sailors, anchored offshore, for vodka. For a price they guided couples to secluded beaches, where women could swim in bathing suits and embrace their boyfriends, activities the clerics had forbidden. The money they earned was swallowed by their addiction.

"I will never be normal again," said one of the men, who spent twenty-three months at the front. "I am nervous. I can't control my anger. If anything disturbs me, like a minor car accident, I explode."

The second man, who was a lieutenant in the war, looked out over the water and said in a monotone, "My battalion was ordered across the flats early one morning. Within a couple of hours four hundred soldiers were dead and hundreds more wounded. It was a stupid, useless waste. When we got back they called us traitors."

In the shade of a stone wall, just in front of the villa, with its collection of drooping cots and dirty shag carpets, a young man, dressed in a black shirt and pants, stared blankly at the water.

"He comes here every day," one of the veterans said. "He just finished his army service, but he has no job and nowhere to go. He smokes hash and watches the surf."

The men said they lived on the margins of existence, sometimes sleeping 75 under grass-roofed huts. The pittance the men earned, the psychological burdens they bore, and their inability to afford a place to live had crushed them.

"All we have left is the sea," a former officer said, "and the sea is what keeps us here. But then one day even the sea isn't enough."

As long as we think abstractly, as long as we find in patriotism and the exuberance of war our fulfillment, we will never understand those who do battle against us, or how we are perceived by them, or finally those who do battle for us and how we should respond to it all. We will never discover who we are. We will fail to confront the capacity we all have for violence. And we will court our own extermination. By accepting the facile cliché that the battle under way against terrorism is a battle against evil, by easily branding those who fight us as the barbarians, we, like them, refuse to acknowledge our own culpability. We ignore real injustices that have led many of those arrayed against us to their rage and despair.

Late one night, unable to sleep during the war in El Salvador, I picked up Shakespeare's *Macbeth*. It was not a calculated decision. I had come that day from a village where about a dozen people had been murdered by the death squads, their thumbs tied behind their backs with wire and their throats slit.

I had read the play before, but in my other life as a student. A thirst for power at the cost of human life was no longer an abstraction to me. It was part of my universe.

I came upon Macduff's wife's speech made when the murderers, sent 80 by Macbeth, arrive to kill her and her small children: "Whither should I fly?" she asks,

> I have done no harm. But I remember now
> I am in this earthly world—where to do harm
> Is often laudable, to do good sometime
> Accounted dangerous folly.

Those words seized me like furies and cried out for the dead I had seen lined up that day in a dusty market square, the dead I have seen since, the dead, including the two thousand children who were killed in Sarajevo. The words cried out for those whom I would see later in unmarked mass graves in Bosnia, Kosovo, Iraq, the Sudan, Algeria, El Salvador, the dead who are my own, who carried notebooks, cameras, and a vanquished idealism and sad addiction into war and never returned. Of course resistance is usually folly, of course power exercised with ruthlessness will win, of course force easily snuffs out gentle people, the compassionate, and the decent. A repentant Lear, who was unable to love because of his thirst for power and self-adulation acknowledges this in the final moments of the play.

Shakespeare celebrates, at his best, this magnificence of failure. When we view our lives honestly from the inside we are all failures, all sinners, all in need of forgiveness. Shakespeare lays bare the myths that blind and deform our souls. He understands that the world of the flesh and the world of the spirit are indivisible, that they coexist in a paradox, ever present.

Shakespeare reminds us that though we may not do what we want, we are responsible for our lives. It does not matter what has been made of us; what matters is what we ourselves make of what has been done to us.

I returned from the Balkans to America in the fall of 1998, to a Nieman Fellowship at Harvard, after fifteen years abroad mostly reporting wars. I no longer had the emotional and physical resilience of youth. The curator of the Nieman program, Bill Kovach, suggested that I see James O. Freedman, the former president of Dartmouth, for advice on how to spend the year. Freedman recommended the classics and urged me to take Greek or Latin.

I had studied Greek in seminary so I opted for Latin. Of course, there is 85 nothing sacred, or necessarily redeeming, about ancient texts. The German and Italian fascists used and misused classical literature, especially Virgil's *Aeneid*, in their propaganda. The Greeks and Romans embraced magic, slavery, the subjugation of women, racial triumphalism, animal sacrifice, and infanticide. The Roman emperors staged elaborate reenactments of battles in and outside the arena that saw hundreds and at times thousands of prisoners and slaves maimed and killed for sport. At lunchtime, in between shows, they publicly executed prisoners. Any democratic participation was the prerogative of male citizens and was snuffed out for long periods by tyrants and near-constant warfare.

But the classics offer a continuum with Western literature, architecture, art, and political systems. Our country's past, our political and social philosophy, and our intellectual achievements and spiritual struggles cannot be connected without great holes in the fabric, and failures of understanding, if we are not conversant in the classics.

"All literature, all philosophical treaties, all the voices of antiquity," Cicero wrote, "are full of examples for imitation, which would all lie unseen in darkness without the light of literature." Thucydides, knowing that Athens was doomed in the war with Sparta, consoled himself with the belief that his city's artistic and intellectual achievements would in the coming centuries overshadow raw Spartan militarism. Beauty and knowledge could, ultimately, triumph over power.

As my year at Harvard progressed, I devoured the classical authors but wasn't always as sure about taking on a dead language. One of my favorite professors, Kathleen Coleman, stopped me one morning and announced that I needed a purpose behind my slog through Latin. Once a week, she instructed, I would appear at her office prepared to do a translation of a poem by Catullus or passage from Virgil. I had never read Catullus, but came to love him.

Carrying my books, I retreated in the afternoons to the Smyth Classical Library within Widener Library, with its huge oak tables and sagging leather chairs. My fondest memories revolve around this sanctuary with its well-thumbed volumes, noisy heating system, and glass cases with dusty displays of items like Roman table legs. I was freed to step outside myself, to struggle with questions the cant of modern culture often allows us to ignore.

All idylls must end. Mine was shattered on March 24, 1999, when 90 NATO began its bombing of Kosovo. I had come to Cambridge from Kosovo. Kosovar Albanians I had known for three years were now missing or found dead along roadsides. I slept little. I was chained to the news reports. My translator in Kosovo, Shukrije Gashi, a poet, vanished. (I returned to Kosovo that summer to find her family was searching for her in mass graves.) The horrors of Kosovo were abstractions to most people in Cambridge. I held a communion, in my final weeks at Harvard, with the long dead.

I had memorized a few poems by Catullus and parts of *The Aeneid*. I woke one morning well before dawn, haunted by a Catullus poem written to Calvus, whose lover Quintilia had died. Calvus had abandoned her, as I felt I had abandoned friends in Kosovo and an array of other conflicts. His grief was mingled with his guilt. In the end, these words give me a balm to my grief, a momentary solace, a little understanding:

> If anything welcome or pleasing, Calvus, can be felt
> by silent tombs in answer to our grief,
> from that painful longing in which we renew old loves
> and weep for friendships we once cast away,
> Surely Quintilia does not lament her early death
> as much as she rejoices in your love.

To survive as a human being is possible only through love. And, when Thanatos is ascendant, the instinct must be to reach out to those we love, to see in them all the divinity, pity, and pathos of the human. And to recognize love in the lives of others—even those with whom we are in conflict—love that is like our own. It does not mean we will avoid war or death. It does not mean that we as distinct individuals will survive. But love, in its mystery, has its own power. It alone gives us meaning that endures. It alone allows us to embrace and cherish life. Love has power both to resist in our nature what we know we must resist, and to affirm what we know we must affirm. And love, as the poets remind us, is eternal.

WHAT DOES HE SAY?

1. As you read, put a straight line in the margin wherever you see Hedges identifying war's attractions. Put a wiggly line in the margin wherever you see the essay identifying war's dangerous or scary aspects.

2. What is "Eros," as you understand it in this essay? Write a paragraph explaining it. Then do the same thing for "Thanatos."

3. Identify one paragraph that, no matter how often you read it, you're still unsure of its meaning. Then identify another paragraph that you fully understand. Be ready to discuss each of these.

4. Write a paragraph that explains why you think—or do not think—that Chris Hedges is a person who can be trusted as an authority. Does his essay carry persuasive weight for you?

5. Identify two assertions that Hedges's essay makes powerfully persuasive. How does the essay do that?

WHAT DO YOU THINK?

6. Consider "Eros and Thanatos" in terms of *logos, ethos,* and *pathos* (pp. 9–10). What means of persuasion does this essay use? Which of these seem to you successful or powerful and which less so? Write an essay that makes this analysis, and make sure that it quotes sections of "Eros and Thanatos" in order to illustrate your points.

7. Write an essay that explains your own reactions to reading and thinking about "Eros and Thanatos." Organize this essay in terms of "your thinking about war before reading the essay" and "your thoughts about war and about what Hedges has to say." Note that we are not assuming Hedges will entirely change your mind. We do assume that reading his essay will have some effects.

8. Focus on one section of Hedges's essay, explain it carefully, quote it as necessary, and then discuss why and how you see it as a significant and important section.

WHAT WOULD THEY SAY?

9. Read "Eros and Thanatos" together with George Orwell's "Politics and the English Language" (p. 461). What reactions do you believe Orwell would have to Hedges's essay?

10. Consider "Eros and Thanatos" together with Andre Dubus's "Giving Up the Gun" (p. 180). How would the authors react to each other's work? Add Michael Levin's "The Case for Torture" (p. 201) into the mix. Would these three essayists tend to agree with each other? Why or why not?

11. Read Jane Goodall's "Compassion and Love" (p. 265). Why or how does that essay change your understanding of Hedges's essay? How does it change your overall response to Hedges's analysis?

JANE GOODALL
Compassion and Love

CHRIS HEDGES'S PIECE (p. 247) ends by affirming love as the one force strong enough to overcome human tendencies toward violence. Here, Jane Goodall (b. 1934) comes to similar conclusions via very different observations—from her forty-plus years of observing chimpanzees in Africa. The world's foremost authority on chimpanzees and a former United Nations Messenger of Peace, Goodall is the author of several books, including In the Shadow of Man *(1971) and* Reason for Hope *(2000), from which "Compassion and Love" is taken.*

From the earliest years at Gombe I had been fascinated and delighted by the friendly and nurturing behavior that I observed so often among the chimpanzees. Peaceful interactions within a community are seen much more often than aggressive ones. Indeed, for hours, even days, one can follow a small group of chimps and see no aggression at all. Of course, these chimpanzees are, as we have seen, capable of violence and brutality. But fights between members of the same community seldom last more than a few seconds and rarely result in wounding. For the most part, relationships between the members of a community are relaxed and friendly, and we see frequent expressions of caring, helping, compassion, altruism, and most definitely a form of love.

Chimpanzees are intensely physical. When friends meet, after a separation, they may embrace and kiss each other. When they are fearful or suddenly terribly excited they reach out to touch each other—sometimes they show a whole orgy of contact-seeking behaviors, embracing, pressing open mouths upon each other, patting each other, holding hands. Friendships are maintained and poor relationships improved by the most important of all friendly behaviors—social grooming. Grooming enables adult chimpanzees to spend long hours in friendly, relaxed physical contact. A session may last more than an hour as the participants work their way, with soothing movements of their fingers, over every inch of each other's bodies. Grooming is used to calm tense or nervous companions, and mothers often quiet restless or distressed infants in the same way. And when chimps play, there is a lot of body contact as they tickle each other, and roll over and over in bouts of rough-and-tumble wrestling matches. Loud chuckles of chimpanzee laughter accompany these joyous play sessions so that even fully adult group members are sometimes compelled to join in.

As the years passed at Gombe and we learned more about who was related to whom in the chimpanzees' complex society it became obvious that ties between family members were particularly strong and enduring, and not just between mothers and their offspring, but also between siblings. I learned a great deal from the hours I spent with old Flo and her family. I watched as she not only rushed to the defense of her juvenile offspring, Flint and Fifi, but also tried to help her adult sons, Figan and Faben. When Flint was born, Fifi soon became utterly preoccupied with the new baby. As soon as she was allowed, she played with him, groomed him, and carried him around. Indeed, she became a real help to her mother. Eventually I realized that all young chimpanzees are fascinated and delighted by new arrivals in their families, and that these sibling relationships persist over many years. Brothers become close friends as they mature and often then become allies, protecting each other in social conflicts or when under attack by other individuals.

These sibling bonds are adaptive in many ways. On one occasion, nine-year-old Pom, leading her family along a forest trail, suddenly saw a big snake coiled up. Uttering a soft call of concern she rushed up a tree. But little brother Prof, still a bit unsteady on his feet at three years old, ignored her warning. Perhaps he did not understand its meaning or simply did not hear it. As he got closer and closer to the snake Pom's hair bristled with alarm, and she grinned hugely in fear. Suddenly, as though she couldn't bear it anymore, she rushed down to Prof, gathered him up, and climbed back up her tree.

One most moving story is about orphan Mel and Spindle, his adolescent 5 protector. Mel was three and a quarter years old when his mother died. He had no elder brother or sister to adopt him. To our amazement (for we had thought he would die), he was adopted by twelve-year-old Spindle. Although all members of the Gombe chimpanzee population have a few genes in common, Spindle was certainly not closely related to Mel. Nevertheless, as the weeks went by, the two became inseparable. Spindle waited for Mel during travel; he permitted the infant to ride on his back, even allowed him to cling beneath, as a mother carries her baby, when Mel was frightened or when it was raining. Most remarkably, if Mel got too close to the big males during social excitement when inhibitions are sometimes swept aside, Spindle would hurry to remove his small charge from danger even though this usually meant he was buffeted himself. For a whole year this close relationship endured, and there can be no doubt that Spindle saved Mel's life. Why did Spindle act that way, burdening himself with the care of a small, sickly youngster who was not even a close relative? Probably we shall never know, but it is interesting to reflect that during the epidemic that claimed Mel's mother, Spindle's ancient mother died also. A typical twelve-year-old male chimpanzee, though perfectly able to fend for himself, will continue to spend much time with his mother, especially if he has been through a stressful time with the adult males, or been hurt in a fight. Is it possible that Spindle's loss of his mother left an empty space in his life? And that the close contact with a small dependent youngster helped to fill that space? Or did Spindle experience an emotion similar to that which we call compassion? Perhaps he felt a mixture of both.

Chimpanzees in zoos are often kept in enclosures surrounded or partially surrounded by water-filled moats. Since they do not swim, death by drowning has been a sadly frequent mishap. But almost always one or more of the victim's companions have attempted to rescue the individual in difficulties. There are a number of accounts of heroic rescues, or rescue attempts. In one instance an adult male lost his life as he tried to rescue a drowning infant who was not his own.

Evolutionary biologists do not count the helping of family members as true altruism. Your kin all share, to a greater or lesser extent, some of the same genes as yourself. So your action, they argue, is just a way of ensuring that as many of those precious genes as possible are preserved. Even if you lose your life through some helping act, your mother or sibling or child who has been saved will ensure that your own genes are still represented in future generations. Thus your behavior can still be seen as fundamentally selfish. And what if you help an individual who is not related to you? This is explained as an example of "reciprocal altruism"—help your companion today in the expectation that he will help you tomorrow. This sociobiological theory, while helpful in understanding the basic mechanism of the evolutionary process, tends to be dangerously reductionist when used as the sole explanation of human—or chimpanzee—behavior. After all, whilst our biological nature and instincts can hardly be denied, we are, and have been for thousands of years, caught up in cultural evolution as well. We do things which are sometimes quite unrelated to any hope for genetic survival in the future. Even Richard Dawkins,° in an interview in the *London Times Magazine*, said, "Most of us, if we see somebody in great distress, weeping—we will go and put an arm around them and try to console them. It's a thing I have an overwhelming impulse to do…and so we know that we can rise above our Darwinian past." When he was asked how this could be, he smiled and said he didn't know. But I gradually came to see that a simple explanation presents itself.

Patterns of caring and helping and reassurance evolved, over thousands of years, in the context of the mother–child and family relationships. In this context they are clearly beneficial to the well-being of the living individuals as well as in the evolutionary sense. So these behaviors have become ever more firmly embedded in the genetic endowment of chimpanzees (and other higher, social animals). And so we would expect an individual who is constantly interacting with other familiar companions—with whom he plays, grooms, travels, and feeds and with whom he forms close relationships—to treat them, at least sometimes, as honorary family members. Obviously, then, he is likely to respond to the distress or pleas of these honorary family members as well as those of his blood relations. In other words, a close but not related companion may be treated as if he or she were biological kin.

Compassion and self-sacrifice are highly valued qualities in many human cultures. If we know that another person, particularly a close personal friend or relative, is suffering, we become upset. Only by doing something,

---

Richard Dawkins (b. 1941): Oxford University biologist particularly interested in genetics and evolution. [All notes are the Editors'.]

by helping (or trying to help) can we alleviate our own discomfort. We may also feel the need to help people we do not know at all. We send money, or clothing, or medical equipment to earthquake victims, refugees, or other suffering people in all corners of the globe, once their plight has been brought to our attention. Do we do these things so that others will applaud our virtuous behavior? Or because the sight of starving children or homeless refugees evokes in us feelings of pity which make us terribly uncomfortable, feelings of guilt because we know we have so much, and they so little?

If our motivation to perform charitable acts is simply to advance our so-   10
cial standing, or to lessen our inner discomfort, should we not conclude that our action, in the final analysis, is nothing more than selfish? Some might argue thus—and in some cases it could be true. But I believe it is wrong—dangerous even—to accept reductionistic arguments of this sort that denigrate all that is most truly noble in our species. History resounds with tales of extraordinarily inspirational acts of courage and self-sacrifice. Good heavens!—the very fact that we can feel distressed by the plight of people we have never met says it all for me. It is, surely, remarkable and heartwarming that we can empathize, and feel truly saddened, when we hear of a child brain-damaged in an accident; an elderly couple losing their life savings to a thief; a family dog stolen and sold to a medical research lab and traced too late to be saved.

So here we are, the human ape, half sinner, half saint, with two opposing tendencies inherited from our ancient past pulling us now toward violence, now toward compassion and love. Are we, forever, to be torn in two different directions, cruel in one instance, kind the next? Or do we have the ability to control these tendencies, choosing the direction we wish to go? During the early 1970s these were the questions that gripped me. Yet here again, my observations of the apes offered at least a glimmer of an answer.

Thus chimpanzees, I realized, although freer to act the way they feel than we are, are not entirely uninhibited. As they get older, they usually give up the frustrated tantrums of childhood, although they may let off steam by charging through the undergrowth, sometimes slapping a bystander who gets in the way. An outburst of swearing and table thumping can sometimes do the same for humans. Chimpanzees have excellent mechanisms for defusing tense situations. Thus the victim in a fight, even though he or she is clearly fearful, often approaches the aggressor, uttering screams or whimpers of fear, and makes some gesture or posture of submission, such as crouching low to the ground, or holding out a pleading hand as though begging for reassurance. And the aggressor will usually respond—touching, patting, or even kissing or embracing the supplicant. The victim visibly relaxes and social harmony is restored. Indeed, for the most part, the chimpanzees follow Danny's° favorite text: they seldom let the sun go down on their wrath.

Danny's: Goodall's grandmother's nickname was Danny.

One female chimpanzee, living in a large captive group in a zoo in Holland, became amazingly skillful at restoring peaceful relations. Whenever two of the adult males were sitting tense after a conflict, avoiding each other's gaze, there would be noticeable agitation running throughout the entire group. This old female would then initiate a grooming session with one of the rivals, during which she gradually moved a little closer to the second male—followed by her grooming partner. Then she would leave him and repeat her maneuver with his rival. Eventually the two males were so close that both could groom her at the same time. When she was thus the only thing separating them she quietly moved away, and, calmed by the grooming, and neither having to be the first to break the deadlock, they started to groom each other.

Surely, I thought, if chimpanzees can control their aggressive tendencies, and diffuse the situation when things get out of hand, so can we. And herein, perhaps, was the hope for our future: we really do have the ability to override our genetic heritage. Like strict parents or schoolteachers, we can reprimand our aggressive tendencies, deny them expression, thwart those selfish genes (unless we are suffering from some physiological or psychological disorder, and major strides have been made in medication for such conditions). Our brains are sufficiently sophisticated; it's a question of whether or not we really *want* to control our instincts.

In point of fact most of us discipline those rebel genes on a day-to-day 15 basis. As did Whitson, a twelve-year-old African American boy, in a little incident which could have escalated into violence, but which was beautifully defused. Young Whitson was one of a group of kids gathered in Colorado for a youth summit. It had just snowed—and Whitson, from San Francisco, had not seen more than about twenty snowflakes in his life. He made a snowball that got bigger and bigger and bigger as he rolled it along the ground. Somehow he managed, with help, to get this large and very heavy mass of impacted snow onto his head. He wanted to see how far he could carry it on the planned hike. I was right close by when a girl from Virginia, white and middle-class, came up behind him and, I suppose as a joke, pushed the snowball off his head. It shattered into many pieces on the hard ground. I was close by when this happened, so I saw Whitson's face, and saw the shock, the horror—and then, unmistakably, the expression of fury. Indeed, he raised a hand as if to strike her, though he was much the smaller. And then she, horrified at what she had all unthinkingly started, cried out, "Oh I am so so sorry. I don't know what made me do that. I'm really, really sorry," and she knelt to try to repair the broken ball. For a moment Whitson went rigid. Slowly he lowered his arm, slowly the rage left his face. And then he too knelt. Together they repaired the snowball. He won out over his aggressive impulse—and I was proud of them both.

Indeed, it is fortunate that we are not *compelled* to obey our aggressive urges. If we did not inhibit feelings of aggression continually, society would be extremely unruly, as is the case when social norms break down during rioting and warfare—when the ugly face of anarchy grins out of the chaos.

And so, as the 1970s came to a close, I began to take heart. Our knowledge of chimpanzee behavior does, indeed, indicate that our aggressive tendencies are deeply embedded in our primate heritage. Yet so too are our caring and altruistic ones. And just as it appears that our wicked deeds can be far, far worse than the aggressive behavior of chimpanzees, so too our acts of altruism and self-sacrifice often involve greater heroism than those performed by apes. Chimpanzees, as we have seen, may respond to the immediate need of a companion in distress, even when this involves a risk to themselves. However I think it is only we humans, with our sophisticated intellect, who are capable of performing acts of self-sacrifice with full knowledge of the costs that we may have to bear, not only at the time, but also, perhaps, at some future date.

Whether or not chimpanzees would choose to die in order to save a companion if they *could* comprehend the stakes, I do not know. It seems highly unlikely that apes have any understanding of the concept of death, or their own mortality: in which case they could not make a *conscious* decision to give up their lives for a friend—although their helping actions might result in just that. But we humans certainly can make conscious decisions of this sort. We find examples of heroic self-sacrifice all the time if we read the newspapers or watch television. A recent example in England was when Pete Goss, who was winning a round-the-world yacht race, turned back, in the teeth of a terrific storm, when he heard the distress signal of a fellow competitor. Unhesitatingly he not only risked his life to rescue a French rival from his yacht that was breaking up in huge seas, but also sacrificed his chance of winning a prestigious award. Some of the most inspiring tales of heroism have come from the battlefields of war when, time and again, men and women have risked—and lost—their lives to help a wounded or endangered companion. The highest award for bravery in England, the Victoria Cross, only too often has to be awarded posthumously. Resistance fighters in occupied countries have, again and again, carried out secret missions against the enemy despite the very real risk of death and, worse, torture; sacrificing themselves and even their families for their beliefs or their country.

Acts of self-sacrifice in the hell of the death camps were frequent. There was a moving incident that took place at Auschwitz when a Pole, facing a death sentence, sobbed and begged that his life might be spared so that he could stay with his two children. At this moment, the great priest Saint Maximilian Kolbe stepped forward and offered his life instead. After surviving two weeks in the starvation bunker, Kolbe was then murdered by the Nazis but the story lived on, serving as an inspiration to surviving prisoners: a beacon of hope and love had been lit in the dark confines of the concentration camp.

Nor was it only in the death camps that such acts took place. The extra- [20] ordinary and selfless deeds of Oskar Schindler, who employed and rescued countless Jews in Poland, have been immortalized in Steven Spielberg's *Schindler's List*. Less well known is the heroic effort of two consuls in Nazi-occupied Lithuania. Jan Zwartendijk, acting Dutch consul, without any authorization wrote out almost two thousand transfer permits for Lithuanian Jews who were trying to escape the approaching Nazi occupation. These documents gave them permission, from the Dutch government, to enter the Dutch colony of Curaçao. Zwartendijk was fortunate to escape himself. Japanese consul Chiune Sugihara, in direct defiance of his superiors in Tokyo, wrote out visas for several thousand Jews to pass through Russia on their way to Curaçao. He knew that this involved personal risk and being disgraced and fired. But he was a samurai who had been taught to help those in need. "I may have to disobey my government," he said, "but if I don't, I would be disobeying God." He was indeed later disgraced in Tokyo, and ended his life in financial ruin and without honor: yet some eight thousand Lithuanian Jews, who would otherwise have been killed in the death camps, escaped. It was the third largest rescue operation in the history of the Holocaust. An estimated forty thousand descendants of the Jewish refugees saved in 1940 are alive today because of the courageous actions of these two remarkable men.

The most significant event for Christians (along with the Resurrection) is that Jesus offered up His life, gave Himself into the hands of His persecutors, knowing only too well the agony He would endure. "Father . . . take this cup from me," he prayed, in the Garden of Gethsemane. "Nevertheless, not my will, but Thine be done." He sacrificed himself because He believed His act would redeem mankind.

It is these undeniable qualities of human love and compassion and self-sacrifice that give me hope for the future. We are, indeed, often cruel and evil. Nobody can deny this. We gang up on one another, we torture each other, with words as well as deeds, we fight, we kill. But we are also capable of the most noble, generous, and heroic behavior.

WHAT DOES SHE SAY?

1. This essay begins with a series of small stories and direct observations that Jane Goodall made as she watched chimpanzees. What do you make of these as you're reading them? Do they surprise you? confuse you? Do they seem to matter in terms of the overall question of this chapter? Write a paragraph in response.

2. Pay particular attention to Goodall's observations of Spindle, an adolescent male, and his relationship with and behavior toward Mel. At one point, the essay says, "Why did Spindle act that way, burdening himself with the care of a small, sickly youngster who was not even a close relative?" What's Goodall's answer? What would yours be?

3. Do you ever send money or other donations to refugees, the homeless, the hungry, or victims of catastrophe? If so, why? If not, why not?

4. What one paragraph of Goodall's essay seems to you to come closest to summarizing the whole? Copy it out by hand, then write a paragraph of your own in response.

WHAT DO YOU THINK?

5. Write an essay about an experience you had when you were tempted to react violently to a situation or person. Explain the experience in detail; then try to explain why you think you acted as you did and what you think of those actions now.

6. As you read and think about Goodall's essay, note those places where she specifically calls attention to differences between chimpanzees and humans. Summarize the most important of these differences (use brief quotations from the essay to help you) and explain why understanding them is crucial to understanding what Goodall says.

7. What personal experience do you have of conflict resolution—of ways that tensions between individuals can be lessened or resolved? Write an essay that presents some of this experience and explain how it is reinforced or contradicted by Goodall's essay. *Or* write an essay that presents your experience of acting violently. What were the circumstances? What did you do? Why? End by comparing this experience to some part of what Goodall says and by explaining why you do, or do not, agree with her assertion that "Our brains are sufficiently sophisticated; it's a question of whether or not we really *want* to control our instincts."

WHAT WOULD THEY SAY?

8. Read Andre Dubus's "Giving Up the Gun" (p. 180); then write an essay explaining how his experience actually illustrates some of what Jane Goodall says in "Compassion and Love."

9. Consider Michael Levin's "The Case for Torture" (p. 201) together with Goodall's essay. Do you see them as contradicting each other? Supporting each other? Write your own essay discussing this, and end it by explaining how your consideration of these two essays leads you to greater or lesser agreement with the argument Levin makes.

10. Consider "Compassion and Love" together with the Dalai Lama's "The Need for Discernment" (p. 205). How does Goodall's essay help make clearer what the Dalai Lama presents? Or are you more confused? Write an essay that discusses and presents your sense of the ways that Goodall and the Dalai Lama agree or disagree. End by explaining why you are, or are not, hopeful about our ability to control our aggressive impulses.

11. Read "Compassion and Love" together with Chris Hedges's "Eros and Thanatos" (p. 247). Write an essay that explains how reading these essays together helps make each of them clearer. End by identifying and explaining the most central shared assertions that Goodall and Hedges make.

For Community Learning and Research

1. Look at cartoons on the editorial pages of a big-city daily for the week of your most recent birthday and the weeks immediately before and after it. What issues do the cartoons address? Photocopy three of these cartoons and use them to anchor a discussion of why you believe such cartoons should, or should not, be taken seriously.

2. Identify two local individuals who have been seriously wounded or killed while in recent military service. How were their stories presented by the local news media? Locate newspaper or magazine reports that discuss their experiences and make photocopies of what you find. Write an essay that summarizes the experiences of these two people. Quote at least three of the sources. End by discussing the impact that this researching and summarizing has had on your beliefs about war.

3. Collect recruiting information—brochures, informational packets, and so on—from at least two branches of the armed forces. What picture of military service emerges from these sources? Explain this carefully and accurately given the information you have. Then consider this information in connection with Dan Baum's "The Casualty" (p. 232). Do you believe that the recruiting information presents a fair picture of the experience of military service? Should it present a fair picture?

4. Interview a combat veteran (someone who actually saw battle). Read your interviewee paragraph 32 in Chris Hedges's essay (p. 247): "War ascendant wipes out Eros. It wipes out all delicacy and tenderness...." Ask for his or her reaction to what Hedges says. Identify four other paragraphs in Hedges's essay and ask for reactions to each of them. Explain what you learn and the extent to which your interview helps you understand Hedges and agree or disagree with his essay.

5. Identify any local organizations—or local chapters of larger organizations—that are centrally committed to the peaceful resolution of conflict (at any level). If they have offices nearby, visit them. Gather whatever informational materials they distribute about themselves. Write an essay that reports on these organizations and ends by explaining why you would, or would not, be inclined to join them.

6. Visit local food banks or other organizations aimed at helping the hungry, and also visit organizations that seek to help the homeless. Gather any information they provide about themselves and their services. Try to speak with members of these organizations. Ask them about the connections—if any—that they perceive between hunger and violence or homelessness and violence. Write an essay that explains what you learn. Variation: Volunteer for ten hours at one of these organizations. Write about what those ten hours have made clearer to you and about what issues now seem more complicated and unclear.

7. Visit a shelter for those fleeing domestic violence. Ask for any information that will help you understand why spouses (usually men) physically attack those they purport to love. Why do those who suffer such attacks stay? What forces them finally to seek shelter? Variation: Volunteer for ten hours at such a shelter. Write about what those ten hours have helped you understand about violence and what issues seem complicated and unclear.

● | ○ 8. Choose one of the questions above, and after doing your research, prepare a speech for your fraternity, sorority, dormitory, church group, or any community of which you are part. The goal of your speech is to persuade the people in this community to take a certain action. For example, based on your research for question 7, give a speech urging your friends to volunteer at a shelter for those fleeing domestic violence. Based on your research for question 3, give a speech urging your friends to join the military, to support a particular war, or to vote for a particular political candidate who supports a war. Conversely, based on the information you gathered for question 2, 4, or 5, give a speech urging your friends to oppose a war, to vote for a certain political candidate who opposes a war, or to participate in a local antiwar rally.

4

Are We Our Bodies?

WHAT WOULD YOU DO?
JUDGING BASED ON APPEARANCE

You're sitting in a classroom on the first day of classes for a new term, watching students walk in and take their seats. One older guy shuffles in the door. He's carrying a backpack, he's wearing old running shoes with no laces, and he hasn't shaved in maybe a week. You notice he limps slightly. Behind him, a petite coed, wearing a jeans skirt and a halter top, walks through the door, smiles briefly, and sits down on the other side of you. You notice that her top reads "Tommy Girl." She's wearing sandals, and her nails are painted the color of plums.

What quick judgments do you make about these two people? Would you talk to either one of them? Would you make any assumptions about them?

Now another man walks in. He looks to be in his early 60s, with long hair pulled back in a ponytail and shirt untucked in back. He goes to the desk in the front of the room, and when he looks up you see that his eyebrows meet in the middle.

This is the teacher, you realize.

What's your first response? What do you assume?

All of us *do* judge books by their covers, at least at first. Our initial infor-mation about something or someone is likely to be visual, and when it's not, we're curious. Suppose you have a brother who's in a new relation-ship. He tells you "it's more than friendship." You agree to meet the two of them for lunch. Aren't you going to look closely at this person your brother brings? And won't you make at least fleeting judgments at first sight? We choose cars, homes, even schools partly on the basis of how they look. And if the advertisements in mass-market magazines are any indication, we care quite a bit about the clothes we wear and the mes-sages they send.

In this chapter, we turn to questions of the body—questions that have much more significance than those fleeting judgments—involving such things as identity, gender, race, health, privacy, as well as the range of some of the most fundamental of our human choices. All of these questions turn, wholly or in part, on the most fundamental fact about us: we each live in a unique human form. Jenefer Shute's narrator ("Life-Size," p. 279) believes she's being treated unfairly simply because she refuses to eat. Brent Staples realizes that just walking down the street can seem menacing to others ("Just Walk on By: Black Men and Public Space," p. 289). Nancy Mairs calls herself a "cripple," in part, she says, because she wants people to see her as "a tough customer" ("On Being a Cripple," p. 333). Sallie Tisdale works—and thinks—in an abortion clinic ("We Do Abortions Here," p. 351), and Bill McKibben ("Designer Genes," p. 360) worries that if given the chance, we might opt to genetically modify our children.

To what extent do our bodies determine our personalities, identify our choices, and make us the individuals that we are? When are we solely and fully responsible for our bodies? When, if ever, should other people intervene and claim some of that responsibility? Should we use the resources of medicine and research to create the offspring we seek? About the body, there are many open questions and a single clear fact: no one can live without one.

Opening the Question

*After reading and discussing several of the selections in this chapter, return to the situation above. **Now** what would you do? Write an essay answering this question, drawing on at least two of the selections. You don't need to have changed your mind, but you do need to demonstrate how the reading has complicated your thinking.*

Do the selections you've read make you any less likely to judge others by their appearance? Explain.

Do the selections you've read in any way change your opinion about what makes a man or woman good-looking or appealing? Explain.

Do the selections here change your attitude about your own body? Explain.

After doing this reading, are you more or less likely to favor genetic modification of the body for purposes of improved appearance or performance?

JENEFER SHUTE
Life-Size

*T*HIS FICTIONAL, FIRST-PERSON ACCOUNT *by a hospitalized anorexic raises specific questions about the extent to which a person ought to have the freedom to starve herself into life-threatening illness. The author, Jenefer Shute (b. 1956), is a professor of creative writing at Hunter College of the City University of New York. She earned a PhD from UCLA and has written several novels, including* Sex Crimes *(1997) and* Free Fall *(2002). This piece is an excerpt from her 1992 novel,* Life-Size, *the story of Josie, an anorexic graduate student who is hospitalized against her will.*

I'm lying here, just occupying space, drifting in and out of a dream, when I hear something clattering and rumbling down the hall. I know what it is; my jaw and stomach muscles tense, but otherwise I remain exactly as I am. Why should I move? The trolley stops outside the door with a faint tinkle of crockery; after a brief knock (giving me no time to respond), she comes in, smiling and pert, brisk and trim in her white tunic and pants. (Trim, but don't think I don't notice the almost-sagging buttocks, the incipient droop of the upper arm.)

As she walks toward me, her blockish, cushiony shoes squeak against the floor, jarring my ears, scraping my brain.

"Hello! Still lying there? It's lunchtime."

I make no response as she puts the tray down next to me and removes some kind of cover from the plate, releasing a sickening, mealy odor.

"Sit up and enjoy your lunch," she says brightly, pushing it closer to the bed. "I'll be back in half an hour to see how you're doing." I say nothing and she leaves (shoes conversing in shrill, rubbering shrieks across the floor).

I'm not planning even to look at this tray, but the smell is so strong that I turn my head and encounter, at eye level, a brown, oily, pimply thing (chicken! as if I would ever eat that) oozing onto a mound of mashed potato and some big green branches of broccoli. I try, and fail, to imagine eating it, like munching on a tree. Everything is heaped, crowded on the plate, everything touching. There's also a glass of milk, beaded with sweat; a puffy roll plus two pats of butter; a dish of flabby yellow stuff growing a skin (custard? are they kidding?); an apple; a little envelope of salt, one of pepper, one of ketchup. The smell is so overpowering that I know I'm going to have to do something.

Reluctantly I roll over on to my side and tip myself so that my feet hang over the edge of the bed. Then, very slowly, I push upward until I'm sitting, curled, with my head on my lap. I rest like this awhile, trying to breathe, and then, tightening my abdominals, raise myself carefully to my feet.

This prevents fainting.

I have to get this tray out of my sight. The smell is entering me as a hollow nausea, and seeing all that...food sends a chilly tingle across my skin. Got to get this thing away! I dump it on the other bed and am about to climb back on mine when I reconsider, go back, and pick off a small piece of the roll, which I put in the drawer of my nightstand: just in case.

Then I roll on the bed, flop my arms wide, wait for everything to stop   10
spinning, and, fixing my eye on the ceiling lightbulb, return its stern, milky stare.

So this is what my world has shrunk to: a ward with two gray metal beds, barred at head and foot, with thin spreads, waffled, that might once have been white. The walls, an institutional cream, are scuffed and scarred: lying here, I trace and retrace each blister, each blemish, each bruise. The cold floor is tiled in beige and khaki, which might once have been lemon and olive, or even vanilla and lime. Through the high, locked windows—is this perhaps the psycho ward, after all?—limp shades diffuse a sooty light. A metal nightstand with a screeching drawer, a locker in which my clothes are locked from me, and a plastic chair—for visitors I assume (though who would come here, I cannot think)—complete the decor.

Since being admitted two days ago, I've spent most of my time lying on this bed, arms apart, hands splayed, eyes fixed on the blind bulb above me. They want me to get up, put on my robe, perhaps wander down to the dayroom to meet the other inmates. But I won't, of course. I'm just going to lie here, drifting through time, dreams washing over me, retinal dots composing themselves pointillist style into a private flow of images.

But then I notice that I'm holding my breath, almost choking: a chemical whiff in the air has stopped my throat. At first I think this is a new symptom—already I'm afraid of running water, of restaurants, of licking a postage stamp—but then it makes sense. The last time I was in a hospital was when I was nine, for a tonsillectomy: in my throat I feel again the dry, violent pain, like swallowing ground glass. Dark clotted stuff in the mouth, salting the ice cream, tinging the vanilla with tinny strawberry.

Vanilla and strawberry and cream. Think about something else. Think about the tonsils, ripped out like tubers.

A brisk knock, and then the door opens immediately (why do they never wait   15
for me to answer?). In comes Squeaky, interrupting my dream—the surgeon is caressing my hair, the anesthetic taking its ecstatic hold—but I don't even move my head. Out of the corner of my eye I can see her taking in the situation: the full tray dumped on the other bed, me flat on my back, arms outspread, my pelvic bones protruding pointedly under the gray-green hospital gown. She shakes her head and says in what she probably takes for a calm, reasonable tone: "Josie, you haven't eaten anything, have you? That's very disappointing: you know the rules. You remember what the doctor said."

"I'm not hungry," I say.

"It was too much," I say.

"Anyway, I did eat something," I say. "I ate some of the roll."

"Josie," she says, "you know the rules, you agreed to them yourself. Do you just want to lie here forever? What's the point of that?"

Her measured yet whiny tone is getting to me and I just want her out. Out! Out of my room! Still staring at the ceiling, I say "I don't like chicken." They say I'm sick, but what about them, all of them, who think nothing of chewing on a carcass, sinking their teeth into muscle and gristle and blood? They say I'm sick, but what about them, who feast on corpses?

"Well, you wouldn't fill out a menu card, so the dietician picked out something for you."

A corpse and a tree; a fluid secreted by bovine mammary glands; gobs of congealed grease.

"Later, if you fill out the card, you can get something you like. A nice fruit salad perhaps, with ice cream? Or a tuna sandwich, with a banana, perhaps, and some cookies . . . ?"

Banana and tuna and cream: the very words, as if secret, obscene, are making me ill, my heart starting to hammer, the same hollow sickness poking at the base of my throat. To get her to stop, I say "Leave the card here and I'll think about it."

"Okay. And we have a busy afternoon planned for you. The endocrinologist is going to stop by to ask you some questions, and then we'll need to take you for some blood samples."

Blood again. They're after my blood.

Sure enough, a chirpy little woman (thin, birdlike, but with a turkey's tired wattle) shows up, armed with a rubber mallet. She asks me a few questions about my periods; that's all anyone seems to care about around here.

"I forget. Maybe when I was seventeen."

"So you've had no periods for eight years now?"

"No, they come and go. Sometimes I won't have any for a year or two, then they'll come back for a while, then go away again."

"And how long have they been gone this time?"

"I forget. Maybe a year or so."

Why do they think I should care, anyway? Who, given the choice, would really opt to menstruate, invite the monthly hemorrhage—a reminder that the body is nothing but a bag of blood, liable to seep or spatter at any moment?

Then I discover what the rubber mallet is for. She asks me to sit on the edge of the bed and starts tapping away at my knees, a sharp, clean crack on the bone. Nothing happens, so I give a little kick to help things along. Then she tickles the soles of my feet and tells me my reflexes are impaired because the electrolytes are out of balance and the neurons aren't firing properly or some such jargon.

Fine with me. I don't want any involuntary responses: soon, in this body, everything will be willed.

So I just look at her blankly and flop back on the bed, because all this sitting up and being hammered is making me light-headed. The minute she leaves, I roll over on to my side and begin my leg lifts, hoping I can complete the full hundred on each side without being interrupted.

I am halfway through the second set when the nurse comes back again, pushing a wheelchair, into which she invites me to climb for some blood tests. (More blood.) I tell her I won't get in the chair, I can walk, thank you— I'm desperate to move: My muscles are turning mushy from lying here. But she insists—says it's "policy"—and wraps a blanket around me when I complain of the cold. So off we go, her shoes conversing squeakily across the tiles.

The assistant who's supposed to take the blood looks startled when she sees me and shakes her head at my arms—my white, well-defined arms, ropy with blue and softly furred. (I hate this hair, this down, which keeps growing all over me, even on my stomach: I have tried bleaching it, but more just keeps growing in, dark, like a pelt.) She comes at me with the needle, jabbing and wiggling; she tries both arms a few times, getting flustered.

"Your veins keep collapsing," she says. "I'm sorry, dear, but I have to keep trying."

It hurts and though I don't look, distancing myself from this piece of 40 meat that's being probed, I start feeling sick, my head suddenly receding from my feet, which in turn have disconnected from my knees. Squeaky, ever vigilant, pushes my head gently down onto my lap, and after a few minutes in this pose, I feel ready to continue.

"Come on, let's get it over with," I say.

More prodding, but eventually she finds a vein, and, while I fix my attention on the far wall, she takes eight tubes of blood: to test potassium, calcium, hemoglobin levels. Sugar too: as if they would find sugar in my blood. Even though I don't watch the blood being sucked out—once I made the mistake of observing the thick, grape-colored stuff rising in the tube, stood up, and passed out—I still feel light-headed, and the shaken blood-sucker makes me lie down and drink some apple juice (130 calories; I take only a sip) before we leave.

My keeper wheels me back and explains, in her professionally patient, reasonable tone (I'd love to hear how she bitches with the other nurses on her coffee break) that, though psychotherapy is part of the treatment plan, "they" have decided that I cannot begin yet because, she says, I am a starving organism and my brain is starving and therefore not working the way it should. I say nothing but it's hard not to sneer: my brain's not working the way it should! On the contrary, it's never been purer and less cluttered, concentrated on essentials instead of distracted by a body clamoring for attention, demanding that its endless appetites be appeased. Stripped down, the brain is closer to the surface, taking in colors, light, sounds, with a fine, vibrating intensity.

One day I will be pure consciousness, traveling unmuffled through the world; one day I will refine myself to the bare wiring, the irreducible circuitry of mind.

She also explains to me, again in what she thinks is a neutral, measured 45 tone, that they're sure I'm going to cooperate, but if not, as a last resort, they might have to consider hyperalimentation. Hyperalimentation: interesting euphemism for force-feeding, for attaching a helpless human body to a tangle of tubes and pumping—what, I wonder?—into its unwilling ducts. Hyperalimentation: isn't that the word, rather, for the way most people eat?

I never feel hungry and despise those who do, whose lives are governed by the peristaltic pulse. Never have they learned to ignore the gaping maw-mouth: its slightest twinge sends them running to the trough. From the first mouthful in the morning to the last at night, their lives are one long foraging. In the morning, hunched over their desks, they munch on soft dough; at noon, they herd out en masse, meat-hungry, to feed; midafternoon, in a circadian slump, they crave sugar; arriving home, they root in the refrigerator's roaring heart and eat upright before an open door. And all this before the serious eating begins, the ever-to-be-repeated hours of shopping and chopping and mixing and cooking and serving, only to wolf down the result in seconds and greet it the next morning transformed into shit.

But I've freed myself from this compulsion. When I wake, I'm empty, light, light-headed; I like to stay this way, free and pure, light on my feet, traveling light. For me, food's only interest lies in how little I need, how strong I am, how well I can resist—each time achieving another small victory of the will: one carrot instead of two, half a cracker, no more peas. Each gain makes me stronger, purer, larger in my exercise of power, until eventually I see no reason to eat at all. Like a plant, surely, the body can be trained to subsist on nothing, to take its nourishment from the air.

Miss Pert—I think her name is Suzanne—finally leaves me, with a cheery reminder to fill out the menu card for dinner. The minute she's gone, I take it out and study it carefully, reading it and rereading it, savoring not the names of the food so much as the knowledge I will never eat them. Some disgust me, the very words filling my mouth with a viscid sickness: pork chops, hamburger, cheese omelette, clam chowder. But others I linger over, imagining their colors and textures, feeding on images, secure in the knowledge that images alone can fill me.

I prepare myself an imaginary feast, taking about forty minutes to decide on the menu—banana with peanut butter, fried rice, pecan pie—and to imagine consuming it lasciviously with a spoon. When it's over, I look at the menu card again, knowing that Squeaky-Pert will harass me if I don't mark something. Some of the dishes frighten me, their names alone quickening my pulse: spaghetti and meatballs! Imagine eating that, a whole, giant plate of it, everything heaped together, oozing oil. My heart is racing now, so I put a check mark next to "mixed salad" on the card and push it away from me, to the far side of the nightstand. I lie back again, trying to relax, wondering how big the salad will be and whether they'll try to make me eat the whole thing. Then panic seizes me: I sit up violently, grab the menu card again, and write in emphatic block letters next to my check mark "NO DRESSING!!" I underline this three times and then lie back, trying to calm my hammering heart.

To collect myself, I start doing leg lifts again, picking up where I was in- 50 terrupted earlier and deciding I will do an extra fifty on each side in case the nurse, my jailer, makes me eat the whole salad. The bed isn't really firm enough for calisthenics, but I'm afraid to get down on the floor in case someone comes in. I'm going to have to get down there eventually, to do my pushups: maybe I can say I'm looking for something on the floor. (A contact lens? A cockroach?) They think they can wear me down by this constant intrusion—I'm supposed to be on an hourly watch—but I know I can outlast them all.

One day I will be thin enough. Just the bones, no disfiguring flesh, just the pure, clear shape of me. Bones. That is what we are, after all, what we're made of, and everything else is storage, deposit, waste. Strip it away, use it up, no deposit, no return.

Every morning the same ritual, the same inventory, the same naming of parts before rising, for fear of what I may have become overnight. Jolting out of sleep—what was that dream, that voice offering me strawberries and cream?—the first thing I do is feel my hip bones, piercingly concave, two naked arcs of bone around an emptiness. Next I feel the wrists, encircling each with the opposite hand, checking that they're still frail and pitiful, like the legs of little birds. There's a deep hollow on the inside of each wrist, suspending delicately striated hands, stringy with tendon and bone. On the outside of the wrist, I follow the bone all the way up to the elbow, where it joins another, winglike, in a sharp point.

Moving down to the thighs, first I feel the hollow behind the knee to check that the tendon is still clean and tight, a naked cord. Then I follow the outside of each thigh up toward the hips: no hint of a bulge, no softening anywhere. Next I grab the inner thigh and pinch hard, feeling almost all the way around the muscle there; finally, turning on one side and then the other, I press each buttock, checking that the bones are still sticking through.

Sitting up in bed, a little more anxiously now, I grasp the collar bones, so prominent that they protrude beyond the edges of the shoulders, like a wire coat hanger suspending this body, these bones. Beneath them, the rows of ribs, deeply corrugated (and the breasts, which I don't inspect). Then I press the back of my neck and as far down my spine as I can, to make sure the vertebrae are all still there, a row of perfect little buttons: as if they held this body together, as if I could unbutton it and step out any time I wanted to.

Dinner is as bad as I was afraid it would be. At precisely six o'clock, Squeaky 55
squeaks in with a big tray, which she puts down next to the bed where I am
floating again, on my back, imaging myself somewhere else altogether, cool
and perfectly hard in a silk-lined gown. Firmly she says "Josie, I hope you're
going to eat your salad tonight, otherwise the medical team will have to make
a decision tomorrow about hyperalimentation."

I look in horror at the huge bowl of salad on the tray. *It's possible to*
slow yourself down by eating too much salad. "This *is* hyperalimentation," I say: a
mound of lettuce with chunks of pale tomato, shards of green pepper, hunks
of purplish raw onion, and—they must be nuts if they think I'm going to eat
any of this—gobs of cheese and hard-boiled egg, with a bruise-colored line
where the white pulls away from the yolk. Even though I didn't ask for
it, there's a big, stale-looking roll and butter, an apple, a dish of vanilla ice
cream, a glass of milk, and a plastic container of some urine-colored oil labeled
"Italian."

"I can't eat if you're watching me," I say, which is true.

"Okay," she says, "I'll be back in half an hour to see how you're doing."

As soon as she leaves, I draw the curtain around my bed: No one must
ever see me eat, no one must ever catch me in the act—especially now that
my appearance excites so much attention, with people always staring at me,
willing me to weaken.

The Trobrianders° eat alone, retiring to their own hearths with their portions, 60
turning their backs on one another and eating rapidly for fear of being observed.

With the curtains drawn, my heart slows down a little and I concentrate
on controlling this food: if I don't deal with it soon, it will exert a magnetic
pull on me, commanding me to eat it, filling my consciousness until the only
way I could escape would be to run shrieking into the street.

There is a big paper napkin on the tray, so I scrape exactly half the salad
out of the bowl and into the napkin, along with half the roll. I bundle this
mess up and start looking for a place to hide it: not easy in this cell. My clothes
locker is locked and I don't have the key—of course not: this is going to be
one of my little "rewards." (Even my shoes have been locked away, my socks.)
Under my pillow would be too risky, because the napkin could leak or break,
making a big lettucey mess that would be hard to explain. So the only place I
can think of is the drawer of the nightstand next to the other bed, the unoccu-
pied one, the one as flat and empty as I would like mine to be.

Once that little bundle is out of the way, I can relax a bit and start working on what's left. I separate the mound of food into piles: lettuce on one side,
tomato on the other, pepper pieces neatly stacked and segregated from the
rank, juicy onion. The egg and cheese I pick right off and banish to the bread

---

Trobrianders: Inhabitants of the Trobriand Islands of New Guinea whose culture traces
family lineage through mothers rather than fathers. [EDS.]

plate: evil. *Cheese is the hardest food to digest, and it contaminates everything you eat it with.* Then I cut the lettuce, tomato, and pepper into tiny pieces, deciding I won't even pretend to eat the onion because lots of people don't like raw onion: it's legitimate, it's "normal." I cut the half-roll into four sections and decide I will eat only one. Of the ice cream, I will eat exactly two spoonfuls, and the apple I will save for another time. So I put it away in my nightstand drawer along with the piece of roll I picked off the lunch tray: just in case.

Now that these decisions have been made, now that the bad stuff has been removed, now that the food is separated, with white space showing on the plate, now I can start eating: one piece at a time, and at least three minutes (timed on a second hand) between mouthfuls, with the fork laid down precisely in the center of the plate after each bite.

Of course the nurse comes back before I'm done and, without even ask- 65 ing, swishes back the bed curtains, revealing me shamefully hunched over the tray, chewing. I freeze, unable to meet her eyes. She says, gently, "There's really no need to close the curtains, dear, when you're alone."

Sullenly I push the tray away and lie back on the pillow, staring up at the mangy acoustic tile.

"Don't stop," she says. "I'll come back in fifteen minutes or so." She leaves, but it's no good: I can't eat any more; I feel sick and upset, with the undigested salad sitting scratchily, bulkily, inside me. My stomach is beginning to swell: I feel it anxiously, palming the dip between my hipbones, sensing a new curvature, a new tightness there. Panicky, before I know what I have done, I have wolfed down three teaspoons of the now almost entirely melted ice cream.

I put the tray on the other bed and draw the bed curtains around it so I don't have to be reminded of my gluttony; climbing back onto my own bed, I draw those curtains too, wanting to be alone, to hide where no one can find me, can tempt me, can torment my will. I want to find a cave or burrow somewhere where the idea of food becomes an abstraction, and this body, ever clearer and purer, evaporates finally into the dark, leaving only consciousness behind.

When the nurse comes back, I ask her to take me to the bathroom (another of these laws under which I now live: I can't leave the ward unaccompanied). This is partly a diversionary tactic, but partly also because I'm desperate to wash my hands and face: my skin feels oily and slimy, as if the fat in the food is oozing out through my pores. She helps me tie on my hospital-issue robe, with a faded blue design that makes my skin look even more cyanotic than it is. I'm cold but she won't let me put on any more clothes. So we walk slowly to the bathroom and she stands near the door while I go into a cubicle, where I'm not allowed to close the door in case I make myself vomit (which I've never been able to do—though not for want of trying). I can't pee under these conditions, so I give up and comb my hair instead (it's still coming out, in dry hanks), tying it back tightly with an elastic band. Then I scrub my face and hands once, and

again, then again, until the nurse says sharply "That's enough now" and we
trudge back to the cell.

She bustles about, making a big deal of flinging back the curtains on 70
both beds, plumping up pillows, straightening the limp covers. Then, tilting
her head to one side, she contemplates the tray and says, "Well, Josie, you did
a good job on your dinner."

Relieved, I climb back on the bed and pick up a *Vogue* that's been lying
around—I got away with it! again!—when she says "I'm going to have to
take a look around, if you don't mind. It's one of the rules."

If I don't mind! What choice do I have, powerless as a child, forced to
lie and scheme simply to exercise the elementary—the alimentary—right
to determine what does and doesn't go into my body?

She looked quickly under both beds and behind the curtains, checks the
lock on the clothes locker, runs her hand between the end of the mattress and
the metal railing at the foot of both beds, and then, of course, opens the
nightstand drawer on the far side.

"What's this?" she says, though she knows.

"I was saving it for later," I say. "I couldn't eat it all now, so I was going 75
to have some more later, before bed."

She says nothing but just stands there, shaking her head, holding the im-
perfectly closed bundle of salad and bread, already soggy in spots. Then she
dumps it on the tray and says, "Anything you don't eat, just leave on the tray."
She seems about to pick up the tray and go, but then, as an afterthought, comes
over to the side of my bed, opens the screeching drawer—is there no place
that's mine?—and finds the apple and the piece of roll I took from lunch. "This
is hoarding," she says. "You can have anything you want to eat at any time—
just ask, but don't hoard."

Angry and humiliated and bereft, I don't answer. I put the *Vogue* over my
face so I won't have to see her, wondering what I must look like, lying here flat
in a faded robe, my fragile limbs sticking out like a grasshopper's, my skin a dry
grayish white, netted with veins, my fingertips and nails blueberry-hued, the
crook of each arm a purplish mess dotted with bloody pinpricks, and on top of
this all, superimposed over my face, the vivid face of the *Vogue* cover, each eyelash alert, each tooth a dazzling, clunky tile like a Chiclet, the skin a sealed and
poreless stretch of pink, and the ripe, shiny lips curved into a radiant smirk.

WHAT DOES SHE SAY?

1. As you read, make a list of exactly ten adjectives that you'd use to accurately and
   fully describe the narrator.

2. Pay particular attention to how "Life-Size" describes food and how it describes
   other people (the person who delivers lunch, for instance). Write a paragraph
   about what you observe.

3. What two or three sections of this selection give you the clearest view of the sort of dangerous trouble that afflicts this narrator? Identify these in the margins, and then write a paragraph that discusses the larger picture they make.

4. What do you make of the last paragraph of this selection? Does it surprise you that this narrator seems to have a clear idea of how she must look?

WHAT DO YOU THINK?

5. Analyze "Life-Size" by trying to figure out what its narrator believes and values. Identify three of these central assumptions or assertions, and use them to explain your own judgments of this narrator's outlook.

6. Buy a new copy or look at a back issue of *Vogue*. Pay attention to the articles and the advertisements. Using examples from a specific issue (indicate which one), write an essay that describes and explains what you see. Do you think that publications like *Vogue* bear responsibility for creating situations like the one in "Life-Size"? End your essay by discussing this question.

7. Write a letter to the narrator in "Life-Size." Explain your reaction to her, and let her know what you think is most centrally important about your responses to her essay.

8. Research the current thinking on the causes of anorexia or bulimia and the physical effects of these conditions. To what extent can you see your research reflected in Shute's selection? Having done this research and comparison, what's clearer to you now about anorexia and about the narrator of "Life-Size"?

WHAT WOULD THEY SAY?

9. Read "Life-Size" together with Scott Russell Sanders's "Looking at Women" (p. 294). How does Sanders's essay help you understand what you've read in "Life-Size"? Now also read "The Beauty Myth" by Naomi Wolf (p. 451). How does that essay add to your understanding?

10. Consider "Life-Size" together with Ellen Goodman's "Who Lives? Who Dies? Who Decides?" (p. 348). To what extent, or not, do you think that Goodman and Shute's narrator are talking about the same issues?

11. Read Bowen H. McCoy's "The Parable of the Sadhu" (p. 102). To what extent, or not, would you view the narrator of "Life-Size" as a kind of sadhu—an ascetic on a pilgrimage? What questions does McCoy raise that might also apply here? How would you respond to the assertion that the narrator in "Life-Size" seems to know exactly what she's doing?

BRENT STAPLES

Just Walk on By: Black Men and Public Space

*D*O YOUR SIZE *and the color of your skin determine who you are? In this essay, Brent Staples (b. 1951) tells how people in public react to his presence as a tall, broad-built black man. Staples earned a PhD in psychology from the University of Chicago in 1982 but left psychology and began a career in journalism. His autobiography,* Parallel Time: Growing Up in Black and White *(1994), won the Anisfield Wolff Book Award. He is currently on the board of the* New York Times *and contributes to several magazines, including* Harper's *and* Ms., *in which "Just Walk on By" appeared in 1986.*

My first victim was a woman—white, well dressed, probably in her early twenties. I came upon her late one evening on a deserted street in Hyde Park, a relatively affluent neighborhood in an otherwise mean, impoverished section of Chicago. As I swung onto the avenue behind her, there seemed to be a discreet, uninflammatory distance between us. Not so. She cast back a worried glance. To her, the youngish black man—a broad six feet two inches with a beard and billowing hair, both hands shoved into the pockets of a bulky military jacket—seemed menacingly close. After a few more quick glimpses, she picked up her pace and was soon running in earnest. Within seconds she disappeared into a cross street.

That was more than a decade ago. I was twenty-two years old, a graduate student newly arrived at the University of Chicago. It was in the echo of that terrified woman's footfalls that I first began to know the unwieldy inheritance I'd come into—the ability to alter public space in ugly ways. It was clear that she thought herself the quarry of a mugger, rapist, or worse. Suffering a bout of insomnia, however, I was stalking sleep, not defenseless wayfarers. As a softy who is scarcely able to take a knife to a raw chicken—let alone hold it to a person's throat—I was surprised, embarrassed, and dismayed all at once. Her flight made me feel like an accomplice in tyranny. It also made it clear that I was indistinguishable from the muggers who occasionally seeped into the area from the surrounding ghetto. That first encounter, and those that followed, signified that a vast, unnerving gulf lay between nighttime pedestrians—particularly women—and me. And I soon gathered that being perceived as dangerous is a hazard in itself. I only needed to turn a corner into a dicey situation, or crowd some frightened, armed person in a foyer somewhere, or make an errant move after being pulled over by a policeman. Where fear and weapons meet—and they often do in urban America—there is always the possibility of death.

In that first year, my first away from my hometown, I was to become thoroughly familiar with the language of fear. At dark, shadowy intersections in Chicago, I could cross in front of a car stopped at a traffic light and elicit the *thunk, thunk, thunk, thunk* of the driver—black, white, male, or female— hammering down the door locks. On less traveled streets after dark, I grew accustomed to but never comfortable with people who crossed to the other side of the street rather than pass me. Then there were the standard unpleas- antries with police, doormen, bouncers, cab drivers, and others whose busi- ness it is to screen out troublesome individuals *before* there is any nastiness.

I moved to New York nearly two years ago and I have remained an avid night walker. In central Manhattan, the near-constant crowd cover minimizes tense one-on-one street encounters. Elsewhere—visiting friends in SoHo, where sidewalks are narrow and tightly spaced buildings shut out the sky— things can get very taut indeed.

Black men have a firm place in New York mugging literature. Norman   5 Podhoretz in his famed (or infamous) 1963 essay, "My Negro Problem—and Ours," recalls growing up in terror of black males; they "were tougher than we were, more ruthless," he writes—and as an adult on the Upper West Side of Manhattan, he continues, he cannot constrain his nervousness when he meets black men on certain streets. Similarly, a decade later, the essayist and novelist Edward Hoagland extols a New York where once "Negro bitterness bore down mainly on other Negroes." Where some see mere panhandlers, Hoagland sees "a mugger who is clearly screwing up his nerve to do more than just *ask* for money." But Hoagland has "the New Yorker's quick-hunch posture for broken-field maneuvering," and the bad guy swerves away.

I often witness that "hunch posture," from women after dark on the war- renlike streets of Brooklyn where I live. They seem to set their faces on neutral and, with their purse straps strung across their chests bandolier style, they forge ahead as though bracing themselves against being tackled. I understand, of course, that the danger they perceive is not a hallucination. Women are particu- larly vulnerable to street violence, and young black males are drastically overrep- resented among the perpetrators of that violence. Yet these truths are no solace against the kind of alienation that comes of being ever the suspect, against being set apart, a fearsome entity with whom pedestrians avoid making eye contact.

It is not altogether clear to me how I reached the ripe old age of twenty- two without being conscious of the lethality nighttime pedestrians attributed to me. Perhaps it was because in Chester, Pennsylvania, the small, angry in- dustrial town where I came of age in the 1960s, I was scarcely noticeable against a backdrop of gang warfare, street knifings, and murders. I grew up one of the good boys, had perhaps a half-dozen fist fights. In retrospect, my shyness of combat has clear sources.

Many things go into the making of a young thug. One of those things is the consummation of the male romance with the power to intimidate. An in- fant discovers that random flailings send the baby bottle flying out of the crib and crashing to the floor. Delighted, the joyful babe repeats those motions again and again, seeking to duplicate the feat. Just so, I recall the points at which some of my boyhood friends were finally seduced by the perception of themselves as tough guys. When a mark cowered and surrendered his money without resistance, myth and reality merged—and paid off. It is, after all, only manly to embrace the power to frighten and intimidate. We, as men, are not supposed to give an inch of our lane on the highway; we are to seize the fighter's edge in work and in play and even in love; we are to be valiant in the face of hostile forces.

Unfortunately, poor and powerless young men seem to take all this nonsense literally. As a boy, I saw countless tough guys locked away; I have since buried several, too. They were babies, really—a teenage cousin, a brother of twenty-two, a childhood friend in his midtwenties—all gone down in episodes of bravado played out in the streets. I came to doubt the virtues of intimidation early on. I chose, perhaps even unconsciously, to remain a shadow—timid, but a survivor.

The fearsomeness mistakenly attributed to me in public places often has a 10 perilous flavor. The most frightening of these confusions occurred in the late 1970s and early 1980s when I worked as a journalist in Chicago. One day, rushing into the office of a magazine I was writing for with a deadline story in hand, I was mistaken for a burglar. The office manager called security and, with an ad hoc posse, pursued me through the labyrinthine halls, nearly to my editor's door. I had no way of proving who I was. I could only move briskly toward the company of someone who knew me.

Another time I was on assignment for a local paper and killing time before an interview. I entered a jewelry store on the city's affluent Near North Side. The proprietor excused herself and returned with an enormous red Doberman pinscher straining at the end of a leash. She stood, the dog extended toward me, silent to my questions, her eyes bulging nearly out of her head. I took a cursory look around, nodded, and bade her good night. Relatively speaking, however, I never fared as badly as another black male journalist. He went to nearby Waukegan, Illinois, a couple of summers ago to work on a story about a murderer who was born there. Mistaking the reporter for the killer, police hauled him from his car at gunpoint and but for his press credentials would probably have tried to book him. Such episodes are not uncommon. Black men trade tales like this all the time.

In "My Negro Problem—and Ours," Podhoretz writes that the hatred he feels for blacks makes itself known to him through a variety of avenues— one being his discomfort with that "special brand of paranoid touchiness" to which he says blacks are prone. No doubt he is speaking here of black men. In time, I learned to smother the rage I felt at so often being taken for a criminal. Not to do so would surely have led to madness—via that special "paranoid touchiness" that so annoyed Podhoretz at the time he wrote the essay.

I began to take precautions to make myself less threatening. I move about with care, particularly late in the evening. I give a wide berth to nervous people on subway platforms during the wee hours, particularly when I have exchanged business clothes for jeans. If I happen to be entering a building behind some people who appear skittish, I may walk by, letting them clear the lobby before I return, so as not to seem to be following them. I have been calm and extremely congenial on those rare occasions when I've been pulled over by the police.

And on late-evening constitutionals along streets less traveled by, I employ what has proved to be an excellent tension-reducing measure: I whistle melodies from Beethoven and Vivaldi and the more popular classical composers. Even steely New Yorkers hunching toward nighttime destinations seem to relax, and occasionally they even join in the tune. Virtually everybody seems to sense that a mugger wouldn't be warbling bright, sunny selections from Vivaldi's *Four Seasons*. It is my equivalent of the cowbell that hikers wear when they know they are in bear country.

WHAT DOES HE SAY?

1. As you read "Just Walk on By," identify and copy out five sentences: two that identify the effects that Staples seems to produce and three that help you identify the person he really is.

2. As he takes his nightly walks, does Staples seem to be in control of the reactions of other people? Either way, what in the essay leads you to think this?

3. Have you ever been perceived as threatening or felt threatened, as described in "Just Walk on By"? Identify the section in Staples's essay that comes closest to your experience. Then write a paragraph about what happened.

WHAT DO YOU THINK?

4. To what extent, or not, would you argue that any of us is capable of altering public space based on how we look? Return to the scenario that opened this chapter. To what extent do the young woman and the older guy change the classroom's public space? How would you describe those changes? How would it make a difference to the scenario if its location were a subway car? a laundromat? a church?

5. Write about a time when you were judged solely on the basis of your outward appearance. Explain the circumstances carefully, and discuss the reasons you believe you were judged in those ways. What was your reaction to such judgments at the time? What is your reaction now? Use Staples's essay to help illustrate your points.

WHAT WOULD THEY SAY?

6. Read Elmaz Abinader's "Profile of an Arab Daughter" (p. 36) and Benjamin Saenz's "Exile: El Paso, Texas" (p. 20) together with "Just Walk on By." What do these three essays have in common? Together, what do they suggest about

American culture? Write an essay that quotes each of these essays as you analyze the ways they inform each other.

7. Read Studs Terkel's interview with C. P. Ellis (p. 568) together with "Just Walk on By." Based on your understanding of C. P. Ellis, as revealed in that interview, what reactions or comments would he make after reading Staples's essay? What reactions or comments do you think Staples would make after reading the Ellis interview?

SCOTT RUSSELL SANDERS
Looking at Women

*T*HE PRINCIPAL QUESTION *of this essay is how a man should look at a woman, though other questions crop up. Quoting from sources that include Simone de Beauvoir, John Berger, D. H. Lawrence, and Kate Millett, Sanders opens questions about the objectification of women, about pornography, about the struggle always "to recall the wholeness of persons, including ourselves."*

Scott Russell Sanders (b. 1945) is a professor of English at Indiana University and a writer in a variety of genres, including science fiction, folktales, children's stories, historical novels, and essays. His works include The Paradise of Bombs *(1987),* Staying Put: Making a Home in a Restless World *(1993), and* The Country of Language *(1999). "Looking at Women" is taken from his 1991 book,* Secrets of the Universe: Scenes from the Journey Home.

On that sizzling July afternoon, the girl who crossed at the stoplight in front of our car looked, as my mother would say, as though she had been poured into her pink shorts. The girl's matching pink halter bared her stomach and clung to her nubbin breasts, leaving little to the imagination, as my mother would also say. Until that moment, it had never made any difference to me how much or little a girl's clothing revealed, for my imagination had been entirely devoted to other mysteries. I was eleven. The girl was about fourteen, the age of my buddy Norman who lounged in the back seat with me. Staring after her, Norman elbowed me in the ribs and murmured, "Check out that chassis."

His mother glared around from the driver's seat. "Hush your mouth."

"I was talking about that sweet Chevy," said Norman, pointing out a souped–up jalopy at the curb.

"I know what you were talking about," his mother snapped.

No doubt she did know, since mothers could read minds, but at first I did not have a clue. Chassis? I knew what it meant for a car, an airplane, a radio, or even a cannon to have a chassis. But could a girl have one as well? I glanced after the retreating figure, and suddenly noticed with a sympathetic twitching in my belly the way her long raven ponytail swayed in rhythm to her walk and the way her fanny jostled in those pink shorts. In July's dazzle of sun, her swinging legs and arms beamed at me a semaphore I could almost read.

As the light turned green and our car pulled away, Norman's mother cast one more scowl at her son in the rearview mirror, saying, "Just think how it makes her feel to have you two boys gawking at her."

How? I wondered.

5

"Makes her feel like hot stuff," said Norman, owner of a bold mouth.

"If you don't get your mind out of the gutter, you're going to wind up in the state reformatory," said his mother.

Norman gave a snort. I sank into the seat, and tried to figure out what power had sprung from that sashaying girl to zap me in the belly.

Only after much puzzling did it dawn on me that I must finally have drifted into the force field of sex, as a space traveler who has lived all his years in free fall might rocket for the first time within gravitational reach of a star. Even as a bashful eleven-year-old I knew the word *sex*, of course, and I could paste that name across my image of the tantalizing girl. But a label for a mystery no more explains a mystery than the word *gravity* explains gravity. As I grew a beard and my taste shifted from girls to women, I acquired a more cagey language for speaking of desire, I picked up disarming theories. First by hearsay and then by experiment, I learned the delicious details of making babies. I came to appreciate the urgency for propagation that litters the road with maple seeds and drives salmon up waterfalls and yokes the newest crop of boys to the newest crop of girls. Books in their killjoy wisdom taught me that all the valentines and violins, the waltzes and glances, the long fever and ache of romance, were merely embellishments on biology's instructions that we multiply our kind. And yet, the fraction of desire that actually leads to procreation is so vanishingly small as to seem irrelevant. In his lifetime a man sways to a million longings, only a few of which, or perhaps none at all, ever lead to the fathering of children. Now, thirty years away from that July afternoon, firmly married, twice a father, I am still humming from the power unleashed by the girl in pink shorts, still wondering how it made her feel to have two boys gawk at her, still puzzling over how to dwell in the force field of desire.

How should a man look at women? It is a peculiarly and perhaps neurotically human question. Billy goats do not fret over how they should look at nanny goats. They look or don't look, as seasons and hormones dictate, and feel what they feel without benefit of theory. There is more billy goat in most men than we care to admit. None of us, however, is pure goat. To live utterly as an animal would make the business of sex far tidier but also drearier. If we tried, like Rousseau,° to peel off the layers of civilization and imagine our way back to some pristine man and woman who have not yet been corrupted by hand-me-down notions of sexuality, my hunch is that we would find, in our speculative state of nature, that men regarded women with appalling simplicity. In any case, unlike goats, we dwell in history. What attracts our eyes and rouses our blood is only partly instinctual. Other forces contend in us as well: the voices of books and religions, the images of art and film and advertising,

---

Rousseau: Jean-Jacques Rousseau (1712–1778), French philosopher who asserted that human beings were naturally good and that education, society, and government undermined this natural state. [All notes are the Editors'.]

the entire chorus of culture. Norman's telling me to relish the sight of females and his mother's telling me to keep my eyes to myself are only two of the many voices quarreling in my head.

If there were a rule book for sex, it would be longer than the one for baseball (that byzantine sport), more intricate and obscure than tax instructions from the Internal Revenue Service. What I present here are a few images and reflections that cling, for me, to this one item in such a compendium of rules: how should a man look at women?

Well before I was to see any women naked in the flesh, I saw a bevy of them naked in photographs, hung in a gallery around the bed of my freshman room-mate at college. A *Playboy* subscriber, he would pluck the centerfold from its staples each month and tape another airbrushed lovely to the wall. The gallery was in place when I moved in, and for an instant before I realized what I was looking at, all that expanse of skin reminded me of a meat locker back in New-ton Falls, Ohio. I never quite shook that first impression, even after I had in-spected the pinups at my leisure on subsequent days. Every curve of buttock and breast was news to me, an innocent kid from the Puritan back roads. Today you would be hard pressed to find a college freshman as ignorant as I was of fe-male anatomy, if only because teenagers now routinely watch movies at home that would have been shown, during my teen years, exclusively on the fly-speckled screens of honky-tonk cinemas or in the basement of the Kinsey Institute.° I studied those alien shapes on the wall with a curiosity that was not wholly sexual, a curiosity tinged with the wonder that astronomers must have felt when they pored over the early photographs of the far side of the moon.

The paper women seemed to gaze back at me, enticing or mocking, yet 15 even in my adolescent dither I was troubled by the phony stare, for I knew this was no true exchange of looks. Those mascaraed eyes were not fixed on me but on a camera. What the models felt as they posed I could only guess—perhaps the boredom of any numbskull job, perhaps the weight of dollar bills, per-haps the sweltering lights of fame, perhaps a tingle of the power that launched a thousand ships.

Whatever their motives, these women had chosen to put themselves on display. For the instant of the photograph, they had become their bodies, as a prizefighter does in the moment of landing a punch, as a weightlifter does in the moment of hoisting a barbell, as a ballerina does in the whirl of a pirouette, as we all do in the crisis of making love or dying. Men, ogling such pho-tographs, are supposed to feel that where so much surface is revealed there can be no depths. Yet I never doubted that behind the makeup and the plump curves and the two dimensions of the image there was an inwardness, a feeling

---

Kinsey Institute: The research institute devoted to the interdisciplinary study of human sexuality, founded by Alfred Kinsey in 1947.

self as mysterious as my own. In fact, during moments when I should have been studying French or thermodynamics, I would glance at my roommate's wall and invent mythical lives for those goddesses. The lives I made up were adolescent ones, to be sure; but so was mine. Without that saving aura of inwardness, these women in the glossy photographs would have become merely another category of objects for sale, alongside the sports cars and stereo systems and liquors advertised in the same pages. If not extinguished, however, their humanity was severely reduced. And if by simplifying themselves they had lost some human essence, then by gaping at them I had shared in the theft.

What did that gaping take from me? How did it affect my way of seeing other women, those who would never dream of lying nude on a fake tiger rug before the million-faceted eye of a camera? The bodies in the photographs were implausibly smooth and slick and inflated, like balloon caricatures that might be floated overhead in a parade. Free of sweat and scars and imperfections, sensual without being fertile, tempting yet impregnable, they were Platonic ideals of the female form, divorced from time and the fluster of living, excused from the perplexities of mind. No actual woman could rival their insipid perfection.

The swains who gathered to admire my roommate's gallery discussed the pinups in the same tones and in much the same language as the farmers back home in Ohio used for assessing cows. The relevant parts of male or female bodies are quickly named—and, the *Kamasutra* and Marquis de Sade notwithstanding, the number of ways in which those parts can be stimulated or conjoined is touchingly small—so these studly conversations were more tedious than chitchat about the weather. I would lie on my bunk pondering calculus or Aeschylus° and unwillingly hear the same few nouns and fewer verbs issuing from one mouth after another, and I would feel smugly superior. Here I was, improving my mind, while theirs wallowed in the notorious gutter. Eventually the swains would depart, leaving me in peace, and from the intellectual heights of my bunk I would glance across at those photographs—and yield to the gravity of lust. Idiot flesh! How stupid that a counterfeit stare and artful curves, printed in millions of copies on glossy paper, could arouse me. But there it was, not the first proof of my body's automatism and not the last.

Nothing in men is more machinelike than the flipping of sexual switches. I have never been able to read with a straight face the claims made by D. H. Lawrence° and lesser pundits that the penis is a god, a lurking dragon. It more nearly resembles a railroad crossing signal, which stirs into life at intervals to announce, "Here comes a train." Or, if the penis must be likened to an animal, let it be an ill-trained circus dog, sitting up and playing dead and heeling whenever it takes a notion, oblivious of the trainer's commands. Meanwhile,

---

Aeschylus (525–456 B.C.): Greek writer of plays, especially tragedies.
D. H. Lawrence (1885–1930): English novelist whose works often explore sexual themes.

heart, lungs, blood vessels, pupils, and eyelids all assert their independence like the members of a rebellious troupe. Reason stands helpless at the center of the ring, cracking its whip.

While he was president, Jimmy Carter raised a brouhaha by confessing 20 in a *Playboy* interview, of all shady places, that he occasionally felt lust in his heart for women. What man hasn't, aside from those who feel lust in their hearts for other men? The commentators flung their stones anyway. Naughty, naughty, they chirped. Wicked Jimmy. Perhaps Mr. Carter could derive some consolation from psychologist Allen Wheelis, who blames male appetite on biology: "We have been selected for desiring. Nothing could have convinced us by argument that it would be worthwhile to chase endlessly and insatiably after women, but something has transformed us from within, a plasmid has invaded our DNA, has twisted our nature so that now this is exactly what we *want* to do." Certainly, by Darwinian logic, those males who were most avid in their pursuit of females were also the most likely to pass on their genes. Consoling it may be, yet it is finally no solution to blame biology. "I am extremely sexual in my desires: I carry them everywhere and at all times," William Carlos Williams° tells us on the opening page of his autobiography. "I think that from that arises the drive which empowers us all. Given that drive, a man does with it what his mind directs. In the manner in which he directs that power lies his secret." Whatever the contents of my DNA, however potent the influence of my ancestors, I still must direct that rebellious power. I still must live with the consequences of my looking and my longing.

Aloof on their blankets like goddesses on clouds, the pinups did not belong to my funky world. I was invisible to them, and they were immune to my gaze. Not so the women who passed me on the street, sat near me in classes, shared a table with me in the cafeteria: it was risky to stare at them. They could gaze back, and sometime did, with looks both puzzling and exciting. It only complicated matters for me to realize that so many of these strangers had taken precautions that men should notice them. The girl in matching pink halter and shorts who set me humming in my eleventh year might only have wanted to keep cool in the sizzle of July. But these alluring college femmes had deeper designs. Perfume, eye shadow, uplift bras (about which I learned in the Sears catalog), curled hair, stockings, jewelry, lipstick, lace—what were these if not hooks thrown out into male waters?

I recall being mystified in particular by spike heels. They looked painful to me, and dangerous. Danger may have been the point, since the spikes would have made good weapons—they were affectionately known, after all, as stilettos. Or danger may have been the point in another sense, because a woman teetering along on such heels is tipsy, vulnerable, broadcasting her need for support.

William Carlos Williams (1883–1963): Noted American poet, he was also a medical doctor.

And who better than a man to prop her up, some guy who clomps around in brogans wide enough for the cornerstones of flying buttresses? (For years after college, I felt certain that spike heels had been forever banned, like bustles and foot-binding, but lately they have come back in fashion, and once more one encounters women teetering along on knife points.)

Back in those days of my awakening to women, I was also baffled by lingerie. I do not mean underwear, the proletariat of clothing, and I do not mean foundation garments, pale and sensible. I mean what the woman who lives in the house behind ours—owner of a shop called "Bare Essentials"—refers to as "intimate apparel." Those two words announce that her merchandise is both sexy and expensive. These flimsy items cost more per ounce than truffles, more than frankincense and myrrh. They are put-ons whose only purpose is in being taken off. I have a friend who used to attend the men's-only nights at Bare Essentials, during which he would invariably buy a slinky outfit or two, by way of proving his serious purpose, outfits that wound up in the attic because his wife would not be caught dead in them. Most of the customers at the shop are women, however, as the models are women, and the owner is a woman. What should one make of that? During my college days I knew about intimate apparel only by rumor, not being that intimate with anyone who would have tricked herself out in such finery, but I could see the spike heels and other female trappings everywhere I turned. Why, I wondered then and wonder still, do so many women decorate themselves like dolls? And does that mean they wish to be viewed as dolls?

On this question as on many others, Simone de Beauvoir° has clarified matters for me, writing in *The Second Sex:* "The 'feminine' woman in making herself prey tries to reduce man, also, to her carnal passivity; she occupies herself in catching him in her trap, in enchaining him by means of the desires she arouses in him in submissively making herself a thing." Those women who transform themselves into dolls, in other words, do so because that is the most potent identity available to them. "It must be admitted," Beauvoir concedes, "that the males find in woman more complicity than the oppressor usually finds in the oppressed. And in bad faith they take authorization from this to declare that she has *desired* the destiny they have imposed on her."

Complicity, oppressor, bad faith: such terms yank us into a moral realm un- 25 known to goats. While I am saddled with enough male guilt to believe three-quarters of Beauvoir's claim, I still doubt that men are so entirely to blame for the turning of women into sexual dolls. I believe human history is more collaborative than her argument would suggest. It seems unlikely to me that one-half the species could have "imposed" a destiny on the other half, unless that other half were far more craven than the females I have known. Some women have expressed their own skepticism on this point. Thus Joan Didion:

Simone de Beauvoir (1908–1986): French novelist, philosopher, and feminist critic.

"That many women are victims of condescension and exploitation and sex-role stereotyping was scarcely news, but neither was it news that other women are not: nobody forces women to buy the package." Beauvior herself recognized that many members of her sex refuse to buy the "feminine" package: "The emancipated woman, on the contrary, wants to be active, a taker, and refuses the passivity man means to impose on her."

Since my college years, back in the murky 1960s, emancipated women have been discouraging their unemancipated sisters from making spectacles of themselves. Don't paint your face like a clown's or drape your body like a mannequin's, they say. Don't bounce on the sidelines in skimpy outfits, screaming your fool head off, while men compete in the limelight for victories. Don't present yourself to the world as a fluff pastry, delicate and edible. Don't waddle across the stage in a bathing suit in hopes of being named Miss This or That.

A great many women still ignore the exhortations. Wherever a crown for beauty is to be handed out, many still line up to stake their claims. Recently, Miss Indiana Persimmon Festival was quoted in our newspaper about the burdens of possessing the sort of looks that snag men's eyes. "Most of the time I enjoy having guys stare at me," she said, "but every once in a while it makes me feel like a piece of meat." The news photograph showed a cheerleader's perky face, heavily made-up, with starched hair teased into a blond cumulus. She put me in mind not of meat but of a plastic figurine, something you might buy from a booth outside a shrine. Nobody should ever be seen as meat, mere juicy stuff to satisfy an appetite. Better to appear as a plastic figurine, which is not meant for eating, and which is a gesture, however crude, toward art. Joyce° described the aesthetic response as a contemplation of form without the impulse to action. Perhaps that is what Miss Indiana Persimmon Festival wishes to inspire in those who look at her, perhaps that is what many women who paint and primp themselves desire: to withdraw from the touch of hands and dwell in the eye alone, to achieve the status of art.

By turning herself (or allowing herself to be turned into) a work of art, does a woman truly escape men's proprietary stare? Not often, says the British critic John Berger. Summarizing the treatment of women in Western painting, he concludes that—with a few notable exceptions, such as works by Rubens and Rembrandt—the woman on canvas is a passive object displayed for the pleasure of the male viewer, especially for the owner of the painting, who is, by extension, owner of the woman herself. Berger concludes: "Men look at women. Women watch themselves being looked at. This determines not only most relations between men and women but also the relation of women to themselves. The surveyor of woman in herself is male: the surveyed female. Thus she turns herself into an object—and most particularly an object of vision: a sight."

James Joyce (1882–1941): Irish novelist.

That sweeping claim, like the one quoted earlier from Beauvoir, also seems to me about three-quarters truth and one-quarter exaggeration. I know men who outdo the peacock for show, and I know women who are so fully possessed of themselves that they do not give a hang whether anybody notices them or not. The flamboyant gentlemen portrayed by Van Dyck° are no less aware of being *seen* than are the languid ladies portrayed by Ingres.° With or without clothes, both gentlemen and ladies may conceive of themselves as objects of vision, targets of envy or admiration or desire. Where they differ is in their potential for action: the men are caught in the midst of a decisive gesture or on the verge of making one; the women wait like fuel for someone else to strike a match.

I am not sure the abstract nudes favored in modern art are much of an advance over the inert and voluptuous ones of the old school. Think of two famous examples: Duchamp's *Nude Descending a Staircase* (1912), where the faceless woman has blurred into a waterfall of jagged shards, or Picasso's *Les Demoiselles d'Avignon* (1907), where the five angular damsels have been hammered as flat as cookie sheets and fitted with African masks. Neither painting invites us to behold a woman, but instead to behold what Picasso or Duchamp can make of one.

The naked women in Rubens, far from being passive, are gleefully active, exuberant, their sumptuous pink bodies like rainclouds or plump nebulae. "His nudes are the first ones that ever made me feel happy about my own body," a woman friend told me in one of the Rubens galleries of the Prado Museum. I do not imagine any pinup or store-window mannequin or bathing-suited Miss Whatsit could have made her feel that way. The naked women in Rembrandt, emerging from the bath or rising from bed, are so private, so cherished in the painter's gaze, that we as viewers see them not as sexual playthings but as loved persons. A man would do well to emulate that gaze.

I have never thought of myself as a sight. How much that has to do with being male and how much with having grown up on the back roads where money was scarce and eyes were few, I cannot say. As a boy, apart from combing my hair when I was compelled to and regretting the patches on my jeans (only the poor wore patches), I took no trouble over my appearance. It never occurred to me that anybody outside my family, least of all a girl, would look at me twice. As a young man, when young women did occasionally glance my way, without any prospect of appearing handsome I tried at least to avoid appearing odd. A standard haircut and the cheapest versions of the standard clothes were camouflage enough. Now as a middle-aged man I have achieved once more that boyhood condition of invisibility, with less hair to comb and fewer patches to humble me.

Van Dyck: Anthony Van Dyck (1599–1641), Dutch painter.
Ingres: Jean-Auguste-Dominique Ingres (1780–1867), French painter.

Many women clearly pass through the world aspiring to invisibility. Many others just as clearly aspire to be conspicuous. Women need not make spectacles of themselves in order to draw the attention of men. Indeed, for my taste, the less paint and fewer bangles the better. I am as helpless in the presence of subtle lures as a male moth catching a whiff of pheromones. I am a sucker for hair ribbons, a scarf at the throat, toes leaking from sandals, teeth bared in a smile. By contrast, I have always been more amused than attracted by the enameled exhibitionists whom our biblical mothers would identify as brazen hussies or painted Jezebels or, in the extreme cases, as whores of Babylon.

To encounter female exhibitionists in their full glory and variety, you need to go to a city. I never encountered ogling as a full-blown sport until I visited Rome, where bands of Italian men joined with gusto in appraising the charms of every passing female, and the passing females vied with one another in demonstrating their charms. In our own cities the most notorious bands of oglers tend to be construction gangs or street crews, men who spend much of their day leaning on the handles of shovels or pausing between bursts of riveting guns, their eyes tracing the curves of passersby. The first time my wife and kids and I drove into Boston we followed the signs to Chinatown, only to discover that Chinatown's miserably congested main street was undergoing repairs. That street also proved to be the city's home for X-rated cinemas and girlie shows and skin shops. LIVE SEX ACTS ON STAGE. PEEP SHOWS. PRIVATE BOOTHS. Caught in a traffic jam, we spent an hour listening to jackhammers and wolf whistles as we crept through the few blocks of pleasure palaces, my son and daughter with their noses hanging out the windows, my wife and I steaming. Lighted marquees peppered by burnt-out bulbs announced the titles of sleazy flicks; life-size posters of naked women flanked the doorways of clubs: leggy strippers in miniskirts, the originals for some of the posters, smoked on the curb between numbers.

After we had finally emerged from the zone of eros, eight-year-old Jesse 35 inquired, "What was *that* place all about?"

"Sex for sale," my wife Ruth explained.

That might carry us some way toward a definition of pornography: making flesh into a commodity, flaunting it like any other merchandise, divorcing bodies from selves. By this reckoning, there is a pornographic dimension to much advertising, where a charge of sex is added to products ranging from cars to shaving cream. In fact, the calculated imagery of advertising may be more harmful than the blatant imagery of the pleasure palaces, that frank raunchiness which Kate Millett refers to as the "truthful explicitness of pornography." One can leave the X-rated zone of the city, but one cannot escape the sticky reach of commerce, which summons girls to the high calling of cosmetic glamor, fashion, and sexual display, while it summons boys to the panting chase.

You can recognize pornography, according to D. H. Lawrence, "by the insult it offers, invariably, to sex, and to the human spirit." He should know,

Millett argues in *Sexual Politics*, for in her view Lawrence himself was a purveyor of patriarchal and often sadistic pornography. I think she is correct about the worst of Lawrence, and that she identifies a misogynist streak in his work; but she ignores his career-long struggle to achieve a more public, tolerant vision of sexuality as an exchange between equals. Besides, his novels and stories all bear within themselves their own critiques. George Steiner° reminds us that "the list of writers who have had the genius to enlarge our actual compass of sexual awareness, who have given the erotic play of the mind a novel focus, an area of recognition previously unknown or fallow, is very small." Lawrence belongs on that brief list. The chief insult to the human spirit is to deny it, to claim that we are merely conglomerations of molecules, to pretend that we exist purely as bundles of appetites or as food for the appetites of others.

Men commit that insult toward women out of ignorance, but also out of dread. Allen Wheelis again: "Men gather in pornographic shows, not to stimulate desire, as they may think, but to diminish fear. It is the nature of the show to reduce the woman, discard her individuality, her soul, make her into an object, thereby enabling the man to handle her with greater safety, to use her as a toy.... As women move increasingly toward equality, the felt danger to men increases, leading to an increase in pornography and, since there are some men whose fears cannot even so be stilled, to an increase also in violence against women."

Make her into an object: all the hurtful ways for men to look at women 40 are variations on this betrayal. "Thus she turns herself into an object," writes Berger. A woman's ultimate degradation is in "submissively making herself a thing," writes Beauvoir. To be turned into an object—whether by the brush of a painter or the lens of a photographer or the eye of a voyeur, whether by hunger or poverty or enslavement, by mugging or rape, bullets or bombs, by hatred, racism, car crashes, fires, or falls—is for each of us the deepest dread; and to reduce another person to an object is the primal wrong.

Caught in the vortex of desire, we have to struggle to recall the wholeness of persons, including ourselves. Beauvoir speaks of the temptation we all occasionally feel to give up the struggle for a self and lapse into the inertia of an object: "Along with the ethical urge of each individual to affirm his subjective existence, there is also the temptation to forgo liberty and become a thing." A woman in particular, given so much encouragement to lapse into thinghood, "is often very well pleased with her role as the *Other*."

Yet one need not forgo liberty and become a thing, without a center or a self, in order to become the Other. In our mutual strangeness, men and women can be doorways one for another, openings into the creative mystery

---

George Steiner (b. 1929): Contemporary critic of language and culture.

that we share by virtue of our existence in the flesh. "To be sensual," James Baldwin writes, "is to respect and rejoice in the force of life, of life itself, and to be *present* in all that one does, from the effort of loving to the breaking of bread." The effort of loving is reciprocal, not only in act but in desire, an *I* addressing a *Thou*, a meeting in that vivid presence. The distance a man stares across at a woman, or a woman at a man, is a gulf in the soul, out of which a voice cries, *Leap, leap*. One day all men may cease to look on themselves as prototypically human and on women as lesser miracles; women may cease to feel themselves the targets for desire; men and women both may come to realize that we are all mere flickerings in the universal fire; and then none of us, male or female, need give up humanity in order to become the *Other*.

Ever since I gawked at the girl in pink shorts, I have dwelt knowingly in the force field of sex. Knowingly or not, it is where we all dwell. Like the masses of planets and stars, our bodies curve the space around us. We radiate signals constantly, radio sources that never go off the air. We cannot help being centers of attraction and repulsion for one another. That is not all we are by a long shot, nor all we are capable of feeling, and yet, even after our much-needed revolution in sexual consciousness, the power of eros will still turn our heads and hearts. In a world without beauty pageants, there will still be beauty, however its definition may have changed. As long as men have eyes, they will gaze with yearning and confusion at women.

When I return to the street with the ancient legacy of longing coiled in my DNA, and the residues from a thousand generations of patriarchs silting my brain, I encounter women whose presence strikes me like a slap of wind in the face. I must prepare a gaze that is worthy of their splendor.

WHAT DOES HE SAY?

1. As you're reading, pay attention to whenever the essay seems to indicate that "desire" and "sex" are biologically driven and whenever it seems to say that such things are learned, cultural behaviors. Mark each of these in a different way in the margin so that you can easily locate them later.

2. Scott Russell Sanders tells us that his college roommate pinned up *Playboy* centerfolds. How does Sanders describe what it meant to look at those pictures? Copy out three sentences that seem centrally important to understanding what Sanders says. Then write a paragraph discussing your reactions.

3. "Looking at Women" says, at one point, that "alluring college femmes had deeper designs." Copy out the sentence that follows this quotation. Later on, the essay quotes Simone de Beauvoir as she speaks of "the 'feminine' woman." Locate that section and copy out the first sentence of that quotation. Finally, locate the section a bit later where Beauvoir characterizes "the emancipated woman" and copy out that sentence. Now write a paragraph in response to the three sentences you have copied.

WHAT DO YOU THINK?

4. Take an inventory of your own clothes closet. What does it contain? What do you wear to classes? What do you wear to go shopping? What do you wear to nicer restaurants? In each case, discuss candidly why you choose to wear the clothes that you pick. Do you dress for yourself? Do your clothing choices send messages to other people? Do you dress for how you will be seen? Write an essay that discusses how you want to be looked at, and make sure that it quotes "Looking at Women" at least twice.

5. Write an imitation of "Looking at Women," but use the word *women* or *men* to fit your sexual orientation. Select the parts of Sanders's essay that come closest to paralleling or contradicting your own experience, and use those parts to help make your own experience clearer to readers (either via comparison or contrast). You'll notice that "Looking at Women" uses extra space to announce shifts in the essay's direction. Use the same tactic in your own essay.

6. Write about an experience when you became only a body—reduced in someone else's eyes to merely a physical exterior or reduced by the circumstances of the moment to simply a biological entity. Contrast that experience with another in which your inner self, your consciousness, and your character made all the difference. Once you've written about these two experiences, tell readers how you can, or cannot, reconcile them: What do you make of their contrasts? What seems clearer to you now that you have explored those contrasts?

WHAT WOULD THEY SAY?

7. Read "Looking at Women" together with Stephen L. Carter's "Welcoming the Stranger" (p. 111) and Brent Staples's "Just Walk on By: Black Men and Public Space" (p. 289). Write an essay that discusses how the issues these essays raise involve, or do not involve, essential questions of freedom.

8. Consider Bernard Cooper's "A Clack of Tiny Sparks: Remembrances of a Gay Boyhood" (p. 314) together with "Looking at Women." To what extent do these essays assert some of the same things? To what extent do they significantly differ?

9. Read "Looking at Women" together with Judith Ortiz Cofer's "The Story of My Body" (p. 323). To what extent do these essays acknowledge and assert the same things? Do they significantly differ?

LYNNE LUCIANO

Male Body Image in America

*W*E MOVE FROM THE ISSUE *of female bodies and body image to the issue of male body image. In this piece, Lynne Luciano (b. 1943) traces recent changes in male body image and what our culture thinks of men and how they should look.*

An assistant professor in the University of California system, Luciano teaches courses in women's history and twentieth century American history. She has worked for the RAND Corporation on international relations and policy planning. The excerpt printed here is from Looking Good: Male Body Image in America *(2001), her first book.*

American men spent $3 billion on grooming aids and fragrances in 1997. They also spent nearly $800 million on hair transplants and $400 million on hairpieces. Sales of exercise equipment and health-club memberships raked in $4 billion. An estimated eighty-five million Americans, mostly male, are doing some kind of weight training. Even serious bodybuilding, once a fringe activity largely relegated to the lower classes, has gained middle-class status as upwardly mobile men of all ages grunt and strain for the blood-vessel-constricting high known as the pump. For men who have more fat than muscle, a lucrative foundation-garment industry offers Butt-Busters and Man-Bands to flatten bulges. Men are dieting in unprecedented numbers, and an estimated one million of them suffer from eating disorders commonly thought to afflict only women.

Also surprising is men's pursuit of beauty through the scalpel: in 1996, the bill for male cosmetic surgery was $500 million. Just under $200 million was spent on the two most popular surgeries, liposuction and rhinoplasty (nose jobs), with the rest going for esoteric surgeries like pectoral implants and the creation of cleft chins, not to mention the ultimate male surgery, penis enlargement. We are clearly witnessing the evolution of an obsession with body image, especially among middle-class men, and a corresponding male appropriation of, in the words of the feminist Barbara Ehrenreich, "status-seeking activities...once seen as feminine."

What, then, does it mean to be a man at the dawn of the twenty-first century? The historian and philosopher Elisabeth Badinter has concluded that models of masculinity haven't changed much over the centuries. She points to four "imperatives" for today's men: first and foremost, men must be men — "no sissy stuff"; second, they must be competitive, constantly demonstrating their success and superiority; third, they must be "detached and impassive"; and, finally, they must be willing to take risks and confront danger, even to the point of violence. These four imperatives have two qualities in common: they are diametrically opposed to what is generally regarded as feminine behavior, and they say nothing about how a man is supposed to *look*.

Until World War II, it is true, male attractiveness was derived from activity; how a man behaved and what he achieved were the true measures of his worth. In the immediate aftermath of World War II, it seemed these ideals would continue along their accustomed track. The American male would provide for his family, succeed at his job, and be strong, rugged, and virile. While women labored at self-beautification, men devoted themselves to more important matters. Men were not exactly indifferent to their bodies, but any man who overly emphasized his physical appearance risked being accused of vanity. Men who wore toupees aroused amused derision at best. Although obesity among Americans had reached alarming proportions by midcentury, men shied away from dieting, despite warnings about heart disease. Exercise, which at least had the cachet of being "masculine" because it was associated with action, didn't get much more strenuous than golf and gardening. Workouts that raised serious sweat had few middle-class adherents, and cosmetic surgery was regarded as the exclusive preserve of women. As for the body's most intimate parts, a cloud of secrecy shrouded them, as well as their function (and dysfunction), from public debate and public view.

What has caused American men to fall into the beauty trap so long assumed to be the special burden of women? Does men's concern about their bodies mean they've become feminized? Have they been so addled by the women's movement that they are responding by becoming more like women? There is no simple, single answer. Rather, a confluence of social, economic, and cultural changes has been instrumental in shaping the new cult of male body image in postwar America.

The changing status of women brought about by second-wave feminism has radically reshaped how women view the male body. As long as men controlled economic resources, their looks were of secondary importance. Though feminism would have many, often conflicting, objectives, the liberal feminism that emerged mainly among professional and upper-middle-class women focused on social and legal constraints that denied women equal access to the workplace. As the role of breadwinner became a shared one, men's economic power and sense of uniqueness would be undermined.

The impetus behind the rising number of college-educated wives entering the workplace came less from the need to contribute to the family income, however, than from the diminishing attractions of the home. Avid middle-class pursuit of higher education, especially at graduate and professional levels, deterred growing numbers of young men and women from early marriage. At the same time, greater latitude for sexual experimentation made it less likely that women would marry just to legitimize sexual relations. An emphasis on the importance of self-fulfillment also undermined marriage as a priority for many young Americans. It was during the 1960s that the term *lifestyle* was first used in reference to being single: its significance lay in its suggestion of choice.

Marriage was no longer expected but a matter of personal taste, as were its alternatives, divorce and cohabitation, which became ever more common.

By the end of the decade, the average age at first marriage had risen, and the marriage rate had begun to drop, and continued to drop through the 1970s. A survey of college students at that time showed that 82 percent of the women rated a career as important to self-fulfillment, whereas only 67 percent believed this was true of marriage. The *Cosmopolitan* editor Helen Gurley Brown, who had spent most of the 1960s trying to create an image of the *Cosmo* girl as mirror image of the sexually uninhibited *Playboy* man, emphatically agreed: marriage, she told her legions of female readers, was nothing more than "insurance for the worst years of your life."

Try as she might to turn men into sex objects, Brown was ahead of her time in 1962. For most women, being single was still stigmatizing rather than stimulating. And as Brown herself was quick to point out, sexual liberation didn't work without economic liberation, and that hadn't arrived yet. But as the decade progressed, single life took on new legitimacy and had wide-ranging social and economic effects. One of the most significant was that in the dating marketplace, single women were as likely to be doing the choosing—and rejecting—as men, elevating the importance of male looks to a whole new level. Why, demands the woman who works out rigorously to keep her body lean and fit, should I put up with a man who spends his leisure time sitting on a couch watching television? Or, as the feminist Germaine Greer inquired with some acerbity in 1971, was it too much to ask that women be spared "the daily struggle for superhuman beauty in order to offer it to the caresses of a subhuman ugly mate"?

Economic change wasn't limited to women's more substantial paychecks. 10 World War II catapulted America into unprecedented power and prosperity. Lavish government spending, corporate expansion, and the development of a vast complex of technological industries based on the postwar symbiosis of military, government, and science created thousands of secure, well-paying white-collar jobs. As union wages rose, stimulated by cost-of-living increases and buffered by national prosperity, millions of working-class Americans could afford middle-class lifestyles and the accoutrements that defined them.

For nearly a quarter century, expectations of continued affluence and material progress were undimmed. But in the 1970s, America's virtually unchallenged global economic preeminence, as well as its internal prosperity, would confront foreign competition, inflation, declining corporate profits, and unemployment. In the ensuing downsizing that persisted well into the 1990s, hardest hit would be those most accustomed to job success and security—white males. To maintain an edge, it became important not just to be qualified for a job but to look as if one were; and that meant looking dynamic, successful, and, above all, young.

These changes are related to a more complex and extremely significant alteration in American life since midcentury: the rise of a culture increasingly based on self-fulfillment and the cultivation of self-esteem. Though many factors brought about this sea change, one of the most compelling was the proliferation of consumerism and its emphasis on the importance of self-image.

America's transformation from a culture of production to one of consumption was well under way by the turn of the nineteenth century. At that time, the basic needs of most middle-class Americans were being met, and manufacturers therefore sought to create desire in place of necessity. They were aided by advertisers who set out to convince consumers that their very identities depended on owning the right products, that they could be whatever they wished, as long as they purchased enough goods.

Advertising agencies appeared on the American landscape as early as the 1850s but remained on a small scale until World War I, when technological and cultural factors converged to create the modern advertising industry. New technologies like arc and neon lighting allowed ads to be displayed in more interesting and enticing ways, while advanced printing methods like lithography made it possible to copy images less expensively and more attractively. During the war, advertising and public relations joined forces with the U.S. government to generate propaganda and unifying symbols as a means of mobilizing support for the war among a fragmented and diverse population—an effort devoted more to popularizing and legitimizing the war than to disseminating real information. Afterward, products poured off booming American assembly lines, and advertisers mobilized consumer enthusiasm in much the same way. Ad agencies created personalities for their products, which were sold not on the basis of what they could do but on the basis of the image they projected—as one advertising mogul put it, they sold the sizzle, not the steak.

Advertising was helped in its crusade by the emergent popularity of psy- 15 chology. Terms like *ego* and *repression* were bandied about in everyday conversation, and by the 1920s, the idea of complexes had moved out of medical circles and into the lives of ordinary people. Americans, buffeted by changes brought about by industrialization and the new public life of cities, had fallen prey to feelings of anxiety and insecurity. Magazines and self-help books asked, "Do you have an inferiority complex?" and emphasized the importance of self-scrutiny. Advertisers seized on the connection between the psychological and the physical, urging consumers to buy their products to overcome deficiencies ranging from dandruff to bad breath.

Well into the twentieth century, women were advertisers' main targets. Consumption—that is, shopping—was defined as women's work. Single women were encouraged to compete for men by buying commodities to make themselves more beautiful, and married women were encouraged to demonstrate their husbands' success by their purchasing power. But as commodities became increasingly central to defining self-worth, men, too, would be pulled into the vortex of consumerism, warned by advertisers that the wrong "look" posed a threat to career, love life, and self-esteem.

In its early days, advertising had been simply a means of linking buyer and seller by presenting basic information about a product—how big it was, for example, or how much it cost. But in an urbanizing and modernizing culture, advertising evolved from selling mere products to selling their benefits. Advertising is about image, self-esteem, and display of the self. It is *not* about what the psychologist Erik Erikson calls, in his studies of human psychological development, "the mature person's developing sense of the importance of giving something back to community and society." In a consumer society, a sense of responsibility to the larger community doesn't develop. As the sociologist Diane Barthel points out, every advertiser knows that the critical attribute of any product is "What will it do for *me*?" The line between commodity and individual has become blurred, so that we *are* what we buy. Americans have been beguiled by marketing acumen, and the body has become the ultimate commodity.

The importance of self-presentation originated early in the century, though initially it was more subtle than it is today. As early as the second decade, social critics were noting that America was shifting from a culture of character to a culture of personality. Character implies self-discipline and a sense of inner direction, whereas personality revolves around the ability to please others—not necessarily through real accomplishment but by winning friends and influencing people. While character is its own reward, personality demands external validation and appreciation.

By midcentury, the ethos of personality had almost entirely displaced older notions of character. Image is described by the historian Daniel Boorstin as "a studiously crafted personality profile of an individual...a value caricature, shaped in three dimensions, of synthetic materials." Like the right personality, it relies on external indicators to proclaim our personal worth and determine how others see and evaluate us. The right clothes, the right car, and even the right body and face—all can be purchased rather than cultivated.

The 1960s brought not only social upheaval but an emphasis on sexuality, 20 self-expression, and youth. Commercial packaging of youth actually began in the 1950s, when marketers recognized teenagers' "purchasing power," a term first used after World War II. By 1959, teenagers controlled ten billion dollars in discretionary income, more than the total sales of General Motors. Teen society was grounded in a sense of acute difference from adult society and was primarily defined in terms of consumer choices, especially in fashion and music. Yet in other respects, adolescents in the 1950s appeared to want the same things as their parents: a mate, a family, a home in the suburbs. They spent a great deal of time practicing for their future by playing courtship games like going steady and getting pinned. Most girls looked forward to taking on the responsibilities of motherhood, and boys wanted to become men. As for adults, though they wanted to look attractive and have that elusive quality known as "sex appeal," they generally didn't wish to look, or behave, like teenagers. The culture of youth was distinctive *because* it was reserved for the young.

The cultural importance of youth surged in the 1970s, as prosperity continued to allow teenagers to pursue their distinctive consumerism and because so many defining aspects of the 1960s—fashion, hair, music, radicalism—had centered on young people, especially those of college age. Even the soldiers who fought in the Vietnam War were younger than those of any previous American war: their average age was nineteen, compared with twenty-four for soldiers in World War II. Although the end of the 1960s was marked by disillusionment over the decade's social and political turmoil, the desirability of being (and looking) young remained undimmed. Growing numbers of Americans, confronting the prospect of turning thirty, became determined never to leave adolescence—at least, not physically. Youth was no longer a stage of life to be passed through but one to be clung to tenaciously.

In the 1970s, the obsession with youthfulness combined with the emphasis on self-expression and acquisitiveness to create an entirely new culture grounded in the importance of self-esteem. Narcissism, identified in the 1960s by Erikson as a modern form of neurosis, was recast by the historian and cultural theorist Christopher Lasch into a theory of modern social history. According to Lasch, the bewildering array of images to which the average American was subjected led to a preoccupation with projecting the "right" image of oneself in order to confirm one's very existence. If the 1950s had been defined by conformity, the 1970s were characterized by a sense of selfhood "hopelessly dependent on the consumption of images" and consequently on relentless self-scrutiny. The marketing of commodities, Lasch cautioned, created a world of insubstantial images difficult to distinguish from reality. Within this world, images were incorporated into Americans' visions of themselves, with important implications for body image for both genders. Advertising and mass marketing held out the promise of self-fulfillment and eternal youth through consumerism—for everyone. Finally, as the historian Margaret Morganroth Gullette has observed, "the system that sells products based on fears of aging...turned its giant voracious maw toward that next great big juicy market, men."

In the 1990s, that "big juicy market" was the largest it had ever been—the baby boomers were entering middle age. These thirty-one million people—12 percent of the population—were beginning to experience the trauma of midlife crisis. In 1993, the National Men's Resource Center declared that all men undergo a midlife crisis and that a major manifestation of this was growing concern about the loss of physical appeal.

It's tempting to surmise that men's interest in body image, and their relatively recent concerns about physical attractiveness, along with sexualization of the male body, means they are becoming feminized. This, however, is decidedly not the case. Looking good is part of a quintessential male strategy whose ultimate aim is to make men more successful, competitive, and powerful. The means of achieving this goal may be new, but the objective is not.

Millions of American men have been transformed into body-conscious 25
consumers of revealing fashions, seductive perfumes, and the services of hair-
stylists, personal trainers, and plastic surgeons. Due credit for this transformation must be given to advertisers, marketers, and self-esteem gurus, who have
sold men—and all of us—a message of self-transfiguration through self-
commodification. The traditional image of women as sexual objects has simply been expanded: *everyone* has become an object to be seen.

WHAT DOES SHE SAY?

1. Before you start reading this essay, make a list of five attributes of a successful
   twenty-something man.

2. Luciano cites several causes for the male pursuit of youth, sex appeal, and success.
   Identify two of these causes that seem particularly accurate to you. Then write a
   paragraph explaining why you chose them.

3. Look at a magazine like *GQ, Esquire,* or *Vanity Fair.* Identify an advertisement that
   seems to illustrate some of the points Luciano makes. Make a copy of the ad and
   bring it to class.

4. Think of men you know. To what extent—or not—would they recognize themselves in Luciano's essay? Write a paragraph that links (via similarity or difference)
   someone you know with a specific section or paragraph of "Male Body Image in
   America."

WHAT DO YOU THINK?

5. Make copies of magazine ads for at least two drugs aimed at helping men with
   erectile dysfunction. Pay attention to the way men are portrayed in these ads. Then
   write an essay that explains how Luciano's essay is, or is not, related to what you're
   seeing in the ads.

6. Page through a magazine like *Cosmopolitan* or *Vogue*, noting how men are portrayed in the advertisements. Of the first fifteen men you see, how many are bald-
   ing? How many look significantly overweight? How many look well muscled?
   Based on what you find, write an essay that explains how your data does, or does
   not, confirm what Luciano asserts. Variation: Do this same activity, except substitute magazines aimed primarily at men.

7. Luciano's essay says at one point that "in 1996, the bill for male cosmetic surgery
   was $500 million." Go onto the Web and identify two plastic surgeons (in your
   state or a neighboring one) who specialize in plastic surgery for men. What do their
   sites tell you about the most frequent procedures? about costs? recovery times?
   Based on what you find and on your reading of Luciano's essay, write your own
   essay discussing your reactions and responses. Make sure your essay quotes Luciano
   at least twice and also quotes Web sources twice.

WHAT WOULD THEY SAY?

8. The last sentence of Luciano's first paragraph asserts that more and more men are suffering from eating disorders "commonly thought to afflict only women." Read Jenefer Shute's "Life-Size" (p. 279) and then do some research on anorexia and bulimia in men. Does your research agree with Luciano's basic analysis that "*everyone* has become an object to be seen"? Do anorexia and bulimia have similar causes in men and women? Write an essay that discusses what you have learned, been surprised by, been alarmed at, or been confused by as you researched eating disorders in men and women and as you read "Life-Size" and "Male Body Image in America."

9. Read "Male Body Image in America" together with Lance Armstrong's "Before and After" (p. 344). To what extent do these two essays inform each other or argue with each other or simply talk about different things? Write an essay that discusses how we should understand Armstrong's essay as illustrating, or not, some of what Luciano says in "Male Body Image in America."

10. In his essay "Looking at Women" (p. 294), Scott Russell Sanders asks the question, "How should a man look at a woman?" In broader terms, how should we look at those to whom we're naturally attracted? Use Sanders's and Luciano's insights in an essay that responds to this question. If you see a gap between what we do and what we should do, how do you explain it? How do these two essays help you explain it?

BERNARD COOPER

A Clack of Tiny Sparks: Remembrances of a Gay Boyhood

Bᴇʀɴᴀʀᴅ Cᴏᴏᴘᴇʀ' s ᴇssᴀʏ *recounts his efforts to change his sexual orientation in vivid, concrete detail. Thus, questions of identity and the body are raised in yet another way.*

Cooper (b. 1951) has taught in several schools, including UCLA's writing program; he is currently an art critic for Los Angeles Magazine. *His books include a collection of essays,* Maps to Anywhere *(1990); a collection of short stories,* Guess Again *(2000); and a novel,* A Year of Rhymes *(1993). "A Clack of Tiny Sparks: Remembrances of a Gay Boyhood" first appeared in the January 1991 issue of* Harper's.

Theresa Sanchez sat behind me in ninth-grade algebra. When Mr. Hubbley faced the blackboard, I'd turn around to see what she was reading; each week a new book was wedged inside her copy of *Today's Equations*. The deception worked; from Mr. Hubbley's point of view, Theresa was engrossed in the value of *X*, but I knew otherwise. One week she perused *The Wisdom of the Orient*, and I could tell from Theresa's contemplative expression that the book contained exotic thoughts, guidelines handed down from high. Another week it was a paperback novel whose title, *Let Me Live My Life*, appeared in bold print atop every page, and whose cover, a gauzy photograph of a woman biting a strand of pearls, head thrown back in an attitude of ecstasy, confirmed my suspicion that Theresa Sanchez was mature beyond her years. She was the tallest girl in school. Her bouffant hairdo, streaked with blond, was higher than the flaccid bouffants of others girls. Her smooth skin, plucked eyebrows, and painted fingernails suggested hours of pampering, a worldly and sensual vanity that placed her within the domain of adults. Smiling dimly, steeped in daydreams, Theresa moved through the crowded halls with a languid, self-satisfied indifference to those around her. "You are merely children," her posture seemed to say. "I can't be bothered." The week Theresa hid *101 Ways to Cook Hamburger* behind her algebra book, I could stand it no longer and, after the bell rang, ventured a question.

"Because I'm having a dinner party," said Theresa. "Just a couple of intimate friends."

No fourteen-year-old I knew had ever given a dinner party, let alone used the word *intimate* in conversation. "Don't you have a mother?" I asked.

Theresa sighed a weary sigh, suffered my strange inquiry. "Don't be so naive," she said. "Everyone has a mother." She waved her hand to indicate the brick school buildings outside the window. "A higher education should have taught you that." Theresa draped an angora sweater over her shoulders,

314

scooped her books from the graffiti-covered desk, and just as she was about to walk away, she turned and asked me, "Are you a fag?"

There wasn't the slightest hint of rancor or condescension in her voice.   5 The tone was direct, casual. Still I was stunned, giving a sidelong glance to make sure no one had heard. "No," I said. Blurted really, with too much defensiveness, too much transparent fear in my response. Octaves lower than usual, I tried a "Why?"

Theresa shrugged. "Oh, I don't know. I have lots of friends who are fags. You remind me of them." Seeing me bristle, Theresa added, "It was just a guess." I watched her erect, angora back as she sauntered out the classroom door.

She had made an incisive and timely guess. Only days before, I'd invited Grady Rogers to my house after school to go swimming. The instant Grady shot from the pool, shaking water from his orange hair, freckled shoulders shining, my attraction to members of my own sex became a matter I could no longer suppress or rationalize. Sturdy and boisterous and gap-toothed, Grady was an inveterate backslapper, a formidable arm wrestler, a wizard at basketball. Grady was a boy at home in his body.

My body was a marvel I hadn't gotten used to; my arms and legs would sometimes act of their own accord, knocking over a glass at dinner or flinching at an oncoming pitch. I was never singled out as a sissy, but I could have been just as easily as Bobby Keagan, a gentle, intelligent, and introverted boy reviled by my classmates. And although I had always been aware of a tacit rapport with Bobby, a suspicion that I might find with him a rich friendship, I stayed away. Instead, I emulated Grady in the belief that being seen with him, being like him, would somehow vanquish my self-doubt, would make me normal by association.

Apart from his athletic prowess, Grady had been gifted with all the trappings of what I imagined to be a charmed life: a fastidious, aproned mother who radiated calm, maternal concern; a ruddy, stoic father with a knack for home repairs. Even the Rogerses' small suburban house in Hollywood, with its spindly Colonial furniture and chintz curtains, was a testament to normalcy.

Grady and his family bore little resemblance to my clan of Eastern Euro- 10 pean Jews, a dark and vociferous people who ate with abandon—matzo and halvah and gefilte fish; foods the goyim couldn't pronounce—who cajoled one another during endless games of canasta, making the simplest remark about the weather into a lengthy philosophical discourse on the sun and the seasons and the passage of time. My mother was a chain-smoker, a dervish in a frowsy housedress. She showed her love in the most peculiar and obsessive ways, like spending hours extracting every seed from a watermelon before she served it in perfectly bite-sized, geometric pieces. Preoccupied and perpetually frantic, my mother succumbed to bouts of absentmindedness so profound she'd forget what she was saying midsentence, smile and blush and walk away. A divorce attorney, my father wore roomy, iridescent suits, and the intricacies, the deceits inherent in his profession, had the effect of making him forever tense and vigilant. He was "all wound up," as my mother put it. But when he relaxed, his laughter was explosive, his disposition prankish: "Walk this way," a waitress would say, leading us to our table, and my father would mimic the way she walked, arms akimbo, hips liquid, while my mother and I were wracked with laughter. Buoyant or brooding, my parents' moods were unpredictable, and in a household fraught with extravagant emotion it was odd and awful to keep my longing secret.

One day I made the mistake of asking my mother what a "fag" was. I knew exactly what Theresa had meant but hoped against hope it was not what I thought; maybe *fag* was some French word, a harmless term like *naive*. My mother turned from the stove, flew at me, and grabbed me by the shoulders. "Did someone call you that?" she cried.

"Not me," I said. "Bobby Keagan."

"Oh," she said, loosening her grip. She was visibly relieved. And didn't answer. The answer was unthinkable.

For weeks after, I shook with the reverberations from that afternoon in the kitchen with my mother, pained by the memory of her shocked expression and, most of all, her silence. My longing was wrong in the eyes of my mother, whose hazel eyes were the eyes of the world, and if that longing continued unchecked, the unwieldy shape of my fate would be cast, and I'd be subjected to a lifetime of scorn.

During the remainder of the semester, I became the scientist of my own desire, plotting ways to change my yearning for boys into a yearning for girls. I had enough evidence to believe that any habit, regardless of how compulsive, how deeply ingrained, could be broken once and for all: the plastic cigarette my mother purchased at the Thrifty pharmacy—one end was red to approximate an ember, the other tan like a filtered tip—was designed to wean her from the real thing. To change a behavior required self-analysis, cold resolve, and the substitution of one thing for another: plastic, say, for tobacco. Could I also find a substitute for Grady? What I needed to do, I figured, was kiss a girl and learn to like it.

This conclusion was affirmed one Sunday morning when my father, seeing me wrinkle my nose at the pink slabs of lox he layered on a bagel, tried to convince me of its salty appeal. "You should try some," he said. "You don't know what you're missing."

"It's loaded with protein," added my mother, slapping a platter of sliced onions onto the dinette table. She hovered above us, cinching her housedress, eyes wet from onion fumes, the mock cigarette dangling from her lips.

My father sat there chomping with gusto, emitting a couple of hearty grunts to dramatize his satisfaction. And still I was not convinced. After a loud and labored swallow, he told me I may not be fond of lox today, but sooner or later I'd learn to like it. One's tastes, he assured me, are destined to change.

"Live," shouted my mother over the rumble of the Mixmaster. "Expand your horizons. Try new things." And the room grew fragrant with the batter of a spice cake.

The opportunity to put their advice into practice, and try out my plan 20 to adapt to girls, came the following week when Debbie Coburn, a member of Mr. Hubbley's algebra class, invited me to a party. She cornered me in the hall, furtive as a spy, telling me her parents would be gone for the evening and slipping into my palm a wrinkled sheet of notebook paper. On it were her address and telephone number, the lavender ink in a tidy cursive. "Wear cologne," she advised, wary eyes darting back and forth. "It's a make-out party. Anything can happen."

The Santa Ana wind blew relentlessly the night of Debbie's party, careening down the slopes of the Hollywood hills, shaking the road signs and stoplights in its path. As I walked down Beachwood Avenue, trees thrashed, surrendered their leaves, and carob pods bombarded the pavement. The sky was a deep but luminous blue, the air hot, abrasive, electric. I had to squint in order to check the number of the Coburns' apartment, a three-story building with glitter embedded in its stucco walls. Above the honeycombed balconies was a sign that read BEACHWOOD TERRACE in lavender script resembling Debbie's.

From down the hall, I could hear the plaintive strains of Little Anthony's "I Think I'm Going Out of My Head." Debbie answered the door bedecked in an Empire dress, the bodice blue and orange polka dots, the rest a sheath of black and white stripes. "Op art," proclaimed Debbie. She turned in a circle, then proudly announced that she'd rolled her hair in orange-juice cans. She patted the huge unmoving curls and dragged me inside. Reflections from the swimming pool in the courtyard, its surface ruffled by wind, shuddered over the ceiling and walls. A dozen of my classmates were seated on the sofa or huddled together in corners, their whispers full of excited imminence, their bodies barely discernible in the dim light. Drapes flanking the sliding glass doors bowed out with every gust of wind, and it seemed that the room might lurch from its foundations and sail with its cargo of silhouettes into the hot October night.

Grady was the last to arrive. He tossed a six-pack of beer into Debbie's arms, barreled toward me, and slapped my back. His hair was slicked back with Vitalis, lacquered furrows left by the comb. The wind hadn't shifted a single hair. "Ya ready?" he asked, flashing the gap between his front teeth and leering into the darkened room. "You bet," I lied.

Once the beers had been passed around, Debbie provoked everyone's attention by flicking on the overhead light. "Okay," she called. "Find a partner." This was the blunt command of a hostess determined to have her guests aroused in an orderly fashion. Everyone blinked, shuffled about, and grabbed a member of the opposite sex. Sheila Garabedian landed beside me—entirely at random, though I wanted to believe she was driven by passion—her timid smile giving way to plain fear as the light went out. Nothing for a moment but the heave of the wind and the distant banter of dogs. I caught a whiff of Sheila's perfume, tangy and sweet as Hawaiian Punch. I probed her face with my own, grazing the small scallop of an ear, a velvety temple, and though Sheila's trembling made me want to stop, I persisted with my mission until I found her lips, tightly sealed as a private letter. I held my mouth over hers and gathered her shoulders closer, resigned to the possibility that, no matter how long we stood there, Sheila would be too scared to kiss me back. Still, she exhaled through her nose, and I listened to the squeak of every breath as though it were a sigh of inordinate pleasure. Diving within myself, I monitored my heartbeat and respiration, trying to will stimulation into being, and all the while an image intruded, an image of Grady erupting from our pool, rivulets of water sliding down his chest. "Change," shouted Debbie, switching on the light. Sheila thanked me, pulled away, and continued her routine of gracious terror with every boy throughout the evening. It didn't matter whom I held—Margaret Sims, Betty Vernon, Elizabeth Lee—my experiment was a failure; I continued to picture Grady's wet chest, and Debbie would bellow "change" with such fervor, it could have been my own voice, my own incessant reprimand.

Our hostess commandeered the light switch for nearly half an hour. 25 Whenever the light came on, I watched Grady pivot his head toward the newest prospect, his eyebrows arched in expectation, his neck blooming with hickeys, his hair, at last, in disarray. All that shuffling across the carpet charged everyone's arms and lips with static, and eventually, between low moans and soft osculations, I could hear the clack of tiny sparks and see them flare here and there in the dark like meager, short-lived stars.

I saw Theresa, sultry and aloof as ever, read three more books—*North American Reptiles, Bonjour Tristesse,* and *MGM: A Pictorial History*—before she vanished early in December. Rumors of her fate abounded. Debbie Coburn swore that Theresa had been "knocked up" by an older man, a traffic cop, she thought, or a grocer. Nearly quivering with relish, Debbie told me and Grady about the home for unwed mothers in the San Fernando Valley, a compound teeming with pregnant girls who had nothing to do but touch their stomachs and contemplate their mistake. Even Bobby Keagan, who took Theresa's place behind me in algebra, had a theory regarding her disappearance colored by his own wish for escape; he imagined that Theresa, disillusioned with society, booked passage to a tropical island, there to live out the rest of her days without restrictions or ridicule. "No wonder she flunked out of school," I overheard Mr. Hubbley tell a fellow teacher one afternoon. "Her head was always in a book."

Along with Theresa went my secret, or at least the dread that she might divulge it, and I felt, for a while, exempt from suspicion. I was, however, to run across Theresa one last time. It happened during a period of torrential rain that, according to reports on the six o'clock news, washed houses from the hillsides and flooded the downtown streets. The halls of Joseph Le Conte Junior

High were festooned with Christmas decorations: crepe-paper garlands, wreaths studded with plastic berries, and one requisite Star of David twirling above the attendance desk. In Arts and Crafts, our teacher, Gerald (he was the only teacher who allowed us—*required* us—to call him by his first name), handed out blocks of balsa wood and instructed us to carve them into bugs. We would paint eyes and antennae with tempera and hang them on a Christmas tree he'd made the previous night. "Voilà," he crooned, unveiling his creation from a burlap sack. Before us sat a tortured scrub, a wardrobe-worth of wire hangers that were bent like branches and soldered together. Gerald credited his inspiration to a Charles Addams cartoon he's seen in which Morticia, grimly preparing for the holidays, hangs vampire bats on a withered pine. "All that red and green," said Gerald. "So predictable. So *boring*."

As I chiseled a beetle and listened to rain pummel the earth, Gerald handed me an envelope and asked me to take it to Mr. Kendrick, the drama teacher. I would have thought nothing of his request if I hadn't seen Theresa on my way down the hall. She was cleaning out her locker, blithely dropping the sum of its contents—pens and textbooks and mimeographs—into a trash can. "Have a nice life," she sang as I passed. I mustered the courage to ask her what had happened. We stood alone in the silent hall, the reflections of wreaths and garlands submerged in brown linoleum.

"I transferred to another school. They don't have grades or bells, and you get to study whatever you want." Theresa was quick to sense my incredulity. "Honest," she said. "The school is progressive." She gazed into a glass cabinet that held the trophies of track meets and intramural spelling bees. "God," she sighed, "this place is so...barbaric." I was still trying to decide whether or not to believe her story when she asked me where I was headed. "Dear," she said, her exclamation pooling in the silence, "that's no ordinary note, if you catch my drift." The envelope was blank and white; I looked up at Theresa, baffled. "Don't be so naive," she muttered, tossing an empty bottle of nail polish into the trash can. It struck bottom with a resolute thud. "Well," she said, closing her locker and breathing deeply, "bon voyage." Theresa swept through the double doors and in seconds her figure was obscured by rain.

As I walked toward Mr. Kendrick's room, I could feel Theresa's insinua- 30 tion burrow in. I stood for a moment and watched Mr. Kendrick through the pane in the door. He paced intently in front of the class, handsome in his shirt and tie, reading from a thick book. Chalked on the blackboard behind him was THE ODYSSEY BY HOMER. I have no recollection of how Mr. Kendrick reacted to the note, whether he accepted it with pleasure or embarrassment, slipped it into his desk drawer or the pocket of his shirt. I have scavenged that day in retrospect, trying to see Mr. Kendrick's expression, wondering if he acknowledged me in any way as his liaison. All I recall is the sight of his mime through a pane of glass, a lone man mouthing an epic, his gestures ardent in empty air.

Had I delivered a declaration of love? I was haunted by the need to know. In fantasy, a kettle shot steam, the glue released its grip, and I read the letter with impunity. But how would such a letter begin? Did the common endearments apply? This was a message between two men, a message for which I had no precedent, and when I tried to envision the contents, apart from a hasty, impassioned scrawl, my imagination faltered.

Once or twice I witnessed Gerald and Mr. Kendrick walk together into the faculty lounge or say hello at the water fountain, but there was nothing especially clandestine or flirtatious in their manner. Besides, no matter how acute my scrutiny, I wasn't sure, short of a kiss, exactly what to look for— what semaphore of gesture, what encoded word. I suspected there were signs, covert signs that would give them away, just as I'd unwittingly given myself away to Theresa.

In the school library, a *Webster's* unabridged dictionary lay on a wooden podium, and I padded toward it with apprehension; along with clues to the bond between my teachers, I risked discovering information that might incriminate me as well. I had decided to consult the dictionary during lunch period, when most of the students would be on the playground. I clutched my notebook, moving in such a way as to appear both studious and nonchalant, actually believing that, unless I took precautions, someone would see me and guess what I was up to. The closer I came to the podium, the more obvious, I thought, was my endeavor; I felt like the model of The Visible Man in our science class, my heart's undulations, my overwrought nerves legible through transparent skin. A couple of kids riffled through the card catalog. The librarian, a skinny woman whose perpetual whisper and rubber-soled shoes caused her to drift through the room like a phantom, didn't seem to register my presence. Though I'd looked up dozens of words before, the pages felt strange beneath my fingers. *Homer* was the first word I saw. *Hominid. Homogenize.* I feigned interest and skirted other words before I found the word I was after. Under the heading HO•MO•SEX•U•AL was the terse definition: *adj. Pertaining to, characteristic of, or exhibiting homosexuality.—n. A homosexual person.* I read the definition again and again, hoping the words would yield more than they could. I shut the dictionary, swallowed hard, and, none the wiser, hurried away.

As for Gerald and Mr. Kendrick, I never discovered evidence to prove or dispute Theresa's claim. By the following summer, however, I had overheard from my peers a confounding amount about homosexuals: they wore green on Thursday, couldn't whistle, hypnotized boys with a piercing glance. To this lore, Grady added a surefire test to ferret them out.

"A test?" I said.

"You ask a guy to look at his fingernails, and if he looks at them like this"—Grady closed his fingers into a fist and examined his nails with manly detachment—"then he's okay. But if he does this"—he held out his hands at arm's length, splayed his fingers, and coyly cocked his head—"you'd better watch out." Once he'd completed his demonstration, Grady peeled off his shirt and plunged into our pool. I dove in after. It was early June, the sky immense,

35

glassy, placid. My father was cooking spareribs on the barbecue, an artist with a basting brush. His apron bore the caricature of a frazzled French chef. Mother curled on a chaise lounge, plumes of smoke wafting from her nostrils. In a stupor of contentment she took another drag, closed her eyes, and arched her face toward the sun.

Grady dog-paddled through the deep end, spouting a fountain of chlorinated water. Despite shame and confusion, my longing for him hadn't diminished; it continued to thrive without air and light, like a luminous fish in the dregs of the sea. In the name of play, I swam up behind him, encircled his shoulders, astonished by his taut flesh. The two of us flailed, pretended to drown. Beneath the heavy press of water, Grady's orange hair wavered, a flame that couldn't be doused.

I've lived with a man for seven years. Some nights, when I'm half-asleep and the room is suffused with blue light, I reach out to touch the expanse of his back, and it seems as if my fingers sink into his skin, and I feel the pleasure a diver feels the instant he enters a body of water.

I have few regrets. But one is that I hadn't said to Theresa, "Of course I'm a fag." Maybe I'd have met her friends. Or become friends with her. Imagine the meals we might have concocted: hamburger Stroganoff, Swedish meatballs in a sweet translucent sauce, steaming slabs of Salisbury steak.

WHAT DOES HE SAY?

1. Pay attention to the parts of Cooper's essay that speak of his first sexual awareness. What two places in the essay can you see this most clearly? Mark each of them. Then write a paragraph about how you are, or are not, surprised by Cooper's first stirrings of sexual feeling.

2. At one point, Cooper says, "I became the scientist of my own desire." Why did he do this? What principle or theory is he trying to follow at this point? Write out this theory in your own words.

3. Some argue that homosexuality is a learned behavior or a chosen behavior or a lifestyle that can be easily changed (like deciding to change the type of clothing one wears). What does Cooper's essay say about this? Based on his experience, could he unlearn or consciously decide to change his homosexual feelings?

WHAT DO YOU THINK?

4. Using Cooper's essay and also drawing on your own experience, write a personal essay that explains why you believe sexual orientation can, or cannot, be changed simply based on conscious decision making.

5. Popular culture abounds in stereotypes of heterosexual and of homosexual desire. Research the serious, authoritative commentary on sexual desire: its origins; what, if anything, is considered normal; and how these ideas have changed in the last twenty or so years. Part of your task is to figure out what voices you—and others— would recognize as "serious" and "authoritative." Write an essay that makes an argument for those you believe merit being called "authoritative" and that reports and summarizes the research you have studied. Whenever possible, link this information to Cooper's essay. End by discussing what, if anything, surprises you about what you learned.

WHAT WOULD THEY SAY?

6. Read "A Clack of Tiny Sparks" together with Scott Russell Sanders's "Looking at Women" (p. 294). In what places do these essays resemble each other (despite the difference in sexual orientation)? Though not very much about the older Bernard Cooper is revealed in his essay, explain how many of Sanders's questions about looking at women also could pertain to a homosexual man looking at men. In other words, translate Sanders's questions so that they correspond to an adult, thoughtful, homosexual man's questions about how to look at other men. Variation: Read these two essays, explain how they echo or overlap, and then discuss how they could be translated to apply to a lesbian looking at other women.

7. Consider Langston Hughes's poem "Theme for English B" (p. 42) and Cooper's "A Clack of Tiny Sparks." Write an essay that explains how, or why, Hughes's poem openly acknowledges his race—his significant difference with his teacher—while Cooper couldn't even mention his own feelings to Theresa, much less share them with a teacher. Explain to what extent, or not, Hughes's narrator and Cooper's narrator are alike and to what extent (or not) Hughes's poem and Cooper's essay are roughly equivalent.

JUDITH ORTIZ COFER
The Story of My Body

COFER'S STORY, told in terms of "skin," "color," "size," and "looks," is essentially the story of how others perceive her and make judgments about her without knowing her as a person. In addition to questions of stereotyping and discrimination, the essay also prompts one to ask whether or not composing such a story of one's body is, or ought to be, a useful exercise for each of us.

Judith Ortiz Cofer (b. 1952) moved to the United States from Puerto Rico when she was eight. Her first novel, The Line of the Sun *(1989), was nominated for the Pulitzer Prize, and her 1990 essay collection,* Silent Dancing: A Partial Remembrance of a Puerto Rican Girlhood, *won a PEN/Martha Albrand special citation for nonfiction. She is a professor of English and creative writing at the University of Georgia. "The Story of My Body" is from Cofer's* The Latin Deli: Prose and Poetry *(1995).*

> Migration is the story of my body.
> — VICTOR HERNANDEZ CRUZ

1. SKIN

I was born a white girl in Puerto Rico, but became a brown girl when I came to live in the United States. My Puerto Rican relatives called me tall; at the American school, some of my rougher classmates called me "skinny-bones" and "the shrimp," because I was the smallest member of my classes all through grammar school until high school, when the midget Gladys was given the honorary post of front-row center for class pictures and score-keeper, bench warmer in PE. I reached my full stature of five feet even in sixth grade.

I started out life as a pretty baby and learned to be a pretty girl from a pretty mother. Then at ten years of age I suffered one of the worst cases of chicken pox I have ever heard of. My entire body, including the inside of my ears and in between my toes, was covered with pustules that, in a fit of panic at my appearance, I scratched off of my face, leaving permanent scars. A cruel school nurse told me I would always have them — tiny cuts that looked as if a mad cat had plunged its claws deep into my skin. I grew my hair long and hid behind it for the first years of my adolescence. This was when I learned to be invisible.

2. COLOR

In the animal world it indicates danger: the most colorful creatures are often the most poisonous. Color is also a way to attract and seduce a mate. In the human world color triggers many more complex and often deadly reactions. As a Puerto Rican girl born of "white" parents, I spent the first years of my life hearing people refer to me as *blanca*, white. My mother insisted that I protect myself from the intense island sun because I was more prone to sunburn than some of my darker, *triqeno* playmates. People were always commenting within my hearing about how my black hair contrasted so nicely with my "pale" skin. I did not think of the color of my skin consciously, except when I heard the adults talking about complexion. It seems to me that the subject is much more common in the conversation of mixed-race peoples than in mainstream U.S. society, where it is a touchy and sometimes even embarrassing topic to discuss, except in a political context. In Puerto Rico I heard many conversations about skin color. A pregnant woman could say "I hope my baby doesn't turn out *prieto* (slang for dark or black) like my husband's grandmother, although she was a good-looking *negra* in her time." I am a combination of both, being olive-skinned—lighter than my mother yet darker than my fair-skinned father. In America, I am a person of color, obviously a Latina. On the island I have been called everything from a *paloma blanca*, after the song (by a black suitor), to *la gringa*.

My first experience of color prejudice occurred in a supermarket in Paterson, New Jersey. It was Christmastime and I was eight or nine years old. There was a display of toys in the store where I went two or three times a day to buy things for my mother who never made lists but sent for milk, cigarettes, a can of this or that, as she remembered from hour to hour. I enjoyed being trusted with money and walking half a city block to the new, modern grocery store. It was owned by three good-looking Italian brothers. I liked the younger one with the crew-cut blond hair. The two older ones watched me and the other Puerto Rican kids as if they thought we were going to steal something. The oldest one would sometimes even try to hurry me with my purchases, although part of my pleasure in these expeditions came from looking at everything in the well-stocked aisles. I was also teaching myself to read English by sounding out the labels on packages: L&M cigarettes, Borden's homogenized milk, Red Devil potted ham, Nestlé's chocolate mix, Quaker oats, and Bustelo coffee, Wonder bread, Colgate toothpaste, Ivory soap, and Goya (makers of products used in Puerto Rican dishes) everything—these are some of the brand names that taught me nouns. Several times this man had come up to me wearing his bloodstained butcher's apron and, towering over me, had asked in a harsh voice whether there was something he could help me find. On the way out I would glance at the younger brother who ran one of the registers and he would often smile and wink at me.

It was the mean brother who first referred to me as "colored." It was a 5 few days before Christmas and my parents had already told my brother and me that since we were in *los estados* now, we would get our presents on December twenty-fifth instead of *Los Reyes, Three Kings Day*, when gifts are exchanged in Puerto Rico. We were to give them a wish list that they would take to Santa Claus, who apparently lived in the Macy's store downtown—at least that's where we had caught a glimpse of him when we went shopping. Since my parents were timid about entering the fancy store, we did not approach the huge man in the red suit. I was not interested in sitting on a stranger's lap anyway. But I did covet Susie, the talking schoolteacher doll that was displayed in the center aisle of the Italian brothers' supermarket. She talked when you pulled a string on her back. Susie had a limited repertoire of three sentences: I think she could say: "Hello, I'm Susie Schoolteacher; two plus two is four," and one other thing I cannot remember. The day the older brother chased me away, I was reaching to touch Susie's blond curls. I had been told many times, as most children have, not to touch anything in a store that I was not buying. But I had been looking at Susie for weeks. In my mind, she was my doll. After all, I had put her on my Christmas wish list. The moment is frozen in my mind as if there were a photograph of it on file. It was not a turning point, a disaster, or an earthshaking revelation. It was simply the first time I considered—if naively— the meaning of skin color in human relations.

I reached to touch Susie's hair. It seems to me that I had to get on tiptoe since the toys were stacked on a table and she sat like a princess on top of the fancy box she came in. Then I heard the booming "Hey, kid, what do you think you're doing!" spoken very loudly from the meat counter. I felt caught although I knew I was not doing anything criminal. I remember not looking at the man, but standing there feeling humiliated because I knew everyone in the store must have heard him yell at me. I felt him approach and when I knew he was behind me, I turned around to face the bloody butcher's apron. His large chest was at my eye level. He blocked my way. I started to run out of the place, but even as I reached the door I heard him shout after me: "Don't come in here unless you gonna buy something. You PR kids put your dirty hands on stuff. You always look dirty. But maybe dirty brown is your natural color." I heard him laugh and someone else too in the back. Outside in the sunlight I looked at my hands. My nails needed a little cleaning as they always did since I liked to paint with watercolors, but I took a bath every night. I thought the man was dirtier than I was in his stained apron. He was also always sweaty—it showed in big yellow circles under his shirt sleeves. I sat on the front steps of the apartment building where we lived and looked closely at my hands, which showed the only skin I could see, since it was bitter cold and I was wearing my quilted play coat, dungarees, and a knitted navy cap of my father's. I was not pink like my friend Charlene and her sister Kathy who had blue eyes and light-brown hair. My skin is the color of the coffee my grandmother made, which was half milk, *leche con café* rather than *café con leche*. My mother is the opposite mix. She has a lot of café in her color. I could not understand how my skin looked like dirt to the supermarket man.

I went in and washed my hands thoroughly with soap and hot water, and, borrowing my mother's nail file, I cleaned the crusted watercolors from underneath my nails. I was pleased with the results. My skin was the same color as before, but I knew I was clean. Clean enough to run my fingers through Susie's fine gold hair when she came home to me.

3. SIZE

My mother is barely four feet eleven inches in height, which is average for women in her family. When I grew to five feet by age twelve, she was amazed and began to use the word tall to describe me, as in: "Since you are tall, this dress will look good on you." As with the color of my skin, I didn't consciously think about my height or size until other people made an issue of it. It is around the preadolescent years that in America the games children play for fun become fierce competitions where everyone is out to "prove" they are better than others. It was in the playground and sports fields that my size-related problems began. No matter how familiar the story is, every child who is the last chosen for a team knows the torment of waiting to be called up. At the Paterson, New Jersey, public schools that I attended, the volleyball or softball game was the metaphor for the battlefield of life to the inner city kids—the black kids vs. the Puerto Rican kids, the whites vs. the blacks vs. the Puerto Rican kids; and I was 4F, skinny, short, bespectacled, and apparently impervious to the blood thirst that drove many of my classmates to play ball as if their lives depended on it. Perhaps they did. I would rather be reading a book than sweating, grunting, and running the risk of pain and injury. I simply did not see the point in competitive sports. My main form of exercise then was walking to the library, many city blocks away from my barrio.

Still, I wanted to be wanted. I wanted to be chosen for the teams. Physical education was compulsory, a class where you were actually given a grade. On my mainly all-*A* report card, the *C* for compassion I always received from the PE teachers shamed me the same as a bad grade in a real class. Invariably, my father would say: "How can you make a low grade *for playing games?*" He did not understand. Even if I had managed to make a hit (it never happened), or get the ball over that ridiculously high net, I already had a reputation as a "shrimp," a hopeless nonathlete. It was an area where the girls who didn't like me for one reason or another—mainly because I did better than they on academic subjects—could lord it over me; the playing field was the place where even the smallest girl could make me feel powerless and inferior. I instinctively understood the politics even then; how the *not* choosing me until the teacher forced one of the team captains to call my name was a coup of sorts—there you little show-off, tomorrow you can beat us in spelling and geography, but this afternoon you are the loser. Or perhaps those were only my own bitter thoughts as I sat or stood in the sidelines while the big girls were grabbed like fish and I, the little brown tadpole, was ignored until Teacher looked over in my general direction and shouted, "Call Ortiz," or worse, "Somebody's *got* to take her."

No wonder I read Wonder Woman comics and had Legion of Super   10 Heroes daydreams. Although I wanted to think of myself as "intellectual," my body was demanding that I notice it. I saw the little swelling around my once-flat nipples; the fine hairs growing in secret places; but my knees were still bigger than my thighs and I always wore long or half-sleeve blouses to hide my bony upper arms. I wanted flesh on my bones—a thick layer of it. I saw a new product advertised on TV. Wate-On. They showed skinny men and women before and after taking the stuff, and it was a transformation like the 97-pound weakling turned into Charles Atlas ads that I saw on the back cover of my comic books. The Wate-On was very expensive. I tried to explain my need for it in Spanish to my mother, but it didn't translate very well, even to my ears—and she said with a tone of finality, eat more of my good food and you'll get fat—anybody can get fat. Right. Except me. I was going to have to join a circus someday as "Skinny Bones," the woman without flesh.

Wonder Woman was stacked. She had a cleavage framed by the spread wings of a golden eagle and a muscular body that has become fashionable with women only recently. But since I wanted a body that would serve me in PE, hers was my ideal. The breasts were an indulgence I allowed myself. Perhaps the daydreams of bigger girls were more glamorous, since our ambitions are filtered through our needs, but I wanted first a powerful body. I daydreamed of leaping up above the gray landscape of the city to where the sky was clear and blue, and in anger and self-pity I fantasized about scooping my enemies up by their hair from the playing fields and dumping them on a barren asteroid. I would put the PE teachers each on their own rock in space too where they would be the loneliest people in the universe since I knew they had no "inner resources," no imagination, and in outer space, there would be no air for them to fill their deflated volleyballs with. In my mind all PE teachers have blended into one large spiky-haired woman with a whistle on a string around her neck and a volleyball under one arm. My Wonder Woman fantasies of revenge were a source of comfort to me in my early career as a shrimp.

I was saved from more years of PE torment by the fact that in my sophomore year of high school I transferred to a school where the midget, Gladys, was the focal point of interest for the people who must rank according to size. Because her height was considered a handicap, there was an unspoken rule about mentioning size around Gladys, but of course there was no need to say anything. Gladys knew her place: front-row center in class photographs. I gladly moved to the left or to the right of her, as far as I could without leaving the picture completely.

4. LOOKS

Many photographs were taken of me as a baby by my mother to send to my father who was stationed overseas during the first two years of my life. With the army in Panama when I was born, he later joined the navy and traveled often on tours of duty. I was a healthy, pretty baby. Recently I read that people are drawn to big-eyed round-faced creatures, like puppies, kittens, and certain other mammals and marsupials, koalas for example, and, of course, infants. I was all eyes, since my head and body, even as I grew older, remained thin and small-boned. As a young child I got a lot of attention from my relatives and many other people we met in our barrio. My mother's beauty may have had something to do with how much attention we got from strangers in stores and on the street. I can imagine it. In the pictures I have seen of us together, she is a stunning young woman by Latino standards: long, curly black hair and round curves in a compact frame. From her I learned how to move, smile, and talk like an attractive woman. I remember going into a bodega for our groceries and being given candy by the proprietor as a reward for being *bonita*, pretty.

I can see in the photographs and I also remember that I was dressed in the pretty clothes, the stiff, frilly dresses, with layers of crinolines underneath, the glossy patent leather shoes, and, on special occasions, the skull-hugging little hats and the white gloves that were popular in the late fifties and early sixties. My mother was proud of my looks, although I was a bit too thin. She could dress me up like a doll and take me by the hand to visit relatives, or go to the Spanish mass at the Catholic church, and show me off. How was I to know that she and the others who called me pretty were representatives of an aesthetic that would not apply when I went out into the mainstream world of school?

In my Paterson, New Jersey, public schools there were still quite a few   15 white children, although the demographics of the city were changing rapidly. The original waves of Italian and Irish immigrants, silk-mill workers and laborers in the cloth industries, had been "assimilated." Their children were now the middle-class parents of my peers. Many of them moved their children to the Catholic schools that proliferated enough to have leagues of basketball teams. The names I recall hearing still ring in my ears: Don Bosco High vs. St. Mary's High, St. Joseph's vs. St. John's. Later I too would be transferred to the safer environment of a Catholic school. But I started school at Public School Number 11. I came there from Puerto Rico, thinking myself a pretty girl, and found that the hierarchy for popularity was as follows: pretty white girl, pretty Jewish girl, pretty Puerto Rican girl, pretty black girl. Drop the last two categories; teachers were too busy to have more than one favorite per class, and it was simply understood that if there was a big part in the school play, or any competition where the main qualification was "presentability" (such as escorting a school visitor to or from the principal's office), the classroom's public address speaker would be requesting the pretty and/or nice-looking white boy or girl. By the time I was in the sixth grade, I was sometimes called by the principal to represent my class because I dressed neatly (I knew this from a progress report sent to my mother, which I translated for her), and because all the "presentable" white girls had moved to the Catholic schools (I later surmised this part). But I was still not one of the popular girls with the boys. I remember one incident where I stepped out into the playground in my baggy gym shorts and one Puerto Rican boy said to the other: "What do you think?" The other one answered: "Her face is okay, but look at the toothpick legs." The next best thing to a compliment I got was when my favorite male teacher, while handing out the class pictures, commented that with my long neck and delicate features I resembled the movie star Audrey Hepburn. But the Puerto Rican boys had learned to respond to a fuller figure: long necks and a perfect little nose were not what they looked for in a girl. That is when I decided I was a "brain." I did not settle into the role easily. I was nearly devastated by what the chicken-pox episode had done to my self-image. But I looked into the mirror less often after I was told that I would always have scars on my face, and I hid behind my long black hair and my books.

After the problems at the public school got to the point where even nonconfrontational little me got beaten up several times, my parents enrolled me at St. Joseph's High School. I was then a minority of one among the Italian and Irish kids. But I found several good friends there—other girls who took their studies seriously. We did our homework together and talked about the Jackies. The Jackies were two popular girls, one blonde and the other red-haired, who had women's bodies. Their curves showed even in the blue jumper uniforms with straps that we all wore. The blond Jackie would often let one of the straps fall off her shoulder, and although she, like all of us, wore a white blouse underneath, all the boys stared at her arm. My friends and I talked about this and practiced letting our straps fall off our shoulders. But it wasn't the same without breasts or hips.

My final two and a half years of high school were spent in Augusta, Georgia, where my parents moved our family in search of a more peaceful environment. There we became part of a little community of our army-connected relatives and friends. School was yet another matter. I was enrolled in a huge school of nearly two thousand students that had just that year been forced to integrate. There were two black girls and there was me. I did extremely well academically. As to my social life, it was, for the most part, uneventful—yet it is in my memory blighted by one incident. In my junior year, I became wildly infatuated with a pretty white boy. I'll call him Ted. Oh, he was pretty: yellow hair that fell over his forehead, a smile to die for, and he was a great dancer. I watched him at Teen Town, the youth center at the base where all the military brats gathered on Saturday nights. My father had retired from the military and we had all our base privileges—one other reason we had moved to Augusta. Ted looked like an angel to me. I worked on him for a year before he asked me out. This meant maneuvering to be within the periphery of his vision at every possible occasion. I took the long way to my classes in school just to pass by his locker, I went to football games that I detested, and I danced (I too was a good dancer) in front of him at Teen Town—this took some fancy footwork since it involved subtly moving my partner toward the right spot on the dance floor. When Ted finally approached me, "A Million to One" was playing on the jukebox, and when he took me into his arms, the odds suddenly turned in my favor. He asked me to go to a school dance the following Saturday. I said yes, breathlessly, I said yes but there were obstacles to surmount at home. My father did not allow me to date casually. I was allowed to go to major events like a prom or a concert with a boy who had been properly screened. There was such a boy in my life, a neighbor who wanted to be a Baptist missionary and was practicing his anthropological skills on my family. If I was desperate to go somewhere and needed a date, I'd resort to Gary. This is the type of religious nut that Gary was: when the school bus did not show up one day, he put his hands over his face and prayed to Christ to get us a way to get to school. Within ten minutes a mother in a station wagon on her way to town stopped to ask why we weren't in school. Gary informed her that the Lord had sent her just in time to get us there for roll call. He assumed that I was impressed. Gary was even good-looking in a bland sort of way, but he kissed me with his lips tightly pressed together. I think Gary probably ended up marrying a native woman from wherever he may have gone to preach the Gospel according to Paul. She probably believes that all white men pray to God for transportation and kiss with their mouths closed. But it was Ted's mouth, his whole beautiful self that concerned me in those days. I knew my father would say no to our date, but I planned to run away from home if necessary. I told my mother how important this date was. I cajoled and pleaded with her from Sunday to Wednesday. She listened to my arguments, and must have heard the note of desperation in my voice. She said very gently to me: "You better be ready for disappointment." I did not ask what she meant. I did not want her fears for me to taint my happiness. I asked her to tell my father about my date. Thursday at breakfast my father looked at me across the table with his eyebrows together. My mother looked at him with her mouth set in a straight line. I looked down at my bowl of cereal. Nobody said anything. Friday I tried on every dress in my closet. Ted would be picking me up at six on Saturday: dinner and then the sock hop at school. Friday night I was in my room doing my nails or something else in preparation for Saturday (I know I groomed myself nonstop all week) when the telephone rang. I ran to get it. It was Ted. His voice sounded funny when he said my name, so funny that I felt compelled to ask: "Is something wrong?" Ted blurted it all out without a preamble. His father had asked who he was going out with. Ted had told him my name. "Ortiz? That's Spanish, isn't it?" the father had asked. Ted had told him yes, then shown him my picture in the yearbook. Ted's father had shaken his head. No. Ted would not be taking me out. Ted's father had known Puerto Ricans in the army. He had lived in

New York City while studying architecture and had seen how the *spics* lived. Like rats. Ted repeated his father's words to me as if I should understand *his predicament* when I heard why he was breaking our date. I don't remember what I said before hanging up. I do recall the darkness of my room that sleepless night, and the heaviness of my blanket in which I wrapped myself like a shroud. And I remember my parents' respect for my pain and their gentleness toward me that weekend. My mother did not say "I warned you," and I was grateful for her understanding silence.

In college, I suddenly became an "exotic" woman to the men who had survived the popularity wars in high school, who were now practicing to be worldly: they had to act liberal in their politics, in their lifestyles, and in the women they went out with. I dated heavily for a while, then married young. I had discovered that I needed stability more than social life. I had brains for sure, and some talent in writing. These facts were a constant in my life. My skin color, my size, and my appearance were variables—things that were judged according to my current self-image, the aesthetic values of the times, the places I was in, and the people I met. My studies, later my writing, the respect of people who saw me as an individual person they cared about, these were the criteria for my sense of self-worth that I would concentrate on in my adult life.

WHAT DOES SHE SAY?

1. Cofer's essay is divided into four numbered sections. As you read along, write a two or three sentence summary of each section.

2. "The Story of My Body" often relates how Judith Ortiz Cofer was judged by others as she grew up. What criteria were used to make these various judgments? That is, what did those who judged her consider good or preferable?

3. "The Story of My Body" begins with an epigraph by Victor Hernandez Cruz: "Migration is the story of my body." Write a paragraph about how the rest of the essay illustrates various kinds of "migration."

WHAT DO YOU THINK?

4. Think about your own childhood experiences as you're reading about Cofer's. Then compare your childhood with hers. Were you also one of the kids picked last for sports teams? Were you singled out because of how you looked? Write an essay explaining where your experience would have fit into the various scenarios and small stories that Cofer tells. End by describing what judgments you made about others when you were in grade school and middle school.

5. Write an essay that roughly imitates Judith Ortiz Cofer's. Use the same title. Tell your story in four numbered sections. But use any subtitles you wish (or keep the

ones Cofer uses). End by adding a paragraph that discusses what is clearer to you as a result of reading Cofer's story and telling your own in this form.

WHAT WOULD THEY SAY?

6. Read "The Story of My Body" together with Winona LaDuke's "Voices from White Earth" (p. 72). Both essays present information having to do with their authors' origins. Given this essential similarity, how would you account for the differences in what these essayists choose to discuss? Write an essay that contrasts and compares these two essays. Don't try to judge one as better than the other; instead, try to understand what accounts for their differences and similarities.

7. Read "The Story of My Body" together with Lynne Luciano's "Male Body Image in America" (p. 306) and Jenefer Shute's "Life-Size" (p. 279). Write an essay that explores how each of these selections defines success. End by discussing the extent to which success and health are, or are not, the same things in these selections.

NANCY MAIRS
On Being a Cripple

IN THIS ESSAY, Nancy Mairs (b. 1943) addresses the title of this chapter directly, and her answer is no, she is not her body, even though her experience with multiple sclerosis (MS) has radically changed her life. This is a lively and unusual personal essay, another "story of a body," written with shocking honesty and humor.

From 1983 to 1985, Mairs served as assistant director of the Southwest Institute for Research on Women, and she has also taught at the University of Arizona and at UCLA. Her works include Carnal Acts: Essays *(1990),* Ordinary Time: Cycles in Marriage, Faith, and Renewal *(1993), and* Waist High in the World: A Life among the Disabled *(1996). "On Being a Cripple" comes from* Plaintext *(1986).*

> To escape is nothing. Not to escape is nothing.
> —LOUIS BOGAN

The other day I was thinking of writing an essay on being a cripple. I was thinking hard in one of the stalls of the women's room in my office building, as I was shoving my shirt into my jeans and tugging up my zipper. Preoccupied, I flushed, picked up my book bag, took my cane down from the hook, and unlatched the door. So many movements unbalanced me, and as I pulled the door open I fell over backward, landing fully clothed on the toilet seat with my legs splayed in front of me: the old beetle-on-its-back routine. Saturday afternoon, the building deserted, I was free to laugh aloud as I wriggled back to my feet, my voice bouncing off the yellowish tiles from all directions. Had anyone been there with me, I'd have been still and faint and hot with chagrin. I decided that it was high time to write the essay.

First, the matter of semantics. I am a cripple. I choose this word to name me. I choose from among several possibilities, the most common of which are *handicapped* and *disabled*. I made the choice a number of years ago, without thinking, unaware of my motives for doing so. Even now, I'm not sure what those motives are, but I recognize that they are complex and not entirely flattering. People—crippled or not—wince at the word *cripple*, as they do not at *handicapped* or *disabled*. Perhaps I want them to wince. I want them to see me as a tough customer, one to whom the fates/gods/viruses have not been kind, but who can face the brutal truth of her existence squarely. As a cripple, I swagger.

But, to be fair to myself, a certain amount of honesty underlies my choice. *Cripple* seems to me a clean word, straightforward and precise. It has an honorable history, having made its first appearance in the Lindisfarne   **333**

Gospel° in the tenth century. As a lover of words, I like the accuracy with which it describes my condition: I have lost the full use of my limbs. *Disabled*, by contrast, suggests any incapacity, physical or mental. And I certainly don't like *handicapped*, which implies that I have deliberately been put at a disadvantage, by whom I can't imagine (my God is not Handicapper General), in order to equalize chances in the great race of life. These words seem to me to be moving away from my condition, to be widening the gap between word and reality. Most remote is the recently coined euphemism *differently abled*, which partakes of the same semantic hopefulness that transformed countries from *undeveloped* to *underdeveloped*, then to *less developed*, and finally to *developing* nations. People have continued to starve in those countries during the shift. Some realities do not obey the dictates of language.

Mine is one of them. Whatever you call me, I remain crippled. But I don't care what you call me, so long as it isn't "differently abled," which strikes me as pure verbal garbage designed, by its ability to describe anyone, to describe no one. I subscribe to George Orwell's° thesis that "the slovenliness of our language makes it easier for us to have foolish thoughts." And I refuse to participate in the degeneration of the language to the extent that I deny that I have lost anything in the course of this calamitous disease; I refuse to pretend that the only differences between you and me are the various ordinary ones that distinguish any one person from another. But call me "disabled" or "handicapped" if you like. I have long since grown accustomed to them; and if they are vague, at least they hint at the truth. Moreover, I use them myself. Society is no readier to accept crippledness than to accept death, war, sex, sweat, or wrinkles. I would never refer to another person as a cripple. It is the word I use to name only myself.

I haven't always been crippled, a fact for which I am soundly grateful. To   5
be whole of limb is, I know from experience, infinitely more pleasant and useful than to be crippled; and if that knowledge leaves one open to bitterness at my loss, the physical soundness I once enjoyed (though I did not enjoy it half enough) is well worth the occasional stab of regret. Though never any good at sports, I was a normally active child and young adult. I climbed trees, played hopscotch, jumped rope, skated, swam, rode my bicycle, sailed. I despised team sports, spending some of the wretchedest afternoons of my life, sweaty and humiliated, behind a field-hockey stick and under a basketball hoop. I tramped alone for miles along the bridle paths that webbed the woods behind the house I grew up in. I swayed through countless dim hours in the arms of one man or another under the scattered shot of light from mirrored balls, and gyrated

---

Lindisfarne Gospel: An intricately designed illuminated manuscript created between 715 and 720 by monks at the Lindisfarne monastery on Holy Island off the coast of northern England. [All notes are the Editors'.]

 George Orwell's (1903–1950): English novelist and essayist, author of "Politics and the English Language" (p. 461).

through countless more as Tab Hunter and Johnny Mathis gave way to the Rolling Stones, Creedence Clearwater Revival, Cream. I walked down the aisle. I pushed baby carriages, changed tires in the rain, marched for peace.

When I was twenty-eight I started to trip and drop things. What at first seemed my natural clumsiness soon became too pronounced to shrug off. I consulted a neurologist, who told me that I had a brain tumor. A battery of tests, increasingly disagreeable, revealed no tumor. About a year and a half later I developed a blurred spot in one eye. I had, at last, the episodes "disseminated in space and time" requisite for a diagnosis: multiple sclerosis. I have never been sorry for the doctor's initial, misdiagnosis, however. For almost a week, until the negative results of the tests were in, I thought that I was going to die right away. Every day for the past nearly ten years, then, has been a kind of gift. I accept all gifts.

Multiple sclerosis is a chronic degenerative disease of the central nervous system, in which the myelin that sheathes the nerves is somehow eaten away and scar tissue forms in its place, interrupting the nerves' signals. During its course, which is unpredictable and uncontrollable, one may lose vision, hearing, speech, the ability to walk, control of bladder and/or bowels, strength in any or all extremities, sensitivity to touch, vibration, and/or pain, potency, coordination of movements—the list of possibilities is lengthy and, yes, horrifying. One may also lose one's sense of humor. That's the easiest to lose and the hardest to survive without.

In the past ten years, I have sustained some of these losses. Characteristic of MS are sudden attacks, called exacerbations, followed by remissions, and these I have not had. Instead, my disease has been slowly progressive. My left leg is now so weak that I walk with the aid of a brace and a cane; and for distances I use an Amigo, a variation on the electric wheelchair that looks rather like an electrified kiddie car. I no longer have much use of my left hand. Now my right side is weakening as well. I still have the blurred spot in my right eye. Overall, though, I've been lucky so far. My world has, of necessity, been circumscribed by my losses, but the terrain left me has been ample enough for me to continue many of the activities that absorb me: writing, teaching, raising children and cats and plants and snakes, reading, speaking publicly about MS and depression, even playing bridge with people patient and honorable enough to let me scatter cards every which way without sneaking a peek.

Lest I begin to sound like Pollyanna, however, let me say that I don't like having MS. I hate it. My life holds realities—harsh ones, some of them— that no right-minded human being ought to accept without grumbling. One of them is fatigue. I know of no one with MS who does not complain of bone weariness; in a disease that presents an astonishing variety of symptoms, fatigue seems to be a common factor. I wake up in the morning feeling the way most people do at the end of a bad day, and I take it from there. As a result, I spend a lot of time *in extremis* and, impatient with limitation, I tend to ignore my fatigue until my body breaks down in some way and forces rest.

Then I miss picnics, dinner parties, poetry readings, the brief visits of old friends from out of town. The offspring of a puritanical tradition of exceptional venerability, I cannot view these lapses without shame. My life often seems a series of small failures to do as I ought.

I lead, on the whole, an ordinary life, probably rather like the one I   10 would have led had I not had MS. I am lucky that my predilections were already solitary, sedentary, and bookish—unlike the world-famous French cellist I have read about, or the young woman I talked with one long afternoon who wanted only to be a jockey. I had just begun graduate school when I found out something was wrong with me, and I have remained, interminably, a graduate student. Perhaps I would not have if I'd thought I had the stamina to return to a full-time job as a technical editor; but I've enjoyed my studies.

In addition to studying, I teach writing courses. I also teach medical students how to give neurological examinations. I pick up freelance editing jobs here and there. I have raised a foster son and sent him into the world, where he has made me two grandbabies, and I am still escorting my daughter and son through adolescence. I go to Mass every Saturday. I am a superb, if messy, cook. I am also an enthusiastic laundress, capable of sorting a hamper full of clothes into five subtly differentiated piles, but a terrible housekeeper. I can do italic writing and, in an emergency, bathe an oil-soaked cat. I play a fiendish game of Scrabble. When I have the time and the money, I like to sit on my front steps with my husband, drinking Amaretto and smoking a cigar, as we imagine our counterparts in Leningrad and make sure that the sun gets down once more behind the sharp childish scrawl of the Tucson Mountains.

This lively plenty has its bleak complement, of course, in all the things I can no longer do. I will never run again, except in dreams, and one day I may have to write that I will never walk again. I like to go camping, but I can't follow George and the children along the trails that wander out of a campsite through the desert or into the mountains. In fact, even on the level I've learned never to check the weather or try to hold a coherent conversation: I need all my attention for my wayward feet. Of late, I have begun to catch myself wondering how people can propel themselves without canes. With only one usable hand, I have to select my clothing with care not so much for style as for ease of ingress and egress, and even so, dressing can be laborious. I can no longer do fine stitchery, pick up babies, play the piano, braid my hair. I am immobilized by acute attacks of depression, which may or may not be physiologically related to MS but are certainly its logical concomitant.

These two elements, the plenty and the privation, are never pure, nor are the delight and wretchedness that accompany them. Almost every pickle that I get into as a result of my weakness and clumsiness—and I get into plenty—is funny as well as maddening and sometimes painful. I recall one May afternoon when a friend and I were going out for a drink after finishing up at school. As we were climbing into opposite sides of my car, chatting, I tripped and fell, flat and hard, onto the asphalt parking lot, my abrupt departure interrupting him in midsentence. "Where'd you go?" he called as he came around the back of the car to find me hauling myself up by the door frame. "Are you all right?" Yes, I told him, I was fine, just a bit rattly, and we drove off to find a shady patio and some beer. When I got home an hour or so later, my daughter greeted me with "What have you done to yourself?" I looked down. One elbow of my white turtleneck with the green froggies, one knee of my white trousers, one white kneesock were blood-soaked. We peeled off the clothes and inspected the damage, which was nasty enough but not alarming. That part wasn't funny: the abrasions took a long time to heal, and one got a little infected. Even so, when I think of my friend talking earnestly, suddenly, to the hot thin air while I dropped from his view as though through a trap door, I find the image as silly as something from a Marx Brothers movie.

I may find it easier than other cripples to amuse myself because I live propped by the acceptance and the assistance and, sometimes, the amusement of those around me. Grocery clerks tear my checks out of my checkbook for me, and sales clerks find chairs to put into dressing rooms when I want to try on clothes. The people I work with make sure I teach at times when I am least likely to be fatigued, in places I can get to, with the materials I need. My students, with one anonymous exception (in an end-of-the-semester evaluation), have been unperturbed by my disability. Some even like it. One was immensely cheered by the information that I paint my own fingernails; she decided, she told me, that if I could go to such trouble over fine details, she could keep on writing essays. I suppose I became some sort of bright-fingered muse. She wrote good essays, too.

The most important struts in the framework of my existence, of course, 15 are my husband and children. Dismayingly few marriages survive the MS test, and why should they? Most twenty-two- and nineteen-year-olds, like George and me, can vow in clear conscience, after a childhood of chicken pox and summer colds, to keep one another in sickness and in health so long as they both shall live. Not many are equipped for catastrophe: the dismay, the depression, the extra work, the boredom that a degenerative disease can insinuate into a relationship. And our society, with its emphasis on fun and its association of fun with physical performance, offers little encouragement for a whole spouse to stay with a crippled partner. Children experience similar stresses when faced with a crippled parent, and they are more helpless, since parents and children can't usually get divorced. They hate, of course, to be different from their peers, and the child whose mother is tacking down the aisle of a school auditorium packed with proud parents like a Cape Cod dinghy in a stiff breeze jolly well stands out in crowd. Deprived of legal divorce, the child can at least deny the mother's disability, even her existence, forgetting to tell her about recitals and PTA meetings, refusing to accompany her to stores or church or the movies, never inviting friends to the house. Many do.

But I've been limping along for ten years now, and so far George and the children are still at my left elbow, holding tight. Anne and Matthew vacuum floors and dust furniture and haul trash and rake up dog droppings and button my cuffs and bake lasagna and Toll House cookies with just enough grumbling so I know that they don't have brain fever. And far from hiding me, they're forever dragging me by racks of fancy clothes or through teeming school corridors, or welcoming gaggles of friends while I'm wandering through the house in Anne's filmy pink baby-doll pajamas. George generally calls before he brings someone home, but he does just as many dumb thankless chores as the children. And they all yell at me, laugh at some of my jokes, write me funny letters when we're apart—in short, treat me as an ordinary human being for whom they have some use. I think they like me. Unless they're faking. . . .

Faking. There's the rub. Tugging at the fringes of my consciousness always is the terror that people are kind to me only because I'm a cripple. My mother almost shattered me once, with that instinct mothers have—blind, I think, in this case, but unerring nonetheless—for striking blows along the fault lines of their children's hearts, by telling me, in an attack on my selfishness, "We all have to make allowances for you, of course, because of the way you are." From the distance of a couple of years, I have to admit that I haven't any idea just what she meant, and I'm not sure that she knew either. She was awfully angry. But at the time, as the words thudded home, I felt my worst fear, suddenly realized. I could bear being called selfish: I am. But I couldn't bear the corroboration that those around me were doing in fact what I'd always suspected them of doing, professing fondness while silently putting up with me because of the way I am. A cripple. I've been a little cracked ever since.

Along with this fear that people are secretly accepting shoddy goods comes a relentless pressure to please—to prove myself worth the burdens I impose, I guess, or to build a substantial account of goodwill against which I may write drafts in times of need. Part of the pressure arises from social expectations. In our society, anyone who deviates from the norm had better find some way to compensate. Like fat people, who are expected to be jolly, cripples must bear their lot meekly and cheerfully. A grumpy cripple isn't playing by the rules. And much of the pressure is self-generated. Early on I vowed that, if I had to have MS, by God I was going to do it well. This is a class act, ladies and gentlemen. No tears, no recriminations, no faintheartedness.

One way and another, then, I wind up feeling like Tiny Tim, peering over the edge of the table at the Christmas goose, waving my crutch, piping down God's blessing on us all. Only sometimes I don't want to play Tiny Tim. I'd rather be Caliban, a most scurvy monster. Fortunately, at home no one much cares whether I'm a good cripple or a bad cripple as long as I make vichyssoise with fair regularity. One evening several years ago, Anne was reading at the dining-room table while I cooked dinner. As I opened a can of tomatoes, the can slipped in my left hand and juice spattered me and the counter with bloody spots. Fatigued and infuriated, I bellowed, "I'm so sick of being crippled!" Anne glanced at me over the top of her book. "There now," she said, "do you feel better?" "Yes," I said, "yes, I do." She went back to her reading. I felt better. That's about all the attention my scurviness ever gets.

Because I hate being crippled, I sometimes hate myself for being a 20 cripple. Over the years I have come to expect—even accept—attacks of violent self-loathing. Luckily, in general our society no longer connects deformity and disease directly with evil (though a charismatic once told me that I have MS because a devil is in me) and so I'm allowed to move largely at will, even among small children. But I'm not sure that this revision of attitude has been particularly helpful. Physical imperfection, even freed of moral disapprobation, still defies and violates the ideal, especially for women, whose confinement in their bodies as objects of desire is far from over. Each age, of course, has its ideal, and I doubt that ours is any better or worse than any other. Today's ideal woman, who lives on the glossy pages of dozens of magazines, seems to be between the ages of eighteen and twenty-five; her hair has body, her teeth flash white, her breath smells minty, her underarms are dry; she has a career but is still a fabulous cook, especially of meals that take less than twenty minutes to prepare; she does not ordinarily appear to have a husband or children; she is trim and deeply tanned; she jogs, swims, plays tennis, rides a bicycle, sails, but does not bowl; she travels widely, even to out-of-the way places like Finland and Samoa, always in the company of the ideal man, who possesses a nearly identical set of characteristics. There are a few exceptions. Though usually white and often blond, she may be black, Hispanic, Asian, or Native American, so long as she is unusually sleek. She may be old, provided she is selling a laxative or is Lauren Bacall. If she is selling a detergent, she may be married and have a flock of strikingly messy children. But she is never a cripple.

Like many women I know, I have always had an uneasy relationship with my body. I was not a popular child, largely, I think now, because I was peculiar: intelligent, intense, moody, shy, given to unexpected actions and inexplicable notions and emotions. But as I entered adolescence, I believed myself unpopular because I was homely: my breasts too flat, my mouth too wide, my hips too narrow, my clothing never quite right in fit or style. I was not, in fact, particularly ugly, old photographs inform me, though I was well off the ideal; but I carried this sense of self-alienation with me into adulthood, where it regenerated in response to the depredations of MS. Even with my brace I walk with a limp so pronounced that, seeing myself on the videotape of a television program on the disabled, I couldn't believe that anything but an inchworm could make progress humping along like that. My shoulders droop and my pelvis thrusts forward as I try to balance myself upright, throwing my frame into a bony *S*. As a result of contractures, one shoulder is higher than the other and I carry one arm bent in front of me, the fingers curled into a claw. My left arm and leg have wasted into pipe stems, and I try always to keep them covered. When I think about how my body must look to others, especially to men, to whom I have been trained to display myself, I feel ludicrous, even loathsome.

At my age, however, I don't spend much time thinking about my appearance. The burning egocentricity of adolescene, which assures one that all the world is looking all the time, has passed, thank God, and I'm generally too caught up in what I'm doing to step back, as I used to, and watch myself as though upon a stage. I'm also too old to believe in the accuracy of self-image. I know that I'm not a hideous crone, that in fact, when I'm rested, well dressed, and well made up, I look fine. The self-loathing I feel is neither physically nor intellectually substantial. What I hate is not me but a disease.

I am not a disease.

And a disease is not—at least not single-handedly—going to determine who I am, though at first it seemed to be going to. Adjusting to a chronic incurable illness, I have moved through a process similar to that outlined by Elisabeth Kübler-Ross in *On Death and Dying*. The major difference—and it is far more significant than most people recognize—is that I can't be sure of the outcome, as the terminally ill cancer patient can. Research studies indicate that, with proper medical care, I may achieve a "normal" life span. And in our society, with its vision of death as the ultimate evil, worse even than decrepitude, the response to such news is, "Oh well, at least you're not going to *die*." Are there worse things than dying? I think that there may be.

I think of two women I know, both with MS, both enough older than 25 I to have served me as models. One took to her bed several years ago and has been there ever since. Although she can sit in a high-backed wheelchair, because she is incontinent she refuses to go out at all, even though incontinence pants, which are readily available at any pharmacy, could protect her from embarrassment. Instead, she stays at home and insists that her husband, a small quiet man, a retired civil servant, stay there with her except for a quick weekly foray to the supermarket. The other woman, whose illness was diagnosed when she was eighteen, a nursing student engaged to a young doctor, finished her training, married her doctor, accompanied him to Germany when he was in the service, bore three sons and a daughter, now grown and gone. When she can, she travels with her husband; she plays bridge, embroiders, swims regularly; she works, like me, as a symptomatic-patient instructor of medical students in neurology. Guess which woman I hope to be.

At the beginning, I thought about having MS almost incessantly. And because of the unpredictable course of the disease, my thoughts were always terrified. Each night I'd get into bed wondering whether I'd get out again the next morning, whether I'd able to see, to speak, to hold a pen between my fingers. Knowing that the day might come when I'd be physically incapable of killing myself, I thought perhaps I ought to do so right away, while I still had the strength. Gradually I came to understand that the Nancy who might one day lie inert under a bedsheet, arms and legs paralyzed, unable to feed or bathe herself, unable to reach out for a gun, a bottle of pills, was not the Nancy I was at present, and that I could not presume to make decisions for that future Nancy, who might well not want in the least to die. Now the only provision I've made for the future Nancy is that when the time comes—and it is likely to come in the form of pneumonia, friend to the weak and the old—I am not to be treated with machines and medications. If she is unable to communicate by then, I hope she will be satisfied with these terms.

Thinking all the time about having MS grew tiresome and intrusive, especially in the large and tragic mode in which I was accustomed to considering my plight. Months and even years went by without catastrophe (at least without one related to MS), and really I was awfully busy, what with George and children and snakes and students and poems, and I hadn't the time, let alone the inclination, to devote myself to being a disease. Too, the richer my life became, the funnier it seemed, as though there were some connection between largesse and laughter, and so my tragic stance began to waver until, even with the aid of a brace and a cane, I couldn't hold it for very long at a time.

After several years I was satisfied with my adjustment. I had suffered my grief and fury and terror, I thought, but now I was at ease with my lot. Then one summer day I set out with George and the children across the desert for a vacation in California. Part way to Yuma I became aware that my right leg felt funny. "I think I've had an exacerbation," I told George. "What shall we do?" he asked. "I think we'd better get the hell to California," I said, "because I don't know whether I'll ever make it again." So we went on to San Diego and then to Orange, up the Pacific Coast Highway to Santa Cruz, across to Yosemite, down to Sequoia and Joshua Tree, and so back over the desert to home. It was a fine two-week trip, filled with friends and fair weather, and I wouldn't have missed it for the world, though I did in fact make it back to California two years later. Nor would there have been any point in missing it, since in MS, once the symptoms have appeared, the neurological damage has been done, and there's no way to predict or prevent that damage.

The incident spoiled my self-satisfaction, however. It renewed my grief and fury and terror, and I learned that one never finishes adjusting to MS. I don't know now why I thought one would. One does not, after all, finish adjusting to life, and MS is simply a fact of my life—not my favorite fact, of course—but as ordinary as my nose and my tropical fish and my yellow Mazda station wagon. It may at any time get worse, but no amount of worry or anticipation can prepare me for a new loss. My life is a lesson in losses. I learn one at a time.

And I had best be patient in the learning, since I'll have to do it like it or 30 not. As any rock fan knows, you can't always get what you want. Particularly when you have MS. You can't, for example, get cured. In recent years researchers and the organizations that fund research have started to pay MS some attention even though it isn't fatal; perhaps they have begun to see that life is something other than a quantitative phenomenon, that one may be very much alive for a very long time in a life that isn't worth living. The researchers have made some progress toward understanding the mechanism of the disease: it may well be an autoimmune reaction triggered by a slow-acting virus. But they are nowhere near its prevention, control, or cure. And most of us want to be cured. Some, unable to accept incurability, grasp at one treatment after another, no matter how bizarre: megavitamin therapy, gluten-free diet, injections of cobra venom, hypothermal suits, lymphocytopharesis, hyperbaric chambers. Many treatments are probably harmless enough, but none are curative.

The absence of a cure often makes MS patients bitter toward their doctors. Doctors are, after all, the priests of modern society, the new shamans, whose business is to heal, and many an MS patient roves from one to another, searching for the "good" doctor who will make him well. Doctors too think of themselves as healers, and for this reason many have trouble dealing with MS patients, whose disease in its intransigence defeats their aims and mocks their skills. Too few doctors, it is true, treat their patients as whole human beings, but the reverse is also true. I have always tried to be gentle with my doctors, who often have more at stake in terms of ego than I do. I may be frustrated, maddened, depressed by the incurability of my disease, but I am not diminished by it, and they are. When I push myself up from my seat in the waiting room and stumble toward them, I incarnate the limitation of their powers. The least I can do is refuse to press on their tenderest spots.

This gentleness is part of the reason that I'm not sorry to be a cripple. I didn't have it before. Perhaps I'd developed it anyway—how could I know such a thing?—and I wish I had more of it, but I'm glad of what I have. It has opened and enriched my life enormously, this sense that my frailty and need must be mirrored in others, that in searching for and shaping a stable core in a life wrenched by change and loss, change and loss, I must recognize the same process, under individual conditions, in the lives around me. I do not deprecate such knowledge, however I've come by it.

All the same, if a cure were found, would I take it? In a minute. I may be a cripple, but I'm only occasionally a loony and never a saint. Anyway, in my brand of theology God doesn't give bonus points for a limp. I'd take a cure; I just don't need one. A friend who also has MS startled me once by asking, "Do you ever say to yourself, 'Why me, Lord?'" "No, Michael, I don't," I told him, "because whenever I try, the only response I can thing of is 'Why not?'" If I could make a cosmic deal, who would I put in my place? What in my life would I give up in exchange for sound limbs and a thrilling rush of energy? No one. Nothing. I might as well do the job myself. Now that I'm getting the hang of it.

WHAT DOES SHE SAY?

1. As you're reading, write five sentences that seem accurate about Nancy Mairs and her essay. For each sentence, mark the place in the essay that prompted you to write.

2. Written in first person, this essay features an *I* narrator who does many things. Identify ten activities that reflect her "crippledness" and ten that do not.

3. Write a paragraph about the experience of reading this essay. Is it discouraging? fun?

4. Find a point in this essay where you're sure that Nancy Mairs asserts that she is not merely her body. Copy out at least two sentences of this part. Then find a section where you're sure Mairs is asserting that she is her body. Copy out at least two sentences from this part too.

WHAT DO YOU THINK?

5. Apply this chapter's question to Nancy Mairs's essay. That is, is Nancy Mairs her body? Write an essay that explains how "On Being a Cripple" makes its responses to this question.

6. As it goes along, Nancy Mairs's essay draws a clear picture of what she understands is the ideal woman. Explain this ideal, as Mairs presents and implies it, and why you agree, or disagree, that it's an accurate reflection of the general view, using current examples from popular culture to support your view. Then discuss the extent to which you've internalized these ideals, too. (It may seem like this is aimed only at women, but it as an assignment both women and men could tackle.)

7. Discuss the Nancy Mairs whom you meet in this essay. What seems clearest to you about her? What interests or surprises you? Then write about how she reminds you of someone else you know. Try to present this other person so clearly (imitate Mairs's techniques) that readers understand this other individual almost as well as you do.

WHAT WOULD THEY SAY?

8. Having read Nancy Mairs's "On Being a Cripple," now read Jenefer Shute's "Life-Size" (p. 279). What do these selections have in common? And what are their greatest differences? What do you learn or understand better as a result of comparing and contrasting them? And what, if anything, do these essays have to do with ethics or ethical behavior?

9. Read "On Being a Cripple" together with Bowen H. McCoy's "The Parable of the Sadhu" (p. 102). Then assume that Nancy Mairs does not have health insurance and cannot pay for her own care. To what extent, or not, do you think McCoy's essay applies here? That is, to what extent do you think that we have some societal obligation to care for someone like Nancy Mairs, despite the fact that she cannot afford or cannot obtain health insurance? Write an essay that uses McCoy's essay to explain your view. Variation: Make this same effort, except use Garrett Hardin's essay "Lifeboat Ethics: The Case against Helping the Poor" (p. 130) instead of McCoy's.

LANCE ARMSTRONG
Before and After

*I*N THIS EXCERPT *from a recent autobiography, cyclist Lance Armstrong (b. 1971) describes his experience with testicular and brain cancer, raising issues about the power of the will and the limitations of the body. A two-time Olympian and six-time Tour de France winner, Armstrong started the Lance Armstrong Foundation for those living with cancer after his recovery. With Sally Jenkins, he has written two autobiographies:* Every Second Counts *(2004) and* It's Not about the Bike *(2000), from which this piece is taken.*

I want to die at a hundred years old with an American flag on my back and the star of Texas on my helmet, after screaming down an Alpine descent on a bicycle at 75 miles per hour. I want to cross one last finish line as my stud wife and my ten children applaud, and then I want to lie down in a field of those famous French sunflowers and gracefully expire, the perfect contradiction to my once-anticipated poignant early demise.

A slow death is not for me. I don't do anything slow, not even breathe. I do everything at a fast cadence: eat fast, sleep fast. It makes me crazy when my wife, Kristin, drives our car, because she brakes at all the yellow caution lights, while I squirm impatiently in the passenger seat.

"Come on, don't be a skirt," I tell her.

"Lance," she says, "marry a man."

I've spent my life racing my bike, from the back roads of Austin, Texas, to the Champs-Elysées, and I always figured if I died an untimely death, it would be because some rancher in his Dodge 4×4 ran me headfirst into a ditch. Believe me, it could happen. Cyclists fight an ongoing war with guys in big trucks, and so many vehicles have hit me, so many times, in so many countries, I've lost count. I've learned how to take out my own stitches: all you need is a pair of fingernail clippers and a strong stomach.

If you saw my body underneath my racing jersey, you'd know what I'm talking about. I've got marbled scars on both arms and discolored marks up and down my legs, which I keep clean shaven. Maybe that's why trucks are always trying to run me over; they see my sissy-boy calves and decide not to brake. But cyclists have to shave, because when the gravel gets into your skin, it's easier to clean and bandage if you have no hair.

One minute you're pedaling along a highway, and the next minute, *boom*, you're facedown in the dirt. A blast of hot air hits you, you taste the acrid, oily exhaust in the roof of your mouth, and all you can do is wave a fist at the disappearing taillights.

5

Cancer was like that. It was like being run off the road by a truck, and I've got the scars to prove it. There's a puckered wound in my upper chest just above my heart, which is where the catheter was implanted. A surgical line runs from the right side of my groin into my upper thigh, where they cut out my testicle. But the real prizes are two deep half-moons in my scalp, as if I was kicked twice in the head by a horse. Those are the leftovers from brain surgery.

When I was 25, I got testicular cancer and nearly died. I was given less than a 40 percent chance of surviving, and frankly, some of my doctors were just being kind when they gave me those odds. Death is not exactly cocktail-party conversation, I know, and neither is cancer, or brain surgery, or matters below the waist. But I'm not here to make polite conversation. I want to tell the truth. I'm sure you'd like to hear about how Lance Armstrong became a Great American and an Inspiration To Us All, how he won the Tour de France, the 2,290-mile road race that's considered the single most grueling sporting event on the face of the earth. You want to hear about faith and mystery, and my miraculous comeback, and how I joined towering figures like Greg LeMond and Miguel Indurain in the record book. You want to hear about my lyrical climb through the Alps and my heroic conquering of the Pyrenees, and how it *felt*. But the tour was the least of the story.

Some of it is not easy to tell or comfortable to hear. I'm asking you 10 now, at the outset, to put aside your ideas about heroes and miracles, because I'm not storybook material. This is not Disneyland, or Hollywood. I'll give you an example: I've read that I *flew* up the hills and mountains of France. But you don't fly up a hill. You struggle slowly and painfully up a hill, and maybe, if you work very hard, you get to the top ahead of everybody else.

Cancer is like that, too. Good, strong people get cancer, and they do all the right things to beat it, and they still die. That is the essential truth that you learn. People die. And after you learn it, all other matters seem irrelevant. They just seem small.

I don't know why I'm still alive. I can only guess. I have a tough constitution, and my profession taught me how to compete against long odds and big obstacles. I like to train hard and I like to race hard. That helped, it was a good start, but it certainly wasn't the determining factor. I can't help feeling that my survival was more a matter of blind luck.

When I was 16, I was invited to undergo testing at a place in Dallas called the Cooper Clinic, a prestigious research lab and birthplace of the aerobic exercise revolution. A doctor there measured my VO_2 max, which is a gauge of how much oxygen you can take in and use, and he says that my numbers are still the highest they've ever come across. Also, I produced less lactic acid than most people. Lactic acid is the chemical your body generates when it's winded and fatigued—it's what makes your lungs burn and your legs ache.

Basically, I can endure more physical stress than most people can, and I don't get as tired while I'm doing it. So I figure maybe that helped me live.

I was lucky—I was born with an above-average capacity for breathing. But even so, I was in a desperate, sick fog much of the time.

My illness was humbling and starkly revealing, and it forced me to sur-   15
vey my life with an unforgiving eye. There are some shameful episodes in it: instances of meanness, unfinished tasks, weakness, and regrets. I had to ask myself, "If I live, who is it that I intend to be?" I found that I had a lot of growing to do as a man.

I won't kid you. There are two Lance Armstrongs, precancer, and post. Everybody's favorite question is "How did cancer change you?" The real question is how didn't it change me? I left my house on October 2, 1996, as one person and came home another. I was a world-class athlete with a mansion on a riverbank, keys to a Porsche, and a self-made fortune in the bank. I was one of the top riders in the world and my career was moving along a perfect arc of success. I returned a different person, literally. In a way, the old me did die, and I was given a second life. Even my body is different, because during the chemotherapy I lost all the muscle I had ever built up, and when I recovered, it didn't come back in the same way.

The truth is that cancer was the best thing that ever happened to me. I don't know why I got the illness, but it did wonders for me, and I wouldn't want to walk away from it. Why would I want to change, even for a day, the most important and shaping event in my life?

People die. That truth is so disheartening that at times I can't bear to articulate it. Why should we go on, you might ask? Why don't we all just stop and lie down where we are? But there is another truth, too. People live. It's an equal and opposing truth. People live, and in the most remarkable ways. When I was sick, I saw more beauty and triumph and truth in a single day than I ever did in a bike race—but they were *human* moments, not miraculous ones. I met a guy in a fraying sweatsuit who turned out to be a brilliant surgeon. I became friends with a harassed and overscheduled nurse named La-Trice, who gave me such care that it could only be the result of the deepest sympathetic affinity. I saw children with no eyelashes or eyebrows, their hair burned away by chemo, who fought with the hearts of Indurains.

I still don't completely understand it.

All I can do is tell you what happened.   20

WHAT DOES HE SAY?

1. As you read, make notes about the precancer Lance Armstrong. What words would you use to describe him? Keep a running list as you read.

2. Find and underline three places in this essay that help you understand why Lance Armstrong achieved his various successes as an athlete.

3. To what extent, or not, do you find that Armstrong fits your stereotype of the male sports star? Write a paragraph explaining this.

4. In the beginning of this selection, Armstrong refers to his "stud wife." Frustrated with her driving, he says, "Come on, don't be a skirt." What is your reaction to these phrases? What do they suggest about Armstrong's attitude toward women and toward men?

WHAT DO YOU THINK?

5. How would you describe Armstrong's voice in this essay? loud? soft? cocky? humble? Does the voice change in these few pages, or does it stay the same? Based on this selection, would you like to have lunch with Lance Armstrong?

6. Armstrong talks about his various scars, both from cycling accidents and from his cancer surgeries. What seems to be his attitude about these scars? Is he proud of them? ashamed of them? What is the relationship between what Armstrong says about scars and his main point in this essay? Write an essay about your own scars, physical or emotional. What do they mean to you?

7. Write an essay about an experience of illness and of cancer specifically—either your own or the illness of someone close to you. How does your experience relate to Armstrong's? Explain.

8. Armstrong says that he wants to "tell the truth" about his experience rather than indulging in the easy "Hollywood" or "Disneyland" clichés about illness and about sports. Explain what he means. Write an essay doing the same: tell the "truth" about an experience of your own and show how it contrasts with the easy Hollywood clichés.

9. Armstrong says that his old self "died" and that he was given "a second life." Write about a radical change in your own life or in the life of someone you know. Give it the same title as this essay: "Before and After."

WHAT WOULD THEY SAY?

10. Read Armstrong's "Before and After" in conjunction with Andre Dubus's "Giving Up the Gun" (p. 180) and Studs Terkel's "C. P. Ellis" (p. 568); then write an essay reflecting on the process of change in the lives of all three of these men. What causes such radical change in a person's life? What are the similarities in these three accounts? What are the differences?

11. Put Lance Armstrong in a room with Scott Russell Sanders, the author of "Looking at Women" (p. 294). Imagine that Armstrong has read Sanders's essay. What would he say to Sanders? How would Sanders respond?

12. Imagine that Armstrong comes to visit the narrator of Jenefer Shute's "Life-Size" (p. 279) in the hospital. What would he say to her?

13. Suppose that Armstrong has read Bill McKibben's "Designer Genes" (p. 360). How would he respond? Would he be in favor of artificially manipulating the human body? Explain. How would McKibben then respond?

ELLEN GOODMAN

Who Lives? Who Dies? Who Decides?

*T*HIS PIECE CAPTURES *the complex debate about euthanasia with clarity and sharpness. Who should decide who lives and dies, and how should that decision be made?*

    Educated at Radcliffe College, Ellen Goodman (b. 1948) began her journalistic career as a researcher for Newsweek. *In 1967 she began writing a column for the* Boston Globe, *which has been syndicated nationally since 1972. Six collections of her columns have been published, including* Making Sense *(1989) and* Value Judgments *(1993). "Who Lives? Who Dies? Who Decides?" was published in 1980, the same year Goodman won a Pulitzer Prize for Distinguished Commentary.*

Some have called it a Right to Die case. Others have labeled it a Right to Live case. One group of advocates has called for "death with dignity." Others have responded accusingly, "euthanasia."

    At the center of the latest controversy about life and death, medicine and law, is a seventy-eight-year-old Massachusetts man whose existence hangs on a court order.

    On one point, everyone agrees: Earle Spring is not the man he used to be. Once a strapping outdoorsman, he is now strapped to a wheelchair. Once a man with a keen mind, he is now called senile by many, and mentally incompetent by the courts. He is, at worst, a member of the living dead; at best, a shriveled version of his former self.

    For more than two years, since his physical and then mental health began to deteriorate, Earle Spring has been kept alive by spending five hours on a kidney dialysis machine three times a week. Since January 1979, his family has pleaded to have him removed from the life-support system.

    They believe deeply that the Earle Spring who was would not want to 5 live as the Earle Spring who is. They believe they are advocates for the right to die in peace.

    In the beginning, the courts agreed. Possibly for the first time, they ruled last month in favor of withdrawing medical care from an elderly patient whose mind had deteriorated. The dialysis was stopped.

    But then, in a sudden intervention, an outside nurse and doctor visited Earle Spring and testified that he was alert enough to "make a weak expression of his desire to live." And so the treatments were resumed.

    Now, while the courts are waiting for new and more through evidence about Spring's mental state, the controversy rages about legal procedures; no judge ever visited Spring, no psychiatrist ever testified. And even more important, we are again forced to determine one person's right to die or to live.

This case makes the Karen Ann Quinlan story seem simple in comparison. Quinlan today hangs onto her "life" long after her "plug was pulled." But when the New Jersey court heard that case, Quinlan had no will. She had suffered brain death by any definition.

The Spring story is different. He is neither competent nor comatose. He 10 lives in a gray area of consciousness. So the questions also range over the gray area of consciences.

What should the relationship be between mental health and physical treatment? Should we treat the incompetent as aggressively as the competent? Should we order heart surgery for one senile citizen? Should we take another off a kidney machine? What is the mental line between a life worth saving and the living dead? Who is to decide?

Until recently, we didn't have the technology to keep an Earle Spring alive. Until recently, the life-and-death decisions about the senile elderly or the retarded or the institutionalized were made privately between families and medical people. Now, increasingly, in states like Massachusetts, they are made publicly and legally.

Clearly there are no absolutes in this case. No right to die. No right to live. We have to take into account many social as well as medical factors. How much of the resources of a society or a family should be allotted to a member who no longer recognizes it? How many sacrifices should the healthy and vital make for the terminally or permanently ill and disabled?

In England, where kidney dialysis machines are scarce, Earle Spring would never have remained on one. In America, one Earle Spring can decimate the energy and income of an entire family.

But the Spring case is a crucial, scary one that could affect all those liv- 15 ing under that dubious sentence "incompetent" or that shaky diagnosis "senile." So it seems to me that if there is one moment a week when the fog lifts and when this man wants to live, if there is any mental activity at all, then disconnecting him from life would be a dangerous precedent, far more dangerous than letting him continue.

The court ruled originally in favor of taking Spring off the machine. It ruled that this is what Earle Spring would have wanted. I have no doubt that his family believes it. I have no doubt of their affection or their pain.

But I remember, too, what my grandfather used to say: no one wants to live to be one hundred until you ask the man who is ninety-nine. Well, no one, including Earle Spring, wants to live to be senile. But once senile, he may well want to live. We simply have to give him the benefit of the doubt. Any doubt.

WHAT DOES SHE SAY?

1. As you read, make a list of the open, unanswered questions that Ellen Goodman asks in this essay. Once you have the list in front of you, write a paragraph as a first response to those questions.

2. What facts are not in dispute in this essay? Make a list of them. Then write two sentences about what you understand as you read this list.

3. Goodman's essay comes to a quite definite conclusion: "disconnecting him from life would be a dangerous precedent." Understand this conclusion as thoroughly as you can: what principles or assumptions lead Goodman to it?

WHAT DO YOU THINK?

4. "Who Lives? Who Dies? Who Decides?" covers a lot of ground very quickly. Write an essay that simply reports the facts as presented and that then tries to understand the various arguments and positions that swirl around those facts. Some of them have to do with costs, some with circumstances, some with the difference between kindness and cruelty, and so on. If there are others that you think of that don't appear in Goodman's essay, include them in yours. In short, dig into these issues and conflicts and explain why what to do with Earle Spring, and others who share his condition, becomes so complex. Don't try to arrive at a conclusion. Rather, try to show why it's so hard to reach a conclusion to which all can agree.

5. Interview a classmate about what she or he privately believes should be done with a relative like Earle Spring. That is, try to comprehend your interviewee's private understanding and position—including any uncertainties or confusion. Take good notes so that you can report this in your paper. Then ask your interviewee if she or he believes this privately held position ought to be adopted as public policy. That is, to what extent, or not, would your interviewee wish to see his or her private views become law for everyone. Again, take careful notes. Then write a two-part summary of your interview. Make sure that you quote your interviewee often and accurately.

WHAT WOULD THEY SAY?

6. Read Nancy Mairs's "On Being a Cripple" (p. 333) together with "Who Lives? Who Dies? Who Decides?" Note that Mairs's essay briefly explains her own wishes for end-of-life care. Also read Jenefer Shute's "Life-Size" (p. 279). Based on your reading of all three of these selections, explain your understanding and confusion about the issue of who ought to be making life-and-death health-care decisions.

7. Read Parker Palmer's "The Community of Truth" (p. 627) and apply what that essay says to the situation Goodman describes. Write your own essay explaining how you would understand and seek to use what Palmer says in order to more fully wrestle with—and perhaps answer—the many questions that Goodman raises.

8. Consider William Stafford's "Traveling through the Dark" (p. 172) together with Goodman's essay. Explain how you understand what Stafford's speaker does in that poem. Then explain why or how you would want to compare the situation and actions of Stafford's poem with the situation and uncertainties Goodman presents.

SALLIE TISDALE
We Do Abortions Here

SALLIE TISDALE (b. 1957) speaks here as a medical worker acutely conscious of the complexities and failures that attend abortion. Her essay aims to help us understand her work's routine and its moral and ethical terrain, but without judging it—thus inviting the readers to judge the narrator.

    Tisdale has been a registered nurse, a profession that influences much of her writing, including her first book, The Sorcerer's Apprentice: Tales of the Modern Hospital *(1986). She has written several other books, including* Talk Dirty to Me: An Intimate Philosophy of Sex *(1994) and* The Best Thing I Ever Tasted: The Secret of Food *(2000). She has also taught writing at the University of Portland and the University of California, Davis. "We Do Abortions Here" was first published in* Harper's *in 1990.*

We do abortions here; that is all we do. There are weary, grim moments when I think I cannot bear another basin of bloody remains, utter another kind phrase of reassurance. So I leave the procedure room in the back and reach for a new chart. Soon I am talking to an eighteen-year-old woman pregnant for the fourth time. I push up her sleeve to check her blood pressure and find row upon row of needle marks, neat and parallel and discolored. She has been so hungry for her drug for so long that she has taken to using the loose skin of her upper arms; her elbows are already a permanent ruin of bruises. She is surprised to find herself nearly four months pregnant. I suspect she is often surprised, in a mild way, by the blows she is dealt. I prepare myself for another basin, another brief and chafing loss.

"How can you stand it?" Even the clients ask. They see the machine, the strange instruments, the blood, the final stroke that wipes away the promise of pregnancy. Sometimes I see that too: I watch a woman's swollen abdomen sink to softness in a few stuttering moments and my own belly flip-flops with sorrow. But all it takes for me to catch my breath is another interview, one more story that sounds so much like the last one. There is a numbing sameness lurking in this job: the same questions, the same answers, even the same trembling tone in the voices. The worst is the sameness of human failure, of inadequacy in the face of each day's dull demands.

In describing this work, I find it difficult to explain how much I enjoy it most of the time. We laugh a lot here, as friends and as professional peers. It's nice to be with women all day. I like the sudden, transient bonds I forge with some clients: moments when I am in my strength, remembering weakness, and a woman in weakness reaches out for my strength. What I offer is not power, but

351

solidness, offered almost eagerly. Certain clients waken in me every tender urge I have—others make me wince and bite my tongue. Both challenge me to find a balance. It is a sweet brutality we practice here, a stark and loving dispassion.

I look at abortion as if I am standing on a cliff with a telescope, gazing at some great vista. I can sweep the horizon with both eyes, survey the scene in all its distance and size. Or I can put my eye to the lens and focus on the small details, suddenly so close. In abortion the absolute must always be tempered by the contextual, because both are real, both valid, both hard. How can we do this? How can we refuse? Each abortion is a measure of our failure to protect, to nourish our own. Each basin I empty is a promise—but a promise broken a long time ago.

I grew up on the great promise of birth control. Like many women my age, I took the pill as soon as I was sexually active. To risk pregnancy when it was so easy to avoid seemed stupid, and my contraceptive success, as it were, was part of the promise of social enlightenment. But birth control fails, far more frequently than laboratory trials predict. Many of our clients take the pill; its failure to protect them is a shocking realization. We have clients who have been sterilized, whose husbands have had vasectomies; each one is a statistical misfit, fine print come to life. The anger and shame of these women I hold in one hand, and the basin in the other. The distance between the two, the length I pace and try to measure, is the size of an abortion.

The procedure is disarmingly simple. Women are surprised, as though the mystery of conception, a dark and hidden genesis, requires an elaborate finale. In the first trimester of pregnancy, it's a mere few minutes of vacuuming, a neat tidying up. I give a woman a small yellow Valium, and when it has begun to relax her, I lead her into the back, into bareness, the stirrups. The doctor reaches in her, opening the narrow tunnel to the uterus with a succession of slim, smooth bars of steel. He inserts a plastic tube and hooks it to a hose on the machine. The woman is framed against white paper that crackles as she moves, the light bright in her eyes. Then the machine rumbles low and loud in the small windowless room; the doctor moves the tube back and forth with an efficient rhythm, and the long tail of it fills with blood that spurts and stumbles along into a jar. He is usually finished in a few minutes. They are long minutes for the woman; her uterus frequently reacts to its abrupt emptying with a powerful, unceasing cramp, which cuts off the blood vessels and enfolds the irritated, bleeding tissue.

I am learning to recognize the shadows that cross the faces of the women I hold. While the doctor works between her spread legs, the paper drape hiding his intent expression, I stand beside the table. I hold the woman's hands in mine, resting them just below her ribs. I watch her eyes, finger her necklace, stroke her hair. I ask about her job, her family; in a haze she answers me; we chatter, faces close, eyes meeting and sliding apart.

I watch the shadows that creep up unnoticed and suddenly darken her face as she screws up her features and pushes a tear out each side to slide down her cheeks. I have learned to anticipate the quiver of chin, the rapid intake of breath, and the surprising sobs that rise soon after the machine starts to drum. I know this is when the cramp deepens, and the tears are partly the tears that follow pain—the sharp, childish crying when one bumps one's head on a cabinet door. But a well of woe seems to open beneath many women when they hear that thumping sound. The anticipation of the moment has finally come to fruit; the moment has arrived when the loss is no longer an imagined one. It has come true.

I am struck by the sameness and I am struck every day by the variety here—how this commonplace dilemma can so display the differences of women. A twenty-one-year-old woman, unemployed, uneducated, without family, in the fifth month of her pregnancy. A forty-two-year-old mother of teenagers, shocked by her condition, refusing to tell her husband. A twenty-three-year-old mother of two having her seventh abortion, and many women in their thirties having their first. Some are stoic, some hysterical, a few giggle uncontrollably, many cry.

I talk to a sixteen-year-old uneducated girl who was raped. She has 10 gonorrhea. She describes blinding headaches, attacks of breathlessness, nausea. "Sometimes I feel like two different people," she tells me with a calm smile, "and I talk to myself."

I pull out my plastic models. She listens patiently for a time, and then holds out her hands wide in front of her stomach.

"When's the baby going to go up into my stomach?" she asks.

I blink. "What do you mean?"

"Well," she says, still smiling, "when women get so big, isn't the baby in your stomach? Doesn't it hatch out of an egg there?"

My first question in an interview is always the same. As I walk down 15 the hall with the woman, as we get settled in chairs and I glance through her files, I am trying to gauge her, to get a sense of the words, and the tone, I should use. With some I joke, and others I chat, sometimes I fall into a brisk, business-like patter. But I ask every woman, "Are you sure you want to have an abortion?" Most nod with grim knowing smiles. "Oh, yes," they sigh. Some seek forgiveness, offer excuses. Occasionally a woman will flinch and say, "Please don't use that word."

Later I describe the procedure to come, using care with my language. I don't say "pain" any more than I would say "baby." So many are afraid to ask how much it will hurt. "My sister told me—" I hear. "A friend of mine said—" and the dire expectations unravel. I prick the index finger of a woman for a drop of blood to test, and as the tiny lancet approaches the skin she averts her eyes, holding her trembling hand out to me and jumping at my touch.

It is when I am holding a plastic uterus in one hand, a suction tube in the other, moving them together in imitation of the scrubbing to come, that women ask the most secret question. I am speaking in a matter-of-fact voice about "the tissue" and "the contents" when the woman suddenly catches my eye and asks, "How big is the baby now?" These words suggest a quiet need for a definition of the boundaries being drawn. It isn't so odd, after all, that she feels relief when I describe the growing bud's bulbous shape, its miniature nature. Again I gauge, and sometimes lie a little, weaseling around its infantile features until its clinging power slackens.

But when I look in the basin, among the curdlike blood clots, I see an elfin thorax, attenuated, its pencilline ribs all in parallel rows with tiny knobs of spine rounding upwards. A translucent arm and hand swim beside.

A sleepy-eyed girl, just fourteen, watched me with a slight and goofy smile all through her abortion. "Does it have little feet and little fingers and all?" she'd asked earlier. When the suction was over she sat up woozily at the end of the table and murmured, "Can I see it?" I shook my head firmly.

"It's not allowed," I told her sternly, because I knew she didn't really 20 want to see what was left. She accepted this statement of authority, and a shadow of confused relief crossed her plain, pale face.

Privately, even grudgingly, my colleagues might admit the power of abortion to provoke emotion. But they seem to prefer the broad view and disdain the telescope. Abortion is a matter of choice, privacy, control. Its uncertainty lies in specific cases: retarded women and girls too young to give consent for surgery, women who are ill or hostile or psychotic. Such common dilemmas are met with both compassion and impatience; they slow things down. We are too busy to chew over ethics. One person might discuss certain concerns, behind closed doors, or describe a particularly disturbing dream. But generally there is to be no ambivalence.

Every day I take calls from women who are annoyed that we cannot see them, cannot do their abortion today, this morning, now. They argue the price, demand that we stay after hours to accommodate their job or class schedule. Abortion is so routine that one expects it to be like a manicure; quick, cheap, and painless.

Still, I've cultivated a certain disregard. It isn't negligence, but I don't always pay attention. I couldn't be here if I tried to judge each case on its merits; after all, we do over a hundred abortions a week. At some point each individual in this line of work draws a boundary and adheres to it. For one physician the boundary is a particular week of gestation; for another, it is a certain number of repeated abortions. But these boundaries can be fluid too: One physician overruled his own limit to abort a mature but severely malformed fetus. For me, the limit is allowing my clients to carry their own burden, shoulder the responsibility themselves. I shoulder the burden of trying not to judge them.

This city has several "crisis pregnancy centers" advertised in the Yellow Pages. They are small offices staffed by volunteers, and they offer free pregnancy testing, glossy photos of dead fetuses, and movies. I had a client recently whose mother is active in the antiabortion movement. The young woman went to the local crisis center and was told that the doctor would make her touch her dismembered baby, that the pain would be the most horrible she could imagine, and that she might, after an abortion, never be able to have children. All lies. They called her at home and at work, over and over and over, but she had been wise enough to give a false name. She came to us a fugitive. We who do abortions are marked, by some, as impure. It's dirty work.

When a deliveryman comes to the sliding glass window by the reception 25 desk and tilts a box toward me, I hesitate. I read the packing slips, assess the shape and weight of the box in the light of its supposed contents. We request familiar faces. The doors are carefully locked; I have learned to half glance around at bags and boxes, looking for a telltale sign. I register with security when I arrive, and I am careful not to bang a door. We are a little on edge here.

Concern about size and shape seem to be natural, and so is the relief that follows. We make the powerful assumption that the fetus is different from us, and even when we admit the similarities, it is too simplistic to be seduced by form alone. But the form is enormously potent—humanoid, powerless, palm-sized, and pure, it evokes an almost fierce tenderness when viewed simply as what it appears to be. But appearance, and even potential, aren't enough. The fetus, in becoming itself, can ruin others; its utter dependence has a sinister side. When I am struck in the moment by the contents in the basin, I am careful to remember the context, to note the tearful teenager and the woman sighing with something more than relief. One kind of question, though, I find considerably trickier.

"Can you tell what it is?" I am asked, and this means gender. This question is asked by couples, not women alone. Always couples would abort a girl and keep a boy. I have been asked about twins, and even if I could tell what race the father was.

An eighteen-year-old woman with three daughters brought her husband to the interview. He glared first at me, then at his wife, as he sank lower and lower in the chair, picking his teeth with a toothpick. He interrupted a conversation with his wife to ask if I could tell whether the baby would be a boy or a girl. I told him I could not.

"Good," he replied in a slow and strangely malevolent voice, " 'cause if it was a boy I'd wring her neck."

In a literal sense, abortion exists because we are able to ask such ques- 30 tions, able to assign a value to the fetus which can shift with changing circumstances. If the human bond to a child were as primitive and unflinchingly narrow as that of other animals, there would be no abortion. There would be no abortion because there would be nothing more important than caring for the young and perpetuating the species, no reason for sex but to make babies. I sense this sometimes, this wordless organic duty, when I do ultrasounds.

We do ultrasound, a sound-wave test that paints a faint, gray picture of the fetus, whenever we're uncertain of gestation. Age is measured by the width of the skull and confirmed by the length of the femur or thighbone; we speak of a pregnancy as being a certain "femur length" in weeks. The usual concern is whether a pregnancy is within the legal limit for an abortion. Women this far along have bellies which swell out round and tight like trim muscles. When they lie flat, the mound rises softly above the hips, pressing the umbilicus upward.

It takes practice to read an ultrasound picture, which is grainy and etched as though in strokes of charcoal. But suddenly a rapid rhythmic motion appears— the beating heart. Nearby is a soft oval, scratched with lines—the skull. The leg is harder to find, and then suddenly the fetus moves, bobbing in the surf. The skull turns away, an arm slides across the screen, the torso rolls. I know the weight of a baby's head on my shoulder, the whisper of lips on ears, the delicate curve of a fragile spine in my hand. I know how heavy and correct a newborn cradled feels. The creature I watch in secret requires nothing from me but to be left alone, and that is precisely what won't be done.

These inadvertently made beings are caught in a twisting web of motive and desire. They are at least inconvenient, sometimes quite literally dangerous in the womb, but most often they fall somewhere in between—consequences never quite believed in come to roost. Their virtue rises and falls outside their own nature: they become only what we make them. A fetus created by acci- dent is the most absolute kind of surprise. Whether the blame lies in a failed IUD, a slipped condom, or a false impression of safety, that fetus is a thing whose creation has been actively worked against. Its existence is an error. I think this is why so few women, even late in a pregnancy, will consider giving a baby up for adoption. To do so means making the fetus real—imagining it as something whole and outside oneself. The decision to terminate a preg- nancy is sometimes so difficult and confounding that it creates an enormous demand for immediate action. The decision is a rejection; the pregnancy has become something to be rid of, a condition to be ended. It is a burden, a weight, a thing separate.

Women have abortions because they are too old, and too young, too poor, and too rich, too stupid, and too smart. I see women who berate them- selves with violent emotions for their first and only abortion, and others who return three times, five times, hauling two or three children, who cannot re- member to take a pill or where they put the diaphragm. We talk glibly about choice. But the choice for what? I see all the broken promises in lives lived like a series of impromptu obstacles. There are the sweet, light promises of love and intimacy, the glittering promise of education and progress, the warm promise of safe families, long years of innocence and community. And there is the promise of freedom: freedom from failure, from faithlessness. Freedom from biology. The early feminist defense of abortion asked many questions, but the one I remember is this: is biology destiny? And the answer is yes, sometimes it is. Women who have the fewest choices of all exercise their right to abortion the most.

Oh, the ignorance. I take a woman to the back room and ask her to 35
undress; a few minutes later I return and find her positioned discreetly behind a drape, still wearing underpants. "Do I have to take these off too?"
she asks, a little shocked. Some swear they have not had sex, many do not
know what a uterus is, how sperm and egg meet, how sex makes babies.
Some late seekers do not believe themselves pregnant; they believe themselves *impregnable*. I was chastised when I began this job for referring
to some clients as girls: it is a feminist heresy. They come so young, snap-
ping gum, sockless and sneakered, and their shakily applied eyeliner smears
when they cry. I call them girls with maternal benignity. I cannot imagine
them as mothers.

The doctor seats himself between the woman's thighs and reaches into the di-
lated opening of a five-month pregnant uterus. Quickly he grabs and crushes
the fetus in several places, and the room is filled with a low clatter and snap of
forceps, the click of the tanaculum, and a pulling, sucking sound. The paper
crinkles as the drugged and sleepy woman shifts, the nurse's low, honey-brown
voice explains each step in delicate words.

I have fetus dreams, we all do here: dreams of abortions one after the
other; of buckets of blood splashed on the walls; trees full of crawling fetuses.
I dreamed that two men grabbed me and began to drag me away: "Let's do
an abortion," they said with a sickening leer, and I began to scream, plunged
into a vision of sucking, scraping pain, of being spread and torn by impartial
instruments that do only what they are bidden. I woke from this dream
barely able to breathe and thought of kitchen tables and coat hangers, knit-
ting needles striped with blood, and women all alone clutching a pillow in
their teeth to keep the screams from piercing the apartment-house walls.
Abortion is the narrowest edge between kindness and cruelty. Done as well
as it can be, it is still violence — merciful violence, like putting a suffering
animal to death.

Maggie, one of the nurses, received a call at midnight not long ago. It
was a woman in her twentieth week of pregnancy; the necessarily gradual
process of cervical dilation begun the day before had stimulated labor, as it
sometimes does. Maggie and one of the doctors met the woman at the office
in the night. Maggie helped her onto the table, and as she lay down the fetus
was delivered into Maggie's hands. When Maggie told me about it the next
day, she cupped her hands into a small bowl — "It was just like a small kit-
ten," she said softly, wonderingly. "Everything was still attached."

At the end of the day I clean out the suction jars, pouring blood into
the sink, splashing the sides with flecks of tissue. From the sink rises a rich and
humid smell, hot, earthy, and moldering; it is the smell of something recently
alive beginning to decay. I take care of the plastic tub on the floor, filled with
pieces too big to be trusted to the trash. The law defines the contents of the
bucket I hold protectively against my chest as "tissue." Some would say my

complicity in filling that bucket gives me no right to call it anything else. I slip the tissue gently into a bag and place it in the freezer, to be burned at another time. Abortion requires of me an entirely new set of assumptions. It requires a willingness to live with conflict, fearlessness, and grief. As I close the freezer door, I imagine a world where this won't be necessary, and then return to the world where it is.

WHAT DOES SHE SAY?

1. Make a list of the clients (describe each one with a phrase or sentence) mentioned in "We Do Abortions Here." Once you've finished the essay and have a complete list, write a paragraph commenting on whatever that list tells you about those who seek abortions.

2. Write down five sentences that suggest to you that Sallie Tisdale approves of abortion and another five that suggest she doesn't. Write down another two or three that suggest how Tisdale confronts these seeming contradictions.

3. Identify the places in this essay where you see Tisdale most directly confronting the moral questions of abortion. Mark them in the margin. Once you've finished reading, write a paragraph summarizing Tisdale's moral position.

4. What surprises you most about "We Do Abortions Here"? Write a paragraph identifying this and explaining it briefly.

WHAT DO YOU THINK?

5. Consider the various clients mentioned in "We Do Abortions Here," and write an essay that explains their motives as you understand them from this essay. What situations, thoughts, or emotions seem to be at work? End by discussing to what extent you do, or do not, see abortion as an issue and decision separable from other issues and circumstances in a person's life.

6. Write a comparison-and-contrast essay that explains your experience with and understanding of abortion before and after reading this essay and thinking hard about it. (If this is too personally difficult an area to write about, say so in private to your teacher.)

7. Write about an issue other than abortion that has provoked intense debate, discussion, and perhaps hurtful argument within your own family or within your closest circle of friends. Explain the issue, including the various sides or responses and your own position, and end by analyzing how, as a group, you have all handled this controversy. What sorts of actions have helped you understand each other's views and beliefs? What actions have shut down communication or made it more painful or difficult? What, ideally, would you hope for the future when this same group of people is confronted with the next large, complex disagreement? Use Tisdale as an example that helps you explain some aspect of your essay.

WHAT WOULD THEY SAY?

8. Read Andrew Sullivan's "The Pursuit of Happiness: Four Revolutionary Words" (p. 217) together with "We Do Abortions Here." What do you think Sullivan would say about abortion as something to be decided by laws? More particularly, how do you think he would respond to Tisdale's essay? Write an essay that discusses this.

9. Read "We Do Abortions Here" together with Maxine Hong Kingston's "No Name Woman" (p. 45) and Bowen H. McCoy's "The Parable of the Sadhu" (p. 102). What relationships do you see between these essays? What new understandings arise as a result of thinking about them as a group?

10. Read Parker Palmer's "The Community of Truth" (p. 627) together with "We Do Abortions Here." Assume that a diverse and divergent group of people were going to discuss abortion—but they'd agreed to try to abide by the principles Palmer suggests. In an essay, explain those principles and propose a discussion format that embodies them.

BILL McKIBBEN
Designer Genes

*J*UST BECAUSE *we shall soon have the technology to genetically engineer a child, should we use it? Bill McKibben (b. 1960) raises this question and many others in this essay, a look at the complexities of genetic engineering.*

    A former New Yorker *staff writer, McKibben has published widely on current issues, including the books* The End of Nature *(1989) and* Enough: Staying Human in an Engineered Age *(2003). He lives with his wife and daughter in the Adirondack Mountains, where he is the Sunday school superintendent for a local Methodist church. "Designer Genes" was first published in the May/June 2003 issue of* Orion.

I grew up in a household where we were very suspicious of dented cans. Dented cans were, according to my mother, a well-established gateway to botulism, and botulism was a bad thing, worse than swimming immediately after lunch. It was one of those bad things measured in extinctions, as in "three tablespoons of botulism toxin could theoretically kill every human on Earth." Or something like that.

    So I refused to believe the early reports, a few years back, that socialites had begun injecting dilute strains of the toxin into their brows in an effort to temporarily remove the vertical furrow that appears between one's eyes as one ages. It sounded like a Monty Python routine, some clinic where they daubed your soles with plague germs to combat athlete's foot. But I was wrong to doubt. As the world now knows, Botox has become, in a few short years, a staple weapon in the cosmetic arsenal—so prevalent that, in the words of one writer, "it is now rare in certain social enclaves to see a woman over the age of thirty-five with the ability to look angry." With their facial muscles essentially paralyzed, actresses are having trouble acting; since the treatment requires periodic booster shots, doctors warn that "you could marry a woman (or a man) with a flawlessly even face and wind up with someone who four months later looks like a shar-pei." But never mind—now you can get Botoxed in strip-mall storefronts and at cocktail parties.

    People, in other words, will do fairly far-out things for less-than-pressing causes. And more so all the time: public approval of "aesthetic surgery" has grown 50 percent in the United States in the last decade. But why stop there? Once you accept the idea that our bodies are essentially plastic, and that it's okay to manipulate that plastic, there's no reason to think that consumers would balk because "genes" were involved instead of, say, "toxins." Especially since genetic engineering would not promote your own vanity, but instead be sold as a boon to your child.

The vision of genetic engineers is to do to humans what we have already done to salmon and wheat, pine trees and tomatoes. That is, to make them better in some way; to delete, modify, or add genes in developing embryos so that the cells of the resulting person will produce proteins that make them taller and more muscular, or smarter and less aggressive, maybe handsome and possibly straight. Even happy. As early as 1993, a March of Dimes poll found that 43 percent of Americans would engage in genetic engineering "simply to enhance their children's looks or intelligence."

Ethical guidelines promulgated by the scientific oversight boards so far   5
prohibit actual attempts at human genetic engineering, but researchers have walked right to the line, maybe even stuck their toes a trifle over. In the spring of 2001, for instance, a fertility clinic in New Jersey impregnated fifteen women with embryos fashioned from their own eggs, their partner's sperm, and a small portion of an egg donated by a second woman. The procedure was designed to work around defects in the would-be mother's egg—but in at least two of the cases, tests showed the resulting babies carried genetic material from all three "parents."

And so the genetic modification of humans is not only possible, it's coming fast; a mix of technical progress and shifting mood means it could easily happen in the next few years. Consider what happened with plants. A decade ago, university research farms were growing small plots of genetically modified grain and vegetables. Sometimes activists who didn't like what they were doing would come and rip the plants up, one by one. Then, all of a sudden in the mid-1990s, before anyone had paid any real attention, farmers had planted half the corn and soybean fields in America with transgenic seed.

Every time you turn your back this technology creeps a little closer. Gallops, actually, growing and spreading as fast as the Internet. One moment you've sort of heard of it; the next moment it's everywhere. But we haven't done it yet. For the moment we remain, if barely, a fully human species. And so we have time yet to consider, to decide, to act. This is arguably the biggest decision humans will ever make.

Right up until this decade, the genes that humans carried in their bodies were exclusively the result of chance—of how the genes of the sperm and the egg, the father and the mother, combined. The only way you could intervene in the process was by choosing who you would mate with—and that was as much wishful thinking as anything else, as generation upon generation of surprised parents have discovered.

But that is changing. We now know two different methods to change human genes. The first, and less controversial, is called somatic gene therapy. Somatic gene therapy begins with an existing individual—someone with, say, cystic fibrosis.° Researchers try to deliver new, modified genes to some of her cells, usually by putting the genes aboard viruses they inject into the patient, hoping that the viruses will infect the cells and thereby transmit the genes. Somatic gene therapy is, in other words, much like medicine. You take an existing patient with an existing condition, and you in essence try and convince her cells to manufacture the medicine she needs.

Germline genetic engineering on the other hand is something very novel   10
indeed. "Germ" here refers not to microbes, but to the egg and sperm cells, the germ cells of the human being. Scientists intent on genetic engineering would probably start with a fertilized embryo a week or so old. They would tease apart the cells of that embryo, and then, selecting one, they would add to, delete, or modify some of its genes. They could also insert artificial chromosomes containing predesigned genes. They would then take the cell, place it inside an egg whose nucleus had been removed, and implant the resulting new embryo inside a woman. The embryo would, if all went according to plan, grow into a genetically engineered child. His genes would be pushing out proteins to meet the particular choices made by his parents, and by the companies and clinicians they were buying the genes from. Instead of coming solely from the combination of his parents, and thus the combination of their parents, and so on back through time, those genes could come from any other person, or any other plant or animal, or out of the thin blue sky. And once implanted they will pass to his children, and on into time.

But all this work will require one large change in our current way of doing business. Instead of making babies by making love, we will have to move conception to the laboratory. You need to have the embryo out there where you can work on it—to make the necessary copies, try to add or delete genes, and then implant the one that seems likely to turn out best. Gregory Stock, a researcher at the University of California and an apostle of the new genetic technologies, says that "the union of egg and sperm from two individuals...would be too unpredictable with intercourse." And once you've got the embryo out on the lab bench, gravity disappears altogether. "Ultimately," says Michael West, CEO of Advanced Cell Technology, the firm furthest out on the cutting edge of these technologies, "the dream of biologists is to have the sequence of DNA, the programming code of life, and to be able to edit it the way you can a document on a word processor."

Does it sound far-fetched? We began doing it with animals (mice) in 1978, and we've managed the trick with most of the obvious mammals, except one. Some of the first germline interventions might be semimedical. You might, say some advocates, start by improving "visual and auditory acuity,"

°*Cystic fibrosis*: A currently incurable inherited genetic disease affecting the lungs and the systems responsible for digestion and reproduction; about 2500 new cases are diagnosed in the United States each year. [All notes are the Editors'.]

first to eliminate nearsightedness or prevent deafness, then to "improve artistic potential." But why stop there? "If something has evolved elsewhere, then it is possible for us to determine its genetic basis and transfer it into the human genome," says Princeton geneticist Lee Silver—just as we have stuck flounder genes into strawberries to keep them from freezing, and jellyfish genes into rabbits and monkeys to make them glow in the dark.

But would we actually do this? Is there any real need to raise these questions as more than curiosities, or will the schemes simply fade away on their own, ignored by the parents who are their necessary consumers?

Anyone who has entered a baby supply store in the last few years knows that even the soberest parents can be counted on to spend virtually unlimited sums in pursuit of successful offspring. What if the *Baby Einstein* video series, which immerses "learning enabled" babies in English, Spanish, Japanese, Hebrew, German, Russian, and French, could be bolstered with a little gene-tweaking to improve memory? What if the Wombsongs prenatal music system, piping in Brahms to your waiting fetus, could be supplemented with an auditory upgrade? One sociologist told the *New York Times* we'd crossed the line from parenting to "product development," and even if that remark is truer in Manhattan than elsewhere, it's not hard to imagine what such attitudes will mean across the affluent world.

Here's one small example. In the 1980s, two drug companies were 15 awarded patents to market human growth hormone to the few thousand American children suffering from dwarfism. The FDA thought the market would be very small, so HGH was given "orphan drug status," a series of special market advantages designed to reward the manufacturers for taking on such an unattractive business. But within a few years, HGH had become one of the largest-selling drugs in the country, with half a billion dollars in sales. This was not because there'd been a sharp increase in the number of dwarves, but because there'd been a sharp increase in the number of parents who wanted to make their slightly short children taller. Before long the drug companies were arguing that the children in the bottom five percent of their normal height range were in fact in need of three to five shots a week of HGH. Take eleven-year-old Marco Oriti. At four foot one, he was about four inches shorter than average, and projected to eventually top out at five foot four. This was enough to convince his parents to start on a six-day-a-week HGH regimen, which will cost them $150,000 over the next four years. "You want to give your child the edge no matter what," said his mother.

A few of the would-be parents out on the current cutting edge of the reproduction revolution—those who need to obtain sperm or eggs for in vitro fertilization—exhibit similar zeal. Ads started appearing in Ivy League college newspapers a few years ago: couples were willing to pay $50,000 for an egg, provided the donor was at least five feet ten inches tall, white, and had scored 1400 on her SATs. There is, in other words, a market just waiting for the first clinic with a catalog of germline modifications, a market that two California artists proved when they opened a small boutique, Gene Genies Worldwide, in a trendy part of Pasadena. Tran Kim-Trang and Karl Mihail wanted to get people thinking more deeply about these emerging technologies, so they outfitted their store with petri dishes and models of the double helix, and printed up brochures highlighting traits with genetic links: creativity, extroversion, thrill-seeking criminality. When they opened the doors, they found people ready to shell out for designer families (one man insisted he wanted the survival ability of a cockroach). The "store" was meant to be ironic, but the irony was lost on a culture so deeply consumer that this kind of manipulation seems like the obvious next step. "Generally, people refused to believe this store was an art project," says Tran. And why not? The next store in the mall could easily have been a Botox salon.

But say you're not ready. Say you're perfectly happy with the prospect of a child who shares the unmodified genes of you and your partner. Say you think that manipulating the DNA of your child might be dangerous, or presumptuous, or icky? How long will you be able to hold that line if the procedure begins to spread among your neighbors? Maybe not so long as you think: if germline manipulation actually does begin, it seems likely to set off a kind of biological arms race. "Suppose parents could add thirty points to their child's IQ," asks MIT economist Lester Thurow. "Wouldn't you want to do it? And if you don't, your child will be the stupidest in the neighborhood." That's precisely what it might feel like to be the parent facing the choice. Individual competition more or less defines the society we've built, and in that context love can almost be defined as giving your kids what they need to make their way in the world. Deciding not to soup them up...well, it could come to seem like child abuse.

Of course, the problem about arms races is that you never really get anywhere. If everyone's adding thirty IQ points, then having an IQ of one hundred fifty won't get you any closer to Stanford than you were at the outset. The very first athlete engineered to use twice as much oxygen as the next guy will be unbeatable in the Tour de France—but in no time he'll merely be the new standard. You'll have to do what he did to be in the race, but your upgrades won't put you ahead, merely back on a level playing field. You might be able to argue that society as a whole was helped, because there was more total brainpower at work, but your kid won't be any closer to the top of the pack. All you'll be able to do is guarantee she won't be left hopelessly far behind.

In fact, the arms-race problem has an extra ironic twist when it comes to genetic manipulation. The United States and the Soviet Union could, and did, keep adding new weapons to their arsenals over the decades. But with germline manipulation, you get only one shot; the extra chromosome you stick in your kid when he's born is the one he carries throughout his life. So let's say baby Sophie has a state-of-the-art gene job: her parents paid for the proteins discovered by, say, 2005 that, on average, yielded ten extra IQ points. By the time Sophie is five, though, scientists will doubtless have discovered ten more genes linked to intelligence. Now anyone with a platinum card can get twenty IQ points, not to mention a memory boost and a permanent wrinkle-free brow. So by the time Sophie is twenty-five and in the job market, she's already more or less obsolete—the kids coming out of college just plain have better hardware.

"For all his billions, Bill Gates could not have purchased a single genetic 20 enhancement for his son Rory John," writes Gregory Stock, at the University of California. "And you can bet that any enhancements a billion dollars can buy Rory's child in 2030 will seem crude alongside those available for modest sums in 2060." It's not, he adds, "so different from upgraded software. You'll want the new release."

The vision of one's child as a nearly useless copy of *Windows 95* should make parents fight like hell to make sure we never get started down this path. But the vision gets lost easily in the gushing excitement about "improving" the opportunities for our kids.

Beginning the hour my daughter came home from the hospital, I spent part of every day with her in the woods out back, showing her trees and ferns and chipmunks and frogs. One of her very first words was "birch," and you couldn't have asked for a prouder papa. She got her middle name from the mountain we see out the window; for her fifth birthday she got her own child-sized canoe; her school wardrobe may not be relentlessly up-to-date but she's never lacked for hiking boots. As I write these words, she's spending her first summer at sleep-away camp, one we chose because the kids sleep in tents and spend days in the mountains. All of which is to say that I have done everything in my power to try and mold her into a lover of the natural world. That is where my deepest satisfactions lie, and I want the same for her. It seems benign enough, but it has its drawbacks; it means less time and money and energy for trips to the city and music lessons and so forth. As time goes on and she develops stronger opinions of her own, I yield more and more, but I keep trying to stack the deck, to nudge her in the direction that's meant something to me. On a Saturday morning, when the question comes up of what to do, the very first words out of my mouth always involve yet another hike. I can't help myself.

In other words, we already "engineer" our offspring in some sense of the word: we do our best, and often our worst, to steer them in particular directions. And our worst can be pretty bad. We all know people whose lives were blighted trying to meet the expectations of their parents. We've all seen the crazed devotion to getting kids into the right schools, the right professions, the right income brackets. Parents try and pass down their prejudices, their politics, their attitude toward the world ("we've got to toughen that kid up—he's going to get walked all over"). There are fathers who start teaching the curveball at the age of four, and sons made to feel worthless if they don't make the Little League traveling team. People move house so that their kids can grow up with the right kind of schoolmates. They threaten to disown them for marrying African Americans, or for not marrying African Americans.

No dictator anywhere has ever tried to rule his subjects with as much attention to detail as the average modern parent.

Why not take this just one small step further? Why not engineer children to up the odds that all that nudging will stick? In the words of Lee Silver, the Princeton geneticist, "Why not seize this power? Why not control what has been left to chance in the past? Indeed, we control all other aspects of our children's lives and identities through powerful social and environmental influences.... On what basis can we reject positive genetic influences on a person's essence when we accept the rights of parents to benefit their children in every other way?" If you can buy your kid three years at Deerfield, four at Harvard, and three more at Harvard Law, why shouldn't you be able to turbocharge his IQ a bit?

But most likely the answer has already occurred to you as well. Because you know plenty of people who managed to rebel successfully against whatever agenda their parents laid out for them, or who took that agenda and bent it to fit their own particular personality. In our society that's often what growing up is all about—the sometimes excruciatingly difficult, frequently liberating break with the expectations of your parents. The decision to join the Peace Corps (or, the decision to leave the commune where you grew up and go to business school). The discovery that you were happiest davening in an Orthodox shul° three hours a day, much to the consternation of your good suburban parents who almost always made it to Yom Kippur services; the decision that, much as you respected the Southern Baptist piety of your parents, the Bible won't be your watchword.

Without the grounding offered by tradition, the search for the "authentic you" can be hard; our generations contain the first people who routinely shop religions, for instance. But the sometimes poignant diffculty of finding yourself merely underscores how essential it is. Silver says the costs of germline engineering and a college education might be roughly comparable; in both cases, he goes on, the point is to "increase the chances the child will become wiser in some way, and better able to achieve success and happiness." But that's half the story, at best. College is where you go to be exposed to a thousand new influences, ideas that should be able to take you in almost any direction. It's where you go to get out from under your parents' thumb, to find out that you actually don't have to go to law school if you don't want to. As often as not, the harder parents try and wrench their kids in one direction, the harder those kids eventually fight to determine their own destiny. I am as prepared as I can be for the possibility—the probability—that Sophie will decide she wants to live her life in the concrete heart of Manhattan. It's her life (and perhaps her kids will have a secret desire to come wander in the woods with me).

------

davening ... shul: Praying in an Orthodox synagogue.

We try and shape the lives of our kids—to "improve" their lives, as we would measure improvement—but our gravity is usually weak enough that kids can break out of it if and when they need to. (When it isn't, when parents manage to bend their children to the point of breaking, we think of them as monstrous.) "Many of the most creative and valuable human lives are the result of particularly difficult struggles" against expectation and influence, writes the legal scholar Martha Nussbaum.

That's not how a genetic engineer thinks of his product. He works to ensure absolute success. Last spring an Israeli researcher announced that he had managed to produce a featherless chicken. This constituted an improvement, to his mind, because "it will be cheaper to produce since its lack of feathers means there is no need to pluck it before it hits the shelves." Also, poultry farmers would no longer have to ventilate their vast barns to keep their birds from overheating. "Feathers are a waste," the scientist explained. "The chickens are using feed to produce something that has to be dumped, and the farmers have to waste electricity to overcome that fact." Now, that engineer was not trying to influence his chickens to shed their feathers because they'd be happier and the farmer would be happier and everyone would be happier. He was inserting a gene that created a protein that made good and certain they would not be producing feathers. Just substitute, say, an even temperament for feathers, and you'll know what the human engineers envision.

"With reprogenetics," writes Lee Silver, "parents can gain *complete control* [emphasis mine] over their destiny, with the ability to guide and enhance the characteristics of their children, and their children's children as well." Such parents would not be calling their children on the phone at annoyingly frequent intervals to suggest that it's time to get a real job; instead, just like the chicken guy, they would be inserting genes that produced proteins that would make their child behave in certain ways throughout his life. You cannot rebel against the production of that protein. Perhaps you can still do everything in your power to defeat the wishes of your parents, but that protein will nonetheless be pumped out relentlessly into your system, defining who you are. You won't grow feathers, no matter how much you want them. And maybe they can engineer your mood enough that your lack of plumage won't even cross your mind.

Such children will, in effect, be assigned a goal by their programmers: 30 "intelligence," "even temper," "athleticism." (As with chickens, the market will doubtless lean in the direction of efficiency. It may be hard to find genes for, say, dreaminess.) Now two possibilities arise. Perhaps the programming doesn't work very well, and your kid spells poorly, or turns moody, or can't hit the inside fastball. In the present world, you just tell yourself that that's who he is. But in the coming world, he'll be, in essence, a defective product. Do you still accept him unconditionally? Why? If your new Jetta got thirty miles to the gallon instead of the forty it was designed to get, you'd take it back. You'd call it a lemon. If necessary, you'd sue.

Or what if the engineering worked pretty well, but you decided, too late, that you'd picked the wrong package, hadn't gotten the best features? Would you feel buyer's remorse if the kid next door had a better ear, a stronger arm?

Say the gene work went a little awry and left you with a kid who had some serious problems; what kind of guilt would that leave you with? Remember, this is not a child created by the random interaction of your genes with those of your partner, this is a child created with specific intent. Does *Consumer Reports* start rating the various biotech offerings?

What if you had a second child five years after the first, and by that time the upgrades were undeniably improved: How would you feel about the first kid? How would he feel about his new brother, the latest model?

The other outcome—that the genetic engineering works just as you had hoped—seems at least as bad. Now your child is a product. You can take precisely as much pride in her achievements as you take in the achievements of your dishwashing detergent. It was designed to produce streak-free glassware, and she was designed to be sweet-tempered, social, and smart. And what can she take pride in? Her good grades? She may have worked hard, but she'll always know that she was spec'ed for good grades. Her kindness to others? Well, yes, it's good to be kind—but perhaps it's not much of an accomplishment once the various genes with some link to sociability have been cataloged and manipulated. I have no doubt that these qualms would be one of the powerful psychological afflictions of the future—at least until someone figures out a fix that keeps the next generations from having such bad thoughts.

Britain's chief rabbi, Jonathan Sacks, was asked, a few years ago, about the announcement that Italian doctors were trying to clone humans. "If there is a mystery at the heart of human condition, it is otherness: the otherness of man and woman, parent and child. It is the space we make for otherness that makes love something other than narcissism." I remember so well the feeling of walking into the maternity ward with Sue, and walking out with Sue and Sophie: where there had been two there were now, somehow, three, each of us our own person, but now commanded to make a family, a place where we all could thrive. She was so mysterious, that Sophie, and in many ways she still is. There are times when, like every parent, I see myself reflected in her, and times when I wonder if she's even related. She's ours to nurture and protect, but she is who she is. That's the mystery and the glory of any child.

Mystery, however, is not one of the words that thrills engineers. They try and deliver solid bridges, unyielding dams, reliable cars. We wouldn't want it any other way. The only question is if their product line should be expanded to include children.

Right now both the genes, and the limits that they set on us, connect us with every human that came before. Human beings can look at rock art carved into African cliffs and French caves thirty thousand years ago and feel an electric, immediate kinship. We've gone from digging sticks to combines, and from drum circles to symphony orchestras (and back again to drum circles), but we still hear in the same range and see in the same spectrum, still produce adrenaline and dopamine in the same ways, still think in many of the same patterns. We are, by the large, the same people, more closely genetically related to one another than we may be to our engineered grandchildren.

These new technologies show us that human meaning dangles by a far thinner thread than we had thought. If germline genetic engineering ever starts, it will accelerate endlessly and unstoppably into the future, as individuals make the calculation that they have no choice but to equip their kids for the world that's being made. The first child whose genes come in part from some corporate lab, the first child who has been "enhanced" from what came before — that's the first child who will glance back over his shoulder and see a gap between himself and human history.

These would be mere consumer decisions — but that also means that they would benefit the rich far more than the poor. They would take the gap in power, wealth, and education that currently divides both our society and the world at large, and write that division into our very biology. A sixth of the American population lacks health insurance of any kind — they can't afford to go to the doctor for a checkup. And much of the rest of the world is far worse off. If we can't afford the fifty cents a person it would take to buy bed nets to protect most of Africa from malaria, it is unlikely we will extend to anyone but the top tax bracket these latest forms of genetic technology. The injustice is so obvious that even the strongest proponents of genetic engineering make little attempt to deny it. "Anyone who accepts the right of affluent parents to provide their children with an expensive private-school education cannot use 'unfairness' as a reason for rejecting the use of reprogenetic technologies," says Lee Silver.

These new technologies, however, are not yet inevitable. Unlike global 40 warming, this genie is not yet out of the bottle. But if germline genetic engineering is going to be stopped, it will have to happen now, before it's quite begun. It will have to be a political choice, that is — one we make not as parents but as citizens, not as individuals but as a whole, thinking not only about our own offspring but about everyone.

So far the discussion has been confined to a few scientists, a few philosophers, a few ideologues. It needs to spread widely, and quickly, and loudly. The stakes are absurdly high, nothing less than the meaning of being human. And given the seductions that we've seen — the intuitively and culturally delicious prospect of a better child — the arguments against must be not only powerful but also deep. They'll need to resonate on the same intuitive and cultural level. We'll need to feel in our gut the reasons why, this time, we should tell Prometheus thanks, but no thanks.

WHAT DOES HE SAY?

1. Write down five significantly important statements of fact that Bill McKibben presents, and also write down five significantly important statements of judgment or opinion that McKibben asserts. In each case, be ready to explain why what you've written down is a fact or an opinion.

2. Write down three sentences that seem on the borderline between fact and fiction—or sentences that you're just not sure how to classify as one or the other.

3. Write a paragraph that tries to summarize what McKibben calls the "biological arms race" problem. Then write another paragraph explaining why you think it makes sense or sounds bogus.

4. Write down two significantly important sentences that have you nodding in agreement as you read them in this essay (choose one from early in the essay and one from later). Also write down two significantly important sentences that have you wondering or unsure.

WHAT DO YOU THINK?

5. Based on your reading of "Designer Genes," explain your understanding of Bill McKibben's views of what parenting is and should be. Make sure your essay quotes his at least three times. Don't try to agree or disagree; simply report clearly and accurately.

6. Write about two or three significant childhood experiences you had with adults (your parents or other influential people) which you remember as efforts to steer your preferences or beliefs. Recount these so that readers will understand them, then use them as evidence (positive, negative, or complicated) to explain responsibilities you believe parents have toward their children. Finally, discuss whether or not those responsibilities would extend to genetically engineering children so that they might be smarter or prettier than nature might have made them.

7. McKibben's essay really discusses many different applications for gene therapy and genetic manipulation. Identify two such applications that interest you. For each one, summarize McKibben's presentation and add to it by quoting and summarizing other authoritative research. For each application, explain why you think McKibben's presentation is fair and accurate, and explain why you're in favor of or opposed to it.

8. Do research on Down syndrome. Also locate some firsthand accounts from parents of Down syndrome children. Based on what you learn, explain what Down syndrome is and why you think the parents of Down syndrome children would tend to favor or oppose genetic modification of human reproduction to eliminate that condition. Make sure that your resulting essay quotes McKibben at least once.

9. Investigate and report on recent world efforts to eradicate polio. Explain the locations of such efforts, their primary strategies or tactics, and the degree of their success. Then explain why, in your opinion, the effort to eradicate polio is, or is not, like the effort to design more perfect children. Make sure you quote McKibben at least twice.

WHAT WOULD THEY SAY?

10. Read Rebecca Mead's "Eggs for Sale" (p. 499) together with McKibben's essay. Based on your understanding of these essays, how do you think Mead would respond to what McKibben says?

11. Read Aldo Leopold's "The Land Ethic" (p. 531) together with "Designer Genes." Use both essays to discuss what these authors would assert as the best definition of what is healthy for the human community.

12. What would Stephen L. Carter, author of "Welcoming the Stranger" (p. 111), have to say about McKibben's essay? Make sure that you explain and support your assertions by quoting both Carter and McKibben.

For Community Learning and Research

1. Locate the chapter or contact person for Overeaters Anonymous closest to where you live. Find out the basics of this organization: What's their mission? Whom do they serve? What's their philosophy and approach? What typical outcomes result? What factors lead to success and what ones often lead to relapses or lack of progress?

2. Investigate the local treatment options, programs, and facilities for those battling anorexia or bulimia. Where would students on your campus go for help with such problems? What information about these conditions can you obtain from these places? Are there classic profiles for those who suffer from these problems? What treatments show promise for what kinds of sufferers? Based on your research, prepare a pamphlet for your dorm, sorority, or fraternity that makes this information quickly and clearly available.

3. Find out what modifications or design features have been built into your campus in the last twenty years to make it possible for those who have mobility problems to access the offices, labs, performance spaces, and classrooms on campus. Interview appropriate campus officials, long-time teachers, alumni (if you know some), and current students. To what extent can it be said that any student who can think and learn at the college level can physically access your campus? End your research report by explaining what you've learned from doing this assignment.

4. Interview someone on campus who is playing a varsity sport. How much time— both for practices and games—does this sport require in a typical week during the season? What is it about this sport that your interviewee finds challenging or difficult? What's rewarding about it? What physical abilities are key to success in this sport? What injuries are common? Which ones are most threatening? What specific physical condition does the sport require? What happens when that athlete gets injured and cannot play—what happens to her or his state of mind? Does winning matter to her sense of self or her sense of the world? What about if she is losing often? To what extent is her identity or sense of self significantly linked to what her body can do as a participant in this sport? End by commenting on what your interview results tell you about this participant's investment in physical success in a varsity sport.

5. Find out where a woman in an abusive relationship could go for help and support either on campus or close to it. Then gather information from that source: Can anything be said about the typical client for such services (other than the abuse itself)? What services are available? Who pays for them? How often are they used? Is the current network of support sufficient given local need? Based on what you learn, write an "in my opinion" piece for your school or local newspaper.

6. What pregnancy counseling and abortion services are available in your area? If a person you knew wanted to get an abortion, where could she go? Find out what local options are available to a person who is twelve weeks pregnant and unsure about whether she wants to continue the pregnancy. Present this information as neutrally as possible. Then add a last page that discusses your own view of such counseling and abortion services.

○ 7. Compose a poster advertising a one-day conference called "Are We Our Bodies?" on your campus. Imagine that five or six of the writers included in this chapter will attend this conference. As you consider what information to include and how that information should be arranged on the page, consider these three questions: Who should come to the conference? What would the purpose of the conference be? How might people be changed if they attended? Consider actually arranging such a conference, inviting local and campus authorities to speak.

5.

Is Honesty the Best Policy?

WHAT WOULD YOU DO?
A CASE OF PLAGIARISM

In the introduction, we talked about a student who plagiarized a paper. Let's look at this scenario again from the point of view of the professor of the class.

The professor is a committed teacher who works hard to encourage classroom participation and develop innovative assignments. She knows all her students by name. And she knows and likes Amy, the student who has plagiarized. Amy has written several good papers for the class so far, has regularly contributed to discussions, and has even come to the professor's office once or twice to talk about the ideas in the course.

Let's say, too, that the university where this happens has an honor code in place, a clear set of standards and a clear procedure for dealing with violations, and that Amy is well aware of this code.

But now, reading Amy's final paper, the professor comes across several whole paragraphs that have been pulled without citation from a scholarly article—an article that the professor knows well. Another student has turned in a plagiarized paper, too, a student who has often come late and who has failed several exams and papers already.

If you were the professor, what would you do? How would you respond to both students?

At first glance, the answer to our chapter's title is obvious: of course, honesty is the best policy. But in practice, in the real worlds of the university, of business, and of politics—in the real worlds of our daily lives—the question is more open because it's more subtle. We steal a grape at the grocery store. The phone rings but it's someone we don't want to talk to: "Tell him I'm not here," you whisper to your roommate. A friend says something negative about another friend, and though you know it's not true, you let it go, sharing in the laugh. We are all a little dishonest now and then and sometimes even more than a little, practicing dishonesty as a conscious strategy. Exaggeration, after all, is the basis of most advertising, as Malcolm Gladwell demonstrates in "Big and Bad" (p. 440), an essay about the marketing of SUVs.

What *is* dishonesty anyway? How has the Internet, for example, changed the nature of composition and authorship and of what might count as cheating? Lawrence Hinman asks in "Virtual Virtues: Reflections on Academic Integrity in the Age of the Internet" (p. 415). Or what about the related issue of privacy? When is a photo newsworthy and when is it intrusive? Nora Ephron ponders in "The Boston Photographs" (p. 433).

Even when there's little doubt about the dishonesty of an act, the question is, What social factors have made this act possible and what can be done to change those factors? Donald McCabe and Linda Klebe Trevino in "Honesty and Honor Codes" (p. 405), for example, argue that honor codes can encourage a culture of honesty on campus. Are they right? Can honesty be taught or encouraged? Can it be legislated?

Opening the Question

After reading and discussing several of the selections in this chapter, return to the situation above. ***Now*** *what would you do? Write an essay answering this question, drawing on at least two of the selections. You don't need to have changed your mind, but you do need to demonstrate how the reading has complicated your thinking.*

Do the readings make you less sure that Amy's action was, or was not, dishonest? Do the readings give the professor strategies for dealing with Amy? Do the readings give Amy strategies for dealing with the professor?

JAMES FREY

How Do You Think It Makes Your Mother Feel?

*W*E OPEN THIS SECTION *with the question of personal honesty: what does it mean to be honest with yourself? In drug rehabilitation, the narrator in this selection faces his addictions and tries to honestly accept responsibility for the choices he's made, even as his family tries to be frank about their role in his problems.*

This piece is an excerpt from the first memoir of James Frey (b. 1970), A Million Little Pieces (2003), the story of his experiences with drug and alcohol addiction and rehabilitation.

Joanne is sitting behind her desk. I say hello to her, she says hello to me. My Mother is sitting on the couch. She stands, says hello, gives me a hug. I hug her back. I am still not comfortable touching her, and I am still not comfortable having her touch me, but I know it's better if I let it happen. She hugs me tight. I wait. She lets go of me. I feel better.
Where's Dad?
My Mother speaks.
He had a call he had to make for work. He'll be here as soon as he's done.
Everything all right?   5
I think so.
I look at Joanne.
What are we doing tonight?
We're going to talk about the source of your addiction and what the root causes might be.
Do we wait for my Dad to do that?   10
Yes.
What do we do till then?
Your Mother was just telling me a story.
About what?
The first time she really believed you might be in trouble.   15
I look at my Mother.
When was it?
Do you remember when I found that bag of marijuana in your jacket pocket?
I chuckle.
Yeah.   20
Why are you laughing?
378   I don't know.

It wasn't funny, James.

I know, Mom.

Joanne speaks.   25

Did you find it funny, James?

Sort of.

Why don't you tell me your version of it.

I look at my Mother, she looks tense. I wait for a moment, collect my memories, speak.

I was fourteen. I had been away at Soccer Camp the Summer before. I had 30 met this Girl there, I think her name was Emily, and we spent all of our time at the Camp sneaking away and smoking dope. When we left, we wrote each other. She was sort of a female version of me, which meant the letters were pretty explicit about drugs and drinking. One afternoon I came home from School and went to my Room and a bunch of my stuff, stuff that I kept hidden, including Emily's letters, was sitting on my dresser. I knew I was in trouble and I was pissed my Mom had gone through my shit, so I went back downstairs to find her and get it over with. When I walked into the Kitchen, she was standing there holding a bag of dope that she found in the pocket of my coat. She asked what's this and I asked her where she got it and she said don't talk back to me young man and I said tell me where you got it and I'll tell you what it is and she said stop mouthing off young man and I laughed.

I look at my Mother. Her face is white beneath her makeup. I look back to Joanne.

She held the dope in front of me and she screamed *what is this where did you get this you tell me right now*. I laughed and she kept screaming. I got sick of her screaming and I was pissed about the invasion of my privacy, so as she was holding the bag up, I reached out and I snatched it from her hand. She was shocked, and as I put the bag in my pocket, she reared back to slap me. I saw it coming, so when she swung I grabbed her hand. That made her swing with the other hand and I grabbed that one too. I had both of her hands and she was struggling and screaming and I was laughing. I guess I was laughing because a bag of dope didn't seem like such a big deal to me and it was ridiculous to watch her freak out over it. She couldn't hit me because I had her arms, so she tried to kick me. As she did, I let go of her hands and she lost her balance and fell to the floor and she started crying, crying really hard. I turned around and walked out the front door. I could hear her crying as I did, but I didn't want to deal with it, so I just walked out. When I came home a few hours later my Dad screamed at me and grounded me for a month.

I look at my Mother. She is staring at the floor. Joanne speaks.

That's an awful story, James.

I know.   35

How did it make you feel as you told it?

Part of me still thinks it's funny, but more of me is just ashamed and embarrassed.

How do you think it makes your Mother feel?
I look at my Mother. She is staring at the floor and she is trying not to cry.
I think it probably makes her feel pretty awful.   40
Why?
Because it must have been humiliating. Trying to confront your Kid about
drugs and having him laugh at you and trying to discipline him and ending up
in a heap on the floor.
Joanne looks at my Mother.
Is that true, Lynne?
My Mother looks up, lips quivering.   45
Yes.
Do you think that was what the incident was really about, drugs and discipline?
I speak.
No.
What do you think it was about?   50
It was about control.
Why do you think that?
Going through my shit and reading my private letters was about knowing what
I was doing so that she could control me. Trying to make me tell her what was
in the bag when she already knew what was in it was about control. When she
fell after she hit me, she wasn't upset because she didn't land her shots, she was
upset because she knew, at that point, I was out of control.
Joanne looks at my Mother.
Do you think that's a valid interpretation?   55
My Mother stares at the floor, thinks. She looks up.
I was upset about the drugs. It was upsetting reading those letters and finding
out about some of the things he had been doing, especially after we sent
him to that Camp to try and get him away from some of that stuff. When I
actually found the bag in his coat, I was scared and horrified. He was fourteen. Fourteen-year-old Boys shouldn't be carrying around bags of drugs. To
a certain extent, though, he's right about the control. His Father and I were
always trying to control him, mainly because he had always been so out of
control.
There is a knock at the door. Joanne says come in and the door opens and my
Father steps into the Office.
My Mother stands and gives him a hug. I do the same. My Father sits next to
my Mother. He holds her hand and he looks at Joanne.
Sorry I'm late.   60
We were talking about an event that happened when James was fourteen, and
that discussion led to one about the issue of control. The goal of this evening's
session is to try and get some idea of a root cause for his addiction. I'm sensing
that there may be some connection between the issue of control and the root
cause.
What was the incident?

My Mother speaks.

When I found that bag of marijuana in his coat pocket.

Which time?   65

The time I fell trying to slap him.

My Father nods.

That was bad. What does control have to do with it?

Joanne speaks.

James said he thought the incident had more to do with control than with 70
drugs.

My Father turns toward me. He looks confused, slightly angry.

That sounds a bit ridiculous, James.

I speak.

Not to me. Going through all my stuff and reading my letters and hunting
through my jacket is about trying to find out what I'm doing so that Mom
could try to control it.

There were drugs in there. Your Mother had every right to go through your 75
jacket. You were fourteen years old.

That's fine if that's what you think, but spying on me and sneaking around
through my private shit was about controlling me, which is something you
guys always tried to do.

My Father's voice rises.

You've been out of control your entire life. We're your Parents, what did
you expect us to do?

My voice rises.

Leave me be. Let me live my own life.   80

When you were fourteen? Where do you think you'd be if we'd done that?

Where the fuck am I now? It couldn't be much worse than this.

Parents don't leave Children alone, James, they raise them. That's all your
Mother and I tried to do with you.

You tried to micromanage me and keep track of me every second of every
day and make me do what you wanted me to do.

My Father clenches his jaw just like I clench my jaw. He's angry, very angry, 85
and he starts to speak. Joanne cuts him off.

Just a second, Mr. Frey.

He takes a breath and he nods. She looks at me.

Why do you think it didn't work?

Same reason that if you keep a dog on a short leash it's more aggressive. Same
reason if you keep a Prisoner in solitary for too long they become violent.
Same reason Dictatorships usually end in Revolution.

Those are nice examples, but what's the reason?   90

I didn't want to be controlled, so I did everything I could to try to break the
pattern of it, which made them want to control me more.

Joanne looks at my Parents.

Do you think there is any validity to what he's saying?

My Father speaks.
No.   95
My Mother speaks.
Yes.
My Father looks at my Mother.
Why do you think that?
You know I always worried about him, even when he was an infant I wor-   100
ried. I probably tried to keep him too close because I didn't want him to get
hurt.
Joanne speaks.
You have another Son, right?
My Mother nods, my Father says yes.
Did you raise him the same way?
My Father nods, speaks.   105
Yes.
My Mother speaks.
No.
What was the difference?
I was much more careful with James than I was with Bob. I knew we weren't   110
going to have any other Children, and I wanted James to be perfect and
healthy and safe. I can't say it any other way. I wanted him to be safe.
That's natural, but do you think you tried to keep him too safe?
My Father speaks.
Too safe? Is that possible with a Child?
Joanne nods.
Yes, it is.   115
My Mother speaks.
How?
Everyone has boundaries. They're different for every Person, but we all have
them. When they're crossed or violated, it is usually upsetting. If they are
crossed or violated repeatedly, especially in the case of a Child, who usually has
no way of controlling whether someone crosses or violates his boundaries, it
can result in negative behaviors, the easiest example being the resentment of
authority.
My Father speaks.
That sounds absurd to me. Children's boundaries are set by their Parents, and   120
the Child learns to respect them, not the other way around.
Joanne speaks.
Not necessarily.
What do you mean?
Children learn more in the first two years of their life than they do in all of
the rest of their years combined, even if they live to be a hundred. Most be-
havioral patterns, including our personal boundaries, are set during those first

two years. Sometimes the pattern of establishment of those behaviors and boundaries is disrupted.

By what? 125

Generally by abuse.

My Father flares.

If you're suggesting—

Joanne holds her hand up.

I'm not suggesting anything, and when I brought up the possibility of abuse 130
with James, he very adamantly insisted that he had not suffered from any. I'm telling you how this sometimes happens.

My Mother speaks.

We did protect James more than our other Son, but I think we had good reason, and I don't think we violated anything.

Joanne looks at her, waits for her to continue.

Bob is three years older than James. Just after Bob was born, my Father retired, and after he retired he started drinking heavily. It was very difficult for my Mother and my Brother and my Sister and me. We tried to stop him, but he just told us to leave him alone, that he had spent his whole life taking care of us and now he wanted to be left alone. I had heard about Alcoholism being passed from generation to generation, so when James was born I was scared to death. I don't know if it was female intuition or what, but for some reason I didn't worry about Bob, I just worried about James.

I speak. 135

Grandpa was an Alcoholic?

My Father looks at my Mother, my Mother speaks.

I don't know if he was an Alcoholic, but he had a drinking problem.

Joanne speaks.

Did you not know that, James? 140

My Father speaks.

It's not something we have ever really spoken about.

Why?

It was a very sad and devastating situation. We try to remember Lynne's Father as he was for the greater part of his life, which was a kind and gentle and generous man, rather than what he was near the end of it.

Joanne speaks. 145

As Lynne mentioned, it has been proven that there is a link between the disease of Alcoholism and genetics. Don't you think it might have helped James to know that he might have, and in my opinion, most probably does have, a genetic predisposition toward addiction?

I speak.

I don't think knowing about my Grandfather would have made any difference. I didn't drink and do drugs because of some genetic flaw.

Joanne speaks.

Why are you so quick to dismiss what has been proven empirically to exist?   150
I think it's bullshit. People don't want to accept the responsibility for their own weakness, so they place the blame on something that they're not responsible for, like disease or genetics. As far as studies go, I could prove I was from Mars if you gave me enough time and enough resources.
My Mother speaks.
It certainly might help explain a lot of these things for us.
I think it's interesting that Grandpa had a drinking problem. I'm surprised to learn it, because I have only heard great things about him. I think it sucks, and it must have been awful for everyone to have to deal with him, just like it has been awful to have to deal with me, but I won't blame him or his genes for my problems.
My Father speaks.   155
What's your explanation?
I was weak and pathetic and I couldn't control myself. An explanation, especially a bullshit one, doesn't alter the circumstances. I need to change, I have to change, and at this point, change is my only option, unless I am ready to die. All that matters is that I make myself something else and someone else for the future.
Joanne speaks.
Don't you think knowing why you are the way you are might help you in the process of that change?
I think I do know why.   160
Would you like to share your ideas with us?
Not really.
Why?
Because it will hurt and upset my Parents, and I think I've done enough of that.
My Mother speaks.   165
I think we'd like to hear, James.
My Father speaks.
We definitely would.
I look at them, take a deep breath, speak.
I've always felt these things. I don't think there are any words that describe   170
them exactly, but they are a combination of rage, anger, extreme pain. They mix together into what I call the Fury. I have known the Fury for as long as I can remember. It is the one thing that has been with me throughout my entire life. I am starting to learn how to deal with it, but until recently, the only way I knew was through drinking and drugs. I took something, whatever it was, and if I took enough of it, the Fury would subside. The problem was that it would always come back, usually stronger, and that would require more and stronger substances to kill it, and that was always the goal, to kill it. From the first time I drank, I knew drinking would kill it. From the first time I took drugs, I knew drugs would kill it. I took them willingly, not because of some genetic link or

some function of some disease, but because I knew they would kill the god-damn Fury. Even though I knew I was killing myself, killing the Fury was more important.

I look at my Parents.

I don't know why, and I don't know if it matters, but whenever you are near me, the Fury gets worse. Whenever you have tried to control me or baby me or take care of me or stop me, the Fury has gotten worse. Whenever we talk on the phone or I hear your voices, the Fury gets worse. I'm not saying you're to blame for it, because I don't think you are to blame. I know you did the best you could with me and I know I'm lucky to have you, and I can't think of anything in my background that would have caused it. Maybe the Fury is genetic, but I highly fucking doubt it, and I won't accept disease and genetics as the cause of it anyway. It makes it too easy to deflect the responsibility for what I have done and what I have done knowing full well I was doing it. Each and every time, I knew full fucking well, whether it was take a drink or snort a line or take a hit from a pipe or get arrested, and I made the decision to do it anyway. Most of the time it was to kill the Fury, some of the time it was to kill myself, and eventually I didn't know the difference. All I knew was that I was killing and that at some point it would end, which would probably be best for everyone involved. For whatever it is worth, I feel it now, sitting here with you, and I will feel it tomorrow morning when I see you again. I will feel it the next time we speak, and the time after that and the time after that, and if there is an explanation for why I am the way I am or for who I am, it is that there is a Fury within me that is uncontrollable without drinking or drugs. How do I get better? I take responsibility for myself and I learn to deal with myself and I learn to control the Fury. It might take a while, but if I hold on long enough and I don't accept excuses for failure or deflect what is essentially a problem I have caused, I can do it.

My Mother and My Father stare at me. My Mother looks as if she's going to cry, my Father looks pale, as if he has just seen a terrible wreck. My Mother starts to speak, stops, wipes her eyes. My Father just stares. Joanne speaks.

Not discounting other factors, I would say there may be some validity to your theory, but I am curious where you think this Fury comes from.

I don't know. 175

She looks at my Parents. There are tears on my Mother's face, my Father still stares. My Mother looks at me, speaks.

Why didn't you tell us this before?

What was I supposed to say?

Do you hate us?

I shake my head. 180

What did we do?

You didn't do anything, Mom. This isn't your fault.

She wipes her face. My Father stares.

I'm sorry, James.

Don't be sorry, Mom. I'm the one who should be sorry.   185

There is a long silence. My Father looks at Joanne, speaks.

Could this feeling, or set of feelings, have been brought on by a Medical
Condition?

Did James have a Medical Condition as an Infant?

He had ear problems.

Were they properly diagnosed and treated?   190

My Mother speaks.

We didn't know.

How did you not know?

My Mother looks at my Father and she takes his hand. She speaks.

We didn't have much money when the Boys were first born. Bob was a   195
Lawyer, but most of his salary went to paying off his school loans. Bob Junior
came out healthy and he was a happy child. He was very quiet and very calm.
When James was born, he was the opposite. He screamed and screamed and
screamed, and no matter what we did, we couldn't get him to stop. It was
awful screaming, long and loud and piercing, and I can still hear it in my memories. We went to the Doctor, and we got the best one we could afford.

The Doctor told us that there was nothing wrong, that James was probably
just a vocal child. We went home and the screaming continued. I'd hold
James, Bob would hold James, we tried giving him little toys and feeding him
more, and nothing worked. Nothing could make him stop.

The tears start flowing. My Mother grips my Father's hand, my Father
watches her as she speaks. I sit and I listen. I have never heard about my
screaming before, though it does not surprise me. I have been screaming for
years. Screaming bloody fucking murder. My Mother cries as she continues.

It went on for almost two years. James just screamed and screamed. Bob started
doing well at his Firm and got a raise, and as soon as we had some extra
money, I took James to see a better Doctor. As soon as he looked at him, he
told me that James had terrible infections in both of his ears that were eating
away his eardrums. He said James had been screaming for all that time because
he was in tremendous pain and that he had been screaming for help. He recommended surgery, and just before he turned two, James had surgery on both
of his ears, which was the first of seven surgeries that he would have on them.
Obviously we felt terrible, but we didn't know.

The tears turn into sobs.   200

If we had known we would have done something.

Sobs.

But we didn't know.

My Father holds her.

He just screamed and screamed and all that time we didn't know that he was   205
screaming because he hurt.

My Mother breaks down, burying her face in my Father's shoulder and shaking
and trembling and quivering. My Father holds her and he patiently waits for

her, stroking her hair and rubbing her back. I sit and I stare, and though I have no memory of what she's talking about, I do remember the pain. That is all that remains. The pain.

My Mother stops crying and she pulls away slightly just slightly from my Father. She looks at me.

I'm sorry, James. We didn't know. We really didn't know.

I reach out and I put my hand on one of my Mother's hands.

You got nothing to be sorry about, Mom. You did the best you could.   210

She pulls away from my Father completely and she stands and she takes two steps toward me and she puts her arms around me and she hugs me. She hugs me strong and tight and I return her hug and I can tell that she is trying to express her remorse and sadness. In a way this hug is her apology, though none is needed.

She lets go and she sits back down next to my Father. Joanne waits for a moment to see if any of us are going to speak. We don't, so she does.

Do you remember any of that, James?

I remember the operations, only because I had them until I was twelve, but I don't remember any of the early stuff.

Was there any long-term damage from them?   215

I have thirty percent hearing loss in my left ear and twenty in the other.

Why didn't you tell me this before?

I don't think it's that big a deal.

It helps explain, or perhaps, entirely explains, why you say your first and earliest memories are of rage and pain.

Why do you think that?   220

When a child is born, it needs food and shelter and a sense of safety and comfort. If it screams, it is usually screaming for a reason, and in your case, it seems you were probably screaming because you were in pain and you wanted help. If those screams went unheeded, whether consciously or unconsciously, they might have ignited a fairly profound sense of rage within you, and might very well have led to some long-term resentments. That rage would help explain both your feelings of what you call the Fury, and also your particular feelings of it in regards to your Parents and in regards to issues of control with them.

I sit and I think. I try to decide if I am willing to accept genetics and ear infections as an explanation for twenty-three years of chaos. It would be easy to do so. To place myself on a pedestal away from what and who I am and to write it all off because of my Grandfather's genes and a Doctor's incompetence. It has been twenty-three years of chaos. Twenty-three years of Hell. I could let it all go with the simple acceptance of that which has been presented to me. I could let it all go.

I look up. My Parents are watching me, Joanne is watching me. They are waiting for a response. I take a breath and I speak.

It's an interesting theory. It probably holds some weight. I can accept it for what I feel it is, which is a possibility. I won't accept it as a root cause, because

I think it's a cop-out, and because I don't think it does me any good to accept anything other than myself and my own weakness as a root cause. I did everything I did. I made the decisions to do it all. The only way I'm going to get better is if I accept responsibility for the decision to either be an Addict or not be an Addict. That's the way it has to be for me. I know you're going to try and convince me otherwise, but you shouldn't bother.

Joanne chuckles, my Mother and Father stare at me. I look at Joanne and I   225
speak.

Why are you chuckling?

She smiles.

Because you are the single most stubborn Person that I've ever met.

I just won't let myself be a victim.

What do you mean by that?   230

People in here, People everywhere, they all want to take their own problems, usually created by themselves, and try to pass them off on someone or something else. I know my Mother and Father did the best they could and gave me the best they could and loved me the best they could and if anything, they are victims of me. I could say I'm flawed in my genetic makeup, that I have this disease and my addictions are caused by the presence of it, but I think that's a load of shit. I'm a victim of nothing but myself, just as I believe that most People with this so-called disease aren't victims of anything other than themselves. If you want to call that philosophy stubbornness, go right ahead. I call it being responsible. I call it the acceptance of my own problems and my own weaknesses with honor and dignity. I call it getting better.

Joanne smiles.

Despite the fact that I can't really endorse or condone your philosophy, I am gradually becoming a Believer.

I smile.

Thank you.   235

My Father speaks.

James.

I turn toward him and my Mother. They are smiling at me.

I have never been more proud of you than I am this moment.

I smile.   240

Thanks, Dad.

My Mother speaks.

Me too, James.

Thanks, Mom.

Joanne looks at her watch.   245

I think we've done some exceptional work tonight and it's getting late.

I stand.

Let's get out of here.

My Parents stand. My Mother speaks.

Can we have another hug before we go?   250

I step forward, put one of my arms around each of them, and they each put one of their arms around me. We pull each of us pulls and we hug each other the three of us hug each other it is strong and easy and full of something maybe love. The Fury flares and I am momentarily uncomfortable, but the strength I am giving and the strength I am taking kills it. Easily and quickly.

The giving and taking kills it.

We separate. My Parents are still smiling. I say good-bye to Joanne and she says good-bye to me. I open the door and I wait. My Parents say good-bye and thank you to Joanne and she smiles and says no problem. They walk out and I follow them. We say good-bye outside the door and they go one way and I go another.

I walk back to the Unit. I know my way the walk is automatic. I am tired and I'm ready for bed. I don't want to deal with anything or anybody. I don't want to think about Prison or genetics or ear infections. I don't know about one and the other two don't matter. I want to sleep. Close my eyes and sleep.

I get to my Room open the door walk inside. Miles is in bed he is already   255
sleeping. The light on my nightstand is on I turn it off get under the covers. They are warm. The pillow is soft.

I am tired.

I go to sleep.

WHAT DOES HE SAY?

1. This is an excerpt from a memoir. The selection presents a long conversation among four people—James Frey (the narrator), his mother and father, and his therapist. It's not immediately obvious what the point of the conversation is. In the margins, mark the moment when you think the major theme of the conversation emerges and the author's point starts to become clear to you. Write a note summarizing that theme in a short phrase. As you continue reading, mark two or three other places where a clear theme emerges. Does the theme change? Does the theme get complicated or modified? When you finish, stop and quickly write what you think the overall theme of the piece might be. Think of this as explaining the "moral" of the story. Don't worry about sounding obvious or clichéd. Just state the theme as best you can. If you're not clear, write a few sentences explaining your confusion.

2. Keep a record of your emotional response to this very intense therapy session. Write in the margins using words like *tense*, *worried*, *resisting*, and *angry*. When you finish, quickly write three or four sentences, giving "a movie of your mind." For example, "I was intrigued at first, but then as the conversation went on I kept getting madder and madder. I really sympathized with the parents. The narrator? What a jerk!" (This doesn't have to be your own response, of course.)

3. Do you trust the narrator? Do you like the narrator? Explain in a short paragraph.

WHAT DO YOU THINK?

4. Why do you think we chose to begin a chapter called "Is Honesty the Best Policy?" with this selection? What does this piece have to do with the theme of honesty?

5. Is the narrator honest with his parents?

6. Should the narrator's parents have been more honest with him about his grandfather's alcoholism? Would that have made any difference in his own struggle with addiction?

7. By the end of this conversation, what do you think is the cause of the narrator's addiction? Who, or what, is responsible? Why do you think this?

8. What do you think of the therapist in this session? Does she seem trustworthy? What does she think? How do you know what she thinks? How does she guide the conversation?

9. Write an essay in the form of a conversation among three or four people. Use the conversation to develop a point or theme, but don't come out and say what that point is.

WHAT WOULD THEY SAY?

10. Assume that the young narrator of this story has read Nora Ephron's "The Boston Photographs" (p. 433). How would he respond to Ephron's argument that these sensational and disturbing photographs should be made widely available? How would Ephron respond to the narrator's sometimes shocking honesty with his parents?

11. Write an essay on the topic of personal change and transformation, drawing on Andre Dubus's "Giving Up the Gun" (p. 180), Lance Armstrong's "Before and After" (p. 344), and Frey's, "How Do You Think It Makes Your Mother Feel?" Does the narrator of the latter selection change in the same ways as these other two men and, if so, for the same reasons? Is his transformation genuine and complete? Are the transformations of the other two writers genuine and complete?

12. Consider "How Do You Think It Makes Your Mother Feel?" together with Jenefer Shute's "Life-Size" (p. 279). Discuss each according to how it treats questions of honesty. Based on these two essays, to what extent would you agree, or disagree, that honesty is the best policy?

STEPHEN L. CARTER
The Best Student Ever

*T*HIS ESSAY, *by Stephen Carter (b. 1954), a Yale Law School professor and a leading black intellectual, uses the problem of inflated praise in letters of recommendation to complicate our thinking about language, advertising, and the university.*

Carter earned his law degree from Yale, served as a law clerk for Supreme Court Justice Thurgood Marshall, and is now the William Cromwell Professor of Law at Yale University. He has written many important works on legal and social issues, including The Culture of Disbelief: How American Law and Politics Trivialize Religious Devotion *(1993),* Civility: Manners, Morals, and the Etiquette of Democracy *(1998), and* Integrity *(1997), from which "The Best Student Ever" is excerpted. (Carter's essay, "Welcoming the Stranger," appears on p. 111 of this book.)*

When we talk of life, we talk of what we have experienced. So as I turn to the practical side of integrity, I will begin with an activity with which I am intimately familiar. I refer to writing letters to potential employers, evaluating the work of my students. Here, the reader may well suppose, is one arena of life in which the rules of integrity...should apply with precision. But as it turns out, the rules of this particular game—performance evaluations—make it all but impossible to act with integrity, not only for me as a law professor but for employers and managers and many others besides.

QUALIFICATION INFLATION

At the Yale Law School, I occasionally teach a seminar on Law, Secrets, and Lying. A few years ago, I asked the class about letters of recommendation that professors often write to help their students gain the judicial clerkships that so many budding lawyers crave. (A clerkship is the chance to spend a year as an assistant to a federal judge.) I observed that the letters—much like letters of recommendation for students seeking admission to law school—are awash in hyperbole: "Mr. X has one of the keenest intellects I have ever encountered." "Ms. Y is as brilliant a student as I have ever known." Nobody is ever just pretty good or even in the top 20 percent: every student earns superlatives. Every one of them is one of the best.

When letters of recommendation read this way, the reader has trouble sorting them out. The purpose of a reference is to assist a potential employer (or college or professional school) in making the often difficult decisions on

391

hiring (or admission). If all the letters are the same, however, they are effectively useless. And nowadays, more and more, all the letters are the same.

You might suppose that the concept of integrity...would apply in a rather straightforward way to letters of recommendation: the writer should reach an honest evaluation of the applicant and should write a letter reflecting that evaluation. If the writer is unable to do so, then the letter should state explicitly the reasons for his or her reluctance. And if the writer is uneasy writing a positive recommendation, perhaps he or she should tell the student. But that is not what happens. It seems as though everybody deserves a letter and everybody deserves a powerful one.

As we discussed whether anything might be wrong with this practice, I   5 told the students a story from the year that I was privileged to spend serving as a law clerk to the late, great Thurgood Marshall at the U.S. Supreme Court. One of the tasks of the clerks was to help the justice sort through applications from law students hoping to clerk for him in the following term of the Court. That year, we received two different letters from a very prominent law professor endorsing two different students for clerkships, and referring to each as the brightest student in his particular law school's graduating class. As this was obviously impossible, the only rational option was to discount both letters entirely.

One thinks here of Hannah Arendt's prediction that although a liar "may get away with any number of single falsehoods," it will be "impossible to get away with lying on principle."[1] For at least one of the letters *must* be a lie, if one conceives of a lie as an intentional misstatement of the truth. Obviously, the case is an extreme one—but the problem of lying in recommendation letters is pervasive. Would not both applicants and potential employers be better served, I asked my seminar, if their professors made more of a stab at honesty?

My students had an interesting take on the matter. The genie, they argued, will not go back into the bottle. Now that the market has set a pattern of letters so drenched with hyperbole that they are effectively useless, everyone who writes a letter must follow that model. If a letter of recommendation calls a student anything less than brilliant, the reader, comparing it with others, will assume that the student is somehow deficient. "She's very bright" simply will not do—not when the reader has become accustomed to learning that everybody else is "one of my best students ever."

Letters of reference, the students told me, are written in a special language, a language in which there are only a few gradations: *brilliant, one of the best,* or *the best.* Once the reader understands this, the terms can be translated: for *brilliant,* read "okay," for *one of the best,* read "pretty good," for *the best,* read "outstanding." Consider the obvious analogy to the phenomenon of grade inflation: just drop every grade a few points, and you should know what a transcript really means. Nowadays, a grade of C, which once indicated average work, is treated like a failure; similarly, a letter stating that a student is "average" would be taken to mean that the student is a disaster.

Thus, in my students' analysis, even the professor who wrote the two letters for two students, each of them his best, was not actually lying; in the special language of recommendation letters, he was not even engaging in hyperbole. He was simply saying, in that peculiar language, what was true. The worst sin he committed, then, was to forget what he had written in one letter when he sat down to write the other. And perhaps he did not even forget. Perhaps the reader was meant to translate the special language of recommendation into ordinary language and conclude that neither student was actually the best but both were very good.

I suppose I understand my students' point. After all, there are other areas   10 of life in which we talk this way. The lover's confident if muddled declaration, "I would do anything for you," is meant to be taken seriously but not to be taken literally: by stating it, the lover signals something else, an allegiance, a certain depth of love. But *not* to say it—to declare instead what is likely true, "I would do many things for you"—somehow loses romantic effect.

For the sake of such effects, we have done terrible violence to—may I say the word?—the integrity of our language. As we spin toward hyperbole, it is harder and harder to trust (or even to understand) the literal meaning of what we say to each other. In our politics, this is particularly true. It is hard to believe that anyone actually considers the 70 percent or so of American adults who favor classroom prayer in the public schools a dangerous fringe, but that is how antiprayer forces often describe them.[2] And the legal scholar Ronald Dworkin, in his book on abortion, counsels pro-choice activists not to take literally the frequent pro-life rhetoric that accuses them of murder: they do not, says Dworkin, really mean it.[3]

Well, maybe they do and maybe they don't. Integrity might seem to require that we be more accurate in our labeling, of both our students and our opponents. But what is clear about our politics, as about our letters of recommendation, is that we have reached the point where hyperbole is often the price of admission.

PUFFERY AND ITS COUSINS

In the law of advertising, there is a word for this strange language of hyperbole. The word is *puffery*. Puffery—the form of words one uses, in the jargon, to "puff" a product—is defined as an advertising claim that is favorable to a product but that nobody would ever believe. The concept is most easily understood by example. Imagine that an automaker markets its new model as THE BEST CAR IN THE WORLD. Does the potential buyer understand this literally? Does she assume that the car is in fact the best in the world, that somebody has tested it, that it holds a specific rank, that it has gained some official stamp of approval? Does she assume that the automaker stands behind it, that if another car turns out to be somehow better, she will get her money back? The law of puffery says *no*.

This *no* matters. Suppose that a reasonable potential buyer, on seeing the advertisement, *would* believe the claim to be true. In that case, if the claim is false, the automaker risks liability for false advertising. But the courts have said that there is no liability for puffing a product, because puffery, by definition, involves a claim that will not be believed.[4]

If, however, nobody believes the claims that are made when products are puffed, then why do advertisers do it? Why do they use words like *best* and *most*? And if, as the courts say, nobody believes the claims, why don't consumers get angry at the terrific lies told in the commercials for the puffed products?

The answer is the same here as in the case of the impossibly glowing recommendation letters. The market has evolved a special puffing language, a set of claims that, as the courts say, no buyer believes, but that, as marketers know, every buyer expects. If a firm fails to puff its product, it at once arouses the consumer's suspicion—assuming that the firm is able to gain the consumer's attention at all. In other words, the consumer, perhaps without being aware of it, wonders *why* the automaker is reluctant to call its car the best in the world, or why a soft-drink maker promises only that the buyer will *like* the soft drink, not that the buyer will *love* it. (Is it any wonder that the experiment with a lemon-lime drink called Like, intended to compete with Seven-Up and armed with the lackluster slogan "You like it, it likes you," was an abysmal failure?) I suspect that is why, even though it sticks in the memory of anyone over the age of about thirty, the WE'RE NUMBER TWO, WE TRY HARDER campaign that Avis ran for years always left me a bit put off. Yes, I always wanted to respond, you might be number two, but you needn't be so proud of it.

In the language of the market, one wants, or at least expects, every company to make the bold proclamation that it is the absolute best. It does not matter whether it actually *is* the best or, indeed, whether a means of measurement even exists. What matters is that the company show the confidence (perhaps brashness is a better word) to *say* that it is the best. In the language in which products are puffed, to claim for one's company anything less is really to stop trying. So the reason that every car rental firm—or every deodorant or every dentist—will claim to be the best is not that every one really *is* the best, or even that every one *believes* itself to be the best, but rather that consumers expect the claim. To be the best is in that sense the *minimum* claim; one must present at least that much to get the consumer's attention so that the rest of the message can get through.

Indeed, grabbing and holding the consumer's attention has grown more and more difficult, and the devices for accomplishing it have grown more and more sophisticated. There are probably not many people left in America who are fooled by those big manila envelopes bearing legends like SWEEPSTAKES PRIZE NOTIFICATION and CONGRATULATIONS, YOU ARE AN OFFICIAL WINNER of a contest you did not even enter. But there are other methods. Lots of direct-mail solicitations are now designed to resemble official government forms or even checks. Not long ago, I received in the mail from one of my credit-card issuers an envelope bearing on the outside the phrase CREDIT ENHANCEMENT

NOTIFICATION, which seemed nice, except that in the past, increases in my credit line had been presented in more subtle envelopes. And, sure enough, the "enhancement" was not an increase in my credit line but some special service that the bank wanted me to purchase.

Trying to fool the customer with such schemes might be clever marketing, but it seems to lack integrity in the most basic sense: the advertisement that is disguised as something else does not meet the third criterion of integrity°, because the firm does not say what it is doing and why. In fact, the pretense is like the Trojan horse, intended to mislead, which means that the firm is disobeying the third criterion quite flagrantly: not only does it not say what it is doing; it claims to be doing something else.

It is easy to imagine, however, the firm's reply: the advertisement that 20 arrives in a disguise is no more than puffery of a very sophisticated kind. Consumers expect it. The day is long past when direct-mail solicitations can be honest about themselves, can look like what they are, because consumers will simply throw them away. In order to grab consumer attention, even for the briefest of instants, they must instead look like something else. The consumer, through experience, fully understands this, which is why so many of the formerly successful schemes — envelopes that vaguely resemble government documents, or little clear windows that seem to show a check nestled inside — no longer work as well as they once did. When an envelope arrives in the mail without any outward signs that it is an advertisement, the consumer in effect must guess whether it is or is not, and thus whether to open it or not. And if the consumer decides to open it, and if the material inside is flashy enough to catch the consumer's attention, then it has done its work.[5]

Something similar is happening in the increasingly wild world of direct-mail fund-raising, where the left and the right both are sacrificing accuracy for the sake of gaining attention. One group I have supported with contributions in the past probably will never get another penny of my money because of its shameful opportunistic efforts to capitalize on the April 1995 Oklahoma City bombing: not an envelope arrives now without the word *militia* somewhere in the return address. (I suppose that integrity requires me to write and say *why* I have stopped giving.) But my being offended is unimportant. An analysis in the *New York Times* reached this depressing conclusion: "fund-raising letters, whether for causes of the right or the left, are designed to reach the gut, not the brain. They are written that way for one reason: it works."[6]

---

third criterion of integrity: In the first chapter of *Integrity*, Carter says that integrity "requires three steps: 1, *discerning* what is right and what is wrong; 2, *acting* on what you have discerned, even at personal cost; and 3, *saying openly* that you are acting on your understanding of right and wrong" (7). As Carter restates his definition a little later, integrity requires "moral reflectiveness," "keeping commitments," and being "unashamed of doing the right" (7). [EDS.]

Reluctance to Judge

It works: that explains the seeming lack of integrity in advertising and fund-raising, perhaps. It cannot quite explain what is going on in this strange, puffing language of recommendations. I fear that the refusal of so many professors to write accurate letters of reference is part of a larger problem in academia today and, from what I understand, in other professions as well: the reluctance, not to say refusal, to judge the performance of others. One sees it in the phenomenon of grade inflation on campus (a phenomenon that some elite universities have finally started to address) and in the routine and utterly useless "He-worked-here-and-caused-no-trouble" letters of reference nowadays supplied by ex-employers. It is as though those of us who are actually charged with evaluating the work of other people would rather not have the responsibility.

Once, during my brief period of private law practice, I was all set to rec-ommend that we hire a particular person who had interviewed well and whose reference letter from the previous job was fine. And then her last boss told me — on the phone, not in writing — that the applicant had been dismissed be-cause of poor work habits and might have been stealing from the firm. Now, you might think that problems of that sort should be part of the reference, that even a minimal integrity would require one employer to warn the next; but you would evidently be wrong. I was fortunate to get the information I did; lots of employers would not have provided it, even on the telephone. As a 1992 study in the *American Business Law Journal* noted, "Most employers today either give no employment reference information, or merely confirm that the (for-mer) employee worked for the employer during specified dates and at a speci-fied rank or position."[7]

Why? A fear of litigation is presumably part of the reason, for lawsuits against former employers for their negative references are said to be on the upswing. Putting aside cases alleging discrimination, which will often, al-though of course not always, involve allegations that deserve to be taken seri-ously, a growing number of lawsuits charge former employers with breach of contract, wrongful interference with business relations, or even *defamation* for revealing the reason for an employee's discharge. A 1993 article in the *Wall Street Journal* warned that more and more courts were applying a bizarre vari-ant of defamation called "compelled self-publication," in which the employee claims that because the ex-employer is going to reveal to potential employers the official reason for the discharge, the employee must reveal it first.[8]

It all sounds very scary. But the *American Business Law Journal* study, which compared reported court decisions in the periods 1965–1970 and 1985–1990, concluded that the fears of employers are generally unfounded. The authors found "that the relative frequency of such litigation probably has not increased, that defamation law still privileges employers so that (former) employees seldom win any award, and that the size of awards has declined over time." The authors speculated that employers who were reluctant to report the true reasons for the discharge of employees were basing their behavior on media reports of jury verdicts awarding damages "in a few atypical cases."

And although everybody hears about lawsuits employing such bizarre theories as "bad-faith grading" by a college professor who awarded a low grade or infliction of emotional distress by an employer who gave a poor performance review, what is less frequently reported is that such cases are usually dismissed.[9] True, employers will want to avoid the cost and bad publicity attending even lawsuits they expect to win, but over time, if employers keep winning, one would expect the number of suits filed to drop. (Moreover, litigation may run the other way: sometimes, the new employer sues the old one for failure to warn that the employee in question is violent or prone to steal.) In short, there is good reason to be skeptical of the claim that the still rare case in which a teacher or an employer is successfully sued for writing the wrong words can quite explain our growing hesitation to evaluate with integrity.

I do not mean to insist that litigation has no effect on how we hire, promote, and fire. In the field with which I am most familiar, the academic world, we are already facing a crisis of confidentiality. Academic tenure debates are traditionally carried on behind closed doors, in the hope that professors will be open in their evaluation of their junior colleagues' work. But this has been growing harder for years. At one well-known law school, a junior member of the faculty up for promotion was given the confidential file of written comments from senior colleagues. Given the file by whom? Probably a senior colleague. At Yale Law School, an account of one closed faculty meeting wound up in the local paper. The account was in important respects inaccurate, but that is not the issue; the problem is that the leak could only have come from a member of the faculty, who deemed the end he or she was seeking far more important than the tradition of confidentiality. (Nope, no points for either leaker's integrity in breaking tradition, because neither one ever came forward and said openly, "I did it and here's why.") In both cases, the effect is to chill the honesty and depth that evaluation of scholarship demands.

Litigation has only complicated matters. The Supreme Court has held that neither the First Amendment nor any special evidentiary privilege allows universities that are facing employment discrimination claims to withhold reviews written by outside evaluators of the candidate's work.[10] One can hardly expect anything else: a university, in the eyes of the law, is simply an employer, and when it faces a lawsuit, it has the same obligation as other employers to open its internal deliberations. At the same time, one can scarcely miss the effect this rule will have—is already having, I suspect—on outside reviewers. The pressure to be less than honest increases with the likelihood that one's comments will become known, because fewer and fewer academics seem to have the integrity to stand behind their criticisms of their colleagues. University officials have complained that the court decisions allowing tenure files to be opened will make it harder and harder to obtain the written evaluations that tenure deliberations have traditionally demanded.[11]

Here again, I make no claim to exemplary behavior. Although I do sometimes agree to write evaluation letters for professors up for tenure at other schools, I rarely do so unless I am comfortably enthusiastic. I do not relish the thought of being at the center of a public battle of the sort that too often breaks out nowadays when tenure is denied. And if my motives seem self-interested and unintegral, well, I suppose I must plead guilty; but I have better things to do with my time. I am far from alone in this. I have colleagues who, citing a fear of publicity, will not write the letters at all. So the integrity of one important process—the adjudication of discrimination complaints—seems to be on the way to destroying the integrity of another—peer review for academic tenure. Probably that is inevitable: we must sometimes establish priorities among our integrities. But we can weep for the demise of the old system even as we try to work out how to build a new one to meet the demands of a new age.

That is what everybody is doing now: working out new ways to perform 30 the evaluations that are necessary in both the workplace and the campus. We need to do this because people are simply less willing than in the past to put the truth to paper—at least when the truth might hurt someone's career. I continue to harbor doubts, however, that litigation is the principal cause. What else might be the source of this unfortunate reluctance to judge others, especially students?

Conservatives sometimes lay the blame for the problem squarely at the door of such fashionable academic theories as deconstruction and multiculturalism, which, because they question established hierarchies, are said to call the authority to evaluate into question. Perhaps there is *something* to the charge—I recall, for example, my conversation a few years ago with a respected white sociologist who told me all the reasons that he graded his black students more leniently than his white students. But the claim that left faddism has somehow done in our standards of judgment is a gross overstatement of the sort that has become common in this era that has linked the fate of the public intellectual to the ability to command television time, which in turn is linked to the ability to shock. There are causes aplenty for the decline of standards, if we would only look.

For example, the old-boy network, under siege but still stumbling along, has created vast spaces for mediocrities who happen to be white and male to move ahead, unjudged, as has the fawning relationship between members of Congress and the PACs that more or less purchase their votes in exchange for favors that those who fund the PACs have not earned. In law enforcement, the notorious "blue wall of silence"—the tradition that police officers do not turn one another in—renders any serious investigation of police incompetence or even corruption extraordinarily difficult, with the rare exception of very public malfeasance (preferably captured on videotape). Across the country, union seniority and work rules often make it impossible for firms to reward their best people with the highest salaries. The problem has become particularly acute on Wall Street, where corporations bring considerable pressure to bear on analysts not to downgrade their stocks. The pressure may include anything from refusing to give information (so that the analysts are at a competitive disadvantage) to refusing to invite them to corporate events. The result, according to the *Wall Street Journal*, is that many savvy traders have come to take stock recommendations as necessarily exaggerations: so *buy* means *hold,* and *hold* means *sell*.[12] In short, we are all a little bit dirty on this one.

So, rather than place blame for our reluctance to judge, let us be satisfied with pointing out that it is antithetical to integrity to give someone an evaluation, a letter, a grade that he or she has not earned. We might have a lively discussion of what it means to earn an evaluation, but my concern is with the teacher or manager who *consciously* decides to avoid trouble by ranking somebody higher than the ranker actually thinks justified; or who refuses to do the work of figuring out where students or employees rank; or who decides not to get involved in evaluation at all. Such acts of unintegrity are corrupting: not only do they ease the path of the doer away from integrity, but they send quite unfortunate signals to those who look to their teachers or managers for models of behavior.

Now let us consider a simple example.

Example 5-1. A college professor receives a telephone call about one of her students from a firm that is thinking of hiring him. The professor never agreed to serve as a reference, and the student did not list her as one. But the employer, suspicious of the glowing tone of the formal reference letters, is making random calls to other faculty members whose names appear on the student's transcript. The student received a B in her course, based on a very fine paper that would have been an easy A, except that it was turned in several weeks late. If the professor decides to tell the employer the truth, which may cost the student a chance at the job because of his poor work habits, will she be acting with integrity?

Observation 5-1(a). The easy answer is yes. She should tell the truth or decline to comment, because to do anything else would be actively misleading. But if she declines to comment, even if she states that it is her policy, the employer might well take it as a negative reference anyway, assuming—in this case, correctly—that she does not want to say anything because she cannot say anything nice.

Observation 5-1(b). The potentially difficult point for the professor is that the student never asked her to serve as a reference. However, it is quite unclear why that decision on the student's part should bind the professor to say nothing about him. We might question the professor's integrity were she to conduct a campaign against the student, contacting potential employers before they even ask, in order to harm his job prospects: a vendetta almost always will lack an integral justification.

I said that the example is simple, and it is. But there is a complicating 35
factor. Were the professor to follow the course of action I propose—the
course that integrity demands—she might very well hear from the student.
The employer, deciding not to give him the job, might let slip the reason.
And even a sanitized version ("We had questions about your work habits")
might supply a sufficient clue for the student to figure out who provided the
derogatory information. Litigation, of course, might follow, or worse: there
are cases of physical assault upon, and even murder of, faculty members by
disgruntled students. But even if none of these horrors occurs, the professor,
in today's world, might well be thrown on the defensive by the student, who
would complain that she had, through telling the truth, ruined his life. I have
heard that very cry from students who were dissatisfied with their grades. I
once had an agonized telephone call from the assistant dean at another school,
one of whose students I had allowed into a seminar: Would I please raise the
young man's grade, because he otherwise would be unable to graduate? The
premise of these complaints is fascinating: if the student gets a bad grade or a
bad reference, it is the fault of the professor, not the student.

Grade Inflation

Although I am loath to be too critical of colleagues I admire, I believe that the
grade inflation about which so many people get so exercised rests on a similar
refusal by faculty members to behave like adults, that is, like people with
enough integrity to disappoint other people. It is as though some professors
want to believe that everybody deserves to be first. But everybody doesn't.

A good deal of grade inflation probably stems from the desire of professors
to avoid the guilty feelings that honest grading might generate, as well as a fear
of being disliked by students, or perhaps simply a fear of arguing with them.
The net effect is that the grades that students work so hard to earn matter a
good deal less. During my undergraduate years at Stanford in the 1970s, graduate students in at least some departments, as I recall, were not permitted to
count grades of C toward their degrees. That meant that many mathematics and
science courses in which both graduate and undergraduate students enrolled
were graded essentially on an A/B curve: except for cases of utter disaster, instructors were loath to award Cs, because too much time was spent arguing
with students desperate to raise their grades and avoid repeating the class.

Grade inflation is a signal that professors are no longer treating grades as
though they matter. But faculty members who are unwilling to say this are
participating wholesale in a breach of our rule 3. And, as with most breaches
of integrity, they are causing great harm. Obviously, grade inflation is bad for
potential employers, who may be unable to evaluate transcripts. It is also unfair to those students who achieve genuinely outstanding work but are tossed
into the vast pool of A averages, not all of which are actually earned. One of

my Yale colleagues, upon hearing that a candidate for a teaching position had nearly straight-As from Harvard Law School, grumbled: "Yeah, but who did he have? I mean, do those grades really count?" Thus we move from the raw data of the transcript to the use of informal sources of information—always a dangerous practice, because of the bias and intense subjectivity that we automatically import.

Indeed, the collapse of grading as a serious enterprise, by forcing potential employers to rely on faculty contacts and other informal sources rather than grades to obtain reliable information, could severely retard the cause of racial justice. Working harder in the classroom and thus earning better grades than the white kids has always been one of the things that minority students have been counseled to do: only by being better, we have told each other for a generation and more, can we hope to avoid the pernicious effects of the old-boy network and other informal means of hiring that have traditionally been closed to us. (And even with better grades there is no guarantee.) But if every student gets the same high grades without doing the hard work, the informal contacts become even more important and the old-boy network is back in business.[13]

But perhaps most important, as one would expect from so patent a breach of integrity, grade inflation is bad for the students who receive inflated grades, because the meaningless grades leave them incapable of judging *their own* performances. I remember receiving an A in an accelerated undergraduate physics course in which I had understood little of what went on. But I did not realize how little I had understood until I tried to apply my "knowledge" in a more advanced course in the subsequent term. Had I received the grade I deserved—perhaps a B, probably a C—I would have worked harder (because I would have known that I was in trouble) or perhaps abandoned the field of physics a good deal sooner. Either one would have been an improvement.

But instead of providing accurate evaluations, we indulge this almost willed refusal to judge our students. So, rather than turn down requests from weaker students for letters of recommendation, we have developed this peculiar language in which so-so students become great and good students become brilliant and no words are left over to describe the truly exceptional students. And the students themselves understand and take advantage of the dilemma in which our own reluctance to appear mean has left us. I have heard more than one student argue quite seriously that faculty members are *obliged* to write letters for any student who asks, as though we are an employment agency—but then, some faculty members behave as though we are, pulling out all the stops, calling in favors all over the country and generally making great nuisances of themselves to get jobs for the students they like the best—using these informal methods because the grades and letters are largely fungible. (Again, let me emphasize for the reader that this practice can have serious racial exclusionary effects.)

I admit that I do not act like an employment counselor. I turn down some of the students who ask me for letters, unless I actually have something interesting to say. I generally limit my endorsements to two categories: the student whom I have supervised in writing a major paper and the student who has served as one of my research assistants. Then, even if I am in principle willing to write a letter, I always explain to the student asking for one that I write long and quite complicated letters, pointing out weaknesses as well as strengths. I point out that some judges or other potential employers might think that since I eschew the usual language in which letters of recommendation are written, I am trying to warn them off—that is, by writing an honest letter instead of lying, I must mean that the student is not good enough to hire.

This prospect saddens me, for I harbor no wish to make more difficult the task of finding a job, but I simply am not capable of writing the dreary succession of "best-student-in-a-decade" letters that so many law faculty members churn out. Some of my students are less saddened than angry, or perhaps offended, for many of them behave as though glowing letters of recommendation are theirs as of right. I cannot really blame them. Years of higher education have trained them to believe it. But I also cannot indulge them. The long and complicated letter, with all its risks, is the only kind I am able comfortably to write.

I do not want to say that professors (or employers) who make a different choice lack integrity, and, indeed, that is not what I believe. I would rather say that they are fluent in a strange but obviously useful language that I am far too old to learn.

Notes

1. Hannah Arendt, "Lying in Politics: Reflections on the Pentagon Papers," in *Crises of the Republic* (New York: Harcourt Brace Jovanovich, 1972), pp. 3, 7.

2. The most recent classroom prayer figure, as of this writing, is a Gallup Poll finding 71 percent in favor of a constitutional amendment to support it. See Mary Beth Marklein, "Discipline Is No. 1 School Concern," *USA Today*, August 23, 1995.

3. See Ronald Dworkin, *Life's Dominion: An Argument about Abortion, Euthanasia, and Individual Freedom* (New York: Knopf, 1993), p. 13.

4. For a fairly simple explanation of puffery and the reasons the courts allow it, see Ivan L. Preston, "The Definition of Deceptiveness in Advertising and Other Commercial Speech," *Catholic Law Review* 39 (1990): 1035. See also Albert Breton and Ronald Wintrobe, "Freedom of Speech v. Efficient Regulation in Market for Ideas," *Journal of Economic Behavior and Organization* 2 (March 1992): 217.

5. This practice may be defended by use of the substantial economic literature on advertising as information. The basic idea is that advertising does not necessarily *persuade* the consumer to make a purchase, but does *inform* the consumer about the products or services that a firm provides. The advertising will keep the brand name before the consumers, so that when they go to make purchases, they will do so with more information. See Phillip Nelson, "The Economic Consequences of Advertising," *Journal of Business* 48 (1975): 213. See also William Landes and Richard Posner, "Trademark Law: An Economic Perspective," *Journal of Law and Economics* 30 (1987): 265.

6. Erik Eckholm, "The Dark Science of Fund-Raising by Mail," *New York Times*, May 28, 1995, sec. 4, p. 6.

7.   Ramona L. Paetzold and Steven L. Willborn, "Employer Irrationality and the Demise of Employment References," *American Business Law Journal* (May 1992): 23.

8.   Junda Woo, "Quirky Slander Actions Threaten Employers," *Wall Street Journal*, November 26, 1993, p. B1.

9.   See, for example, *Clements v. County of Nassau*, 835 F.2d 1000 (2d Cir. 1987) (dismissing bad-faith grading suit); and *Wallen v. Domm*, 532 F. Supp. 73 (E.D. Va. 1982) (dismissing infliction-of-distress suit).

10.   *University of Pennsylvania v. Equal Employment Opportunity Commission*, 493 U.S. 182 (1990).

11.   See Stephen Wermiel, "Colleges Lose Case on Secrecy of Tenure Files," *Wall Street Journal*, January 10, 1990.

12.   See Michael Sicouolfi, "Many Companies Press Analysts to Steer Clear of Negative Ratings," *Wall Street Journal*, July 19, 1995, p. A1.

13.   I discuss the old-boy network and its modern derivation, the "star system," in Stephen L. Carter, *Reflections of an Affirmative Action Baby* (New York: Basic Books, 1991), chap. 2.

WHAT DOES HE SAY?

1.   Stephen L. Carter talks about a number of related subjects here, from the university to language to advertising, as well as several others. As you read, mark these shifts from one world or realm to another, writing *university* or *language* or some other descriptive word or phrase in the margins.

2.   Explain what Carter means by "the integrity of language" and how this applies to the argument that he is making.

3.   You have, no doubt, asked for letters of recommendation for college or for a job. How did you feel about asking? What did you imagine these people saying in their letters? Did you read any of these letters, and if so, what was your reaction? Given your experience, how do you feel "going behind the scenes," hearing what a writer of such letters actually thinks about them? Does Carter's reflection make you uneasy? Why or why not? Do you think that your recommenders engaged in what Carter calls "hyperbole," deliberately exaggerating for effect, and if so, how does that make you feel?

WHAT DO YOU THINK?

4.   Carter argues that inflated grades are bad for students—that students who get unrealistically high grades are harmed by these grades. Explain what he means; then write an essay agreeing or disagreeing. Draw on your own experience of receiving grades—some of which, no doubt, seemed fair to you, while others, perhaps, did not.

5.   Carter argues that advertising actually works. Does it? Do you think that you are influenced by advertising? Explain, supporting your claims with examples.

6. Would you take a course from Stephen L. Carter (assuming that he taught a subject that was relevant to your education)? Would you ask him for a letter of recommendation afterward? Explain why or why not.

7. Think of "The Best Student Ever" both in terms of what it presents and in terms of the ethos it establishes for Carter. Write a letter of recommendation for Stephen L. Carter. Assume that he is being nominated for an award. Variation: Base your recommendation on this essay and on the other Stephen L. Carter essay, "Welcoming the Stranger" (p. 111), included in chapter 2 of this text.

8. Is your reaction to this essay in any way influenced by the fact that Carter is African American? that he teaches at a prestigious Ivy League school, Yale University?

WHAT WOULD THEY SAY?

9. Carter describes what he calls a "simple example" of the problem he's exploring in this essay, the college professor who receives a telephone call from a potential employer about a problematic student. Write an essay explaining how Lawrence Hinman ("Virtual Virtues," p. 415) and Naomi Wolf ("The Beauty Myth," p. 451) would respond to this situation. What would they do if they were the professor? In your essay, also explain how you think you would respond.

10. Read Annie Dillard's "Singing with the Fundamentalists" (p. 583). How would she respond to Carter's argument? How would he respond to her? Obviously, these two essays deal with different subjects, but only superficially. What are the underlying issues? How do these two different subjects shed light on each other?

11. Write an essay on the theme of the "integrity of language." Draw on Carter's "Best Student Ever," Naomi Wolf's "The Beauty Myth" (p. 451), and George Orwell's "Politics and the English Language" (p. 461).

DONALD McCABE AND
LINDA KLEBE TREVINO
Honesty and Honor Codes

In this carefully worded academic argument that uses statistical research, Donald McCabe and Linda Klebe Trevino expand the issue of honesty to the larger question of cheating and academic integrity in general. McCabe, a professor in the Business School at Rutgers University, is the founder of the Center for Academic Integrity. Trevino, an expert on corporate ethics, is a professor of business administration at Pennsylvania State University. "Honesty and Honor Codes" was first published in Academe *in 2002.*

A recent editorial in the *Cavalier Daily*, the University of Virginia's student newspaper, opened with the statement, "The honor system at the university needs to go. Our honor system routinely rewards cheaters and punishes honesty." In the wake of a highly publicized cheating scandal in an introductory physics course at the university, it was easy to understand the frustration and concern surrounding Virginia's long-standing practice of trusting students to honor the university's tradition of academic integrity.

We could not disagree more, however, with the idea that it's time for Virginia or any other campus to abandon the honor system. We believe instead that America's institutions of higher education need to recommit themselves to a tradition of integrity and honor. Asking students to be honest in their academic work should not fall victim to debates about cultural relativism. Certainly, such recommitment seems far superior to throwing up our hands in despair and assuming that the current generation of students has lost all sense of honor. Fostering integrity may not be an easy task, but we believe an increasing number of students and campuses are ready to meet the challenge.

Although our belief may be rooted in idealism—some might argue naiveté—it is supported by a decade of research in which we have surveyed over fourteen thousand students on fifty-eight different campuses, from small liberal-arts colleges to large comprehensive universities. Much of this work has focused on traditional academic codes of honor—the kind that routinely reward cheaters in the view of the *Cavalier Daily*—and their impact on student dishonesty in the classroom. Although the details of these codes vary from campus to campus, they resemble Virginia's in that they place the primary responsibility for cheating on students.

Traditional codes often mandate unproctored exams, a judicial process over which students have majority or complete control, and a written pledge requiring students to affirm they have completed their work honestly. Many traditional codes also place some level of obligation on students to report incidents of cheating they may observe among their peers, although such clauses are infrequently enforced.

Some schools use rituals and ceremonies to generate greater student commitment to their honor codes. Vanderbilt University, for example, has instituted a unique signing-in ceremony. Following an honor code orientation, each first-year student signs a class banner indicating a personal commitment to the Vanderbilt code. The signed banners for each of the four classes currently enrolled at the university hang in a prominent location in Vanderbilt's student center as a constant reminder to students of the commitment they made.

Modified honor codes, a more recent innovation, have appeared on some campuses in the past decade. Recognizing the difficulty of developing a campus culture that can support a traditional code, these codes aim to develop a sense of community responsibility for academic integrity, particularly among students. Unproctored exams and the use of a pledge are usually at the instructor's option (and often found only in smaller upper-division courses, if at all).

But two elements, common to all modified codes, are critical. First, a campus must communicate to its students that academic integrity is a major institutional priority. Typical strategies for doing so include "integrity seminars" and presidential or other high-level involvement with the issue of academic integrity. Some campuses have even staged "pep rallies." The University of Maryland at College Park held such rallies to focus student attention on its new modified honor code. The participation of the state's governor and the university's president in the inaugural rally sent a clear signal to the campus community of the institution's level of commitment to the principle of academic integrity.

Student participation in campus judicial or hearing bodies review alleged infringements of the honor code is the second critical component of modified codes. Students should also have a voice on task forces or committees charged with informing other students about the purposes and philosophy of the code, and they should play a major role in its development and implementation. But the support of faculty and top administrators is also essential. As we have noted, academic integrity must be promoted as a basic campus priority.

The impact of honor codes, both traditional and modified, is surprisingly strong on many campuses, suggesting that an ethical appeal to students—rooted in a sense of community responsibility—can help reduce cheating. Although high levels of cheating are found on many campuses, we know of institutions at which cheating is simply not a fact of everyday student life. And some of these campuses, from small private schools like Elizabethtown College in Pennsylvania to large public universities like Kansas State, have only recently implemented honor codes or similar initiatives. These experiences suggest that such efforts can succeed—that it is still possible to develop cultures that instill academic integrity. Certainly, at least one of the students we surveyed thinks so: "I believe [my school] to be a rare example of integrity in college.... The biggest factor...is our honor code. By signing the honor code...we all agree to conduct our studies, as well as our social lives, in an ethical manner. This results in an atmosphere of trust between students and faculty."

RISE IN CHEATING

The evidence that academic dishonesty among college students is frequent, and growing, is compelling. In the early 1960s, sociologist William Bowers conducted a landmark study of cheating among college students for his doctoral dissertation at Columbia University. Bowers surveyed over five thousand students on ninety-nine campuses and reported that at least half of those in his sample engaged in some form of academic dishonesty since coming to college; he believed this estimate was conservative. And although he acknowledged the importance of factors such as students' high school experience and value orientation and institutional size and selectivity, Bowers felt that students' college peers had perhaps the most powerful effect on their attitude toward cheating. He argued that "students are less apt to cheat as the campuswide climate of disapproval [of cheating] increases." Indeed, Bowers believed it was peer pressure that explained why schools with honor systems generally had lower levels of cheating.

Our research has corroborated Bowers's major conclusions, but it has also documented significant increases in student cheating over the past three decades. For example, in a 1993 survey of students on nine campuses included in the Bowers study, we found disturbing increases in the level of serious cheating on tests and exams. In 1963, 26 percent of the students on the nine campuses, none of which had honor codes, acknowledged copying from another student on a test or exam; by 1993, the percentage had grown to 52. In addition, we observed a fourfold increase in the use of crib notes, from 6 to 27 percent.

Given this rise in cheating, it is more important than ever for faculty and administrators to understand the potential of honor codes to reduce it. The research results are clear. The level of self-reported cheating by students on honor-code campuses, even those with unproctored exams, is significantly lower than that on campuses without codes, where exams are often carefully monitored. For example, almost half of the students we surveyed on seventeen noncode campuses reported one or more instances of serious cheating on tests or exams, compared with fewer than one in three on fourteen code campuses surveyed. The difference was even more dramatic among students who admitted to more than three incidents of serious test cheating—one in six students did so on noncode campuses versus one in sixteen at code schools. Not only do more students cheat on noncode campuses, but those that do, cheat more often.

Research suggests that many faculty members fail to take adequate precautions to deter cheating or ignore suspected incidents, so perhaps these results are not surprising. Often, a low level of peer disapproval is the only thing standing between a student on a noncode campus and the decision to engage in academic dishonesty. Unlike their peers on code campuses, these students compete in a culture that attaches little or no social stigma to cheating.

CULTURE OF INTEGRITY

Simply having an honor code means little if students don't know about it. It must be introduced to new students and made a topic of ongoing campus dialogue. The level of trust placed in students on honor-code campuses establishes academic integrity as a clear institutional priority. The high value attached to honesty and, perhaps more important, the privileges accorded to students under traditional honor-code systems creates a culture that makes cheating socially unacceptable among most students—Bowers's concept of peer disapproval.

Like Vanderbilt, some honor-code schools use rituals or ceremonies to 15 develop such cultures. These strategies are particularly popular at traditional women's colleges that have honor codes, including Mount Holyoke, Smith, and Wellesley. At Washington and Lee University, prospective students are informed of their expected obligations under the campus honor code as part of the admissions process. Even in this day of intense competition for the best students, the university's admissions literature suggests that if applicants cannot abide by the provisions of the campus code, Washington and Lee is probably not the right school for them. Members of the student honor committee at Rice University orient new faculty to the student honor code and keep department chairs apprised of any changes in the committee's emphasis.

Although such strategies may work on campuses that already have strong honor codes, they mean little on those that do not, especially large campuses and those at which many students attend part time or live off campus. Developing a shared culture of any kind is more difficult on such campuses, because many students cannot, or do not, participate in campus life. We surveyed 1,800 students on nine campuses fitting this general description in 1993 and found very high levels of cheating. Almost two-thirds of our respondents acknowledged one or more incidents of serious test cheating in the previous year, and one in four admitted to more than three incidents of serious test cheating.

Although many, and probably most, students, faculty, and administrators at noncode campuses seem convinced that an honor code would never work on their campus, we believe such attitudes are overly pessimistic. In affiliation with the Center for Academic Integrity at Duke University, we recently surveyed 2,200 students on twenty-one different campuses. Nine of these institutions did not have an honor code, eight had traditional honor codes, one used a code that is a hybrid between a traditional and a modified code, and three (large public universities) had modified honor codes.

Based on their size and the greater percentage of their students who were enrolled part time or who lived off campus, we normally would have expected to find the highest levels of self-reported cheating on these three large campuses. But self-reported cheating was actually lower at these three schools compared with the nine noncode campuses surveyed. One-third of the students at the large universities acknowledged one or more instances of serious cheating compared with almost half of the students at the noncode schools. One in ten students at the universities acknowledged repetitive serious test cheating versus one in six at the noncode schools.

We believe such data suggest that most schools can develop strategies to reduce the level of student cheating. The data also underscore the importance of bringing students into campus conversations about academic integrity and involving them in any effort to change institutional culture. Success depends on getting students to accept responsibility for academic integrity, both their own and that of their peers. They do not necessarily have to monitor and report on their peers, but they do have to help create and sustain an environment where most students view cheating as socially unacceptable.

Pressing Issue

Right now is a critical time for colleges and universities to address the issue of 20 academic integrity. Recent research suggests that cheating in American high schools is on the rise. In particular, new technologies are raising difficult questions, for both students and teachers, about what is and is not appropriate behavior. For example, a recent survey of 4,500 high school students suggests that the Internet is creating new dilemmas for students concerning plagiarism. The same survey reports that many students are dealing with what they perceive as unreasonable workloads by collaborating on assignments, even when they are asked for individual work, or by copying someone else's work. The students say they feel that some teachers simply give too much homework even though they know many students have jobs, extracurricular activities, and active social lives.

Now more than ever, students arriving at our colleges and universities need guidance to help them think about academic integrity. We know that moral development can advance dramatically over the four years of college, but such advancement depends on a student's experience both in and outside the classroom. We believe that student engagement in an environment that values honesty can contribute significantly to moral development.

Faculty members have an important role to play in creating such an environment, but students report wide variations in how faculty address academic integrity in the classroom. Many students who cheat blame faculty for their transgressions, especially professors who fail to respond to what students consider obvious incidents of cheating that occur in their courses. In today's highly competitive environment, otherwise honest students can persuade themselves that they must cheat to keep the playing field level. The following student comments are not unusual:

> I think the cutthroat competition of getting good grades, getting into a good grad school, are the two most important factors in what drives students to cheat. Pressure from parents/family/professors...makes you think about cheating. It really is such a shame that society has turned us into such deceitful people.

> I feel that there is so much cheating going on, the only way to remain competitive is by cheating. I don't think it's fair that students with better GPAs than myself because of cheating deserve getting into grad schools over people who don't cheat.

> Although dealing with student cheating is difficult, faculty can address some concerns simply through good teaching—by, for example, challenging academic dishonesty when it occurs in their courses and fostering an environment of trust in their classrooms.

We understand that skeptics, many of them faculty on our own campuses, feel little can be done to improve student integrity in the classroom. But the data are clear: faculty and administrators can work with students to create a campus culture where trust is higher, cheating is lower, and students learn to behave more ethically. Honor codes, both traditional and modified, seem to be an effective approach. But we also know of several noncode schools that have reduced academic dishonesty among students. Although they lack a formal code, they subscribe to the basic strategy we have suggested: they communicate the campus's commitment to academic integrity and make it an active topic of discussion among students and faculty to help them understand that every member of the campus community is responsible for promoting it.

The Massachusetts Institute of Technology is a good example. In the early 1990s, some upper-class students developed "bibles" for selected courses that included solutions for homework problems and other information that could allow students to improve their grades inappropriately. Rather than ignore the problem, MIT used it as an opportunity to reexamine the issue of cheating. And after surveying students and faculty, the institution initiated a yearlong discussion of the state of academic integrity on campus. The discussion led to several policy revisions and a heightened state of understanding among students and faculty about the importance of academic integrity.

Of course, simply having a code or updating your policy will not guarantee reduced student cheating. Creating a culture of academic integrity takes years to achieve and demands the commitment of all members of the campus community. Once attained, such a culture requires constant attention and renewal. Rules must be developed when new issues, such as those raised by the Internet, present themselves, and the rules must be enforced. Moreover, the greatest benefit of a culture of integrity may not be reduced student cheating. Instead, it may be the lifelong benefit of learning the value of living in a community of trust.

WHAT DO THEY SAY?

1. This is a clear, straightforward, conventionally organized piece of academic writing. Outline it. Without necessarily following the structure of a formal outline, somehow indicate the thesis, the subpoints, and the main pieces of supporting evidence.

2. As you read, underline the major transitional words and phrases, the language that indicates the essay's structure and flow (such as, *that is, for example, first, second,* and so on).

3. This essay was originally published in a journal called *Academe,* a journal written not for students but for faculty members and administrators at colleges and universities. As you read, mark the words and phrases that suggest this intended audience, words and phrases that you might not understand or that indicate the kind of shared experience that this audience has and so need not be explained in detail.

4. How does it feel to be reading an article that does not have you as its intended audience. Do you feel excluded? as if you were eavesdropping? put off? attracted? Write a quick paragraph discussing this.

WHAT DO YOU THINK?

5. The authors assert that cheating is on the rise at colleges and universities. Do you agree? Why or why not? Check with the office on your campus that handles cases involving cheating: do they agree that cheating is increasing? Write an essay discussing this. Make sure it includes your own knowledge, opinions, and reactions to "Honesty and Honor Codes" and whatever information about cheating on your campus you can gather.

6. The authors suggest that sometimes otherwise honest and well-intentioned students find themselves in situations that lead to plagiarism or other kinds of cheating. Often, they say, the problem is that students don't leave themselves enough time and so cheat as a last resort. Is this true? Do honest students sometimes cheat? Is this kind of cheating less problematic than systematic and repeated cheating?

7. The main claim of this essay is that explicit honor codes cut down on the amount of cheating. Does your university practice some of the strategies that the authors recommend, and if so, how do they work? If your institution doesn't have an honor code, how would you respond personally to the establishment of such a code? Would you be less inclined to cheat?

8. One of the strengths of this essay is that the authors draw on extensive sociological and statistical research, both their own and that of others. Find and read at least two of the research studies that the authors cite, and compare those studies to what the authors say about them in this essay. Evaluate the methods of these studies. Do you find them reliable? convincing?

9. Reflect on your own experience as a student in light of the authors' claims about the rise of cheating and the effect of honor codes. We realize that this can be tricky, particularly if you're one of those students who has cheated over the years

or if your friends have cheated. If you need to, fictionalize. The question is whether your own experience supports or refutes the authors' argument.

10. How would the authors of this article respond to the scenario that opens this chapter? What would they advise the professor to do? Explain, quoting at least once from "Honesty and Honor Codes." Then end by explaining why and on what points you would agree or disagree with McCabe and Klebe Trevino.

WHAT WOULD THEY SAY?

11. Though Adrienne Rich in "Claiming an Education" (p. 608) and Parker Palmer in "The Community of Truth" (p. 627) do not talk about cheating and plagiarism directly, what they say about education has implications for this issue. (Both these selections are in chapter 7, "Why Change Your Mind?") Explore those issues. Write an essay imagining what Rich and Palmer would say in response to this article.

12. How would Lawrence Hinman ("Virtual Virtues: Reflections on Academic Integrity in the Age of the Internet," p. 415) respond to this essay? Do the kinds of honor codes that the authors describe answer to the problems of cyberspace as Hinman outlines them? Would a different honor code have to be devised for cyberspace? Write an essay exploring these questions, bringing in as well Esther Dyson's "Cyberspace: If You Don't Love It, Leave It" (p. 141).

BILL WATTERSON

"Today at school, I tried to decide whether to cheat on my test or not."

T*HE* C*REATOR* *of the* Calvin and Hobbes *comic strip, Bill Watterson (b. 1958) refused to merchandise his characters.* Calvin and Hobbes *appeared in more than 2,300 newspapers around the world, and ran from November 1985 through December 1995.*

WHAT DOES IT SAY?

1. There are two figures in this comic strip, Calvin and his tiger, Hobbes. Track what each one says. Calvin obviously does most of the talking. What does Hobbes say and when does he say it? What is your reaction to Hobbes's final statement? How

does Hobbes's body language—his facial expressions, his gestures—contribute to your understanding of what he says?

2. It doesn't take long to read a comic strip like this, and first reactions are usually quick, too. Describe yours. As soon as you stop reading, jot down a quick four sentence response. Did you laugh? Why? What made this funny? If you didn't laugh, what was your reaction and why?

WHAT DO YOU THINK?

3. Bill Watterson, the cartoonist, doesn't come out and say what he wants this comic to mean. He is neither Calvin nor Hobbes. What do you think Watterson is getting at? Write a brief essay that presents your understanding of the thesis statement of this cartoon, and explain the evidence that supports your analysis.

4. Though Watterson is neither Calvin nor Hobbes, one of these characters may serve as his spokesperson. Which do you think does? Which of these characters comes closest to representing Watterson's own views, and how do you know? What details in the comic lead to this conclusion? Or do you think that neither character represents Watterson?

5. People often send their friends and families copies of cartoons they like. Who would you send this cartoon to, and why?

6. Hobbes says that "Anymore, simply acknowledging the issue is a moral victory." Write an essay agreeing or disagreeing with that statement, explaining your position.

WHAT WOULD THEY SAY?

7. Read Lawrence Hinman's "Virtual Virtues: Reflections on Academic Integrity in the Age of the Internet" (p. 415). How would Watterson have to adapt this particular cartoon to reflect Hinman's analysis of ethical behavior and the Internet? Would the cartoon have to be any different? Is there something about cyberspace that changes the ethical dilemma that Calvin is describing?

8. Based on your reading of Hinman's "Virtual Virtues: Reflections on Academic Integrity in the Age of the Internet" (p. 415), do you think he would put a copy of this cartoon on his office door or on his syllabus for one of his courses? (Hinman is an ethicist who teaches courses in ethics and ethical reasoning.) Explain why or why not.

9. Write an essay explaining how you think Stephen L. Carter, in "The Best Student Ever" (p. 391), and Donald McCabe and Linda Klebe Trevino, in "Honesty and Honor Codes" (p. 405), would respond to this cartoon. What would they say? Would they agree with its premise? Why or why not?

10. Out of all the essays you've read in this book, which writer comes closest to embodying Calvin's position in this comic? Which writer comes closest to embodying Hobbes's position? Explain.

LAWRENCE HINMAN

Virtual Virtues: Reflections on Academic Integrity in the Age of the Internet

*T*HIS ARTICLE *narrows the focus of the previous selection to the particular issue of plagiarism and the Internet, arguing that technology has radically changed the nature of
authorship. Without preaching, and with a sympathetic analysis of student behavior,
this piece organizes the facts and opens up the questions.*

 *Lawrence Hinman is director of the Values Institute and professor of philoso-
phy at the University of San Diego, where he has been teaching since 1975. He has
published widely on ethical issues, including two textbooks,* Ethics: A Pluralistic
Approach to Moral Theory *(3rd ed., 2003) and* Contemporary Moral Issues
(3rd ed., 2003).

INTRODUCTION

When I was an undergraduate in the sixties, many things were different. Vacuum tubes were still common, even in computers not associated with air-traffic
control. Xeroxing was possible, but still considered extravagant. And plagiarism
was different as well. We would hear rumors that certain fraternities had files of
term papers that members could access. Occasionally we heard of someone who
used a book or journal in the library and typed portions of it into a term paper.
Once in a while a friend would write or rewrite a paper for someone else, usually a girlfriend for a boyfriend. But that was about it. Plagiarism was tedious,
time-consuming, and required some forethought in most cases.

 The academic community in which we lived was also different then. In
many ways, the academic community for many of us was akin to Aristotle's
description of the polis in Book III of the *Politics*:

> This is obvious; for suppose distinct places, such as Corinth and
> Megara, to be brought together so that their walls touched, still they
> would not be one city, not even if the citizens had the right to inter-
> marry, which is one of the rights peculiarly characteristic of states.
> Again, if men dwelt at a distance from one another, but not so far off as
> to have no intercourse, and there were laws among them that they
> should not wrong each other in their exchanges, neither would this be
> a state. Let us suppose that one man is a carpenter, another a husband-
> man, another a shoemaker, and so on, and that their number is ten
> thousand: nevertheless, if they have nothing in common but exchange,
> alliance, and the like, that would not constitute a state. Why is this?

Surely not because they are at a distance from one another: for even supposing that such a community were to meet in one place, but that each man had a house of his own, which was in a manner his state, and that they made alliance with one another, but only against evildoers; still an accurate thinker would not deem this to be a state, if their intercourse with one another was of the same character after as before their union. It is clear then that a state is not a mere society, having a common place, established for the prevention of mutual crime and for the sake of exchange. These are conditions without which a state cannot exist; but all of them together do not constitute a state, which is a community of families and aggregations of families in well-being, for the sake of a perfect and self-sufficing life. Such a community can only be established among those who live in the same place and intermarry. Hence arise in cities family connections, brotherhoods, common sacrifices, amusements which draw men together. But these are created by friendship, for the will to live together is friendship. The end of the state is the good life, and these are the means towards it. And the state is the union of families and villages in a perfect and self-sufficing life, by which we mean a happy and honorable life.

Our conclusion, then, is that political society exists for the sake of noble actions, and not of mere companionship.[1]

The academic community, while not a city-state in all the ways Aristotle describes, nonetheless possesses the distinguishing characteristic of the academic community at its best: the coming together of individuals for noble actions, in this case for the advancement of knowledge through research and scholarship, the transmission of knowledge through undergraduate education and the formation of future scholars and researchers through graduate education.

The situation today is very different. Although the life of the academic community remains, this life now intersects with the lives we lead on the Internet. If the traditional academic community is akin to the Aristotelian polis, the world of the Internet is closer to Hobbes's° state of nature. While it would be an exaggeration to say, following Hobbes's description of the state of nature, that "the notions of right and wrong, justice and injustice...have no place," this description fits life on the Internet more closely than the Aristotelian one does. To be sure, pockets of genuine community exist on the Net, and the Net has made distance a much less relevant [issue] than was the case in Aristotle's view. Genuine scholarly communities thrive on the Web, often around moderated listservers that are based on some specific noble goals. However, the Web as a whole has an anarchical structure much closer to Hobbes's state of nature than Aristotle's polis, a structure (or perhaps, more precisely, the absence of a structure) in which right and wrong, justice and injustice have little or no place.

Thomas Hobbes (1588–1679): English philosopher who viewed human beings as essentially self-interested—hence naturally prone to conflict with each other. [EDS.]

The world of the Web has not supplanted the academic world, but each has changed the other in important ways. They exist, not in identity or opposition, but like overlapping circles in a Venn diagram, partially sharing the same space but each in itself a larger world.

In this new world, plagiarism is fast and easy—just a few clicks away on   5
the Web—although it is often costly. A Google search on *term papers* yields over 1.7 million results. A few are free, many are recycled papers that have been turned in before in other classes, and these seem to sell from $25 and up to $15 per page. Browsing through the ethics section of a typical site, I found papers on common topics such as "Kant's Moral Law and Mill's Utilitarianism" and much more obscure themes such as "Air Traffic Controllers Dismissal and Its Relation to the Works of Kant." You can also have custom papers written just for you, although there is something ironic about a site guaranteeing that it is a newly written paper for your plagiaristic pleasure. Some sites even offer to write masters theses and doctoral dissertations, and presumably the price for that would be quite high. It is also hard to imagine what kind of relationship would exist between a student and a thesis or dissertation director that this would even be possible. Some sites even advertise for writers, requiring at least a master's degree and claiming writers can earn as much as $2,000 per week writing full-time. Plagiarism has not become big business, but it has certainly become at least small business.

The rise of term-paper mills is not the only factor that influences the increased ease with which assignments can be plagiarized from the Web. Newspapers, magazines, and organizations of all kinds put materials on the Web, and students can sometimes use these as sources from which to plagiarize. (They can also, of course, use them to do research, and in many cases they offer excellent resources for the serious student.) Professors often put their own papers online, some journal[s are] now online, and in some cases students put their own assignments online as part of a course requirement. In many cases, these resources are not in a password-protected area and thus they become additional free resources for students who are intent on plagiarizing.

Just as plagiarism has become a business, so too has the detection of plagiarism. A Google search on *plagiarism* returns 462,000 entries, and we can easily see that there has been an expansive attempt to fight technological fire with more technological fire. Some sites offer tips on how to spot plagiarism.[2] Other sites offer plagiarism-detection software programs.[3] Still other sites provide plagiarism-detection services. The best-known of these is TurnItIn.com, which began as Plagiarism.org.[4] This service works by matching submitted papers against its database of available papers and then producing a color-coded report showing what percentage of the paper appears to be taken from other sources. The submitted paper is then added to the database for future reference.

Technological responses to the challenge of plagiarism often elicit technological countermeasures. Recognizing that antiplagiarism software relies on matching word patterns, students turn to Microsoft *Word*'s AutoSummarize

function in the hope of fooling the detection software. My suspicion is that
there is other software out there that is dedicated to changing papers sufficiently
to avoid being flagged by plagiarism-detection software. We've come a long
way from vacuum tubes!

In the following remarks, I want to explore some of the ways in which
we can respond to the moral challenges posed by ease of plagiarism on the
Web. We will see that this is an interesting and complex moral terrain, shaped
in part by technological innovations and in part by nontechnological considerations. As I map out this terrain, a single figure—Aristotle—will hover in
the background, providing guidance and insight. In particular, Aristotle's account of virtues as excellences of character will offer us the philosophical framework within which we can most fruitfully sketch out the full issue of academic
integrity. In order to show this, I would first like to sketch out some background information about who cheats, and then turn [to] a framework for understanding academic integrity, and then look in depth at the issue of
intellectual property rights and academic integrity, offering some practical suggestions for reducing the lack of clarity in this area.

PART ONE: WHO PLAGIARIZES?

One of the pioneers in empirical research in this area, Donald McCabe,[5] a pro-   10
fessor of management at the Business School at Rutgers University, has suggested a very useful typology for grouping students in regard to the issue of
academic integrity.[6] He suggests that students can be divided into three groups:
those who never cheat, at one end of the spectrum; those who routinely cheat
as their preferred choice, at the other end of the spectrum; and, in the middle,
those who cheat occasionally....About 20 percent of the students never
cheated, about 60 percent cheated occasionally, and about 20 percent habitually
tried to cheat. In recent years, that has changed somewhat, with the "never
cheat" category shrinking in size while the "habitually cheat" category has
grown. These numbers vary, depending on the type of school, selectivity of the
admissions process, school culture, etc. Schools with honor codes typically have
the lowest overall rates of cheating.[7]

If we wished to minimize plagiarism, each of these three groups needs to
be approached differently. The first group, the one that never cheats, obviously
does not need to be deterred from cheating. The most important thing in regard to this group is to provide a campus culture that is as supportive as possible of their commitment to academic integrity. They will not be influenced by
the ready accessibility of term papers on the Internet, but they may well falter
in their commitment if they find wide-spread plagiarism around them going
unpunished.

The third group, the habitual cheaters, certainly find their life is made
easier by the easy accessibility of Web-based resources for plagiarism, but

generally speaking they do not plagiarize *because* these resources are available. If they were not available, they would find some other way of plagiarizing. It is here that antiplagiarism software can be very helpful, for these are students whose papers ought to be checked regularly. It should be noted, furthermore, that these are the students who are often best at cheating and plagiarizing. They have done it before. They are not usually encumbered by guilt. Among those who cheat, these are the pros.

The middle group, those who occasionally cheat or plagiarize, are the most interesting and the most likely to be affected by the easy availability of Web-based resources. McCabe has suggested that the challenge of academic integrity today is to figure out how best to work with this group. The first group will take care of itself, at least in a minimally supportive environment. The third group can only be detected and caught, and in some cases it might be deterred by very aggressive monitoring. The middle group, however, is most influenced by the easy availability of Web resources, since their plagiarism is more likely to be a spur-of-the-moment decision. Let me give two examples.

First, I have sat on a number of hearing committees as a faculty representative. This is the accused student's "day in court." The professor presents the complaint. The student presents his or her side of the case separately. Each is questioned by committee members. Typical scenarios in such hearings are students who have failed to manage their time well. They have a paper due, realize they cannot complete the assignment on time, and turn the night before to the Web to get a paper or portions of a paper which they then turn in as their own work the next day. (I also realize, sitting on these committees, that I am often looking at the students who do not cheat well, in part because they do not cheat often; the hard-core cheaters, the third group, are often more skilled and consequently harder to catch.) Had the Web resources not been available, some of these students would probably have not handed in a paper or handed in some very minimal assignment. The Web offers them another possibility, not previously available at that late date.

Let me share a second example, changing a few incidental details to insure that the actual student is not recognizable. I was teaching an ethics course, and one of the assignments was for students to do a weekly journal of personal reflections on the readings. One class, when I was away at a conference, my grad assistant showed the movie *Mississippi Burning* at my request, since we were covering moral issues about racism that week. During the last week of class, a student asked if they were required to write a journal entry on the movie. I said they were not, but if they wanted to write about it, I would give them some extra credit. One of the students, who was rarely present in class, turned in his journal with an entry on the movie—and it turned out to be a movie review from a well-known American movie critic. It took me about thirty seconds to track it down (the second entry on an MSN search), and my guess is that it took the student approximately the same amount of time to find it as well. (There are in fact a number of good, critical resources available on the Web about this movie, even if this review did not happen to be one of them.) I am not sure if this student belonged in the second or third category, but my assumption is that this student would never have bothered to plagiarize this extra-credit assignment if it had not been so easy — and, in this case, free.

The data on whether this assumption is justified are inconclusive. In McCabe's most recent research with high school students and cheating, he found that "90 percent of the students using the Internet to plagiarize have also plagiarized from written sources.... [in other words,] The Web has 'created' few new cheaters — 6 percent of all students."[8] As more data become available, we should get a clearer empirical picture of the extent to which the Web is encouraging students who cheat occasionally to do so more often.

We can place these three groups of students within the context of Aristotle's discussion of the virtues and vices.[9] Aristotle draws a helpful distinction between two kinds of goodness: the temperate person and the continent person. Let me illustrate this first in terms of food (one of my favorite subjects), and then apply this distinction to academic integrity issues.

A temperate person is one who not only does the good, but also desires it for its own sake. I know people, although I do not count myself as a member of this group, who not only eat foods that are good for them, but do so because they *like* those foods. These are *temperate* people in regard to food. They have, in Aristotle's phrase, rightly-ordered desires. Others, and on my good days I count myself a member of this group, eat foods that are good for them, but they do not enjoy doing so. They do it because they know they should, but it is not enjoyable for them. These are *continent* people, individuals who do the right thing even though on some level they do not *desire* the right thing.

Individuals who fail to do good may also be divided into two groups, although this has been a much more contentious issue in moral theory. On the one hand, we have those who want to do the right thing but are weak and thus fall to temptation. How one explains weakness of will (*akrasia* was Aristotle's term) is a matter of dispute, but we all recognize the phenomenon. On the other hand, there are those who seem consciously to choose the bad or the evil. (There is a debate about whether one can really know the good and not choose it, but we do not need to settle that debate here.) Unfortunately, we probably all recognize this phenomenon as well.

We can apply this set of distinctions [to the] ... McCabe research. The [20] third group of students, those who habitually cheat, belong in this final category, those who choose the bad. The first group, those who never cheat, are in all likelihood temperate individuals who are honest because they find that rewarding in itself; they desire the good. The middle group, the one for whom we are battling, is the group of individuals who are either continent or else weak-willed. It is this group that we must support and educate in the virtues of the academic life.

Part Two: The Fundamental Virtues
of Academic Integrity

In 1998, at the request of my dean, I became involved in revising the document that eventually was named "The Fundamental Values of Academic Integrity,"[10] and which is now available from the Center for Academic Integrity, which is affiliated with the Kenan Institute for Ethics at Duke University. The process of working with faculty and administrators on this issue was an enlightening one in several ways, and I gradually came to have a much richer notion of academic integrity than I originally had.

A Minimalist Concept of Academic Integrity. Before I became involved in the Fundamental Values Project, I had what one might call a minimalist conception of academic integrity: don't cheat and don't copy. It was simple, and easy for everyone to remember.

A Rich Concept of Academic Integrity. As I began working with the Fundamental Values Project, I encountered a different, far richer concept of academic integrity. Basically, the question that the original authors of this document asked was this: what values are necessary to a flourishing academic life? Their answer was that there were five such fundamental values:

- honesty
- trust
- fairness
- respect
- responsibility

Taken together, these five values comprise what I would call the rich definition of academic integrity.

From Values to Virtues. The Fundamental Values Project framed the issue of academic integrity in terms of values, but I would like to recast it in a more Aristotelian light by considering these values as the fundamental *virtues* of academic life.

Aristotle on the Virtues. Aristotle's virtues approach is particularly helpful here because of its strong focus on the importance of flourishing. Aristotle's general question about the virtues was straightforward: what are the strengths of character necessary to human flourishing? The focus is a positive one, since for Aristotle the payoff of the virtues, to put the matter more crudely than Aristotle did, is that the individual's life is better because of them. So, too, about the vices: they are weakness of character which diminish our lives. Vices are not only objectionable because they harm other people, but our vices are also harmful to ourselves. Our lives are diminished because of our vices.

Aristotle also sees the ways in which specific virtues are responses to particular challenges in life. Courage, for example, is the strength of character that we need to face danger and the possibility of death. Similarly, we can ask the question: what strengths of character do we need to flourish in the academic life, both as students and as professors? The virtues of honesty, trust, fairness, respect, and responsibility, when taken together, provide the foundation of a flourishing academic life. Let me comment on each of these virtues.

Honesty.   Honesty is the bedrock virtue on which the academic life rests. Consider research in the sciences. If researchers are not honest in reporting their findings, there is little chance that science can make any progress. Either scientists will be forced to reinvent the wheel every time they design an experiment or else they will find themselves relying on data that proves to be inaccurate. To be sure, sometimes mistakes happen; no one is infallible. Being honest is not equivalent to being right. However, as long as researchers report their results accurately and honestly, we can assume that in most cases the results are at least as accurate as they can make them.

Honesty is a strength of character, and it does not begin just with honesty toward others. It is also honesty with oneself. Whether scientist or philosopher, whether student or professor, in order to have a flourishing intellectual life, each of us must be rigorously honest with ourselves, always trying to insure that we see in our work what is actually there, not what we either hope or fear to see. Such honesty is akin to a spiritual discipline, requiring precisely the kind of strength of character that Aristotle describes as "virtue."

Of course, we have to be honest with students as well as with ourselves. We have to exhibit honesty to them by telling the truth, even when the truth contradicts our own cherished beliefs. The professor who is an ideologue falls short of this ideal, and is likely to be surrounded by people who are either true believers or vociferous atheists. Professors who hold themselves to a standard of intellectual honesty and rigor provide a model for students and other faculty alike.

We as teachers need to be honest with our students in other ways as well. 30 We need to share our mistakes as well as our insights. The college environment is all too often dominated by textbooks, which give the impression of timeless truths. Students often feel a pressure to look like they always know the answer—even if the only way they can accomplish this is by being quiet—and rarely do we value mistakes for what they can teach us. My experience is that students are often very interested in hearing about situations in which I have changed my views on an issue, and this often gives them permission to see their own intellectual journey in developmental terms.

Similarly, we need to be honest with students, faculty, and administrators in difficult areas such as evaluations and recommendations. We live in an era of inflation, including inflation of grades and recommendations. One of the ways in which professors can model the virtue of honesty for their students is to provide them with honest feedback and evaluation.

The Web is having an impact on honesty in several ways, some positive, some negative. We have already discussed the impact on plagiarism, which is the area in which its impact is most visible. However, the Web has had an influence on honesty issues in other ways as well. Let me mention two of them here.

First, some students find it easier to be honest in Web-based communications (online class forums, etc.) than they do in face-to-face classroom situations. This sounds paradoxical, since one thinks of honesty as a paradigmatically face-to-face virtue, but in fact those students who find direct communication uncomfortable sometimes flourish in online chat rooms and in other virtual venues.

Second, as we shall see in more detail in part 3 of this article, students are increasingly likely to be placed in learning situations where there is in fact no teacher as computer-based teaching becomes more common. It is precisely here where Aristotle's emphasis on the importance of virtues *for the self* becomes so important. Students engaged in computer-based learning often have no one else to be honest *to*; after all, they are responding primarily to a computer program. The incentive for being honest in these contexts must be primarily self-referential: without honesty, the student simply will not benefit from that particular educational experience. Dishonesty, in this context, harms the student first and foremost.

Trust. If honesty is the foundation of the academic life, trust is the natural result of such honesty. Just as professors may trust students, so too students must be able to trust their professors. The virtue of trust is the glue which holds the academic life together.   35

The paradigm case of trust is found in a relationship between two people, where one (A) trusts the other (B) to do or be a certain thing (x). Thus there are three elements in trust: the one who is doing the trusting, the one who is being trusted, and the trusted matter that is at stake. Typically, this trusted matter must be important and there must be an objective element of uncertainty about it. I can trust a good friend to watch out for my children if anything suddenly happened to me, but I cannot trust that friend to know that $2 + 2 = 4$. That is something that I can know on my own, and there is no element of uncertainty attached to it.

One of the most interesting implications of the Web for academic integrity issues turns on the issue of trust. As was mentioned in the beginning of this paper, antiplagiarism software can be used to automatically screen all incoming assignments and rate them for possible plagiarism. But what is the impact of doing this on the relationship of trust between student and professor, especially when all incoming papers are automatically tested for possible plagiarism? It seems that this is an indication of a lack of trust, and no different in principle from, say, urine testing for Olympic athletes. We test precisely because we do not trust.

Let me contrast two ways of responding to the possibility of Web-based plagiarism. The first way is to fight fire with more technological fire. Here the example of TurnItIn.com is most relevant. Individual instructors can purchase the services on a per-course basis, but they typically sell their services to larger groups—departments, colleges, and universities—as a package. (Since the papers that are submitted for screening are also added to the database, there is a double incentive to sign up entire departments or institutions.) If a university subscribes to this service, then individual professors can send all papers in a given course to TurnItIn.com for screening.

Let me suggest an alternative approach to Web-based plagiarism, both low tech and old-fashioned: better teaching. Typically, it is easiest to plagiarize a term paper from the Web when you simply have an assignment to turn the paper in at the end of the semester. If, on the other hand, professors meet with students to discuss topics, choose highly individualized topics, then plagiarism becomes more difficult. If professors require that, at regular intervals, students submit a topic, an initial outline, a preliminary bibliography, a short rough draft, and then the final paper, the possibility of plagiarism plummets: it is simply too much trouble to take a plagiarized paper and work back to each of the preceding steps. Moreover, if professors require that students respond to comments at each stage and incorporate that response into the next stage, then plagiarism becomes even less possible. If students present their work in class, this further reduces the odds.

Web-based plagiarism often arises in a vacuum, when students feel that 40 they are not really seen or respected. There is much to be said for resisting the tendency to respond to this by additional technological means. We are much more likely, I think, to be able to do this by trusting our students and engaging them directly in the challenges of the material we are teaching.

There is, however, a good technological fix for what sometimes appears to be "inadvertent" plagiarism, that is, cases in which people lose track of the sources for their data.[11] This is particularly easy to have happen in a drag-and-drop environment, and I am sure faculty are often plagued by this problem as well. The fix is straightforward: an option (yes, one more checkbox under Tools|Options) that would enable your word-processing program and your browser to work together, so that every time you drag and drop something from the Web into a document, the reference is automatically created with it.

There is yet another aspect to the issue of trust and the Web. One of the skills we have to teach our students is how to determine which sources of information are trustworthy. The virtue of trust has an element of *phronesis* in it, what Aristotle called practical wisdom. In the case of trust, we find that this has both cognitive and volitional elements to it, which again is characteristic of Aristotle's account of the virtues. We have to be willing to trust (that's the volitional element), and we have to know what is worth trusting (the cognitive element).

This is particularly a problem on the Web, where peer review is rare. Students are often *too* willing to trust, and lack the discrimination necessary to distinguish sources worth trusting from those that ought not to be trusted. Aristotle tells us that vices can be excesses or deficiencies. Here too much trust is a vice, making students overcredulous and gullible. In my experience, the other end of the spectrum, the overly skeptical student, is much less common. Typically, students know that they can trust articles they find in mainstream journals and in books published by major university presses, but they have much less sense about what they can trust in Web sites.

Fairness. Fairness is an intellectual virtue, akin to justice in many ways. It is certainly crucial to the academic life. For the academic life to flourish, we need to be fair to people and fair to ideas as well. This latter kind of fairness is an intellectual virtue, consisting of giving each idea its due, being open to the implications of an argument, judging claims on the basis of their merit rather than on the basis of their source, being—in Martha Nussbaum's° beautiful phrase, "finely aware and richly responsible."

Fairness in this sense is akin to what Aristotle called justice, and just as 45 justice is the fundamental virtue of the well-functioning polis, so too fairness is one of the most important virtues in the interactions of the academic community. Fairness is a virtue of interaction, of relationship regarding the way in which we assess one another and also apportion the goods and burdens of the academic life.

The impact of the Web in regard to fairness is primarily found in the way in which certain groups will typically have less access to the Web. Increasingly, professors make Web access a mandatory part of their courses, but some students simply do not have the financial resources to have their own computers and high-speed Internet access. This "digital divide" disadvantages some students and gives an unfair boost to others who have had long familiarity with the Web. But this is not just an economic issue. There is certainly a percentage of students—rich, poor, and in between—who are just not comfortable with computers and computer-mediated instruction. The fairness issue extends to them as well, for they may be students who in many other ways are quite talented.

Teachers often feel caught between the proverbial rock and a hard place in regard to this issue. Until two years ago, I made sure that everything in my course was accessible to those without computers, but I gradually found my policy changing on this. I became increasingly concerned that those who did not use computers in fact needed to be helped (and perhaps pushed) in this direction, and now my courses regularly require Web access. However, one

---

Martha Nussbaum (b. 1947): A distinguished professor of law and ethics at the University of Chicago Law School. [EDS.]

of the things that made this possible is that our university provides very good computer-lab facilities, so students without their own computers can get online for as long as they want and do so without a wait. In addition, I found myself conducting minicourses for those who were not yet comfortable with using computers, to try to reduce ways in which they might otherwise have been disadvantaged because of this requirement.

Respect.   Respect manifests itself in many different ways. One of the most important ways in the academic life that we can show respect for other people is to take their ideas seriously. Lack of respect will often undermine trust and the other fundamental values.

The impact of the Web on respect seems, at best, indirect. Respect is an interpersonal virtue, so it seems that insofar as the Web establishes contexts in which individuals are less likely to recognize one another as persons, there may be some undermining of respect, but this typically only occurs in situations of high anonymity (online groups, flaming, etc.), but in educational contexts these are exceptions.

The other context in which issues of respect arise is respect for prop- 50 erty, and here the Web has had an impact. All too often, we just fail to respect copyright restrictions and the like, even when this is not a matter of plagiarism. I will discuss this in more detail in part 4.

Responsibility.   The final fundamental value of academic integrity is responsibility. In its most basic sense here, to show responsibility means to take control of one's own educational career and to make it one's own—to say, in effect, "This is me," rather than to say, "This is a GE requirement" or "This is something my parents want me to take."

The impact of the Web in this area is less easy to discern. The relevant variable here is anonymity. Insofar as some Web-based structures increase anonymity, they may diminish responsibility. This is particularly an issue in courses that are taught without an instructor. We will discuss this issue in part 3.

Thus, the five fundamental virtues are the strengths of character necessary to a flourishing academic community. While the impact of the Web on some of them (especially respect and responsibility) is minimal, its impact on others of those virtues (honesty and trust, most notably) is much greater. Let's now turn to another area in which the Web is increasingly influential: distance education.

PART THREE: VIRTUE AT A DISTANCE

Much of the preceding discussion has been confined to the impact of the Web on academic integrity within the traditional classroom. Interesting though that may be, the most interesting changes are going to occur as the Web transforms the traditional classroom into new and challenging configurations.

WHAT THE FUTURE HOLDS

There are several ways in which the traditional classroom will be transformed 55 by the Web. These are not mutually exclusive, alternative futures but rather parallel developments, and they have important implications for academic integrity in the rich sense discussed above. Let's examine several of these.

The Hybrid Course. Increasingly, many traditional courses will be taught as a combination of the traditional face-to-face classroom and the virtual classroom. This can occur in many configurations. Consider three. First, online discussions may simply be added to the regular class meetings. However, this quickly gives rise to the question: if we are spending more and more time online together, then can't we reduce the amount of actual classroom time? This leads to the next possibilities. Second, following the model of lecture/lab in the sciences, some courses may have the main presentation of material on the Web and then schedule small-group face-to-face interactions that deal with applications of the lecture. This is particularly useful when a single professor is offering a course that meets on several campuses simultaneously. The lecture occurs online, and then grad assistants conduct the discussion on the various campuses. Third, in some cases the main presentation may actually be a live lecture, followed by online meetings that function like discussion sections.

The hybrid character of such courses will not of itself have a significant impact on academic integrity.

The "Rent-a-Course" Option. Consider the following scenario. A university is doing well. Enrollments are increasing every year and are now constrained only by the capacity of the current campus. But administrators are cautious; they know that if they begin building additional facilities, they could open themselves to long-term liabilities that would be difficult to meet if enrollments began to drop. They realize that if they add classroom space, they must make a number of other additions as well, including parking spaces, dormitory rooms, cafeteria space, etc. Yet the present moment seems to be a golden opportunity to increase enrollment and income, and they are hesitant to keep enrollments capped at previous levels.

Into this situation comes a new factor. A company, which in the past only published books, has now decided to take the next step and sell courses as well. It has formed a for-profit online university, but it markets its products in a unique way. It approaches administrators in precisely the situation described above and offers to sell them, say, five sections of Intro to World Civilization. These courses could be taken online by the university's students, listed in the regular course schedule, etc. Similarly with a range of other basic courses. The company offers to sell these courses to the university at, perhaps, $3,000 per section and a set cost per student—carefully calculated to be slightly less than the salary of a part-timer and slightly less than the tuition paid per student.[12]

To many administrators, this may seem to be the answer to their prayers. 60
Suddenly they are able to offer a sufficient number of basic courses that can
increase enrollment without adding classroom space. In fact, they can even
make a bit of money in the process. This can be a very attractive proposition to
those who are charged with guarding the financial well-being of the university.
The attraction is not greed but caution.

This development has serious implications for academic integrity for
several reasons. First, these are typically very standardized courses that in large
measure "teach themselves," that is, there is a standard set of readings and assignments that students are taken through no matter who is the actual teacher
of record. There is little room for individualized interaction or even personal
contact between the student and the instructor.

Second, such courses typically will not be integrated into the life of the
department. There is no discussion between the faculty who teach the online
courses and the regular departmental faculty. The courses meet a requirement,
but fail to be part of the undergraduate experience that universities hope to
deliver.

Third, introductory courses are often quite important in terms of recruiting majors in a particular area. Often that process involves a student identifying with a particular professor. It is not simply a matter of becoming
interested in American history, but of wanting to be like a particular professor
who is teaching that course. As we all know from our own experience in the
classroom, students start coming to office hours, asking questions about the
subject matter, and generally trying on the identity of a person who works in
this particular area. Insofar as we have online courses for meeting general education requirements, we may well lose this valuable opportunity for helping
students to gain a sense of what they want to pursue academically.

Finally, in most universities there is a well-defined process for approving
both courses and teachers. This type of online course could still be approved
for its content, but there would be little or no opportunity for departments to
screen those who would be teaching the course, whereas departments would
typically screen adjunct faculty who teach in their department. This under-
mines faculty autonomy in a very crucial area.

The Professor-less Course.[13] The next step in this process is easy to see. 65
Once someone has developed a set of assignments and activities and tests and
has also developed a way in which students' progress can be automatically assessed, it becomes possible to eliminate the instructor completely. This seems
to be a reasonable scenario in certain types of courses that aim at developing
a proficiency or skill in a given area. (I sometimes think my students could
take my introductory logic course without me: lectures are available on the
Web, assignments and tests could be automatically scored, and I could spend
my time doing something more interesting than teaching intro logic for the
fiftieth time.)

The implications of this for academic integrity are quite significant. When we recall the five values of academic integrity, we see that most of them are relational, that is, they define the optimal relationship between student and professor. What happens when the professor is removed from this equation? Consider, for example, the value of trust. Presumably students will still trust the accuracy of the material presented, but there will be no opportunity to develop a relationship of trust with a professor who might then guide one's academic progress. Trust in the *person* disappears. Similarly with respect. There is little room for respect to arise, simply because there may not be a professor to respect—or, for that matter, to manifest respect for the students.

PART FOUR: THE END OF PRIVATE PROPERTY?

Let me conclude with a brief discussion of one of the additional ways in which the Web has affected academic integrity issues, and this has to do with private property. There is something about the Web that breeds disrespect for private property, almost as though it were an irrelevant concept. Let me offer some examples.

File sharing has become popular on the Web. Napster certainly made the biggest splash in this area, but there were other, less well known but more radical competitors. The best known of these is Gnutella.[14] In many cases, and this is clearly true in regard to Gnutella, sharing is voluntary, although sometimes individuals may share material to which they have no rights.

Let me offer a personal example. On a number of occasions, I have found myself wanting to grab copies of photos off the Web without asking permission. (This is particularly true if I am doing a *PowerPoint* and need something visual for a particular slide.) If I were in a colleague's office and that colleague had a picture of Rawls on his desk, and I needed a picture of Rawls, I would never just take the picture without asking. I would ask and, if refused, would not pursue the matter. If, however, I found that same photo on my colleague's Web site, I might well grab the picture, even without asking.

What's the relevant difference here? In the case of a physical picture, my taking the picture diminishes the person to whom it belongs. On the other hand, with a virtual photo, the person who originally had the photo is not thereby deprived of his or her possession, although its value may be reduced by the production of copies. The math of copying and duplicating with virtual files is very different from what it has been in the past, for we can now make identical copies—indeed, it's unclear whether the concept of the "original" still has relevance here—instantaneously and without taking anything away from the original.

There is another relevant difference here as well. When colleagues put pictures on their desks, they are not thereby giving implicit permission to others to take the picture if they want it. However, when something is put on the Web, many people—perhaps incorrectly—believe that the act of putting it on the Web implies that it is available for everyone for free. Certainly much ambiguity could be eliminated if items on the Web had XML tags that indicated whether they were (a) available for free viewing but not download and reuse [say a tag like this: <PermissionFreeNoDownloadNoReuse> and then <EndPermission>] or (b) available for download and reuse as well as viewing [with a tag like this: <PermissionFreeDownloadOKReuseOK> and then <EndPermission>]. Other tags could be added to indicate whether citation is necessary, if reuse is possible but requires either permission or notification, etc. Furthermore, information about the permission holder [<PermissionHolder> and <EndPermissionHolder>] could be embedded on each page or through a server-side include file. All of the tags, furthermore, could be made machine readable for the new standards of the Semantic Web.[15] At that point, the intent of the author of the Web page would be unambiguous and that intent could be communicated in a highly efficient manner.

The XML/RDF solution is a reasonable way of responding to the kind of "policy vacuum," first described by Jim Moor,[16] that is so common in computer ethics. It offers a clear and efficient way of demarcating the difference between what is merely publicly viewable and what is not only publicly viewable but also free for download and reuse.

The advantage of doing this in the realm of academic integrity is clear. It would clearly label authors' work as their own, provide an efficient mechanism for obtaining permission, and greatly reduce the size of the policy vacuum we are currently facing in regard to academic integrity and the World Wide Web.[17]

Notes

1. Aristotle, *The Politics*, Book III, Jowett translation.

2. See, for example, http://alexia.lis.uiuc.edu/~janicke/plagiary.htm

3. See, for example, http://www.plagiarism.com/, which sells plagiarism-detection software.

4. The site, http://www.plagiarism.org, still exists, but primarily points to the services offered at www.TurnItIn.com.

5. See http://rbsweb2.rutgers.edu/display.cfm?IDNumber=104; also see http://www.academicintegrity.org/cai_research.asp for a brief overview of McCabe's research.

6. See, for example, McCabe's presentation at the Tenth Annual Meeting of the Center for Academic Integrity: http://ethics.sandiego.edu/video/CAI/2000/Research/index.html.

7. See Donald L. McCabe, Linda Klebe Trevino, and Kenneth D. Butterfield, "Academic Integrity in Honor Code and Non-Honor Code Environments: A Qualitative Investigation," *Journal of Higher Education* 70, no. 2 (1999): 211 ff.; also see Donald L. McCabe and Linda Klebe Trevino, "Dishonesty in Academic Environments: The Influence of Peer Reporting Requirements," *Journal of Higher Education* 72, no. 1 (2001): 29.

8. See http://ethics.sandiego.edu/video/CAI/2001/McCabe/index_files/slide0006.html.

9. The principal source of Aristotle's account of the virtues is to be found in Aristotle's *Nichomachean Ethics*, but important additional material is to be found in the *Eudemian Ethics*, the *Politics*, and the *Rhetoric*. I have dealt in greater detail with Aristotle's ethics in chapter 9 of my *Ethics: A Pluralistic Approach to Ethical Theory*, 3rd ed. (Belmont: Wadsworth, 2002). This chapter also includes an extensive bibliographical essay.

10. A PDF copy is available at http://www.academicintegrity.org/pdf/FVProject.pdf.

11. I am indebted to Michael Lissack for this suggestion at the Faculty Institute on Academic Integrity and the World Wide Web, sponsored by the Center for Academic Integrity. For information on the workshop, see http://ethics.sandiego.edu/Resources/cai/webwork-shop/.

12. Lest this sound implausible, let me mention that I was actually present during precisely this kind of sales pitch. In that particular instance, it was unsuccessful.

13. I am particularly indebted to Jon Dorbolo for initially pointing this out during a presentation at CAP 2000.

14. See http://www.gnutella.com/.

15. On the Semantic Web, see http://www.w3.org/2001/sw/ and Tim Berners-Lee, James Hendler, Ora Lassila, "The Semantic Web," *Scientific American,* May 2001. http://www.scientificamerican.com/article.cfm?articleID=00048144-10D2-1C7084A9809EC588EF21&catID=2.

16. See James H. Moor, "What Is Computer Ethics?", online at http://www.southernct.edu/organizations/rccs/resources/teaching/teaching_mono/moor/moor_definition.1.

17. Some of these ideas were developed in a much shorter version and without the emphasis on virtues and Aristotle and without many of the policy recommendations in "Academic Integrity and the World Wide Web," *Computers and Society* 31, no. 1 (2002): 33–42 and "The Impact of the Internet on Our Moral Lives in Academia," *Ethics and Information Technology* 4, no. 1 (2002): 31–35.

WHAT DOES HE SAY?

1. In the course of this essay, Hinman draws on the ideas of the Greek philosopher Aristotle and the English political philosopher Thomas Hobbes. As you read, mark Hinman's summaries of these philosophies and write several phrases in the margins summarizing further in your own words. Without reading Aristotle and Hobbes, using only what Hinman tells us about their views, be prepared to summarize in a few sentences the thinking of each.

2. Like Donald McCabe and Linda Klebe Trevino in the essay "Honesty and Honor Codes" (p. 405), Hinman supports his claims with a variety of research and statistics. As you read, underline his main arguments, then draw a circle or square around those passages that support the arguments with data or research studies.

3. This essay is organized into parts that are separated with subheadings. In a few words, summarize the argument of each subsection and indicate how it follows from the previous section or leads into the next.

WHAT DO YOU THINK?

4. Hinman argues for a 20:60:20 split to represent those who cheat rarely, those who sometimes cheat, those who always cheat. Does this fit your experience? Do you agree that those who habitually cheat cannot be reformed or stopped?

5. Hinman alludes to Aristotle's view that virtue makes us happy and vice makes us unhappy. Do you think this is true? If it is, why do so many people cheat on exams or papers?

6. Hinman suggests that plagiarism is more common in courses that are mainly lecture based and that assign papers or give exams without opportunities for drafting, feedback, and revision. In other words (to take this to an extreme), plagiarism can be seen as the failure not of the student but of the course structure. What do you think? If courses were more personally meaningful and engaging, would cheating decline? Write an essay explaining this, drawing on your own experiences as a student.

7. One of the keys to the question of virtual ethics, Hinman says, is learning how to evaluate your sources, deciding which are credible and which are not. Take the topic of UFO sightings in your part of the country in the last year and do a Web search. Find at least five sources and print out at least one page from each site. Now, do a Web search on the sources, finding out all you can about the organizations or groups behind the Web sites. Which groups are to be trusted? Which ones are not to be trusted? On what basis do you make these judgments? What is there in the construction of the Web site itself that gives clues to its credibility? Write an essay that presents your evidence and explains your judgments.

8. Hinman makes the particular recommendation that our Web browsers automatically mark the text whenever we "drag and drop," whenever, that is, we copy a part of a Web site into our own text. Recommend or oppose this idea.

WHAT WOULD THEY SAY?

9. Write an essay listing your own version of what Hinman calls "the values necessary to a flourishing academic life." You can borrow Hinman's own list, add to it, or develop a list of your own. In your essay, draw also on the Adrienne Rich speech "Claiming an Education" (p. 608) and Parker Palmer's "The Community of Truth" (p. 627). Although you are developing a list, be sure that the essay itself is not organized as a string of unrelated ideas. Subordinate your list to a single controlling idea and organize the items on the list in climactic order, from least to most important.

10. Hinman suggests that the world of the Internet is inherently chaotic and "anarchic." Esther Dyson, in "Cyberspace: If You Don't Love It, Leave It" (p. 141), would certainly agree, though her response to this anarchy is very different from Hinman's: she likes it, she celebrates it. Write an essay explaining how Hinman and Dyson differ (quote each of their essays at least once). Also reflect on your own position. Is community impossible on the Web? If not, what technical or legal reforms would be necessary to make it possible? Should cyberspace be regulated at all?

NORA EPHRON
The Boston Photographs

*T*HIS ESSAY *complicates the question of honesty by relating it to the issue of censorship, of how explicit a writer or photographer should be. Are there pictures and stories that people shouldn't be allowed to see or hear? In this case at least, Ephron argues, no.*

Nora Ephron (b. 1941) worked as a reporter for the New York Post *before becoming a columnist and then senior editor for* Esquire. *Ephron has written screenplays and directed movies, including* Sleepless in Seattle *(1993), and continues to write essays on many subjects. "The Boston Photographs" appears in her 1978 collection,* Scribble, Scribble: Notes on the Media.

"I made all kinds of pictures because I thought it would be a good rescue shot over the ladder...never dreamed it would be anything else....I kept having to move around because of the light set. The sky was bright and they were in deep shadow. I was making pictures with a motor drive and he, the fire fighter, was reaching up and, I don't know, everything started falling. I followed the girl down taking pictures....I made three or four frames. I realized what was going on and I completely turned around, because I didn't want to see her hit."

You probably saw the photographs. In most newspapers, there were three of them. The first showed some people on a fire escape—a fireman, a woman, and a child. The fireman had a nice strong jaw and looked very brave. The woman was holding the child. Smoke was pouring from the building behind them. A rescue ladder was approaching, just a few feet away, and the fireman had one arm around the woman and one arm reaching out toward the ladder. The second picture showed the fire escape slipping off the building. The child had fallen on the escape and seemed about to slide off the edge. The woman was grasping desperately at the legs of the fireman, who had managed to grab the ladder. The third picture showed the woman and child in midair, falling to the ground. Their arms and legs were outstretched, horribly distended. A potted plant was falling too. The caption said that the woman, Diana Bryant, nineteen, died in the fall. The child landed on the woman's body and lived.

The pictures were taken by Stanley Forman, thirty, of the *Boston Herald American*. He used a motor-driven Nikon F set at 1/250, f5.6-S. Because of the motor, the camera can click off three frames a second. More than four hundred newspapers in the United States alone carried the photographs: the tear sheets from overseas are still coming in. The *New York Times* ran them on the first page of its second section; a paper in south Georgia gave them nineteen columns; the *Chicago Tribune*, the *Washington Post*, and the *Washington*

433

Star filled almost half their front pages, the *Star* under a somewhat redundant headline that read: SENSATIONAL PHOTOS OF RESCUE ATTEMPT THAT FAILED.

The photographs are indeed sensational. They are pictures of death in action, of that split second when luck runs out, and it is impossible to look at them without feeling their extraordinary impact and remembering, in an almost subconscious way, the morbid fantasy of falling, falling off a building, falling to one's death. Beyond that, the pictures are classics, old-fashioned but perfect examples of photojournalism at its most spectacular. They're throwbacks, really, fire pictures, 1930s tabloid shots; at the same time they're technically superb and thoroughly modern—the sequence could not have been taken at all until the development of the motor-driven camera some sixteen years ago.

Most newspaper editors anticipate some reader reaction to photographs   5 like Forman's; even so, the response around the country was enormous, and almost all of it was negative. I have read hundreds of the letters that were printed in letters-to-the-editor sections, and they repeat the same points. "Invading the privacy of death." "Cheap sensationalism." "I thought I was reading the *National Enquirer*." "Assigning the agony of a human being in terror of imminent death to the status of a side-show act." "A tawdry way to sell newspapers." The *Seattle*

Times received sixty letters and calls; its managing editor even got a couple of them at home. A reader wrote the *Philadelphia Inquirer*: "*Jaws* and *Towering Inferno* are playing downtown; don't take business away from people who pay good money to advertise in your own paper." Another reader wrote the *Chicago Sun-Times*: "I shall try to hide my disappointment that Miss Bryant wasn't wearing a skirt when she fell to her death. You could have had some award-winning photographs of her underpants as her skirt billowed over her head, you voyeurs." Several newspaper editors wrote columns defending the pictures: Thomas Keevil of the *Costa Mesa* (California) *Daily Pilot* printed a ballot for readers to vote on whether they would have printed the pictures; Marshall L. Stone of Maine's *Bangor Daily News*, which refused to print the famous assassination picture of the Vietcong prisoner in Saigon, claimed that the Boston pictures showed the dangers of fire escapes and raised questions about slumlords. (The burning building was a five-story brick apartment house on Marlborough Street in the Back Bay section of Boston.)

For the last five years, the *Washington Post* has employed various journalists as ombudsmen, whose job is to monitor the paper on behalf of the public. The *Post*'s current ombudsman is Charles Seib, former managing editor of the *Washington Star*; the day the Boston photographs appeared, the paper received over seventy calls in protest. As Seib later wrote in a column about the pictures, it was "the largest reaction to a published item that I have experienced in eight months as the *Post*'s ombudsman. . . .

"In the *Post*'s newsroom, on the other hand, I found no doubts, no second thoughts . . . the question was not whether they should be printed but how they should be displayed. When I talked to editors . . . they used words like 'interesting' and 'riveting' and 'gripping' to describe them. The pictures told of something about life in the ghetto, they said (although the neighborhood where the tragedy occurred is not a ghetto, I am told). They dramatized the need to check on the safety of fire escapes. They dramatically conveyed something that had happened, and that is the business we're in. They were news. . . .

"Was publication of that [third] picture a bow to the same taste for the morbidly sensational that makes gold mines of disaster movies? Most papers will not print the picture of a dead body except in the most unusual circumstances. Does the fact that the final picture was taken a millisecond before the young woman died make a difference? Most papers will not print a picture of a bare female breast. Is that a more inappropriate subject for display than the picture of a human being's last agonized instant of life?" Seib offered no answers to the questions he raised, but he went on to say that although as an editor he would probably have run the pictures, as a reader he was revolted by them.

In conclusion, Seib wrote: "Any editor who decided to print those pictures without giving at least a moment's thought to what purpose they served and what their effect was likely to be on the reader should ask another question: have I become so preoccupied with manufacturing a product according

to professional traditions and standards that I have forgotten about the consumer, the reader?"

It should be clear that the phone calls and letters and Seib's own reaction 10 were occasioned by one factor alone: the death of the woman. Obviously, had she survived the fall, no one would have protested; the pictures would have had a completely different impact. Equally obviously, had the child died as well— or instead—Seib would undoubtedly have received ten times the phone calls he did. In each case, the pictures would have been exactly the same—only the captions, and thus the responses, would have been different.

But the questions Seib raises are worth discussing—though not exactly for the reasons he mentions. For it may be that the real lesson of the Boston photographs is not the danger that editors will be forgetful of reader reaction, but that they will continue to censor pictures of death precisely because of that reaction. The protests Seib fielded were really a variation on an old theme—and we saw plenty of it during the Nixon–Agnew years—the "Why doesn't the press print the good news?" argument. In this case, of course, the objections were all dressed up and cleverly disguised as righteous indignation about the privacy of death. This is a form of puritanism that is often justifiable; just as often it is merely puritanical.

Seib takes it for granted that the widespread though fairly recent newspaper policy against printing pictures of dead bodies is a sound one; I don't know that it makes any sense at all. I recognize that printing pictures of corpses raises all sorts of problems about taste and titillation and sensationalism; the fact is, however, that people die. Death happens to be one of life's main events. And it is irresponsible—and more than that, inaccurate—for newspapers to fail to show it, or to show it only when an astonishing set of photos comes in over the Associated Press wire. Most papers covering fatal automobile accidents will print pictures of mangled cars. But the significance of fatal automobile accidents is not that a great deal of steel is twisted but that people die. Why not show it? That's what accidents are about. Throughout the Vietnam War, editors were reluctant to print atrocity pictures. Why *not* print them? That's what that was about. Murder victims are almost never

photographed; they are granted their privacy. But their relatives are relentlessly pictured on their way in and out of hospitals and morgues and funerals.

I'm not advocating that newspapers print these things in order to teach their readers a lesson. The *Post* editors justified their printing of the Boston pictures with several arguments in that direction; every one of them is irrelevant. The pictures don't show anything about slum life; the incident could have happened anywhere, and it did. It is extremely unlikely that anyone who saw them rushed out and had his fire escape strengthened. And the pictures were not news—at least they were not national news. It is not news in Washington, or New York, or Los Angeles that a woman was killed in a Boston fire. The only newsworthy thing about the pictures is that they were taken. They deserve to be printed because they are great pictures, breathtaking pictures of something that happened. That they disturb readers is exactly as it should be: that's why photojournalism is often more powerful than written journalism.

WHAT DOES SHE SAY?

1. Without reading Ephron's essay itself, look at the photographs that she includes. In a short paragraph, quickly write down your first response to them.

2. Now read the essay once through. At the end, write a paragraph summarizing Ephron's main argument. Write this quickly. Don't worry about sounding fancy. Just get the essence of Ephron's main point, as clearly and directly as you can.

3. Now reread the essay and record in the margins your personal and emotional reactions to what Ephron is saying. Make at least three marginal notations at three different points in the essay. Do you find her writing repulsive? scary? fascinating? Explain. Do you find your reaction to Ephron's prose to be very different from your reaction to the photographs? Explain.

WHAT DO YOU THINK?

4. Write an essay explaining how or why you would respond differently to written descriptions of scenes in contrast to photographs of those same scenes. Use "The Boston Photographs" as your first example. Explain how Ephron's essay would have a different impact if the photographs were not included. Then go to your local newspaper. Choose either a recent and controversial photograph or a recent story without a photograph. Use this second example to help explain your main assertions about how we respond to photographs and how we respond to print descriptions.

5. Agree or disagree with Ephron's argument. Should photographs like this be made public? Why or why not? Is censorship of images ever justified? Why or why not?

6. Why do you think this essay is included in a section called "Is Honesty the Best Policy?" Explain.

WHAT WOULD THEY SAY?

7. Say that Chris Hedges, war journalist and author of "Eros and Thanatos" (p. 247), has read Ephron's "The Boston Photographs." What would he say? Write an essay in the form of a dialogue between Hedges and Ephron, with Hedges starting by making a comment on "The Boston Photographs." Write the dialogue back and forth for four pages, and make sure that at some point it addresses the question of whether or not war photographs ought to be published. Make sure each speaker quotes Ephron's essay at least once. Then on a fifth page, explain why you've written the dialogue as you have.

8. Say that Naomi Wolf ("The Beauty Myth," p. 451) has read this article. How would she agree or disagree with Ephron? Does her argument about the popular image of the American woman in any way apply to the woman pictured in these photographs or to the fact of the photographs themselves? Explain.

9. Assume that Cornel West, the author of "The Moral Obligations of Living in a Democratic Society" (p. 123), has read this essay. How would he respond? What value might he see in the publication of such images?

MALCOLM GLADWELL
Big and Bad

*I*N THIS PIECE, *Malcolm Gladwell (b. 1963) complicates the question of honesty by re-lating it to the issue of advertising and big business, demonstrating through interviews and statistics that SUVs are not safer than other vehicles. A staff writer for the* New Yorker, *where he has worked since 1996, Gladwell spent nine years as business and science writer for the* Washington Post. *He is the author of* The Tipping Point: How Little Things Can Make Big Differences *(2000). "Big and Bad" was first printed in the* New Yorker *in 2004.*

In the summer of 1996, the Ford Motor Company began building the Expedition, its new, full-sized SUV, at the Michigan Truck Plant, in the Detroit suburb of Wayne. The Expedition was essentially the F-150 pickup truck with an extra set of doors and two more rows of seats—and the fact that it was a truck was critical. Cars have to meet stringent fuel-efficiency regulations. Trucks don't. The handling and suspension and braking of cars have to be built to the demanding standards of drivers and passengers. Trucks only have to handle like, well, trucks. Cars are built with what is called unit-body construction. To be light enough to meet fuel standards and safe enough to meet safety standards, they have expensive and elaborately engineered steel skeletons, with built-in crumple zones to absorb the impact of a crash. Making a truck is a lot more rudimentary. You build a rectangular steel frame. The engine gets bolted to the front. The seats get bolted to the middle. The body gets lowered over the top. The result is heavy and rigid and not particularly safe. But it's an awfully inexpensive way to build an automobile. Ford had planned to sell the Expedition for thirty-six thousand dollars, and its best estimate was that it could build one for twenty-four thousand—which, in the automotive industry, is a terrifically high profit margin. Sales, the company predicted, weren't going to be huge. After all, how many Americans could reasonably be expected to pay a twelve-thousand-dollar premium for what was essentially a dressed-up truck? But Ford executives decided that the Expedition would be a highly profitable niche product. They were half right. The "highly profitable" part turned out to be true. Yet, almost from the moment Ford's big new SUVs rolled off the assembly line in Wayne, there was nothing "niche" about the Expedition.

Ford had intended to split the assembly line at the Michigan Truck Plant between the Expedition and the Ford F-150 pickup. But, when the first flood of orders started coming in for the Expedition, the factory was entirely given over to SUVs. The orders kept mounting. Assembly-line workers were put on sixty- and seventy-hour weeks. Another night shift was added. The plant was now running twenty-four hours a day, six days a week. Ford executives decided to build a luxury version of the Expedition, the Lincoln Navigator. They bolted a new grille on the Expedition, changed a few body panels, added some sound insulation, took a deep breath, and charged forty-five thousand dollars—and soon Navigators were flying out the door nearly as fast as Expeditions. Before long, the Michigan Truck Plant was the most profitable of Ford's fifty-three assembly plants. By the late 1990s, it had become the most profitable factory of any industry in the world. In 1998, the Michigan Truck Plant grossed eleven billion dollars, almost as much as McDonald's made that year. Profits were $3.7 billion. Some factory workers, with overtime, were making two hundred thousand dollars a year. The demand for Expeditions and Navigators was so insatiable that even when a blizzard hit the Detroit region in January of 1999—burying the city in snow, paralyzing the airport, and stranding hundreds of cars on the freeway—Ford officials got on their radios and commandeered parts bound for other factories so that the Michigan Truck Plant assembly line wouldn't slow for a moment. The factory that had begun as just another assembly plant had become the company's crown jewel.

In the history of the automotive industry, few things have been quite as unexpected as the rise of the SUV. Detroit is a town of engineers, and engineers like to believe that there is some connection between the success of a vehicle and its technical merits. But the SUV boom was like Apple's bringing back the Macintosh, dressing it up in colorful plastic, and suddenly creating a new market. It made no sense to them. Consumers said they liked four-wheel drive. But the overwhelming majority of consumers don't need four-wheel drive. SUV buyers said they liked the elevated driving position. But when, in focus groups, industry marketers probed further, they heard things that left them rolling their eyes. As Keith Bradsher writes in *High and Mighty*—perhaps the most important book about Detroit since Ralph Nader's *Unsafe at Any Speed*—what consumers said was "If the vehicle is up high, it's easier to see if something is hiding underneath or lurking behind it." Bradsher brilliantly captures the mixture of bafflement and contempt that many auto executives feel toward the customers who buy their SUVs. Fred J. Schaafsma, a top engineer for General Motors, says, "Sport-utility owners tend to be more like 'I wonder how people view me,' and are more willing to trade off flexibility or functionality to get that." According to Bradsher, internal industry market research concluded that SUVs tend to be bought by people who are insecure, vain, self-centered, and self-absorbed, who are frequently nervous about their marriages, and who lack confidence in their driving skills. Ford's SUV designers took their cues from seeing "fashionably dressed women wearing hiking boots or even work boots while walking through expensive malls." Toyota's top marketing executive in the United States, Bradsher writes, loves to tell the story of how at a focus group in Los Angeles "an elegant woman in the group said that she needed her full-sized Lexus LX 470 to drive up over the curb and onto lawns to park at large parties in Beverly Hills." One of Ford's senior marketing executives was even blunter: "The only time those SUVs are going to be off-road is when they miss the driveway at 3 AM."

The truth, underneath all the rationalizations, seemed to be that SUV buyers thought of big, heavy vehicles as safe: they found comfort in being surrounded by so much rubber and steel. To the engineers, of course, that didn't make any sense, either: if consumers really wanted something that was big and heavy and comforting, they ought to buy minivans, since minivans, with their unit-body construction, do much better in accidents than SUVs. (In a thirty-five-mph crash test, for instance, the driver of a Cadillac Escalade—the GM counterpart to the Lincoln Navigator—has a 16 percent chance of a life-threatening head injury, a 20 percent chance of a life-threatening chest injury, and a 35 percent chance of a leg injury. The same numbers in a Ford Windstar minivan—a vehicle engineered from the ground up, as opposed to simply being bolted onto a pickup-truck frame—are, respectively, 2 percent, 4 percent, and 1 percent.) But this desire for safety wasn't a rational calculation. It was a *feeling*. Over the past decade, a number of major automakers in America have relied on the services of a French-born cultural anthropologist, G. Clotaire Rapaille, whose speciality is getting beyond the rational—what he calls "cortex"—impressions of consumers and tapping into their deeper, "reptilian" responses. And what Rapaille concluded from countless, intensive sessions with car buyers was that when SUV buyers thought about safety they were thinking about something that reached into their deepest unconscious. "The No. 1 feeling is that everything surrounding you should be round and soft, and should give," Rapaille told me. "There should be air bags everywhere. Then there's this notion that you need to be up high. That's a contradiction, because the people who buy these SUVs know at the cortex level that if you are high there is more chance of a rollover. But at the reptilian level they think that if I am bigger and taller I'm safer. You feel secure because you are higher and dominate and look down. That you can look down is psychologically a very powerful notion. And what was the key element of safety when you were a child? It was that your mother fed you, and there was warm liquid. That's why cup holders, are absolutely crucial for safety. If there is a car that has no cup holder, it is not safe. If I can put my coffee there, if I can have my food, if everything is round, if it's soft, and if I'm high, then I feel safe. It's amazing that intelligent, educated women will look at a car and the first thing they will look at is how many cup holders it has." During the design of Chrysler's PT Cruiser, one of the things Rapaille learned was that car buyers felt unsafe when they thought that an outsider could easily see inside their vehicles. So Chrysler made the back window of the PT Cruiser smaller. Of course, making windows smaller—and thereby reducing visibility—makes driving *more* dangerous, not less so. But that's the puzzle of what has happened to the automobile world: feeling safe has become more important than actually being safe.

One day this fall, I visited the automobile-testing center of Consumers Union,   5
the organization that publishes *Consumer Reports*. It is tucked away in the
woods, in south-central Connecticut, on the site of the old Connecticut Speed-
way. The facility has two skid pads to measure cornering, a long straightaway
for braking tests, a meandering "handling" course that winds around the back
side of the track, and an accident-avoidance obstacle course made out of a row
of orange cones. It is headed by a trim, white-haired Englishman named David
Champion, who previously worked as an engineer with Land Rover and with
Nissan. On the day of my visit, Champion set aside two vehicles: a silver 2003
Chevrolet TrailBlazer—an enormous five-thousand-pound SUV—and a shiny
blue two-seater Porsche Boxster convertible.

We started with the TrailBlazer. Champion warmed up the Chevrolet
with a few quick circuits of the track, and then drove it hard through the twists
and turns of the handling course. He sat in the bucket seat with his back straight
and his arms almost fully extended, and drove with practiced grace: every
movement smooth and relaxed and unhurried. Champion, as an engineer, did
not much like the TrailBlazer. "Cheap interior, cheap plastic," he said, batting
the dashboard with his hand. "It's a little bit heavy, cumbersome. Quiet. Bit
wallowy, side to side. Doesn't feel that secure. Accelerates heavily. Once it gets
going, it's got decent power. Brakes feel a bit spongy." He turned onto the
straightaway and stopped a few hundred yards from the obstacle course.

Measuring accident avoidance is a key part of the Consumers Union evaluation. It's a simple setup. The driver has to navigate his vehicle through two
rows of cones eight feet wide and sixty feet long. Then he has to steer hard to
the left, guiding the vehicle through a gate set off to the side, and immediately
swerve hard back to the right, and enter a second sixty-foot corridor of cones
that are parallel to the first set. The idea is to see how fast you can drive through
the course without knocking over any cones. "It's like you're driving down a
road in suburbia," Champion said. "Suddenly, a kid on a bicycle veers out in
front of you. You have to do whatever it takes to avoid the kid. But there's a
tractor-trailer coming toward you in the other lane, so you've got to swing
back into your own lane as quickly as possible. That's the scenario."

Champion and I put on helmets. He accelerated toward the entrance to
the obstacle course. "We do the test without brakes or throttle, so we can just
look at handling," Champion said. "I actually take my foot right off the ped-
als." The car was now moving at forty mph. At that speed, on the smooth
tarmac of the raceway, the TrailBlazer was very quiet, and we were seated so
high that the road seemed somehow remote. Champion entered the first row
of cones. His arms tensed. He jerked the car to the left. The TrailBlazer's tires
squealed. I was thrown toward the passenger-side door as the truck's body
rolled, then thrown toward Champion as he jerked the TrailBlazer back to
the right. My tape recorder went skittering across the cabin. The whole maneuver had taken no more than a few seconds, but it felt as if we had been
sailing into a squall. Champion brought the car to a stop. We both looked

back: the TrailBlazer had hit the cone at the gate. The kid on the bicycle was probably dead. Champion shook his head. "It's very rubbery. It slides a lot. I'm not getting much communication back from the steering wheel. It feels really ponderous, clumsy. I felt a little bit of tail swing."

I drove the obstacle course next. I started at the conservative speed of thirty-five mph. I got through cleanly. I tried again, this time at thirty-eight mph, and that small increment of speed made a dramatic difference. I made the first left, avoiding the kid on the bicycle. But, when it came time to swerve back to avoid the hypothetical oncoming eighteen-wheeler, I found that I was wrestling with the car. The protests of the tires were jarring. I stopped, shaken. "It wasn't going where you wanted it to go, was it?" Champion said. "Did you feel the weight pulling you sideways? That's what the extra weight that SUVs have tends to do. It pulls you in the wrong direction." Behind us was a string of toppled cones. Getting the TrailBlazer to travel in a straight line, after that sudden diversion, hadn't been easy. "I think you took out a few pedestrians," Champion said with a faint smile.

Next up was the Boxster. The top was down. The sun was warm on 10 my forehead. The car was low to the ground; I had the sense that if I dangled my arm out the window my knuckles would scrape on the tarmac. Standing still, the Boxster didn't feel safe: I could have been sitting in a go-cart. But when I ran it through the handling course I felt that I was in perfect control. On the straightaway, I steadied the Boxster at forty-five mph, and ran it through the obstacle course. I could have balanced a teacup on my knee. At fifty mph, I navigated the left and right turns with what seemed like a twitch of the steering wheel. The tires didn't squeal. The car stayed level. I pushed the Porsche up into the midfifties. Every cone was untouched. "Walk in the park!" Champion exclaimed as we pulled to a stop.

Most of us think that SUVs are much safer than sports cars. If you asked the young parents of America whether they would rather strap their infant child in the backseat of the TrailBlazer or the passenger seat of the Boxster, they would choose the TrailBlazer. We feel that way because in the Trail-Blazer our chances of surviving a collision with a hypothetical tractor-trailer in the other lane are greater than they are in the Porsche. What we forget, though, is that in the TrailBlazer you're also much more likely to hit the tractor-trailer because you can't get out of the way in time. In the parlance of the automobile world, the TrailBlazer is better at "passive safety." The Boxster is better when it comes to "active safety," which is every bit as important.

Consider the set of safety statistics compiled by Tom Wenzel, a scientist at Lawrence Berkeley National Laboratory, in California, and Marc Ross, a physicist at the University of Michigan. The numbers are expressed in fatalities per million cars, both for drivers of particular models and for the drivers of the cars they hit. (For example, in the first case, for every million Toyota Avalons on the road, forty Avalon drivers die in car accidents every year, and twenty people die in accidents involving Toyota Avalons.) The numbers [in the table] have been rounded.

Make/Model	Type	Driver Deaths	Other Deaths	Total
Toyota Avalon	large	40	20	60
Chrysler Town & Country	minivan	31	36	67
Toyota Camry	midsize	41	29	70
Volkswagen Jetta	subcompact	47	23	70
Ford Windstar	minivan	37	35	72
Nissan Maxima	midsize	53	26	79
Honda Accord	midsize	54	27	82
Chevrolet Venture	minivan	51	34	85
Buick Century	midsize	70	23	93
Subaru Legacy/Outback	compact	74	24	98
Mazda 626	compact	70	29	99
Chevrolet Malibu	midsize	71	34	105
Chevrolet Suburban	SUV	46	59	105
Jeep Grand Cherokee	SUV	61	44	106
Honda Civic	subcompact	84	25	109
Toyota Corolla	subcompact	81	29	110
Ford Expedition	SUV	55	57	112
GMC Jimmy	SUV	76	39	114
Ford Taurus	midsize	78	39	117
Nissan Altima	compact	72	49	121
Mercury Marquis	large	80	43	123
Nissan Sentra	subcompact	95	34	129
Toyota 4Runner	SUV	94	43	137
Chevrolet Tahoe	SUV	68	74	141
Dodge Stratus	midsize	103	40	143
Lincoln Town Car	large	100	47	147
Ford Explorer	SUV	88	60	148
Pontiac Grand Am	compact	118	39	157
Toyota Tacoma	pickup	111	59	171
Chevrolet Cavalier	subcompact	146	41	186
Dodge Neon	subcompact	161	39	199
Pontiac Sunfire	subcompact	158	44	202
Ford F-Series	pickup	110	128	238

Are the best performers the biggest and heaviest vehicles on the road? Not at all. Among the safest cars are the midsize imports, like the Toyota Camry and the Honda Accord. Or consider the extraordinary performance of some subcompacts, like the Volkswagen Jetta. Drivers of the tiny Jetta die at a rate of just forty-seven per million, which is in the same range as drivers of the five-thousand-pound Chevrolet Suburban and almost half that of popular SUV models like the Ford Explorer or the GMC Jimmy. In a head-on crash, an Explorer or a Suburban would crush a Jetta or a Camry. But, clearly, the drivers of Camrys and Jettas are finding a way to avoid head-on crashes with Explorers and Suburbans. The benefits of being nimble—of being in an automobile that's capable of staying out of trouble—are in many cases greater than the benefits of being big.

I had another lesson in active safety at the test track when I got in the TrailBlazer with another Consumers Union engineer, and we did three emergency-stopping tests, taking the Chevrolet up to sixty mph and then slamming on the brakes. It was not a pleasant exercise. Bringing five thousand pounds of rubber and steel to a sudden stop involves lots of lurching, screeching, and protesting. The first time, the TrailBlazer took 146.2 feet to come to a halt, the second time 151.6 feet, and the third time 153.4 feet. The Boxster can come to a complete stop from sixty mph in about 124 feet. That's a difference of about two car lengths, and it isn't hard to imagine any number of scenarios where two car lengths could mean the difference between life and death.

The SUV boom represents, then, a shift in how we conceive of safety—from 15 active to passive. It's what happens when a larger number of drivers conclude, consciously or otherwise, that the extra thirty feet that the TrailBlazer takes to come to a stop don't really matter, that the tractor-trailer will hit them anyway, and that they are better off treating accidents as inevitable rather than avoidable. "The metric that people use is size," says Stephen Popiel, a vice president of Millward Brown Goldfarb, in Toronto, one of the leading automotive market-research firms. "The bigger something is, the safer it is. In the consumer's mind, the basic equation is, If I were to take this vehicle and drive it into this brick wall, the more metal there is in front of me the better off I'll be."

This is a new idea, and one largely confined to North America. In Europe and Japan, people think of a safe car as a nimble car. That's why they build cars like the Jetta and the Camry, which are designed to carry out the driver's wishes as directly and efficiently as possible. In the Jetta, the engine is clearly audible. The steering is light and precise. The brakes are crisp. The wheelbase is short enough that the car picks up the undulations of the road. The car is so small and close to the ground, and so dwarfed by other cars on the road, that an intelligent driver is constantly reminded of the necessity of driving safely and defensively. An SUV embodies the opposite logic. The driver is seated as high and far from the road as possible. The vehicle is designed to overcome its environment, not to respond to it. Even four-wheel drive, seemingly the most beneficial feature of the SUV, serves to reinforce this isolation. Having the engine provide power to all four wheels, safety experts point out, does nothing to improve braking, although many SUV owners erroneously believe this to be the case. Nor does the feature necessarily make it safer to turn across a slippery surface: that is largely a function of how much friction is generated by the vehicle's tires. All it really does is improve what engineers call tracking—that is, the ability to accelerate without slipping in perilous conditions or in deep snow or mud. Champion says that one of the occasions when he came closest to death was a snowy day, many years ago, just after he had bought a new Range Rover. "Everyone around me was slipping, and I was thinking, *Yeahhh.* And I came to a stop sign on a major road, and I was driving probably twice as fast as I should have been, because I could. I had traction. But I also weighed probably twice as much as most cars. And I still had only four brakes and four tires on the road. I slid right across a four-lane road." Four-wheel drive robs the driver of feedback. "The car driver whose wheels spin once or twice while backing out of the driveway knows that the road is slippery," Bradsher writes. "The SUV driver who navigates the driveway and street without difficulty until she tries to brake may not find out that the road is slippery until it is too late." Jettas are safe because they make their drivers feel unsafe. SUVs are unsafe because they make their drivers feel safe. That feeling of safety isn't the solution; it's the problem.

Perhaps the most troublesome aspect of SUV culture is its attitude toward risk. "Safety, for most automotive consumers, has to do with the notion that they aren't in complete control," Popiel says. "There are unexpected events that at any moment in time can come out and impact them—an oil patch up ahead, an eighteen-wheeler turning over, something falling down. People feel that the elements of the world out of their control are the ones that are going to cause them distress."

Of course, those things really aren't outside a driver's control: an alert driver, in the right kind of vehicle, can navigate the oil patch, avoid the truck, and swerve around the thing that's falling down. Traffic-fatality rates vary strongly with driver behavior. Drunks are 7.6 times more likely to die in accidents than nondrinkers. People who wear their seat belts are almost half as likely to die as those who don't buckle up. Forty-year-olds are ten times less likely to get into accidents than sixteen-year-olds. Drivers of minivans, Wenzel and Ross's statistics tell us, die at a fraction of the rate of drivers of pickup trucks. That's clearly because minivans are family cars, and parents with children in the backseat are less likely to get into accidents. Frank McKenna, a safety expert at the University of Reading, in England, has done experiments where he shows drivers a series of videotaped scenarios—a child running out the front door of his house and onto the street, for example, or a car approaching an intersection at too great a speed to stop at the red light—and asks people to press a button the minute they become aware of the potential for an accident. Experienced drivers press the button between half a second and a second faster than new drivers, which, given that car accidents are events measured in milliseconds, is a significant difference. McKenna's work shows that, with experience, we all learn how to exert some degree of control over what might otherwise appear to be uncontrollable events. Any conception of safety that revolves entirely around the vehicle, then, is incomplete. Is the Boxster safer than the TrailBlazer? It depends on who's behind the wheel. In the hands of, say, my very respectable and prudent middle-aged mother, the Boxster is by far the safer car. In my hands, it probably isn't. On the open road, my reaction to the Porsche's extraordinary road manners and the sweet, irresistible wail of its engine would be to drive much faster than I should. (At the end of my day at Consumers Union, I parked the Boxster, and immediately got into my own car to drive home. In my mind, I was still at the wheel of the Boxster. Within twenty minutes, I had a $271 speeding ticket.) The trouble with the SUV ascendancy is that it excludes the really critical component of safety: the driver.

In psychology, there is a concept called learned helplessness, which arose from a series of animal experiments in the 1960s at the University of Pennsylvania. Dogs were restrained by a harness, so that they couldn't move, and then repeatedly subjected to a series of electrical shocks. Then the same dogs were shocked again, only this time they could easily escape by jumping over a low hurdle. But most of them didn't; they just huddled in the corner, no longer believing that there was anything they could do to influence their own fate. Learned helplessness is now thought to play a role in such phenomena as depression and the failure of battered women to leave their husbands, but one could easily apply it more widely. We live in an age, after all, that is strangely fixated on the idea of helplessness: we're fascinated by hurricanes and terrorist acts and epidemics like SARS—situations in which we feel powerless to affect our own destiny. In fact, the risks posed to life and limb by forces outside our control are dwarfed by the factors we can control. Our fixation with helplessness distorts our perceptions of risk. "When you feel safe, you can be passive," Rapaille says of the fundamental appeal of the SUV. "Safe means I can sleep. I can give up control. I can relax. I can take off my shoes. I can listen to music." For years, we've all made fun of the middle-aged man who suddenly trades in his sedate family sedan for a shiny red sports car. That's called a midlife crisis. But at least it involves some degree of engagement with the act of driving. The man who gives up his sedate family sedan for an SUV is saying something far more troubling—that he finds the demands of the road to be overwhelming. Is acting out really worse than giving up?

On August 9, 2000, the Bridgestone Firestone tire company announced one of   20
the largest product recalls in American history. Because of mounting concerns about safety, the company said, it was replacing some fourteen million tires that

had been used primarily on the Ford Explorer SUV. The cost of the recall—and of a follow-up replacement program initiated by Ford a year later—ran into billions of dollars. Millions more were spent by both companies on fighting and settling lawsuits from Explorer owners, who alleged that their tires had come apart and caused their SUVs to roll over. In the fall of that year, senior executives from both companies were called to Capitol Hill, where they were publicly berated. It was the biggest scandal to hit the automobile industry in years. It was also one of the strangest. According to federal records, the number of fatalities resulting from the failure of a Firestone tire on a Ford Explorer SUV, as of September 2001, was 271. That sounds like a lot, until you remember that the total number of tires supplied by Firestone to the Explorer from the moment the SUV was introduced by Ford, in 1990, was fourteen million, and that the average life span of a tire is forty-five thousand miles. The allegation against Firestone amounts to the claim that its tires failed, with fatal results, 271 times in the course of 630 billion vehicle miles. Manufacturers usually win prizes for failure rates that low. It's also worth remembering that during that same ten-year span almost half a million Americans died in traffic accidents. In other words, during the 1990s hundreds of thousands of people were killed on the roads because they drove too fast or ran red lights or drank too much. And, of those, a fair proportion involved people in SUVs who were lulled by their four-wheel drive into driving recklessly on slick roads, who drove aggressively because they felt invulnerable, who disproportionately killed those they hit because they chose to drive trucks with inflexible steel-frame architecture, and who crashed because they couldn't bring their five-thousand-pound vehicles to a halt in time. Yet, out of all those fatalities, regulators, the legal profession, Congress, and the media chose to highlight the .0005 percent that could be linked to an alleged defect in the vehicle.

But should that come as a surprise? In the age of the SUV, this is what people worry about when they worry about safety—not risks, however commonplace, involving their own behavior but risks, however rare, involving some unexpected event. The Explorer was big and imposing. It was high above the ground. You could look down on other drivers. You could see if someone was lurking behind or beneath it. You could drive it up on someone's lawn with impunity. Didn't it seem like the safest vehicle in the world?

WHAT DOES HE SAY?

1. As you read, look for the sentence or sentences that clearly summarize Malcolm Gladwell's main point in this essay. (This passage doesn't appear right away.) Copy out at least one sentence from it.

2. It's not immediately obvious why we have included this piece in an ethics reader. It becomes clearer as the essay goes on. As you read, mark the sentence or sentences

that seem to describe what the moral or ethical problem might be in the situation that Gladwell is exploring.

3. As you read, mark the evidence or illustration or detail that seems most convincing to you.

WHAT DO YOU THINK?

4. What is the ethical problem implicit in this essay? Who or what is acting in a way that isn't right? Who is getting hurt and for what reason?

5. Go to three different large-circulation magazines and from each one photocopy an advertisement for an SUV. Then write an essay that compares and contrasts what you see in the ads with what you're reading and understanding in Gladwell's essay.

6. Write an essay in the form of three distinct sections and a conclusion. In the first section, argue that Ford Motor Company is at fault. In the second, argue that the consumer is at fault. In the third argue that no one is at fault. Conclude by explaining your own assertions and analysis.

7. Talk about your attitude about SUVs. Maybe you own one. How does your prior attitude about the subject influence your reading of this article? Did the article confirm your thinking or change your mind?

WHAT WOULD THEY SAY?

8. Read George Orwell's "Politics and the English Language" (p. 461) and apply Orwell's analysis of political language to the problem that Gladwell describes. In other words, explain what Orwell would say about Gladwell's essay.

9. Read Adrienne Rich's "Claiming an Education" (p. 608) in chapter 7, "Why Change Your Mind?", and apply her notion of education to the situation that Gladwell describes. Who in this situation needs to "claim" an education, and what would that education be about? In other words, what would Rich say about Gladwell's essay?

NAOMI WOLF
The Beauty Myth

*T*HIS PIECE TAKES THE THEME *of disparity between appearance and reality and applies it to the image our society projects about women, through advertising and propaganda, an image no truer to reality than the myth of the SUV.*

   A prominent feminist, Naomi Wolf (b. 1962) is the author of several books, including Fire with Fire *(1993),* Promiscuities *(1997), and* Misconceptions: Truth, Lies, and the Unexpected on the Journey to Motherhood *(2001). This piece is an excerpt from her 1991 book,* The Beauty Myth.

At last, after a long silence, women took to the streets. In the two decades of radical action that followed the rebirth of feminism in the early 1970s, Western women gained legal and reproductive rights, pursued higher education, entered the trades and the professions, and overturned ancient and revered beliefs about their social role. A generation on, do women feel free?

   The affluent, educated, liberated women of the first world, who can enjoy freedoms unavailable to any woman ever before, do not feel as free as they want to. And they can no longer restrict to the subconscious their sense that this lack of freedom has something to do with—with apparently frivolous issues, things that really should not matter. Many are ashamed to admit that such trivial concerns—to do with physical appearance, bodies, faces, hair, clothes— matter so much. But in spite of shame, guilt, and denial, more and more women are wondering if it isn't that they are entirely neurotic and alone but rather that something important is indeed at stake that has to do with the relationship between female liberation and female beauty.

   The more legal and material hindrances women have broken through, the more strictly and heavily and cruelly images of female beauty have come to weigh upon us. Many women sense that women's collective progress has stalled; compared with the heady momentum of earlier days, there is a dispiriting climate of confusion, division, cynicism, and above all, exhaustion. After years of much struggle and little recognition, many older women feel burned out; after years of taking its light for granted, many younger women show little interest in touching new fire to the torch.

   During the past decade, women breached the power structure; meanwhile, eating disorders rose exponentially and cosmetic surgery became the fastest-growing medical specialty. During the past five years, consumer spending doubled, pornography became the main media category, ahead of legitimate films and records combined, and thirty-three thousand American women told researchers that they would rather lose ten to fifteen pounds than achieve any other goal. More women have more money and power and scope and legal recognition than we have ever had before; but in terms of how we feel about ourselves *physically*, we may actually be worse off than our unliberated grandmothers. Recent research consistently shows that inside the majority of the West's controlled, attractive, successful working women, there is a secret "underlife" poisoning our freedom; infused with notions of beauty, it is a dark vein of self-hatred, physical obsessions, terror of aging, and dread of lost control.

It is no accident that so many potentially powerful women feel this way.   5
We are in the midst of a violent backlash against feminism that uses images of female beauty as a political weapon against women's advancement: the beauty myth. It is the modern version of a social reflex that has been in force since the Industrial Revolution. As women released themselves from the feminine mystique of domesticity, the beauty myth took over its lost ground, expanding as it waned to carry on its work of social control.

The contemporary backlash is so violent because the ideology of beauty is the last one remaining of the old feminine ideologies that still has the power to control those women whom second-wave feminism would have otherwise made relatively uncontrollable: it has grown stronger to take over the work of social coercion that myths about motherhood, domesticity, chastity, and passivity no longer can manage. It is seeking right now to undo psychologically and covertly all the good things that feminism did for women materially and overtly.

This counterforce is operating to checkmate the inheritance of feminism on every level in the lives of Western women. Feminism gave us laws against job discrimination based on gender; immediately case law evolved in Britain and the United States that institutionalized job discrimination based on women's appearances. Patriarchal religion declined; new religious dogma, using some of the mind-altering techniques of older cults and sects, arose around age and weight to functionally supplant traditional ritual. Feminists, inspired by Betty Friedan, broke the stranglehold on the women's popular press of advertisers for household products, who were promoting the feminine mystique; at once, the diet and skin care industries became the new cultural censors of women's intellectual space, and because of their pressure, the gaunt, youthful model supplanted the happy housewife as the arbiter of successful womanhood. The sexual revolution promoted the discovery of female sexuality; "beauty pornography"—which for the first time in women's history artificially links a commodified "beauty" directly and explicitly to sexuality—invaded the mainstream to undermine women's new and vulnerable sense of sexual self-worth. Reproductive rights gave Western women control over our own bodies; the weight of fashion models plummeted to 23 percent below that of ordinary women, eating disorders rose exponentially, and a mass neurosis was promoted that used food and weight to strip women of that sense of control. Women insisted on politicizing health; new technologies of invasive, potentially deadly "cosmetic" surgeries developed apace to reexert old forms of medical control of women.

Every generation since about 1830 has had to fight its version of the beauty myth. "It is very little to me," said the suffragist Lucy Stone in 1855, "to have the right to vote, to own property, etcetera, if I may not keep my body, and its uses, in my absolute right." Eighty years later, after women had won the vote, and the first wave of the organized women's movement had subsided, Virginia Woolf wrote that it would still be decades before women could tell the truth about their bodies. In 1962, Betty Friedan quoted a young woman trapped in the feminine mystique: "Lately, I look in the mirror, and I'm so afraid that I'm going to look like my mother." Eight years after that, heralding the cataclysmic second wave of feminism, Germaine Greer described "the Stereotype": "To her belongs all that is beautiful, even the very word beauty itself...she is a doll...I'm sick of the masquerade." In spite of the great revolution of the second wave, we are not exempt. Now we can look out over ruined barricades: a revolution has come upon us and changed everything in its path, enough time has passed since then for babies to have grown into women, but there still remains a final right not fully claimed.

The beauty myth tells a story: the quality called "beauty" objectively and universally exists. Women must want to embody it and men must want to possess women who embody it. This embodiment is an imperative for women and not for men, which situation is necessary and natural because it is biological, sexual, and evolutionary: strong men battle for beautiful women, and beautiful women are more reproductively successful. Women's beauty must correlate to their fertility, and since this system is based on sexual selection, it is inevitable and changeless.

None of this is true. "Beauty" is a currency system like the gold stan-   10 dard. Like any economy, it is determined by politics, and in the modern age in the West it is the last, best belief system that keeps male dominance intact. In assigning value to women in a vertical hierarchy according to a culturally imposed physical standard, it is an expression of power relations in which women must unnaturally compete for resources that men have appropriated for themselves.

"Beauty" is not universal or changeless, though the West pretends that all ideals of female beauty stem from one platonic ideal woman; the Maori° admire a fat vulva, and the Padung,° droopy breasts. Nor is "beauty" a function of evolution: its ideals change at a pace far more rapid than that of the evolution of species, and Charles Darwin was himself unconvinced by his own explanation that "beauty" resulted from a "sexual selection" that deviated from the rule of natural selection; for women to compete with women through "beauty" is a reversal of the way in which natural selection affects all

---

Maori: The indigenous people and culture of New Zealand. [All notes are the Editors'.]
Padung: A tribal people native to Northern Thailand.

other mammals. Anthropology has overturned the notion that females must be "beautiful" to be selected to mate: Evelyn Reed,° Elaine Morgan,° and others have dismissed sociobiological assertions of innate male polygamy and female monogamy. Female higher primates are the sexual initiators; not only do they seek out and enjoy sex with many partners, but "every nonpregnant female takes her turn at being the most desirable of all her troop. And that cycle keeps turning as long as she lives." The inflamed pink sexual organs of primates are often cited by male sociobiologists as analogous to human arrangements relating to female "beauty," when in fact that is a universal, nonhierarchical female primate characteristic.

Nor has the beauty myth always been this way. Though the pairing of the older rich men with young, "beautiful" women is taken to be somehow inevitable, in the matriarchal goddess religions that dominated the Mediterranean from about 25,000 B.C.E. to about 700 B.C.E., the situation was reversed: "In every culture, the Goddess has many lovers. . . . The clear pattern is of an older woman with a beautiful but expendable youth—Ishtar and Tammuz, Venus and Adonis, Cybele and Attis, Isis and Osiris . . . their only function the service of the divine 'womb.' " Nor is it something only women do and only men watch: among the Nigerian Wodaabes, the women hold economic power and the tribe is obsessed with male beauty; Wodaabe men spend hours together in elaborate makeup sessions, and compete—provocatively painted and dressed, with swaying hips and seductive expressions—in beauty contests judged by women. There is no legitimate historical or biological justification for the beauty myth; what it is doing to women today is a result of nothing more exalted than the need of today's power structure, economy, and culture to mount a counteroffensive against women.

If the beauty myth is not based on evolution, sex, gender, aesthetics, or God, on what is it based? It claims to be about intimacy and sex and life, a celebration of women. It is actually composed of emotional distance, politics, finance, and sexual repression. The beauty myth is not about women at all. It is about men's institutions and institutional power.

The qualities that a given period calls beautiful in women are merely symbols of the female behavior that that period considers desirable: *the beauty myth is always actually prescribing behavior and not appearance.* Competition between women has been made part of the myth so that women will be divided from one another. Youth and (until recently) virginity have been "beautiful" in women since they stand for experiential and sexual ignorance. Aging in women is "unbeautiful" since women grow more powerful with time, and since the links between generations of women must always be newly broken: older women fear young ones, young women fear old, and the beauty myth

---

Evelyn Reed (1905–1979): A pioneering sociologist and feminist critic.
Elaine Morgan: British science writer who has focused on theories of human origins.

truncates for all the female life span. Most urgently, women's identity must be premised upon our "beauty" so that we will remain vulnerable to outside approval, carrying the vital sensitive organ of self-esteem exposed to the air.

Though there has, of course, been a beauty myth in some form for as 15 long as there has been patriarchy, the beauty myth in its modern form is a fairly recent invention. The myth flourishes when material constraints on women are dangerously loosened. Before the Industrial Revolution, the average woman could not have had the same feelings about "beauty" that modern women do who experience the myth as continual comparison to a mass-disseminated physical ideal. Before the development of technologies of mass production—daguerreotypes, photographs, etc.—an ordinary woman was exposed to few such images outside the church. Since the family was a productive unit and women's work complemented men's, the value of women who were not aristocrats or prostitutes lay in their work skills, economic shrewdness, physical strength, and fertility. Physical attraction, obviously, played its part; but "beauty" as we understand it was not, for ordinary women, a serious issue in the marriage marketplace. The beauty myth in its modern form gained ground after the upheavals of industrialization, as the work unit of the family was destroyed, and urbanization and the emerging factory system demanded what social engineers of the time termed the "separate sphere" of domesticity, which supported the new labor category of the "breadwinner" who left home for the workplace during the day. The middle class expanded, the standards of living and of literacy rose, the size of families shrank; a new class of literate, idle women developed, on whose submission to enforced domesticity the evolving system of industrial capitalism depended. Most of our assumptions about the way women have always thought about "beauty" date from no earlier than the 1830s, when the cult of domesticity was first consolidated and the beauty index invented.

For the first time new technologies could reproduce—in fashion plates, daguerreotypes, tintypes, and rotogravures—images of how women should look. In the 1840s the first nude photographs of prostitutes were taken; advertisements using images of "beautiful" women first appeared in midcentury. Copies of classical artworks, postcards of society beauties and royal mistresses, Currier and Ives prints, and porcelain figurines flooded the separate sphere to which middle-class women were confined.

Since the Industrial Revolution, middle-class Western women have been controlled by ideals and stereotypes as much as by material constraints. This situation, unique to this group, means that analyses that trace "cultural conspiracies" are uniquely plausible in relation to them. The rise of the beauty myth was just one of several emerging social fictions that masqueraded as natural components of the feminine sphere, the better to enclose those women inside it. Other such fictions arose contemporaneously: a version of childhood that required continual maternal supervision; a concept of female biology that required middle-class women to act out the roles of hysterics and hypochondriacs;

a conviction that respectable women were sexually anesthetic; and a definition of women's work that occupied them with repetitive, time-consuming, and painstaking tasks such as needlepoint and lacemaking. All such Victorian inventions as these served a double function—that is, though they were encouraged as a means to expend female energy and intelligence in harmless ways, women often used them to express genuine creativity and passion.

But in spite of middle-class women's creativity with fashion and embroidery and child rearing, and, a century later, with the role of the suburban housewife that devolved from these social fictions, the fictions' main purpose was served: during a century and a half of unprecedented feminist agitation, they effectively counteracted middle-class women's dangerous new leisure, literacy, and relative freedom from material constraints.

Though these time- and mind-consuming fictions about women's natural role adapted themselves to resurface in the postwar feminine mystique, when the second wave of the women's movement took apart what women's magazines had portrayed as the "romance," "science," and "adventure" of home-making and suburban family life, they temporarily failed. The cloying domestic fiction of "togetherness" lost its meaning and middle-class women walked out of their front doors in masses.

So the fictions simply transformed themselves once more: since the 20 women's movement had successfully taken apart most other necessary fictions of femininity, all the work of social control once spread out over the whole network of these fictions had to be reassigned to the only strand left intact, which action consequently strengthened it a hundredfold. This reimposed onto liberated women's faces and bodies all the limitations, taboos, and punishments of the repressive laws, religious injunctions and reproductive enslavement that no longer carried sufficient force. Inexhaustible but ephemeral beauty work took over from inexhaustible but ephemeral housework. As the economy, law, religion, sexual mores, education, and culture were forcibly opened up to include women more fairly, a private reality colonized female consciousness. By using ideas about "beauty," it reconstructed an alternative female world with its own laws, economy, religion, sexuality, education, and culture, each element as repressive as any that had gone before.

Since middle-class Western women can best be weakened psychologically now that we are stronger materially, the beauty myth, as it has resurfaced in the last generation, has had to draw on more technological sophistication and reactionary fervor than ever before. The modern arsenal of the myth is a dissemination of millions of images of the current ideal; although this barrage is generally seen as a collective sexual fantasy, there is in fact little that is sexual about it. It is summoned out of political fear on the part of male-dominated institutions threatened by women's freedom, and it exploits female guilt and apprehension about our own liberation—latent fears that we might be going too far. This frantic aggregation of imagery is a collective reactionary hallucination willed into being by both men and women stunned and disoriented by the rapidity with which gender relations have been transformed: a bulwark of reassurance against the flood of change. The mass depiction of the modern woman as a "beauty" is a contradiction: where modern women are growing, moving, and expressing their individuality, as the myth has it, "beauty" is by definition inert, timeless, and generic. That this hallucination is necessary and deliberate is evident in the way "beauty" so directly contradicts women's real situation.

And the unconscious hallucination grows ever more influential and pervasive because of what is now conscious market manipulation: powerful industries—the $33-billion-a-year diet industry, the $20-billion cosmetics industry, the $300-million cosmetic surgery industry, and the $7-billion pornography industry—have arisen from the capital made out of unconscious anxieties, and are in turn able, through their influence on mass culture, to use, stimulate, and reinforce the hallucination in a rising economic spiral.

This is not a conspiracy theory; it doesn't have to be. Societies tell themselves necessary fictions in the same way that individuals and families do. Henrik Ibsen° called them "vital lies," and psychologist Daniel Goleman describes them working the same way on the social level that they do within families: "The collusion is maintained by directing attention away from the fearsome fact, or by repackaging its meaning in an acceptable format." The costs of these social blind spots, he writes, are destructive communal illusions. Possibilities for women have become so open-ended that they threaten to destabilize the institutions on which a male-dominated culture has depended, and a collective panic reaction on the part of both sexes has forced a demand for counterimages.

The resulting hallucination materializes, for women, as something all too real. No longer just an idea, it becomes three-dimensional, incorporating within itself how women live and how they do not live: it becomes the iron maiden. The original iron maiden was a medieval German instrument of torture, a body-shaped casket painted with the limbs and features of a lovely, smiling young woman. The unlucky victim was slowly enclosed inside her; the lid fell shut to immobilize the victim, who died either of starvation or, less cruelly, of the metal spikes embedded in her interior. The modern hallucination in which women are trapped or trap themselves is similarly rigid, cruel, and euphemistically painted. Contemporary culture directs attention to imagery of the iron maiden, while censoring real women's faces and bodies.

Why does the social order feel the need to defend itself by evading the 25 fact of real women, our faces and voices and bodies, and reducing the meaning of women to these formulaic and endlessly reproduced "beautiful" images? Though unconscious personal anxieties can be a powerful force in the creation of a vital lie, economic necessity practically guarantees it. An economy that depends on slavery needs to promote images of slaves that "justify" the institution of slavery. Western economics are absolutely dependent now on the continued

---

Henrik Ibsen (1828–1906): Norwegian playwright.

underpayment of women. An ideology that makes women feel "worth less" was urgently needed to counteract the way feminism had begun to make us feel worth more. This does not require a conspiracy; merely an atmosphere. The contemporary economy depends right now on the representation of women within the beauty myth. Economist John Kenneth Galbraith offers an economic explanation for "the persistence of the view of homemaking as a 'higher calling'": the concept of women as naturally trapped within the feminine mystique, he feels, "has been forced on us by popular sociology, by magazines, and by fiction to disguise the fact that woman in her role of consumer has been essential to the development of our industrial society....Behavior that is essential for economic reasons is transformed into a social virtue." As soon as a woman's primary social value could no longer be defined as the attainment of virtuous domesticity, the beauty myth redefined it as the attainment of virtuous beauty. It did so to substitute both a new consumer imperative and a new justification for economic unfairness in the workplace where the old ones had lost their hold over newly liberated women.

Another hallucination arose to accompany that of the iron maiden: the caricature of the ugly feminist was resurrected to dog the steps of the women's movement. The caricature is unoriginal; it was coined to ridicule the feminists of the nineteenth century. Lucy Stone herself, whom supporters saw as "a prototype of womanly grace...fresh and fair as the morning," was derided by detractors with "the usual report" about Victorian feminists: "a big masculine woman, wearing boots, smoking a cigar, swearing like a trooper." As Betty Friedan put it presciently in 1960, even before the savage revamping of that old caricature: "The unpleasant image of feminists today resembles less the feminists themselves than the image fostered by the interests who so bitterly opposed the vote for women in state after state." Thirty years on, her conclusion is more true than ever: that resurrected caricature, which sought to punish women for their public acts by going after their private sense of self, became the paradigm for new limits placed on aspiring women everywhere. After the success of the women's movement's second wave, the beauty myth was perfected to checkmate power at every level in individual women's lives. The modern neuroses of life in the female body spread to woman after woman at epidemic rates. The myth is undermining—slowly, imperceptibly, without our being aware of the real forces of erosion—the ground women have gained through long, hard, honorable struggle.

The beauty myth of the present is more insidious than any mystique of femininity yet: a century ago, Nora slammed the door of the doll's house; a generation ago, women turned their backs on the consumer heaven of the isolated multiappliance home; but where women are trapped today, there is no door to slam. The contemporary ravages of the beauty backlash are destroying women physically and depleting us psychologically. If we are to free ourselves from the dead weight that has once again been made out of femaleness, it is not ballots or lobbyists or placards that women will need first; it is a new way to see.

WHAT DOES SHE SAY?

1. Wolf works at a high level of abstraction in this essay, using a number of powerful phrases to advance her argument: for example, "the ideology of beauty," "beauty pornography," and "the beauty story." Mark these three particular phrases in the text and write a short note in the margins trying to define what they mean. If you can't define what they mean, ask a question about them in the margins. Mark three more phrases and write similar notes in the margins.

2. Because this essay tends toward abstraction, Wolf's details—her use of examples and statistics—are very important. As you read, mark three places in the text where she uses such particulars.

3. Would you describe the tone of this essay as sad? angry? loud? soft? What image of the writer do the words imply?

WHAT DO YOU THINK?

4. Wolf suggests that beneath the surface of the modern, successful woman there is "a dark vein of self-hatred, physical obsessions, terror of aging, and dread of lost control." Do you agree or disagree? Does this apply to most women you know? If you are a woman, does it apply to you? Write a personal essay that uses your experience or experience you have witnessed in order to discuss these questions.

5. "[T]he diet and skin care industries became the new cultural censors of women's intellectual space." What does Wolf mean by this statement? What does she mean by the phrase "intellectual space"? How do the diet and skin care industries "censor" such a space?

6. What is the role of technology, according to Wolf, in the creation of the "beauty myth"?

7. Wolf says that the "beauty myth" is not based on "evolution, sex, gender, aesthetics, or God." What does she think it is based on? Why does she think that the beauty myth has been created and maintained? Who is behind it? Who benefits, and how?

8. Collect at least three so-called women's magazines that you can find at the checkout counter of your local grocery store (your library might also carry similar magazines). Find three advertisements that relate to what you've read in "The Beauty Myth." Make photocopies of these ads, and write an essay explaining why you selected those ads and how they connect to Wolf's essay.

WHAT WOULD THEY SAY?

9. Write an essay that explores the common underlying assumptions in Malcolm Gladwell's "Big and Bad" (p. 440), George Orwell's "Politics and the English Language" (p. 461), and Wolf's "The Beauty Myth."

10. Write an essay that explores the common underlying assumptions in Wolf's "The Beauty Myth" and Ruth Benedict's "The Case for Moral Relativism" (p. 619), in chapter 7, "Why Change Your Mind?"

11. Write an essay applying Wolf's analysis to any two essays in chapter 4, "Are We Our Bodies?"

GEORGE ORWELL
Politics and the English Language

*I*N THIS CLASSIC ESSAY, *George Orwell (1903–1950) raises the question of language and political intent. Without pointing to a particular politician or scandal, this essay encourages readers to apply the complicating lessons of the previous readings to the public policies being debated all around them.*

A writer of essays, satires, novels, and articles, Orwell was well known for the political positions he laid out in his works. Despite suffering from tuberculosis, he wrote ten books and more than seven hundred articles and reviews. His best-known novels are Animal Farm *(1945) and* 1984 *(1949). "Politics and the English Language" is taken from* Shooting an Elephant and Other Essays *(1950).*

Most people who bother with the matter at all would admit that the English language is in a bad way, but it is generally assumed that we cannot by conscious action do anything about it. Our civilization is decadent and our language—so the argument runs—must inevitably share in the general collapse. It follows that any struggle against the abuse of language is a sentimental archaism, like preferring candles to electric light or hansom cabs to aeroplanes. Underneath this lies the half-conscious belief that language is a natural growth and not an instrument which we shape for our own purposes.

Now, it is clear that the decline of a language must ultimately have political and economic causes: it is not due simply to the bad influence of this or that individual writer. But an effect can become a cause, reinforcing the original cause and producing the same effect in an intensified form, and so on indefinitely. A man may take to drink because he feels himself to be a failure, and then fail all the more completely because he drinks. It is rather the same thing that is happening to the English language. It becomes ugly and inaccurate because our thoughts are foolish, but the slovenliness of our language makes it easier for us to have foolish thoughts. The point is that the process is reversible. Modern English, especially written English, is full of bad habits which spread by imitation and which can be avoided if one is willing to take the necessary trouble. If one gets rid of these habits one can think more clearly, and to think clearly is a necessary first step toward political regeneration: so that the fight against bad English is not frivolous and is not the exclusive concern of professional writers. I will come back to this presently, and I hope that by that time the meaning of what I have said here will have become clearer. Meanwhile, here are five specimens of the English language as it is now habitually written.

These five passages have not been picked out because they are especially bad—I could have quoted far worse if I had chosen—but because they illustrate various of the mental vices from which we now suffer. They are a little below the average, but are fairly representative samples. I number them so that I can refer back to them when necessary:

(1) I am not, indeed, sure whether it is not true to say that the Milton who once seemed not unlike a seventeenth-century Shelley had not become, out of an experience ever more bitter in each year, more alien [*sic*] to the founder of that Jesuit sect which nothing could induce him to tolerate.

—PROFESSOR HAROLD LASKI
(Essay in *Freedom of Expression*)

(2) Above all, we cannot play ducks and drakes with a native battery of idioms which prescribes such egregious collocations of vocables as the basic *put up with* for *tolerate* or *put at a loss* for *bewilder*.

—PROFESSOR LANCELOT HOGBEN (*Interglossa*)

(3) On the one side we have the free personality: by definition it is not neurotic, for it has neither conflict nor dream. Its desires, such as they are, are transparent, for they are just what institutional approval keeps in the forefront of consciousness; another institutional pattern would alter their number and intensity; there is little in them that is natural, irreducible, or culturally dangerous. But *on the other side*, the social bond itself is nothing but the mutual reflection of these self-secure integrities. Recall the definition of love. Is not this the very picture of a small academic? Where is there a place in this hall of mirrors for either personality or fraternity?

Essay on psychology in *Politics* (New York)

(4) All the "best people" from the gentlemen's clubs, and all the frantic fascist captains, united in common hatred of Socialism and bestial horror of the rising tide of the mass revolutionary movement, have turned to acts of provocation, to foul incendiarism, to medieval legends of poisoned wells, to legalize their own destruction of proletarian organizations, and rouse the agitated petty-bourgeoisie to chauvinistic fervor on behalf of the fight against the revolutionary way out of the crisis.

Communist pamphlet

(5) If a new spirit *is* to be infused into this old country, there is one thorny and contentious reform which must be tackled, and that is the humanization and galvanization of the BBC. Timidity here will bespeak canker and atrophy of the soul. The heart of Britain may be sound and of strong beat, for instance, but the British lion's roar at present is like that of Bottom in Shakespeare's *Midsummer Night's Dream*—as gentle as any sucking dove. A virile new Britain cannot continue indefinitely to be traduced in the eyes, or rather ears, of the

world by the effete languors of Langham Place, brazenly masquerading as "standard English." When the Voice of Britain is heard at nine o'clock, better far and infinitely less ludicrous to hear aitches honestly dropped than the present priggish, inflated, inhibited, school-ma'amish arch braying of blameless bashful mewing maidens!

Letter in *Tribune*

Each of these passages has faults of its own, but, quite apart from avoidable ugliness, two qualities are common to all of them. The first is staleness of imagery; the other is lack of precision. The writer either has a meaning and cannot express it, or he inadvertently says something else, or he is almost indifferent as to whether his words mean anything or not. This mixture of vagueness and sheer incompetence is the most marked characteristic of modern English prose, and especially of any kind of political writing. As soon as certain topics are raised, the concrete melts into the abstract and no one seems able to think of turns of speech that are not hackneyed: prose consists less and less of *words* chosen for the sake of their meaning, and more and more of *phrases* tacked together like the sections of a prefabricated henhouse. I list below, with notes and examples, various of the tricks by means of which the work of prose construction is habitually dodged:

Dying metaphors. A newly invented metaphor assists thought by evoking a visual image, while on the other hand a metaphor which is technically "dead" (e.g., *iron resolution*) has in effect reverted to being an ordinary word and can generally be used without loss of vividness. But in between these two classes there is a huge dump of worn-out metaphors which have lost all evocative power and are merely used because they save people the trouble of inventing phrases for themselves. Examples are: *Ring the changes on, take up the cudgels for, toe the line, ride roughshod over, stand shoulder to shoulder with, play into the hands of, no ax to grind, grist to the mill, fishing in troubled waters, on the order of the day, Achilles' heel, swan song, hotbed.* Many of these are used without knowledge of their meaning (what is a "rift," for instance?), and incompatible metaphors are frequently mixed, a sure sign that the writer is not interested in what he is saying. Some metaphors now current have been twisted out of their original meaning without those who use them ever being aware of the fact. For example, *toe the line* is sometimes written *tow the line.* Another example is *the hammer and the anvil*, now always used with the implication that the anvil gets the worst of it. In real life it is always the anvil that breaks the hammer, never the other way about: a writer who stopped to think what he was saying would be aware of this, and would avoid perverting the original phrase.

Operators or *verbal false limbs.* These save the trouble of picking out appropriate verbs and nouns, and at the same time pad each sentence with extra syllables which give it an appearance of symmetry. Characteristic phrases are *render inoperative, militate against, make contact with, be subjected to, give rise to, give*

5

grounds for, have the effect of, play a leading part (role) in, make itself felt, take effect, exhibit a tendency to, serve the purpose of, etc., etc. The keynote is the elimination of simple verbs. Instead of being a single word, such as *break, stop, spoil, mend, kill,* a verb becomes a *phrase,* made up of a noun or adjective tacked on to some general-purpose verb such as *prove, serve, form, play, render.* In addition, the passive voice is wherever possible used in preference to the active, and noun constructions are used instead of gerunds (*by examination of* instead of *by examining*). The range of verbs is further cut down by means of the *-ize* and *de-* formations, and the banal statements are given an appearance of profundity by means of the *not un-* formation. Simple conjunctions and prepositions are replaced by such phrases as *with respect to, having regard to, the fact that, by dint of, in view of, in the interests of, on the hypothesis that*; and the ends of sentences are saved from anticlimax by such resounding commonplaces as *greatly to be desired, cannot be left out of account, a development to be expected in the near future, deserving of serious consideration, brought to a satisfactory conclusion,* and so on and so forth.

Pretentious diction. Words like *phenomenon, element, individual* (as noun), *objective, categorical, effective, virtual, basic, primary, promote, constitute, exhibit, exploit, utilize, eliminate, liquidate,* are used to dress up simple statements and give an air of scientific impartiality to biased judgments. Adjectives like *epoch-making, epic, historic, unforgettable, triumphant, age-old, inevitable, inexorable, veritable,* are used to dignify the sordid process of international politics, while writing that aims at glorifying war usually takes on an archaic color, its characteristic words being: *realm, throne, chariot, mailed fist, trident, sword, shield, buckler, banner, jackboot, clarion.* Foreign words and expressions such as *cul de sac, ancien régime, deus ex machina, mutatis mutandis, status quo, gleichschaltung, weltanschauung,* are used to give an air of culture and elegance. Except for the useful abbreviations *i.e., e.g.,* and *etc.,* there is no real need for any of the hundreds of foreign phrases now current in English. Bad writers, and especially scientific, political, and sociological writers, are nearly always haunted by the notion that Latin or Greek words are grander than Saxon ones, and unnecessary words like *expedite, ameliorate, predict, extraneous, deracinated, clandestine, subaqueous,* and hundreds of others constantly gain ground from their Anglo-Saxon opposite numbers.[1] The jargon peculiar to Marxist writing (*hyena, hangman, cannibal, petty bourgeois, these gentry, lackey, flunkey, mad dog, White Guard,* etc.) consists largely of words and phrases translated from Russian, German, or French; but the normal way of coining a new word is to use a Latin or Greek root with the appropriate affix and, where

---

[1]An interesting illustration of this is the way in which the English flower names which were in use till very recently are being ousted by Greek ones, *snapdragon* becoming *antirrhinum, forget-me-not* becoming *myosotis,* etc. It is hard to see any practical reason for this change of fashion: it is probably due to an instinctive turning away from the more homely word and a vague feeling that the Greek word is scientific. [All notes are the author's.]

necessary, the *-ize* formation. It is often easier to make up words of this kind (*deregionalize, impermissible, extramarital, nonfragmentary* and so forth) than to think up the English words that will cover one's meaning. The result, in general, is an increase in slovenliness and vagueness.

Meaningless words. In certain kinds of writing, particularly in art criticism and literary criticism, it is normal to come across long passages which are almost completely lacking in meaning.[2] Words like *romantic, plastic, values, human, dead, sentimental, natural, vitality,* as used in art criticism, are strictly meaningless, in the sense that they not only do not point to any discoverable object, but are hardly ever expected to do so by the reader. When one critic writes, "The outstanding feature of Mr. X's work is its living quality," while another writes, "The immediately striking thing about Mr. X's work is its peculiar deadness," the reader accepts this as a simple difference of opinion. If words like *black* and *white* were involved, instead of the jargon words *dead* and *living,* he would see at once that language was being used in an improper way. Many political words are similarly abused. The word *Fascism* has now no meaning except insofar as it signifies "something not desirable." The words *democracy, socialism, freedom, patriotic, realistic, justice,* have each of them several different meanings which cannot be reconciled with one another. In the case of a word like *democracy,* not only is there no agreed definition, but the attempt to make one is resisted from all sides. It is almost universally felt that when we call a country democratic we are praising it: consequently the defenders of every kind of regime claim that it is a democracy, and fear that they might have to stop using the word if it were tied down to any one meaning. Words of this kind are often used in a consciously dishonest way. That is, the person who uses them has his own private definition, but allows his hearer to think he means something quite different. Statements like *Marshal Pétain was a true patriot, The Soviet press is the freest in the world, The Catholic Church is opposed to persecution,* are almost always made with intent to deceive. Other words used in variable meanings, in most cases more or less dishonestly, are: *class, totalitarian, science, progressive, reactionary, bourgeois, equality.*

Now that I have made this catalog of swindles and perversions, let me give another example of the kind of writing that they lead to. This time it must of its nature be an imaginary one. I am going to translate a passage of good English into modern English of the worst sort. Here is a well-known verse from Ecclesiastes:

---

[2]Example: "Comfort's catholicity of perception and image, strangely Whitmanesque in range, almost the exact opposite in aesthetic compulsion, continues to evoke that trembling atmospheric accumulative hinting at a cruel, an inexorably serene timelessness.... Wrey Gardiner scores by aiming at simple bull's-eyes with precision. Only they are not so simple, and through this contented sadness runs more than the surface bittersweet of resignation." (*Poetry Quarterly.*)

I returned and saw under the sun, that the race is not to the swift, nor the battle to the strong, neither yet bread to the wise, nor yet riches to men of understanding, nor yet favor to men of skill; but time and chance happeneth to them all.

Here it is in modern English: 10

Objective consideration of contemporary phenomena compels the conclusion that success or failure in competitive activities exhibits no tendency to be commensurate with innate capacity, but that a considerable element of the unpredictable must invariably be taken into account.

This is a parody, but not a very gross one. Exhibit (3), above, for instance, contains several patches of the same kind of English. It will be seen that I have not made a full translation. The beginning and ending of the sentence follow the original meaning fairly closely, but in the middle the concrete illustration—race, battle, bread—dissolve into the vague phrase "success or failure in competitive activities." This had to be so, because no modern writer of the kind I am discussing—no one capable of using phrases like "objective consideration of contemporary phenomena"—would ever tabulate his thoughts in that precise and detailed way. The whole tendency of modern prose is away from concreteness. Now analyze these two sentences a little more closely. The first contains forty-nine words but only sixty syllables, and all its words are those of everyday life. The second contains thirty-eight words of ninety syllables: eighteen of its words are from Latin roots and one from Greek. The first sentence contains six vivid images, and only one phrase ("time and chance") that could be called vague. The second contains not a single fresh, arresting phrase, and in spite of its ninety syllables it gives only a shortened version of the meaning contained in the first. Yet without a doubt it is the second kind of sentence that is gaining ground in modern English. I do not want to exaggerate. This kind of writing is not yet universal, and outcrops of simplicity will occur here and there in the worst-written page. Still, if you or I were told to write a few lines on the uncertainty of human fortunes, we should probably come much nearer to my imaginary sentence than to the one from Ecclesiastes.

As I have tried to show, modern writing at its worst does not consist in picking out words for the sake of their meaning and inventing images in order to make the meaning clearer. It consists in gumming together long strips of words which have already been set in order by someone else, and making the results presentable by sheer humbug. The attraction of this way of writing is that it is easy. It is easier—even quicker, once you have the habit—to say *In my opinion it is not an unjustifiable assumption that* than to say *I think.* If you use ready-made phrases, you not only don't have to hunt about for words; you also don't have to bother with the rhythms of your sentences, since these phrases are generally so arranged as to be more or less euphonious. When you are composing in a hurry—when you are dictating to a stenographer, for instance, or making a public speech—it is natural to fall into a pretentious,

Latinized style. Tags like *a consideration which we should do well to bear in mind* or *a conclusion to which all of us would readily assent* will save many a sentence from coming down with a bump. By using stale metaphors, similes, and idioms, you save much mental effort, at the cost of leaving your meaning vague, not only for your reader but for yourself. This is the significance of mixed metaphors. The sole aim of a metaphor is to call up a visual image. When these images clash—as in *The Fascist octopus has sung its swan song, the jackboot is thrown into the melting pot*—it can be taken as certain that the writer is not seeing a mental image of the objects he is naming; in other words he is not really thinking. Look again at the examples I gave at the beginning of this essay. Professor Laski (1) uses five negatives in fifty-three words. One of these is superfluous, making nonsense of the whole passage, and in addition there is the slip—*alien* for akin—making further nonsense, and several avoidable pieces of clumsiness which increase the general vagueness. Professor Hogben (2) plays ducks and drakes with a battery which is able to write prescriptions, and, while disapproving of the everyday phrase *put up with*, is unwilling to look *egregious* up in the dictionary and see what it means; (3), if one takes an uncharitable attitude towards it, is simply meaningless: probably one could work out its intended meaning by reading the whole of the article in which it occurs. In (4), the writer knows more or less what he wants to say, but an accumulation of stale phrases chokes him like tea leaves blocking a sink. In (5), words and meaning have almost parted company. People who write in this manner usually have a general emotional meaning—they dislike one thing and want to express solidarity with another—but they are not interested in the detail of what they are saying. A scrupulous writer, in every sentence that he writes, will ask himself at least four questions, thus: What am I trying to say? What words will express it? What image or idiom will make it clearer? Is this image fresh enough to have an effect? And he will probably ask himself two more: Could I put it more shortly? Have I said anything that is avoidably ugly? But you are not obliged to go to all this trouble. You can shirk it by simply throwing your mind open and letting the ready-made phrases come crowding in. They will construct your sentences for you—even think your thoughts for you, to a certain extent—and at need they will perform the important service of partially concealing your meaning even from yourself. It is at this point that the special connection between politics and the debasement of language becomes clear.

In our time it is broadly true that political writing is bad writing. Where it is not true, it will generally be found that the writer is some kind of rebel, expressing his private opinions and not a "party line." Orthodoxy, of whatever color, seems to demand a lifeless, imitative style. The political dialects to be found in pamphlets, leading articles, manifestos, white papers and the speeches of undersecretaries do, of course, vary from party to party, but they are all alike in that one almost never finds in them a fresh, vivid, homemade turn of speech. When one watches some tired hack on the platform mechanically repeating the familiar phrases—*bestial atrocities, iron heel, bloodstained tyranny, free peoples of the world, stand shoulder to shoulder*—one often has a curious feeling that one is not watching a live human being but some kind of dummy: a feeling which suddenly becomes stronger at moments when the light catches the speaker's spectacles and turns them into blank discs which seem to have no eyes behind them. And this is not altogether fanciful. A speaker who uses that kind of phraseology has gone some distance towards turning himself into a machine. The appropriate noises are coming out of his larynx, but his brain is not involved as it would be if he were choosing his words for himself. If the speech he is making is one that he is accustomed to make over and over again, he may be almost unconscious of what he is saying, as one is when one utters the responses in church. And this reduced state of consciousness, if not indispensable, is at any rate favorable to political conformity.

In our time, political speech and writing are largely the defense of the indefensible. Things like the continuance of British rule in India, the Russian purges and deportations, the dropping of the atom bombs on Japan, can indeed be defended, but only by arguments which are too brutal for most people to face, and which do not square with the professed aims of political parties. Thus political language has to consist largely of euphemism, question begging and sheer cloudy vagueness. Defenseless villages are bombarded from the air, the inhabitants driven out into the countryside, the cattle machine-gunned, the huts set on fire with incendiary bullets: this is called *pacification*. Millions of peasants are robbed of their farms and sent trudging along the roads with no more than they can carry: this is called *transfer of population* or *rectification of frontiers*. People are imprisoned for years without trial, or shot in the back of the neck or sent to die of scurvy in Arctic lumber camps: this is called *elimination of unreliable elements*. Such phraseology is needed if one wants to name things without calling up mental pictures of them. Consider for instance some comfortable English professor defending Russian totalitarianism. He cannot say outright, "I believe in killing off your opponents when you can get good results by doing so." Probably, therefore, he will say something like this:

"While freely conceding that the Soviet regime exhibits certain features   15
which the humanitarian may be inclined to deplore, we must, I think, agree that a certain curtailment of the right to political opposition is an unavoidable concomitant of transitional periods, and that the rigors which the Russian people have been called upon to undergo have been amply justified in the sphere of concrete achievement."

The inflated style is itself a kind of euphemism. A mass of Latin words falls upon the facts like soft snow, blurring the outlines and covering up all the details. The great enemy of clear language is insincerity. When there is a gap between one's real and one's declared aims, one turns as it were instinctively to long words and exhausted idioms, like a cuttlefish squirting out ink. In our age there is no such thing as "keeping out of politics." All issues are political issues, and politics itself is a mass of lies, evasions, folly, hatred, and schizophrenia. When the general atmosphere is bad, language must suffer. I should expect to find—this is a guess which I have not sufficient knowledge to verify—that the German, Russian, and Italian languages have all deteriorated in the last ten or fifteen years, as a result of dictatorship.

But if thought corrupts language, language can also corrupt thought. A bad usage can spread by tradition and imitation, even among people who should and do know better. The debased language that I have been discussing is in some ways very convenient. Phrases like *a not unjustifiable assumption, leaves much to be desired, would serve no good purpose, a consideration which we should do well to bear in mind,* are a continuous temptation, a packet of aspirins always at one's elbow. Look back through this essay, and for certain you will find that I have again and again committed the very faults I am protesting against. By this morning's post I have received a pamphlet dealing with conditions in Germany. The author tells me that he "felt impelled" to write it. I open it at random, and here is almost the first sentence that I see: "[The Allies] have an opportunity not only of achieving a radical transformation of Germany's social and political structure in such a way as to avoid a nationalistic reaction in Germany itself, but at the same time of laying the foundations of a cooperative and unified Europe." You see, he "feels impelled" to write—feels, presumably, that he has something new to say—and yet his words, like cavalry horses answering the bugle, group themselves automatically into the familiar dreary pattern. This invasion of one's mind by ready-made phrases (*lay the foundations, achieve a radical transformation*) can only be prevented if one is constantly on guard against them, and every such phrase anesthetizes a portion of one's brain.

I said earlier that the decadence of our language is probably curable. Those who deny this would argue, if they produced an argument at all, that language merely reflects existing social conditions, and that we cannot influence its development by any direct tinkering with words and constructions. So far as the general tone or spirit of a language goes, this may be true, but it is not true in detail. Silly words and expressions have often disappeared, not through any evolutionary process but owing to the conscious action of a minority. Two recent examples were *explore every avenue* and *leave no stone unturned,* which were killed by the jeers of a few journalists. There is a long list of flyblown metaphors which could similarly be got rid of if enough people would interest themselves in the job; and it should also be possible to laugh the *not un-* formation out of existence,[3] to reduce the amount of Latin and Greek in the average sentence, to drive out foreign phrases and strayed scientific words, and, in general, to make pretentiousness unfashionable. But all these are minor points. The defense of the English language implies more than this, and perhaps it is best to start by saying what it does *not* imply.

---

[3]One can cure oneself of the *not un-* formation by memorizing this sentence: *A not unblack dog was chasing a not unsmall rabbit across a not ungreen field.*

To begin with it has nothing to do with archaism, with the salvaging of obsolete words and turns of speech, or with the setting up of a "standard English" which must never be departed from. On the contrary, it is especially concerned with the scrapping of every word or idiom which has outworn its usefulness. It has nothing to do with correct grammar and syntax, which are of no importance so long as one makes one's meaning clear, or with the avoidance of Americanisms, or with having what is called a "good prose style." On the other hand it is not concerned with fake simplicity and the attempt to make written English colloquial. Nor does it even imply in every case preferring the Saxon word to the Latin one, though it does imply using the fewest and shortest words that will cover one's meaning. What is above all needed is to let the meaning choose the word, and not the other way about. In prose, the worst thing one can do with words is to surrender to them. When you think of a concrete object, you think wordlessly, and then, if you want to describe the thing you have been visualizing you probably hunt about till you find the exact words that seem to fit it. When you think of something abstract you are more inclined to use words from the start, and unless you make a conscious effort to prevent it, the existing dialect will come rushing in and do the job for you, at the expense of blurring or even changing your meaning. Probably it is better to put off using words as long as possible and get one's meaning as clear as one can through pictures or sensations. Afterward one can choose—not simply *accept*—the phrases that will best cover the meaning, and then switch round and decide what impression one's words are likely to make on another person. This last effort of the mind cuts out all stale or mixed images, all prefabricated phrases, needless repetitions, and humbug and vagueness generally. But one can often be in doubt about the effect of a word or a phrase, and one needs rules that one can rely on when instinct fails. I think the following rules will cover most cases:

    (i) Never use a metaphor, simile, or other figure of speech which you are used to seeing in print.
   (ii) Never use a long word where a short one will do.
  (iii) If it is possible to cut a word out, always cut it out.
  (iv) Never use the passive where you can use the active.
   (v) Never use a foreign phrase, a scientific word, or a jargon word if you can think of an everyday English equivalent.
  (vi) Break any of these rules sooner than say anything outright barbarous.

These rules sound elementary, and so they are, but they demand a deep change of attitude in anyone who has grown used to writing in the style now fashionable. One could keep all of them and still write bad English, but one could not write the kind of stuff that I quoted in those five specimens at the beginning of this article.

    I have not here been considering the literary use of language, but 20 merely language as an instrument for expressing and not for concealing or preventing thought. Stuart Chase and others have come near to claiming that all abstract words are meaningless, and have used this as a pretext for advocating a kind of political quietism. Since you don't know what Fascism is, how can you struggle against Fascism? One need not swallow such absurdities as this, but one ought to recognize that the present political chaos is connected with the decay of language, and that one can probably bring about some improvement by starting at the verbal end. If you simplify your English, you are freed from the worst follies of orthodoxy. You cannot speak any of the necessary dialects, and when you make a stupid remark its stupidity will be obvious, even to yourself. Political language—and with variations this is true of all political parties, from conservatives to anarchists—is designed to make lies sound truthful and murder respectable, and to give an appearance of solidity to pure wind. One cannot change this all in a moment, but one can at least change one's own habits, and from time to time one can even, if one jeers loudly enough, send some worn-out and useless phrase—some *jackboot, Achilles' heel, hotbed, melting pot, acid test, veritable inferno*, or other lump of verbal refuse— into the dustbin where it belongs.

WHAT DOES HE SAY?

1. George Orwell includes a number of examples of what he considers bad English. Make a list of at least three things that he believes are wrong with all of these examples. What "bad habits" do these examples illustrate?

2. "In our time, political speech and writing are largely the defense of the indefensible." Explain what Orwell means and how it relates to the point of this essay.

3. "In prose, the worst thing one can do with words is to surrender to them." What does Orwell mean by this?

WHAT DO YOU THINK?

4. Orwell believes that there is a connection between language and thought. Explain this connection, and identify two contemporary examples to help illustrate your analysis.

5. Orwell believes that good, clear writing can make a political difference—that good writing can improve not just our political discussion but our policies and even our ways of life. Explain why and how he thinks this could be so. Do you agree?

6. "The great enemy of clear language is insincerity." Explain what Orwell means by this. Also explain why you agree or disagree.

7. At the end of this essay, Orwell lists six rules for writing well. What do you think of these rules? If you followed these rules on your next paper for a class at the university, explain how you think you would do.

8. Orwell's essay is over fifty years old, so his examples of bad writing are also over fifty years old. Update these examples. Find three examples of bad academic and

political writing in your textbooks, in the newspaper, or in your other reading, and write an essay analyzing these examples from Orwell's perspective.

9. Apply Orwell's analysis, using his understanding of language to interpret the phraseology of a contemporary politician talking about a current political situation. Somewhere in the essay, quote this statement: "In our time, political speech and writing are largely the defense of the indefensible."

WHAT WOULD THEY SAY?

10. Apply Orwell's analysis of language to any two essays in this, or any other, chapter. What would Orwell say about the authenticity and effectiveness of the language of these writers?

11. Imagine that Orwell has read Naomi Wolf's "The Beauty Myth" (p. 451). What would he say about it?

12. Imagine that Orwell has read Parker Palmer's "The Community of Truth" (p. 627). What would he say about the notion that truth is constructed by community? What would he say about the notion that final clarity is never possible because the "great things" that are the object of our study are too great to be known completely and definitively? Write an essay explaining your responses to these questions.

For Community Learning and Research

1. Investigate the honor code or the student conduct code at your university. (You can usually find it on the university's Web site.) Interview faculty members involved in the creation of the code. If they are unavailable, interview those currently entrusted with its administration. Also consult university archives for past versions of the code or other statements on academic honesty and civility. How has the issue evolved over the years? What effect has the current code had, if any? If there isn't an honor code at your university, try to determine why. As part of your research, interview one or two other faculty members. Ask them about their own experience with cheating and plagiarism and whether these behaviors are on the rise. What do these faculty members think can, or should, be done about cheating?

   On the basis of this research, write a feature article about the problem of cheating on campus for your school newspaper or alumni magazine. Be sure to quote McCabe and Klebe Trevino's "Honesty and Honor Codes" (p. 405) and Hinman's "Virtual Virtues: Reflections on Academic Integrity in the Age of the Internet" (p. 415). Or use this research to argue—in a letter to the campus newspaper or the dean—that the honor code should be modified, that students should read and follow the honor code, or that professors should take certain steps in their classes to make sure that the honor code is read and understood. Or use this research to write a speech for the people in your dormitory or living community explaining why they shouldn't cheat and what will happen if they do.

2. If you research the word *plagiarism* on the Web, Hinman says in "Virtual Virtues: Reflections on Academic Integrity in the Age of the Internet" (p. 415), you get 462,000 citations. Narrow the search. Experiment with ways of narrowing your research parameters for a Web search until you get under one hundred hits, writing down in a notebook all the moves you make. Now step back and generalize: What does this exercise tell you about the best techniques for successful Web searches? What kind of thinking is required? On the basis of this research, write a one-page handout briefly illustrating the key to good Web research, which can be distributed at your campus library or put on its Web page.

3. Return to Hinman's argument in "Virtual Virtues: Reflections on Academic Integrity in the Age of the Internet (p. 415)" that sometimes the problem of plagiarism is a reflection of the quality of a course—that students cheat more in boring or conventional lecture courses. Reflect on whether this is true in your own experience. Think in particular about a course that was designed in such a way, or that you liked so much, that you wouldn't have dreamed of cheating in it. What was it about that course that made cheating so unlikely? Then write a letter to your university president, provost, or department chair of your major, arguing that he or she needs to see the growing cheating problem in light of student dissatisfaction with certain kinds of classes (specify which kinds) and inferior educational techniques.

4. Select several examples of inauthentic, overgeneralized, and dishonest political language about any subject you care about—environmental or abortion issues, the problem of hunger, the funding for education. Look at the speeches of government officials or at government documents or at op-ed pieces by leading politicians from either party. Take each abstraction or vague pronouncement and

○   research the facts behind it. Find the real truth. Then write a pamphlet that you could distribute on the commons or over the Internet debunking each false statement in turn. Design this document so that the vague political language is on one side and a clear, straightforward "translation" of it on the other, with facts to back up each translation. In other words, research and write a document that exposes the falseness of someone's language on an important issue.

5. Interview a number of faculty members on your campus about their way of writing letters of recommendation—about the kinds of language they use to describe students, about the qualities they look for in students, about how they like to be asked for a letter, and at what point. On the basis of this research, write a brief document to be posted on the university's Web site or somehow distributed to interested students. Call it "A Student's Guide to Asking for Letters of Recommendation." In it be clear about the right way to ask a professor for a letter and about what professors are looking for in the students they recommend. The idea is to distribute this document early in a student's career so that the student can do what is necessary for a letter of recommendation to be generated that is genuine and effective. Somewhere in this document quote both Stephen L. Carter's "The Best Student Ever" (p. 391) and George Orwell's "Politics and the English Language" (p. 461).

6

What Is This Worth?

WHAT WOULD YOU DO?
MAKING A QUESTIONABLE BARGAIN

Let's suppose there's a young woman, Alice, living down the hall, and she has a new roommate, Mary. Alice notices pretty quickly that Mary likes beer. Mary's moved a minifridge into the room, and there's half a case inside it. Alice and Mary are taking two of the same classes. Alice comes to Mary and says, "Listen, since we're taking two classes together, how about if we share the books? You buy your books, I'll make sure the fridge is stocked with beer, and I can borrow your books the day before a test or before a paper is due."

What do you think of this arrangement? Would you adopt a similar arrangement with your roommate? Why or why not?

Daily life asks us to weigh various kinds of worth all the time: Is it worth it to go see that movie or not? Should I study instead? Should I take a walk and save my money? Should I work at a job with good hours even though it means tolerating a boss who tells me I'm stupid for going to college? Should I take the minimum-wage day-care job because I think I have something to offer those kids even though it means I won't have as much spending money? What's it worth to me to major in something I really like and want to engage in rather than something with a clearer path to a job? Should I worry about where my clothes are made or by whom or under what conditions? And really, are eggs from free-range chickens better than those from chickens kept in cages?

The selections in this chapter tackle questions similar to these, only harder. Cindy Schiller, in Rebecca Mead's "Eggs for Sale" (p. 499), is paying for college by inducing her body into producing multiple eggs that she's selling to an infertile couple. Is that ok? She's not so sure. Alice Walker, in "Am I Blue?" (p. 478) sees her neighbor's treatment of his horse as though the animal is just an owned thing. Should that bother her? Eric Schlosser ("What We Eat," p. 491) has deep misgivings about the fast-food industry. Barbara Ehrenreich finds that minimum-wage jobs don't pay for much of a life, as she relates in "Serving in Florida" (p. 483). And Milton Friedman argues that business is about making profits for shareholders, not making society better (p. 518). So, what is business for? What are natural resources for? What's the worth—or cost—of clean water or clean air? What right has the snowy plover or the blue crab to a healthy place to live? At issue here is what we mean by words like *worth, cost, ownership, property*, and *value*. And wondering about those meanings leads us to wonder also about *responsibility*—for what? to what? to whom?

Opening the Question

After reading and discussing several of the selections in this chapter, return to the situation above. Now what would you do? Write an essay answering this question, drawing on at least two of the selections. You don't need to have changed your mind, but you do need to demonstrate how the reading has complicated your thinking.

Do the readings make you think that the textbooks are more or less valuable than you thought they were before? Do they lead you to rethink the relative worth of the minifridge and the beer? Do they make you more or less inclined to say something to Mary and Alice, to actually get involved somehow?

ALICE WALKER
Am I Blue?

*T*HIS SECTION BEGINS *with a brief and lyrical essay about a horse and its beauty—an essay not just about animal rights but about the much larger question of what we think animals are worth, what we think nature is worth, how we see and think about the world outside of us.*

Alice Walker (b. 1944) is a well-known essay and fiction writer, whose second novel, The Color Purple *(1982), received a Pulitzer Prize and the American Book Award and was made into a popular movie. Her recent books include* The Same River Twice *(1996),* Anything We Love Can Be Saved: A Writer's Activism *(1997),* By the Light of My Father's Smile: A Novel *(1988), and* The Way Forward Is with a Broken Heart *(2000). "Am I Blue?" is from her collection* Living by the Word: Selected Writings, 1973–1987 *(1986).*

> *"Ain't these tears in these eyes tellin' you?"*°

For about three years my companion and I rented a small house in the country that stood on the edge of a large meadow that appeared to run from the end of our deck straight into the mountains. The mountains, however, were quite far away, and between us and them there was, in fact, a town. It was one of the many pleasant aspects of the house that you never really were aware of this.

It was a house of many windows, low, wide, nearly floor to ceiling in the living room, which faced the meadow, and it was from one of these that I first saw our closest neighbor, a large white horse, cropping grass, flipping its mane, and ambling about—not over the entire meadow, which stretched well out of sight of the house, but over the five or so fenced-in acres that were next to the twenty-odd that we had rented. I soon learned that the horse, whose name was Blue, belonged to a man who lived in another town, but was boarded by our neighbors next door. Occasionally, one of the children, usually a stocky teenager, but sometimes a much younger girl or boy, could be seen riding Blue. They would appear in the meadow, climb up on his back, ride furiously for ten or fifteen minutes, then get off, slap Blue on the flanks, and not be seen again for a month or more.

There were many apple trees in our yard, and one by the fence that Blue could almost reach. We were soon in the habit of feeding him apples, which he relished, especially because by the middle of summer the meadow grasses—so green and succulent since January—had dried out from lack of rain, and Blue stumbled about munching the dried stalks halfheartedly. Sometimes he would stand very still just by the apple tree, and when one of us came out he would whinny, snort loudly, or stamp the ground. This meant, of course: I want an apple.

It was quite wonderful to pick a few apples, or collect those that had fallen to the ground overnight, and patiently hold them, one by one, up to his large, toothy mouth. I remained as thrilled as a child by his flexible dark lips, huge, cubelike teeth that crunched the apples, core and all, with such finality, and his high, broad-breasted *enormity*; beside which, I felt small indeed. When I was a child, I used to ride horses, and was especially friendly with one named Nan until the day I was riding and my brother deliberately spooked her and I was thrown, head first, against the trunk of a tree. When I came to, I was in bed and my mother was bending worriedly over me; we silently agreed that perhaps horseback riding was not the safest sport for me. Since then I have walked, and prefer walking to horseback riding—but I had forgotten the depth of feeling one could see in horses' eyes.

I was therefore unprepared for the expression in Blue's. Blue was lonely.   5
Blue was horribly lonely and bored. I was not shocked that this should be the case; five acres to tramp by yourself, endlessly, even in the most beautiful of meadows—and his was—cannot provide many interesting events, and once rainy season turned to dry that was about it. No, I was shocked that I had forgotten that human animals and nonhuman animals can communicate quite well; if we are brought up around animals as children we take this for granted. By the time we are adults we no longer remember. However, the animals have not changed. They are in fact *completed* creations (at least they seem to be, so much more than we) who are not likely *to* change; it is their nature to express themselves. What else are they going to express? And they do. And, generally speaking, they are ignored.

After giving Blue the apples, I would wander back to the house, aware that he was observing me. Were more apples not forthcoming then? Was that to be his sole entertainment for the day? My partner's small son had decided he wanted to learn how to piece a quilt; we worked in silence on our respective squares as I thought...

Well, about slavery: about white children, who were raised by black people, who knew their first all-accepting love from black women, and then, when they were twelve or so, were told they must "forget" the deep levels of communication between themselves and "mammy" that they knew. Later they would be able to relate quite calmly, "My old mammy was sold to another good family." "My old mammy was _____." Fill in the blank. Many more years later a white woman would say: "I can't understand these Negroes, these blacks. What do they want? They're so different from us."

And about the Indians, considered to be "like animals" by the "settlers" (a very benign euphemism for what they actually were), who did not understand their description as a compliment.

And about the thousands of American men who marry Japanese, Korean, Filipina, and other non-English-speaking women and of how happy they report they are, "*blissfully*," until their brides learn to speak English, at which point the marriages tend to fall apart. What then did the men see, when they looked into the eyes of the women they married, before they could speak English? Apparently only their own reflections.

I thought of society's impatience with the young. "Why are they playing 10 the music so loud?" Perhaps the children have listened to much of the music of oppressed people their parents danced to before they were born, with its passionate but soft cries for acceptance and love, and they have wondered why their parents failed to hear.

I do not know how long Blue had inhabited his five beautiful, boring acres before we moved into our house; a year after we had arrived—and had also traveled to other valleys, other cities, other worlds—he was still there.

But then, in our second year at the house, something happened in Blue's life. One morning, looking out the window at the fog that lay like a ribbon over the meadow, I saw another horse, a brown one, at the other end of Blue's field. Blue appeared to be afraid of it, and for several days made no attempt to go near. We went away for a week. When we returned, Blue had decided to make friends and the two horses ambled or galloped along together, and Blue did not come nearly as often to the fence underneath the apple tree.

When he did, bringing his new friend with him, there was a different look in his eyes. A look of independence, of self-possession, of inalienable *horse*ness. His friend eventually became pregnant. For months and months there was, it seemed to me, a mutual feeling between me and the horses of justice, of peace. I fed apples to them both. The look in Blue's eyes was one of unabashed "this is *it*ness."

It did not, however, last forever. One day, after a visit to the city, I went out to give Blue some apples. He stood waiting, or so I thought, though not beneath the tree. When I shook the tree and jumped back from the shower of apples, he made no move. I carried some over to him. He managed to half-crunch one. The rest he let fall to the ground. I dreaded looking into his eyes—because I had of course noticed that Brown, his partner, had gone—but I did look. If I had been born into slavery, and my partner had been sold or killed, my eyes would have looked like that. The children next door explained that Blue's partner had been "put with him" (the same expression that old people used, I had noticed, when speaking of an ancestor during slavery who had been impregnated by her owner) so that they could mate and she conceive. Since that was accomplished, she had been taken back by her owner, who lived somewhere else.

Will she be back? I asked.   15

They didn't know.

Blue was like a crazed person. Blue *was*, to me, a crazed person. He galloped furiously, as if he were being ridden, around and around his five beautiful acres. He whinnied until he couldn't. He tore at the ground with his hooves. He butted himself against his single shade tree. He looked always and always toward the road down which his partner had gone. And then, occasionally, when he came up for apples, or I took apples to him, he looked at me. It was a look so piercing, so full of grief, a look so *human*, I almost laughed (I felt too sad to cry) to think there are people who do not know that animals suffer. People like me who have forgotten, and daily forget, all that animals try to tell us. "Everything you do to us will happen to you; we are your teachers, as you are ours. We are one lesson" is essentially it, I think. There are those who never once have even considered animals' rights: those who have been taught that animals actually want to be used and abused by us, as small children "love" to be frightened, or women "love" to be mutilated and raped.... They are the great-grandchildren of those who honestly thought, because someone taught them this: "Women can't think," and "niggers can't faint." But most disturbing of all, in Blue's large brown eyes was a new look, more painful than the look of despair: the look of disgust with human beings, with life; the look of hatred. And it was odd what the look of hatred did. It gave him, for the first time, the look of a beast. And what that meant was that he had put up a barrier within to protect himself from further violence; all the apples in the world wouldn't change that fact.

And so Blue remained, a beautiful part of our landscape, very peaceful to look at from the window, white against the grass. Once a friend came to visit and said, looking out on the soothing view: "And it *would* have to be a *white* horse; the very image of freedom." And I thought, yes, the animals are forced to become for us merely "images" of what they once so beautifully expressed. And we are used to drinking milk from containers showing "contented" cows, whose real lives we want to hear nothing about, eating eggs and drumsticks from "happy" hens, and munching hamburgers advertised by bulls of integrity who seem to command their fate.

As we talked of freedom and justice one day for all, we sat down to steaks. I am eating misery, I thought, as I took the first bite. And spit it out.

WHAT DOES SHE SAY?

1. As you're reading, pay attention to the first place that this essay mentions slavery. Somehow, the narrator's thinking about Blue and how he's treated leads to this shift. Write a paragraph about how you follow this or what confuses you about it.

2. At one point in this essay, the narrator says, "For months and months there was, it seemed to me, a mutual feeling between me and the horses of justice, of peace." Write a paragraph explaining your understanding of what the narrator means.

3. Copy out three sentences that capture the reasons for the narrator's outrage and sadness at how Blue was treated. These could be three consecutive sentences or three separate ones.

4. This essay uses comparisons to make its points. Identify two of the most important comparisons you see and write them down.

WHAT DO YOU THINK?

5. Identify the most significant moral question in this essay. Phrase it as a question. Write an essay that explains how "Am I Blue?" makes this question clear and significant (more significant than other questions it might also raise). Explain how you think "Am I Blue?" answers this moral question. End by discussing why and how you are, or are not, persuaded.

6. Write a personal essay that uses "Am I Blue?" to help clarify your sense of what human beings owe animals like Blue. Compare or contrast this with what you think human beings owe a family pet, like a dog or cat. If you're not sure of your answers here, explain why you're not sure.

7. In one sense, "Am I Blue?" is an essay about what we should not forget. Write an essay that explains how this works in "Am I Blue?" and that also draws on some element of your own life experience. This could be some experience or truth that you knew once and forgot, or it could be some experience or truth that you know now and want to be careful not to forget in the future.

WHAT WOULD THEY SAY?

8. First, read Richard Rodriguez's essay "The Achievement of Desire" (p. 597) together with "Am I Blue?" Then write a dialogue in which you assume that Rodriguez is talking to Alice Walker about "Am I Blue?" and she is answering. Both writers have both essays in front of them, so each quotes the other and sometimes themselves. As the writer of this imagined dialogue, decide what they would discuss and what each would say. The dialogue should run to roughly 1,000 words. Then write another 250 words that explain why you wrote the dialogue as you did.

9. Consider "Am I Blue?" together with Barbara Ehrenreich's "Serving in Florida" (p. 483). Then write an essay explaining to what extent, or not, human treatment of domestic animals (like horses) is similar to corporate treatment of minimum-wage workers. Make sure your own analysis quotes from Walker and Ehrenreich at least once.

BARBARA EHRENREICH
Serving in Florida

*T*HE TONE SHIFTS *from the lyrical to the wryly documentary, the focus from animal rights to economics, in this essay describing the author's experience working as a waitress in a Florida restaurant and raises the question, What are people worth?*

    Barbara Ehrenreich (b. 1941) has brought a decidedly liberal viewpoint to much of her social commentary and criticism. She has written several books of nonfiction, including Fear of Falling: The Inner Life of the Middle Class *(1989),* The Worst Years of Our Lives: Irreverent Notes on a Decade of Greed *(1990), and* Blood Rites: The Origins and History of the Passions of War *(1998). "Serving in Florida" is an excerpt from her 2001 book,* Nickel and Dimed: On (Not) Getting by in America, *a firsthand report on the working poor in the United States, which Ehrenreich researched by trying to live on income from the jobs she writes about.*

I could drift along like this, in some dreamy proletarian idyll, except for two things. One is management. If I have kept this subject to the margins so far it is because I still flinch to think that I spent all those weeks under the surveillance of men (and later women) whose job it was to monitor my behavior for signs of sloth, theft, drug abuse, or worse. Not that managers and especially "assistant managers" in low-wage settings like this are exactly the class enemy. Mostly, in the restaurant business, they are former cooks still capable of pinch-hitting in the kitchen, just as in hotels they are likely to be former clerks, and paid a salary of only about $400 a week. But everyone knows they have crossed over to the other side, which is, crudely put, corporate as opposed to human. Cooks want to prepare tasty meals, servers want to serve them graciously, but managers are there for only one reason—to make sure that money is made for some theoretical entity, the corporation, which exists far away in Chicago or New York, if a corporation can be said to have a physical existence at all. Reflecting on her career, Gail tells me ruefully that she swore, years ago, never to work for a corporation again. "They don't cut you no slack. You give and you give and they take."

    Managers can sit—for hours at a time if they want—but it's their job to see that no one else ever does, even when there's nothing to do, and this is why, for servers, slow times can be as exhausting as rushes. You start dragging out each little chore because if the manager on duty catches you in an idle moment he will give you something far nastier to do. So I wipe, I clean, I consolidate catsup bottles and recheck the cheesecake supply, even tour the tables to make sure the customer evaluation forms are all standing perkily in their places—wondering all the time how many calories I burn in these strictly theatrical exercises. In desperation, I even take the desserts out of their glass display case and freshen them up with whipped cream and bright new maraschino cherries; anything to look busy. When, on a particularly dead afternoon, Stu finds me glancing at a *USA Today* a customer has left behind, he assigns me to vacuum the entire floor with the broken vacuum cleaner, which has a handle only two feet long, and the only way to do that without incurring orthopedic damage is to proceed from spot to spot on your knees.

On my first Friday at Hearthside there is a "mandatory meeting for all restaurant employees," which I attend, eager for insight into our overall marketing strategy and the niche (your basic Ohio cuisine with a tropical twist?) we aim to inhabit. But there is no "we" at this meeting. Phillip, our top manager except for an occasional "consultant" sent out by corporate headquarters, opens it with a sneer: "The break room—it's disgusting. Butts in the ashtrays, newspapers lying around, crumbs." This windowless little room, which also houses the time clock for the entire hotel, is where we stash our bags and civilian clothes and take our half-hour meal breaks. But a break room is not a right, he tells us, it can be taken away. We should also know that the lockers in the break room and whatever is in them can be searched at any time. Then comes gossip; there has been gossip; gossip (which seems to mean employees talking among themselves) must stop. Off-duty employees are henceforth barred from eating at the restaurant, because "other servers gather around them and gossip." When Phillip has exhausted his agenda of rebukes, Joan complains about the condition of the ladies' room and I throw in my two bits about the vacuum cleaner. But I don't see any backup coming from my fellow servers, each of whom has slipped into her own personal funk; Gail, my role model, stares sorrowfully at a point six inches from her nose. The meeting ends when Andy, one of the cooks, gets up, muttering about breaking up his day off for this almighty bullshit.

Just four days later we are suddenly summoned into the kitchen at 3:30 PM, even though there are live tables on the floor. We all—about ten of us—stand around Phillip, who announces grimly that there has been a report of some "drug activity" on the night shift and that, as a result, we are now to be a "drug-free" workplace, meaning that all new hires will be tested and possibly also current employees on a random basis. I am glad that this part of the kitchen is so dark because I find myself blushing as hard as if I had been caught toking up in the ladies' room myself: I haven't been treated this way—lined up in the corridor, threatened with locker searches, peppered with carelessly aimed accusations—since at least junior high school. Back on the floor, Joan cracks, "Next they'll be telling us we can't have *sex* on the job." When I ask Stu what happened to inspire the crackdown, he just mutters about "management decisions" and takes the opportunity to upbraid Gail and me for being too generous with the rolls. From now on there's to be only one per customer and it goes out with the dinner, not with the salad. He's also been riding the cooks, prompting Andy to come out of the kitchen and observe — with the serenity of a man whose customary implement is a butcher knife — that "Stu has a death wish today."

Later in the evening, the gossip crystallizes around the theory that Stu is   5
himself the drug culprit, that he uses the restaurant phone to order up marijuana and sends one of the late servers out to fetch it for him. The server was caught and she may have ratted out Stu, at least enough to cast some suspicion on him, thus accounting for his pissy behavior. Who knows? Personally, I'm ready to believe anything bad about Stu, who serves no evident function and presumes too much on our common ethnicity, sidling up to me one night to engage in a little nativism directed at the Haitian immigrants: "I feel like I'm the foreigner here. They're taking over the country." Still later that evening, the drug in question escalates to crack. Lionel, the busboy, entertains us for the rest of the shift standing just behind Stu's back and sucking deliriously on an imaginary joint or maybe a pipe.

The other problem, in addition to the less-than-nurturing management style, is that this job shows no sign of being financially viable. You might imagine, from a comfortable distance, that people who live, year in and year out, on $6 to $10 an hour have discovered some survival stratagems unknown to the middle class. But no. It's not hard to get my coworkers talking about their living situations, because housing, in almost every case, is the principal source of disruption in their lives, the first thing they fill you in on when they arrive for their shifts. After a week, I have compiled the following survey:

> Gail is sharing a room in a well-known downtown flophouse for $250 a week. Her roommate, a male friend, has begun hitting on her, driving her nuts, but the rent would be impossible alone.

> Claude, the Haitian cook, is desperate to get out of the two-room apartment he shares with his girlfriend and two other, unrelated people. As far as I can determine, the other Haitian men live in similarly crowded situations.

> Annette, a twenty-year-old server who is six months pregnant and abandoned by her boyfriend, lives with her mother, a postal clerk.

> Marianne, who is a breakfast server, and her boyfriend are paying $170 a week for a one-person trailer.

> Billy, who at $10 an hour is the wealthiest of us, lives in the trailer he owns, paying only the $400-a-month lot fee.

> The other white cook, Andy, lives on his dry-docked boat, which, as far as I can tell from his loving descriptions, can't be more than twenty feet long. He offers to take me out on it once it's repaired, but the offer comes with inquiries as to my marital status, so I do not follow up on it.

> Tina, another server, and her husband are paying $60 a night for a room in the Days Inn. This is because they have no car and the Days

Inn is in walking distance of the Hearthside. When Marianne is tossed out of her trailer for subletting (which is against trailer park rules), she leaves her boyfriend and moves in with Tina and her husband.

Joan, who had fooled me with her numerous and tasteful outfits (hostesses wear their own clothes), lives in a van parked behind a shopping center at night and showers in Tina's motel room. The clothes are from thrift shops.[1]

It strikes me, in my middle-class solipsism, that there is gross improvidence in some of these arrangements. When Gail and I are wrapping silverware in napkins—the only task for which we are permitted to sit—she tells me she is thinking of escaping from her roommate by moving into the Days Inn herself. I am astounded: how she can even think of paying $40 to $60 a day? But if I was afraid of sounding like a social worker, I have come out just sounding like a fool. She squints at me in disbelief: "And where am I supposed to get a month's rent and a month's deposit for an apartment?" I'd been feeling pretty smug about my $500 efficiency, but of course it was made possible only by the $1,300 I had allotted myself for start-up costs when I began my low-wage life: $1,000 for the first month's rent and deposit, $100 for initial groceries and cash in my pocket, $200 stuffed away for emergencies. In poverty, as in certain propositions in physics, starting conditions are everything.

There are no secret economies that nourish the poor; on the contrary, there are a host of special costs. If you can't put up the two months' rent you need to secure an apartment, you end up paying through the nose for a room by the week. If you have only a room, with a hot plate at best, you can't save by cooking up huge lentil stews that can be frozen for the week ahead. You eat fast food or the hot dogs and Styrofoam cups of soup that can be microwaved in a convenience store. If you have no money for health insurance—and the Hearthside's niggardly plan kicks in only after three months—you go without routine care or prescription drugs and end up paying the price. Gail, for example, was doing fine, healthwise anyway, until she ran out of money for estrogen pills. She is supposed to be on the company health plan by now, but they claim to have lost her application form and to be beginning the paperwork all over again. So she spends $9 a pop for pills to control the migraines she wouldn't have, she insists, if her estrogen supplements were covered. Similarly, Marianne's boyfriend lost his job as a roofer because he missed so much time after getting a cut on his foot for which he couldn't afford the prescribed antibiotic.

My own situation, when I sit down to assess it after two weeks of work, would not be much better if this were my actual life. The seductive thing

---

[1] I could find no statistics on the number of employed people living in cars or vans, but according to a 1997 report of the National Coalition for the Homeless, "Myths and Facts about Homelessness," nearly one-fifth of all homeless people (in twenty-nine cities across the nation) are employed in full- or part-time jobs. [Author's note.]

about waitressing is that you don't have to wait for payday to feel a few bills in your pocket, and my tips usually cover meals and gas, plus something left over to stuff into the kitchen drawer I use as a bank. But as the tourist business slows in the summer heat, I sometimes leave work with only $20 in tips (the gross is higher, but servers share about 15 percent of their tips with the busboys and bartenders). With wages included, this amounts to about the minimum wage of $5.15 an hour. The sum in the drawer is piling up but at the present rate of accumulation will be more than $100 short of my rent when the end of the month comes around. Nor can I see any expenses to cut. True, I haven't gone the lentil stew route yet, but that's because I don't have a large cooking pot, potholders, or a ladle to stir with (which would cost a total of about $30 at Kmart, somewhat less at a thrift store), not to mention onions, carrots, and the indispensable bay leaf. I do make my lunch almost every day—usually some slow-burning, high-protein combo like frozen chicken patties with melted cheese on top and canned pinto beans on the side. Dinner is at the Hearthside, which offers its employees a choice of BLT, fish sandwich, or hamburger for only $2. The burger lasts longest, especially if it's heaped with gutpuckering jalapeños, but by midnight my stomach is growling again.

So unless I want to start using my car as a residence, I have to find a sec- 10 ond or an alternative job. I call all the hotels I'd filled out housekeeping applications at weeks ago—the Hyatt, Holiday Inn, Econo Lodge, HoJo's, Best Western, plus a half dozen locally run guest houses. Nothing. Then I start making the rounds again, wasting whole mornings waiting for some assistant manager to show up, even dipping into places so creepy that the front-desk clerk greets you from behind bullet-proof glass and sells pints of liquor over the counter. But either someone has exposed my real-life housekeeping habits— which are, shall we say, mellow—or I am at the wrong end of some infallible ethnic equation: most, but by no means all, of the working housekeepers I see on my job searches are African Americans, Spanish speaking, or refugees from the Central European post-Communist world, while servers are almost invariably white and monolingually English speaking. When I finally get a positive response, I have been identified once again as server material. Jerry's—again, not the real name—which is part of a well-known national chain and physically attached here to another budget hotel, is ready to use me at once. The prospect is both exciting and terrifying because, with about the same number of tables and counter seats, Jerry's attracts three or four times the volume of customers as the gloomy old Hearthside.

Picture a fat person's hell, and I don't mean a place with no food. Instead there is everything you might eat if eating had no bodily consequences—the cheese fries, the chicken-fried steaks, the fudge-laden desserts—only here every bite must be paid for, one way or another, in human discomfort. The kitchen is a cavern, a stomach leading to the lower intestine that is the garbage and dishwashing area, from which issue bizarre smells combining the edible and the offal: creamy carrion, pizza barf, and that unique and enigmatic Jerry's scent, citrus fart. The floor is slick with spills, forcing us to walk through the kitchen with tiny steps, like Susan McDougal in leg irons. Sinks everywhere are clogged with scraps of lettuce, decomposing lemon wedges, water-logged toast crusts. Put your hand down on any counter and you risk being stuck to it by the film of ancient syrup spills, and this is unfortunate because hands are utensils here, used for scooping up lettuce onto the salad plates, lifting out pie slices, and even moving hash browns from one plate to another. The regulation poster in the single unisex rest room admonishes us to wash our hands thoroughly, and even offers instructions for doing so, but there is always some vital substance missing—soap, paper towels, toilet paper—and I never found all three at once. You learn to stuff your pockets with napkins before going in there, and too bad about the customers, who must eat, although they don't realize it, almost literally out of our hands.

The break room summarizes the whole situation: there is none, because there are no breaks at Jerry's. For six to eight hours in a row, you never sit except to pee. Actually, there are three folding chairs at a table immediately adjacent to the bathroom, but hardly anyone ever sits in this, the very rectum of the gastroarchitectural system. Rather, the function of the peritoilet area is to house the ashtrays in which servers and dishwashers leave their cigarettes burning at all times, like votive candles, so they don't have to waste time lighting up again when they dash back here for a puff. Almost everyone smokes as if their pulmonary well-being depended on it—the multinational mélange of cooks; the dishwashers, who are all Czechs here; the servers, who are American natives—creating an atmosphere in which oxygen is only an occasional pollutant. My first morning at Jerry's, when the hypoglycemic shakes set in, I complain to one of my fellow servers that I don't understand how she can go so long without food. "Well, I don't understand how *you* can go so long without a cigarette," she responds in a tone of reproach. Because work is what you do for others; smoking is what you do for yourself. I don't know why the anti-smoking crusaders have never grasped the element of defiant self-nurturance that makes the habit so endearing to its victims—as if, in the American workplace, the only thing people have to call their own is the tumors they are nourishing and the spare moments they devote to feeding them.

Now, the Industrial Revolution is not an easy transition, especially, in my experience, when you have to zip through it in just a couple of days. I have gone from craft work straight into the factory, from the air-conditioned morgue of the Hearthside directly into the flames. Customers arrive in human waves, sometimes disgorged fifty at a time from their tour buses, peckish and whiny. Instead of two "girls" on the floor at once, there can be as many as six of us running around in our brilliant pink-and-orange Hawaiian shirts. Conversations, either with customers or with fellow employees, seldom last more than twenty seconds at a time. On my first day, in fact, I am hurt by my sister servers' coldness. My mentor for the day is a supremely competent, emotionally uninflected twenty-three-year-old, and the others, who gossip a little among themselves about the real reason someone is out sick today and the size of the bail bond someone else has had to pay, ignore me completely. On my second day, I find out why. "Well, it's good to see *you* again," one of them says in greeting. "Hardly anyone comes back after the first day." I feel powerfully vindicated—a survivor—but it would take a long time, probably months, before I could hope to be accepted into this sorority.

I start out with the beautiful, heroic idea of handling the two jobs at once, and for two days I almost do it: working the breakfast/lunch shift at Jerry's from 8:00 till 2:00, arriving at the Hearthside a few minutes late, at 2:10, and attempting to hold out until 10:00. In the few minutes I have between jobs, I pick up a spicy chicken sandwich at the Wendy's drive-through window, gobble it down in the car, and change from khaki slacks to black, from Hawaiian to rust-colored polo. There is a problem, though. When, during the 3:00–4:00 o'clock dead time, I finally sit down to wrap silver, my flesh seems to bond to the seat. I try to refuel with a purloined cup of clam chowder, as I've seen Gail and Joan do dozens of times, but Stu catches me and hisses "No *eating!*" although there's not a customer around to be offended by the sight of food making contact with a server's lips. So I tell Gail I'm going to quit, and she hugs me and says she might just follow me to Jerry's herself.

But the chances of this are minuscule. She has left the flophouse and her 15 annoying roommate and is back to living in her truck. But, guess what, she reports to me excitedly later that evening, Phillip has given her permission to park overnight in the hotel parking lot, as long as she keeps out of sight, and the parking lot should be totally safe since it's patrolled by a hotel security guard! With the Hearthside offering benefits like that, how could anyone think of leaving? This must be Phillip's theory, anyway. He accepts my resignation with a shrug, his main concern being that I return my two polo shirts and aprons.

Gail would have triumphed at Jerry's, I'm sure, but for me it's a crash course in exhaustion management. Years ago, the kindly fry cook who trained me to waitress at a Los Angeles truck stop used to say: never make an unnecessary trip; if you don't have to walk fast, walk slow; if you don't have to walk, stand. But at Jerry's the effort of distinguishing necessary from unnecessary and urgent from whenever would itself be too much of an energy drain. The only thing to do is to treat each shift as a one-time-only emergency: you've got fifty starving people out there, lying scattered on the battlefield, so get out there and feed them! Forget that you will have to do this again tomorrow, forget that you will have to be alert enough to dodge the drunks on the drive home tonight— just burn, burn, burn! Ideally, at some point you enter what servers call a "rhythm" and psychologists term a "flow state," where signals pass from the sense organs directly to the muscles, bypassing the cerebral cortex, and a Zen-like emptiness sets in. I'm on a 2:00–10:00 PM shift now, and a male server from the morning shift tells me about the time he "pulled a triple"—three shifts in a row, all the way around the clock—and then got off and had a drink and met this girl, and maybe he shouldn't tell me this, but they had sex right then and there and it was like *beautiful....*

WHAT DOES SHE SAY?

1. As you read this essay, keep two lists: "good guys" and "bad guys." Each time a new person is introduced, figure out which list she or he qualifies for based on your sense of how each is presented. Then write a paragraph about how you decided "good" from "bad."

2. What do the people in this essay do for themselves? What do they do for others? Make two lists.

3. Identify three things in this essay that, as you think about them seriously, bother your conscience or offend your sense of what's right.

WHAT DO YOU THINK?

4. Based only on the evidence Barbara Ehrenreich offers, write an essay that characterizes and explains the corporate philosophy. What are its aims? How does it achieve them? End by discussing whether or not you've experienced this corporate philosophy.

5. Identify five tasks that you know are done for you over a typical week and that you suspect might be done by people paid minimum wage (for example, someone empties the trash in professors' offices). For each of these tasks, try to find out the actual wage paid, the typical hours, and so on. Then write an essay that compares and contrasts what you've learned with what Ehrenreich presents in "Serving in Florida."

6. Compare and contrast your own experience of working minimum-wage jobs with the experiences in "Serving in Florida." Based on your discussion, explain why you would, or would not, favor raising the minimum wage. If you'd raise that wage, what do you think the new rate ought to make possible for those who earn it?

WHAT WOULD THEY SAY?

7. Consider Adrienne Rich's "Claiming an Education" (p. 608) together with "Serving in Florida." Based on these two essays and on your own experiences and beliefs, explain the purpose of a college education—for its individual graduates and for society overall. Variation: add Richard Rodriguez's essay "The Achievement of Desire" (p. 597) to the mix.

8. Read "Serving in Florida" together with Milton Friedman's "The Social Responsibility of Business Is to Increase Its Profits" (p. 518). Considering these two essays, write about why they are, or are not, unavoidably opposed. Said another way, use these two essays to explain why you think that a corporation and its workers are, or are not, unavoidably at odds with each other. If you have relevant personal experience here, add it to your discussion.

ERIC SCHLOSSER
What We Eat

E_{RIC} $S_{CHLOSSER}$ *(b. 1961) writes about the theme of food and economics not as a personal essayist or as a reporter but as a social critic, exploring through statistics, interviews, and sociological research what fast food has come to mean in America. A correspondent for the* Atlantic Monthly, *Schlosser has won numerous awards for his articles and essays about contemporary American life, including a National Magazine Award for a piece he wrote on marijuana.* Fast Food Nation: The Dark Side of the All-American Meal *(2002), Schlosser's first book (from which this selection is excerpted), has led people to reexamine the fast-food industry.*

Over the last three decades, fast food has infiltrated every nook and cranny of American society. An industry that began with a handful of modest hot dog and hamburger stands in southern California has spread to every corner of the nation, selling a broad range of foods wherever paying customers may be found. Fast food is now served at restaurants and drive-throughs, at stadiums, airports, zoos, high schools, elementary schools, and universities, on cruise ships, trains, and airplanes, at Kmarts, Wal-Marts, gas stations, and even at hospital cafeterias. In 1970, Americans spent about $6 billion on fast food; in 2001, they spent more than $110 billion. Americans now spend more money on fast food than on higher education, personal computers, computer software, or new cars. They spend more on fast food than on movies, books, magazines, newspapers, videos, and recorded music — combined.

Pull open the glass door, feel the rush of cool air, walk in, get on line, study the backlit color photographs above the counter, place your order, hand over a few dollars, watch teenagers in uniforms pushing various buttons, and moments later take hold of a plastic tray full of food wrapped in colored paper and cardboard. The whole experience of buying fast food has become so routine, so thoroughly unexceptional and mundane, that it is now taken for granted, like brushing your teeth or stopping for a red light. It has become a social custom as American as a small, rectangular, hand-held, frozen, and re-heated apple pie.

This is... about fast food, the values it embodies, and the world it has made. Fast food has proven to be a revolutionary force in American life; I am interested in it both as a commodity and as a metaphor. What people eat (or don't eat) has always been determined by a complex interplay of social, economic, and technological forces. The early Roman Republic was fed by its citizen-farmers; the Roman Empire, by its slaves. A nation's diet can be more revealing than its art or literature. On any given day in the United States about one-quarter of the adult population visits a fast-food restaurant. During a relatively brief period of time, the fast-food industry has helped to transform not only the American diet, but also our landscape, economy, workforce, and popular culture. Fast food and its consequences have become inescapable, regardless of whether you eat it twice a day, try to avoid it, or have never taken a single bite.

The extraordinary growth of the fast-food industry has been driven by fundamental changes in American society. Adjusted for inflation, the hourly wage of the average U.S. worker peaked in 1973 and then steadily declined for the next twenty-five years. During that period, women entered the workforce in record numbers, often motivated less by a feminist perspective than by a need to pay the bills. In 1975, about one-third of American mothers with young children worked outside the home; today almost two-thirds of such mothers are employed. As the sociologists Cameron Lynne Macdonald and Carmen Sirianni have noted, the entry of so many women into the workforce has greatly increased demand for the types of services that housewives traditionally perform: cooking, cleaning, and child care. A generation ago, three-quarters of the money used to buy food in the United States was spent to prepare meals at home. Today about half of the money used to buy food is spent at restaurants—mainly at fast-food restaurants.

The McDonald's Corporation has become a powerful symbol of America's service economy, which is now responsible for 90 percent of the country's new jobs. In 1968, McDonald's operated about one thousand restaurants. Today it has about thirty thousand restaurants worldwide and opens almost two thousand new ones each year. An estimated one out of every eight workers in the United States has at some point been employed by McDonald's. The company annually hires about one million people, more than any other American organization, public or private. McDonald's is the nation's largest purchaser of beef, pork, and potatoes—and the second largest purchaser of chicken. The McDonald's Corporation is the largest owner of retail property in the world. Indeed, the company earns the majority of its profits not from selling food but from collecting rent. McDonald's spends more money on advertising and marketing than any other brand. As a result it has replaced Coca-Cola as the world's most famous brand. McDonald's operates more playgrounds than any other private entity in the United States. It is responsible for the nation's best-selling line of children's clothing (McKids) and is one of the largest distributors of toys. A survey of American schoolchildren found that 96 percent could identify Ronald McDonald. The only fictional character with a higher degree of recognition was Santa Claus. The impact of McDonald's on the way we live today is hard to overstate. The golden arches are now more widely recognized than the Christian cross.

In the early 1970s, the farm activist Jim Hightower warned of "the McDonaldization of America." He viewed the emerging fast food industry as a threat to independent businesses, as a step toward a food economy dominated

5

by giant corporations, and as a homogenizing influence on American life. In *Eat Your Heart Out* (1975), he argued that "bigger is *not* better." Much of what Hightower feared has come to pass. The centralized purchasing decisions of the large restaurant chains and their demand for standardized products have given a handful of corporations an unprecedented degree of power over the nation's food supply. Moreover, the tremendous success of the fast-food industry has encouraged other industries to adopt similar business methods. The basic thinking behind fast food has become the operating system of today's retail economy, wiping out small businesses, obliterating regional differences, and spreading identical stores throughout the country like a self-replicating code.

America's main streets and malls now boast the same Pizza Huts and Taco Bells, Gaps and Banana Republics, Starbucks and Jiffy-Lubes, Foot Lockers, Snip N' Clips, Sunglass Huts, and Hobbytown USAs. Almost every facet of American life has now been franchised or chained. From the maternity ward at a Columbia/HCA hospital to an embalming room owned by Service Corporation International—"the world's largest provider of death-care services," based in Houston, Texas, which since 1968 has grown to include 3,823 funeral homes, 523 cemeteries, and 198 crematoriums, and which today handles the final remains of one out of every nine Americans—a person can now go from the cradle to the grave without spending a nickel at an independently owned business.

The key to a successful franchise, according to many texts on the subject, can be expressed in one word: "uniformity." Franchises and chain stores strive to offer exactly the same product or service at numerous locations. Customers are drawn to familiar brands by an instinct to avoid the unknown. A brand offers a feeling of reassurance when its products are always and everywhere the same. "We have found out...that we cannot trust some people who are non-conformists," declared Ray Kroc, one of the founders of McDonald's, angered by some of his franchisees. "We will make conformists out of them in a hurry.... The organization cannot trust the individual; the individual must trust the organization."

One of the ironies of America's fast-food industry is that a business so dedicated to conformity was founded by iconoclasts and self-made men, by entrepreneurs willing to defy conventional opinion. Few of the people who built fast-food empires ever attended college, let alone business school. They worked hard, took risks, and followed their own paths. In many respects, the fast food industry embodies the best and the worst of American capitalism at the start of the twenty-first century—its constant stream of new products and innovations, its widening gulf between rich and poor. The industrialization of the restaurant kitchen has enabled the fast-food chains to rely upon a low-paid and unskilled workforce. While a handful of workers manage to rise up the corporate ladder, the vast majority lack full-time employment, receive no benefits, learn few skills, exercise little control over their workplace, quit after a few months, and float from job to job. The restaurant industry is now America's largest private employer, and it pays some of the lowest wages.

During the economic boom of the 1990s, when many American workers enjoyed their first pay raises in a generation, the real value of wages in the restaurant industry continued to fall. The roughly 3.5 million fast food workers are by far the largest group of minimum-wage earners in the United States. The only Americans who consistently earn a lower hourly wage are migrant farm workers.

A hamburger and french fries became the quintessential American meal in   10
the 1950s, thanks to the promotional efforts of the fast-food chains. The typical American now consumes approximately three hamburgers and four orders of french fries every week. But the steady barrage of fast-food ads, full of thick juicy burgers and long golden fries, rarely mentions where these foods come from nowadays or what ingredients they contain. The birth of the fast-food industry coincided with Eisenhower-era glorifications of technology, with optimistic slogans like "Better Living through Chemistry" and "Our Friend the Atom." The sort of technological wizardry that Walt Disney promoted on television and at Disneyland eventually reached its fulfillment in the kitchens of fast-food restaurants. Indeed, the corporate culture of McDonald's seems inextricably linked to that of the Disney empire, sharing a reverence for sleek machinery, electronics, and automation. The leading fast food chains still embrace a boundless faith in science—and as a result have changed not just what Americans eat, but also how their food is made.

The current methods for preparing fast food are less likely to be found in cookbooks than in trade journals such as *Food Technologist* and *Food Engineering*. Aside from the salad greens and tomatoes, most fast food is delivered to the restaurant already frozen, canned, dehydrated, or freeze-dried. A fast food kitchen is merely the final stage in a vast and highly complex system of mass production. Foods that may look familiar have in fact been completely reformulated. What we eat has changed more in the last forty years than in the previous forty thousand. Like Cheyenne Mountain, today's fast food conceals remarkable technological advances behind an ordinary-looking facade. Much of the taste and aroma of American fast food, for example, is now manufactured at a series of large chemical plants off the New Jersey Turnpike.

In the fast-food restaurants of Colorado Springs, behind the counters, amid the plastic seats, in the changing landscape outside the window, you can see all the virtues and destructiveness of our fast-food nation. I chose Colorado Springs as a focal point for this...because the changes that have recently swept through the city are emblematic of those that fast food—and the fast-food mentality—have encouraged throughout the United States. Countless other suburban communities, in every part of the country, could have been used to illustrate the same points. The extraordinary growth of Colorado Springs neatly parallels that of the fast-food industry: during the last few decades, the city's population has more than doubled. Subdivisions, shopping malls, and chain restaurants are appearing in the foothills of Cheyenne Mountain and the plains rolling to the east. The Rocky Mountain region as a whole has the fastest-growing economy in the United States, mixing high-tech and service industries in a way that may define America's workforce for years to come. And new restaurants are opening there at a faster pace than anywhere else in the nation.

Fast food is now so commonplace that it has acquired an air of inevitability, as though it were somehow unavoidable, a fact of modern life. And yet the dominance of the fast-food giants was no more preordained than the march of Colonial split-levels, golf courses, and man-made lakes across the deserts of the American West. The political philosophy that now prevails in so much of the West—with its demand for lower taxes, smaller government, an unbridled free market—stands in total contradiction to the region's true economic underpinnings. No other region of the United States has been so dependent on government subsidies for so long, from the nineteenth-century construction of its railroads to the twentieth-century financing of its military bases and dams. One historian has described the federal government's 1950s highway-building binge as a case study in "interstate socialism"— a phrase that aptly describes how the West was really won. The fast food industry took root alongside that interstate highway system, as a new form of restaurant sprang up beside the new off-ramps. Moreover, the extraordinary growth of this industry over the past quarter-century did not occur in a political vacuum. It took place during a period when the inflation-adjusted value of the minimum wage declined by about 40 percent, when sophisticated mass-marketing techniques were for the first time directed at small children, and when federal agencies created to protect workers and consumers too often behaved like branch offices of the companies that were supposed to be regulated. Ever since the administration of President Richard Nixon, the fast-food industry has worked closely with its allies in Congress and the White House to oppose new worker safety, food safety, and minimum-wage laws. While publicly espousing support for the free market, the fast-food chains have quietly pursued and greatly benefited from a wide variety of government subsidies. Far from being inevitable, America's fast-food industry in its present form is the logical outcome of certain political and economic choices.

In the potato fields and processing plants of Idaho, in the ranch lands east of Colorado Springs, in the feedlots and slaughterhouses of the High Plains, you can see the effects of fast food on the nation's rural life, its environment, its workers, and its health. The fast-food chains now stand atop a huge food-industrial complex that has gained control of American agriculture. During the 1980s, large multinationals—such as Cargill, ConAgra, and IBP— were allowed to dominate one commodity market after another. Farmers and cattle ranchers are losing their independence, essentially becoming hired hands for the agribusiness giants or being forced off the land. Family farms are now being replaced by gigantic corporate farms with absentee owners. Rural communities are losing their middle class and becoming socially stratified, divided between a small, wealthy elite and large numbers of the working poor. Small towns that seemingly belong in a Norman Rockwell painting are being turned into rural ghettos. The hardy, independent farmers whom Thomas Jefferson considered the bedrock of American democracy are a truly vanishing breed. The United States now has more prison inmates than full-time farmers.

The fast-food chains' vast purchasing power and their demand for a uni- 15 form product have encouraged fundamental changes in how cattle are raised, slaughtered, and processed into ground beef. These changes have made meatpacking—once a highly skilled, highly paid occupation—into the most dangerous job in the United States, performed by armies of poor, transient immigrants whose injuries often go unrecorded and uncompensated. And the same meat industry practices that endanger these workers have facilitated the introduction of deadly pathogens, such as *E. coli* 0157:H7°, into America's hamburger meat, a food aggressively marketed to children. Again and again, efforts to prevent the sale of tainted ground beef have been thwarted by meat-industry lobbyists and their allies in Congress. The federal government has the legal authority to recall a defective toaster oven or stuffed animal—but still lacks the power to recall tons of contaminated, potentially lethal meat.

I do not mean to suggest that fast food is solely responsible for every social problem now haunting the United States. In some cases (such as the malling and sprawling of the West) the fast-food industry has been a catalyst and a symptom of larger economic trends. In other cases (such as the rise of franchising and the spread of obesity) fast food has played a more central role. By tracing the diverse influences of fast food I hope to shed light not only on the workings of an important industry, but also on a distinctively American way of viewing the world.

Elitists have always looked down at fast food, criticizing how it tastes and regarding it as another tacky manifestation of American popular culture. The aesthetics of fast food are of much less concern to me than its impact upon the lives of ordinary Americans, both as workers and consumers. Most of all, I am concerned about its impact on the nation's children. Fast food is heavily marketed to children and prepared by people who are barely older than children. This is an industry that both feeds and feeds off the young. During the two years spent researching this book, I ate an enormous amount of fast food. Most of it tasted pretty good. That is one of the main reasons people buy fast food; it has been carefully designed to taste good. It's also inexpensive and convenient. But the value meals, two-for-one deals, and free refills of soda give a distorted sense of how much fast food actually costs. The real price never appears on the menu.

The sociologist George Ritzer has attacked the fast-food industry for celebrating a narrow measure of efficiency over every other human value, calling

---

E. coli 0157:H7: One of many strains of the bacterium *Escherichia coli*, which causes severe intestinal problems and has been associated with undercooked hamburger. [EDS.]

the triumph of McDonald's "the irrationality of rationality." Others consider the fast-food industry proof of the nation's great economic vitality, a beloved American institution that appeals overseas to millions who admire our way of life. Indeed, the values, the culture, and the industrial arrangements of our fast-food nation are now being exported to the rest of the world. Fast food has joined Hollywood movies, blue jeans, and pop music as one of America's most prominent cultural exports. Unlike other commodities, however, fast food isn't viewed, read, played, or worn. It enters the body and becomes part of the consumer. No other industry offers, both literally and figuratively, so much insight into the nature of mass consumption.

Hundreds of millions of people buy fast food every day without giving it much thought, unaware of the subtle and not so subtle ramifications of their purchases. They rarely consider where this food came from, how it was made, what it is doing to the community around them. They just grab their tray off the counter, find a table, take a seat, unwrap the paper, and dig in. The whole experience is transitory and soon forgotten. I've written this . . . out of a belief that people should know what lies behind the shiny, happy surface of every fast-food transaction. They should know what really lurks between those sesame-seed buns. As the old saying goes: you are what you eat.

WHAT DOES HE SAY?

1. In this introduction to his book *Fast Food Nation*, Schlosser says he's writing about fast food and "the values it embodies." Write down some of what he means by "values."

2. Jot down five facts about the McDonald's Corporation. Draw two conclusions from them and write those down.

3. In your own words, what do you think Jim Hightower means when he warns about "the McDonaldization of America"?

4. Once you've finished reading this essay, write four sentences that try to capture your response.

WHAT DO YOU THINK?

5. Using Schlosser's "What We Eat" as your principal source, write an essay that defines what success is as it's presented here. If you're not sure what constitutes success here, write an essay explaining why you can't be sure.

6. Choose one paragraph in "What We Eat" and write an essay that analyzes, explains, and reacts to the various statements, assertions, and evidence contained in that paragraph. Start your paper by reproducing the paragraph you've chosen.

7. Write a "before and after" paper about your own reactions and responses to reading this essay. The "before" part of your paper should identify your opinions, understandings, and so on, about the matters Schlosser discusses; the "after" should discuss how those original understandings, opinions, and so on, have been in any way affected by reading "What We Eat."

8. Write an essay that analyzes and discusses the various ways Schlosser uses the words *price, value*, and *cost*. End by discussing how this analysis helps you arrive at your response to "What We Eat."

9. Have you worked in a fast-food franchise? If so, write an essay that explains your experience and puts it alongside what you've read in "What We Eat." End by discussing how "What We Eat" changes or reinforces any of what you've thought about fast-food jobs.

WHAT WOULD THEY SAY?

10. Read "What We Eat" together with Malcolm Gladwell's "Big and Bad" (p. 440). What do these two essays on American products suggest about American consumer values? Explain that with some care. End by explaining why you are, or are not, more inclined to want an SUV and fast-food lunches.

11. What would Cornel West, author of "The Moral Obligations of Living in a Democratic Society" (p. 123), and Barbara Ehrenreich, author of "Serving in Florida" (p. 483), have to say about "What We Eat"? What about Milton Friedman, author of "The Social Responsibility of Business Is to Increase Its Profits" (p. 518)? Write an essay that takes the form of a round-table discussion. Start with West saying something in response to "What We Eat" (he should quote it as part of his response). Follow with Ehrenreich saying something (quoting either West or Schlosser). Follow her comments with something you believe Friedman would say (quoting either Schlosser, West, or Ehrenreich). Follow Friedman's comments with a response from Schlosser. End with your own comment on the round-table discussion.

REBECCA MEAD
Eggs for Sale

*T*HIS NEW YORKER *PROFILE about women who sell their eggs moves us from the topic of food to the topic of bioethics. This piece raises the question, What are a woman's eggs worth?*

Rebecca Mead (b. 1966) began her writing career for London's Sunday Times *before moving to the United States, where she joined the staff of the* New Yorker *in 1997. Her articles for that magazine focus on a wide variety of subjects, from blogs to legalized prostitution to the wedding industry. "Eggs for Sale" originally appeared in the August 1999 issue.*

The first time I met Cindy Schiller, at the Hungarian Pastry Shop on Amsterdam Avenue and 111th Street one morning this winter, she told me that she wasn't feeling quite herself, on account of what she called "the whole menopause thing." Her short-term memory was out of whack, she was lethargic, and she'd been finding herself suddenly drenched in sweat. "Hot flashes sound like they're no big deal, but hot flashes kick your ass," she said.

Schiller is a student at Columbia University Law School, and at twenty-six she should be only halfway to menopause. But she had been undergoing an artificially induced change of life over the previous weeks, which was precipitated by an array of drugs and an unusually relaxed attitude about sticking needles into herself. For three weeks, she had injected her stomach with a drug called Lupron, which shut down her ovaries, so that none of her eggs ripened and none of her egg follicles developed that month. Then menopause was suddenly over; she switched medications, and started injecting a combination of Pergonal and Metrodin—follicle-stimulating hormones—into her hip every morning. This kicked her quiescent ovaries into overdrive, swelling them to the size of oranges, and brought a cluster of her eggs to the brink of ripeness. After eight days, Schiller took a final shot of a hormone called human chorionic gonadotropin, or HCG, and exactly thirty-six hours later she went to the office of a fertility doctor on Central Park West. There she was put under general sedation, and an ultrasound probe was introduced into her vagina and threaded up through her uterus, so that a needle could be inserted into each of her ovaries and the eggs sucked out, one by one. Twelve eggs were whisked away, to be fertilized in a petri dish with the sperm of a man Schiller wasn't especially fond of, in preparation for transfer to the uterus of a woman she didn't really know, in the hope that at least one would grow into a child whom Schiller would probably never see.

499

Schiller, whose name has been changed in this article at her request, is a lively young woman with blue eyes, long light-brown hair, and very pale skin, unmarked except for five tattoos — tattoos that her mother, back home in the Southwest, has been begging her to remove with laser surgery. She also has sixteen piercings, including several of the kind that only real intimates or fertility doctors get to see.

If she were your daughter, you, too, would probably want her to have the tattoos removed, because in other respects Schiller is such a nice girl: she doesn't drink, she doesn't smoke, she doesn't take drugs, she's pretty and quick to laugh, and she has a lovely singing voice....

Not long after she arrived at Columbia last fall, Schiller read a notice   5
pinned to a bulletin board in the law school by an infertile couple who were seeking an egg donor. For a woman who is trying to get pregnant and has no viable eggs of her own, donor eggs are a last resort. Schiller had signed up with an egg-donor agency while she was an undergraduate in her home state and had twice donated eggs there. She was now eager to do it again, even though the last time she had "hyperstimulated," which means that she had produced too many eggs (more than thirty, in her case) and had suffered so much abdominal pain and nausea that she could hardly get out of bed for two days. On both occasions, she had been selected as a donor immediately, no doubt because she is fair and blue eyed and has a good academic record.

Schiller donates her eggs because she thinks that it's a worthy thing to do, and because it's a worthy thing to do for which she can be paid in sums that seem handsome to a heavily indebted student. Schiller's parents, who are divorced, know that she donates eggs, and they are not opposed to her doing it, though they are concerned about its effect on her health. They aren't especially wealthy, and Schiller says she would rather support herself with eggs than ask them to help her out.

She does, however, have the political objections to the trade.... She thinks it would be "really cool" to donate to a gay couple, say, rather than to the upper-middle-class wives and husbands who are the typical recipients of donor eggs. She also disapproves of the preference for egg donation over adoption. "It's the fact that I'm helping a white-supremacist system work," she told me earnestly. "People are getting these fair, blue-eyed children, and that does bother me philosophically." Still, she had earned twenty-five hundred dollars for each of her earlier donations, and by last fall the going rate in New York was five thousand dollars, so when she saw the ad she called the couple and arranged to meet them at a café on Broadway.

They turned out to be a professional Manhattan couple old enough to be Schiller's parents, and they bought her lunch and quizzed her about her interests and skills. She told them about her expertise in martial arts and music, and about the fact that she was really good at math and science and was also a decent writer. It was a bit like a job interview, she told me, though she hadn't done some of the things that a career counselor might have advised, like removing her nose ring or the stud in her tongue. The hardest part of the interview came when it was time to negotiate the fee, and the couple asked her to name her price. "The husband wouldn't, like, name a figure, so I had to," she said. "Five thousand was the amount that I needed to make in this period of time, and he jumped at it. I probably could have asked for more and got it."

This past February, in the middle of Schiller's fertility-drug regimen, she heard about an advertisement that had been placed in several Ivy League school newspapers offering fifty thousand dollars to a donor who was athletic, had SAT scores of 1,400 or more, and was at least five feet ten inches tall. She was a few inches too short to apply, but it made her think that there might be someone who was willing to pay such a premium for her eggs, thereby making her next year at Columbia a whole lot easier. "I'm only now beginning to realize that I could tap into some cash here," she said.

In 1984, a woman gave birth to a child who was genetically unrelated to her for 10 the first time, after a donor's egg had been fertilized in a petri dish in the laboratory of Dr. Alan Trounson, an embryologist at Monash University, in Melbourne, Australia, and transferred to another woman's womb. This year, there will probably be around five thousand egg donations in the United States.

In the early days of egg donation, very few patients could take advantage of the procedure. These recipients were given whatever eggs clinics could lay their hands on: some were leftover eggs donated by women who had undergone in-vitro fertilization, which involves the same kind of ovary-stimulating hormonal regimen as egg donation; a few came from women who were having their tubes tied and agreed to give away the eggs they would no longer be using. Some infertile women were helped by their younger sisters, or by friends. There was little concern about matching donors and recipients beyond the broadest categories of race. One recipient I spoke with, who is dark-haired, olive-skinned, and Jewish, received donor eggs ten years ago from a woman who was tall, blond, and Nordic.

These days, such a match would be unlikely, although if a dark, Jewish recipient wanted to introduce a little Nordic blood into her family stock, she would certainly be able to find an egg-donor agency happy to oblige. Nowadays, donors and recipients are matched with remarkable precision, right down to tanning ability and hair texture. There are around two hundred private egg-donation agencies and clinics in the United States, and they are intensely competitive, offering patients donor databases that may include as many as three hundred women. . . .

Marketing strategies are ingenious. A New York egg-donation program advertises in movie theaters, inviting would-be donors to dial 1-877-BABY-MAKERS. A new company in Los Angeles called the Center for Egg Options hired a hip advertising agency to write catchy ad copy. Instead of variations on the usual "give the gift of life" theme, one ad reads simply, "Pay your tuition with eggs." Another, which appeared in the magazine *Backstage*, says, "Get paid $4,000 for a small part." The same company is known for sending fertility doctors promotional giveaways that consist of shrink-wrapped egg cartons filled with chocolate eggs.

Many agencies direct would-be recipients to log on to Internet sites and browse through pictures of willing donors which are accompanied by detailed profiles that include the donors' health history, educational background, ambitions, and interests....

The United States is the only country in the world in which the rules of the 15 marketplace govern the trade in gametes and genes. In parts of Europe, and in most of South America, egg donation is illegal, often because of the influence of the Catholic Church, which holds that only intercourse should lead to conception. (Muslim law also forbids egg donation; Judaism generally has a more flexible view toward methods of assisted reproduction.) In other countries, egg donation is legal only under certain circumstances. A recent British law allows patients of in-vitro fertilization to sell their leftover eggs, thereby offsetting the cost of the original IVF procedure, but it is against the law to pay women to undergo voluntary egg retrieval....

Escalating fees are causing doctors in this country, somewhat belatedly, to express reservations about the commercial traffic in eggs. At a recent conference on infertility that I attended in Sydney, Australia, Dr. Mark V. Sauer, who is the director of reproductive endocrinology at Columbia Presbyterian Medical Center, in New York, addressed the issue. "First of all, we have to recognize that we have a problem," he said. "It is like saying at AA meetings, 'I am an alcoholic.' Well, I am an egg-donor man, and I do pay my donors, and I pay them too much, and I recognize that, so what are we going to do about it?"

Doctors are concerned that high prices are attracting women who aren't mature enough to be able to make the kind of philosophical decision implicit in donating eggs; but they are also worried about the interests of their infertility patients, many of whom are being priced out of the market. Egg donation is generally not covered by insurance, and the price for one retrieval (known as a cycle) in New York City, including donor fees and medications for both participants, is currently twenty thousand dollars, with the chances of success being around 50 percent. Some patients undergo as many as three cycles in their efforts to become parents.

The ethical quandary that doctors now find themselves in, however, is one of their own making. It has long been accepted that gametes have a monetary value, ever since commercial sperm donation took off in the 1960s. (Although there are laws against the commodification of body parts, a curious legislative loophole has enabled a market in eggs and sperm to emerge. There is no doubt that if such a loophole existed for the market in, say, kidneys, you would be able to order them on the Internet from donors who would provide detailed accounts of their families' excellent urological history.) The average sperm-donor fee is fifty dollars per deposit, which works out to about

0.00001 cent per spermatozoon. Part of the reason that egg-donor fees are higher than sperm-donor fees is that the effort required is so much greater. Being an egg donor can be inconvenient, because, unlike sperm, eggs cannot easily be frozen, so there are no "egg banks"; instead, the donor takes drugs to synchronize her reproductive system with the recipient's. What's more, as Cindy Schiller found out, the process can be painful, and it can be dangerous as well: hyperstimulation can, in very rare instances, lead to stroke. Donating eggs does not deplete a donor's own reserves, since the eggs that are taken would otherwise have been wasted that month; but it is too early in the history of egg donation to know what the long-term side effects might be. Ovarian scarring may compromise a donor's own fertility, and one medical study, which has since been disputed, has suggested that there might be an association between fertility drugs and ovarian cancer.

All of these factors have led some doctors to argue that egg donors are actually underpaid. Dr. Jamie Grifo, who heads New York University's infertility clinic, says, "If you consider the hourly wage for a sperm donor and the hourly wage for an egg donor—my God, five thousand dollars is about ten times too little."

In its egg-donor guidelines, the American Society for Reproductive 20 Medicine stipulates that donors be paid not for the actual eggs but for the "inconvenience, time, discomfort, and for the risk undertaken." Agencies reject potential donors who say they are doing it just for the money, in part because most recipients wouldn't want a donor who appears to be mercenary; they would prefer a donor who has chosen to perform this service out of the goodness of her heart. (In the euphemistic parlance of the industry, eggs are "donated," never "sold.") The ideal egg donor embodies all sorts of paradoxes: she is compassionate toward an infertile stranger but feels no necessary attachment to her own genetic kin; she is fecund but can easily divorce the reproductive from the maternal.

Before Cindy Schiller was allowed to become an egg donor, she underwent psychological counseling and testing. Egg-donor programs generally reject any young women who view their eggs as protochildren. "They always ask what you are going to do when in eighteen years' time someone comes knocking at your door," Schiller told me, her tone implying that she thought the question was a silly one to ask of someone her age. "How would I know what I'm going to do?"

In the weeks after we first met, Schiller had sent away for an application form from a large West Coast agency called Options. Most agencies do not allow women to donate eggs more than four or five times, because of the health risks, and Schiller was approaching her limit; she hoped that Options would help her market herself for what might be the last time. She was asked to provide head shots, and was taken aback by a number of other details that Options expected.

"They even ask whether your grandparents had acne," she marveled. "I can see why you would want to know about diseases and stuff, but acne? *Please*. I know they're paying top dollar here for the genes, but if acne is your biggest problem you're good to go."

Options is one of the largest egg-brokering agencies in the country: it can offer around two hundred and fifty donors to recipients worldwide at any given moment, and it conducts almost all of its business on the Internet. I went to visit the Options offices, which are located in a nondescript building on an anonymous street in the Los Angeles area; before I was provided with the address, I was required to sign a nondisclosure agreement stating that I would not reveal it. Teri Royal, who runs the company, said that she kept her address secret in order to preserve the security of her records, some of which deal with high-profile clients in Hollywood and in Washington.

The place had the feeling of a cottage industry that needs to move into a mansion: partitions had been set up to divide small spaces into even smaller ones, and there was hardly room to turn around without bumping into another woman with a phone clamped to her ear and a computer screen glowing in front of her. Royal is a stout thirty-nine-year-old woman with strawberry-blond hair. She explained that Options donors are carefully selected for their marketability as well as for their general health; Options does not accept donors older than thirty, for instance, because recipients shy away from them. But when it comes to accepting recipients into the program, Royal practices reproductive free trade.

"We would never turn somebody down," she said. "It is none of my 25 business how someone wants to make her baby, so long as all parties are informed and give their consent. So I'm not going to turn away homosexuals, bisexuals, transracials, single parents, older couples."...

Using Options is expensive. The agency charges $1,865 for bringing donors and recipients together. Administrative and legal costs are close to another thousand dollars. Then there is the compensation for the donor. Options donors are among the best paid in the country: those who appear on the Internet database receive between thirty-five hundred and five thousand dollars, and others who are recruited through private advertisements placed for specific couples earn still more. Last year, Options placed a cap of sixty-five hundred dollars on payments, because would-be recipients were trying to outbid one another in the pages of the same college newspapers....

As egg donation has changed from being an experimental procedure to being just one of a range of infertility treatments, consumers have begun to demand more from agencies like Options. They expect to be offered donors who are not just healthy but bright and accomplished and attractive. One recent morning, I attended a matching session at Saint Barnabas Medical Center, in New Jersey, where the members of the egg-donation team were going over the wish lists of various recipients. (Like all the New York–area egg-donation programs, Saint Barnabas practices anonymous donation, in which recipients and donors are matched by nurses and psychologists; the recipients never see a picture of the woman who is chosen for them.) It felt like a good-humored, girls-only swap meet, although the scarcity of the right kinds of donors was obvious.... A...participant read a wish list of characteristics: "She wants no cat allergies. 'Tall, dark-haired, healthy, athletic, animal-loving.' And a partridge in a pear tree."

...[I]t is not surprising that egg recipients are particularly choosy before conception even takes place. Lyne Macklin, the administrator of an agency in Beverly Hills, the Center for Surrogate Parenting and Egg Donation, told me that there's a great temptation among recipients to engage in a kind of genetic upgrading. "It's like shopping," she said. "If you have the option between a Volkswagen and a Mercedes, you'll select the Mercedes."

It is impossible to determine just how likely a child is to inherit such characteristics as academic ability or athleticism or musicality. Still, would-be parents can play the odds. Robert Plomin, a behavioral geneticist at the University of London, says that a recipient probably ought to pay attention to such characteristics as cognitive ability, which is about 50 percent heritable. "I generally try to be a scientist and say, 'These are populations and averages, and we can't make very good predictions for an individual,'" he told me. "But I do let friends know that some of these things are heritable."

...Egg donation makes it possible, for the first time, for a woman's procreative 30 capacity to be detached from any maternal investment on her part. Though men have always been able to father children they may never meet, the fact that an egg donor might, by semantic equivalence, mother a child she will never know confounds both the dictionary and an ingrained assumption about the maternal instinct.

One day, I asked Schiller whether she had any idea how she would be raising the money for law school if she weren't selling her eggs. "Some idea," she said. "I might be working at Hooters." In an earlier era, Schiller's youth and her fertility would have served her well in the matrimonial marketplace. Because she can now choose an education and a career, deferring marriage and children, her reproductive capital has been made otherwise available — to women who have themselves preferred an education and a career over early childbearing. Schiller told me that she couldn't imagine being ready to have children for at least a decade, if then, and it had occurred to her that she might need reproductive assistance herself one day. "What a sweet irony that would be," she said.

In the years before the birth-control pill and *Roe v. Wade*, a woman like Schiller might have provided an infertile couple not with eggs but with an actual baby — the product of an unwanted pregnancy, given up for adoption. Indeed, the rising demand for donor eggs — most of which come from white, middle-class women—coincides with a decline in the number of adoptable American infants born to white, middle-class women. Some donors have undergone abortions, and they may see egg donation as a way of making amends....

[E]ggs are even more desirable [than adoptions] because they allow a recipient couple to have a baby who is genetically related to one parent. And with egg donation, as opposed to adoption, there is no extraneous birth mother to deal with—as long as [the donor] continues to have no interest in her genetic offspring, that is, and as long as no law is introduced to give donor children the right to track down their genetic mothers.

As the egg-donation industry grows, however, legal changes are expected. "There is currently no controlling federal legislation," Sean Tipton, a spokesman for the American Society for Reproductive Medicine, explains. Donors sign a consent form saying that they are relinquishing any claim to their retrieved eggs. Five states—Florida, North Dakota, Oklahoma, Texas, and Virginia—have passed legislation that releases donors from responsibility for the children born from their eggs. "In most cases, people should be confident that they are giving up those rights," Tipton says. "But it is not clear whether it would survive a court challenge."

Legal scholars expect that, in years to come, lawsuits will be brought by 35 donors who develop regrets about having sold their eggs back in their student days. Karen Synesiou, the co-owner of the Center for Surrogate Parenting and Egg Donation, told me, "If you get an eighteen- or nineteen-year-old who has been stimulated four or five times and her ovaries stop functioning because of all the scarring, she is going to want to sue someone for being infertile." At least one donor has threatened to sue a fertility clinic after being hyperstimulated, but the suit was dropped when the clinic agreed to pay her medical expenses.

Schiller, who as a law student might be expected to be aware of her rights and responsibilities concerning her eggs, seemed vague when I asked her whether she had made any legal arrangement with the couple who had just bought her eggs. She had signed the consent form waiving her rights, she said, but she had not come to any agreement about whether she would have future contact with the family. She seemed to have very little idea of what the couple expected from her; she had never discussed with them whether they planned to tell the child of its origins, and she did not know whether they expected her to be available to the child if it later wanted to know its genetic mother. She wasn't even sure whether they would notify her of a pregnancy, or of a baby's birth, and said that she had never felt that she could ask about these issues. "Ultimately, until it's over and you get paid you feel, 'I had better not say anything,'" she told me.

... This reasoning—the idea that intent trumps biology—makes for some remarkably slippery values. A woman who bears an egg-donor child is encouraged to believe that carrying the fetus is the crucial component of motherhood. But a woman who hires a surrogate to carry her fertilized egg to term for her is encouraged to believe the opposite: that the important thing is the genetic link to the baby, and not the womb out of which the baby came. Biologically, an egg donor's situation is identical to that of a woman who uses a surrogate. But egg donors are encouraged to believe that what makes a woman into a mother is the wish to be a mother—to be what is known in the infertility business as "the social parent."

The American fertility industry is based upon the conviction that a person is the agent of his or her own destiny—that fate and fortune are fashioned, not inflicted. Effective contraception has made it possible for people to believe that all pregnancies can be planned, and that children are chosen. The corollary of that belief is the conviction that choosing to have a child is a right, and that the desire to have one, even when pregnancy is against the odds, should command the utmost attention and effort and resources. The jargon of the reproductive-services industry, which talks about "nontraditional family-building" and "creating families," illustrates this very American idea: that sleeves-rolled-up diligence is what makes people into parents—rather than anything as unreliable as chance, or fate, or luck, or God.

In late June, Schiller finally heard from the couple who had received her eggs four months earlier: the woman had failed to conceive. So far, they hadn't asked her to donate eggs a second time, but they seemed to want to stay in touch, and she wondered whether they might call upon her to repeat the process.

As of July, only a month before fall registration, Schiller had not been chosen 40 by one of Pinkerton's recipients, and she had begun to investigate the possibility of putting up her own classified advertisement on one of the Internet's egg-donor sites. She browsed the advertisements that had been placed by couples who were looking for donors. "Gosh, these ads are really sad," she told me. "Most people have to be really desperate before they will even try something like this." There was one couple who had lost many family members in the Holocaust and wanted a Jewish donor to continue the bloodline; another woman had suffered serious damage to her reproductive organs after being in a car accident.

Schiller had recently heard from Columbia's Financial Aid office that she'd be receiving more funds than she expected this academic year, so she hadn't yet decided whether to go through with a fourth donation. But just in case, she had looked into taking a Mensa test in order to have proof of her intelligence, and she had decided one thing. "If someone offers me something really high, and they are an asshole, I won't do it." In any case, Schiller has no regrets about her adventures in the egg marketplace. "It's almost like a hobby now," she said. "This is weird, isn't it? But it is a very interesting experience. I don't think I would trade it for anything."

WHAT DOES SHE SAY?

1. As you're reading this essay, write down five facts that surprise you or that make you stop and wonder. Write a paragraph about these.

2. What are the ethical questions that the essay specifically mentions about egg donation? Identify two places that capture those questions clearly for you, and write down those questions in your own words.

3. Write down five things that seem to you to be accurate descriptions of Cindy Schiller's situation, thinking, and the like.

4. Make notes of the places where Rebecca Mead describes laws that influence "the egg-donation industry." Then write a paragraph in response to those notes.

WHAT DO YOU THINK?

5. Write an essay that identifies, explains, and tries to answer the three most significant questions that this essay raises for you. End by explaining what you are more sure of, or still unsure of, after these analyses.

6. Go to the Internet and print out at least one page from two different advertisements placed by couples seeking egg donations or by businesses that specialize in selling donated eggs. Write an essay that summarizes, analyzes, and explains the arguments, values, and reasons that these ads use in order to try to make egg donation attractive, positive, and worthwhile. End by discussing your reactions to what you've found.

7. Summarize your understanding of the character and motivations of Cindy Schiller as she is presented in "Eggs for Sale." Be fair, making your presentation of her accurate and complete. Then explain why or how you would judge her choices.

8. Write an opinion piece that uses "Eggs for Sale" as its primary evidence in support of some significant comment or judgment of American culture. This piece needs to be as reasonably close to 750 words as possible, and it must include at least three quotations from the essay itself.

WHAT WOULD THEY SAY?

9. You can bet that Bill McKibben, author of "Designer Genes" (p. 360), might have something to say in response to "Eggs for Sale." Based on your reading of what he favors and what worries him, how would he react to Mead's essay? Write your own essay presenting his response (quote "Designer Genes" at least twice), and end by indicating your response to McKibben and to Mead.

10. Barbara Kingsolver's essay "Stone Soup" (p. 64) discusses many different kinds of families. Based on your reading of her essay, what response do you think she would have to "Eggs for Sale"? Write your own essay predicting her response (quote

"Stone Soup" at least twice), and end by indicating your response to Kingsolver and to Mead.

11. Sallie Tisdale's "We Do Abortions Here" (p. 351) and Rebecca Mead's "Eggs for Sale" both approach questions of human reproduction. Read those two essays together. Then write your own essay explaining how much, or how little, these two essays have in common.

12. Read "Eggs for Sale" together with Helen Prejean's "Executions Are Too Costly— Morally" (p. 614). Then write an essay that discusses the various ways these two essays identify and define *costs, payments,* and *value.* End by explaining your definitions and understandings of these terms.

TONI CADE BAMBARA

The Lesson

*I*N THE VIVID VOICE *of a young black girl, Toni Cade Bambara (1939–1995) takes us on a field trip from the slums of New York to a Fifth Avenue department store. What does this young narrator learn through her experience about how she is valued and what she is worth? What do we learn?*

Born in New York, Bambara was a civil rights activist, and her concern for racial equality is reflected in her writing. She published several books, including The Seabirds Are Still Alive *(1977),* The Salt Eaters *(1980), and* Raymond's Run *(1990). "The Lesson" is from her short-story collection* Gorilla, My Love *(1972).*

Back in the days when everyone was old and stupid or young and foolish and me and Sugar were the only ones just right, this lady moved on our block with nappy hair and proper speech and no makeup. And quite naturally we laughed at her, laughed the way we did at the junk man who went about his business like he was some big-time president and his sorry-ass horse his secretary. And we kinda hated her too, hated the way we did the winos who cluttered up our parks and pissed on our handball walls and stank up our hallways and stairs so you couldn't halfway play hide-and-seek without a goddamn gas mask. Miss Moore was her name. The only woman on the block with no first name. And she was black as hell, cept for her feet, which were fish-white and spooky. And she was always planning these boring-ass things for us to do, us being my cousin, mostly, who lived on the block cause we all moved North the same time and to the same apartment then spread out gradual to breathe. And our parents would yank our heads into some kinda shape and crisp up our clothes so we'd be presentable for travel with Miss Moore, who always looked like she was going to church, though she never did. Which is just one of the things the grown-ups talked about when they talked behind her back like a dog. But when she came calling with some sachet she'd sewed up or some gingerbread she'd made or some book, why then they'd all be too embarrassed to turn her down and we'd get handed out all spruced up. She'd been to college and said it only right that she should take responsibility for the young ones' education, and she not even related by marriage or blood. So they'd go for it. Specially Aunt Gretchen. She was the main gofer in the family. You got some ole dumb shit foolishness you want somebody to go for, you send for Aunt Gretchen. She been screwed into the go-along for so long, it's a blood-deep natural thing with her. Which is how she got saddled with me and Sugar and Junior in the first place while our mothers were in a la-de-da apartment up the block having a good ole time.

So this one day Miss Moore rounds us all up at the mailbox and it's puredee hot and she's knockin herself out about arithmetic. And school suppose to let up in summer I heard, but she don't never let up. And the starch in my pinafore scratching the shit outta me and I'm really hating this nappy-head bitch and her goddamn college degree. I'd much rather go to the pool or to the show where it's cool. So me and Sugar leaning on the mailbox being surly, which is a Miss Moore word. And Flyboy checking out what everybody brought for lunch. And Fat Butt already wasting his peanut-butter-and-jelly sandwich like the pig he is. And Junebug punchin on Q.T.'s arm for potato chips. And Rosie Giraffe shifting from one hip to the other waiting for somebody to step on her foot or ask her if she from Georgia so she can kick ass, preferably Mercedes'. And Miss Moore asking us do we know what money is, like we a bunch of re-tards. I mean real money, she say, like it's only poker chips or monopoly papers we lay on the grocer. So right away I'm tried of this and say so. And would much rather snatch Sugar and go to the Sunset and terrorize the West Indian kids and take their hair ribbons and their money too. And Miss Moore files that remark away for next week's lesson on brotherhood, I can tell. And finally I say we oughta get to the subway cause it's cooler and besides we might meet some cute boys. Sugar done swiped her mama's lipstick, so we ready.

So we heading down the street and she's boring us silly about what things cost and what our parents make and how much goes for rent and how money ain't divided up right in this country. And then she gets to the part about we all poor and live in the slums, which I don't feature. And I'm ready to speak on that, but she steps out in the street and hails two cabs just like that. Then she hustles half the crew in with her and hands me a five-dollar bill and tells me to calculate 10 percent tip for the driver. And we're off. Me and Sugar and Junebug and Flyboy hangin out the window and hollering to everybody, putting lipstick on each other cause Flyboy a faggot anyway, and making farts with our sweaty armpits. But I'm mostly trying to figure how to spend this money. But they all fascinated with the meter ticking and Junebug starts laying bets as to how much it'll read when Flyboy can't hold his breath no more. Then Sugar lays bets as to how much it'll be when we get there. So I'm stuck. Don't nobody want to go for my plan, which is to jump out at the next light and run off to the first bar-b-que we can find. Then the driver tells us to get the hell out cause we are there already. And the meter reads eighty-five cents. And I'm stalling to figure out the tip and Sugar say give him a dime. And I de-cide he don't need it bad as I do, so later for him. But then he tries to take off with Junebug foot still in the door so we talk about his mama something fero-cious. Then we check out that we on Fifth Avenue and everybody dressed up in stockings. One lady in a fur coat, hot as it is. White folks crazy.

"This is the place," Miss Moore say, presenting it to us in the voice she uses at the museum. "Let's look in the windows before we go in."

"Can we steal?" Sugar asks very serious like she's getting the ground rules square away before she plays. "I beg your pardon," say Miss Moore, and we fall   5 out. So she leads us around the windows of the toy store and me and Sugar screamin, "This is mine, that's mine, I gotta have that, that was made for me, I was born for that," till Big Butt drowns us out.

"Hey, I'm goin to buy that there."

"That there? You don't even know what it is, stupid."

"I do so," he say punchin on Rosie Giraffe. "It's a microscope."

"Whatcha gonna do with a microscope, fool?"

"Look at things."

"Like what, Ronald?" ask Miss Moore. And Big Butt ain't got the first notion. So here go Miss Moore gabbing about the thousands of bacteria in a drop of water and the somethinorother in a speck of blood and the million and one living things in the air around us is invisible to the naked eye. And what she say that for? Junebug go to town on that "naked" and we rolling. Then Miss Moore ask what it cost. So we all jam into the window smudgin it up and the price tag say $300. So then she ask how long'd take for Big Butt and Junebug to save up their allowances. "Too long," I say. "Yeh," adds Sugar, "outgrown it by that time." And Miss Moore say no, you never out-grow learning instruments. "Why, even medical students and interns and," blah, blah, blah. And we ready to choke Big Butt for bringing it up in the first damn place.

"This here costs four hundred eighty dollars," say Rosie Giraffe. So we pile up all over her to see what she pointin out. My eyes tell me it's a chunk of glass cracked with something heavy, and different-color inks dripped into the splits, then the whole thing put into a oven or something. But for $480 it don't make sense.

"That's a paperweight made of semi-precious stones fused together under tremendous pressure," she explains slowly, with her hands doing the mining and all the factory work.

"So what's a paperweight?" asks Rosie Giraffe.

"To weigh paper with, dumbbell," say Flyboy, the wise man from the East.

"Not exactly," say Miss Moore, which is what she say when you warm or way off too. "It's to weigh paper down so it won't scatter and make your desk untidy." So right away me and Sugar curtsy to each other and then to Mercedes who is more the tidy type.

"We don't keep paper on top of the desk in my class," say Junebug, fig-uring Miss Moore crazy or lyin one.

"At home, then," she say. "Don't you have a calendar and a pencil case and a blotter and a letter-opener on your desk at home where you do your homework?" And she know damn well what our homes look like cause she nosys around in them every chance she gets.

"I don't even have a desk," say Junebug. "Do we?"

"No. And I don't get no homework neither," say Big Butt.

"And I don't even have a home," say Flyboy like he do at school to keep the white folks off his back and sorry for him. Send this poor kid to camp posters, is his speciality.

"I do," say Mercedes. "I have a box of stationery on my desk and a picture of my cat. My godmother bought the stationery and the desk. There's a big rose on each sheet and the envelopes smell like roses."

"Who want to know about your smelly-ass stationery," say Rosie Giraffe fore I can get my two cents in.

"It's important to have a work area all your own so that..."

"Will you look at this sailboat, please," say Flyboy, cuttin her off and 25 pointin to the thing like it was his. So once again we tumble all over each other to gaze at this magnificent thing in the toy store which is just big enough to maybe sail two kittens across the pond if you strap them to the posts tight. We all start reciting the price tag like we in assembly. "Handcrafted sailboat of fiberglass at one thousand one hundred ninety-five dollars."

"Unbelievable," I hear myself say and am really stunned. I read it again for myself just in case the group recitation put me in a trance. Same thing. For some reason this pisses me off. We look at Miss Moore and she lookin at us, waiting for I dunno what.

"Who'd pay all that when you can buy a sailboat set for a quarter at Pop's, a tube of glue for a dime, and a ball of string for eight cents? It must have a motor and a whole lot else besides," I say. "My sailboat cost me about fifty cents."

"But will it take water?" say Mercedes with her smart ass.

"Took mine to Alley Pond Park once," say Flyboy. "String broke. Lost it. Pity."

"Sailed mine in Central Park and it keeled over and sank. Had to ask 30 my father for another dollar."

"And you got the strap," laugh Big Butt. "The jerk didn't even have a string on it. My old man wailed on his behind."

Little Q.T. was staring hard at the sailboat and you could see he wanted it bad. But he too little and somebody'd just take it from him. So what the hell. "This boat for kids, Miss Moore?"

"Parents silly to buy something like that just to get all broke up," say Rosie Giraffe.

"That much money it should last forever," I figure.

"My father'd buy it for me if I wanted it."   35

"Your father, my ass," say Rosie Giraffe getting a chance to finally push Mercedes.

"Must be rich people shop here," say Q.T.

"You are a very bright boy," say Flyboy. "What was your first clue?" And he rap him on the head with the back of his knuckles, since Q.T. the only one he could get away with. Though Q.T. liable to come up behind you years later and get his licks in when you half expect it.

"What I want to know is," I says to Miss Moore though I never talk to her, I wouldn't give the bitch that satisfaction, "is how much a real boat costs? I figure a thousand'd get you a yacht any day."

"Why don't you check that out," she says, "and report back to the 40 group?" Which really pains my ass. If you gonna mess up a perfectly good swim day least you could do is have some answers. "Let's go in," she say like she got something up her sleeve. Only she don't lead the way. So me and Sugar turn the corner to where the entrance is, but when we get there I kinda hang back. Not that I'm scared, what's there to be afraid of, just a toy store. But I feel funny, shame. But what I got to be shamed about? Got as much right to go in as anybody. But somehow I can't seem to get hold on the door, so I step away for Sugar to lead. But she hangs back too. And I look at her and she looks at me and this is ridiculous. I mean, damn, I have never ever been shy about doing nothing or going nowhere. But then Mercedes steps up and then Rosie Giraffe and Big Butt crowd in behind and shove, and next thing we all stuffed into the doorway with only Mercedes squeezing past us, smoothing out her jumper and walking right down the aisle. Then the rest of us tumble in like a glued-together jigsaw done all wrong. And people lookin at us. And it's like the time me and Sugar crashed into the Catholic church on a dare. But once we got in there and everything so hushed and holy and the candles and the bowin and the handkerchiefs on all the drooping heads, I just couldn't go through with the plan. Which was for me to run up to the altar and do a tap dance while Sugar played the nose flute and messed around in the holy water. And Sugar kept givin me the elbow. Then later teased me so bad I tied her up in the shower and turned it on and locked her in. And she'd be there till this day if Aunt Gretchen hadn't finally figured I was lying about the boarder takin a shower.

Same thing in the store. We all walkin on tiptoe and hardly touchin the games and puzzles and things. And I watched Miss Moore who is steady watchin us like she waitin for a sign. Like Mama Drewery watches the sky and sniffs the air and takes note of just how much slant is in the bird formation. Then me and Sugar bump smack into each other, so busy gazing at the toys, 'specially the sail-boat. But we don't laugh and go into our fat-lady bump-stomach routine. We just stare at that price tag. Then Sugar run a finger over the whole boat. And I'm jealous and want to hit her. Maybe not her, but I sure want to punch somebody in the mouth.

"Watcha bring us here for, Miss Moore?"

"You sound angry, Sylvia. Are you mad about something?" Give me one of them grins like she tellin a grown-up joke that never turns out to be funny. And she's lookin very closely at me like maybe she plannin to do my portrait from memory. I'm mad, but I won't give her that satisfaction. So I slouch around the store bein very bored and say, "Let's go."

Me and Sugar at the back of the train watchin' the tracks whizzin by large then small then gettin gobbled up in the dark. I'm thinkin about this tricky toy I saw in the store. A clown that somersaults on a bar then does chin-ups just cause you yank lightly at his leg. Cost $35. I could see me askin my mother for a $35 birthday clown. "You wanna who that costs what?" she'd say, cockin her head to the side to get a better view of the hole in my head. Thirty-five dollars could buy new bunk beds for Junior and Gretchen's boy. Thirty-five dollars and the whole household could go visit Granddaddy Nelson in the country. Thirty-five dollars would pay for the rent and the piano bill too. Who are these people that spend that much for performing clowns and $1,000 for toy sailboats? What kinda work they do and how they live and how come we ain't in on it? Where we are is who we are, Miss Moore always pointin out. But it don't necessarily have to be that way, she always adds then waits for somebody to say that poor people have to wake up and demand their share of the pie and don't none of us know what kind of pie she talkin about in the first damn place. But she ain't so smart cause I still got her four dollars from the taxi and she sure ain't gettin it. Messin up my day with this shit. Sugar nudges me in my pocket and winks.

Miss Moore lines us up in front of the mailbox where we started from, 45 seem like years ago, and I got a headache for thinkin so hard. And we lean all over each other so we can hold up under the draggy-ass lecture she always finishes us off with at the end before we thank her for borin us to tears. But she just looks at us like she readin tea leaves. Finally she say, "Well, what did you think of F.A.O. Schwarz?"

Rosie Giraffe mumbles, "White folks crazy."

"I'd like to go in there again when I get my birthday money," says Mercedes, and we shove her out the pack so she has to lean on the mailbox by herself.

"I'd like a shower. Tiring day," say Flyboy.

Then Sugar surprises me by saying, "You know, Miss Moore, I don't think all of us here put together eat in a year what that sailboat costs." And Miss Moore lights up like somebody goosed her. "And?" she say, urging Sugar on. Only I'm standin on her foot so she don't continue.

"Imagine for a minute what kind of society it is in which some people 50 can spend on a toy what would cost to feed a family of six or seven. What do you think?"

"I think," say Sugar pushing me off her feet like she never done before, cause I whip her ass in a minute, "that this is not much of a democracy if you ask me. Equal chance to pursue happiness means an equal crack at the dough, don't it?" Miss Moore is besides herself and I am disgusted with Sugar's treachery. So I stand on her foot one more time to see if she'll shove me. She shuts up, and Miss Moore looks at me, sorrowfully I'm thinkin. And somethin weird is going on, I can feel it in my chest.

"Anybody else learn anything today?" lookin dead at me. I walk away and Sugar has to run to catch up and don't even seem to notice when I shrug her arm off my shoulder.

"Well, we got four dollars anyway," she says.

"Uh hunh."

"We could go to Hascombs and get half a chocolate layer and then go 55
to the Sunset and still have plenty money for potato chips and ice-cream
sodas."

"Uh hunh."

"Race you to Hascombs," she say.

We start down the block and she gets ahead which is O.K. by me cause
I'm goin to the West End and then over to the Drive to think this day through.
She can run if she want to and even run faster. But ain't nobody gonna beat me
at nuthin.

WHAT DOES SHE SAY?

1. This story begins, "Back in the days…". As you read, make a list of the clues or
   details that help you guess roughly when this story is set.

2. As you're reading, make some notes about what you're learning about the narrator. Once you're finished, write a paragraph about her.

3. Copy out four sentences that are essential to understanding the point of the story.

4. At one point, the narrator hangs back for a moment. She says, "But I feel funny,
   shame. But what I got to be shamed about?" Write a paragraph about why you
   think she hesitates.

WHAT DO YOU THINK?

5. View this story from Miss Moore's perspective. What lessons is she trying to teach?
   What's her method and her likely reasons for it? How much of what she wants to
   teach Sylvia, Sugar, and the rest do they seem to learn? Based on Sylvia's telling of
   the story, has Miss Moore wasted her time?

6. Compare some incident in your own life to the story presented in "The Lesson."
   Recall the day or part of that day and how your experience helped you understand
   money. End by comparing the lesson (or lessons) you learned with those you think
   Sylvia, Sugar, and the rest learned.

7. Write an analysis and interpretation of only the second-to-last paragraph of this
   story. Explain how and why understanding that paragraph is essential to this story.

WHAT WOULD THEY SAY?

8. Read Benjamin Saenz's "Exile: El Paso, Texas" (p. 20) together with Bambara's
   "The Lesson." Then write an essay discussing the ways that each author addresses

location and the causes of poverty. Variation: add Barbara Ehrenreich's "Serving in Florida" (p. 483) to the mix.

9. Read the Dalai Lama's "The Need for Discernment" (p. 205) together with "The Lesson." Then write an essay explaining how Bambara and the Dalai Lama might agree or disagree about what children should be taught or what adults should understand.

MILTON FRIEDMAN

The Social Responsibility of Business Is to Increase Its Profits

THIS CLASSIC ESSAY again shifts tone and point of view, from experience to ideas, from child to adult, from poor to privileged. But the topic is the same, as if Friedman is reinterpreting the meaning of Bambara's story: the businessperson's responsibility isn't to care for the children on the field trip but to make as much money as possible.

Milton Friedman (b. 1912) won a Nobel Prize in economics in 1976 and has been a Distinguished Professor at the University of Chicago. This essay originally appeared in the September 13, 1970, issue of the New York Times Magazine.

When I hear businessmen speak eloquently about the "social responsibilities of business in a free-enterprise system," I am reminded of the wonderful line about the Frenchman who discovered at the age of seventy that he had been speaking prose all his life. The businessmen believe that they are defending free enterprise when they declaim that business is not concerned "merely" with profit but also with promoting desirable "social" ends; that business has a "social conscience" and takes seriously its responsibilities for providing employment, eliminating discrimination, avoiding pollution, and whatever else may be the catchwords of the contemporary crop of reformers. In fact they are—or would be if they or anyone else took them seriously—preaching pure and unadulterated socialism. Businessmen who talk this way are unwitting puppets of the intellectual forces that have been undermining the basis of a free society these past decades. The discussion of the "social responsibilities of business" are notable for their analytical looseness and lack of rigor. What does it mean to say that "business" has responsibilities? Only people can have responsibilities. A corporation is an artificial person and in this sense may have artificial responsibilities, but "business" as a whole cannot be said to have responsibilities, even in this vague sense. The first step toward clarity to examining the doctrine of the social responsibility of business is to ask precisely what it implies for whom.

Presumably, the individuals who are to be responsible are businessmen, which means individual proprietors or corporate executives. Most of the discussion of social responsibility is directed at corporations, so in what follows I shall mostly neglect the individual proprietors and speak of corporate executives.

In a free-enterprise, private-property system, a corporate executive is an employee of the owners of the business. He has direct responsibility to his employers. That responsibility is to conduct the business in accordance with their desires, which generally will be to make as much money as possible while conforming to the basic rules of the society, both those embodied in law and those embodied in ethical custom. Of course, in some cases his employers may have a different objective. A group of persons might establish a corporation for an eleemosynary° purpose—for example, a hospital or a school. The manager of such a corporation will not have money profit as his objectives but the rendering of certain services.

In either case, the key point is that, in his capacity as a corporate executive, the manager is the agent of the individuals who own the corporation or establish the eleemosynary institution, and his primary responsibility is to them.

Needless to say, this does not mean that it is easy to judge how well he is   5
performing his task. But at least the criterion of performance is straightforward, and the persons among whom a voluntary contractual arrangement exists are clearly defined.

Of course, the corporate executive is also a person in his own right. As a person, he may have many other responsibilities that he recognizes or assumes voluntarily—to his family, his conscience, his feelings of charity, his church, his clubs, his city, his country. He may feel impelled by these responsibilities to devote part of his income to causes he regards as worthy, to refuse to work for particular corporations, even to leave his job, for example, to join his country's armed forces. If we wish, we may refer to some of these responsibilities as "social responsibilities." But in these respects he is acting as a principal, not an agent; he is spending his own money or time or energy, not the money of his employers or the time or energy he has contracted to devote to their purposes. If these are "social responsibilities," they are the social responsibilities of individuals, not of business.

What does it mean to say that the corporate executive has a "social responsibility" in his capacity as businessman? If this statement is not pure rhetoric, it must mean that he is to act in some way that is not in the interest of his employers. For example, that he is to refrain from increasing the price of the product in order to contribute to the social objective of preventing inflation, even though a price increase would be in the best interests of the corporation. Or that he is to make expenditures on reducing pollution beyond the amount that is in the best interests of the corporation or that is required by law in order to contribute to the social objective of improving the environment. Or that, at the expense of corporate profits, he is to hire "hardcore" unemployed instead of better qualified available workmen to contribute to the social objective of reducing poverty.

In each of these cases, the corporate executive would be spending someone else's money for a general social interest. Insofar as his actions in accord with his "social responsibility" reduce returns to stockholders, he is spending their money. Insofar as his actions raise the price to customers, he

---

eleemosynary: Related to charity. [EDS.]

is spending customers' money. Insofar as his actions lower the wages of some employees, he is spending their money.

The stockholders or the customers or the employees could separately spend their own money on the particular action if they wished to do so. The executive is exercising a distinct "social responsibility," rather than serving as an agent of the stockholders or the customers or the employees, only if he spends the money in a different way than they would have spent it.

But if he does this, he is in effect imposing taxes, on the one hand, and 10 deciding how the tax proceeds shall be spent, on the other.

This process raises political questions on two levels: principle and consequences. On the level of political principle, the imposition of taxes and the expenditure of tax proceeds are governmental functions. We have established elaborate constitutional, parliamentary, and judicial provisions to control these functions, to assure that taxes are imposed so far as possible in accordance with the preferences and desires of the public—after all, "taxation without representation" was one of the battle cries of the American Revolution. We have a system of checks and balances to separate the legislative function of imposing taxes and enacting expenditures from the executive function of collecting taxes and administering expenditure programs and from the judicial function of mediating disputes and interpreting the law.

Here the businessman—self-selected or appointed directly or indirectly by stockholders—is to be simultaneously legislator, executive, and jurist. He is to decide whom to tax by how much and for what purpose, and he is to spend the proceeds—all this guided only by general exhortations from on high to restrain inflation, improve the environment, fight poverty, and so on and on.

The whole justification for permitting the corporate executive to be selected by the stockholders is that the executive is an agent serving the interests of his principal. This justification disappears when the corporate executive imposes taxes and spends the proceeds for "social" purposes. He becomes in effect a public employee, a civil servant, even though he remains in name an employee of a private enterprise. On grounds of political principle, it is intolerable that such civil servants—insofar as their action in the name of social responsibility are real and not just window dressing—should be selected as they are now. If they are to be civil servants, then they must be elected through a political process. If they are to impose taxes and make expenditures to foster "social" objectives, then political machinery must be set up to make the assessment of taxes and to determine through a political process the objectives to be served.

This is the basic reason why the doctrine of "social responsibility" involves the acceptance of the socialist view that political mechanisms, not market mechanisms, are the appropriate way to determine the allocation of scarce resources to alternative uses.

On the grounds of consequences, can the corporate executive in fact dis- 15 charge his alleged "social responsibilities"? On the one hand, suppose he could get away with spending the stockholders' or customers' or employees' money. How is he to know how to spend it? He is told that he must contribute to fighting inflation. How is he to know what action of his will contribute to that end? He is presumably an expert in running his company—in producing a product or selling it or financing it. But nothing about his selection makes him an expert on inflation. Will his holding down the price of his product reduce inflationary pressure? Or, by leaving more spending power in the hands of his customers, simply divert it elsewhere? Or, by forcing him to produce less because of the lower price, will it simply contribute to shortages? Even if he could answer these questions, how much cost is he justified in imposing on his stockholders, customers, and employees for this social purpose? What is his appropriate share and what is the appropriate share of others?

And, whether he wants to or not, can he get away with spending his stockholders', customers', or employees' money? Will not the stockholders fire him? (Either the present ones or those who take over when his actions in the name of social responsibility have reduced the corporation's profits and the price of its stock.) His customers and his employees can desert him for other producers and employers less scrupulous in exercising their social responsibilities.

This facet of "social responsibility" doctrine is brought into sharp relief when the doctrine is used to justify wage restraint by trade unions. The conflict of interest is naked and clear when union officials are asked to subordinate the interest of their members to some more general purpose. If union officials try to enforce wage restraint, the consequence is likely to be wildcat strikes, rank-and-file revolts, and the emergence of strong competitors for their jobs. We thus have the ironic phenomenon that union leaders—at least in the United States—have objected to government interference with the market far more consistently and courageously than have business leaders. The difficulty of exercising "social responsibility" illustrates, of course, the great virtue of private competitive enterprise—it forces people to be responsible for their own actions and makes it difficult for them to "exploit" other people for either selfish or unselfish purpose. They can do good—but only at their own expense.

Many a reader who has followed the argument this far may be tempted to remonstrate that it is all well and good to speak of government's having the responsibility to impose taxes and determine expenditures for such "social" purposes as controlling pollution or training the hard-core unemployed, but that the problems are too urgent to wait on the slow course of political processes, that the exercise of social responsibility by businessmen is a quicker and surer way to solve pressing current problems.

Aside from the question of fact—I share Adam Smith's skepticism about the benefits that can be expected from "those who affect to trade for the public good"—this argument must be rejected on the grounds of principle. What it amounts to is an assertion that those who favor the taxes and expenditures in question have failed to persuade a majority of their fellow citizens to be of like mind and that they are seeking to attain by undemocratic procedures what they cannot attain by democratic procedures. In a free society it is hard for "evil" people to do "evil," especially since one man's good is another's evil.

I have, for simplicity, concentrated on the special case of the corporate 20 executive, except only for the brief digression on trade unions. But precisely the same argument applies to the newer phenomenon of calling upon stockholders to require corporations to exercise social responsibility (the recent GM crusade for example). In most of these cases, what is in effect involved is some stockholders trying to get other stockholders (or customers or employees) to contribute against their will to "social" causes favored by the activists. Insofar as they succeed, they are again imposing taxes and spending the proceeds.

The situation of the individual proprietor is somewhat different. If he acts to reduce the returns of his enterprise in order to exercise his "social responsibility," he is spending his own money, not someone else's. If he wishes to spend his money on such purposes, that is his right, and I cannot see that there is any objection to his doing so. In the process, he, too, may impose costs on employees and customers. However, because he is far less likely than a large corporation or union to have monopolistic power, any such side effects will tend to be minor.

Of course, in practice the doctrine of social responsibility is frequently a cloak for actions that are justified on other grounds rather than a reason for those actions.

To illustrate, it may well be in the long-run interest of a corporation that is a major employer in a small community to devote resources to providing amenities to that community or to improving its government. That may make it easier to attract desirable employees, it may reduce the wage bill or lessen losses from pilferage and sabotage or have other worthwhile effects. Or it may be that, given the laws about the deductibility of corporate charitable contributions, the stockholders can contribute more to charities they favor by having the corporation make the gift than by doing it themselves, since they can in that way contribute an amount that would otherwise have been paid as corporate taxes.

In each of these—and many similar—cases, there is a strong temptation to rationalize these actions as an exercise of "social responsibility." In the present climate of opinion, with its widespread aversion to "capitalism," "profits," and the "soulless corporation" and so on, this is one way for a corporation to generate goodwill as a by-product of expenditures that are entirely justified in its own self-interest.

It would be inconsistent of me to call on corporate executives to re- 25 frain from this hypocritical window-dressing because it harms the foundations of a free society. That would be to call on them to exercise a "social responsibility"! If our institutions, and the attitudes of the public make it in their self-interest to cloak their actions in this way, I cannot summon much indignation to renounce them. At the same time, I can express admiration for those individual proprietors or owners of closely held corporations or stockholders of more broadly held corporations who disdain such tactics as approaching fraud.

Whether blameworthy or not, the use of the cloak of social responsibility, and the nonsense spoken in its name by influential and prestigious businessmen, does clearly harm the foundations of a free society. I have been impressed time and again by the schizophrenic character of many businessmen. They are capable of being extremely farsighted and clearheaded in matters that are internal to their businesses. They are incredibly shortsighted and muddle-headed in matters that are outside their businesses but affect the possible survival of business in general. This shortsightedness is strikingly exemplified in the calls from many businessmen for wage and price guidelines or controls or income policies. There is nothing that could do more in a brief period to destroy a market system and replace it by a centrally controlled system than effective governmental control of prices and wages.

The shortsightedness is also exemplified in speeches by businessmen on social responsibility. This may gain them kudos in the short run. But it helps to strengthen the already too prevalent view that the pursuit of profits is wicked and immoral and must be curbed and controlled by external forces. Once this view is adopted, the external forces that curb the market will not be the social consciences, however highly developed, of the pontificating executives; it will be the iron fist of government bureaucrats. Here, as with price and wage controls, businessmen seem to me to reveal a suicidal impulse.

The political principle that underlies the market mechanism is unanimity. In an ideal free market resting on private property, no individual can coerce any other, all cooperation is voluntary, all parties to such cooperation benefit or they need not participate. There are no values, no "social" responsibilities in any sense other than the shared values and responsibilities of individuals. Society is a collection of individuals and of the various groups they voluntarily form.

The political principle that underlies the political mechanism is conformity. The individual must serve a more general social interest—whether that be determined by a church or a dictator or a majority. The individual may have a vote and say in what is to be done, but if he is overruled, he must conform. It is appropriate for some to require others to contribute to a general social purpose whether they wish to or not.

Unfortunately, unanimity is not always feasible. There are some respects 30 in which conformity appears unavoidable, so I do not see how one can avoid the use of the political mechanism altogether.

But the doctrine of "social responsibility" taken seriously would extend the scope of the political mechanism to every human activity. It does not differ in philosophy from the most explicitly collectivist doctrine. It differs only by professing to believe that collectivist ends can be attained without collectivist means. That is why, in my book *Capitalism and Freedom*, I have called it a "fundamentally subversive doctrine" in a free society, and I have said that in such a society, "there is one and only one social responsibility of business—to use its resources and engage in activities designed to increase its profits so long as it stays within the rules of the game, which is to say, engages in open and free competition without deception or fraud."

WHAT DOES HE SAY?

1. Before you even begin reading this essay, write down three things business should do besides increase profits.

2. As you read along, mark in the margin any assertions that seem fundamental or essential to the argument this essay makes. Once you've finished reading, copy out four that seem significant.

3. As you read along, identify four or five short passages that you're pretty sure are important but that you don't fully understand. Mark these with wiggly lines in the margin.

WHAT DO YOU THINK?

4. Identify four centrally important assertions that Milton Friedman makes. Explain each one, and explain why you agree, or disagree, with it. End by explaining how your agreements, or disagreements, help you arrive at an overall response to what Friedman says.

5. As Friedman sees it, what is the role of government as it pertains to business? For example, does this essay suggest Friedman would be for or against mandatory minimum wages? Would he be for or against workplace safety laws? Once you've seen the role(s) that Friedman would assign to government, discuss to what extent, or not, you're ready to agree with Friedman's assertions.

6. Assume that Friedman's essay accurately describes how businesses work: they work to make money for their shareholders. Investigate a company that makes a product you use or wear. Where do the raw materials for this product come from? Where are the components manufactured or assembled? How far must the product travel from where it's made to the store where you bought it? In short, what set of business decisions were made about how this particular product could be assembled or manufactured most cheaply in order to yield the highest profit? Once you understand at least some of these decisions, explain what you think about them. Are you happy to endorse them? Uneasy about some of them? Explain.

7. Interview someone you know (not a full-time student) who is employed by a for-profit business. Explain that you've read Friedman's essay, and explain his three main assertions (clearly, you must decide what these are). For each of these assertions, ask whether or not it holds true in your interviewee's business experience. Report the answers you hear (quote often). End by explaining why and how your interview supports, or challenges, Friedman's understanding of business and its responsibility.

WHAT WOULD THEY SAY?

8. Write an essay in dialogue form featuring Friedman and Barbara Ehrenreich, author of "Serving in Florida" (p. 483). Begin with Ehrenreich. Assume she's just finished reading "The Social Responsibility of Business Is to Increase Its Profits." Give Ehrenreich and Friedman at least two opportunities to speak. You have the last word: explain how or why you believe these two essayists would agree or agree to disagree.

9. Consider Friedman's essay together with Paul Hawken's "A Teasing Irony" (p. 547). Explain the basic assertions each essay makes. End by explaining why or how you're encouraged, or discouraged, by what you've read and analyzed.

ROBERT HAAS

Ethics: A Global Business Challenge

*I*N THIS SHORT SPEECH, *Robert Haas (b. 1941) argues for an understanding of the social role of business quite different from Milton Friedman's. Business should be ethical, he says, and he claims further that ethical practices are actually good for business, increasing profits in the long run. In 1991, Haas, the Chair/CEO of Levi Strauss & Company, made that business the first multinational to adopt guidelines for issues such as child labor and the environment. This selection is part of a speech he delivered at a business conference in May 1994.*

Because Levi Strauss & Company operates in many countries and diverse cultures, we take special care in selecting contractors and those countries where our goods are produced. We do this to ensure that our products are being made in a manner consistent with our values and that protects our brand image and corporate reputation. So, in 1991, we developed a set of Global Sourcing Guidelines.

Our guidelines describe the business conduct we require of our contractors. For instance, the guidelines ban the use of child or prison labor. They stipulate certain environmental requirements. They limit working hours and mandate regularly scheduled days off. Workers must have the right of free association and not be exploited. At a minimum, wages must comply with the law and match prevailing local practice, and working conditions must be safe and healthy. We also expect our business partners to be law abiding and to conduct all of their business affairs in an ethical way.

In developing our guidelines, we also recognized that there are certain issues beyond the control of our contractors, so we produced a list of "country selection" criteria. For example, we will not source in countries where conditions, such as the human rights climate, would run counter to our values and have an adverse effect on our global brand image or damage our corporate reputation.

Similarly, we will not source in countries where circumstances threaten our employees while traveling, where the legal climate makes it difficult or jeopardizes our trademarks, and where political or social turmoil threatens our commercial interest.

Since adopting our guidelines, we've terminated our business relationships with about 5 percent of our contractors and required workplace improvements of another 25 percent. Likewise, we announced a phased withdrawal from contracting in China and exited Burma due to human rights concerns, although we remain hopeful that the human rights climate in these countries will improve so we can alter these decisions.

In the process of creating our guidelines, we formed a working group of 15 employees from a broad cross section of the company. The working group spent nine months formulating our guidelines. In crafting these guidelines, they used our principle-based decision-making model to guide their deliberations.

Drafting these guidelines was difficult. Applying them has proven even more challenging.

When we were rolling out our guidelines—which included extensive on-site audits of each of our 700 contractors worldwide—we discovered that two of our manufacturing contractors in Bangladesh and one in Turkey employed underage workers. This was a clear violation of our guidelines, which prohibit the use of child labor. At the outset, it appeared that we had two options:

- Instruct our contractors to fire these children, knowing that many are the sole wage earners for their families and that if they lost their jobs, their families would face extreme hardships; or we could
- Continue to employ underage children, ignoring our stance against the use of child labor.

By referencing our ethical guidelines to decision making we came up with a different approach and one that we believe helped to minimize adverse ethical consequences.

The contractors agreed to pay the underage children their salaries and 10 benefits while they go to school full-time. We agreed to pay for books, tuition, and uniforms. When the children reach legal working age, they will be offered jobs in the plant. Due to these efforts, thirty-five children have attended school in Bangladesh, while another six are currently in school in Turkey.

And how did we benefit from this situation?

We were able to retain quality contractors that play an important role in our worldwide sourcing strategy. At the same time, we were able to honor our values and protect our brands.

Applying our sourcing guidelines has forced us to find creative solutions to vexing ethical dilemmas. Clearly, at times, adhering to these standards has added costs. To continue working for us, some contractors have added emergency exits and staircases, increased ventilation, reduced crowding, improved bathroom facilities, and invested in water-treatment systems. The costs of these requirements have been passed on to us—at least in part—in the form of higher product prices. In other cases, we have foregone less expensive sources of production due to unsatisfactory working conditions or concerns about the country of origin.

Conventional wisdom holds that these added costs put us at a competitive disadvantage. Yes, they limit our options somewhat and squeeze profit margins in the near term. But over the years, we've found that decisions which emphasize cost to the exclusion of all other factors don't serve a company's and its shareholders' long-term interests.

Moreover, as a company that invests hundreds of millions of advertising 15
dollars each year to create consumer preference for our products, we have a
huge stake in protecting that investment. In today's world, a television exposé
on working conditions can undo years of effort to build brand loyalty. Why
squander your investment when, with foresight and commitment, reputational
problems can be prevented?

But you don't have to take my word for it.

There is a growing body of evidence that shows a positive correlation between good corporate citizenship and financial performance. Studies by leading
research groups such as Opinion Research Corporation and Yankelovich Partners, respected scholars and socially responsible investment firms underscore the
point that companies which look beyond solely maximizing wealth and profits
and are driven by values and a sense of purpose outperform those companies
that focus only on short-term gain.

Companies with strong corporate reputations have been shown to outperform the S&P 500,° have higher sales, sustain greater profits, and have stocks
that outperform the market. These are results that no bottom-line fixated manager can ignore.

Similarly, a recent study suggests that how a company conducts itself affects consumer purchasing decisions and customer loyalty. A vast majority—
84 percent—of the American public agrees that a company's reputation can
well be the deciding factor in terms of what product or service they buy.

These findings mirror our own experience. Our values-driven approach 20
has helped us

- Identify contractors who want to work for Levi Strauss & Company to
  achieve our "blue ribbon" certification, enhancing their own business
  stature;
- We have gained retailer and consumer loyalty. Retailers feel good about
  having us as business partners because of our commitment to ethical practices. Today's consumer has more products to choose from and more information about those products. A company's reputation forms a part of the
  consumer's perceptions of the product and influences purchasing decisions.

At the same time,

- We're better able to attract, retain, and motivate the most talented employees, because the company's values more closely mirror their own personal values.
- Because government and community leaders view us as a responsible
  corporate citizen we have been welcomed to do business in established
  and emerging markets.

S&P 500: Standard & Poor's 500, an index of stocks commonly used to measure stock
market fluctuations. [EDS.]

Let me conclude with a few last thoughts.

We are living in an environment in which ethical standards and behaviors are being increasingly challenged. Addressing these dilemmas becomes even more difficult when you overlay the complexities of different cultures and values systems that exist throughout the world. For example, in some cultures honesty will take precedence over caring—"tell the truth even if it hurts"; whereas other cultures find caring, or "saving face," as the predominant value.

As you grapple with some fictitious ethical quandaries over the next two days, I encourage you to ask yourselves these questions:

- How much am I willing to compromise my principles?
- Are there times when I'm willing to risk something I value for doing the right thing?

For me and my associates at Levi Strauss & Company I think the answers have become clear: ethics must trump all other considerations. Ultimately, there are important commercial benefits to be gained from managing your business in a responsible and ethical way that best serves your enterprise's long-term interests. The opposite seems equally clear: the dangers of not doing so are profound.

Michael Josephson, a noted ethics expert, defined ethics this way: "Ethics is about character and courage and how we meet the challenge when doing the right thing will cost more than we want to pay."

The good news is that courage carries with it a great reward—the prospect of sustained responsible commercial success. I think that's what each of us wants our legacy to be. And I believe ultimately our key stakeholders—all of them—will accept nothing less.

WHAT DOES HE SAY?

1. As you're reading this essay, jot down five reasons that Robert Haas gives for Levi Strauss & Company's development of their Global Sourcing Guidelines.

2. What criticisms or accusations do you think that Levi Strauss & Company is trying to address or to prevent by developing their Global Sourcing Guidelines and applying them as Haas indicates?

3. Write a paragraph that captures your first reaction to reading Haas's essay.

WHAT DO YOU THINK?

4. Visit the Levi Strauss & Company corporate Web site. Print out at least one page that updates or otherwise addresses the company's current ethical views. Then

write a brief analysis that explains how this more current information reinforces, alters, or otherwise compares to what Haas said in 1994.

5. Visit the Levi Strauss & Company Web site and a Web site for Wrangler (parent company VF Corporation), Calvin Klein (parent company Phillips-Van Heusen Corporation), Nike, or a similar apparel company. See what you can determine about the company's business practices in comparison to those of Levi Strauss. Print out at least one page from each site you visit, and write a comparison of what these companies say about ethical business practices.

6. Terms like *globalization*, *outsourcing*, *free trade*, and the like are often reported in the news as controversial. What are such arguments about? Research one or more of these terms in sufficient depth so that you can write an accurate introduction to the controversies of global trade and a global economy.

7. Identify four things that you've purchased recently which cost more than $20 each and which you bought voluntarily. Explain each item—why you wanted it, how you went about selecting it over its competitors, and how much, or little, you thought about any ethical considerations connected with these purchases. Did you concern yourself with how, where, or by whom this item was made? Did you think at all about manufacturing processes or labor practices? Based on this analysis, what conclusions can you draw about corporate ethics and retail purchases?

WHAT WOULD THEY SAY?

8. Read "Ethics: A Global Business Challenge" together with Milton Friedman's "The Social Responsibility of Business Is to Increase Its Profits" (p. 518). Explain how these two essays differ and overlap. Then speculate a little about what changes in business, technology, politics, or culture might account for the ideological shift in Friedman's essay of 1970 to that in Haas's essay of 1994.

9. Assume that Barbara Ehrenreich, author of "Serving in Florida" (p. 483), has just read "Ethics: A Global Business Challenge." What would Ehrenreich have to say in response? What would she applaud? What would she criticize? What would she say goes unaddressed? Write an essay explaining all of this.

10. Assume that Robert Haas has just read "The Singer Solution to World Poverty," by Peter Singer (p. 661). How do you think that Haas would react to Singer's essay? Write your own essay explaining how and why you think these two would agree or disagree.

ALDO LEOPOLD
The Land Ethic

*T*HIS JUSTLY FAMOUS AND INFLUENTIAL ESSAY *invites readers to understand "worth" not just in economic terms but in the sense of intrinsic worth and intrinsic rights. Nature is valuable, Aldo Leopold (1886–1948) suggests, not just because of what we can do with it but in and of itself: in its beauty, in its otherness.*

A naturalist and wildlife biologist, Leopold worked for the forest service for nearly twenty years, pioneering an ecological approach to land and wildlife management. After leaving the forest service, he was on the faculty at the University of Wisconsin until his death. He is best known for A Sand County Almanac *(1949), a collection of essays that focuses on the natural world and the human need for wilderness, from which "The Land Ethic" is taken.*

When godlike Odysseus returned from the wars in Troy, he hanged all on one rope a dozen slave girls of his household whom he suspected of misbehavior during his absence.

This hanging involved no question of propriety. The girls were property. The disposal of property was then, as now, a matter of expediency, not of right and wrong.

Concepts of right and wrong were not lacking from Odysseus's Greece: witness the fidelity of his wife through the long years before at last his black-prowed galleys clove the wine-dark seas for home. The ethical structure of that day covered wives, but had not yet been extended to human chattels. During the three thousand years which have since elapsed, ethical criteria have been extended to many fields of conduct, with corresponding shrinkages in those judged by expediency only.

THE ETHICAL SEQUENCE

This extension of ethics, so far studied only by philosophers, is actually a process in ecological evolution. Its sequences may be described in ecological as well as in philosophical terms. An ethic, ecologically, is a limitation on freedom of action in the struggle for existence. An ethic, philosophically, is a differentiation of social from antisocial conduct. These are two definitions of one thing. The thing has its origin in the tendency of interdependent individuals or groups to evolve modes of cooperation. The ecologist calls these symbioses. Politics and economics are advanced symbioses in which the original

531

free-for-all competition has been replaced, in part, by cooperative mechanisms with an ethical content.

The complexity of cooperative mechanisms has increased with population   5
density, and with the efficiency of tools. It was simpler, for example, to define
the antisocial uses of sticks and stones in the days of the mastodons than of bullets and billboards in the age of motors.

The first ethics dealt with the relation between individuals; the Mosaic
Decalogue° is an example. Later accretions dealt with the relation between
the individual and society. The Golden Rule tries to integrate the individual
to society; democracy to integrate social organization to the individual.

There is as yet no ethic dealing with man's relation to land and to the animals and plants which grow upon it. Land, like Odysseus's slave girls, is still
property. The land relation is still strictly economic, entailing privileges but not
obligations.

The extension of ethics to this third element in human environment is, if
I read the evidence correctly, an evolutionary possibility and an ecological necessity. It is the third step in a sequence. The first two have already been taken.
Individual thinkers since the days of Ezekiel and Isaiah have asserted that the despoliation of land is not only inexpedient but wrong. Society, however, has not
yet affirmed their belief. I regard the present conservation movement as the embryo of such an affirmation.

An ethic may be regarded as a mode of guidance for meeting ecological
situations so new or intricate, or involving such deferred reactions, that the path
of social expediency is not discernible to the average individual. Animal instincts are modes of guidance for the individual in meeting such situations.
Ethics are possibly a kind of community instinct in the making.

The Community Concept

All ethics so far evolved rest upon a single premise: that the individual is a   10
member of a community of interdependent parts. His instincts prompt him to
compete for his place in the community, but his ethics prompt him also to cooperate (perhaps in order that there may be a place to compete for).

The land ethic simply enlarges the boundaries of the community to include soils, waters, plants, and animals, or collectively: the land.

This sounds simple: do we not already sing our love for and obligation to
the land of the free and the home of the brave? Yes, but just what and whom do
we love? Certainly not the soil, which we are sending helter-skelter downriver.
Certainly not the waters, which we assume have no function except to turn tur-
bines, float barges, and carry off sewage. Certainly not the plants, of which we

---

Mosaic Decalogue: The Ten Commandments. [All notes are the Editors'.]

exterminate whole communities without batting an eye. Certainly not the animals, of which we have already extirpated many of the largest and most beautiful species. A land ethic of course cannot prevent the alteration, management, and use of these "resources," but it does affirm their right to continued existence, and, at least in spots, their continued existence in a natural state.

In short, a land ethic changes the role of Homo sapiens from conqueror of the land-community to plain member and citizen of it. It implies respect for his fellow members, and also respect for the community as such.

In human history, we have learned (I hope) that the conqueror role is eventually self-defeating. Why? Because it is implicit in such a role that the conqueror knows, ex cathedra, just what makes the community clock tick, and just what and who is valuable, and what and who is worthless, in community life. It always turns out that he knows neither, and this is why his conquests eventually defeat themselves.

In the biotic community, a parallel situation exists. Abraham knew exactly   15 what the land was for: it was to drip milk and honey into Abraham's mouth. At the present moment, the assurance with which we regard this assumption is inverse to the degree of our education.

The ordinary citizen today assumes that science knows what makes the community clock tick; the scientist is equally sure that he does not. He knows that the biotic mechanism is so complex that its workings may never be fully understood.

That man is, in fact, only a member of a biotic team is shown by an ecological interpretation of history. Many historical events, hitherto explained solely in terms of human enterprise, were actually biotic interactions between people and land. The characteristics of the land determined the facts quite as potently as the characteristics of the men who lived on it.

Consider, for example, the settlement of the Mississippi Valley. In the years following the Revolution, three groups were contending for its control: the native Indian, the French and English traders, and the American settlers. Historians wonder what would have happened if the English at Detroit had thrown a little more weight into the Indian side of those tipsy scales which decided the outcome of the colonial migration into the cane lands of Kentucky. It is time now to ponder the fact that the cane lands, when subjected to the particular mixture of forces represented by the cow, plow, fire, and ax of the pioneer, became bluegrass. What if the plant succession inherent in this dark and bloody ground had, under the impact of these forces, given us some worthless sedge, shrub, or weed? Would Boone and Kenton have held out? Would there have been any overflow into Ohio, Indiana, Illinois, and Missouri? Any Louisiana Purchase? Any transcontinental union of new states? Any Civil War?

Kentucky was one sentence in the drama of history. We are commonly told what the human actors in this drama tried to do, but we are seldom told that their success, or the lack of it, hung in large degree on the reaction of particular soils to the impact of the particular forces exerted by their occupancy. In the

case of Kentucky, we do not even know where the bluegrass came from—
whether it is a native species, or a stowaway from Europe.

Contrast the cane lands with what hindsight tells us about the Southwest, 20
where the pioneers were equally brave, resourceful, and persevering. The impact of occupancy here brought no bluegrass, or other plant fitted to withstand
the bumps and buffetings of hard use. This region, when grazed by livestock,
reverted through a series of more and more worthless grasses, shrubs, and weeds
to a condition of unstable equilibrium. Each recession of plant types bred erosion; each increment to erosion bred a further recession of plants. The result
today is a progressive and mutual deterioration, not only of plants and soils,
but of the animal community subsisting thereon. The early settlers did not expect this: on the ciénegas of New Mexico some even cut ditches to hasten it.
So subtle has been its progress that few residents of the region are aware of it. It
is quite invisible to the tourist who finds this wrecked landscape colorful and
charming (as indeed it is, but it bears scant resemblance to what it was in 1848).

This same landscape was "developed" once before, but with quite different results. The Pueblo Indians settled the Southwest in pre-Columbian
times, but they happened *not* to be equipped with range livestock. Their civilization expired, but not because their land expired.

In India, regions devoid of any sod-forming grass have been settled, apparently without wrecking the land, by the simple expedient of carrying the
grass to the cow, rather than vice versa. (Was this the result of some deep wisdom, or was it just good luck? I do not know.)

In short, the plant succession steered the course of history; the pioneer
simply demonstrated, for good or ill, what successions inhered in the land. Is
history taught in this spirit? It will be, once the concept of land as a community
really penetrates our intellectual life.

THE ECOLOGICAL CONSCIENCE

Conservation is a state of harmony between men and land. Despite nearly a
century of propaganda, conservation still proceeds at a snail's pace; progress
still consists largely of letterhead pieties and convention oratory. On the back
forty we still slip two steps backward for each forward stride.

The usual answer to this dilemma is "more conservation education." No 25
one will debate this, but is it certain that only the *volume* of education needs
stepping up? Is something lacking in the *content* as well?

It is difficult to give a fair summary of its content in brief form, but, as I
understand it, the content is substantially this: obey the law, vote right, join
some organizations, and practice what conservation is profitable on your own
land; the government will do the rest.

Is not this formula too easy to accomplish anything worthwhile? It defines no right or wrong, assigns no obligation, calls for no sacrifice, implies no

change in the current philosophy of values. In respect of land use, it urges only enlightened self-interest. Just how far will such education take us? An example will perhaps yield a partial answer.

By 1930 it had become clear to all except the ecologically blind that southwestern Wisconsin's topsoil was slipping seaward. In 1933 the farmers were told that if they would adopt certain remedial practices for five years, the public would donate CCC labor to install them, plus the necessary machinery and materials. The offer was widely accepted, but the practices were widely forgotten when the five-year contract period was up. The farmers continued only those practices that yielded an immediate and visible economic gain for themselves.

This led to the idea that maybe farmers would learn more quickly if they themselves wrote the rules. Accordingly the Wisconsin legislature in 1937 passed the Soil Conservation District Law. This said to farmers, in effect: *We, the public, will furnish you free technical service and loan you specialized machinery, if you will write your own rules for land use. Each county may write its own rules, and these will have the force of law.* Nearly all the counties promptly organized to accept the proffered help, but after a decade of operation, *no county has yet written a single rule.* There has been visible progress in such practices as strip cropping, pasture renovation, and soil liming, but none in fencing woodlots against grazing, and none in excluding plow and cow from steep slopes. The farmers, in short, have selected those remedial practices which were profitable anyhow, and ignored those which were profitable to the community, but not clearly profitable to themselves.

When one asks why no rules have been written, one is told that the community is not yet ready to support them; education must precede rules. But the education actually in progress makes no mention of obligations to land over and above those dictated by self-interest. The net result is that we have more education but less soil, fewer healthy woods, and as many floods as in 1937. 30

The puzzling aspect of such situations is that the existence of obligations over and above self-interest is taken for granted in such rural community enterprises as the betterment of roads, schools, churches, and baseball teams. Their existence is not taken for granted, nor as yet seriously discussed, in bettering the behavior of the water that falls on the land, or in the preserving of the beauty or diversity of the farm landscape. Land-use ethics are still governed wholly by economic self-interest, just as social ethics were a century ago.

To sum up: we asked the farmer to do what he conveniently could to save his soil, and he has done just that, and only that. The farmer who clears the woods of a 75 percent slope, turns his cows into the clearing, and dumps its rainfall, rocks, and soil into the community creek, is still (if otherwise decent) a respected member of society. If he puts lime on his fields and plants his crops on contour, he is still entitled to all the privileges and emoluments of his Soil Conservation District. The district is a beautiful piece of social machinery, but it is coughing along on two cylinders because we have been too timid, and too anxious for quick success, to tell the farmer the true magnitude of his obligations. Obligations have no meaning without conscience, and the problem we face is the extension of the social conscience from people to land.

No important change in ethics was ever accomplished without an internal change in our intellectual emphasis, loyalties, affections, and convictions. The proof that conservation has not yet touched these foundations of conduct lies in the fact that philosophy and religion have not yet heard of it. In our attempt to make conservation easy, we have made it trivial.

Substitutes for a Land Ethic

When the logic of history hungers for bread and we hand out a stone, we are at pains to explain how much the stone resembles bread. I now describe some of the stones which serve in lieu of a land ethic.

One basic weakness in a conservation system based wholly on economic 35 motives is that most members of the land community have no economic value. Wildflowers and songbirds are examples. Of the 22,000 higher plants and animals native to Wisconsin, it is doubtful whether more than 5 percent can be sold, fed, eaten, or otherwise put to economic use. Yet these creatures are members of the biotic community, and if (as I believe) its stability depends on its integrity, they are entitled to continuance.

When one of these noneconomic categories is threatened, and if we happen to love it, we invent subterfuges to give it economic importance. At the beginning of the century songbirds were supposed to be disappearing. Ornithologists jumped to the rescue with some distinctly shaky evidence to the effect that insects would eat us up if birds failed to control them. The evidence had to be economic in order to be valid.

It is painful to read these circumlocutions today. We have no land ethic yet, but we have at least drawn nearer the point of admitting that birds should continue as a matter of biotic right, regardless of the presence or absence of economic advantage to us.

A parallel situation exists in respect of predatory mammals, raptorial birds, and fish-eating birds. Time was when biologists somewhat overworked the evidence that these creatures preserve the health of game by killing weaklings, or that they control rodents for the farmer, or that they prey only on "worthless" species. Here again, the evidence had to be economic in order to be valid. It is only in recent years that we hear the more honest argument that predators are members of the community, and that no special interest has the right to exterminate them for the sake of a benefit, real or fancied, to itself. Unfortunately this enlightened view is still in the talk stage. In the field the extermination of predators goes merrily on: witness the impending erasure of the timber wolf by fiat of Congress, the Conservation Bureaus, and many state legislatures.

Some species of trees have been "read out of the party" by economics-minded foresters because they grow too slowly, or have too low a sale value to pay as timber crops: white cedar, tamarack, cypress, beech, and hemlock are examples. In Europe, where forestry is ecologically more advanced, the noncommercial tree species are recognized as members of the native forest community, to be preserved as such, within reason. Moreover some (like beech) have been found to have a valuable function in building up soil fertility. The interdependence of the forest and its constituent tree species, ground flora, and fauna is taken for granted.

Lack of economic value is sometimes a character not only of species or 40 groups, but of entire biotic communities: marshes, bogs, dunes, and "deserts" are examples. Our formula in such cases is to relegate their conservation to government as refuges, monuments, or parks. The difficulty is that these communities are usually interspersed with more valuable private lands; the government cannot possibly own or control such scattered parcels. The net effect is that we have relegated some of them to ultimate extinction over large areas. If the private owner were ecologically minded, he would be proud to be the custodian of a reasonable proportion of such areas, which add diversity and beauty to his farm and to his community.

In some instances, the assumed lack of profit in these "waste" areas has proved to be wrong, but only after most of them had been done away with. The present scramble to reflood muskrat marshes is a case in point.

There is a clear tendency in American conservation to relegate to government all necessary jobs that private landowners fail to perform. Government ownership, operation, subsidy, or regulation is now widely prevalent in forestry, range management, soil and watershed management, park and wilderness conservation, fisheries management, and migratory bird management, with more to come. Most of this growth in governmental conservation is proper and logical, some of it is inevitable. That I imply no disapproval of it is implicit in the fact that I have spent most of my life working for it. Nevertheless the question arises: What is the ultimate magnitude of the enterprise? Will the tax base carry its eventual ramifications? At what point will governmental conservation, like the mastodon, become handicapped by its own dimensions? The answer, if there is any, seems to be in a land ethic, or some other force which assigns more obligation to the private landowner.

Industrial landowners and users, especially lumbermen and stockmen, are inclined to wail long and loudly about the extension of government ownership and regulation to land, but (with notable exceptions) they show little disposition to develop the only visible alternative: the voluntary practice of conservation on their own lands.

When the private landowner is asked to perform some unprofitable act for the good of the community, he today assents only with outstretched palm. If the act costs him cash this is fair and proper, but when it costs only forethought, open-mindedness, or time, the issue is at least debatable. The overwhelming growth of land-use subsidies in recent years must be ascribed, in large part, to the government's own agencies for conservation education: the land bureaus, the agricultural colleges, and the extension services. As far as I can detect, no ethical obligation toward land is taught in these institutions.

To sum up: a system of conservation based solely on economic self- 45 interest is hopelessly lopsided. It tends to ignore, and thus eventually to eliminate, many elements in the land community that lack commercial value, but that are (as far as we know) essential to its healthy functioning. It assumes, falsely, I think, that the economic parts of the biotic clock will function without the uneconomic parts. It tends to relegate to government many functions eventually too large, too complex, or too widely dispersed to be performed by government.

An ethical obligation on the part of the private owner is the only visible remedy for these situations.

THE LAND PYRAMID

An ethic to supplement and guide the economic relation to land presupposes the existence of some mental image of land as a biotic mechanism. We can be ethical only in relation to something we can see, feel, understand, love, or otherwise have faith in.

The image commonly employed in conservation education is "the balance of nature." For reasons too lengthy to detail here, this figure of speech fails to describe accurately what little we know about the land mechanism. A much truer image is the one employed in ecology: the biotic pyramid. I shall first sketch the pyramid as a symbol of land, and later develop some of its implications in terms of land use.

Plants absorb energy from the sun. This energy flows through a circuit called the biota, which may be represented by a pyramid consisting of layers. The bottom layer is the soil. A plant layer rests on the soil, an insect layer on the plants, a bird and rodent layer on the insects, and so on up through various animal groups to the apex layer, which consists of the larger carnivores.

The species of a layer are alike not in where they came from, or in what 50 they look like, but rather in what they eat. Each successive layer depends on those below it for food and often for other services, and each in turn furnishes food and services to those above. Proceeding upward, each successive layer decreases in numerical abundance. Thus, for every carnivore there are hundreds of his prey, thousands of their prey, millions of insects, uncountable plants. The pyramidal form of the system reflects this numerical progression from apex to base. Man shares an intermediate layer with the bears, raccoons, and squirrels which eat both meat and vegetables.

The lines of dependency for food and other services are called food chains. Thus soil-oak-deer-Indian is a chain that has now been largely converted to soil-corn-cow-farmer. Each species, including ourselves, is a link in many chains. The deer eats a hundred plants other than oak, and the cow a hundred plants other than corn. Both, then, are links in a hundred chains. The pyramid is a tangle of chains so complex as to seem disorderly, yet the stability of the system proves it to be a highly organized structure. Its functioning depends on the cooperation and competition of its diverse parts.

In the beginning, the pyramid of life was low and squat; the food chains short and simple. Evolution has added layer after layer, link after link. Man is one of thousands of accretions to the height and complexity of the pyramid. Science has given us many doubts, but it has given us at least one certainty: the trend of evolution is to elaborate and diversify the biota.

Land, then, is not merely soil; it is a fountain of energy flowing through a circuit of soils, plants, and animals. Food chains are the living channels which conduct energy upward; death and decay return it to the soil. The circuit is not closed; some energy is dissipated in decay, some is added by absorption from the air, some is stored in soils, peats, and long-lived forests; but it is a sustained circuit, like a slowly augmented revolving fund of life. There is always a net loss by downhill wash, but this is normally small and offset by the decay of rocks. It is deposited in the ocean and, in the course of geological time, raised to form new lands and new pyramids.

The velocity and character of the upward flow of energy depend on the complex structure of the plant and animal community, much as the upward flow of sap in a tree depends on its complex cellular organization. Without this complexity, normal circulation would presumably not occur. Structure means the characteristic numbers, as well as the characteristic kinds and functions, of the component species. This interdependence between the complex structure of the land and its smooth functioning as an energy unit is one of its basic attributes.

When a change occurs in one part of the circuit, many other parts must 55 adjust themselves to it. Change does not necessarily obstruct or divert the flow of energy; evolution is a long series of self-induced changes, the net result of which has been to elaborate the flow mechanism and to lengthen the circuit. Evolutionary changes, however, are usually slow and local. Man's invention of tools has enabled him to make changes of unprecedented violence, rapidity, and scope.

One change is in the composition of floras and faunas. The larger predators are lopped off the apex of the pyramid; food chains, for the first time in history, become shorter rather than longer. Domesticated species from other lands are substituted for wild ones, and wild ones are moved to new habitats. In this worldwide pooling of faunas and floras, some species get out of bounds as pests and diseases, others are extinguished. Such effects are seldom intended or foreseen; they represent unpredicted and often untraceable readjustments in the structure. Agricultural science is largely a race between the emergence of new pests and the emergence of new techniques for their control.

Another change touches the flow of energy through plants and animals and its return to the soil. Fertility is the ability of soil to receive, store, and release energy. Agriculture, by overdrafts on the soil, or by too radical a substitution of domestic for native species in the superstructure, may derange the channels of flow or deplete storage. Soils depleted of their storage, or of the organic matter which anchors it, wash away faster than they form. This is erosion.

Waters, like soil, are part of the energy circuit. Industry, by polluting waters or obstructing them with dams, may exclude the plants and animals necessary to keep energy in circulation.

Transportation brings about another basic change: the plants or animals grown in one region are now consumed and returned to the soil in another. Transportation taps the energy stored in rocks, and in the air, and uses it elsewhere; thus we fertilize the garden with nitrogen gleaned by the guano birds from the fishes of seas on the other side of the equator. Thus the formerly localized and self-contained circuits are pooled on a worldwide scale.

The process of altering the pyramid for human occupation releases stored 60 energy, and this often gives rise, during the pioneering period, to a deceptive exuberance of plant and animal life, both wild and tame. These releases of biotic capital tend to becloud or postpone the penalties of violence.

This thumbnail sketch of land as an energy circuit conveys three basic ideas:

1. That land is not merely soil.
2. That the native plants and animals kept the energy circuit open; others may or may not.
3. That man-made changes are of a different order than evolutionary changes, and have effects more comprehensive than is intended or foreseen.

These ideas, collectively, raise two basic issues: Can the land adjust itself to the new order? Can the desired alterations be accomplished with less violence?

Biotas seem to differ in their capacity to sustain violent conversion. Western Europe, for example, carries a far different pyramid than Caesar found there. Some large animals are lost; swampy forests have become meadows or plowland; many new plants and animals are introduced, some of which escape as pests; the remaining natives are greatly changed in distribution and abundance. Yet the soil is still there and, with the help of imported nutrients, still fertile; the waters flow normally; the new structure seems to function and to persist. There is no visible stoppage or derangement of the circuit.

Western Europe, then, has a resistant biota. Its inner processes are tough, elastic, resistant to strain. No matter how violent the alterations, the pyramid, so far, has developed some new modus vivendi° which preserves its habitability for man, and for most of the other natives.

Japan seems to present another instance of radical conversion without 65 disorganization.

Most other civilized regions, and some as yet barely touched by civilization, display various stages of disorganization, varying from initial symptoms to advanced wastage. In Asia Minor and North Africa diagnosis is confused by climatic changes, which may have been either the cause or the effect of advanced wastage. In the United States the degree of disorganization varies locally; it is worst in the Southwest, the Ozarks, and parts of the South, and least in New England and the Northwest. Better land uses may still arrest it in the less advanced regions. In parts of Mexico, South America, South Africa, and Australia a violent and accelerating wastage is in progress, but I cannot assess the prospects.

This almost worldwide display of disorganization in the land seems to be similar to disease in an animal, except that it never culminates in complete disorganization or death. The land recovers, but at some reduced level of complexity, and with a reduced carrying capacity for people, plants, and animals. Many biotas currently regarded as "lands of opportunity" are in fact already subsisting on exploitative agriculture, i.e., they have already exceeded their sustained carrying capacity. Most of South America is overpopulated in this sense.

In arid regions we attempt to offset the process of wastage by reclamation, but it is only too evident that the prospective longevity of reclamation projects is often short. In our own West, the best of them may not last a century.

The combined evidence of history and ecology seems to support one general deduction: the less violent the man-made changes, the greater the probability of successful readjustment in the pyramid. Violence, in turn, varies with human population density; a dense population requires a more violent conversion. In this respect, North America has a better chance for permanence than Europe, if she can contrive to limit her density.

This deduction runs counter to our current philosophy, which assumes 70 that because a small increase in density enriched human life, that an indefinite increase will enrich it indefinitely. Ecology knows of no density relationship that holds for indefinitely wide limits. All gains from density are subject to a law of diminishing returns.

Whatever may be the equation for men and land, it is improbable that we as yet know all its terms. Recent discoveries in mineral and vitamin nutrition reveal unsuspected dependencies in the up circuit: incredibly minute quantities of certain substances determine the value of soils to plants, of plants to animals. What of the down circuit? What of the vanishing species, the preservation of

---

modus vivendi: Latin for "way of working."

which we now regard as an esthetic luxury? They helped build the soil; in what unsuspected ways may they be essential to its maintenance? Professor Weaver proposes that we use prairie flowers to reflocculate the wasting soils of the dust bowl; who knows for what purpose cranes and condors, otters and grizzlies may some day be used?

LAND HEALTH AND THE A–B CLEAVAGE

A land ethic, then, reflects the existence of an ecological conscience, and this in turn reflects a conviction of individual responsibility for the health of the land. Health is the capacity of the land for self-renewal. Conservation is our effort to understand and preserve this capacity.

Conservationists are notorious for their dissensions. Superficially these seem to add up to mere confusion, but a more careful scrutiny reveals a single plane of cleavage common to many specialized fields. In each field one group (A) regards the land as soil, and its function as commodity production; another group (B) regards the land as a biota, and its function as something broader. How much broader is admittedly in a state of doubt and confusion.

In my own field, forestry, Group A is quite content to grow trees like cabbages, with cellulose as the basic forest commodity. It feels no inhibition against violence; its ideology is agronomic. Group B, on the other hand, sees forestry as fundamentally different from agronomy because it employs natural species, and manages a natural environment rather than creating an artificial one. Group B prefers natural reproduction on principle. It worries on biotic as well as economic grounds about the loss of species like chestnut, and the threatened loss of the white pines. It worries about a whole series of secondary forest functions: wildlife, recreation, watersheds, wilderness areas. To my mind, Group B feels the stirrings of an ecological conscience.

In the wildlife field, a parallel cleavage exists. For Group A the basic 75 commodities are sport and meat; the yardsticks of production are ciphers of take in pheasants and trout. Artificial propagation is acceptable as a permanent as well as a temporary recourse—if its unit costs permit. Group B, on the other hand, worries about a whole series of biotic side issues. What is the cost in predators of producing a game crop? Should we have further recourse to exotics? How can management restore the shrinking species, like prairie grouse, already hopeless as shootable game? How can management restore the threatened rarities, like trumpeter swan and whooping crane? Can management principles be extended to wildflowers? Here again it is clear to me that we have the same A–B cleavage as in forestry.

In the larger field of agriculture I am less competent to speak, but there seem to be somewhat parallel cleavages. Scientific agriculture was actively developing before ecology was born, hence a slower penetration of ecological concepts might be expected. Moreover the farmer, by the very nature of his techniques, must modify the biota more radically than the forester or the wildlife manager. Nevertheless, there are many discontents in agriculture which seem to add up to a new vision of "biotic farming."

Perhaps the most important of these is the new evidence that poundage or tonnage is no measure of the food value of farm crops; the products of fertile soil may be qualitatively as well as quantitatively superior. We can bolster poundage from depleted soils by pouring on imported fertility, but we are not necessarily bolstering food value. The possible ultimate ramifications of this idea are so immense that I must leave their exposition to abler pens.

The discontent that labels itself "organic farming," while bearing some of the earmarks of a cult, is nevertheless biotic in its direction, particularly in its insistence on the importance of soil flora and fauna.

The ecological fundamentals of agriculture are just as poorly known to the public as in other fields of land use. For example, few educated people realize that the marvelous advances in technique made during recent decades are improvements in the pump, rather than the well. Acre for acre, they have barely sufficed to offset the sinking level of fertility.

In all of these cleavages, we see repeated the same basic paradoxes: man 80 the conqueror *versus* man the biotic citizen; science the sharpener of his sword *versus* science the searchlight on his universe; land the slave and servant *versus* land the collective organism. Robinson's injunction to Tristram may well be applied, at this juncture, to Homo sapiens as a species in geological time:

> Whether you will or not
> You are a King, Tristram, for you are one
> Of the time-tested few that leave the world,
> When they are gone, not the same place it was.
> Mark what you leave.

THE OUTLOOK

It is inconceivable to me that an ethical relation to land can exist without love, respect, and admiration for land, and a high regard for its value. By value, I of course mean something far broader than mere economic value; I mean value in the philosophical sense.

Perhaps the most serious obstacle impeding the evolution of a land ethic is the fact that our educational and economic system is headed away from, rather than toward, an intense consciousness of land. Your true modern is separated from the land by many middlemen, and by innumerable physical gadgets. He has no vital relation to it; to him it is the space between cities on which crops grow. Turn him loose for a day on the land, and if the spot does not happen to be a golf links or a "scenic" area, he is bored stiff. If crops could be raised by hydroponics instead of farming, it would suit him very well. Synthetic substitutes for wood, leather, wool, and other natural land products suit him better than the originals. In short, land is something he has "outgrown."

Almost equally serious as an obstacle to a land ethic is the attitude of the farmer for whom the land is still an adversary, or a taskmaster that keeps him in slavery. Theoretically, the mechanization of farming ought to cut the farmer's chains, but whether it really does is debatable.

One of the requisites for an ecological comprehension of land is an understanding of ecology, and this is by no means coextensive with "education"; in fact, much higher education seems deliberately to avoid ecological concepts. An understanding of ecology does not necessarily originate in courses bearing ecological labels; it is quite as likely to be labeled geography, botany, agronomy, history, or economics. This is as it should be, but whatever the label, ecological training is scarce.

The case for a land ethic would appear hopeless but for the minority 85 which is in obvious revolt against these "modern" trends.

The "key log" which must be moved to release the evolutionary process for an ethic is simply this: quit thinking about decent land use as solely an economic problem. Examine each question in terms of what is ethically and esthetically right, as well as what is economically expedient. A thing is right when it tends to preserve the integrity, stability, and beauty of the biotic community. It is wrong when it tends otherwise.

It of course goes without saying that economic feasibility limits the tether of what can or cannot be done for land. It always has and it always will. The fallacy the economic determinists have tied around our collective neck, and which we now need to cast off, is the belief that economics determines *all* land use. This is simply not true. An innumerable host of actions and attitudes, comprising perhaps the bulk of all land relations, is determined by the land users' tastes and predilections, rather than by his purse. The bulk of all land relations hinges on investments of time, forethought, skill, and faith rather than on investments of cash. As a land user thinketh, so is he.

I have purposely presented the land ethic as a product of social evolution because nothing so important as an ethic is ever "written." Only the most superficial student of history supposes that Moses "wrote" the Decalogue; it evolved in the minds of a thinking community, and Moses wrote a tentative summary of it for a "seminar." I say tentative because evolution never stops.

The evolution of a land ethic is an intellectual as well as emotional process. Conservation is paved with good intentions which prove to be futile, or even dangerous, because they are devoid of critical understanding either of the land, or of economic land use. I think it is a truism that as the ethical frontier advances from the individual to the community, its intellectual content increases.

The mechanism of operation is the same for any ethic: social approba- 90 tion for right actions: social disapproval for wrong actions.

By and large, our present problem is one of attitudes and implements. We are remodeling the Alhambra° with a steam shovel, and we are proud of our yardage. We shall hardly relinquish the shovel, which after all has many good points, but we are in need of gentler and more objective criteria for its successful use.

WHAT DOES HE SAY?

1. Aldo Leopold begins by making a distinction between "propriety" and "property." What's the difference, as you understand it? Can you do anything you want with property? Write a paragraph about this.

2. In this essay, Leopold tries to propose two large notions. The first is, roughly, a summary of our old view of land and what it was for. The second is that this view needs to change. Identify three places in "The Land Ethic" where you're pretty sure Leopold is arguing for a change. Mark each of these. Write a paragraph about the one that's clearest to you; try to explain it in your own words.

3. You'll see that this essay is divided into sections, each with its own title (except for the first). For each of these sections, copy out two sentences that seem important to what that section is trying to say. Thus, by the time you've finished reading, you'll have copied out sixteen sentences.

4. Pay special attention to each time this essay mentions questions of value or worth. Underline these or mark the margins for later reference.

WHAT DO YOU THINK?

5. Write an essay that summarizes "The Land Ethic." Stress what Leopold argues should be the case or what he argues we should do. Anticipate readers' misunderstandings. Quote carefully. Your summary cannot exceed one thousand words. Try not to judge what you're summarizing; instead, try to be accurate to what Leopold says.

6. Write an essay that uses "The Land Ethic" as your primary example in the effort to explain your own view of the relationship people ought to have with land. If you have local or personal experience to bring to this essay, do so. But keep "The Land Ethic" as your defining example.

7. Write an analysis of "The Land Ethic" that divides what Leopold says into two categories: what he objects to and what he hopes for. Explain each category. Then apply this framework to some local land-use issue. Explain the issue, explain how Leopold's framework might view it, and end by asserting and explaining your own views.

Alhambra: Thirteenth-century palace located in Grenada, Spain; famous for its delicate Moorish architecture.

8. Write a personal essay about some valued connection that you have to a natural place. Describe the place with care. Explain why you have this connection, what the place means to you, and why or how you would, or would not, be able to put a dollar value on it. Make sure your essay quotes Leopold at least once.

WHAT WOULD THEY SAY?

9. Read Milton Friedman's "The Social Responsibility of Business Is to Increase Its Profits" (p. 518) together with "The Land Ethic." In particular, pay attention to how each writer defines *profit* or *benefit*. On this basis, would you find these authors in fundamental agreement? Write an essay explaining why or why not.

10. Read "The Earth Charter" (p. 158) together with "The Land Ethic." Then compose a document that selects parts of "The Earth Charter" and annotates them with quotations from "The Land Ethic." Overall, the document you make should run about five pages.

11. Consider "The Land Ethic" together with Joy Williams's "Save the Whales, Screw the Shrimp" (p. 146). How would these two essayists agree or disagree? Assume that each has read the other's essay and that now they're talking. Write their dialogue. Then skip several spaces and write—in about one page—why you've constructed this dialogue as you have.

12. Read Wendell Berry's "Out of Your Car, Off Your Horse" (p. 672) together with "The Land Ethic." Choose three of Berry's numbered sections and match each to a portion of "The Land Ethic" to show the extent to which these essayists agree—or not. End by explaining how understanding Berry makes "The Land Ethic" easier to grasp.

PAUL HAWKEN
A Teasing Irony

THIS SECTION CONCLUDES *by returning to the issue of business, though with an econo-mist's surprising claim that ecology and commerce are not at odds but mutually dependent. What's good for the environment is good for business, Paul Hawken (b. 1946) claims.*

An environmentalist, economist, and educator, Hawken is cochair of TNS-International, a nonprofit organization that helps businesses create a commitment to envi-ronmental sustainability, and has served on the boards of the National Audubon Society and Friends of the Earth. He has founded several companies and written six books, in-cluding The Next Economy *(1983),* Growing a Business *(1987), and* The Ecol-ogy of Commerce *(1993), from which "A Teasing Irony" is taken.*

I have come to believe that we in America and in the rest of the industrialized West do not know what business really is, or, therefore, what it can become. Perhaps this is a strange remark, given that free-market capitalism is now largely unchallenged as the economic and social credo of just about every so-ciety on earth, but I believe it's correct. Despite our management schools, despite the thousands of books written about business, despite the legions of economists who tinker with the trimtabs of the $21 trillion world economy, despite and maybe because of the victory of free-market capitalism over so-cialism worldwide, our understanding of business—what makes for healthy commerce, what the role of such commerce should be within society as a whole—is stuck at a primitive level.

The ultimate purpose of business is not, or should not be, simply to make money. Nor is it merely a system of making and selling things. The promise of business is to increase the general well-being of humankind through service, a creative invention and ethical philosophy. Making money is, on its own terms, totally meaningless, an insufficient pursuit for the complex and decaying world we live in. We have reached an unsettling and portentous turning point in industrial civilization. It is emblematic that the second animal ever to be "patented" is a mouse with no immune system that will be used to research diseases of the future, and that mother's milk would be banned by the food safety laws of industrialized nations if it were sold as a packaged good. What's in the milk besides milk and what's suppressing our immune system is literally industry—its by-products, wastes, and toxins. Facts like this lead to an inevitable conclusion: businesspeople must either dedicate them-selves to transforming commerce to a restorative undertaking, or march society to the undertaker.

547

I believe business *is* on the verge of such a transformation, a change brought on by social and biological forces that can no longer be ignored or put aside, a change so thorough and sweeping that in the decades to come business will be unrecognizable when compared to the commercial institutions of today. We have the capacity and ability to create a remarkably different economy, one that can restore ecosystems and protect the environment while bringing forth innovation, prosperity, meaningful work, and true security. As long as we continue to ignore the evolutionary thrust and potential of the existing economy, the world of commerce will continue to be in a state of disorder and constant restructuring. This is not because the worldwide recession has been so deep and long, but because there is a widening gap between the rapid rate at which society and the natural world are decaying and the agonizingly slow rate at which business is effecting any truly fundamental change.

This turbulent, transformative period we now face might be thought of as a system shedding its skin; it signals the first attempts by commerce to adapt to a new era. Many people in business, the media, and politics do not perceive this evolutionary step, while others who do understand fight it. Standing in the way of change are corporations who want to continue worldwide deforestation and build coal-fired power plants, who see the storage or dumping of billions of tons of waste as a plausible strategy for the future, who imagine a world of industrial farms sustained by chemical feedstocks. They can slow the process down, make it more difficult, but they will not stop it. Like a sunset effect, the glories of the industrial economy may mask the fact that it is poised at a declining horizon of options and possibilities. Just as internal contradictions brought down the Marxist and socialist economies, so do a different set of social and biological forces signal our own possible demise. Those forces can no longer be ignored or put aside.

That the title of this book, *The Ecology of Commerce*, reads today as an   5 oxymoron speaks to the gap between how the earth lives and how we now conduct our commercial lives. We don't usually think of ecology and commerce as compatible subjects. While much of our current environmental policy seeks a "balance" between the needs of business and the needs of the environment, common sense says there is only one critical balance and one set of needs: the dynamic, ever-changing interplay of the forces of life. The restorative economy envisioned and described in this book respects this fact. It unites ecology and commerce into one sustainable act of production and distribution that mimics and enhances natural processes. It proposes a newborn literacy of enterprise that acknowledges that we are all here together, at once, at the service of and at the mercy of nature, each other, and our daily acts.

A hundred years ago, even fifty years ago, it did not seem urgent that we understand the relationship between business and a healthy environment, because natural resources seemed unlimited. But on the verge of a new millennium we know that we have decimated 97 percent of the ancient forests in North America; every day our farmers and ranchers draw out 20 billion more gallons of water from the ground than are replaced by rainfall; the Ogalala

Aquifer, an underwater river beneath the Great Plains larger than any body of fresh water on earth, will dry up within thirty to forty years at present rates of extraction; globally we lose 25 billion tons of fertile topsoil every year, the equivalent of all the wheat fields in Australia. These critical losses are occurring while the world population is increasing at the rate of 90 million people per year. Quite simply, our business practices are destroying life on earth. Given current corporate practices, not one wildlife reserve, wilderness, or indigenous culture will survive the global market economy. We know that every natural system on the planet is disintegrating. The land, water, air, and sea have been functionally transformed from life-supporting systems into repositories for waste. There is no polite way to say that business is destroying the world.

Having served on the boards of several environmental organizations, I thought I understood the nature and extent of the problems we face. But as I prepared to write this book, I reviewed much of the new literature in the field and discovered that the more I researched the issues, the more disquieting I found the information. The rate and extent of environmental degradation is far in excess of anything I had previously imagined. The situation was like the textbook illusion in which the viewer is presented with a jumble of halftone dots that reveals the image of Abraham Lincoln only when seen from a distance. Each of the sources I worked with was one such dot, not meaningless in itself, but only a part of the picture. The problem we face is far greater than anything portrayed by the media. I came to understand well the despair of one epidemiologist who, after reviewing the work in her field and convening a conference to examine the effects of chlorinated compounds on embryonic development, went into a quiet mourning for six months. The implications of that conference were worse than any single participant could have anticipated: the immune system of every unborn child in the world may soon be adversely and irrevocably affected by the persistent toxins in our food, air, and water.

A subtler but similarly disquieting development was reported by the *New York Times* in 1992 in an article entitled "The Silence of the Frogs." At an international conference on herpetology (the study of amphibians and reptiles), while 1,300 participants gave hundreds of official papers on specialized subjects, none had focused on the total picture. Pieced together informally in the hallways and in the lunch lines at the conference was the fact that frogs are disappearing from the face of the earth at an inexplicably rapid rate. Even more disturbing was the conclusion that these populations are crashing not merely in regions where there are known industrial toxins, but also in pristine wilderness areas where there is abundant food and no known sources of pollution. The implications of such a die-off go beyond frogs. The human endocrine system is remarkably similar to that of fish, birds, and wildlife; it is, from an evolutionary point of view, an ancient system. If endocrine and immune systems are failing and breaking down at lower levels of the animal kingdom, we may be similarly vulnerable. The reason we may not yet be experiencing the same types of breakdown seen in other species is because we gestate and breed comparatively rather slowly. On complex biological levels such as ours, bad news travels un-hurriedly, but it eventually arrives. In other words, something unusual and in-auspicious may be occurring globally at all levels of biological development: a fundamental decline that we are only beginning to comprehend and that our efforts at "environmentalism" have failed to address.

From this perspective, recycling aluminum cans in the company cafeteria and ceremonial tree plantings are about as effective as bailing out the *Titanic* with teaspoons. While recycling and tree planting are good and necessary ideas, they are woefully inadequate. How can business itself survive a continued pat-tern of worldwide degradation in living systems? What is the logic of extracting diminishing resources in order to create capital to finance more consumption and demand on those same diminishing resources? How do we imagine our fu-ture when our commercial systems conflict with everything nature teaches us?

Constructive changes in our relationship to the environment have thus   10 far been thwarted primarily because business is not properly designed to adapt to the situation we face. Business is the practice of the possible: highly devel-oped and intelligent in many respects, it is, however, not a science. In many ways business economics makes itself up as it progresses, and essentially lacks any guiding principles to relate it to such fundamental and critical concepts as evolution, biological diversity, carrying capacity, and the health of the com-mons. Business is designed to break through limits, not to respect them, espe-cially when the limits posed by ecological constraints are not always as glaring as dead rivers or human birth defects, but are often expressed in small, refined relationships and details.

The past one hundred years have seen waves of enterprise sweep across the world, discovering, mining, extracting, and processing eons' worth of stored wealth and resources. This flood of commerce has enriched capital cities, ruling families, powerful governments, and corporate elites. It has, therefore, quite nat-urally produced a dominant commercial culture that believes all resource and social inequities can be resolved through development, invention, high finance, and growth—always growth. For centuries, business has been able to claim that it is the organizational key to "unlocking the hidden wealth of creation for dis-tribution to the masses." By and large that has been true. But now, rather than distributing the wealth of the present, we are stealing the wealth of the future to enrich a society that seems nonetheless deeply troubled about its "good for-tune." While democratic capitalism still emanates an abundant and optimistic vision of humankind and its potential, it also retains the means to negate this vi-sion in ways that are as harmful as any war.

It is lamentable to extinguish a species by predation and killing, whether the perceived gain is leather, feather, pelt, or horn. But how will we explain that the disappearance of songbirds, frogs, fireflies, wildflowers, and the hun-dreds of thousands of other species that will become extinct in our lifetime had no justification other than ignorance and denial? How will we explain to our children that we knew they would be born with compromised immune systems, but we did nothing? When will the business world look honestly at itself and ask whether it isn't time to change?

Having expropriated resources from the natural world in order to fuel a rather transient period of materialistic freedom, we must now restore no small measure of those resources and accept the limits and discipline inherent in that relationship. Until business does this, it will continue to be maladaptive and predatory. In order for free-market capitalism to transform itself in the century to come, it must fully acknowledge that the brilliant monuments of its triumph cast the darkest of shadows. Whatever possibilities business once represented, whatever dreams and glories corporate success once offered, the time has come to acknowledge that business as we know it is over. Over because it failed in one critical and thoughtless way: it did not honor the myriad forms of life that secure and connect its own breath and skin and heart to the breath and skin and heart of our earth.

Although the essential nature of commerce has not altered since the very first exchange of coin for corn, the power and impact of corporate capitalism have increased so dramatically as to dwarf all previous forms of international power. No empire—Greek, Roman, Byzantine, British, or any other—has had the reach of the modern global corporation, which glides easily across borders, cultures, and governments in search of markets, sales, assets, and profits. This institutional concentration of human energy and creativity is unparalleled in history.

But if capitalism has pillaged, it also delivered the goods, and in quanti-   15 ties that could not have been imagined just two generations ago. Providing that abundance is one of the central goals of doing business, and those who believe in capitalism believe that goal must be facilitated at every opportunity. Government is key to this strategy. The conservative view of free-market capitalism asserts that nothing should be allowed to hinder commerce. Sacrifices might be called for here and there, but in the end, the environment, the poor, the third world will all benefit as business more fully realizes its potential. In the new world order of the post-communist age, free-market capitalism promises to be the secular savior, echoing theologian Michael Novak's homage: "No system has so revolutionized ordinary expectations of human life— lengthened the life span, made the elimination of poverty and famine thinkable, enlarged the range of human choice—as democratic capitalism." This view of business was fervently embraced by the recent Republican administrations, who found in Novak's words an unimpeachable affirmation of many of their programs of deregulation.

Invoking the sanctity of the free market to prove that present business practices are sound and constructive, and using it to rebut every charge of ecological malfeasance is, at its heart, dishonest. Historically, we have given industry great latitude for its miscalculations because there was no science sufficiently developed to inform society of industrialism's effects. One hundred years ago, industrial cities were coated with grime and cut off from the sun by permanent palls of smoke; the citizens were beset by disease; the very conditions under which workers toiled and died were inhumane and exploitative. These conditions had their analog in the industrial processes of waste and despoliation, and were the direct costs of the Industrial Revolution. It took many decades before an appreciation of the social and environmental damage spread beyond a small circle of Marxists and muckrakers to society as a whole. Today, businesspeople readily concede the abuses of the early days of this revolution, but they do not wholly and genuinely acknowledge the more threatening abuses perpetuated by current practices. Troubling untruths lie uneasily within a colossal economic system that denies what we all know while it continues to degrade our world, our society, and our bodies. Business economists can explain in detail the workings of the modern corporation, its complex interrelation with financial markets, how its holdings might be valued on a discounted cash-flow basis, or the dynamics of global competitive advantages. These pronouncements and equations promise hope but they cannot explain—much less justify—the accelerating extinction of species, the deterioration of human health, the stress and anguish of the modern worker, the loss of our air, water, and forests. In short, they cannot explain the consequences of their actions.

Why, then, do we accept the excuses? Why do we hand business a blank check and exempt enterprise from the responsibility for maintaining social values? One reason might be that like the conferees, we have only a piecemeal view of events. We have no hallways to congregate in and so accumulate the overall image of cumulative destruction. Furthermore, their actions are defended—I daresay *have* to be defended—because most of us are dependent upon them for our livelihood. Even a declining General Motors still employs nearly 600,000 people. A supermarket chain such as American Stores employs 200,000 or more. The 400 companies profiled in *Everybody's Business Almanac* employ or support one-fourth of the U.S. population. The largest 1,000 companies in America account for over 60 percent of the GNP, leaving the balance to 11 million small businesses. The average large business is 16,500 times larger than the average small business. And since much of the population is now employed by these large corporations, they naturally see their interest as being linked to the success and growth of their employers. Such fealty resembles the allegiance that sustained feudal baronies; the vassal serfs believed that the lord who exploited them was better than the uncertainty of no lord at all. But in the competitive world of modern commerce, loyalty to the system prevents an objective examination of how market capitalism can also work against those who serve it.

Tinkering with the system will not bring species back to life, profit-sharing schemes do not restore our wetlands, donating money for a new production of *Don Giovanni* will not purify our water, nor will printing annual reports on recycled paper save us. The dilemma that confronts business is the contradiction that a commercial system that works well, by its own definitions, violates the greater and more profound ethic of biology. Succeeding in business today is like winning a battle and then discovering that the war was unjust. Of course, the discovery that a loyalty which has served so well can betray so badly is a troubling concept for any culture.

From my observations, most people involved with commerce who are also educated about environmental issues care deeply about commerce's effects. At the same time, such people feel anxious about their jobs, the economy, and the future in general. The environment becomes just one more thing to worry about. It looms in the future at a time when we are beset with many other, more immediate, concerns. It is like being a single parent when the dog has run away, the children are fighting, the dinner is burning, the babysitter hasn't shown up, we are late for the PTA meeting, and have just spilled gravy on the carpet when someone doing a survey knocks at the door and wants to know how we feel about the proposed landfill at the edge of town. Although the landfill will affect our lives in the future, we are afflicted with pressing problems today. Similarly, when environmental issues are presented to businesspeople as one more cost and one more regulation, "doing the right thing" becomes burdensome and intrusive. And the way our economy is organized today, businesspeople are right: doing the right thing might indeed put them out of business.

We should not be surprised, then, that there is a deep-seated unwilling- 20
ness to face the necessary reconstruction of our commercial institutions so that they function on behalf of our lives. Business believes that if it does not continue to grow and instead cuts back and retreats, it will destroy itself. Ecologists believe that if business continues its unabated expansion it will destroy the world around it. This book will discuss a third way, a path that restores the natural communities on earth but uses many of the historically effective organizational and market techniques of free enterprise.

The act of doing business carries with it ethical import, so given the dominance of business in our time, we must ask the question: How do we want our principal economic organism to conduct its commerce? Is it to be as a marauder, high on the food chain, pinning its prey with ease? If business is based on the notion that it can call upon nature without constraint to submit to the objectives of commerce, it will destroy the foundation on which rests the society it has pledged to serve. Though "nothing seems foul to those that win," the cultures that have been previously harmed and the lands we have forfeited must now be reincorporated into the body economic. Business must judge its goals and behavior, not from inherited definitions of the corporate culture, but from the perspective of the world and society beyond its self-referential borders.

If business is prepared to reexamine its underlying assumptions and listen to ecologists, botanists, toxicologists, zoologists, wildlife management experts, endocrinologists, indigenous cultures, and victims of industrial processes, without the selective filter of its internal rationale and biases, it will not only fulfill its own agenda of contributing to society by providing products, jobs, and prosperity, but also initiate a new era of ecological commerce, more promising and ultimately more fulfilling than the industrial age that preceded it.

While business teaches us effective forms of human organization, environmental science reveals that those forms do not necessarily preserve the natural resources that are the basis of our well-being. While business teaches how to gain financial wealth, ecological understanding demonstrates that wealth to be ultimately illusory unless it is based on the principles and cyclical processes of nature. The dialogue reconciling these dichotomies will be the fundamental basis for economic transformation.

In order for this dialogue to succeed, business needs a new language, a new role, a new way of seeing itself within the larger environment. Business parlance is a specific, rarefied, and, for most of us, borrowed language. It is useful when it describes the mechanics of commerce, but fails when we try to connect it with biology, society, or feeling, yet this specialized dialect has established itself as the planetary lingua franca. In the language and accounting of classical economics, resources do not technically exist until they are drilled, extracted, pumped, or cut; in biological accounting, the principle is reversed. Business language reduces living transactions to costs and exchange value. From this semantic strait emerges the talk of trade-offs and compromises between growth and conservation, jobs and ecology, society and biodiversity, American competitiveness and resource pricing.

The language of commerce sounds specific, but in fact it is not explicit 25 enough. If Hawaiians had 138 different ways to describe falling rain, we can assume that rain had a profound importance in their lives. Business, on the other hand, only has two words for profit—*gross* and *net*. The extraordinarily complex manner in which a company recovers profit is reduced to a single numerically neat and precise concept. It makes no distinctions as to how the profit was made. It does not factor in whether people or places were exploited, resources depleted, communities enhanced, lives lost, or whether the entire executive suite was in such turmoil as to require stress consultants and outplacement services for the victims. In other words, business does not discern whether the profit is one of quality, or mere quantity.

It is understandable that a more meticulous language has not developed in this area because, until relatively recently in history, business has not been central to how societies and cultures defined themselves. In fact, its hegemony is still debated, especially by politicians who cling to the outdated vanity that government is in control. While governments still retain the power to wage war, defend territory, and issue currency, they can do little to create wealth except to work with business. Given that power, the modern corporation needs to expand and widen its vocabulary to become more environmentally accurate and culturally enduring. Without this new vocabulary, capitalism will become the commercial equivalent of the Holy Roman Empire: an amorphous global-corporate state taking what it needs and forcing smaller governments into financial subjugation, since no governing body can retain political legitimacy without money, credits, investment, and the sanction of the international business community. Biologically speaking, such unbalanced dominance will precipitate the demise of global capitalism, just as it brought down Rome.

Free-market purists believe that their system works so perfectly that even without an overarching vision the marketplace will attain the best social and environmental outcome. The restorative economy is organized in a profoundly different way. It does not depend upon a transformed human nature, but it does require that people accept that business is an ethical act and attempt to extend to commerce the interwoven, complex, and efficient models of natural systems. Current commercial practices are guided by the promise that we can stay the way we are, live the way we have, think the thoughts of old, and do business unburdened by real connections to cycles, climate, earth, or nature. Restorative economics challenges each of these assumptions.

The economics of restoration is the opposite of industrialization. Industrial economics separated production processes from the land, the land from people, and, ultimately, economic values from personal values. In an industrial, extractive economy, businesses are created to make money. Their financing and ability to grow are determined by their capacity to produce money. In a restorative economy, viability is determined by the ability to integrate with or replicate cyclical systems, in its means of production and distribution. The restorative economy would invert many fundamentals of the present system. In such an economy, there is the prospect that restoring the environment and making money would be the same process. As in nature, business and restoration should be part of a seamless web. Environmental protection should not be carried out at the behest of charity, altruism, or legislative fiats. As long as it is done so, it will remain a decorous subordinate to finance, growth, and technology.

Business has three basic issues to face: what it takes, what it makes, and what it wastes, and the three are intimately connected. First, business takes too much from the environment and does so in a harmful way; second, the products it makes require excessive amounts of energy, toxins, and pollutants; and finally, the method of manufacture and the very products themselves produce extraordinary waste and cause harm to present and future generations of all species including humans.

The solution for all three dilemmas are three fundamental principles that 30 govern nature. First, waste equals food. In nature, detritus is constantly recycled to nourish other systems with a minimum of energy and inputs. We call ourselves consumers, but the problem is that we do not consume. Each person in America produces twice his weight per day in household, hazardous, and industrial waste, and an additional half-ton per week when gaseous wastes such as carbon dioxide are included. An ecological model of commerce would imply that all waste have value to other modes of production so that everything is either reclaimed, reused, or recycled. Second, nature runs off of current solar income. The only input into the closed system of the earth is the sun. Last, nature depends on diversity, thrives on differences, and perishes in the imbalance of uniformity. Healthy systems are highly varied and specific to time and place. Nature is not mass-produced.

Many industries are now trying to re-source their raw materials to take into account sustainability, methods of extraction, means of processing, and impact on local cultures and ecosystems. For example, Herman Miller, the Knoll Group, and Wal-Mart have all committed themselves to paying higher prices for sustainably produced timber. They join many thousands of businesses, most much smaller, in recognizing their responsibility to initiate an ecological commerce. They should not have to pay more for raw materials that are produced in a sustainable manner. They should pay less. It should be possible to secure sustainably produced raw materials without the extraordinary expense and effort that is required today. Preserving life should be the natural result of commerce, not the exception.

In order to accomplish this, we need to rethink our markets entirely, asking ourselves how it is that products which harm and destroy life can be sold more cheaply than those that don't. Markets, so extremely effective at setting prices, are not currently equipped to recognize the true costs of producing goods. Because of this, business has two contradictory forces operating upon it: the need to achieve the lowest price in order to thrive if not survive in the marketplace, and the increasingly urgent social demand that it internalize the expense of acting more responsibly toward the environment.

Without doubt, the single most damaging aspect of the present economic system is that the expense of destroying the earth is largely absent from the prices set in the marketplace. A vital and key piece of information is therefore missing in all levels of the economy. This omission extends the dominance of industrialism beyond its useful life and prevents a restorative economy from emerging.

Despite that disadvantage, the restorative economy is beginning to prosper. In the United States alone, an estimated 70,000 companies are already committed to some form of environmental commerce that competes with businesses that are not willing to adapt. The impulse to enhance the economic viability of life on earth *through* the recognition and preservation of all living systems is one that is becoming increasingly central to religion, science, medicine, literature, the arts, and women. It should be the dominant theme of generations to come.

Because the restorative economy inverts ingrained beliefs about how 35 business functions, it may precipitate unusual changes in the economy. As will be discussed in later chapters, the restorative economy will be one in which some businesses get smaller but hire more people, where money can be made by selling the *absence* of a product or service, as is the case where public utilities sell efficiency rather than additional power, and where profits increase when productivity is lowered. Corporations can compete to conserve and increase resources rather than deplete them. Complex and onerous regulations will be replaced by motivating standards.

Author Ivan Illich° has pointed out that the average American is involved with his or her automobile—working in order to buy it, actually driving it, getting it repaired, and so on—for sixteen hundred hours a year. This means when all car mileage in a given year is divided by the time spent supporting the car, the average car owner is traveling at an average speed of five miles per hour. To attain the speed of a bicycle, we are devastating our cities, air, lungs, and lives, while bringing on the threat of global warming. It is the restorative, not the industrial economy, that can and will address such aberrations. Restorative entrepreneurs may not be as mediagenic as Wall Street tycoons, because their companies will be smaller, quieter, and less glamorous. However, it is the former who challenge the economic superstitions and fantasies that determine our concept of what a business should be.

A business works best when it has a positive vision, good morale, definite standards, and high goals. Such an organization is receptive to ideas that reinforce corporate growth as it is currently defined, but may be hostile to ideas that are critical of the basic system. After all, a successful business is in effect an advertisement that so much *is* working, that so many people have done a good job. This intolerance of seemingly irrelevant advice and information allows a company to concentrate single-mindedly on carving out market niches, but it also creates a yawning chasm between business economics and good ecology. If corporations were to take worldwide environmental degradation as seriously as they take demographic changes in consumer tastes, they would discover that the remedies for their depredation are more profound and transformative than the measures currently proposed by a few businesses, or even by many of the large environmental organizations. Perhaps that is why they have not delved more deeply.

On the other hand, it is important to understand that we consumers are accessories before and after the fact. We create businesses just as much as businesses create our wants. We have been enthralled by the opportunities, wealth, image, and power offered by business success. We like our comfortable lifestyles if we have them and want them if we don't. Business has intrinsic flaws, but they are created and reinforced by our own desires. "However destructive may be the policies of the government and the methods and products of the corporation," writes essayist and farmer Wendell Berry, "the root of the problem is always to be found in private life. We must learn to see that every problem that concerns us...always leads straight to the question of how we live. The world is being destroyed—no doubt about it—by the greed of the rich and powerful. It is also being destroyed by popular demand. There are not enough rich and powerful people

---

Ivan Illich (1926–2002): Radical political and social thinker. [EDS.]

to consume the whole world; for that, the rich and powerful need the help of countless ordinary people."

The restorative economy comes down to this: we need to imagine a prosperous commercial culture that is so intelligently designed and constructed that it mimics nature at every step, a symbiosis of company and customer and ecology. This book, then, is ultimately about redesigning our commercial systems so that they work for owners, employees, customers, and life on earth without requiring a complete transformation of humankind. Much has been written linking our environmental crises to everything from patriarchal values to a spiritual malaise that has accompanied industrial riches. But we may be trying to accomplish too much. Science does teach us that everything is interdependent: the respiration of the blossom of a lily in the backwaters of the Rio Negro in the Amazon basin affects the weather in New York. However, if we are to be effective in our lives, we have to find workable techniques and programs that can be put into practice soon, tools for change that are easily grasped and understood, and that conform naturally to the landscape of human nature.

If this scenario sounds dreamy and Arcadian it is because we assume that 40 economic forces only exploit and destroy. *The Ecology of Commerce* will try to demonstrate that while this has been largely true up until now, and will continue to be true for some time in the future, this behavior is not the inherent nature of business, nor the inevitable outcome of a free-market system. It is merely the result of the present commercial system's design and use. The human matures from a state of grasping ego gratification to some degree of ethical awareness. Our species is not perfect, but is certainly not depraved, either. Like individuals, societies also mature, albeit more slowly and haltingly. America ended institutionalized slavery, for example, but is only now beginning to address its many forms of racism. I believe our economic system can also mature in a similar fashion.

In *The Merchant of Prato*, Iris Origo's recent account of a fourteenth-century Tuscan merchant, Francisco di Marco Datini, we recognize in Datini all the anxiety and daily vicissitudes of a contemporary businessman. Datini was worried about his investments, taxes, and penalties. As his successes grew, so, too, did his insecurity. He devoted increasing amounts of his riches to acts of piety, from penance to munificent acts for the church, but largess could not alleviate Datini's guilt and *maninconia* (the stress of constant worry and doubt). Datini sounds like every modern businessperson who, approaching death, ponders not the deals that got away, but the humanity and society forsaken in the rush to profit.

Annie Dillard recounts a story with a similar moral in *Pilgrim at Tinker Creek*. A nineteenth-century French physician, having perfected the first procedure to remove cataracts safely, traveled throughout his country restoring sight to people blinded from birth. He witnessed two distinct reactions when people saw the world for the first time: some were appalled at the squalor and ugliness (one person blinded himself in order to forget what he had seen and return to what he imagined the world to be); the greater number were overwhelmed by the beauty, vastness, and colors of the world, their senses flooded with the newness and variety of a creation that had heretofore lacked its most beautiful dimension.

We who are in business today are like these fortunate French men and women. Scientists, naturalists, essayists, and poets are offering us vision, a means with which to see and understand the splendor and sacredness of life. They help us understand that we, as Whitman wrote, "are nature, long have we been absent, but now we return." Will we tear out our eyes, ignore what we are being shown, and continue commercial practices that demean the earth and hasten that day when everything we hold precious has been destroyed? Will we die burdened with Datini's many regrets, or will we exult and exclaim, grateful for the possibilities, the newness, the knowledge offered us to transform our world and our relationship to it?

Many believe that it is too late, that at this moment in our history we cannot be redeemed through existing institutions. It is true that in our lifetime we cannot restore felled ancient forests, vanished wetlands, ghostly strip mines, or the ruined lives of toxic waste victims. Contemporary events support Goldsmith's longstanding declaration, "Honor sinks where commerce long prevails." It takes a serious leap of faith to imagine a transformed Fortune 500, a restorative sustainable economy that will offer full employment, more security, better education, less fear, more stability, and a higher quality of life. But I believe this will happen because prior forms of economic behavior no longer produce the desired results. Even though the GNP of the United States grew considerably during the 1980s, three-fourths of the gain in pretax income went to the richest 1 percent. The majority of Americans had less money and lower incomes than they did when the decade began. Primarily, what growth in the 1980s produced was higher levels of apprehension, violence, dislocation, and environmental degradation.

Gordon Sherman, the founder of Midas Muffler, once wrote: "There is 45 a teasing irony: we spend our lives evading our own redemption. And this is naturally so because something in us knows that to be fully human we must experience pain and loss. Therefore, we are at ceaseless effort to elude this high cost, whatever the price, until at last it overtakes us. And then in spite of ourselves we do realize our humanity. We are put in worthier possession of our souls. Then we look back and know that even our grief contained our blessing."

Ironically, business contains our blessing. It must, because no other institution in the modern world is powerful enough to foster the necessary changes. Perhaps during the many battles between environmentalists and businesspeople we have been asking the wrong question all these years. As generally proposed the question is "How do we save the environment?" As ridiculous as it may first sound to both sides, the question may be "How do we save business?"

Business is the problem and it must be a part of the solution. Its power is more crucial than ever if we are to organize and efficiently meet the world's needs. This book contains quite a few horror stories perpetrated by large, respected, well-managed businesses. I do not cite them to demonize corporations, but to lay the foundation and basis of understanding that will allow us to re-create these companies. Commerce can be one of the most creative endeavors available to us, but it is not worthy of business to be the convenient and complicit bedfellow to a culture divorced from nature. While commerce at its worst sometimes appears to be a shambles of defilement compared to the beauty and complexity of the natural world, the ideas and much of the technology required for the redesign of our businesses and the restoration of the world are already in hand. What is wanting is collective will.

WHAT DOES HE SAY?

1. Write a quick response to this sentence from the second paragraph: "Making money is, on its own terms, totally meaningless, an insufficient pursuit for the complex and decaying world we live in."

2. As you're reading this essay, copy out five sentences that seem to you especially provocative—that is, especially likely to provoke a response.

3. As you're reading, simply make a list of the questions that this essay asks. What's your reaction to the finished list?

4. Write a paragraph that, in your words, explains what Paul Hawken means by "the restorative economy."

WHAT DO YOU THINK?

5. Do you agree that the current economy hurts people and the planet even as it tries to provide jobs and deliver consumer goods? Explore this by writing a short history of the car you drive (or the car you borrow when you need to drive). Where was it made? By whom? What were they paid? What fuel drives it? Where did that fuel come from? What comes out of its tailpipe? Based on your research and Hawken's essay, is this car doing its bit to, in Hawken's words, "help destroy the world"?

6. This essay is the introduction to Hawken's book *The Ecology of Commerce*. What about the "ecology of education"? Investigate the ways that your university impacts the environment. What does it need in terms of energy? Does it make efforts to conserve that energy? What are the sources of that energy, and are they renewable? This may be too large a topic for a complete analysis, so pick one aspect of your campus and how it operates. Report what you find, and end by giving that aspect of campus operation a grade based on the criteria that Hawken suggests.

WHAT WOULD THEY SAY?

7. Read "A Teasing Irony" together with George Orwell's "Politics and the English Language" (p. 461). At what points do these essays seem to overlap or inform each other? Write an essay that focuses on these areas, showing that understanding Orwell's points helps to understand Hawken's (or vice versa).

8. Read "A Teasing Irony" together with "Ethics: A Global Business Challenge" (p. 526), by Robert Haas. Then write an essay explaining how these two readings relate to each other in terms of their major assertions about what constitutes business success.

9. Aldo Leopold's "The Land Ethic" was published in 1949; Hawken's essay was published in 1994. Write an essay that argues that Hawken's essay shows the influence of Leopold's "The Land Ethic" (p. 531). End by explaining why Leopold would, or would not, be pleased by what Hawken says.

For Community Learning and Research

1. Visit your local Humane Society facility and write an essay telling the story of your visit. Where is the facility? What did you see there? How did you react? What did the visit make you think about? Based on this trip and on your own interactions with animals, what conclusions can you come to about how we treat our pets and about how we should treat our pets?

2. Go to the meat section of a local grocery store. Identify the company that markets the chickens you find in the cold cases. Then see what you can find out about that company's policies for the chickens it raises. How are the chickens sheltered during their lifetimes? What are they fed? What sort of daily life does a chicken bound for your grocery store live? Write a factual report on what you learn. Following the factual report, write a letter to the store manager. Compliment or criticize the store's decision to stock this brand of chicken. Variation: instead of chicken, investigate the beef stocked by your store.

3. Gather statistics or any other information on current minimum-wage workers in your state. What jobs do they have? What skills are required for those jobs? What are the typical working conditions? Go on to research the cost of living in your community—the cost of housing, food, and transportation in particular. What does it take to live where you live? Then investigate when your state legislature last considered the question of a minimum wage. Based on your results, write an open letter to your local state representative about your state's current minimum wage. Quote some of the information you gathered. Send the letter to the state representative, and send a copy to your campus newspaper.

4. Research the economic history of your local area. What industries or occupations were most prominent and significant in 1900? in 1950? Which ones are most prominent and significant today? Write a paper that summarizes this economic history and tries to weigh what's been lost, what's been gained, and what significant challenges the present offers in terms of local economic prosperity. Somewhere in your discussion, quote the title of Milton Friedman's essay from this chapter. Assume that your paper might also become the basis for a presentation to a local service club (Zonta, Rotary, and so on) or chamber of commerce.

5. Identify a part of your town and research its history in terms of the land itself: what was its condition and how was it used in 1800? 1850? 1900? 1950? 2000? Summarize your research in a series of posters that could be placed in the foyer of a public building where land-use decisions are discussed (city hall, perhaps, or the county courthouse) as an informational display. Make sure that your posters quote at least two of the essays presented in this chapter.

6. Follow the instructions for question 5, but research a local river instead.

7. Research the nonprofit economy in your area. Discuss the most significant of these businesses or organizations—what they do, whom they employ, how they sustain themselves, and what they count as success. If possible, make on-site visits or volunteering part of your research. Analyze what would be lost to the community if every one of these enterprises shut down.

7.

Why Change Your Mind?

WHAT WOULD YOU DO? RETHINKING A DECISION

With the money you saved from a summer job, and a little help from your parents, you've bought a used SUV, a big one with a V-8. You love everything about it. But several of your friends are taking a course in environmental studies and they're suddenly after you about all the environmental damage that cars do, particularly SUVs. SUVs are not necessary, these friends tell you. It's unethical to drive one. Sell it!

You respect these people. They're not fools, or at least they haven't been in the past. But however valid their opinions, in the end you think it's none of their business what you drive or what anyone drives. It's a free country, and besides, what difference can one SUV make? Why should you sell your car? Why should you change your mind?

What would it take in this situation for your friends to convince you to sell your SUV? What kinds of evidence would they have to find? What strategies or reasons do you think could eventually persuade you?

Ethical thinking always involves openness to change — to the possibility that we are wrong or only partially right. We come to college with certain values and beliefs in place, and these may be valid for us. We may leave with them, too. But the world of ideas is a big place with many points of view. The more we look, the more complicated things turn out to be, the less black and white. If all goes the way it should, we leave the university changed in one way at least, as Parker Palmer argues in "The Community of Truth" (p. 627): we are less arrogant, less sure that we possess the sole truth.

This is the subject of all the essays that follow: change as the basis of education, whether in the university, as in Adrienne Rich's "Claiming an Education" (p. 608), or in life, as in Studs Terkel's "C. P. Ellis" (p. 568). In fact, change, growth, vision, and revision — this has all been the underlying subject of the chapters in this book, an idea reflected in the move from the ethical scenario at the beginning of each chapter to the reexamination of that scenario at the end, in light of the readings. This chapter asks you to look at that process itself, inquiring not so much into a particular issue but into the nature of thinking about issues. Where can we find reasons for making ethical choices? What are sufficient grounds for rethinking, for that willingness to look again at old questions and earlier decisions? And how do we encourage others toward such flexibility, such willingness to listen and reconsider? What language is effective in persuading others to change? Is it really possible to change anyone's mind? And, finally, can we ever be sure? Do grounds for belief really exist?

Opening the Question

*After reading and discussing several of the selections in this chapter, return to the situation above. **Now** what do you think? Write an essay answering this question, drawing on at least two of the selections.*

We're not asking whether you would give up your SUV. We're asking you to think about how you would come to that decision. Do any of the readings suggest what kinds of evidence or reasoning or language or experience would be necessary to convince you?

SCOTT ADAMS

"I teach my kids that these things are right and these things are wrong."

Scott Adams (b. 1957) earned an MBA from the University of California at Berkeley and worked at various businesses before launching his syndicated comic strip, Dilbert, *in 1989. The character Dilbert, Adams says, is a composite of various coworkers.*

WHAT DOES HE SAY?

1. With a few quick details, Scott Adams implies something about the character of the person sitting on the bench in this cartoon: his hair, for example, or the expression on his face. Based just on these details, what kind of person do you think this character is? Do you like him or dislike him? Now, take into account the character's two short statements. What do they imply about the kind of person he is? Do you think that Adams wants us to approve or disapprove of him? Why?

2. Paraphrase what this man says in a short paragraph, making it sound as reasonable and persuasive and positive as you can. After all, many people *do* seriously argue the point that he is making. In your paraphrase, try to be clear about what this point is. What philosophical or moral position does this figure embody?

3. Dogbert is the other character in this three-panel cartoon. Paraphrase what he says in a short paragraph, making it sound as reasonable and persuasive and positive as you can. What philosophical position does Dogbert embody?

4. Dogbert gets the last word here. In fact, that's just what it is: a single word, "Duh." Explain what you think Adams is implying in this single word. What finally is the point of the cartoon? Whose side is Adams on, and how do you know?

WHAT DO YOU THINK?

5. Look at the two paraphrases you've written for questions 2 and 3 above. Which position—that of the unnamed man or that of Dogbert—is closest to your own? Explain.

6. Adams has obviously exaggerated the positions of the two characters in this cartoon in order to make his point. Discuss in small groups or as a whole class what other positions are possible between the extreme view of the man on the bench and the extreme view of Dogbert. What other attitudes might a person take to the issue that the cartoon raises?

7. Plot out another three panel cartoon that might capture some of the views that emerge from the discussion in question 2 above. You could, for example, introduce two new characters into the discussion, or you could have the man on the bench reply to Dogbert's "Duh."

8. Discuss a person in your life who has said something like what the man on the bench says here, who shares his basic philosophy. Describe this person's background, profession, and relationship to you. The man is a parent, for example. Have you ever heard one of your parents say something like what he says here? How did you react?

WHAT WOULD THEY SAY?

9. Imagine that Lance Armstrong ("Before and After," p. 344) happens to sit down on this bench and that the man next to him says exactly what he says to Dogbert. What would Armstrong say?

10. Imagine that Helen Prejean ("Executions Are Too Costly — Morally," p. 614) sits down on this bench and engages this man and Dogbert in an extended conversation. How would she respond to the idea that kids need to know what's right and what's wrong, period, end of story?

11. Imagine that the Dalai Lama ("The Need for Discernment," p. 205) reads this cartoon and is strongly affected by it. He decides to sit down and write a letter to the editor arguing that the cartoon embodies many dominant attitudes in contemporary culture and expressing his reaction to these attitudes. What would he say? Whose side would he be on, Dogbert's or the man's?

STUDS TERKEL
C. P. Ellis

C. P. Ellis is a former member of the Ku Klux Klan who tells Studs Terkel (b. 1912) the story of how he came to change his mind: through experiencing black people in their particulars and their humanity. Terkel, who began his career in radio, is best known for his oral-history interviews. He has published several compilations of these interviews on a variety of social issues, beginning with Division Street: America *(1966). His latest work is* Will the Circle Be Unbroken: Reflections on Death, Rebirth, and Hunger for a Faith *(2001). "C. P. Ellis" is from his 1992 book,* Race: How Blacks and Whites Feel about the American Obsession.

My father worked in a textile mill in Durham. He died at forty-eight years old. It was probably from cotton dust. Back then, we never heard of brown lung. I was about seventeen years old and had a mother and sister depending on somebody to make a livin'. It was just barely enough insurance to cover his burial. I had to quit school and go to work. I was about eighth grade when I quit.

My father worked hard but never had enough money to buy decent clothes. When I went to school, I never seemed to have adequate clothes to wear. I always left school late afternoon with a sense of inferiority. The other kids had nice clothes, and I just had what Daddy could buy. I still got some of those inferiority feelin's now that I have to overcome once in a while.

I loved my father. He would go with me to ball games. We'd go fishin' together. I was really ashamed of the way he'd dress. He would take this money and give it to me instead of putting it on himself. I always had the feeling about somebody looking at him and makin' fun of him and makin' fun of me. I think it had to do somethin' with my life.

My father and I were very close, but we didn't talk about too many intimate things. He did have a drinking problem. During the week, he would work every day, but weekend he was ready to get plastered. I can understand when a guy looks at his paycheck and looks at his bills, and he's worried hard all the week, and his bills are larger than his paycheck. He'd done the best he could the entire week, and there seemed to be no hope. It's an illness thing. Finally you just say: "The heck with it. I'll just get drunk and forget it."

My father was out of work during the depression, and I remember going with him to the finance company uptown, and he was turned down. That's something that's always stuck. 5

My father never seemed to be happy. It was a constant struggle with him just like it was for me. It's very seldom I'd see him laugh. He was just tryin' to figure out what he could do from one day to the next.

After several years pumping gas at a service station, I got married. We had to have children. Four. One child was born blind and retarded, which was a real additional expense to us. He's never spoken a word. He doesn't know me when I go to see him. But I see him, I hug his neck, I talk to him, tell him I love him. I don't know whether he knows me or not, but I know he's well taken care of. All my life, I had work, never a day without work, worked all the overtime I could get and still could not survive financially. I began to say there's somethin' wrong with this country. I worked my butt off and just never seemed to break even.

I had some real great ideas about this great nation. (Laughs.) They say to abide by the law, go to church, do right and live for the Lord, and everything'll work out. But it didn't work out. It just kept gettin' worse and worse.

I was workin' a bread route. The highest I made one week was seventy-five dollars. The rent on our house was about twelve dollars a week. I will never forget: outside of this house was a 265-gallon oil drum, and I never did get enough money to fill up that oil drum. What I would do every night, I would run up to the store and buy five gallons of oil and climb up the ladder and pour it in that 265-gallon drum. I could hear that five gallons when it hits the bottom of that oil drum, splatters, and it sounds like it's nothin' in there. But it would keep the house warm for the night. Next day you'd have to do the same thing.

I left the bread route with fifty dollars in my pocket. I went to the bank 10 and I borrowed four thousand dollars to buy the service station. I worked seven days a week, open and close, and finally had a heart attack. Just about two months before the last payments of that loan. My wife had done the best she could to keep it runnin'. Tryin' to come out of that hole, I just couldn't do it.

I really began to get bitter. I didn't know who to blame. I tried to find somebody. I began to blame it on black people. I had to hate somebody. Hatin' America is hard to do because you can't see it to hate it. You gotta have somethin' to look at to hate. (Laughs.) The natural person for me to hate would be black people, because my father before me was a member of the Klan. As far as he was concerned, it was the savior of the white people. It was the only organization in the world that would take care of the white people. So I began to admire the Klan.

I got active in the Klan while I was at the service station. Every Monday night, a group of men would come by and buy a Coca-Cola, go back to the car, take a few drinks, and come back and stand around talkin'. I couldn't help but wonder: why are these dudes comin' out every Monday? They said they were with the Klan and have meetings close by. Would I be interested? Boy, that was an opportunity I really looked forward to! To be part of somethin'. I joined the Klan, went from member to chaplain, from chaplain to vice president, from vice president to president. The title is exalted cyclops.

The first night I went with the fellas, they knocked on the door and gave the signal. They sent some robed Klansmen to talk to me and give me some instructions. I was led into a large meeting room, and this was the time of my life! It was thrilling. Here's a guy who's worked all his life and struggled all his life to be something, and here's the moment to be something. I will never forget it. Four robed Klansmen led me into the hall. The lights were dim, and the only thing you could see was an illuminated cross. I knelt before the cross. I had to make certain vows and promises. We promised to uphold the purity of the white race, fight communism, and protect white womanhood. After I had taken my oath, there was loud applause goin' throughout the buildin', musta been at least four hundred people. For this one little ol' person. It was a thrilling moment for C. P. Ellis.

It disturbs me when people who do not really know what it's all about are so very critical of individual Klansmen. The majority of 'em are low-income whites, people who really don't have a part in something. They have been shut out as well as the blacks. Some are not very well educated either. Just like myself. We had a lot of support from doctors and lawyers and police officers.

Maybe they've had bitter experiences in this life and they had to hate 15 somebody. So the natural person to hate would be the black person. He's beginnin' to come up, he's beginnin' to learn to read and start votin' and run for political office. Here are white people who are supposed to be superior to them, and we're shut out.

I can understand why people join extreme right-wing or left-wing groups. They're in the same boat I was. Shut out. Deep down inside, we want to be part of this great society. Nobody listens, so we join these groups....

This was the time when the civil rights movement was really beginnin' to peak. The blacks were beginnin' to demonstrate and picket downtown stores. I never will forget some black lady I hated with a purple passion. Ann Atwater. Every time I'd go downtown, she'd be leadin' a boycott. How I hated—pardon the expression, I don't use it much now—how I just hated that black nigger. (Laughs.) Big, fat, heavy woman. She'd pull about eight demonstrations, and first thing you know they had two, three blacks at the check-out counter. Her and I have had some pretty close confrontations.

I felt very big, yeah. (Laughs.) We're more or less a secret organization. We didn't want anybody to know who we were, and I began to do some thinkin'. What am I hidin' for? I've never been convicted of anything in my life. I don't have any court record. What am I, C. P. Ellis, as a citizen and a member of the United Klansmen of America? Why can't I go to the city council meeting and say: "This is the way we feel about the matter? We don't want you to purchase mobile units to set in our school yards. We don't want niggers in our schools."

We began to come out in the open. We would go to the meetings, and the blacks would be there and we'd be there. It was a confrontation every time. I didn't hold back anything. We began to make some inroads with the city councilmen and county commissioners. They began to call us friend. Call us at night on the telephone: "C. P., glad you came to that meeting last night." They didn't want integration either, but they did it secretively, in order to get elected. They couldn't stand up openly and say it, but they were glad somebody was sayin' it. We visited some of the city leaders in their home and talk to 'em privately. It wasn't long before councilmen would call me up: "The blacks are comin' up tonight and makin' outrageous demands. How about some of you people showin' up and have a little balance?" I'd get on the telephone: "The niggers is comin' to the council meeting tonight. Persons in the city's called me and asked us to be there."

We'd load up our cars and we'd fill up half the council chambers, and 20 the blacks the other half. During these times, I carried weapons to the meetings, outside my belt. We'd go there armed. We would wind up just hollerin' and fussin' at each other. What happened? As a result of our fightin' one another, the city council still had their way. They didn't want to give up control to the blacks nor the Klan. They were usin' us.

I began to realize this later down the road. One day I was walkin' downtown and a certain city-council member saw me comin'. I expected him to shake my hand because he was talkin' to me at night on the telephone. I had been in his home and visited with him. He crossed the street. Oh shit, I began to think, somethin's wrong here. Most of 'em are merchants or maybe an attorney, an insurance agent, people like that. As long as they kept low-income whites and low-income blacks fightin', they're gonna maintain control.

I began to get that feeling after I was ignored in public. I thought: Bullshit, you're not gonna use me any more. That's when I began to do some real serious thinkin'.

The same thing is happening in this country today. People are being used by those in control, those who have all the wealth. I'm not espousing communism. We got the greatest system of government in the world. But those who have it simply don't want those who don't have it to have any part of it. Black and white. When it comes to money, the green, the other colors make no difference. (Laughs.)

I spent a lot of sleepless nights. I still didn't like blacks. I didn't want to associate with 'em. Blacks, Jews, or Catholics. My father said: "Don't have anything to do with 'em." I didn't until I met a black person and talked with him, eyeball to eyeball, and met a Jewish person and talked to him, eyeball to eyeball. I found out they're people just like me. They cried, they cussed, they prayed, they had desires. Just like myself. Thank God, I got to the point where I can look past labels. But at that time, my mind was closed.

I remember one Monday night Klan meeting. I said something was 25 wrong. Our city fathers were using us. And I didn't like to be used. The reactions of the others was not too pleasant: "Let's just keep fightin' them niggers."

I'd go home at night and I'd have to wrestle with myself. I'd look at a black person walkin' down the street, and the guy'd have ragged shoes or his clothes would be worn. That began to do somethin' to me inside. I went through this for about six months. I felt I just had to get out of the Klan. But I wouldn't get out.

Then something happened. The state AFL-CIO° received a grant from the Department of HEW°, a $78,000 grant: how to solve racial problems in the school system. I got a telephone call from the president of the state AFL-CIO. "We'd like to get some people together from all walks of life." I said: "All walks of life? Who you talkin' about?" He said: "Blacks, whites, liberals, conservatives, Klansmen, NAACP people."

I said: "No way am I comin' with all those niggers. I'm not gonna be associated with those type of people." A White Citizens Council guy said: "Let's go up there and see what's goin' on. It's tax money bein' spent." I walk in the door, and there was a large number of blacks and white liberals. I knew most of 'em by face 'cause I seen 'em demonstratin' around town. Ann Atwater was there. (Laughs.) I just forced myself to go in and sit down.

The meeting was moderated by a great big black guy who was bushy headed. (Laughs.) That turned me off. He acted very nice. He said: "I want you all to feel free to say anything you want to say." Some of the blacks stand up and say it's white racism. I took all I could take. I asked for the floor and I cut loose. I said: "No, sir, it's black racism. If we didn't have niggers in the schools, we wouldn't have the problems we got today."

I will never forget. Howard Clements, a black guy, stood up. He said: 30 "I'm certainly glad C. P. Ellis come because he's the most honest man here tonight." I said: "What's that nigger tryin' to do?" (Laughs.) At the end of that meeting, some blacks tried to come up shake my hand, but I wouldn't do it. I walked off.

Second night, same group was there. I felt a little more easy because I got some things off my chest. The third night, after they elected all the committees, they want to elect a chairman. Howard Clements stood up and said: "I suggest we elect two cochairpersons." Joe Beckton, executive director of the Human Relations Commission, just as black as he can be, he nominated me. There was a reaction from some blacks. Nooo. And, of all things, they nominated Ann Atwater, that big old fat black gal that I had just hated with a purple passion, as cochairman. I thought to myself: Hey, ain't no way I can work with that gal. Finally, I agreed to accept it, 'cause at this point, I was tired of fightin', either for survival or against black people or against Jews or against Catholics.

A Klansman and a militant black woman, cochairmen of the school committee. It was impossible. How could I work with her? But after about two or three days, it was in our hands. We had to make it a success. This give me

AFL-CIO: American Federation of Labor-Congress of Industrial Organizations; the largest organization of labor unions in the United States. [All notes are the Editors'.]

Department of HEW: Department of Health, Education, and Welfare.

another sense of belongin', a sense of pride. This helped this inferiority feelin' I had. A man who has stood up publicly and said he despised black people, all of a sudden he was willin' to work with 'em. Here's a chance for a low-income white man to be somethin'. In spite of all my hatred for blacks and Jews and liberals, I accepted the job. Her and I began to reluctantly work together. (Laughs.) She had as many problems workin' with me as I had workin' with her.

One night, I called her. "Ann, you and I should have a lot of differences and we got 'em now. But there's somethin' laid out here before us, and if it's gonna be a success, you and I are gonna have to make it one. Can we lay aside some of these feelin's?" She said: "I'm willing if you are." I said: "Let's do it."

My old friends would call me at night: "C. P., what the hell is wrong with you? You're sellin' out the white race." This begin to make me have guilt feelin's. Am I doin' right? Am I doin' wrong? Here I am all of a sudden makin' an about-face and tryin' to deal with my feelin's, my heart. My mind was beginnin' to open up. I was beginnin' to see what was right and what was wrong. I don't want the kids to fight forever.

We were gonna go ten nights. By this time, I had went to work at Duke 35 University, in maintenance. Makin' very little money. Terry Sanford give me this ten days off with pay. He was president of Duke at the time. He knew I was a Klansman and realized the importance of blacks and whites getting along.

I said: "If we're gonna make this thing a success, I've got to get to my kind of people." The low-income whites. We walked the streets of Durham, and we knocked on doors and invited people. Ann was goin' into the black community. They just wasn't respondin' to us when we made these house calls. Some of 'em were cussin' us out. "You're sellin' us out, Ellis, get out of my door. I don't want to talk to you." Ann was gettin' the same response from blacks: "What are you doin' messin' with that Klansman?"

One day, Ann and I went back to the school and we sat down. We began to talk and just reflect. Ann said: "My daughter came home cryin' every day. She said her teacher was makin' fun of me in front of the other kids." I said: "Boy, the same thing happened to my kid. White liberal teacher was makin' fun of Tim Ellis's father, the Klansman. In front of other peoples. He came home cryin'." At this point—(he pauses, swallows hard, stifles a sob)—I begin to see, here we are, two people from the far ends of the fence, havin' identical problems, except hers bein' black and me bein' white. From that moment on, I tell ya, that gal and I worked together good. I began to love the girl, really. (He weeps.)

The amazing thing about it, her and I, up to that point, had cussed each other, bawled each other, we hated each other. Up to that point, we didn't know each other. We didn't know we had things in common.

We worked at it, with the people who came to these meetings. They talked about racism, sex education, about teachers not bein' qualified. After seven, eight nights of real intense discussion, these people, who'd never talked to each other before, all of a sudden came up with resolutions. It was really somethin', you had to be there to get the tone and feelin' of it.

At that point, I didn't like integration, but the law says you do this and 40 I've got to do what the law says, okay? We said: "Let's take these resolutions to the school board." The most disheartening thing I've ever faced was the school system refused to implement any one of these resolutions. These were recommendations from the people who pay taxes and pay their salaries. (Laughs.)

I thought they were good answers. Some of 'em I didn't agree with, but I been in this thing from the beginning, and whatever comes of it, I'm gonna support it. Okay, since the school board refused, I decided I'd just run for the school board.

I spent eighty-five dollars on the campaign. The guy runnin' against me spent several thousand. I really had nobody on my side. The Klan turned against me. The low-income whites turned against me. The liberals didn't particularly like me. The blacks were suspicious of me. The blacks wanted to support me, but they couldn't muster up enough to support a Klansman on the school board. (Laughs.) But I made up my mind that what I was doin' was right, and I was gonna do it regardless what anybody said.

It bothered me when people would call and worry my wife. She's always supported me in anything I wanted to do. She was changing, and my boys were too.

I was invited to the Democratic women's social hour as a candidate. Didn't have but one suit to my name. Had it six, seven, eight years. I had it cleaned, put on the best shirt I had and a tie. Here were all this high-class wealthy candidates shakin' hands. I walked up to the mayor and stuck out my hand. He give me that handshake with that rag type of hand. He said: "C. P., I'm glad to see you." But I could tell by his handshake he was lyin' to me. This was botherin' me. I know I'm a low-income person. I know I'm not wealthy. I know they were sayin': "What's this little ol' dude runnin' for school board?" Yet they had to smile and make like they're glad to see me. I begin to spot some black people in that room. I automatically went to 'em and that was a firm handshake. They said: "I'm glad to see you, C. P." I knew they meant it—you can tell about a handshake.

Every place I appeared, I said I will listen to the voice of the people. I 45 will not make a major decision until I first contacted all the organizations in the city. I got 4,640 votes. The guy beat me by two thousand. Not bad for eighty-five bucks and no constituency.

The whole world was openin' up, and I was learnin' new truths that I had never learned before. I was beginnin' to look at a black person, shake hands with him, and see him as a human bein'. I hadn't got rid of all this stuff. I've still got a little bit of it. But somethin' was happenin' to me.

It was almost like bein' born again. It was a new life. I didn't have these sleepless nights I used to have when I was active in the Klan and slippin' around at night. I could sleep at night and feel good about it. I'd rather live now than at any other time in history. It's a challenge.

Back at Duke, doin' maintenance, I'd pick up my tools, fix the commode, unstop the drains. But this got in my blood. Things weren't right in this country, and what we done in Durham needs to be told. I was so miserable at Duke, I could hardly stand it. I'd go to work every morning just hatin' to go.

My whole life had changed. I got an eighth-grade education, and I wanted to complete high school. Went to high school in the afternoons on a program called PEP—Past Employment Progress. I was about the only white in class, and the oldest. I begin to read about biology. I'd take my books home at night, 'cause I was determined to get through. Sure enough, I graduated. I got the diploma at home....

Last year, I ran for business manager of the union. He's elected by the 50 workers. The guy that ran against me was black, and our membership is 75 percent black. I thought: Claiborne, there's no way you can beat that black guy. People know your background. Even though you've made tremendous strides, those black people are not gonna vote for you. You know how much I beat him? Four to one. (Laughs.)

The company used my past against me. They put out letters with a picture of a robe and a cap: would you vote for a Klansman? They wouldn't deal with the issues. I immediately called for a mass meeting. I met with the ladies at an electric component plant. I said: "Okay, this is Claiborne Ellis. This is where I come from. I want you to know right now, you black ladies here, I was at one time a member of the Klan. I want you to know, because they'll tell you about it."

I invited some of my old black friends. I said: "Brother Joe, Brother Howard, be honest now and tell these people how you feel about me." They done it. (Laughs.) Howard Clements kidded me a little bit. He said: "I don't know what I'm doin' here, supportin' an ex-Klansman." (Laughs.) He said: I know what C. P. Ellis come from. I knew him when he was. I knew him as he grew, and growed with him. I'm tellin' you now: follow, follow this Klansman." (He pauses, swallows hard.) "Any questions?" "No," the black ladies said. "Let's get on with the meeting, we need Ellis." (He laughs and weeps.) Boy, black people sayin' that about me. I won one thirty-four to forty-one. Four to one.

It makes you feel good to go into a plant and butt heads with professional union busters. You see black people and white people join hands to defeat the racist issues they use against people. They're tryin' the same things with the Klan. It's still happenin' today. Can you imagine a guy who's got an adult high school diploma runnin' into professional college graduates who are union busters? I gotta compete with 'em. I work seven days a week, nights and on Saturday and Sunday. The salary's not that great, and if I didn't care, I'd quit. But I care and I can't quit. I got a taste of it. (Laughs.)

I tell people there's a tremendous possibility in this country to stop wars, the battles, the struggles, the fights between people. People say: "That's an impossible dream. You sound like Martin Luther King." An ex-Klansman who sounds like Martin Luther King. (Laughs.) I don't think it's an impossible dream. It's happened in my life. It's happened in other people's lives in America.

I don't know what's ahead of me. I have no desire to be a big union official. I want to be right out here in the field with the workers. I want to walk through their factory and shake hands with that man whose hands are dirty. I'm gonna do all that one little ol' man can do. I'm fifty-two years old, and I ain't got many years left, but I want to make the best of 'em. 55

When the news came over the radio that Martin Luther King was assassinated, I got on the telephone and begin to call other Klansmen. We just had a real party at the service station. Really rejoicin' 'cause that son of a bitch was dead. Our troubles are over with. They say the older you get, the harder it is for you to change. That's not necessarily true. Since I changed, I've set down and listened to tapes of Martin Luther King. I listen to it and tears come to my eyes 'cause I know what he's sayin' now. I know what's happenin'.

WHAT DOES HE SAY?

1. In this profile, Terkel transcribes C. P. Ellis's own way of talking, his word choices and sentence rhythms. After the first few paragraphs, looking just at these qualities of language, make an informed guess about Ellis's level of education. What about his income? his age? Write a paragraph that describes him in these terms.

2. What is your reaction to Ellis as you go along? Tell the story of this reaction: whether you resist him or feel attracted to him, like or dislike him, believe or disbelieve him, and how your reaction changes as he continues to tell his story. Mark the turning points in the margins.

3. Mark the passage where it becomes clear to you why we have included this profile in a book on ethical thinking and in a chapter called "Why Change Your Mind?"

WHAT DO YOU THINK?

4. Make a list of at least three significant things that cause Ellis to change his mind—three things in his environment and experience or within himself. Write an essay explaining these significant causes and how they affected Ellis. Then explain to what extent—or not—you believe that Ellis is a good example of how someone significantly changes attitudes and outlook. Could you reproduce this process of change for someone else? If so, what key things would you have to do? Or is this change made possible by something intrinsic to Ellis's character, something in him that another person might not necessarily possess?

5. Assume for the sake of discussion or writing that the process that Ellis goes through is representative for all education. His is the model of how all people should learn. Construct a college curriculum and a college experience that reproduces this model

for everyone else. How long, for example, would people have to be in school? What would they read, or would they read at all? What classes, if any, would they take? What would be the role of teachers?

6. What, if any, is the role of government in C. P. Ellis's change of mind? What is the influence of government agencies and programs?

7. Right now do you know anyone like the racist C. P. Ellis? Talk about this person. What conditions make this racism possible, even now, in the twenty-first century? Or is racism more subtle? Would you argue that racism doesn't exist?

8. Write an essay arguing carefully and persuasively that C. P. Ellis, by the end of this story, embodies what it means to be an ethical person.

WHAT WOULD THEY SAY?

9. Read Adrienne Rich's "Claiming an Education" (p. 608), an essay originally delivered as a speech. Imagine that C. P. Ellis is sitting in the audience for that speech. What parts of it would particularly resonate with him? What would he say in response? Imagine that Rich has heard Ellis's story. What would she say? Write an essay explaining how Rich and Ellis would react to and discuss each other's essay.

10. Read Jenefer Shute's "Life-Size" (p. 279) in chapter 4, "Are We Our Bodies?" Imagine that C. P. Ellis comes to visit her narrator in the hospital. What does he say? How does Shute's narrator respond?

11. Suppose C. P. Ellis meets and has coffee with Lance Armstrong, author of "Before and After" (p. 344) in chapter 4, "Are We Our Bodies?" What do the two say to each other? Would they get along? Why or why not?

12. Write an essay in the form of a dialogue between Brent Staples, author of "Just Walk on By: Black Men and Public Space" (p. 289) and C. P. Ellis. Assume that Ellis has read Staples's essay, and assume that Staples has read Ellis's interview. Give Staples the first comment and give Ellis the last one. The dialogue should run about four pages. Then skip a line and write a page explaining why you wrote the dialogue as you did.

NAOMI SHIHAB NYE
Long Overdue

*T*HE PERSPECTIVE SHIFTS NOW, *from someone changing his mind to someone trying to change the minds of others. In this brief personal essay, Arab American poet Naomi Shihab Nye (b. 1952) describes her encounters with anti-Arab prejudice and her struggle to know what to say in response.*

Nye, the daughter of an American mother and a Palestinian father, has won many awards, including four Pushcart Prizes, the Jane Addams Children's Book Award, and the Paterson Poetry Prize. Her books include Never in a Hurry *(1996),* Fuel *(1998),* What Have You Lost? *(1999), and* The Flag of Childhood: Poems from the Middle East *(2002).*

A gardener stares at our raggedy front yard. More weeds than grass. The star jasmine vine has died in the drought, leaving its bony spine woven through the frets of the wire fence. A young hackberry presses too close to the house. A bedraggled pomegranate tree crowds the banana palms.

The gardener shakes his head. Hands on hips. He is large and blond as a Viking. He wears no shirt. When I ask what he thinks about laying flat stones on the beaten path from driveway to porch so we don't track in mud when it rains, he nods silently, then puts his arms out to embrace this troubled yard. "Long overdue."

Excuse me? And the trimming? What would he charge to take out that tree? Could he edge this flowerbed with smooth rounded river rocks while he's at it? He stares into my face.

Long, long, long overdue.

I laugh out loud.   5

His few well-chosen words come back to me for days.

That's how I feel about lives bereft of poetry.

That's how I feel about the whole Middle East.

The words we didn't say. How many times? Stones stuck in the throat. Endlessly revised silence. *What was wrong with me? How could I, a person whose entire vocation has been dedicated one way or another to "the use of words," lose words completely when I needed them? Where does vocal paralysis come from? Why does regret have such a long life span?* My favorite poet William Stafford used to say, "Think of something you said. Now write what you *wish you* had said."

But I am always thinking of the times I said nothing.   10

In England, attending a play by myself, I was happy when the elderly woman next to me began speaking at intermission. Our arms had been touching lightly on the arm rest between our seats.

"Smashingly talented," she said of Ben Kingsley, whose brilliant monologue we'd been watching. "I don't know how he does it—transporting us so effortlessly, he's a genius. Not many in the world like him." I agreed. But then she sighed and made an odd turn. "You know what's wrong with the world today? It's Arabs. I blame it all on the Arabs. Most world problems can really be traced to them."

My blood froze. Why was she saying this? The play wasn't about Arabs. Ben Kingsley was hardly your blue-blooded Englishman, either, so what brought it up? Nothing terrible relating to Arabs had happened lately in the news. I wasn't wearing a kef'fiyeh° around my neck.

But my mouth would not open.

"Why *did so* many of them come to England?" she continued, mutter-   15
ing as if we were sharing a confidence. "A ruination, that's what it is."

It struck me then she might be a landlady having trouble with tenants. I tried and tried to part my lips. *Where is the end of the tangled thread? How will we roll it into a ball if we can't find an end?*

She chitted on about something less consequential, never seeming to mind our utterly one-sided conversation, till the lights went down. Of course I couldn't concentrate on the rest of the play. My precious ticket felt wasted. I twisted my icy hands together while my cheeks burned.

Even worse, she and I rode the same train afterwards. I had plenty of time to respond, to find a vocabulary for prejudice and fear. The dark night buildings flew by. I could have said, "Madam, I am half Arab. I pray your heart grows larger someday." I could have sent her off, stunned and embarrassed, into the dark.

My father would say, *People like that can't be embarrassed.*

But what would he say *back to her?*   20

Oh I was ashamed for my silence and I have carried that shame across oceans, through a summer when it never rained, in my secret pocket, till now. I will never feel better about it. Like my reckless angry last words to the one who took his own life.

Years later my son and I were sitting on an American island with a dear friend, the only African American living among eighty or so residents. A brilliant artist and poet in his seventies, he has made a beautiful lifetime of painting picture books, celebrating expression, encouraging the human spirit, reciting poems of other African American heroes, delighting children and adults alike.

---

kef'fiyeh: Arab cloth headdress. [All notes are the Editors'.]

We had spent a peaceful day riding bicycles, visiting the few students at the schoolhouse, picking up rounded stones on the beach, digging peat moss in the woods. We had sung hymns together in the resonant little church. Our friend had purchased a live lobster down at the dock for supper. My son and I became sad when it seemed to be knocking on the lid of the pot of boiling water. "Let me out!" We vowed quietly to one another never to eat a lobster again.

After dinner a friend of our friend dropped in, returned to the island from her traveling life as an anthropologist. We asked if she had heard anything about the elections in Israel—that was the day Shimon Peres and Benjamin Netanyahu vied for prime minister and we had been unable to pick up a final tally on the radio.

She thought Netanyahu had won. The election was very close. But then 25 she said, "Good thing! He'll put those Arabs in their places. Arabs always want more than they deserve."

My face froze. Was it possible I had heard incorrectly? *An anthropologist speaking. Not a teenager, not a blithering idiot.* I didn't speak another word during her visit. I wanted to, I should have, but I couldn't. My plate littered with red shells.

After she left, my friend put his gentle hand on my shoulder. He said simply, "Now you know a little more what it feels like to be black."

So what happens to my words when the going gets rough? In a world where certain equities for human beings seem long, long, long, overdue, where is the magic sentence to act as a tool? Where is the hoe, the tiller, the rake?

Pontificating, proving, proselytizing leave me cold. So do endless political debates over coffee after dinner. I can't listen to talk radio, drowning in jabber.

The poetic impulse—to suggest, hint, shape a little picture, to find a 30 story, metaphor, scene—abides as a kind of music inside. Nor can I forget the journalist in Dubai who called me a donkey for talking about vegetables when there was injustice in the world.

I can talk about sumac too. When a friend asks what's that purple spice in the little shake-up jar at the Persian restaurant, tears cloud my eyes.

Is it good for you?

Are vegetables, in some indelible way, smarter than we are? Are animals?

But then the headlines take the power. The fanatical behavior.

Problem is, we can't hear the voices of the moderates, said the Israeli man, who 35 assured me his home was built on a spot where Arabs had never lived. Where are *they*? Why *don't* they *speak louder*?

(They don't like to raise their voices.)

(Maybe they can't hear you either.)

The men haven't fixed it. Lose their turn. Their turn was long enough. Hanan stepped back. Anyone can understand why. Too many men. Pass the power to the women. And the children. And the eggplants. But it *was women who said stupid things both times to me*. No one exempt from stupidity. Is there a cure?

I love when the poet Wislawa said we have to honor anew those humble words *I don't know*.

Then we start out fresh. Like the soft dampness of a new morning.   40

I don't know. How. To tell the whole story. No one tells the whole story. No one knows it! *Still, don't those guys seem to talk forever?*

EVERY VIOLENT ACT SETS US BACK. SETS US BACK. Say it louder.

What to contain. To honor, leave unspoken. People will talk and talk while the almond tree is blooming. But something crucial is always too big, or too obvious, to say. Obviously, it is the thing which could save people, if we could only learn its name.

The gardener laid the stones. He cut the trees back. He turned over the soil around the plants so their roots could breathe. He used no language doing it. His skin glistened in the sun.

What he has suffered in his life remains a mystery to me. Rumors in the 45 neighborhood say it has been much, and extreme. What did Aldous Huxley° say toward the end of his life when someone asked him for advice? *After so much study, after so much research and discussion, it comes to this: be a little kinder to one another.*

Before leaving, the gardener mentioned the grass would grow up soon between the stepping stones to help them look much nicer, as if they had been there for years.

WHAT DOES SHE SAY?

1. Nye begins with a brief scene that doesn't at first seem to have anything to do with the subject of the Middle East and the treatment of Arabs. When you've finished reading the essay the first time, go back to this opening and write a note in the margins explaining how it applies to Nye's purpose. What does "long overdue" mean?

2. This essay is a collage, moving from one short piece to another using blank space as a visual cue to signal the change. Would you be able to follow the essay if the blank space were removed and the pieces blended together? Write a short paragraph explaining why or why not.

3. Mark what you think is the crucial scene in this essay, the piece of the collage that organizes and makes sense of all the others. (Though it is central, it may not appear in the middle.)

Aldous Huxley (1894–1963): British novelist and essayist.

4. *"Where is the end of the tangled thread?"* What does Nye mean by this?

5. The quote in the question above is written in italics. A number of other sentences in this piece are written in italics. Why italicize these sentences? What is their function in the essay? How do they relate to each other?

WHAT DO YOU THINK?

6. "I pray your heart grows larger someday," Nye imagines she tells the woman from the play. Assume that this sentence contains the main point of the essay. (There may be other sentences that do this, too.) Explain and interpret what Nye says.

7. "EVERY VIOLENT ACT SETS US BACK. SETS US BACK. Say it louder." What's the importance of this passage in the essay? Why is it in capital letters? Why does Nye repeat part of it? Why does she prompt, "Say it louder"? Why is this passage isolated on the page as a separate piece of the collage?

8. Write a brief essay about the idea of language in "Long Overdue." Explain how Nye feels about the power of language and the relation of language to the problem that she is experiencing. What can language do to change things, according to the author?

9. Write a personal essay describing and discussing one or more times when you found yourself in the position of someone in Nye's essay—either as someone hearing a comment that was offensive (whether the offense is intended or not) or as someone saying something offensive (whether intended or not). Explain the circumstances, how they were similar to and different from those in Nye's essay, and what you think about this incident (or these incidents) now.

WHAT WOULD THEY SAY?

10. Say that Nye has read the Studs Terkel profile of C. P. Ellis (p. 568). What would she learn from this about the possibilities and means of change in America? Would she be encouraged or discouraged? Write your own essay addressing these questions. Make sure that it quotes from Nye and from Ellis as least once.

11. In "Politics and the English Language" (p. 461), George Orwell argues that clear language can change the political landscape. Based on "Long Overdue," how would Nye respond to this argument? Write your own essay explaining this.

ANNIE DILLARD
Singing with the Fundamentalists

*T*HIS UNDERSTATED ESSAY *describes the narrator's experience singing with a group of fundamentalist students on the campus where she teaches. What Annie Dillard (b. 1945) demonstrates here is a willingness to engage real particulars rather than remain content with stereotypes.*

Dillard, a professor emeritus at Wesleyan University, has written numerous books, including the Pulitzer Prize–winning Pilgrim at Tinker Creek *(1974),* Holy the Firm *(1977),* Teaching a Stone to Talk *(1982), and* An American Childhood *(1989). "Singing with the Fundamentalists" was first published in the Winter 1985 issue of the* Yale Review.

It is early spring. I have a temporary office at a state university on the West Coast. The office is on the third floor. It looks down on the Square, the enormous open courtyard at the center of campus. From my desk I see hundreds of people moving between classes. There is a large circular fountain in the Square's center.

Early one morning, on the first day of spring quarter, I hear singing. A pack of students has gathered at the fountain. They are singing something which, at this distance, and through the heavy window, sounds good.

I know who these singing students are: they are the Fundamentalists. This campus has a lot of them. Mornings they sing on the Square; it is their only perceptible activity. What are they singing? Whatever it is, I want to join them, for I like to sing; whatever it is, I want to take my stand with them, for I am drawn to their very absurdity, their innocent indifference to what people think. My colleagues and students here, and my friends everywhere, dislike and fear Christian fundamentalists. You may never have met such people, but you've heard what they do: they pile up money, vote in blocs, and elect right-wing crazies; they censor books; they carry handguns; they fight fluoride in the drinking water and evolution in the schools; probably they would lynch people if they could get away with it. I'm not sure my friends are correct. I close my pen and join the singers on the Square.

There is a clapping song in progress. I have to concentrate to follow it:

Come on, rejoice,
And let your heart sing,
Come on, rejoice,
Give power to the king.

> Singing alleluia —
> He is the king of kings;
> Singing alleluia —
> He is the king of kings.

Two song leaders are standing on the broad rim of the fountain; the   5
water is splashing just behind them. The boy is short, hard faced, with a
moustache. He bangs his guitar with the backs of his fingers. The blond girl,
who leads the clapping, is bouncy; she wears a bit of makeup. Both are wearing blue jeans.

The students beside me are wearing blue jeans, too — and athletic jerseys,
parkas, football jackets, turtlenecks, and hiking shoes or jogging shoes. They all
have canvas or nylon book bags. They look like any random batch of seventy
or eighty students at this university. They are grubby or scrubbed, mostly
scrubbed; they are tall, fair, or redheaded in large proportions. Their parents are
white-collar workers, blue-collar workers, farmers, loggers, orchardists, merchants, fishermen; their names are, I'll bet, Olsen, Jensen, Seversen, Hansen,
Klokker, Sigurdsen.

Despite the vigor of the clapping song, no one seems to be giving it much
effort. And no one looks at anyone else; there are no sentimental glances and
smiles, no glances even of recognition. These kids don't seem to know each
other. We stand at the fountain's side, out on the broad, bricked Square in front
of the science building, and sing the clapping song through three times.

It is quarter to nine in the morning. Hundreds of people are crossing the
Square. These passersby — faculty, staff, students — pay very little attention to
us; this morning singing has gone on for years. Most of them look at us directly,
then ignore us, for there is nothing to see: no animal sacrifices, no lynchings, no
collection plate for Jesse Helms,° no seizures, snake handling, healing, or glosso-
lalia. There is barely anything to hear. I suspect the people glance at us to learn
if we are really singing: how could so many people make so little sound? My
fellow singers, who ignore each other, certainly ignore passersby as well. Within
a week, most of them will have their eyes closed anyway.

We move directly to another song, a slower one.

> He is my peace
> Who has broken down every wall;
> He is my peace,
> He is my peace.
>
> Cast all your cares on him,
> For he careth for you — oo — oo
> He is my peace,
> He is my peace.

Jesse Helms (b. 1921): Conservative and controversial U.S. Senator from North Carolina;
retired in 2002. [EDS.]

I am paying strict attention to the song leaders, for I am singing at the top 10 of my lungs and I've never heard any of these songs before. They are not the old American low-church Protestant hymns; they are not the old European high-church Protestant hymns. These hymns seem to have been written just yesterday, apparently by the same people who put out lyrical Christian greeting cards and bookmarks.

"Where do these songs come from?" I ask a girl standing next to me. She seems appalled to be addressed at all, and startled by the question. "They're from the praise albums!" she explains, and moves away.

The songs' melodies run dominant, subdominant, dominant, tonic, dominant. The pace is slow, about the pace of "Tell Laura I Love Her," and with that song's quavering, long notes. The lyrics are simple and repetitive; there are very few of them to which a devout Jew or Mohammedan could not give wholehearted assent. These songs are similar to the things Catholics sing in church these days. I don't know if any studies have been done to correlate the introduction of contemporary songs into Catholic churches with those churches' decline in membership, or with the phenomenon of Catholic converts' applying to enter cloistered monasteries directly, without passing through parish churches.

> I'm set free to worship,
> I'm set free to praise him,
> I'm set free to dance before the Lord...

At nine o'clock sharp we quit and scatter. I hear a few quiet "see you's." Mostly the students leave quickly, as if they didn't want to be seen. The Square empties.

The next day we show up again, at twenty to nine. The same two leaders stand on the fountain's rim; the fountain is pouring down behind them.

After the first song, the boy with the moustache hollers, "Move on up! Some of you guys aren't paying attention back there! You're talking to each other. I want you to concentrate!" The students laugh, embarrassed for him. He sounds like a teacher. No one moves. The girl breaks into the next song, which we join at once:

> In my life, Lord,
> Be glorified, be glorified, be glorified;
> In my life, Lord,
> Be glorified, be glorified, today.

At the end of this singularly monotonous verse, which is straining my tolerance for singing virtually anything, the boy with the moustache startles me by shouting, "Classes!"

At once, without skipping a beat, we sing, "In my classes, Lord, be glori- 15 fied, be glorified..." I give fleet thought to the class I'm teaching this afternoon. We're reading a little "Talk of the Town" piece called "Eggbag," about a cat in a magic store on Eighth Avenue. "Relationships!" the boy calls. The students seem to sing "In my relationships, Lord," more easily than they sang "classes." They seemed embarrassed by "classes." In fact, to my fascination, they seem embarrassed by almost everything. Why are they here? I will sing with the Fundamentalists every weekday morning all spring; I will decide, tentatively, that they come pretty much for the same reasons I do: each has a private relationship with "the Lord" and will put up with a lot of junk for it.

I have taught some Fundamentalist students here, and know a bit of what they think. They are college students above all, worried about their love lives, their grades, and finding jobs. Some support moderate Democrats; some support moderate Republicans. Like their classmates, most support nuclear freeze, ERA, and an end to the draft. I believe they are divided on abortion and busing. They are not particularly political. They read *Christianity Today* and *Campus Life* and *Eternity*—moderate, sensible magazines, I think; they read a lot of C. S. Lewis. (One such student, who seemed perfectly tolerant of me and my shoddy Christianity, introduced me to C. S. Lewis's critical book on Charles Williams.) They read the Bible. I think they all "believe in" organic evolution. The main thing about them is this; there isn't any "them." Their views vary. They don't know each other.

Their common Christianity puts them, if anywhere, to the left of their classmates. I believe they also tend to be more able than their classmates to think well in the abstract, and also to recognize the complexity of moral issues. But I may be wrong.

In 1980, the media were certainly wrong about television evangelists. Printed estimates of Jerry Falwell's television audience ranged from 18 million to 30 million people. In fact, according to Arbitron's actual counts, fewer than 1.5 million people were watching Falwell. And, according to an Emory University study, those who did watch television evangelists didn't necessarily vote with them. Emory University sociologist G. Melton Mobley reports, "When that message turns political, they cut it off." Analysis of the 1982 off-year elections turned up no Fundamentalist bloc voting. The media were wrong, but no one printed retractions.

The media were wrong, too, in a tendency to identify all fundamentalist Christians with Falwell and his ilk, and to attribute to them, across the board, conservative views.

Someone has sent me two recent issues of *Eternity: The Evangelical* 20 *Monthly*. One lead article criticizes a television preacher for saying that the United States had never used military might to take land from another nation. The same article censures Newspeak, saying that government rhetoric would have us believe in a "clean bomb," would have us believe that we "defend" America by invading foreign soil, and would have us believe that the dictatorships we support are "democracies." "When the President of the United States says that one reason to support defense spending is because it creates jobs," this lead article says, "a little bit of *1984* begins to surface." Another article criticizes a "heavy-handed" opinion of Jerry Falwell Ministries—in this case a broadside attack on artificial insemination, surrogate motherhood, and lesbian motherhood. Browsing through *Eternity*, I find a double crosstic. I find an intelligent, analytical, and enthusiastic review of the new London Philharmonic recording of Mahler's second symphony—a review which stresses the "glorious truth" of the Jewish composer's magnificent work, and cites its recent performance in Jerusalem to celebrate the recapture of the Western Wall following the Six Day War. Surely, the evangelical Christians who read this magazine are not book-burners. If by chance they vote with the magazine's editors, then it looks to me as if they vote with the American Civil Liberties Union and Americans for Democratic Action.

Every few years some bold and sincere Christian student at this university disagrees with a professor in class—usually about the professor's out-of-hand dismissal of Christianity. Members of the faculty, outraged, repeat the stories of these rare and uneven encounters for years on end, as if to prove that the crazies are everywhere, and gaining ground. The notion is, apparently, that these kids can't think for themselves. Or they wouldn't disagree.

Now again the moustached leader asks us to move up. There is no harangue, so we move up. (This will be a theme all spring. The leaders want us closer together. Our instinct is to stand alone.) From behind the tall fountain comes a wind; on several gusts we get sprayed. No one seems to notice.

We have time for one more song. The leader, perhaps sensing that no one likes him, blunders on. "I want you to pray this one through," he says. "We have a lot of people here from a lot of different fellowships, but we're all one body. Amen?" They don't like it. He gets a few polite Amens. We sing:

> Bind us together, Lord,
> With a bond that can't be broken;
> Bind us together, Lord,
> With love.

Everyone seems to be in a remarkably foul mood today. We don't like this song. There is no one here under seventeen, and, I think, no one here who believes that love is a bond that can't be broken. We sing the song through three times; then it is time to go.

The leader calls after our retreating backs. "Hey, have a good day! Praise Him all day!" The kids around me roll up their eyes privately. Some groan; all flee.

The next morning is very cold. I am here early. Two girls are talking on the fountain's rim; one is part Indian. She says, "I've got all the Old Testament, but I can't get the New. I screw up the New." She takes a breath and rattles off a long list, ending with "Jonah, Micah, Nahum, Habakkuk, Zephaniah,

Haggai, Zechariah, Malachi." The other girl produces a slow, sarcastic applause. I ask one of the girls to help me with the words to a song. She is agreeable, but says, "I'm sorry, I can't. I just became a Christian this year, so I don't know all the words yet."

The others are coming; we stand and separate. The boy with the moustache is gone, replaced by a big, serious fellow in a green down jacket. The bouncy girl is back with her guitar; she's wearing a skirt and wool knee socks. We begin, without any preamble, by singing a song that has so few words that we actually stretch one syllable over eleven separate notes. Then we sing a song in which the men sing one phrase and the women echo it. Everyone seems to know just what to do. In the context of our vapid songs, the lyrics of this one are extraordinary:

> I was nothing before you found me.
> Heartache! Broken people! Ruined lives
> Is why you died on Calvary.

The last line rises in a regular series of half-notes. Now at last some people are actually singing; they throw some breath into the business. There is a seriousness and urgency to it: "Heartache! Broken people! Ruined lives...I was nothing."

We don't look like nothing. We look like a bunch of students of every stripe, ill shaven or well shaven, dressed up or down, but dressed warmly against the cold: jeans and parkas, jeans and heavy sweaters, jeans and scarves and blow-dried hair. We look ordinary. But I think, quite on my own, that we are here because we know this business of nothingness, brokenness, and ruination. We sing this song over and over.

Something catches my eye. Behind us, up in the science building, professors are standing alone at opened windows.

The long brick science building has three upper floors of faculty offices, thirty-two windows. At one window stands a bearded man, about forty; his opening his window is what caught my eye. He stands full in the open window, his hands on his hips, his head cocked down toward the fountain. He is drawn to look, as I was drawn to come. Up on the building's top floor, at the far right window, there is another: an Asian American professor, wearing a white shirt, is sitting with one hip on his desk, looking out and down. In the middle of the row of windows, another one, an old professor in a checked shirt, stands sideways to the opened window, stands stock-still, his long, old ear to the air. Now another window cranks open, another professor—or maybe a graduate student—leans out, his hands on the sill.

We are all singing, and I am watching these five still men, my colleagues, 30 whose office doors are surely shut—for that is the custom here: five of them alone in their offices at the science building who have opened their windows on this very cold morning, who motionless hear the Fundamentalists sing, utterly unknown to each other.

We sing another four songs, including the clapping song, and one which repeats, "This is the day which the Lord hath made; rejoice and be glad in it." All the professors but one stay still by their opened windows, figures in a frieze. When after ten minutes we break off and scatter, each cranks his windows shut. Maybe they have nine o'clock classes too.

I miss a few sessions. One morning of the following week, I rejoin the Fundamentalists on the Square. The wind is blowing from the north; it is sunny and cold. There are several new developments.

Someone has blown up rubber gloves and floated them in the fountain. I saw them yesterday afternoon from my high office window, and couldn't quite make them out: I seemed to see hands in the fountain waving from side to side, like those hands wagging on springs which people stick in the back windows of their cars. I saw these many years ago in Quito and Guayaquil, where they were a great fad long before they showed up here. The cardboard hands said, on their palms, HOLA GENTE, hello people. Some of them just said HOLA, hello, with a little wave to the universe at large, in case anybody happened to be looking. It is like our sending radio signals to planets in other galaxies: HOLA, if anyone is listening. Jolly folk, these Ecuadorians, I thought.

Now, waiting by the fountain for the singing, I see that these particular hands are long surgical gloves, yellow and white, ten of them, tied off at the cuff. They float upright and they wave, *hola, hola, hola*; they mill around like a crowd, bobbing under the fountain's spray and back again to the pool's rim, *hola*. It is a good prank. It is far too cold for the university's maintenance crew to retrieve them without turning off the fountain and putting on rubber boots.

From all around the Square, people are gathering for the singing. There 35 is no way I can guess which kids, from among the masses crossing the Square, will veer off to the fountain. When they get here, I never recognize anybody except the leaders.

The singing begins without ado as usual, but there is something different about it. The students are growing prayerful, and they show it this morning with a peculiar gesture. I'm glad they weren't like this when I first joined them, or I never would have stayed.

Last night there was an educational television special, part of *Middletown*. It was a segment called "Community of Praise," and I watched it because it was about Fundamentalists. It showed a Jesus-loving family in the Midwest; the treatment was good and complex. This family attended the prayer meetings, healing sessions, and church services of an unnamed sect—a very low-church sect, whose doctrine and culture were much more low-church than those of the kids I sing with. When the members of this sect prayed, they held their arms over their heads and raised their palms, as if to feel or receive a blessing or energy from above.

Now today on the Square there is a new serious mood. The leaders are singing with their eyes shut. I am impressed that they can bang their guitars, keep their balance, and not fall into the pool. It is the same bouncy girl and earnest boy. Their eyeballs are rolled back a bit. I look around and see that almost everyone in this crowd of eighty or so has his eyes shut and is apparently praying the words of this song or praying some other prayer.

Now as the chorus rises, as it gets louder and higher and simpler in melody —

> I exalt thee,
> I exalt thee,
> I exalt thee,
> Thou art the Lord —

then, at this moment, hands start rising. All around me, hands are going up — that tall girl, that blond boy with his head back, the redheaded boy up front, the girl with the McDonald's jacket. Their arms rise as if pulled on strings. Some few of them have raised their arms very high over their heads and are tilting back their palms. Many, many more of them, as inconspicuously as possible, have raised their hands to the level of their chins.

What is going on? Why are these students today raising their palms in 40 this gesture, when nobody did it last week? Is it because the leaders have set a prayerful tone this morning? Is it because this gesture always accompanies this song, just as clapping accompanies other songs? Or is it, as I suspect, that these kids watched the widely publicized documentary last night just as I did, and are adopting, or trying out, the gesture?

It is a sunny morning, and the sun is rising behind the leaders and the fountain, so those students have their heads tilted, eyes closed, and palms upraised toward the sun. I glance up at the science building and think my own prayer: thank God no one is watching this.

The leaders cannot move around much on the fountain's rim. The girl has her eyes shut; the boy opens his eyes from time to time, glances at the neck of the guitar, and closes his eyes again.

When the song is over, the hands go down, and there is some desultory chatting in the crowd, as usual; can I borrow your library card? And, as usual, nobody looks at anybody.

All our songs today are serious. There is a feudal theme to them, or a feudal analogue:

> I will eat from abundance of your household.
> I will dream beside your streams of righteousness.
> You are my king.
> Enter his gates
> with thanksgiving in your heart;
> come before his courts with praise.
> He is the king of kings.
> Thou art the Lord.

All around me, eyes are closed and hands are raised. There is no social 45
pressure to do this, or anything else. I've never known any group to be less cohesive, imposing fewer controls. Since no one looks at anyone, and since
passersby no longer look, everyone out here is inconspicuous and free. Perhaps
the palm-raising has begun because the kids realize by now that they are not
on display; they're praying in their closets, right out here on the Square. Over
the course of the next weeks, I will learn that the palm-raising is here to stay.

The sun is rising higher. We are singing our last song. We are praying.
We are alone together.

> He is my peace
> Who has broken down every wall...

When the song is over, the hands go down. The heads lower, the eyes
open and blink. We stay still a second before we break up. We have been
standing in a broad current; now we have stepped aside. We have dismantled
the radar cups; we have closed the telescope's vault. Students gather their book
bags and go. The two leaders step down from the fountain's rim and pack
away their guitars. Everyone scatters. I am in no hurry, so I stay after everyone
is gone. It is after nine o'clock, and the Square is deserted. The fountain is
playing to an empty house. In the pool the cheerful hands are waving over the
water, bobbing under the fountain's veil and out again in the current, *hola*.

WHAT DOES SHE SAY?

1. Before reading this essay, write a short paragraph describing your own associations with the word *fundamentalist*. What does it call to mind?

2. Before reading this essay, conjecture: What do you think Annie Dillard might say about the fundamentalists? What do you assume this essay is about?

3. Read the essay through once, and mark at least three passages that either confirm or overturn your first assumptions about it. In other words, mark at least three passages where Dillard seems to be stating or implying her attitude about the fundamentalist students on her campus. How do these passages match up with your expectations?

4. As an essayist, Dillard uses image, scene, and implication rather than explicit statement; she shows rather than tells. It may not be entirely clear what she thinks or is getting at. Mark two passages where this seems to be the case—where you're not entirely sure what the point is.

WHAT DO YOU THINK?

5. "The notion is, apparently, that these kids can't think for themselves. Or they wouldn't disagree." Explain the context for this statement and what you think

Dillard means by it, then apply it to your own experience at the university. When or how have you been treated as if you can't think for yourself? Have you ever tried to disagree with a professor? On what grounds? How does this experience help you understand the point that Dillard is making? Write an essay explaining how your analysis of the quotation and your own experiences help you understand Dillard's implications and assertions.

6. Why does Dillard decide to sing with the fundamentalists on her campus? What motivates her? Mark the passage where this seems to become clear and use it in an essay that explains what this action on her part implies about the kind of person Dillard is and her habits of thinking. Then explain your reaction to and judgments of her.

7. Argue that Dillard's behavior and ways of thinking in this essay are exemplary; all people at the university should do what she does here. Explain.

8. Argue that Dillard's essay isn't a defense of religion but a critique of the university. Write an essay spelling out at least three elements of this critique. To support your claim, find three scenes or images from the essay.

9. What do you think of the ending? What does the scene imply—the deserted square, the fountain, the inflated rubber gloves? What's the significance of the final word, *hola*? Why that word? Why at the end?

WHAT WOULD THEY SAY?

10. Read Ruth Benedict's "The Case for Moral Relativism" (p. 619). What would Benedict say about Dillard's methods as a researcher? about her way of writing? about her conclusions? about her apparent attitude toward religion? Write an essay addressing these questions and explaining how "The Case for Moral Relativism" helps you understand "Singing with the Fundamentalists."

11. What would Helen Prejean, the author of "Executions Are Too Costly—Morally" (p. 614), say about Dillard's methods, conclusions, and attitudes toward religion?

12. Write an essay showing how Dillard's "Singing with the Fundamentalists" illustrates the philosophy that Parker Palmer proposes in "The Community of Truth" (p. 627). Include in your essay one selection from anywhere in this book that illustrates the opposite of what Palmer proposes—a closed mind, an overinsistent or narrow argument.

DAVID DENBY

Passion at Yale

*T*HIS BRIEF ESSAY *reflects on a protest lodged by Orthodox Jewish students at Yale who are upset by the university's requirements that all first-year students live in coed dorms. Here, David Denby raises the issues of sex on campus, the limits of the First Amendment, the role of religion in democracy, and the nature of the university.*

  Denby is a staff writer and film critic for the New Yorker *and has published two books:* Great Books *(1997) and* American Sucker *(2004). "Passion at Yale" was first published in the* New Yorker *in 1997.*

DOES THE CONSTITUTION CARE ABOUT COED DORMS?

As college students gather in the opening weeks of a new semester, there is, we hear, a scandal brewing, a dirty secret spreading its stain through the life of undergraduates, whose life is conducted, at many campuses, in coed dormitories. The secret (which, of course, is not very new and not entirely secret) is that there isn't very much sex going on. There's *some*, of course: some students are very active sexually (and become either famous or notorious for it), and a few may even have the grace or the misfortune to experience what would have been known in another era as passion. But many students "hook up" only now and then, and others may be defiantly chaste, or perhaps lonely or indifferent, and spend the best part of four years in a state of bluesy sexual withdrawal, rarely experiencing so much as the dip of a window shade.

  All this serves as the necessary ironic background for the recent announcement by a group of five Yale freshmen and sophomores of the Orthodox Jewish faith that they may begin a lawsuit against the university in order to fight the requirement that they spend their first two years at Yale living in coed dormitories. (At Yale, freshmen generally live on all-male or all-female floors but share some bathrooms; sophomores live in single-sex suites joined by bathrooms. It may, on occasion, be necessary to knock.) Such a residence requirement, the students declare, contradicts religious rules that demand privacy and modesty as well as sexual abstinence prior to marriage. So far, Yale has refused to waive its requirement that the students live in the dormitories, and, in response, the Yale Five (as they style themselves) have asked for the assistance of a prominent lawyer—Nathan Lewin, of Washington—who describes the affair as a constitutional issue in which the students' rights to free religious expression have been infringed. In the past, Mr. Lewin has successfully sued for the rights of Orthodox Jews in public jobs to maintain elements of religious

593

observance — the right of an air force psychologist, say, to wear a yarmulke at work. But no one is prohibiting the exercise of religious observance at Yale, and the students can maintain a kosher diet in an off-campus dining hall. What's at stake for the Yale Five is the *atmosphere* of undergraduate life — the threat it poses to their purity of conduct. But temptations must surround the orthodox of any faith when they leave family and community and enter the world. Though the sensibilities of these students may be affronted, have their constitutional rights been abrogated?

One remains puzzled by the students' notion that dormitory life is a parade of licentious goings on — or, at least, a series of remorseless intrusions. "There is no way to keep female visitors away," one of the Five is quoted as saying. ("I should be so lucky," his dorm mates may be thinking.) Yes, every dorm resident does have to put up with occasional annoyances — a floor mate, say, who won't turn down a CD player. But no one is forcing the students to do anything in particular. No one is requiring of them — as certain heretical Christian sects were accused of requiring of members — that they lie next to young virgins as a test of their resolve. One of the Five did complain that during freshman orientation he was subjected to a lecture on condoms. It strikes one as exceedingly curious, however, that any university student should be shocked by mere information. Furthermore, students need not avail themselves of the condoms that Yale — continuing to operate in loco parentis° — offers to its charges to prevent the spread of sexually transmitted diseases and, of course, unwanted pregnancies. Doors can always be locked. It is hard to believe that if a student wants to live quietly and privately in a Yale dormitory others will not, after a while, respect the signals he is sending out.

In a *Times* Op-Ed piece that appeared last Tuesday, Elisha Dov Hack, one of the Yale Five, complained of a sign he spied during an orientation tour which touted "100 ways to make love without having sex." One of the advertised ways that offended Mr. Hack was "Take a nap together." The sign, of course, was a joking nudge to behave responsibly. Yet even the notion of a mere coed snooze strikes Mr. Hack as heresy. Unmarried intimacy of any kind — or even proximity — seems to be what disturbs the Yale Five. "We cannot, in good conscience," Mr. Hack writes, "live in a place where women are permitted to stay overnight in men's rooms." In that case, Mr. Hack should avoid living in big-city apartment buildings as well.

The students' grievance appears to be produced by a combination of   5
harsh medieval ardor and culture-of-complaint hypersensitivity. If the students care so much for modesty and chastity, they could, of course, attend a seminary. But it's the Yale degree they want, and they can hardly accuse the university of

---

in loco parentis: Latin for "in the place of a parent." [EDS.]

false advertising. Living in a coed dorm for two years is now part of the known Yale experience, just as taking certain required courses, like the Literature, Humanities, and the Contemporary Civilization courses at Columbia, is part of the life of other schools.

No modern university can be asked to spare its observant students the chagrins of a secular existence, for almost every aspect of the curriculum itself has been formed by secular assumptions. In class, the students may hear religion discussed in historical, political, and military—rather than sacred—terms; they may even hear religion discussed as a system of illusion. In every discipline, the disenchanted modern world awaits them. One of the Yale Five is a biology major. The Hebrew Bible says nothing about evolution. Will the student boycott his courses? One thing that separates a faith community from a learning community is that in the latter one's preconceptions are constantly, and productively, under duress. The experience of confronting both new ideas and people who think differently from oneself has traditionally formed the heart of a liberal education.

It's bad enough that the dormitories at Berkeley are partly balkanized by special-interest groups and that at many universities African Americans congregate at meals (often to the dismay of white students who would like to mingle with them and make friends). Such self-imposed separations attack the very idea of a university. By not giving in, Yale no doubt wants to avoid a situation in which separatist communities increase their demands on the university. And Yale is right. If universities continue to humor every group's sensitivities, then what is to stop blacks from demanding protection from exposure to white students, gays from exposure to straights, fundamentalist Christians from exposure to Jews and Muslims? In this society, existence is rarely free from jostling: we all, every day, find our deepest convictions offended, even traduced by *something*. In that respect, the Yale Five, whether they get their way or not, will have to take their chances along with the rest of us.

WHAT DOES HE SAY?

1. Put a wiggly line by at least one place in this essay where you don't understand what David Denby is saying, don't agree with what he's saying, or strongly disagree with what he's saying.

2. Denby reflects on a particular problem in a particular place, much as we ask you to do in the ethical scenarios that begin each chapter of this book. Summarize the facts of the case he discusses in this essay.

3. Write a quick paragraph explaining what this essay is about. Is it about religion? the university? sex? the Constitution? What's Denby's main point, and where does he make it?

WHAT DO YOU THINK?

4. If you were the president of Yale University, how would you respond to the "Yale Five," the five students who are protesting Yale's policies in this essay? Assuming the role of the university president—someone deeply committed to higher education—write a letter to these students.

5. Write an essay discussing a situation on your campus that is similar to that of the the Yale Five. There are always situations like this, conflicts and people objecting, often on the same grounds, that a particular group's values have been offended or threatened. Describe and discuss such a conflict in your college or university. Does Denby's argument apply here as well? Has your university responded as Yale has to the Yale Five? Should it?

6. "One thing that separates a faith community from a learning community is that in the latter one's preconceptions are constantly, and productively, under duress." Write an essay that explains what Denby means by this statement and how or why you agree or disagree. Have you found this to be true in your own experience?

7. "In this society, existence is rarely free from jostling: we all, every day, find our deepest convictions offended, even traduced by *something*." Explain what Denby means, and write an essay exploring this idea in your own experience. Denby seems to think that this "jostling" is a good thing. Do you?

WHAT WOULD THEY SAY?

8. "The experience of confronting both new ideas and people who think differently from oneself has traditionally formed the heart of a liberal education." Write an essay using this as your thesis statement and incorporating passages from at least two other essays in this chapter.

9. Use the quote in question 8 as your thesis statement for an essay incorporating passages from Langston Hughes's "Theme for English B" (p. 42), Bowen H. McCoy's "The Parable of the Sadhu" (p. 102), and Andre Dubus's "Giving Up the Gun" (p. 180).

RICHARD RODRIGUEZ
The Achievement of Desire

*T*HE CONTROVERSIAL ARGUMENT *of this selection is that education in some way alienates us from our parents, our class and our origins, inevitably changing our minds and thus changing us. Richard Rodriguez (b. 1944) earned a doctorate in literature from the University of California, Berkeley, and has been a commentator on PBS's* MacNeil/Lehrer News Hour. *Among his published books are* Days of Obligation: An Argument with My Father *(1992) and* Brown: The Last Discovery of America *(2002). "The Achievement of Desire" is from his first book,* The Hunger of Memory *(1982), the story of how his education distanced him from the native culture of his parents.*

I stand in the ghetto classroom—"the guest speaker"—attempting to lecture on the mystery of the sounds of our words to rows of diffident students. "Don't you hear it? Listen! The music of our words. *'Sumer is i-cumen in. . . .'* And songs on the car radio. We need Aretha Franklin's voice to fill plain words with music—her life." In the face of their empty stares, I try to create an enthusiasm. But the girls in the back row turn to watch some boy passing outside. There are flutters of smiles, waves. And someone's mouth elongates heavy, silent words through the barrier of glass. Silent words—the lips straining to shape each voiceless syllable: *"Meet meee late err."* By the door, the instructor smiles at me, apparently hoping that I will be able to spark some enthusiasm in the class. But only one student seems to be listening. A girl, maybe fourteen. In this gray room her eyes shine with ambition. She keeps nodding and nodding at all that I say; she even takes notes. And each time I ask a question, she jerks up and down in her desk like a marionette, while her hand waves over the bowed heads of her classmates. It is myself (as a boy) I see as she faces me now (a man in my thirties).

The boy who first entered a classroom barely able to speak English, twenty years later concluded his studies in the stately quiet of the reading room in the British Museum. Thus with one sentence I can summarize my academic career. It will be harder to summarize what sort of life connects the boy to the man.

With every award, each graduation from one level of education to the next, people I'd meet would congratulate me. Their refrain always the same: "Your parents must be very proud." Sometimes then they'd ask me how I managed it—my "success." (How?) After a while, I had several quick answers to give in reply. I'd admit, for one thing, that I went to an excellent grammar school. (My earliest teachers, the nuns, made my success their ambition.) And my brother and both my sisters were very good students. (They often brought home the shiny school trophies I came to want.) And my mother and father always encouraged me. (At every graduation they were behind the stunning flash of the camera when I turned to look at the crowd.)

As important as these factors were, however, they account inadequately for my academic advance. Nor do they suggest what an odd success I managed. For although I was a very good student, I was also a very bad student. I was a "scholarship boy," a certain kind of scholarship boy. Always successful, I was always unconfident. Exhilarated by my progress. Sad. I became the prized student—anxious and eager to learn. Too eager, too anxious—an imitative and unoriginal pupil. My brother and two sisters enjoyed the advantages I did, and they grew to be as successful as I, but none of them ever seemed so anxious about their schooling. A second-grade student, I was the one who came home and corrected the "simple" grammatical mistakes of our parents. ("Two negatives make a positive.") Proudly I announced—to my family's startled silence—that a teacher had said I was losing all trace of a Spanish accent. I was oddly annoyed when I was unable to get parental help with a homework assignment. The night my father tried to help me with an arithmetic exercise, he kept reading the instructions, each time more deliberately, until I pried the textbook out of his hands, saying, "I'll try to figure it out some more by myself."

When I reached the third grade, I outgrew such behavior. I became   5
more tactful, careful to keep separate the two very different worlds of my day. But then, with ever-increasing intensity, I devoted myself to my studies. I became bookish, puzzling to all my family. Ambition set me apart. When my brother saw me struggling home with stacks of library books, he would laugh, shouting: "Hey, Four Eyes!" My father opened a closet one day and was startled to find me inside, reading a novel. My mother would find me reading when I was supposed to be asleep or helping around the house or playing outside. In a voice angry or worried or just curious, she'd ask: "What do you see in your books?" It became the family's joke. When I was called and wouldn't reply, someone would say I must be hiding under my bed with a book.

(How did I manage my success?)

What I am about to say to you has taken me more than twenty years to admit: *A primary reason for my success in the classroom was that I couldn't forget that schooling was changing me and separating me from the life I enjoyed before becoming a student.* That simple realization! For years I never spoke to anyone about it. Never mentioned a thing to my family or my teachers or classmates. From a very early age, I understood enough, just enough about my classroom experiences to keep what I knew repressed, hidden beneath layers of embarrassment. Not until my last months as a graduate student, nearly thirty years old, was it possible for me to think much about the reasons for my academic success. Only then. At the end of my schooling, I needed to determine how far I had moved from my past. The adult finally confronted, and now must publicly say, what the child shuddered from knowing and could never admit to himself or to those many faces that smiled at his every success. ("Your parents must be very proud....")

At the end, in the British Museum (too distracted to finish my dissertation) for weeks I read, speed-read, books by modern educational theorists, only to find infrequent and slight mention of students like me. (Much more is written about the more typical case, the lower-class student who barely is helped by his schooling.) Then one day, leafing through Richard Hoggart's *The Uses of Literacy*, I found, in his description of the scholarship boy, myself. For the first time I realized that there were other students like me, and so I was able to frame the meaning of my academic success, its consequent price—the loss.

Hoggart's description is distinguished, at least initially, by deep understanding. What he grasps very well is that the scholarship boy must move between environments, his home and the classroom, which are at cultural extremes, opposed. With his family, the boy has the intense pleasure of intimacy, the family's consolation in feeling public alienation. Lavish emotions texture home life. *Then,* at school, the instruction bids him to trust lonely reason primarily. Immediate needs set the pace of his parents' lives. From his mother and father the boy learns to trust spontaneity and nonrational ways of knowing. *Then,* at school, there is mental calm. Teachers emphasize the value of a reflectiveness that opens a space between thinking and immediate action.

Years of schooling must pass before the boy will be able to sketch the cultural differences in his day as abstractly as this. But he senses those differences early. Perhaps as early as the night he brings home an assignment from school and finds the house too noisy for study. 10

> He has to be more and more alone, if he is going to "get on." He will have, probably unconsciously, to oppose the ethos of the hearth, the intense gregariousness of the working-class family group. Since everything centers upon the living room, there is unlikely to be a room of his own; the bedrooms are cold and inhospitable, and to warm them or the front room, if there is one, would not only be expensive, but would require an imaginative leap—out of the tradition—which most families are not capable of making. There is a corner of the living-room table. On the other side Mother is ironing, the wireless is on, someone is singing a snatch of song or Father says intermittently whatever comes into his head. The boy has to cut himself off mentally, so as to do his homework, as well as he can.[1]

The next day, the lesson is as apparent at school. There are even rows of desks. Discussion is ordered. The boy must rehearse his thoughts and raise his hand before speaking out in a loud voice to an audience of classmates. And there is time enough, and silence, to think about ideas (big ideas) never considered at home by his parents.

Not for the working-class child alone is adjustment to the classroom difficult. Good schooling requires that any student alter early childhood habits.

---

[1]All quotations...are from Richard Hoggart, *The Uses of Literacy* (London: Chatto and Windus, 1957), chapter 10. [Author's note.]

But the working-class child is usually least prepared for the change. And, unlike many middle-class children, he goes home and sees in his parents a way of life not only different but starkly opposed to that of the classroom. (He enters the house and hears his parents talking in ways his teachers discourage.)

Without extraordinary determination and the great assistance of others—at home and at school—there is little chance for success. Typically most working-class children are barely changed by the classroom. The exception succeeds. The relative few become scholarship students. Of these, Richard Hoggart estimates, most manage a fairly graceful transition. Somehow they learn to live in the two very different worlds of their day. There are some others, however, those Hoggart pejoratively terms "scholarship boys," for whom success comes with special anxiety. Scholarship boy: good student, troubled son. The child is "moderately endowed," intellectually mediocre, Hoggart supposes—though it may be more pertinent to note the special qualities of temperament in the child. High-strung child. Brooding. Sensitive. Haunted by the knowledge that one *chooses* to become a student. (Education is not an inevitable or natural step in growing up.) Here is a child who cannot forget that his academic success distances him from a life he loved, even from his own memory of himself.

Initially, he wavers, balances allegiance. ("The boy is himself [until he reaches, say, the upper forms] very much of *both* the worlds of home and school. He is enormously obedient to the dictates of the world of school, but emotionally still strongly wants to continue as part of the family circle.") Gradually, necessarily, the balance is lost. The boy needs to spend more and more time studying, each night enclosing himself in the silence permitted and required by intense concentration. He takes his first step toward academic success, away from his family.

From the very first days, through the years following, it will be with his parents—the figures of lost authority, the persons toward whom he feels deepest love—that the change will be most powerfully measured. A separation will unravel between them. Advancing in his studies, the boy notices that his mother and father have not changed as much as he. Rather, when he sees them, they often remind him of the person he once was and the life he earlier shared with them. He realizes what some Romantics also know when they praise the working class for the capacity for human closeness, qualities of passion and spontaneity, that the rest of us experience in like measure only in the earliest part of our youth. For the Romantic, this doesn't make working-class life childish. Working-class life challenges precisely because it is an *adult* way of life.

The scholarship boy reaches a different conclusion. He cannot afford to 15 admire his parents. (How could he and still pursue such a contrary life?) He permits himself embarrassment at their lack of education. And to evade nostalgia for the life he has lost, he concentrates on the benefits education will bestow upon him. He becomes especially ambitious. Without the support of old certainties and consolations, almost mechanically, he assumes the procedures and doctrines of the classroom. The kind of allegiance the young student might have given his mother and father only days earlier, he transfers to the teacher, the new figure of authority. "[The scholarship boy] tends to make a father-figure of his form-master," Hoggart observes.

But Hoggart's calm prose only makes me recall the urgency with which I came to idolize my grammar school teachers. I began by imitating their accents, using their diction, trusting their every direction. The very first facts they dispensed, I grasped with awe. Any book they told me to read, I read— then waited for them to tell me which books I enjoyed. Their every casual opinion I came to adopt and to trumpet when I returned home. I stayed after school "to help"—to get my teacher's undivided attention. It was the nun's encouragement that mattered most to me. (She understood exactly what— my parents never seemed to appraise so well—all my achievements entailed.) Memory gently caressed each word of praise bestowed in the classroom so that compliments teachers paid me years ago come quickly to mind even today.

The enthusiasm I felt in second-grade classes I flaunted before both my parents. The docile, obedient student came home a shrill and precocious son who insisted on correcting and teaching his parents with the remark: "My teacher told us...."

I intended to hurt my mother and father. I was still angry at them for having encouraged me toward classroom English. But gradually this anger was exhausted, replaced by guilt as school grew more and more attractive to me. I grew increasingly successful, a talkative student. My hand was raised in the classroom; I yearned to answer any question. At home, life was less noisy than it had been. (I spoke to classmates and teachers more often each day than to family members.) Quiet at home, I sat with my papers for hours each night. I never forgot that schooling had irretrievably changed my family's life. That knowledge, however, did not weaken ambition. Instead, it strengthened resolve. Those times I remembered the loss of my past with regret, I quickly reminded myself of all the things my teachers could give me. (They could make me an educated man.) I tightened my grip on pencil and books. I evaded nostalgia. Tried hard to forget. But one does not forget by trying to forget. One only remembers. I remembered too well that education had changed my family's life. I would not have become a scholarship boy had I not so often remembered.

Once she was sure that her children knew English, my mother would tell us, "You should keep up your Spanish." Voices playfully groaned in response. "¡*Pochos!*" my mother would tease. I listened silently.

After a while, I grew more calm at home. I developed tact. A fourth-grade student, I was no longer the show-off in front of my parents. I became a conventionally dutiful son, politely affectionate, cheerful enough, even—for reasons beyond choosing—my father's favorite. And much about my family life was easy then, comfortable, happy in the rhythm of our living together: hearing my father getting ready for work; eating the breakfast my mother had made me; looking up from a novel to hear my brother or one of my sisters playing with friends in the backyard; in winter, coming upon the house all lighted up after dark.   20

But withheld from my mother and father was any mention of what most mattered to me: the extraordinary experience of first-learning. Late afternoon: in the midst of preparing dinner, my mother would come up behind me while I was trying to read. Her head just over mine, her breath warmly scented with food. "What are you reading?" Or, "Tell me all about your new courses." I would barely respond, "Just the usual things, nothing special." (A half smile, then silence. Her head moving back in the silence. Silence! Instead of the flood of intimate sounds that had once flowed smoothly between us, there was this silence.) After dinner, I would rush to a bedroom with papers and books. As often as possible, I resisted parental pleas to "save lights" by coming to the kitchen to work. I kept so much, so often, to myself. Sad. Enthusiastic. Troubled by the excitement of coming upon new ideas. Eager. Fascinated by the promising texture of a brand-new book. I hoarded the pleasures of learning. Alone for hours. Enthralled. Nervous. I rarely looked away from my books— or back on my memories. Nights when relatives visited and the front rooms were warmed by Spanish sounds, I slipped quietly out of the house.

It mattered that education was changing me. It never ceased to matter. My brother and sisters would giggle at our mother's mispronounced words. They'd correct her gently. My mother laughed girlishly one night, trying not to pronounce *sheep* as *ship*. From a distance I listened sullenly. From that distance, pretending not to notice on another occasion, I saw my father looking at the title pages of my library books. That was the scene on my mind when I walked home with a fourth-grade companion and heard him say that his parents read to him every night. (A strange-sounding book— *Winnie the Pooh*.) Immediately, I wanted to know, "What is it like?" My companion, however, thought I wanted to know about the plot of the book. Another day, my mother surprised me by asking for a "nice" book to read. "Something not too hard you think I might like." Carefully I chose one, Willa Cather's *My Ántonia*. But when, several weeks later, I happened to see it next to her bed unread except for the first few pages, I was furious and suddenly wanted to cry. I grabbed up the book and took it back to my room and placed it in its place, alphabetically on my shelf.

"Your parents must be very proud of you." People began to say that to me about the time I was in sixth grade. To answer affirmatively, I'd smile. Shyly I'd smile, never betraying my sense of the irony: I was not proud of my mother and father. I was embarrassed by their lack of education. It was not that I ever thought they were stupid, though stupidly I took for granted their enormous native intelligence. Simply, what mattered to me was that they were not like my teachers.

But, "Why didn't you tell us about the award?" my mother demanded, her frown weakened by pride. At the grammar school ceremony several weeks after, her eyes were brighter than the trophy I'd won. Pushing back the hair from my forehead, she whispered that I had "shown" the *gringos*. A few minutes later, I heard my father speak to my teacher and felt ashamed of his labored, accented words. Then guilty for the shame. I felt such contrary feelings. (There is no simple road map through the heart of the scholarship boy.) My teacher was so soft-spoken and her words were edged sharp and clean. I admired her until it seemed to me that she spoke too carefully. Sensing that she was condescending to them, I became nervous. Resentful. Protective. I tried to move my parents away. "You both must be very proud of Richard," the nun said. They responded quickly. (They were proud.) "We are proud of all our children." Then this afterthought: "They sure didn't get their brains from us." They all laughed. I smiled.

Tightening the irony into a knot was the knowledge that my parents were al- 25 ways behind me. They made success possible. They evened the path. They sent their children to parochial schools because the nuns "teach better." They paid a tuition they couldn't afford. They spoke English to us.

For their children my parents wanted chances they never had—an easier way. It saddened my mother to learn that some relatives forced their children to start working right after high school. To *her* children she would say, "Get all the education you can." In schooling she recognized the key to job advancement. And with the remark she remembered her past.

As a girl new to America my mother had been awarded a high school diploma by teachers too careless or busy to notice that she hardly spoke English. On her own, she determined to learn how to type. That skill got her jobs typing envelopes in letter shops, and it encouraged in her an optimism about the possibility of advancement. (Each morning when her sisters put on uniforms, she chose a bright-colored dress.) The years of young womanhood passed, and her typing speed increased. She also became an excellent speller of words she mispronounced. "And I've never been to college," she'd say, smiling, when her children asked her to spell words they were too lazy to look up in a dictionary.

Typing, however, was dead-end work. Finally frustrating. When her youngest child started high school, my mother got a full-time office job once again. (Her paycheck combined with my father's to make us—in fact—what we had already become in our imagination of ourselves—middle class.) She worked then for the (California) state government in numbered civil-service positions secured by examinations. The old ambition of her youth was rekindled. During the lunch hour, she consulted bulletin boards for announcements of openings. One day she saw mention of something called an "anti-poverty agency." A typing job. A glamorous job, part of the governor's staff. "A knowledge of Spanish required." Without hesitation she applied and became nervous only when the job was suddenly hers.

"Everyone comes to work all dressed up," she reported at night. And didn't need to say more than that her coworkers wouldn't let her answer the phones. She was only a typist, after all, albeit a very fast typist. And an excellent speller. One morning there was a letter to be sent to a Washington cabinet officer. On the dictating tape, a voice referred to urban guerrillas. My mother typed (the wrong word, correctly): "gorillas." The mistake horrified the antipoverty bureaucrats who shortly after arranged to have her returned to her previous position. She would go no further. So she willed her ambition to her children. "Get all the education you can; with an education you can do anything." (With a good education *she* could have done anything.)

When I was in high school, I admitted to my mother that I planned to become a teacher someday. That seemed to please her. But I never tried to explain that it was not the occupation of teaching I yearned for as much as it was something more elusive: I wanted to *be* like my teachers, to possess their knowledge, to assume their authority, their confidence, even to assume a teacher's persona.

In contrast to my mother, my father never verbally encouraged his children's academic success. Nor did he often praise us. My mother had to remind him to "say something" to one of his children who scored some academic success. But whereas my mother saw in education the opportunity for job advancement, my father recognized that education provided an even more startling possibility: it could enable a person to escape from a life of mere labor.

In Mexico, orphaned when he was eight, my father left school to work as an "apprentice" for an uncle. Twelve years later, he left Mexico in frustration and arrived in America. He had great expectations then of becoming an engineer. ("Work for my hands and my head.") He knew a Catholic priest who promised to get him money enough to study full time for a high school diploma. But the promises came to nothing. Instead there was a dark succession of warehouse, cannery, and factory jobs. After work he went to night school along with my mother. A year, two passed. Nothing much changed, except that fatigue worked its way into the bone; then everything changed. He didn't talk anymore of becoming an engineer. He stayed outside on the steps of the school while my mother went inside to learn typing and shorthand.

By the time I was born, my father worked at "clean" jobs. For a time he was a janitor at a fancy department store. ("Easy work; the machines do it all.") Later he became a dental technician. ("Simple.") But by then he was pessimistic about the ultimate meaning of work and the possibility of ever escaping its claims. In some of my earliest memories of him, my father already seems aged by fatigue. (He has never really grown old like my mother.) From boyhood to manhood, I have remembered him in a single image: seated, asleep on the sofa, his head thrown back in a hideous corpselike grin, the evening newspaper spread out before him. "But look at all you've accomplished," his best friend said to him once. My father said nothing. Only smiled.

It was my father who laughed when I claimed to be tired by reading and writing. It was he who teased me for having soft hands. (He seemed to sense that some great achievement of leisure was implied by my papers and books.) It was my father who became angry while watching on television some woman at the Miss America contest tell the announcer that she was going to college. ("Majoring in fine arts.") "College!" he snarled. He despised the trivialization of higher education, the inflated grades and cheapened diplomas, the half education that so often passed as mass education in my generation.

It was my father again who wondered why I didn't display my awards 35 on the wall of my bedroom. He said he liked to go to doctors' offices and see their certificates and degrees on the wall. ("Nice.") My citations from school got left in closets at home. The gleaming figure astride one of my trophies was broken, wingless, after hitting the ground. My medals were placed in a jar of loose change. And when I lost my high school diploma, my father found it as it was about to be thrown out with the trash. Without telling me, he put it away with his own things for safekeeping.

These memories slammed together at the instant of hearing that refrain familiar to all scholarship students: "Your parents must be very proud...." Yes, my parents were proud. I knew it. But my parents regarded my progress with more than mere pride. They endured my early precocious behavior—but with what private anger and humiliation? As their children got older and would come home to challenge ideas both of them held, they argued before submitting to the force of logic or superior factual evidence with the disclaimer, "It's what we were taught in our time to believe." These discussions ended abruptly, though my mother remembered them on other occasions when she complained that our "big ideas" were going to our heads. More acute was her complaint that the family wasn't close anymore, like some others she knew. Why weren't we close, "more in the Mexican style"? Everyone is so private, she added. And she mimicked the yes and no answers she got in reply to her questions. Why didn't we talk more? (My father never asked.) I never said.

I was the first in my family who asked to leave home when it came time to go to college. I had been admitted to Stanford, one hundred miles away. My departure would only make physically apparent the separation that had occurred long before. But it was going too far. In the months preceding my leaving, I heard the question my mother never asked except indirectly. In the hot kitchen, tired at the end of her workday, she demanded to know, "Why aren't the colleges here in Sacramento good enough for you? They are for your brother and sister." In the middle of a car ride, not turning to face me, she wondered, "Why do you need to go so far away?" Late at night, ironing, she said with disgust, "Why do you have to put us through this big expense? You know your scholarship will never cover it all." But when September came there was a rush to get everything ready. In a bedroom that last night I packed the big brown valise, and my mother sat nearby sewing initials onto the clothes I would take. And she said no more about my leaving.

Months later, two weeks of Christmas vacation: the first hours home were the hardest. ("What's new?") My parents and I sat in the kitchen for a conversation. (But, lacking the same words to develop our sentences and to shape our interests, what was there to say? What could I tell them of the term paper I had just finished on the "universality of Shakespeare's appeal"?) I mentioned only small, obvious things: my dormitory life; weekend trips I had taken; random events. They responded with news of their own. (One was almost grateful for a family crisis about which there was much to discuss.) We tried to make our conversation seem like more than an interview.

WHAT DOES HE SAY?

1. Early on in this essay Rodriguez highlights his main point by putting it in italics. Summarize this statement in the margins, in your own words.

2. As you read the rest of the essay, mark at least three important passages and explain briefly in the margins how they relate to this main, italicized statement.

3. What is the "desire" that Rodriguez achieves? Desire for what? How is it achieved?

4. Make a list of at least three negative consequences of education, according to Rodriguez.

5. What does Rodriguez mean by the term *scholarship boy*? Is this a positive or a negative term?

WHAT DO YOU THINK?

6. Make a list of at least three positive things that education makes possible, according to Rodriguez. Explain these things and Rodriguez's reasons for valuing them. Then construct your own such list. What has Rodriguez left out, if anything? Or would you simply agree with him? Either way, use your educational experience to explain your own position as clearly as you do Rodriguez's.

7. Write an essay discussing how your family views your education. In light of your education, how do you view your family? For example, like Rodriguez, are you a first-generation college student? If so, how does this affect your relationship with your family? If your parents did go to college, how does that affect your attitude toward your education? What about the role of race and ethnicity in these questions? Rodriguez is Latino. Is the estrangement he feels from his family the necessary result of education for Latinos? Is estrangement any less of a danger for students of other races and ethnicities?

8. Do you agree that education necessarily estranges us from our origins? Write your own personal essay more or less in the manner of Richard Rodriguez. Address the ways that your own education has changed the relationships you've had with home and family.

WHAT WOULD THEY SAY?

9. How would Adrienne Rich ("Claiming an Education," p. 608) respond to Rodriguez? How is the status of women in education like and unlike the status of

people of color? Would Rich lament the negative consequences of education for women? Write an essay explaining what Rich would hear in "The Achievement of Desire" and how she would comment on it.

10. How would Parker Palmer, author of "The Community of Truth" (p. 627), interpret Rodriguez's essay? In particular, how would Palmer understand the role of Rodriguez's parents in the "community of truth"?

11. Assume that Benjamin Saenz, in "Exile: El Paso, Texas" (p. 20), has read Rodriguez's essay. (Saenz's essay is the first in this book.) Assume that Rodriguez has read Saenz. What would they say to each other? Explain their responses; then explain what is clearer to you now that you have read these essays together.

ADRIENNE RICH
Claiming an Education

*I*N THIS IMPORTANT ESSAY, *Adrienne Rich (b. 1929) argues that education entails being responsible for oneself—not just for women, but for all students. Her emphasis is on clear thinking, active discussion, and the intellectual and imaginative capacity to be persuaded that new ideas might be true.*

Rich, a well-known feminist, has written numerous essays and many volumes of poetry, including The Necessities of Life *(1966),* Leaflets *(1969),* The Will to Change *(1971), and* An Atlas of the Difficult World *(1991). "Claiming an Education," a talk given at the Douglass College convocation in 1977, was first printed in the magazine* The Common Woman *in 1977.*

For this convocation, I planned to separate my remarks into two parts: some thoughts about you, the woman students here, and some thoughts about us who teach in a women's college. But ultimately, those two parts are indivisible. If university education means anything beyond the processing of human beings into expected roles, through credit hours, tests, and grades (and I believe that in a women's college especially it *might* mean much more), it implies an ethical and intellectual contract between teacher and student. This contract must remain intuitive, dynamic, unwritten; but we must turn to it again and again if learning is to be reclaimed from the depersonalizing and cheapening pressures of the present-day academic scene.

The first thing I want to say to you who are students, is that you cannot afford to think of being here to *receive* an education; you will do much better to think of yourselves as being here to *claim* one. One of the dictionary definitions of the verb "to claim" is: *to take as the rightful owner; to assert in the face of possible contradiction.* "To receive" is *to come into possession of; to act as receptacle or container for; to accept as authoritative or true.* The difference is that between acting and being acted-upon, and for women it can literally mean the difference between life and death.

One of the devastating weaknesses of university learning, of the store of knowledge and opinion that has been handed down through academic training, has been its almost total erasure of women's experience and thought from the curriculum, and its exclusion of women as members of the academic community. Today, with increasing numbers of women students in nearly every branch of higher learning, we still see very few women in the upper levels of faculty and administration in most institutions. Douglass College itself is a women's college in a university administered overwhelmingly by men, who in turn are answerable to the state legislature, again composed predominantly of men. But the most significant fact for you is that what you learn here, the very texts you read, the lectures you hear, the way your studies are divided into categories and fragmented one from the other—all this reflects, to a very large degree, neither objective reality, nor an accurate picture of the past, nor a group of rigorously tested observations about human behavior. What you can learn here (and I mean not only at Douglass but any college in any university) is how *men* have perceived and organized their experience, their history, their ideas of social relationships, good and evil, sickness and health, etc. When you read or hear about "great issues," "major texts," "the mainstream of Western thought," you are hearing about what men, above all white men, in their male subjectivity, have decided is important.

Black and other minority peoples have for some time recognized that their racial and ethnic experience was not accounted for in the studies broadly labeled human; and that even the sciences can be racist. For many reasons, it has been more difficult for women to comprehend our exclusion, and to realize that even the sciences can be sexist. For one thing, it is only within the last hundred years that higher education has grudgingly been opened up to women at all, even to white, middle-class women. And many of us have found ourselves poring eagerly over books with titles like: *The Descent of Man; Man and His Symbols; Irrational Man; The Phenomenon of Man; The Future of Man; Man and the Machine; From Man to Man; May Man Prevail?; Man, Science, and Society;* or *One-Dimensional Man*—books pretending to describe a "human" reality that does not include over one-half the human species.

Less than a decade ago, with the rebirth of a feminist movement in this country, women students and teachers in a number of universities began to demand and set up women's studies courses—to *claim* a woman-directed education. And, despite the inevitable accusations of "unscholarly," "group therapy," "faddism," etc., despite backlash and budget cuts, women's studies are still growing, offering to more and more women a new intellectual grasp on their lives, new understanding of our history, a fresh vision of the human experience, and also a critical basis for evaluating what they hear and read in other courses, and in the society at large.

But my talk is not really about women's studies, much as I believe in their scholarly, scientific, and human necessity. While I think that any Douglass student has everything to gain by investigating and enrolling in women's studies courses, I want to suggest that there is a more essential experience that you owe yourselves, one which courses in women's studies can greatly enrich, but which finally depends on you, in all your interactions with yourself and your world. This is the experience of *taking responsibility toward yourselves.* Our upbringing as women has so often told us that this should come second to our relationships and responsibilities to other people. We have been offered ethical models of the self-denying wife and mother; intellectual models of the brilliant but slapdash dilettante who never commits herself to anything

5

the whole way, or the intelligent woman who denies her intelligence in order to seem more "feminine," or who sits in passive silence even when she disagrees inwardly with everything that is being said around her.

Responsibility to yourself means refusing to let others do your thinking, talking, and naming for you; it means learning to respect and use your own brains and instincts; hence, grappling with hard work. It means that you do not treat your body as a commodity with which to purchase superficial intimacy or economic security; for our bodies and minds are inseparable in this life, and when we allow our bodies to be treated as objects, our minds are in mortal danger. It means insisting that those to whom you give your friendship and love are able to respect your mind. It means being able to say, with Charlotte Brontë's Jane Eyre: "I have an inward treasure born with me, which can keep me alive if all the extraneous delights should be withheld or offered only at a price I cannot afford to give."

Responsibility to yourself means that you don't fall for shallow and easy solutions—predigested books and ideas, weekend encounters guaranteed to change your life, taking "gut" courses instead of ones you know will challenge you, bluffing at school and life instead of doing solid work, marrying early as an escape from real decisions, getting pregnant as an evasion of already existing problems. It means that you refuse to sell your talents and aspirations short, simply to avoid conflict and confrontation. And this, in turn, means resisting the forces in society which say that women should be nice, play safe, have low professional expectations, drown in love and forget about work, live through others, and stay in the places assigned to us. It means that we insist on a life of meaningful work, insist that work be as meaningful as love and friendship in our lives. It means, therefore, the courage to be "different"; not to be continuously available to others when we need time for ourselves and our work; to be able to demand of others—parents, friends, roommates, teachers, lovers, husbands, children—that they respect our sense of purpose and our integrity as persons. Women everywhere are finding the courage to do this, more and more, and we are finding that courage both in our study of women in the past who possessed it, and in each other as we look to other women for comradeship, community, and challenge. The difference between a life lived actively, and a life of passive drifting and dispersal of energies, is an immense difference. Once we begin to feel committed to our lives, responsible to ourselves, we can never again be satisfied with the old, passive way.

Now comes the second part of the contract. I believe that in a women's college you have the right to expect your faculty to take you seriously. The education of women has been a matter of debate for centuries, and old, negative attitudes about women's role, women's ability to think and take leadership, are still rife both in and outside the university. Many male professors (and I don't mean only at Douglass) still feel that teaching in a women's college is a second-rate career. Many tend to eroticize their women students—to treat them as sexual objects—instead of demanding the best of their minds. (At Yale a legal suit

[*Alexander v. Yale*] has been brought against the university by a group of women students demanding a stated policy against sexual advances toward female students by male professors.) Many teachers, both men and women, trained in the male-centered tradition, are still handing the ideas and texts of that tradition on to students without teaching them to criticize its antiwoman attitudes, its omission of women as part of the species. Too often, all of us fail to teach the most important thing, which is that clear thinking, active discussion, and excellent writing are all necessary for intellectual freedom, and that these require *hard work.* Sometimes, perhaps in discouragement with a culture which is both anti-intellectual and antiwoman, we may resign ourselves to low expectations for our students before we have given them half a chance to become more thoughtful, expressive human beings. We need to take to heart the words of Elizabeth Barrett Browning, a poet, a thinking woman, and a feminist, who wrote in 1845 of her impatience with studies which cultivate a "passive recipiency" in the mind, and asserted that "women want to be made to *think actively*: their apprehension is quicker than that of men, but their defect lies for the most part in the logical faculty and in the higher mental activities." Note that she implies a defect which can be remedied by intellectual training, *not* an inborn lack of ability.

I have said that the contract on the student's part involves that you de- 10 mand to be taken seriously so that you can also go on taking yourself seriously. This means seeking out criticism, recognizing that the most affirming thing anyone can do for you is demand that you push yourself further, show you the range of what you *can* do. It means rejecting attitudes of "take-it-easy," "why-be-so-serious," "why-worry-you'll-probably-get-married-anyway." It means assuming your share of responsibility for what happens in the classroom, because that affects the quality of your daily life here. It means that the student sees herself engaged *with* her teachers in an active, ongoing struggle for a real education. But for her to do this, her teachers must be committed to the belief that women's minds and experience are intrinsically valuable and indispensable to any civilization worthy the name; that there is no more exhilarating and intellectually fertile place in the academic world today than a women's college — *if* both students and teachers in large enough numbers are trying to fulfill this contract. The contract is really a pledge of mutual seriousness about women, about language, ideas, methods, and values. It is our shared commitment toward a world in which the inborn potentialities of so many women's minds will no longer be wasted, raveled-away, paralyzed, or denied.

WHAT DOES SHE SAY?

1. This essay is a famous statement of feminist ideas. Quickly and without censoring, make a list of the first five things that come to mind when you hear the word *feminism*. How do you think your assumptions will influence your reading of "Claiming an Education"? What will you be looking for? What do you expect to find?

2. As you read the essay, mark three passages that don't fit your expectations, that in some way are counter to what you think of when you hear the word *feminism*. Come to class prepared to read one of these aloud.

3. Rich talks about the "ethical and intellectual contract" that exists between teacher and student. As you read, mark this and any other passage that talks explicitly about ethics and the connection between ethics and intellectual life. Why is this essay included in a book about ethics?

WHAT DO YOU THINK?

4. Rich argues that the use of the word *man* as a synonym for *all people*, as in *mankind* or *humanity*, implies a bias against women and ultimately harms their status. Explain why you agree or disagree. Does the use of a single word make that much difference? Does language matter? If you are a man, how would you react if the word *woman* was used as a synonym for *all people*?

5. Explain what Rich means by the "ethical and intellectual contract" that exists between teacher and student. In groups, develop a list of three further elements of such a contract. What do students agree to do in a class? What do teachers agree to do? What is the larger, ethical goal of these agreements? What is the connection between ethical and intellectual concerns, for Rich and for you?

6. Rich's essay is the text of a speech that she delivered to an audience of students at an all-female college. Do you think that the speech applies only to women? Would the essay make sense if every reference to women were changed to include men and women both? Would the argument still hold? Would the argument hold if every reference to women were changed to refer to men only?

7. Rich implicitly criticizes what she calls the "ethical model" of the "self-denying wife and mother." Write an essay responding to this criticism, based on your experience and reading as a college student. You can write this essay as a portrait of a particular woman you know—your mother or grandmother perhaps—or you can focus on a famous figure in our culture. As you reflect, consider whether "self-denial" is necessarily a bad thing. Shouldn't men be "self-denying," too? Why or why not? How does the issue of "self-denial" look in the twenty-first century, after decades of women working and assuming many of the roles once reserved for men?

WHAT WOULD THEY SAY?

8. Imagine that Adrienne Rich and two other authors in this chapter are teachers at your college or university. Write an essay considering whether you would take a course from any, or all, of these people based on the essays you've read. Why would, or wouldn't, you choose these people as teachers? Have you taken courses from someone like Rich? Rodriguez? Palmer? What was it like? What were the challenges and rewards?

9. While Rich celebrates the transformative power of education, Richard Rodriguez, in "The Achievement of Desire" (p. 597), seems to lament it, at least a little. Get these two into conversation. Yes, education changes us. But what are the dangers as well as the benefits of such transformation? Would Rich see any negatives? What might be lost?

10. What would David Denby, author of "Passion at Yale" (p. 593), say about Rich's essay, and what would Rich say about his? Do they agree or disagree? Explain.

HELEN PREJEAN

Executions Are Too Costly—Morally

*H*ELEN *P*REJEAN *(b. 1939) is a Catholic nun made famous by the movie* Dead Man Walking. *Her discourse about capital punishment explicitly reflects on how we make arguments and on what basis people can be persuaded. Prejean has been involved in prison ministry since 1981, and is active in the campaign to abolish the death penalty. Her first book,* Dead Man Walking: An Eyewitness Account of the Death Penalty in the United States *(1993), was on the national best-seller list for thirty-one weeks. "Executions Are Too Costly—Morally" is an excerpt from that work.*

I think of the running debate I engage in with "church" people about the death penalty. "Proof texts" from the Bible usually punctuate these discussions without regard for the cultural context or literary genre of the passages invoked. (Will D. Campbell, a Southern Baptist minister and writer, calls this use of scriptural quotations "biblical quarterbacking.")

It is abundantly clear that the Bible depicts murder as a crime for which death is considered the appropriate punishment, and one is hard-pressed to find a biblical "proof text" in either the Hebrew Testament or the New Testament which unequivocally refutes this. Even Jesus' admonition "Let him without sin cast the first stone," when he was asked the appropriate punishment for an adulteress (John 8:7)—the Mosaic law prescribed death—should be read in its proper context. This passage is an "entrapment" story, which sought to show Jesus' wisdom in besting his adversaries. It is not an ethical pronouncement about capital punishment.

Similarly, the "eye for eye" passage from Exodus, which pro–death penalty advocates are fond of quoting, is rarely cited in its original context, in which it is clearly meant to limit revenge.

The passage, including verse 22, which sets the context reads:

> If, when men come to blows, they hurt a woman who is pregnant and she suffers a miscarriage, though she does not die of it, the man responsible must pay the compensation demanded of him by the woman's master; he shall hand it over after arbitration. But should she die, you shall give life for life, eye for eye, tooth for tooth, hand for hand, foot for foot, burn for burn, wound for wound, stroke for stroke. (Exodus 21:22–25)

In the example given (patently patriarchal: the woman is considered the negotiable property of her male master), it is clear that punishment is to be

5

measured out according to the seriousness of the offense. If the child is lost but not the mother, the punishment is less grave than if both mother and child are lost. *Only* an eye for an eye, *only* a life for a life is the intent of the passage. Restraint was badly needed. It was not uncommon for an offended family or clan to slaughter entire communities in retaliation for an offense against one of their members.

Even granting the call for restraint in this passage, it is nonetheless clear—here and in numerous other instances throughout the Hebrew Bible—that the punishment for murder was death.

But we must remember that such prescriptions of the Mosaic law were promulgated in a seminomadic culture in which the preservation of a fragile society—without benefit of prisons and other institutions—demanded quick, effective, harsh punishment of offenders. And we should note the numerous other crimes for which the Bible prescribes death as punishment:

- contempt of parents (Exodus 21:15, 17; Leviticus 24:17);
- trespass upon sacred ground (Exodus 19:12–13; Numbers 1:51; 18:7);
- sorcery (Exodus 22:18; Leviticus 20:27);
- bestiality (Exodus 22:19; Leviticus 20:15–16);
- sacrifice to foreign gods (Exodus 22:20; Deuteronomy 13:1–9);
- profaning the Sabbath (Exodus 31:14);
- adultery (Leviticus 20:10; Deuteronomy 22:22–24);
- incest (Leviticus 20:11–13);
- homosexuality (Leviticus 20:13);
- and prostitution (Leviticus 21:19; Deuteronomy 22:13–21).

And this is by no means a complete list.

But no person with common sense would dream of appropriating such a moral code today, and it is curious that those who so readily invoke the "eye for an eye, life for life" passage are quick to shun other biblical prescriptions which also call for death, arguing that modern societies have evolved over the three thousand or so years since biblical times and no longer consider such exaggerated and archaic punishments appropriate.

Such nuances are lost, of course, in "biblical quarterbacking," and more 10 and more I find myself steering away from such futile discussions. Instead, I try to articulate what I personally believe about Jesus and the ethical thrust he gave to humankind: an impetus toward compassion, a preference for disarming enemies without humiliating and destroying them, and a solidarity with poor and suffering people.

So, what happened to the impetus of love and compassion Jesus set blazing into history?

The first Christians adhered closely to the way of life Jesus had taught. They died in amphitheaters rather than offer homage to worldly emperors. They refused to fight in emperors' wars. But then a tragic diversion happened, which Elaine Pagels has deftly explored in her book *Adam, Eve, and the Serpent*: in 313 C.E. (Common Era) the Emperor Constantine entered the Christian church.

Pagels says, "Christian bishops, once targets for arrest, torture, and execution, now received tax exemptions, gifts from the imperial treasury, prestige, and even influence at court; the churches gained new wealth, power, and prominence."

Unfortunately, the exercise of power practiced by Christians in alliance with the Roman Empire—with its unabashed allegiance to the sword—soon bore no resemblance to the purely moral persuasion that Jesus had taught.

In the fifth century, Pagels points out, Augustine provided the theologi- 15 cal rationale the church needed to justify the use of violence by church and state governments. Augustine persuaded church authorities that "original sin" so damaged every person's ability to make moral choices that external control by church and state authorities over people's lives was necessary and justified. The "wicked" might be "coerced by the sword" to "protect the innocent," Augustine taught. And thus was legitimated for Christians the authority of secular government to "control" its subjects by coercive and violent means— even punishment by death.

In the latter part of the twentieth century, however, two flares of hope— Mohandas K. Gandhi and Martin Luther King—have demonstrated that Jesus' counsel to practice compassion and tolerance even toward one's enemies can effect social change. Susan Jacoby, analyzing the moral power that Gandhi and King unleashed in their campaigns for social justice, finds a unique form of aggression:

"'If everyone took an eye for an eye,' Gandhi said, 'the whole world would be blind.' But Gandhi did not want to take anyone's eye; he wanted to force the British out of India....'"

> Nonviolence and nonaggression are generally regarded as interchangeable concepts—King and Gandhi frequently used them that way— but nonviolence, as employed by Gandhi in India and by King in the American South, might reasonably be viewed as a highly disciplined form of aggression. If one defines aggression in the primary dictionary sense of "attack," nonviolent resistance proved to be the most powerful attack imaginable on the powers King and Gandhi were trying to overturn. The writings of both men are filled with references to love as a powerful force against oppression, and while the two leaders were not using the term *force* in the military sense, they certainly regarded nonviolence as a tactical weapon as well as an expression of high moral principle. The root meaning of Gandhi's concept of *satyagraha*...is "holding on to truth."...Gandhi also called *satyagraha* the "love force" or "soul force" and explained that he had discovered "in the earliest stages that pursuit of truth did not permit violence being inflicted on one's opponent, but that he must be weaned from error by patience and sympathy.... And patience means self-suffering." So the doctrine

came to mean vindication of truth, not by the infliction of suffering on the opponent, but on one's self.

King was even more explicit on this point: the purpose of civil disobedience, he explained many times, was to force the defenders of segregation to commit brutal acts in public and thus arouse the conscience of the world on behalf of those wronged by racism. King and Gandhi did not succeed because they changed the hearts and minds of southern sheriffs and British colonial administrators (although they did, in fact, change some minds) but because they *made the price of maintaining control too high for their opponents* [emphasis mine].

That, I believe, is what it's going to take to abolish the death penalty in this country: we must persuade the American people that government killings are too costly for us, not only financially, but — more important — morally.

The death penalty *costs* too much. Allowing our government to kill citizens compromises the deepest moral values upon which this country was conceived: the inviolable dignity of human persons.

I have no doubt that we will one day abolish the death penalty in America. It will come sooner if people like me who know the truth about executions do our work well and educate the public. It will come slowly if we do not. Because, finally, I know that it is not a question of malice or ill will or meanness of spirit that prompts our citizens to support executions. It is, quite simply, that people don't know the truth of what is going on. That is not by accident. The secrecy surrounding executions makes it possible for executions to continue. I am convinced that if executions were made public, the torture and violence would be unmasked, and we would be shamed into abolishing executions. We would be embarrassed at the brutalization of the crowds that would gather to watch a man or woman be killed. And we would be humiliated to know that visitors from other countries — Japan, Russia, Latin America, Europe — were watching us kill our own citizens — we, who take pride in being the flagship of democracy in the world.

WHAT DOES SHE SAY?

1. As you read, focus not on the content of Prejean's argument against capital punishment but on the *way* she makes that argument — what she sees as the best grounds for supporting her claim. Explain. What kind of evidence *doesn't* work on this question, according to Prejean, and why? What kind of evidence and reasoning *does* work, and why?

2. The essay makes its key point near the end. Mark this passage. What has come before this passage? What comes afterward?

3. Reread the quotation from Gandhi that Prejean uses near the end of the essay and write a three-to-four-sentence summary. What's the function of this quotation in the essay? How does Prejean use this quotation to make her argument?

WHAT DO YOU THINK?

4. Explain Prejean's reasons for opposing capital punishment. Don't try to agree or disagree; instead, try to explain clearly by quoting and interpreting key passages.

5. Explain what Prejean means by "biblical quarterbacking."

6. Are you for or against capital punishment? Explain your reasons and use Prejean's essay in any way you choose in order to help readers understand your points.

7. Why does Prejean think that discussions based on the Bible are "futile"? Do you agree or disagree?

8. How does the fact that Helen Prejean is a Catholic nun—a Sister of St. Joseph—influence your response to this essay? Does it make you more or less willing to trust her argument, and why? Prejean's book *Dead Man Walking* was made into a successful movie starring Susan Sarandon and Sean Penn. If you have seen the movie, how does it influence your reading of her essay? Why?

WHAT WOULD THEY SAY?

9. Read Ruth Benedict's "The Case for Moral Relativism" (p. 619). How would Helen Prejean respond to Benedict's argument that morality is relative, varying from culture to culture? Explain how or why Prejean would agree or disagree. End by explaining your own responses to these two essays.

10. Read Annie Dillard's "Singing with the Fundamentalists" (p. 583) in this chapter. How would Prejean respond to Dillard's story? What would she make of Dillard's willingness to leave her office and enter the world of the students singing around the fountain in the university's square?

11. Read Garrett Hardin's "Lifeboat Ethics: The Case against Helping the Poor" (p. 130). How would Prejean respond to Hardin's argument that some people need to be sacrificed for the greater good?

RUTH BENEDICT
The Case for Moral Relativism

*I*N THIS ESSAY, *anthropologist Ruth Benedict (1887–1948) argues that there is no objective moral standard on which to make judgments. What we think "abnormal" is in fact normal in many other cultures. How, then, do we change our minds? Through the close examination of actual facts, culture to culture, the author suggests.*

Benedict taught at Columbia University and is best known for her book Patterns of Culture *(1934). This piece is excerpted from "Anthropology and the Abnormal," which was first published in the* Journal of General Psychology *in 1934.*

Modern social anthropology has become more and more a study of the varieties and common elements of cultural environment and the consequences of these in human behavior. For such a study of diverse social orders primitive peoples fortunately provide a laboratory not yet entirely vitiated by the spread of a standardized worldwide civilization. Dyaks and Hopis, Fijians and Yakuts are significant for psychological and sociological study because only among these simpler peoples has there been sufficient isolation to give opportunity for the development of localized social forms. In the higher cultures the standardization of custom and belief over a couple of continents has given a false sense of the inevitability of the particular forms that have gained currency, and we need to turn to a wider survey in order to check the conclusions we hastily base upon this near-universality of familiar customs. Most of the simpler cultures did not gain the wide currency of the one which, out of our experience, we identify with human nature, but this was for various historical reasons, and certainly not for any that gives us as its carriers a monopoly of social good or of social sanity. Modern civilization, from this point of view, becomes not a necessary pinnacle of human achievement but one entry in a long series of possible adjustments.

These adjustments, whether they are in mannerisms like the ways of showing anger, or joy, or grief in any society, or in major human drives like those of sex, prove to be far more variable than experience in any one culture would suggest. In certain fields, such as that of religion or of formal marriage arrangements, these wide limits of variability are well known and can be fairly described. In others it is not yet possible to give a generalized account, but that does not absolve us of the task of indicating the significance of the work that has been done and of the problems that have arisen.

One of these problems relates to the customary modern normal-abnormal categories and our conclusions regarding them. In how far are such categories culturally determined, or in how far can we with assurance regard them as absolute?

In how far can we regard inability to function socially as diagnostic of abnormality, or in how far is it necessary to regard this as a function of the culture?

As a matter of fact, one of the most striking facts that emerge from a study of widely varying cultures is the ease with which our abnormals function in other cultures. It does not matter what kind of "abnormality" we choose for illustration, those which indicate extreme instability, or those which are more in the nature of character traits like sadism or delusions of grandeur or of persecution, there are well-described cultures in which these abnormals function at ease and with honor, and apparently without danger or difficulty to the society....

The most notorious of these is trance and catalepsy. Even a very mild mystic is aberrant in our culture. But most peoples have regarded even extreme psychic manifestations not only as normal and desirable, but even as characteristic of highly valued and gifted individuals. This was true even in our own cultural background in that period when Catholicism made the ecstatic experience the mark of sainthood. It is hard for us, born and brought up in a culture that makes no use of the experience, to realize how important a role it may play and how many individuals are capable of it, once it has been given an honorable place in any society....

Cataleptic and trance phenomena are, of course, only one illustration of the fact that those whom we regard as abnormals may function adequately in other cultures. Many of our culturally discarded traits are selected for elaboration in different societies. Homosexuality is an excellent example, for in this case our attention is not constantly diverted, as in the consideration of trance, to the interruption of routine activity which it implies. Homosexuality poses the problem very simply. A tendency toward this trait in our culture exposes an individual to all the conflicts to which all aberrants are always exposed, and we tend to identify the consequences of this conflict with homosexuality. But these consequences are obviously local and cultural. Homosexuals in many societies are not incompetent, but they may be such if the culture asks adjustments of them that would strain any man's vitality. Wherever homosexuality has been given an honorable place in any society, those to whom it is congenial have filled adequately the honorable roles society assigns to them. Plato's *Republic* is, of course, the most convincing statement of such a reading of homosexuality. It is presented as one of the major means to the good life, and it was generally so regarded in Greece at that time.

The cultural attitude toward homosexuals has not always been on such a high ethical plane, but it has been very varied. Among many American Indian tribes there exists the institution of the berdache, as the French called them. These men-women were men who at puberty or thereafter took the dress and the occupations of women. Sometimes they married other men and lived with them. Sometimes they were men with no inversion, persons of weak sexual endowment who chose this role to avoid the jeers of the women. The berdaches were never regarded as of first-rate supernatural power, as similar men-women were in Siberia, but rather as leaders in women's occupations, good healers in certain diseases, or, among certain tribes, as the genial organizers of social affairs. In any case, they were socially placed. They were not left exposed to the conflicts that visit the deviant who is excluded from participation in the recognized patterns of his society.

The most spectacular illustrations of the extent to which normality may be culturally defined are those cultures where an abnormality of our culture is the cornerstone of their social structure. It is not possible to do justice to these possibilities in a short discussion. A recent study of an island of northwest Melanesia by Fortune° describes a society built upon traits which we regard as beyond the border of paranoia. In this tribe the exogamic° groups look upon each other as prime manipulators of black magic, so that one marries always into an enemy group which remains for life one's deadly and unappeasable foes. They look upon a good garden crop as a confession of theft, for everyone is engaged in making magic to induce into his garden the productiveness of his neighbors'; therefore no secrecy in the island is so rigidly insisted upon as the secrecy of a man's harvesting of his yams. Their polite phrase at the acceptance of a gift is, "And if you now poison me, how shall I repay you this present?" Their preoccupation with poisoning is constant; no woman ever leaves her cooking pot for a moment untended. Even the great affinal economic exchanges that are characteristic of this Melanesian culture area are quite altered in Dobu since they are incompatible with this fear and distrust that pervades the culture. They go farther and people the whole world outside their own quarters with such malignant spirits that all-night feasts and ceremonials simply do not occur here. They have even rigorous religiously enforced customs that forbid the sharing of seed even in one family group. Anyone else's food is deadly poison to you, so that communality of stores is out of the question. For some months before harvest the whole society is on the verge of starvation, but if one falls to the temptation and eats up one's seed yams, one is an outcast and a beachcomber for life. There is no coming back. It involves, as a matter of course, divorce and the breaking of all social ties.

Now in this society where no one may work with another and no one may share with another, Fortune describes the individual who was regarded by all his fellows as crazy. He was not one of those who periodically ran amok and, beside himself and frothing at the mouth, fell with a knife upon anyone he could reach. Such behavior they did not regard as putting anyone outside the pale. They did not even put the individuals who were known to be liable to these attacks under any kind of control. They merely fled when they saw the attack coming on and kept out of the way. "He would be all right tomorrow." But there was one man of sunny, kindly disposition who liked work

---

Fortune: Reo Franklin Fortune (1903–1979), social anthropologist and author of *The Sorcerors of Dobu: The Social Anthropology of the Dobu Islanders of the Western Pacific.* [All notes are the Editors'.]

exogamic: The practice of marrying outside one's tribe or family group.

and liked to be helpful. The compulsion was too strong for him to repress it in favor of the opposite tendencies of his culture. Men and women never spoke of him without laughing; he was silly and simple and definitely crazy. Nevertheless, to the ethnologist used to a culture that has, in Christianity, made his type the model of all virtue, he seemed a pleasant fellow....

   ...Among the Kwakiutl° it did not matter whether a relative had died 10 in bed of disease, or by the hand of an enemy, in either case death was an affront to be wiped out by the death of another person. The fact that one had been caused to mourn was proof that one had been put upon. A chief's sister and her daughter had gone up to Victoria, and either because they drank bad whiskey or because their boat capsized they never came back. The chief called together his warriors, "Now I ask you, tribes, who shall wail? Shall I do it or shall another?" The spokesman answered, of course, "Not you, Chief. Let some other of the tribes." Immediately they set up the war pole to announce their intention of wiping out the injury, and gathered a war party. They set out, and found seven men and two children asleep and killed them. "Then they felt good when they arrived at Sebaa in the evening."

   The point which is of interest to us is that in our society those who on that occasion would feel good when they arrived at Sebaa that evening would be the definitely abnormal. There would be some, even in our society, but it is not a recognized and approved mood under the circumstances. On the Northwest Coast those are favored and fortunate to whom that mood under those circumstances is congenial, and those to whom it is repugnant are unlucky. This latter minority can register in their own culture only by doing violence to their congenial responses and acquiring others that are difficult for them. The person, for instance, who, like a Plains Indian whose wife has been taken from him, is too proud to fight, can deal with the Northwest Coast civilization only by ignoring its strongest bents. If he cannot achieve it, he is the deviant in that culture, their instance of abnormality.

   This head-hunting that takes place on the Northwest Coast after a death is no matter of blood revenge or of organized vengeance. There is no effort to tie up the subsequent killing with any responsibility on the part of the victim for the death of the person who is being mourned. A chief whose son has died goes visiting wherever his fancy dictates, and he says to his host, "My prince has died today, and you go with him." Then he kills him. In this, according to their interpretation, he acts nobly because he has not been downed. He has thrust back in return. The whole procedure is meaningless without the fundamental paranoid reading of bereavement. Death, like all the other untoward accidents of existence, confounds man's pride and can only be handled in the category of insults.

   Behavior honored upon the Northwest Coast is one which is recognized as abnormal in our civilization, and yet it is sufficiently close to the attitudes of

Kwakiutl: Native people of coastal British Columbia.

our own culture to be intelligible to us and to have a definite vocabulary with which we may discuss it. The megalomaniac paranoid trend is a definite danger in our society. It is encouraged by some of our major preoccupations, and it confronts us with a choice of two possible attitudes. One is to brand it as abnormal and reprehensible, and is the attitude we have chosen in our civilization. The other is to make it an essential attribute of ideal man, and this is the solution in the culture of the Northwest Coast.

These illustrations, which it has been possible to indicate only in the briefest manner, force upon us the fact that normality is culturally defined. An adult shaped to the drives and standards of either of these cultures, if he were transported into our civilization, would fall into our categories of abnormality. He would be faced with the psychic dilemmas of the socially unavailable. In his own culture, however, he is the pillar of society, the end result of socially inculcated mores, and the problem of personal instability in his case simply does not arise.

No one civilization can possibly utilize in its mores the whole potential 15
range of human behavior. Just as there are great numbers of possible phonetic articulations, and the possibility of language depends on a selection and standardization of a few of these in order that speech communication may be possible at all, so the possibility of organized behavior of every sort, from the fashions of local dress and houses to the dicta of a people's ethics and religion, depends upon a similar selection among the possible behavior traits. In the field of recognized economic obligations or sex taboos this selection is as nonrational and subconscious a process as it is in the field of phonetics. It is a process which goes on in the group for long periods of time and is historically conditioned by innumerable accidents of isolation or of contact of peoples. In any comprehensive study of psychology, the selection that different cultures have made in the course of history within the great circumference of potential behavior is of great significance.

Every society, beginning with some slight inclination in one direction or another, carries its preference farther and farther, integrating itself more and more completely upon its chosen basis, and discarding those types of behavior that are uncongenial. Most of those organizations of personality that seem to us most uncontrovertibly abnormal have been used by different civilizations in the very foundations of their institutional life. Conversely the most valued traits of our normal individuals have been looked on in differently organized cultures as aberrant. Normality, in short, within a very wide range, is culturally defined. It is primarily a term for the socially elaborated segment of human behavior in any culture; and abnormality, a term for the segment that that particular civilization does not use. The very eyes with which we see the problem are conditioned by the long traditional habits of our own society.

It is a point that has been made more often in relation to ethics than in relation to psychiatry. We do not any longer make the mistake of deriving the morality of our locality and decade directly from the inevitable constitution of human nature. We do not elevate it to the dignity of a first principle. We recognize that morality differs in every society, and is a convenient term for socially approved habits. Mankind has always preferred to say, "It is morally good," rather than "It is habitual," and the fact of this preference is matter enough for a critical science of ethics. But historically the two phrases are synonymous.

The concept of the normal is properly a variant of the concept of the good. It is that which society has approved. A normal action is one which falls well within the limits of expected behavior for a particular society. Its variability among different peoples is essentially a function of the variability of the behavior patterns that different societies have created for themselves, and can never be wholly divorced from a consideration of culturally institutionalized types of behavior.

Each culture is a more or less elaborate working-out of the potentialities of the segment it has chosen. Insofar as a civilization is well integrated and consistent within itself, it will tend to carry farther and farther, according to its nature, its initial impulse toward a particular type of action, and from the point of view of any other culture those elaborations will include more and more extreme and aberrant traits.

Each of these traits, in proportion as it reinforces the chosen behavior pat-   20
terns of that culture, is for that culture normal. Those individuals to whom it is congenial either congenitally, or as the result of childhood sets, are accorded prestige in that culture, and are not visited with the social contempt or disapproval which their traits would call down upon them in a society that was differently organized. On the other hand, those individuals whose characteristics are not congenial to the selected type of human behavior in that community are the deviants, no matter how valued their personality traits may be in a contrasted civilization.

The Dobuan who is not easily susceptible to fear of treachery, who enjoys work and likes to be helpful, is their neurotic and regarded as silly. On the Northwest Coast the person who finds it difficult to read life in terms of an insult contest will be the person upon whom fall all the difficulties of the culturally unprovided for. The person who does not find it easy to humiliate a neighbor, nor to see humiliation in his own experience, who is genial and loving, may, of course, find some unstandardized way of achieving satisfactions in his society, but not in the major patterned responses that his culture requires of him. If he is born to play an important role in a family with many hereditary privileges, he can succeed only by doing violence to his whole personality. If he does not succeed, he has betrayed his culture; that is, he is abnormal.

I have spoken of individuals as having sets toward certain types of behavior, and of these sets as running sometimes counter to the types of behavior which are institutionalized in the culture to which they belong. From all that we know of contrasting cultures it seems clear that differences of temperament occur in every society. The matter has never been made the subject of investigation, but from the available material it would appear that these temperament types are very likely of universal recurrence. That is, there is an ascertainable range of human behavior that is found wherever a sufficiently large series of individuals is observed. But the proportion in which behavior types stand to one another in different societies is not universal. The vast majority of individuals in any group are shaped to the fashion of that culture. In other words, most individuals are plastic to the molding force of the society into which they are born. In a society that values trance, as in India, they will have supernormal experience. In a society that institutionalizes homosexuality, they will be homosexual. In a society that sets the gathering of possessions as the chief human objective, they will amass property. The deviants, whatever the type of behavior the culture has institutionalized, will remain few in number, and there seems no more difficulty in molding the vast malleable majority to the "normality" of what we consider an aberrant trait, such as delusions of reference, than to the normality of such accepted behavior patterns as acquisitiveness. The small proportion of the number of the deviants in any culture is not a function of the sure instinct with which that society has built itself upon the fundamental sanities, but of the universal fact that, happily, the majority of mankind quite readily take any shape that is presented to them....

WHAT DOES SHE SAY?

1. Modern civilization, Ruth Benedict says, is not "a necessary pinnacle of human achievement but one entry in a long series of possible adjustments." Explain what she means and give an example.

2. Mark at least three examples that Benedict uses to support her claim. Do you find these examples convincing? Why or why not?

3. Summarize in your own words what Benedict says about homosexuality in other cultures.

WHAT DO YOU THINK?

4. "One of the most striking facts that emerge from a study of widely varying cultures is the ease with which our abnormals function in other cultures." Explain what Benedict means by "our abnormals" and how they function in other cultures. Discuss. What do you think of this idea?

5. On what basis could you agree or disagree with Benedict's conclusions? Would you have to have traveled to all the different places she's been to and studied all the cultures she's studied? What is her authority, and what kind of authority would you need to disagree? How would you gain this authority?

6. Take any issue that you feel strongly about, either for or against. Say you feel very strongly that same-sex marriage is immoral and wrong. How would Benedict respond? Say you feel very strongly that capital punishment is wrong. How would Benedict respond?

7. Write an essay explaining how Benedict might respond to the scenario that opened this chapter. Explain how you would value or disagree with this response as a way to help explain how you would react to this scenario.

WHAT WOULD THEY SAY?

8. How would the Dalai Lama ("The Need For Discernment," p. 205) respond to Ruth Benedict?

9. How would Aldo Leopold ("The Land Ethic," p. 531) respond to Ruth Benedict?

10. Apply Ruth Benedict's argument and assumptions to Ellen Goodman's "Who Lives? Who Dies? Who Decides?" (p. 348).

11. Write an essay arguing that Parker Palmer, in "The Community of Truth" (p. 627), does *not* agree with Ruth Benedict in "The Case for Moral Relativism." Use another selection from any chapter of this book to illustrate Palmer's point, and another essay to illustrate Benedict's. Call this essay, "The Case for and against Moral Relativism."

PARKER J. PALMER
The Community of Truth

*I*N THIS PIECE, *Parker Palmer (b. 1939) urges us to remain open-minded and humble before what he calls the "grace of great things." Thus, a change of mind is always possible. A widely respected writer, teacher, and activist, Palmer works independently on issues in education, community, leadership, spirituality, and social change. His books include* To Know as We Are Known: Education as Spiritual Journey *(1992) and* Let Your Life Speak: Listening for the Voice of Vocation *(1999). "The Community of Truth" is from his landmark work on education,* The Courage to Teach: Exploring the Inner Landscape of a Teacher's Life *(1999).*

TRUTH REVISITED

Truth is not a word much spoken in educational circles these days. It suggests an earlier, more naive era when people were confident they could know the truth. But we are confident we cannot, so we refuse to use the word for fear of embarrassing ourselves.

Of course, the fact that we do not use the word does not mean that we have freed ourselves from the concept, let alone the possibilities to which it points. On the contrary, the less we talk about truth, the more likely that our knowing, teaching, and learning will be dominated by a traditional—and mythical—model of truth, the objectivist model so deeply embedded in our collective unconscious that to ignore it is to give it power.

Because the community of truth is an alternative to this unconscious and mythical objectivism, it will be easier to describe my vision of educational community and how it works if I first raise the objectivist myth to visible form, which I do in Figure 1.

This mythical but dominant model of truth-knowing and truth-telling has four major elements:

1. *Objects* of knowledge that reside "out there" somewhere, pristine in physical or conceptual space, as described by the "facts" in a given field.

2. *Experts,* people trained to know these objects in their pristine form without allowing their own subjectivity to slop over onto the purity of the objects themselves. This training transpires in a far-off place called graduate school, whose purpose is so thoroughly to obliterate one's sense of self that one becomes a secular priest, a safe bearer of the pure objects of knowledge.

3. *Amateurs,* people without training and full of bias, who depend on the experts for objective or pure knowledge of the pristine objects in question.

Figure 1.   *The Objectivist Myth of Knowing.*

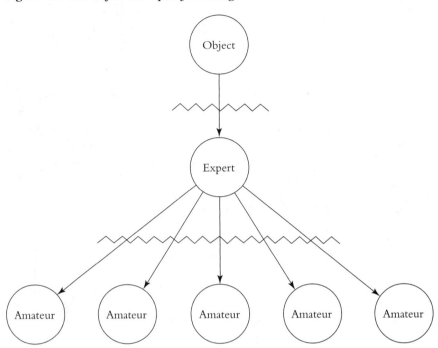

4. *Baffles* at every point of transmission—between objects and experts, be-
    tween experts and amateurs—that allow objective knowledge to flow
    downstream while preventing subjectivity from flowing back up.

The image of baffles came to me on overhearing a marvelous remark: 5
"We don't seem to mind if civilization goes down the drain, as long as the
drain doesn't back up!" Objectivism, obsessed with the purity of knowledge,
wants to avoid the mess of subjectivity at all costs—even if the cost is the "de-
civilizing" kind of knowledge that renders us unfit for the messiness of life.

In the objectivist myth, truth flows from the top down, from experts
who are qualified to know truth (including some who claim that truth is an
illusion) to amateurs who are qualified only to receive truth. In this myth,
truth is a set of propositions about objects; education is a system for delivering
those propositions to students; and an educated person is one who can remember and repeat the experts' propositions. The image is hierarchical, linear, and compulsive-hygienic, as if truth came down an antiseptic conveyer
belt to be deposited as pure product at the end.

There are only two problems with this myth: it falsely portrays how we
know, and it has profoundly deformed the way we educate. I know a thousand
classrooms where the relationships of teacher, students, and subject look exactly

like this image. But I know of no field—from astronomy to literature to political science to theology—where the continuing quest to know truth even vaguely resembles this mythical objectivism.

The community of truth represents knowing quite differently (see Figure 2). In the community of truth, as in real life, there are no pristine objects of knowledge and no ultimate authorities. In the community of truth, as in real life, truth does not reside primarily in propositions, and education is more than delivering propositions about objects to passive auditors. In the community of truth, knowing and teaching and learning look less like General Motors and more like a town meeting, less like a bureaucracy and more like bedlam.

The community of truth is, in fact, many communities, far-flung across space and ever-changing through time. I name it with a singular noun because in any given field, the many are made one by the fact that they gather around a common subject and are guided by shared rules of observation and

Figure 2.   *The Community of Truth.*

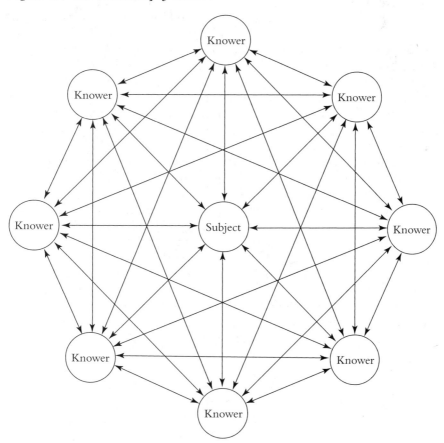

interpretation that require them to approach the subject in the same way. Thus biologists in twentieth-century America and Linnaeus and his colleagues in eighteenth-century Sweden, despite their vast differences in theory and technique, are one, giving this form of community a longevity and reach that make it one of our most powerful social forms.

At the center of this communal circle, there is always a subject—as contrasted with the object at the top of the objectivist ladder. This distinction is crucial to knowing, teaching, and learning: *a subject is available for relationship; an object is not.* When we know the other as a subject, we do not merely hold it at arm's length. We know it in and through relationship, the kind of relationship Barbara McClintock° had with the corn plants that she studied.

This relationship begins when we allow the subject to occupy the center of our attention, exactly as the diagram suggests. This contrasts sharply with objectivism, which puts the expert at the center of our attention: in objectivism, the objects of knowing are so far beyond our reach that the expert is the only party with whom we can connect.

When we make the subject the center of our attention, we give it the respect and authority that we normally give only to human beings. We give it ontological significance, the significance that Barbara McClintock gave to an ear of corn, acknowledging its unique identity and integrity.[1] In the community of truth, the connective core of all our relationships is the significant subject itself—not intimacy, not civility, not accountability, not the experts, but the power of the living subject.

As we try to understand the subject in the community of truth, we enter into complex patterns of communication—sharing observations and interpretations, correcting and complementing each other, torn by conflict in this moment and joined by consensus in the next. The community of truth, far from being linear and static and hierarchical, is circular, interactive, and dynamic.

At its best, the community of truth advances our knowledge through conflict, not competition. Competition is a secretive, zero-sum game played by individuals for private gain; conflict is open and sometimes raucous but always communal, a public encounter in which it is possible for everyone to win by learning and growing. Competition is the antithesis of community, an acid that can dissolve the fabric of relationships. Conflict is the dynamic by which we test ideas in the open, in a communal effort to stretch each other and make better sense of the world.

This communal dynamic is governed by rules of observation and interpretation that help define us as a community by bringing focus and discipline to our discourse. To be in the community of truth, we must abide by its norms and procedures, which differ from one field to another, from art history to chemistry to philosophy. These standards are strong but not chiseled in stone:

Barbara McClintock (1902–1992): Geneticist; winner of the 1983 Nobel Prize in medicine. [EDS.]

they evolve, even as our understanding of a subject evolves. We can challenge and change the norms, but we must be able to justify any deviation from them in a public and compelling way.

Implicit in this exploration of how we know is an image of truth that can now be made explicit: *truth is an eternal conversation about things that matter, conducted with passion and discipline.*

Unlike the objectivist, I do not understand truth to be lodged in the conclusions we reach about objects of knowledge. How could it be, since the conclusions keep changing? I understand truth as the passionate and disciplined process of inquiry and dialogue itself, as the dynamic conversation of a community that keeps testing old conclusions and coming into new ones.

We need to know the current conclusions in order to get in on the conversation. But it is not our knowledge of conclusions that keeps us in the truth. It is our commitment to the conversation itself, our willingness to put forward our observations and interpretations for testing by the community and to return the favor to others. To be in the truth, we must know how to observe and reflect and speak and listen, with passion and with discipline, in the circle gathered around a given subject.

If truth is an eternal conversation whose conclusions and norms keep changing, what happens to the idea of objective knowledge? I do not think that my image of truth alters anything about the nature of objectivity—except the objectivist myth.

As far as I can tell, the only "objective" knowledge we possess is the 20 knowledge that comes from a community of people looking at a subject and debating their observations within a consensual framework of procedural rules. I know of no field, from science to religion, where what we regard as objective knowledge did not emerge from long and complex communal discourse that continues to this day, no field where the facts of the matter were delivered fully formed from on high.

The firmest foundation of all our knowledge is the community of truth itself. This community can never offer us ultimate certainty—not because its process is flawed but because certainty is beyond the grasp of finite hearts and minds. Yet this community can do much to rescue us from ignorance, bias, and self-deception if we are willing to submit our assumptions, our observations, our theories—indeed, ourselves—to its scrutiny.

In rejecting the objectivist model, I have not embraced a relativism that reduces truth to whatever the community decides, for the community of truth includes a transcendent dimension of truth-knowing and truth-telling that takes us beyond relativism and absolutism alike. The clearest and most compelling naming of that dimension is found in a couplet by Robert Frost: "We dance round in a ring and suppose, / But the Secret sits in the middle and knows."[2]

Frost honors the transcendent secret of the subject at the center of the community of truth, a secret that is equally obscured by absolutism, which claims that we can know the full reality of things, and by relativism, which claims that things have no reality save what we know. The subject knows itself better than we can ever know it, and it forever evades our grasp by keeping its own secrets.

If this were not the case, the process of knowing would have long ago come to a halt. Why did we not settle for the pre-Socratic view of the nature of the physical world or the medieval view or the view of early modern science? Why are we pressing, even now, on the view we hold today? Because at the center of our attention is a subject that continually calls us deeper into its secret, a subject that refuses to be reduced to our conclusions about it.

The idea of a subject that calls to us is more than metaphor. In the community of truth, the knower is not the only active agent—the subject itself participates in the dialectic of knowing. It is as Mary Oliver says: "The world offers itself to your imagination, / calls to you like the wild geese..., /...announcing your place / in the family of things."[3]

We say that knowing begins in our intrigue about some subject, but that intrigue is the result of the subject's action upon us: geologists are people who hear rocks speak, historians are people who hear the voices of the long dead, writers are people who hear the music of words. The things of the world call to us, and we are drawn to them—each of us to different things, as each is drawn to different friends.

Once we have heard that call and responded, the subject calls us out of ourselves and into its own selfhood. At the deepest reaches, knowing requires us to imagine the inner standpoint of the subject—of that historical moment, of that literary character, of that rock, or of that ear of corn. As one research scientist has said, "If you want to really understand about a tumor, you've got to *be* a tumor."[4]

We cannot know the subject well if we stand only in our own shoes. We must believe in the subject's inner life and enter with empathy into it, an empathy unavailable to us when we neither believe in nor cultivate an inner life of our own. When we deny or disparage the knower's inner life, as is the objectivist habit, we have no capacity to intuit, let alone inhabit, the inwardness of the known.

The sort of science done by Barbara McClintock requires one to fathom the mystery of self in order to fathom the mystery of the world, to become—as a colleague said of McClintock—"someone who understands where the mysteries lie" rather "than someone who mystifies."[5]

As we gather around the subject in the community of truth, it is not only we who correct each other's attempts at knowing, rejecting blurry observations and false interpretations. The subject itself corrects us, resisting our false framings with the strength of its own identity, refusing to be reduced to our self-certain ways of naming its otherness.

Eventually, as our insight deepens, the subject yields to a certain naming, and we conclude that we know it. But the transcendent subject always stands ready to take us by surprise, calling us into new observations, interpretations, and namings and into the mystery that can never be fully named.

Openness to transcendence is what distinguishes the community of truth from both absolutism and relativism. In this community, the process of truth-knowing and truth-telling is neither dictatorial nor anarchic. Instead, it is a complex and eternal dance of intimacy and distance, of speaking and listening, of knowing and not knowing, that makes collaborators and coconspirators of the knowers and the known.

THE GRACE OF GREAT THINGS

The community of truth is an image that can carry the educational mission because it embraces an essential fact: the reality we belong to, the reality we long to know, extends far beyond human beings interacting with one another. In the community of truth, we interact with nonhuman forms of being that are as important and powerful as the human and sometimes even more so. This is a community held together not only by our personal powers of thought and feeling but also by the power of "the grace of great things."[6]

That phrase comes from an essay by Rilke. When I read it, I realized that our conventional images of educational community ignore our relationships with the great things that call us together—the things that call us to know, to teach, to learn. I saw how diminished the educational community becomes when it excludes the grace of great things and relies entirely on our own quite limited graces.

By *great things*, I mean the subjects around which the circle of seekers has 35 always gathered—not the disciplines that study these subjects, not the texts that talk about them, not the theories that explain them, but the things themselves.

I mean the genes and ecosystems of biology, the symbols and referents of philosophy and theology, the archetypes of betrayal and forgiveness and loving and loss that are the stuff of literature. I mean the artifacts and lineages of anthropology, the materials of engineering with their limits and potentials, the logic of systems in management, the shapes and colors of music and art, the novelties and patterns of history, the elusive idea of justice under law.

Great things such as these are the vital nexus of community in education. It is in the act of gathering around them and trying to understand them—as the first humans must have gathered around fire—that we become who we are as knowers, teachers, and learners. When we are at our best, it is because the grace of great things has evoked from us the virtues that give educational community its finest form:

- We invite *diversity* into our community not because it is politically correct but because diverse viewpoints are demanded by the manifold mysteries of great things.

- We embrace *ambiguity* not because we are confused or indecisive but because we understand the inadequacy of our concepts to embrace the vastness of great things.

- We welcome *creative conflict* not because we are angry or hostile but because conflict is required to correct our biases and prejudices about the nature of great things.

- We practice *honesty* not only because we owe it to one an other but because to lie about what we have seen would be to betray the truth of great things.

- We experience *humility* not because we have fought and lost but because humility is the only lens through which great things can be seen—and once we have seen them, humility is the only posture possible.

- We become *free* men and women through education not because we have privileged information but because tyranny in any form can be overcome only by invoking the grace of great things.

Of course, the educational community is not always at its best! We can easily cite instances when the community of truth has been driven by the antithesis of virtues such as these. *The Double Helix* is a book that chronicles such a case: the discovery of DNA by James Watson and Francis Crick, a case in which ego and competition, pigheadedness and greed, are shown to lie at the heart of the academic enterprise.[7]

So it intrigues me that the two principals in that story, interviewed on the fortieth anniversary of their discovery, spoke about the way certain virtues have overtaken them since they first encountered the great thing called DNA.

James Watson said, "The molecule is so beautiful. Its glory was reflected on Francis and me. I guess the rest of my life has been spent trying to prove that I was almost equal to being associated with DNA, which has been a hard task."

Then Francis Crick—of whom Watson once said, "I have never seen him in a modest mood"—replied, "We were upstaged by a molecule."[8]

Crick's humility may be uncharacteristic and strained, but that only makes it a more compelling example of the power of the community of truth—a community in which even our own agendas are sometimes upstaged by the grace of great things. When the great things disappear, when they lose their gravitational pull on our lives, we fall out of the communal orbit into the black hole of posturing, narcissism, and arrogance.

How do the great things disappear? They dim, if they do not disappear altogether, when the image of community that forms (or deforms) education has more to do with intimacy, majority rule, or marketing than with knowing, teaching, and learning. But there is a deeper threat to great things: they are killed off by an intellectual arrogance that tries to reduce them to nothing more than the machinations of our minds.

The great things disappear in the face of both absolutism and relativism. With absolutism, we claim to know precisely the nature of great things, so there is no need to continue in dialogue with them—or with each other. The experts possess the facts, and all that remains is for them to transmit those facts to those who do not know. With relativism, we claim that knowledge depends wholly on where one stands, so we cannot know anything with any certainty beyond our personal point of view. Once again, there is no need to continue in dialogue with great things or with each other: one truth for you, another for me, and never mind the difference.

Of course, the great things do not disappear in reality—they only disap- 45 pear from our view. The great things themselves survive all the assaults of human arrogance, for they are the irreducible elements of life itself and of the life of the mind. The question is, will we abandon the arrogance that claims either to know the world perfectly or to invent the world at will? Will we acknowledge the independent reality of great things and their power to work on our lives?

We will experience the power of great things only when we grant them a life of their own—an inwardness, identity, and integrity that make them more than objects, a quality of being and agency that does not rely on us and our thoughts about them.

To understand this more fully, we need only look at what happens when we rob great things of their integrity. In the study of literature, it is now common to teach classic texts through analytical lenses that show how riddled they are with the biases of their authors and their times. From this standpoint, it does not matter that *Moby-Dick* reaches deep into such great things in the human experience as hubris and destiny. It matters only that Melville was a patriarchal bigot.

David Denby has shown the hubris of this posture itself: it gives us, teachers and students alike, feelings of superiority to the text, thereby depriving us of the chance to learn anything from it except how superior we are.[9] It is impossible to be in a learning relationship with a text or a person that one regards as morally bankrupt. When we reduce great things to such dismissive categories, we rob them of their selfhood and deprive them of their voice.

It is not cheap mysticism to claim that all great things have inner lives that will speak to our own—if we let them. Literary texts are merely the clearest example of such voices, voices that reach us with astonishing clarity across huge gaps of space and time. The history of the Third Reich speaks a voice of evil that if I listen carefully to it, will find echoes in my own soul.

A marine biologist can pick up a seashell and, through careful listening, 50 learn much about what happened in the lifetime of its inhabitant and in the evolution of its species. Every geologist knows that even the rocks speak, telling tales across gaps of time far wider than recorded history, stories we would not know if human vocalization were the only speech we could hear.

Annie Dillard titled one of her books *Teaching a Stone to Talk*, but the real issue, as Dillard knows, is teaching ourselves to listen.[10] The inner life of any great thing will be incomprehensible to me until I develop and deepen an inner life of my own. I cannot know in another being what I do not know in myself.

The conclusion seems clear: we cannot know the great things of the universe until we know ourselves to be great things. Absolutism and relativism have ravaged not only the things of the world but our sense of the knowing self as well. We are whiplashed between an arrogant overestimation of ourselves and a servile underestimation of ourselves, but the outcome is always the same: a distortion of the humble yet exalted reality of the human self, a paradoxical pearl of great price.

I once heard this Hasidic tale: "We need a coat with two pockets. In one pocket there is dust, and in the other pocket there is gold. We need a coat with two pockets to remind us who we are."[11] Knowing, teaching, and learning under the grace of great things will come from teachers who own such a coat and who wear it to class every day.

Notes

1. Evelyn Fox Keller, *A Feeling for the Organism: The Life and Work of Barbara McClintock* (New York: Freeman, 1983), 200.

2. Robert Frost, "The Secret Sits," in *The Poetry of Robert Frost,* ed. Edward Connery Lathem (New York: Henry Holt, 1979), 362. Copyright 1942 by Robert Frost, © 1970 by Lesley Frost Ballantine, © 1969 by Henry Holt & Co. Reprinted by permission of Henry Holt and Co., Inc.

3. Mary Oliver, "Wild Geese," in *Dream Work* (New York: Atlantic Monthly Press, 1986), 14.

4. Keller, *A Feeling for the Organism,* 207.

5. James Shapiro, University of Chicago, quoted in "Dr. Barbara McClintock, 90, Gene Research Pioneer Dies," *New York Times,* Sept. 4, 1992, C16.

6. Rainer Maria Rilke, *Rodin and Other Prose Pieces* (London: Quartet Books, 1986), 4.

7. James D. Watson, *The Double Helix* (New York: Atheneum, 1968).

8. Leon Jaroff, "Happy Birthday, Double Helix," *Time,* Mar. 15, 1993, 58–59.

9. David Denby, *Great Books* (New York: Simon & Schuster, 1996).

10. Annie Dillard, *Teaching a Stone to Talk* (New York: HarperCollins, 1982).

11. A rabbi told me this Hasidic tale. I have not found it in print.

WHAT DOES HE SAY?

1. Parker Palmer takes great pains to be clear in this selection, using a number of graphic and rhetorical devices. Make a list of these devices, and mark where they occur in the essay. Do you find Palmer easy or hard to understand? Explain.

2. Explain what Palmer means by the "objectivist myth of knowing" and what he calls "the community of truth." What does he mean by "community" and what does he mean by "truth"? Write a paragraph explaining what's clear or what's confusing to you.

3. What does Palmer mean by the "grace of great things"?

4. Why, according to Palmer, should we always be open to changing our minds? What is it about the nature of reality and of our relationships with others that requires humility and openness?

WHAT DO YOU THINK?

5. Recall some truly significant learning experience that you have had. Use this experience to help explain why or how you find Palmer's theory of knowledge interesting and compelling.

6. In your experience at college, have classes more often reflected the "objectivist myth" of knowledge or the idea of a "community of truth"? Explain, giving specific examples. Which courses have been the most significant to you? What's clearer about Palmer's essay once you have brought this experience to it?

7. "[T]ruth," Palmer says, "is an eternal conversation about things that matter, conducted with passion and discipline." Discuss this idea. Give an example from your own experience, in or out of school.

WHAT WOULD THEY SAY?

8. Based on "Politics and the English Language" (p. 461), how do you think George Orwell would respond to Palmer's idea that truth is multiple and communal? Write an essay discussing this. Start by explaining your understanding of Parker's idea. Then explain what reaction you believe Orwell would have. Quote Orwell in order to make your assertions clearer.

9. Based on "Lifeboat Ethics: The Case against Helping the Poor" (p. 130) and "Cyberspace: If You Don't Love It, Leave It" (p. 141), how would Garrett Hardin and Esther Dyson respond to Palmer's essay?

10. Assume that Parker Palmer and Joan Didion, author of "On Morality" (p. 167), have read each other's essay and agreed to conduct a discussion about it. What would Didion say in response to "The Community of Truth"? What would Palmer say in response to "On Morality"? Would they find areas of agreement? of disagreement? Write an essay explaining how they would react to each other's essay, and end by explaining your own stance.

For Community Learning and Research

1. Write an essay called "Singing with the ____." Fill in the blank with any group that represents the opposite of what you believe, any group that you normally wouldn't join. For example, say that you're someone who strongly supports gay rights. Attend several meetings of a politically conservative group on campus. Say that you're someone who strongly opposes clear-cutting in national forests. Attend several meetings of a logging or pro–forest-management group on campus. In other words, choose a group that is "foreign" or "other," join it for a few days, and take lots of notes. In the end, use this field experience as the basis for an essay that does what Dillard's essay ("Singing with the Fundamentalists," p. 583) does.

2. Adrienne Rich's "Claiming an Education" (p. 608) was written in the 1970s. Many things have changed. Research how things have changed in one or more of these particular areas: the ratio of male and female faculty members at universities, the ratio of male to female students, the status of women's sports programs, the inclusion of works by women authors in literature and other classes, and so on. On the basis of your research, write a feature article for your campus paper arguing that things have gotten better, stayed the same, or gotten worse. Quote "Claiming an Education" at least twice.

3. Find copies of the last three graduation addresses given at your college or university and compare them to any two essays about education in this chapter. Write an essay reflecting on what you've found. Are the values in the two essays reflected in the graduation addresses? Are the graduation addresses at odds with the essays?

4. Look at your college or university Web site for its statement of goals or mission. Does this statement say anything about change or personal transformation? Is there any statement that implies an ethical value for education? If not, rewrite the mission statement, incorporating any of the ideas you've found useful in the readings in this chapter. For a model, use Parker Palmer's list of educational values or attitudes in "The Community of Truth" (p. 627)—humility, open-mindedness, and so on.

5. Interview a leading spokesperson for an important religious, political, or civic organization in your community. Write a profile of this person in the style of Studs Terkel's "C. P. Ellis" (p. 568), letting the person speak for himself or herself. Shape the final profile to emphasize the theme of education, transformation, and change.

6. Choose any subject that you feel very strongly about and write a letter to the editor arguing for it. Argue as strongly and persuasively as you can. Make sure your letter quotes from at least one reading in this chapter.

7. Interview several students who are close to graduating from your college or university. Ask about their most important learning experiences in the last four years, in or out of college. Write up the results in the form of a speech to be delivered to your faculty senate. The purpose of the speech is to praise the faculty and/or argue for major changes in the way courses are taught.

8.

What Should You Do?

WHAT WOULD YOU DO? TAKING A STAND

You've decided to quit your fraternity. Partying is fine, but half the house is drunk half the time. And now it's finals week, and because they haven't kept up with their classes, too many of your fraternity brothers are plagiarizing their final papers, stealing from the Net or from files of term papers that the fraternity keeps. You know at least a dozen guys who are cheating. Enough! You've made some good friends, you've had some good experiences, but it's time to go.

(We're not suggesting that all fraternities are like this, just this one.)

When you confide in an older person you trust—a minister or rabbi, a relative, a family friend—she surprises you. Don't run, she says. Stay. Try to make things better somehow.

What do you say? What do you do?

It's not enough to *think* ethically. Finally, we have to *act* ethically.

Yes, we have to acknowledge the complexity of life. Yes, we have to be open to other points of view. All the readings we've included up to this point, and all our questions about these readings, and all the real-life ethical scenarios that frame these readings—everything we've done in this book has been intended to complicate and deepen your thinking. No, the answer isn't black and white. No, there isn't a single answer. And realizing that is the beginning of humility and so of compassion and wisdom.

But in the end, we have to live life here and now, in practical terms. Ultimately, we have to make choices—specific choices—even when it's not obvious how our decisions make a difference in the larger scheme of things. The challenge is both to act and to believe that our action matters. The challenge is to act even in the face of uncertainty. The challenge is to act even when the problems of the world seem vast and insurmountable, something that the writers in this section urge us to do. Rebecca Solnit asks us to be careful about what we buy ("The Silence of the Lambswool Cardigans," p. 668). Wendell Berry asks us to give up our cars ("Out of Your Car, Off Your Horse," p. 672). Martin Luther King asks us to join a social movement and change the world ("Letter from Birmingham Jail," p. 682).

All the writers in this chapter reflect on the question of ethical action, from small to large, and so challenge you to think about your own next step, your own given life. Now that you've read some of the readings in this book, now that you've written and revised several papers, now that you've spent this term in college—*now* what do you think? *Now* what do you *do*?

Opening the Question

After reading and discussing several of the selections in this chapter, return to the situation above. Write an essay exploring your second and third thoughts, drawing on at least several of the selections. You don't need to have changed your mind, but you do need to demonstrate how the reading has complicated your thinking.

Do the readings inspire you to act when you wouldn't have before? Do they provide specific strategies and models for action? Do any of the readings justify leaving the fraternity and getting on with your life?

U.S. DEPARTMENT OF HOMELAND SECURITY
"Get Ready Now."

*A*VAILABLE IN POST OFFICES *throughout the United States as late as May of 2004 and online as late as fall of 2004, this brochure was published by the Department of Homeland Security in partial response to the September 11, 2001, terrorist attacks.*

"Terrorism forces us to make a choice."

— Secretary Tom Ridge, U.S. Department of Homeland Security

Preparing makes sense.

The likelihood that you and your family will survive a house fire depends as much on having a working smoke detector and an exit strategy, as on a well-trained fire department. The same is true for surviving a terrorist attack. We must have the tools and plans in place to make it on our own, at least for a period of time, no matter where we are when disaster strikes. Just like having a working smoke detector, preparing for the unexpected makes sense. **Get ready now.**

We can be afraid.
Or, we can be ready.

1

Be prepared to improvise and use what you have on hand to make it on your own for at least three days, or longer.

While there are many things that might make you more comfortable, think first about fresh water, food and clean air.

Consider putting together two kits. In one, put everything needed to stay where you are and make it on your own.

The other should be a lightweight, smaller version if you have to get away.

www.ready.gov

Make an Emergency Supply Kit

You'll need a gallon of **water** per person per day. Include in the kits canned and dried **foods** that are easy to store and prepare. If you live in a cold weather climate, include **warm clothes** and a sleeping bag for each member of the family.

Start now by gathering basic **emergency supplies** and setting them aside — a flashlight, a battery-powered radio, extra batteries, a first-aid kit, toilet articles and other special things your family may need.

Many potential terrorist attacks could send tiny microscopic "junk" into the air. Many of these materials can only hurt you if they get into your body, so think about creating a barrier between yourself and any contamination. It's smart to have something for each member of the family that **covers their mouth and nose.**

Plan to use two to three layers of a cotton t-shirt, handkerchief or towel. Or, consider **filter masks,** readily available in hardware stores, which are rated based on how small a particle they filter. It is very important that the mask or other material fit your face snugly so that most of the air you breathe comes through the mask, not around it. Do whatever you can to make the best fit possible for children.

Also, include **duct tape and heavyweight garbage bags or plastic sheeting** that can be used to seal windows and doors if you need to create a barrier between yourself and any potential contamination outside.

2

Plan in advance what you will do in an emergency.

Be prepared to assess the situation. Use common sense and whatever you have on hand to take care of yourself and your loved ones.

Depending on your circumstances and the nature of the attack, the first important decision is whether you stay put or get away.

You should understand and plan for both possibilities.

Make a Family Communications Plan

Develop a Family Communications Plan: Your family may not be together when disaster strikes, so **plan how you will contact one another and review what you will do in different situations.** Consider a plan where each family member calls, or e-mails, the same friend or relative in the event of an emergency. It may be easier to make a long-distance phone call than to call across town, so an out-of-state contact may be in a better position to communicate among separated family members. You may have trouble getting through, or the phone system may be down altogether, but be patient.

Create a Plan to "Shelter-in-Place": There are circumstances when staying put and creating a barrier between yourself and potentially contaminated air outside, a process known as "shelter-in-place," can be a matter of survival. **Choose an interior room or one with as few windows and doors as possible. Consider precutting plastic sheeting to seal windows, doors and air vents.** Each piece should be several inches larger than the space you want to cover so that you can duct tape it flat against the wall. Label each piece with the location of where it fits.

If you see large amounts of debris in the air or if local authorities say the air is badly contaminated, you may want to "shelter-in-place." Quickly bring your family and pets inside, lock doors, and close windows, air vents and fireplace dampers. Immediately turn off air conditioning, forced air heating systems, exhaust fans and clothes dryers. Take your emergency supplies and go into the room you have designated. Seal all windows, doors and vents. Watch TV, listen to radio or check the Internet for instructions.

Create a Plan to Get Away: Plan in advance how you will assemble your family and anticipate where you will go. **Choose several destinations in different directions so you have options in an emergency.** If you have a car, keep a half tank of gas in it at all times. **Become familiar with alternate routes as well as other means of transportation out of your area.** If you do not have a car, plan how you will leave if you have to. **Take your emergency supply kit** and lock the door behind you. If you believe the air may be contaminated, drive with your windows and vents closed and keep the air conditioning and heater turned off. Listen to the radio for instructions.

Plan at School and Work: Think about the places where your family spends time: school, work and other places your family frequents. **Talk to your children's schools and your employer about emergency plans.** Find out how they will communicate with families during an emergency. If you are an employer, be sure you have an emergency preparedness plan. Review and practice it with your employees. A community working together during an emergency also makes sense. **Talk to your neighbors about how you can work together.**

3

Be Informed

Some of the things you can do to prepare for the unexpected, such as assembling a supply kit and developing a family communications plan, are the same for both a natural or man-made emergency. However there are important differences among potential terrorist threats, such as biological, chemical, explosive, nuclear and radiological, that will impact the decisions you make and the actions you take.

Call:
1-800-BE-READY
(1-800-237-3239)
for a free brochure, or

Go to:
www.ready.gov
to learn about potential terrorist threats.

4

Remain Calm

Be prepared to adapt this information to your personal circumstances and make every effort to follow instructions received from authorities on the scene. Above all, stay calm, be patient and think before you act. With these simple preparations, you can be ready for the unexpected. If you have a working smoke detector, you have already understand that preparing makes sense.

Get ready now.

WHAT DOES IT SAY?

1. This pamphlet was available in U.S. post offices across the country as recently as April 2004. As you look it over, determine its purpose and write a short paragraph explaining it.

2. Make a list of the threats or situations for which this pamphlet urges that we prepare.

3. Write out one recommendation you understand fully and a second that seems vague or less clear. Explain why the one is clear while the other is not.

4. As you look over this pamphlet, what does it assume that you can do about terrorism? What does it leave out or not mention?

WHAT DO YOU THINK?

5. How do you react to reading this pamphlet? Does it calm your concerns about terrorist attacks? Write a 750-word response, explaining your analysis of the effectiveness of this publication. Make sure you use at least one quotation from it.

6. This pamphlet quotes Secretary of Homeland Security Tom Ridge as saying, "We can be afraid. Or, we can be ready." What's your reaction to this quotation? Do you agree that those are our choices about terrorism?

7. Consider this pamphlet in terms of *logos, ethos*, and *pathos* as ways to understand the challenge of those who had to write it. Explain how each of these analytical tools helps you understand the pamphlet. Given your analyses, explain what grade you would give this pamphlet as an effort at persuasion.

8. Consider the writing, publication, and distribution of this pamphlet as one example of something the government can do in the face of terrorist threats. Explain briefly why you do, or do not, believe that this pamphlet is an effective strategy, and then add three more strategies you would also recommend. Make sure that your resulting essay quotes the pamphlet at least once; make sure it also includes quotations from two additional sources that discuss terrorism or terrorist threats and that you find useful in helping to explain your assertions.

WHAT WOULD THEY SAY?

9. Consider this pamphlet together with "Why I Volunteer" (p. 697). In what ways do the basic assumptions of these two works overlap? How do they differ? Write an essay discussing this. End by explaining what's clearer to you as a result of your comparison.

10. Consider this pamphlet together with Tracy Kidder's "The Good Doctor" (p. 645). See full directions following that essay.

TRACY KIDDER
The Good Doctor

IN THIS PROFILE of an American doctor working in Haiti, Tracy Kidder (b. 1945) shows us a hero, someone selflessly devoting himself to helping others. In answering the chapter question, Dr. Farmer shows that one person can do a lot.

The author of several books, including The Soul of a New Machine *(1982),* Among Schoolchildren *(1989), and* Old Friends *(1993), Kidder has been awarded both a Pulitzer Prize and a National Book Award. He is a frequent contributor to the* New Yorker, *where this piece was first published in 2000. Kidder has since completed an entire book about Dr. Farmer,* Mountains beyond Mountains *(2003).*

On maps of Haiti, National Highway 3 looks like a major thoroughfare. And, indeed, it is the *gwo wout la*, the biggest road across the Central Plateau, a dirt track where trucks of various sizes, overfilled with passengers, sway in and out of giant potholes, raising clouds of dust, their engines whining in low gear. A more numerous traffic plods along on donkeys and on foot, including a procession of the sick. They are headed for the village of Cange and the medical complex called Zanmi Lasante, Creole for Partners in Health. In an all but treeless landscape, it stands out like a fortress on a hillside, a large collection of concrete buildings half covered by tropical greenery. Now and then on the road, a bed moves slowly toward it, a bearer at each corner, a patient on the mattress.

Zanmi Lasante is famous in the Central Plateau, in part for its medical director, Dr. Paul Farmer, known as Doktè Paul, or Polo, or, occasionally, Blan Paul. The women in Zanmi Lasante's kitchen call him *ti blan mwen*— "my little white guy." Peasant farmers like to remember how, during the violent years of the coup that deposed President Aristide, the unarmed Doktè Paul faced down a soldier who tried to enter the complex carrying a gun. One peasant told me, "God gives everyone a gift, and his gift is healing." A former patient once declared, "I believe he is a god." It was also said, in whispers, "He works with both hands"—that is, both with science and with the magic necessary to remove ensorcellments, to many Haitians the deep cause of illnesses. Most of the encomiums seem to embarrass and amuse Farmer. But this last has a painful side. The Haitian belief in illness sent by sorcery thrives on deprivation, on the long absence of effective medicine. Farmer has dozens of voodoo priests among his patients.

On an evening last January, Farmer sat in his office at Zanmi Lasante, dressed in his usual Haiti clothes, black pants and a T-shirt. He was holding aloft a large white plastic bottle. It contained indinavir, one of the new protease   **645** inhibitors for treating AIDS—the kind of magic he believes in. A sad-faced young man sat in the chair beside him. Patients never sat on the other side of his desk. He seemed bound to get as close to them as possible.

Farmer is an inch or two over six feet and thin, unusually long-legged and long-armed, and he has an agile way of folding himself into a chair and arranging himself around a patient he is examining that made me think of a grasshopper. He is about forty. There is a vigorous quality about his thinness. He has a narrow face and a delicate nose, which comes almost to a point. He peered at his patient through the little round lenses of wire-rimmed glasses.

The young man was looking at his feet. He wore ragged sneakers. They   5
were probably Kennedys. Back in the 1960s, Farmer explained to me, J.F.K. had sponsored a program that sent industrial-grade oil to Haiti. The Haitians considered it of inferior quality, and the president's name ever since has been synonymous with shoddy or hand-me-down goods. The young man had AIDS. Farmer had been treating him with antibacterials, but his condition had worsened. The young man said he was ashamed.

"Anybody can catch this—I told you that already," Farmer said in Creole. He shook the bottle, and the pills inside rattled. He asked the young man if he'd heard of this drug and the other new ones for AIDS. The man hadn't.

Well, Farmer said, the drugs didn't cure AIDS, but they would take away his symptoms and, if he was lucky, let him live for many years as if he'd never caught the virus. Farmer would begin treating him soon. He had only to promise that he would never miss a dose. The young man was still looking at his shoes. Farmer leaned closer to him. "I don't want you to be discouraged."

The young man looked up. "Just talking to you makes me feel better. Now I know I'll sleep tonight." Clearly, he wanted to speak to Farmer some more, and just as clearly he was welcome to do so. Farmer likes to tell medical students that to be a good clinician you must never let a patient know that you have problems or that you're in a hurry. "And the rewards are so great for just those simple things!" Of course, this means that some patients wait most of a day to see him, and that he rarely leaves his office before stars shiver in the louvred windows. There is a price for everything, especially virtue.

"My situation is so bad," the young man said. "I keep injuring my head, because I'm living in such a crowded house. We have only one bed, and I let my children sleep on it, so I have to sleep under the bed, and I forget, and I hit my head when I sit up." He went on, "I don't forget what you did for me, Doktè Paul. When I was sick and no one would touch me, you used to sit on my bed with your hand on my head. I would like to give you a chicken or a pig."

When Farmer is relaxed, his skin is pale, with a suggestion of freckles   10
underneath. Now it reddened instantly, from the base of his neck to his forehead. "You've already given me a lot. Stop it!"

The young man was smiling. "I am going to sleep well tonight."

"OK, *neg pa* (my man)."

Farmer put the bottle of pills back in his desk drawer. No one else is treating impoverished Haitians with the new antiretroviral drugs. Even some of his allies in the Haitian medical establishment think he's crazy to try. The drugs could cost as much as eighteen thousand dollars a year per patient. But the fact that the poor are dying of illnesses for which effective treatments exist is, like many global facts of life, unacceptable to Farmer. Indeed, to him it is a sin.

Last fall, he gave a speech to a group in Massachusetts called Cambridge Cares About AIDS and said, "Cambridge cares about AIDS, but not nearly enough." He wondered if he'd gone too far, but afterward, at his suggestion, health-care workers in the audience and people with AIDS collected a bunch of unused drugs, and he ended up with enough to begin triple therapy for several of his Haitian patients. He is working on grant proposals to obtain a larger, more reliable supply. He doesn't seem to think there is a chance he'll fail. In his experience, when he begs for medicines someone always comes through. Begging of one sort or another is the main way in which he and others managed to create Zanmi Lasante. They didn't borrow, but he did a little stealing—the first microscope in Cange was one he had appropriated from Harvard Medical School.

Farmer graduated from Duke in 1982, summa cum laude and with a 15 major in anthropology. He started coming to Haiti the following spring. On an early visit, he met an Episcopal priest named Fritz Lafontant, who became, and remains, the patriarch of Zanmi Lasante. In 1984, Farmer enrolled at Harvard Medical School, and two years later he enrolled in Harvard's graduate program in anthropology. He received both degrees simultaneously, in 1990. He worked hard at his studies, but often far away from Harvard, while helping to create, piece by piece, the medical complex that would become Zanmi Lasante and serving as an unlicensed doctor in Cange. By the time he got his M.D., he had dealt with more varieties of illness than most American physicians see in a lifetime. With several American friends, he had also founded Partners in Health, Zanmi Lasante's sponsoring organization, with headquarters in Cambridge.

Farmer had chosen to work in one of Haiti's poorest regions. His idea was to bring Boston medicine to the Central Plateau, and in some respects he has succeeded. About a million peasant farmers rely on the medical complex now. About a hundred thousand live in its catchment area—the area for which the organization provides community health workers. On many nights, a hundred people camp out in the courtyard beside the ambulatory clinic; by morning, three hundred, sometimes more, are waiting for treatment. Unlike almost every other hospital in Haiti, Zanmi Lasante charges only nominal fees, and women and children and the seriously ill pay nothing. Partners in Health pays the bills, which are remarkably small. My local hospital, in Massachusetts, which treats about 175,000 patients a year, has an annual operating budget of sixty million dollars. Zanmi Lasante spends only about one and a half million dollars to treat 40,000 patients a year. (Farmer spends about two hundred dollars to cure an uncomplicated case of TB in Haiti. The same cure in the United States costs between fifteen and twenty thousand dollars.)

Sometimes the pharmacy muddles a prescription or runs out of a drug. Now and then, the lab technicians lose a specimen. Seven doctors work at the complex, not all of them fully competent—Haitian medical training is mediocre at best. But Zanmi Lasante has built schools and communal water systems for most of the villages in its catchment area. A few years back, when Haiti suffered an outbreak of typhoid resistant to the drugs usually used to treat it, Partners in Health imported an effective but expensive antibiotic, cleaned up the water supply, and stopped the outbreak in the Central Plateau. The medical complex has launched programs in its catchment area for both the prevention and the treatment of AIDS, and has reduced the vertical transmission rate (from mothers to babies) to 4 percent—about half the current rate in the United States. In Haiti, tuberculosis kills more adults than any other disease, but no one from the catchment area has died from it since 1988.

Farmer now has these titles, among others: associate professor in two different departments at Harvard Medical School; member of the senior staff in Infectious Disease at the Brigham and Women's Hospital, in Boston; chief consultant on tuberculosis in Russian prisons for the World Bank (unpaid, at his insistence—he deplores some of the World Bank's policies); and founding director of Partners in Health, which has outposts not only in Cange but in Mexico, Cambodia, Peru, and Roxbury, Massachusetts. The organization is perennially overextended, perennially just getting by financially. It raised about three million dollars last year, from grants and private donations—the largest from one of the founders, a Boston developer named Tom White, who has donated millions over the years. Farmer contributed, too, though he didn't know exactly how much.

In 1993, the MacArthur Foundation gave Farmer one of its so-called genius grants. He had the entire sum sent to Partners in Health—in this case, some $220,000. During his medical-school years, Farmer camped out in Roxbury, in a garret in the rectory of St. Mary of the Angels. Later, during sojourns in Boston, he stayed in the basement of Partners in Health headquarters, and he went on staying there after he got married—to Didi Bertrand, the daughter of the schoolmaster in Cange, and "the most beautiful woman in Cange," people at Zanmi Lasante say. When a daughter was born, two years ago, Farmer saw no reason to change their Boston digs, but his wife did. Now they have an apartment in Eliot House, at Harvard. He never sees his paychecks from Harvard and the Brigham. The bookkeeper at Partners in Health cashes them, pays his family's bills, and puts the rest away in the treasury. One day not long ago, Farmer tried to use his credit card and was told he'd reached his limit, so he called the bookkeeper. She told him, "Honey, you are the hardest-working broke man I know."

By any standard, Farmer's life is complicated. Didi, who is thirty-one, 20 and their daughter spend the academic year in Paris, where Didi is finishing her own studies in anthropology. Several friends have told Farmer that he should visit his family more often. "But I don't have any patients in Paris," he says forlornly. In theory, he works four months in Boston and the rest of the year in Haiti. In fact, those periods are all chopped up. Years ago, he got a letter from American Airlines welcoming him to its million-mile club. He has traveled at least two million miles since. I spent a month with Farmer: a little more than two weeks in Haiti, with a short trip to South Carolina wedged in; five days in Cuba, at a conference on AIDS; and the rest in Moscow, on TB business. He called this "a light month for travel." It had a certain roundness. A church group was, in effect, paying for his flight to South Carolina; the Cuban government covered his travel to Havana; and the Soros Foundation financed his trip to Moscow. "Capitalists, Commies, and Jesus Christers are paying," he said.

When Paul Farmer goes on a long trip, he carries medicines and carrousels of slides and gifts of Haitian art for his hosts, and ends up with room for only three shirts. He owns one suit, which is black, so that he can, for example, wipe the fuzz off the tip of his pen on his pant leg while writing up orders at the Brigham, catch a night flight to Lima or Moscow, and still look presentable when he arrives. En route to South Carolina, the zipper on his suit pants came apart. "Oh well, I'll button my coat," he said before his speech. "That's what a gentleman does when his zipper is broken."

He addressed a meeting of the Anderson County Medical Society. Some of its members visit Cange every year to treat patients free. Some in this particular audience were also church people—the Episcopal Diocese of Upper South Carolina has been making donations to Zanmi Lasante for almost two decades. It was a jacket-and-tie crowd. Farmer gave them his Haiti talk, a compendium of harsh statistics (per-capita incomes of about $230 a year and consequent burdens of preventable, treatable illnesses, which kill 25 percent of Haitians before the age of forty) and cheerful photographs that showed what contributions from places like South Carolina could do. Here was a photograph of a girl who had come to Zanmi Lasante with extra-pulmonary TB. She was bald, her limbs were wasted. And here was the same girl, with a full head of hair and chubby cheeks, smiling at the camera. Cries of surprise from the crowd, followed by applause. No matter who the audience, that pair of photographs always had the same effect. Farmer had felt jubilant, too, when he treated the girl, but the fact was that the "before" picture more nearly represented the Haitian norm. When the applause died away, Farmer made a little grin. "It's *almost* as if she had a treatable infectious disease."

Throughout the world, the poor stand by far the greatest chances of contracting treatable diseases and of dying from them. Not just simple poverty but even relative poverty in affluent countries is associated with large burdens of disease and untimely death. Medicine can address only some symptoms of poverty. Farmer likes to say that he and his colleagues will make common cause with anyone who is sincerely trying to change the "political economies" of countries like Haiti. In the meantime, though, the poor are suffering. They are "dying like smelt," as Farmer puts it. Partners in Health believes in providing services to them—directly, now. "We call it pragmatic solidarity," he told the audience in South Carolina. "It's probably a goofy term, but we mean it."

Farmer showed a slide with a quotation from the World Health Organization: "In developing countries, people with multi-drug-resistant TB usually die, because effective treatment is often impossible in poor settings." He asked, "Why is it impossible? Because adequate resources have not been brought to bear in places like Haiti and Peru." He showed another photograph of a child —a child who "did not want to be declared cost-ineffective." He said, "Cost-effectiveness analysis is good if you use it in order not to waste money. But what's so great about reducing health expenditures?" He told the audience, "We need to oppose this push for lower standards of care for the poor. We are physicians. I don't mean we should do bone-marrow transplants in Cange, but proven therapies. Equity is the only acceptable goal."

"He always kind of holds your feet to the fire," the MC said when Farmer 25 was done, and, indeed, the applause sounded only slightly more than polite.

Like much of the audience, Farmer is himself religious. He subscribes to the Catholic doctrine called liberation theology, and to its central imperative— to provide "a preferential option for the poor." But, he told me, "I hang on to my Catholicism by a tiny thread. I'm still looking for something in the sacred texts that prohibits using condoms." Some of his beliefs, ones he hadn't openly expressed that night—for example, "I think there should be a massive redistribution of wealth to places like Haiti"—would have seemed extreme to this sedate audience. Yet he liked these people a great deal.

Farmer's politics are complex. He has problems with groups that on the surface would seem to be allies. With, for example, what he calls "WLs"— "white liberals," some of whose most influential spokespeople are black. "I love WLs, love 'em to death. They're on our side," Farmer once said. "But WLs think all the world's problems can be fixed without any cost to themselves. We don't believe that. There's a lot to be said for sacrifice, remorse, even pity. It's what separates us from roaches." As often as not, he prefers religious groups and what he calls "church ladies."

We stayed at the house of a church lady that night, an impeccably genteel Southerner. She lived in a retirement community. When we arrived, one of her neighbors, a retired dentist, was repainting the movable flags on all the residents' mailboxes. Of our hostess, Farmer had said, "She is a very good person. I'll take her over a Harvard smart-ass any day. I love her, actually." I was a little puzzled. This woman wasn't a person you'd suspect of threatening the world order. An hour before dawn the next morning, we climbed into her big new car and she turned on her headlights. They lit up her garage, which was filled to the rafters with boxes and crates—all the equipment Farmer had requested for a new ophthalmology clinic in Cange.

As we flew back toward Haiti, via Miami, Farmer worked on thank-you notes to patrons of Partners in Health. During the descent into Miami, Farmer said he had a fantasy that one day he'd look out at the skyline and at the count of ten all the buildings erected with drug money would collapse. He glanced out the window, disappointed once again. He had other Miami rituals. Depending on its length, a layover at the airport was either "a Miami day" or "a Miami day plus," and included a haircut from his favorite Cuban barber (they'd chat in Spanish) and a thorough reading of *People*, which he called the Journal of Popular Studies, or the JPS (it took him fifty-five minutes, "about as long as Mass in the States"). And then it was up to the Admirals' Club, which he was in the habit of calling "Amirales." There he'd take a hot shower and then stake out a section of lounge (this was "making a cave" or "getting cavaceous at Amirales") and answer e-mail. He had a message from one of the staff in Cange:

> Dear Polo, we are so glad we will see you in a mere matter of hours.
> We miss you. We miss you as the cracked, dry earth misses the rain.

"After thirty-six hours?" Farmer said to his computer. "Haitians, man. 30 They're totally over the top. My kind of people."

Days and nights ran together. He has a small house in Cange, the closest thing in his life to a home, perched on a cliff across the road from the medical complex. It's a modified *ti kay*, the better sort of peasant house, with a metal roof and concrete floors, and is exceptional in that it has a bathroom, albeit without hot water. Farmer told me that he slept about five hours a night, but, many times when I looked inside his house, his bed seemed unused. Once he told me, "I can't sleep. There's always somebody not getting treatment. I can't stand that." I suppose he slept some nights. His days usually began around dawn. He'd spend an hour or so among the people who had camped out in the lower courtyard, to make sure the staff hadn't missed someone critically ill, and another hour gobbling a little breakfast while answering e-mail, from Peru and other Partners in Health outposts, and Harvard students, and colleagues at the Brigham, and the various warring factions involved in the effort to stop the Russian TB epidemic. Then he saw patients in his office.

Most of the patients were indeed the poor and the maimed and the halt and the blind. For consolation, there was the man he called Lazarus, who had first arrived on a stretcher, wasted by AIDS and TB to about ninety pounds, and now weighed a hundred and fifty. There was a healthy-looking young woman with AIDS whose father only a month before had been saving for her coffin. But there was also a tiny old woman whose backbone had been eaten by TB bacilli, and who hobbled around with her torso at right angles to her legs. A sixteen-year-old boy who weighed only sixty pounds. ("His body has got used to starvation. We're gonna buff him up.") A lovely young woman being treated for drug-resistant TB, now in the midst of a sickle-cell crisis and moaning in pain. ("OK, *doudou*. OK, *cheri*," Farmer cooed. He gave her morphine.) An elderly man with drug-resistant TB who was totally blind. (He'd wanted a pair of glasses anyway; Farmer had found him a pair.) He called the old women "Mother," and the old men "Father." He exchanged quips with most of his patients while he examined them. He turned to me. "It's so awful you might as well be cheerful."

Off and on during those two weeks in Cange, he conducted what he called "a sorcery consult." A woman had decided that one of her sons had "sent" the sickness that killed another son. Farmer was trying to make peace in the family. This would probably take months, because, for one thing, it was useless to try to convince any of the parties that sorcery didn't exist. Farmer said he felt "86 percent amused." But he saw suffering behind these accusations. Saying that one son had "sold" the other, the mother had used an old Creole word once applied to slaves, and such charges, which often tore friends and families apart, always seemed to spring from the jealousies that great scarcity inspires—in this case, the accused son lived in a better *ti kay* than his mother. Farmer said, "It's not enough that the Haitians get destroyed by everything else, but they also have an exquisite openness to being injured by words."

After office hours, he went on rounds, first to the general hospital and then, with trepidation, to the children's pavilion upstairs, where there always seemed to be a baby with the sticklike limbs, the bloated belly, the reddish hair of kwashiorkor, a form of starvation. Just two weeks earlier, on his first morning back in Cange this year, he'd lost a baby to meningitis, in its ghastly *purpura fulminans* presentation. And, only days later, another baby, from beyond the catchment area—within it, all children are vaccinated free—had died of tetanus. Farmer saved rounds at the TB hospital for last, because just now everyone there was getting better. Most of the patients were sitting on the beds in one of the rooms watching a soccer game on a wavy, snowy TV screen. "Look at you bourgeois people watching TV!" Farmer said.

Everyone laughed. One of the young men looked up at him. "No, Doktè 35 Paul, not bourgeois. If we were bourgeois, we would have an antenna."

"It cheers me up," Farmer said on the way out. "It's not all bad. We're failing on seventy-one levels, but not on one or two." Then it was across the road to his *ti kay*, where he worked with a young American woman from Partners in Health who had been dispatched to help him—on his thank-you notes and upcoming speeches and grant proposals. But on many nights Ti Jean, a handyman, would appear out of the dark, with news that would take Farmer back to the hospital.

A thirteen-year-old girl with meningitis had arrived by donkey ambulance. The young doctors on duty hadn't done a spinal tap, to find out which type of meningitis, and thus which drugs to give her. "Doctors, doctors, what is wrong with you?" Farmer said. Then he did the tap himself. Wild cries from the child: *"Li fe-m mal, mwen grangou."* Farmer looked up from his work and said, "She's crying, 'It hurts, I'm hungry.' Can you believe it? Only in Haiti would a child cry out that she's hungry during a spinal tap."

Two days before we left for Cuba, Farmer took a hike to the village of Morne Michel, the most distant of all the settlements in the catchment area. "And beyond the mountains, more mountains" is an old Haitian saying. It appeared to describe the location of Morne Michel. A TB outpatient from the town had missed an appointment. So—this was a rule at Zanmi Lasante—someone had to go and find him. The annals of international health contain many stories of adequately financed projects that failed because "noncompliant" patients didn't take all their medicines. Farmer said, "Only physicians are noncompliant. If the patient doesn't get better, it's your own fault. Fix it." A favorite Doktè Paul story in the village of Kay Epin was of the time, many years earlier, when he chased a man into a field of cane, calling to him plaintively to come out and be treated. He still went after patients occasionally. To inspire the staff, he said. Hence the trip to Morne Michel.

He drove the first leg in a pickup truck, past dirt-floored huts with banana-frond roofs, which leak during the rainy season, so that the dirt floors turn to mud; and little granaries on stilts, which don't prevent rats from taking a third of every farmer's meager harvest; and yellow dogs so skinny, Haitian peasants say, that they have to lean against trees in order to bark. In a little while, the reservoir that feeds the Péligre Dam came into view, a mountain lake far below the road. The scene looked beautiful: blue waters set among steep, arid mountainsides. But if you saw with peasant eyes, Farmer said, the scene looked violent and ugly—a lake that had buried the good farmland and ravaged the mountainsides.

We parked near the rusted hulk of a small cement factory, beside the 40 concrete dam. In every speech and in all his books, Farmer is at pains to assert the interconnectedness of the rich and poor parts of the world, and here in the dam he had his favorite case study. The dam was planned by engineers from the United States Army during the rather brutal American occupation of Haiti early in the twentieth century, and was built in the midfifties, during the reign of one of America's client dictators, by Brown & Root, of Texas, among others, with money from the U.S. Export-Import Bank. The dam had drowned the peasants' farms and driven them into the hills, where farming meant erosion, all in order to improve irrigation for American-owned agribusinesses downstream and, eventually, to supply electricity to Port-au-Prince, especially to the homes of the wealthy elite and the foreign-owned assembly plants, in which peasant girls and boys from Cange still work as servants and laborers, more than a few of them nowadays returning home with AIDS. Most of the peasants didn't get paid for their land. As they liked to say, the project hadn't even brought them electricity or water.

On the other side of the dam, a footpath—loose dirt and stones, slippery looking—went straight up. Farmer has a slipped disk from eighteen years of traveling the *gwo wout la*. He also suffers from high blood pressure and mild asthma, which developed after he'd recovered from a possible case of tuberculosis. His left leg was surgically repaired after he was hit by a car and turns out at a slight angle—like a kickstand, as one of his brothers says. But when I got to the top of that first hill, sweating and panting, he was sitting on a rock, writing a letter. It was the first of many hills. We passed smiling children carrying water jugs that must have weighed half as much as they did, and the children had no shoes. We passed groups of laughing women washing clothes in the muddy rivulets of gullies. Haitians, Farmer had said, are a fastidious people. "I know. I've been in all their nooks and crannies. But they blow their noses into dresses because they don't have tissues, wipe their asses with leaves, and have to apologize to their children for not having enough to eat."

"Misery," I said.

"And don't think they don't know it," Farmer said. "There's a WL line—the 'They're poor but they're happy' line. They do have nice smiles and good senses of humor, but that's entirely different."

We stopped awhile at a cockfight, the national sport, and passed beside many fields of millet, the national dish, which seemed to be growing out of rocks, not soil. We passed small stands of banana trees and, now and then, other tropical species, Farmer pausing to apply the Latin and familiar names: papaw, soursop, mango—a gloomy litany, because there were so many fewer of each variety than there should have been. We paused on hilltops, where the wind was strong and cold on my sweaty skin. Curtains of rain and swaths of sunlight swept across the vast reservoir far below and across the yellow mountains, which, I realized, could never look pretty again to me. I wondered how Haitians avoided hopelessness. I wondered how Farmer did. After about two and a half hours, we arrived at the hut of the noncompliant patient, another shack made of rough-sawn palm wood with a roof of banana fronds and a cooking fire of the kind Haitians call "three rocks." The patient, it turned out, had been given confusing instructions by the staff at Zanmi Lasante, and he hadn't received the money, about ten dollars a month, that all Zanmi Lasante's TB patients get—for extra nutrition, to boost their immune systems. He hadn't missed any doses of his TB drugs, however.

Farmer gave him the money, and we started back through the moun- 45 tains. I slipped and slid down the paths behind him. "Some people would argue this wasn't worth a five-hour walk," he said over his shoulder. "But you can never invest too much in making sure this stuff works."

"Sure," I said. "But some people would ask, 'How can you expect others to replicate what you're doing here?' What would be your answer to that?"

He turned back and, smiling sweetly, said, "Fuck you."

Then, in a stentorian voice, he corrected himself: "No. I would say, 'The objective is to inculcate in the doctors and nurses the spirit to dedicate themselves to the patients, and especially to having an outcome-oriented view of t.b.'" He was grinning, his face alight. He looked very young just then. "In other words, 'Fuck you.'"

WHAT DOES HE SAY?

1. Much of this profile consists of description and narration without explicit commentary from the author. As you read, mark at least three scenes where you think Tracy Kidder is implicitly portraying Paul Farmer, his subject, in either a positive or negative light.

2. At several points Kidder does briefly come out and interpret the action directly, suggesting what he thinks about his subject. Mark those places.

3. After your first reading of this story, write a paragraph in which you explain what you think Kidder wants us to believe as a result of reading about Paul Farmer. Kidder doesn't spell out the moral of the story. Based on the clues, what do you think it is?

WHAT DO YOU THINK?

4. Write a character summary of Paul Farmer as you understand him. What traits does he possess? What beliefs or values do you see as fundamental to his character? Don't try to judge Farmer; simply try to summarize your understandings of who he is.

5. What do you think of Paul Farmer and why? Cite details from the story to back up your response.

6. In what ways can Paul Farmer be seen as a role model, for you or anybody else? Is it possible for the average person to do what he has done? Why or why not?

7. Write an essay explaining what Kidder means for us to understand. Quote "The Good Doctor" in several places to help make your assertions clearer.

8. How would Paul Farmer respond to the scenario that we include in the introduction to this chapter? What would he advise? How would Kidder respond? Would his response be different from Farmer's?

WHAT WOULD THEY SAY?

9. Assume that Paul Farmer, the subject of Kidder's essay, has read the pamphlet from the Homeland Security Office, "Get Ready Now" (p. 642). How might he respond? Bring Peter Singer, of "The Singer Solution to World Poverty" (p. 661) into this conversation, too. How would Singer respond to the pamphlet and how would he respond to Farmer? (A way of getting started on this would be to recognize that Singer would probably say that one response to terrorism is to consider the social and economic conditions that make it possible.) Now, assume that Kofi Annan, whose "Nobel Lecture" (p. 225) we include in chapter 3, has come in on the conversation. With whom would he align himself? What would he say to the others in the group, and why? How would Paul Farmer respond to Annan?

10. Both Ruth Benedict, in "The Case for Moral Relativism" (p. 619), and Paul Farmer, the subject of Kidder's profile, travel to exotic places and interact with the peoples

and cultures they find there. Write an essay in which you compare and contrast their different methods. Explain their different aims, different agendas, and different ways of going about their work. Would Benedict endorse Farmer's actions? What would Farmer say about Benedict? Variation: Also consider and explain how Kidder, the author of the profile (as distinct from Farmer, his subject), compares to Benedict in approach and underlying value system.

11. Assume that Paul Farmer has read Garrett Hardin's essay, "Lifeboat Ethics: The Case against Helping the Poor" (p. 130). What would Farmer say in response? What would Hardin say about Farmer? Write an essay explaining these responses. End by discussing your own views as you consider these questions.

BARBARA LAZEAR ASCHER
On Compassion

A FORMER ATTORNEY, Barbara Lazear Ascher (b. 1946) is the author of two collections of essays, Playing After Dark *(1986) and* The Habit of Loving *(1989). She has also written a memoir about her brother's death from AIDS,* Landscape Without Gravity: A Memoir of Grief *(1993), and a book about romance,* Dancing in the Dark: Romance, Yearning, and the Search for the Sublime *(1999). Her essays have been published in a wide variety of periodicals, including* National Geographic, Elle, The New York Times Book Review, *and* Vogue. *She has taught writing at several workshops and schools, and is currently on the board of directors for the Academy of American Poets.*

The man's grin is less the result of circumstance than dreams or madness. His buttonless shirt, with one sleeve missing, hangs outside the waist of his baggy trousers. Carefully plaited dreadlocks bespeak a better time, long ago. As he crosses Manhattan's Seventy-ninth Street, his gait is the shuffle of the forgotten ones held in place by gravity rather than plans. On the corner of Madison Avenue, he stops before a blond baby in an Aprica stroller. The baby's mother waits for the light to change and her hands close tighter on the stroller's handle as she sees the man approach.

The others on the corner, five men and women waiting for the crosstown bus, look away. They daydream a bit and gaze into the weak rays of November light. A man with a briefcase lifts and lowers the shiny toe of his right shoe, watching the light reflect, trying to catch and balance it, as if he could hold and make it his, to ease the heavy gray of coming January, February, and March. The winter months that will send snow around the feet, calves, and knees of the grinning man as he heads for the shelter of Grand Central or Pennsylvania Station.

But for now, in this last gasp of autumn warmth, he is still. His eyes fix on the baby. The mother removes her purse from her shoulder and rummages through its contents: lipstick, a lace handkerchief, an address book. She finds what she's looking for and passes a folded dollar over her child's head to the man who stands and stares even though the light has changed and traffic navigates about his hips.

His hands continue to dangle at his sides. He does not know his part. He does not know that acceptance of the gift and gratitude are what make this transaction complete. The baby, weary of the unwavering stare, pulls its blanket over its head. The man does not look away. Like a bridegroom waiting at the altar, his eyes pierce the white veil.

657

The mother grows impatient and pushes the stroller before her, bearing   5
the dollar like a cross. Finally, a black hand rises and closes around green.

Was it fear or compassion that motivated the gift?

Up the avenue, at Ninety-first Street, there is a small French bread shop
where you can sit and eat a buttery, overpriced croissant and wash it down with
rich cappuccino. Twice when I have stopped here to stave hunger or stay the
cold, twice as I have sat and read and felt the warm rush of hot coffee and milk,
an old man has wandered in and stood inside the entrance. He wears a stained
blanket pulled up to his chin, and a woolen hood pulled down to his gray,
bushy eyebrows. As he stands, the scent of stale cigarettes and urine fills the
small, overheated room.

The owner of the shop, a moody French woman, emerges from the
kitchen with steaming coffee in a Styrofoam cup, and a small paper bag of…of
what? Yesterday's bread? Today's croissant? He accepts the offering as silently as
he came, and is gone.

Twice I have witnessed this, and twice I have wondered, what compels
this woman to feed this man? Pity? Care? Compassion? Or does she simply
want to rid her shop of his troublesome presence? If expulsion were her motivation she would not reward his arrival with gifts of food. Most proprietors
do not. They chase the homeless from their midst with expletives and threats.

As winter approaches, the mayor of New York City is moving the home-   10
less off the streets and into Bellevue Hospital. The New York Civil Liberties
Union is watchful. They question whether the rights of these people who live
in our parks and doorways are being violated by involuntary hospitalization.

I think the mayor's notion is humane, but I fear it is something else as
well. Raw humanity offends our sensibilities. We want to protect ourselves
from an awareness of rags with voices that make no sense and scream forth in
inarticulate rage. We do not wish to be reminded of the tentative state of our
own well-being and sanity. And so, the troublesome presence is removed from
the awareness of the electorate.

Like other cities, there is much about Manhattan now that resembles
Dickensian London. Ladies in high-heeled shoes pick their way through
poverty and madness. You hear more cocktail party complaints than usual, "I
just can't take New York anymore." Our citizens dream of the open spaces of
Wyoming, the manicured exclusivity of Hobe Sound.

And yet, it may be that these are the conditions that finally give birth to
empathy, the mother of compassion. We cannot deny the existence of the
helpless as their presence grows. It is impossible to insulate ourselves against
what is at our very doorstep. I don't believe that one is born compassionate.
Compassion is not a character trait like a sunny disposition. It must be learned,
and it is learned by having adversity at our windows, coming through the gates
of our yards, the walls of our towns, adversity that becomes so familiar that we
begin to identify and empathize with it.

For the ancient Greeks, drama taught and reinforced compassion within a society. The object of Greek tragedy was to inspire empathy in the audience so that the common response to the hero's fall was: "There, but for the grace of God, go I." Could it be that this was the response of the mother who offered the dollar, the French woman who gave the food? Could it be that the homeless, like those ancients, are reminding us of our common humanity? Of course, there is a difference. This play doesn't end—and the players can't go home.

WHAT DOES SHE SAY?

1. Read this essay until you get to the question, "Was it fear or compassion that motivated the gift?" Stop at that point and write a paragraph that's your answer. If you don't like your two choices ("fear or compassion"), write about whatever you think might more accurately describe the woman's motives.

2. Once you've finished this essay, make two lists: in one, put those in the essay who are not offended by what Ascher calls "raw humanity," and in the other put those who are.

WHAT DO YOU THINK?

3. Pay attention to what the narrator of this essay does. Based on all you can glean, explain your understanding of the narrator's response to the two individuals who appear to be among those "who live in our parks and doorways."

4. "On Compassion" seems to announce a large theme. Yet it really only offers two quite specific examples, neither of which is discussed at length. Write a critique of this essay explaining why you believe it is or is not effective. (Clearly, to do this you will need to decide what you believe the essay tries to do.)

5. Write an essay that tells the story of your own experience in giving a needy stranger money. Be as specific in your descriptions as Ascher is in her essay. Give the details of your experience, comment on it, and quote from "On Compassion" at least once. Explain whether or not this was a new experience for you, explain what the experience felt like at the time, and explain how you view it now as you try to understand how and to whom we ought to extend compassion.

6. Write an essay that starts by aggressively arguing with Ascher's implication that it's compassionate simply to hand people money or coffee or food. Make the strongest such argument you can. Then skip some extra space and explain to what extent you do or do not agree with what the essay presented to that point.

WHAT WOULD THEY SAY?

7. Write an essay that discusses how "On Compassion" might or might not work as an essay that could be translated from person-to-person action to nation-to-nation action. Use the Earth Charter (p. 158) in some fashion to help make your discussion clearer.

8. Explain how Garrett Hardin's "Lifeboat Ethics: The Case against Helping the Poor" (p. 130) would translate to the personal level of "On Compassion." From that point of view, should the woman give the man a dollar? Should the coffee-shop proprietor give out free coffee and pastry? Follow that analysis by discussing the extent to which you think most people (including yourself) do or do not follow their own version of Hardin's lifeboat ethics. End by explaining why you will, or will not, give to the needy on a city street.

9. In one sense, "On Compassion" is an essay about empathy. So consider this essay together with "Profile of an Arab Daughter" (p. 36) by Elmaz Abinader, Bernard Cooper's "A Clack of Tiny Sparks: Remembrances of a Gay Boyhood" (p. 314), and Sarah Vowell's "Shooting Dad" (p. 29). Use these four essays to discuss your sense of how we develop empathy. To what extent, or not, are we empathetic only toward those who are most like us? End by discussing what is clearer to you now about empathy, about action, about compassion, and about education.

PETER SINGER
The Singer Solution to World Poverty

*L*IKE D*R.* F*ARMER in the Kidder profile, Peter Singer (b. 1946) makes a radical de-*
mand: that we give away all the money we make above whatever is necessary for our sur-
vival. Singer, chair of bioethics at Princeton University, is devoted to ending human
"speciesism"—valuing human rights above the rights of other species. His works include
Should the Baby Live? The Problem of Handicapped Infants *(1985),* Animal
Factories *(1990),* How Are We to Live? *(1994), and* Rethinking Life and Death
(1995). "The Singer Solution to World Poverty" originally appeared in the September
1999 issue of the New York Times Magazine.

In the Brazilian film *Central Station*, Dora is a retired schoolteacher who makes
ends meet by sitting at the station writing letters for illiterate people. Suddenly
she has an opportunity to pocket $1,000. All she has to do is persuade a home-
less nine-year-old boy to follow her to an address she has been given. (She is
told he will be adopted by wealthy foreigners.) She delivers the boy, gets the
money, spends some of it on a television set and settles down to enjoy her new
acquisition. Her neighbor spoils the fun, however, by telling her that the boy
was too old to be adopted—he will be killed and his organs sold for transplan-
tation. Perhaps Dora knew this all along, but after her neighbor's plain speaking,
she spends a troubled night. In the morning Dora resolves to take the boy back.

Suppose Dora had told her neighbor that it is a tough world, other
people have nice new TVs too, and if selling the kid is the only way she can
get one, well, he was only a street kid. She would then have become, in the
eyes of the audience, a monster. She redeems herself only by being prepared
to bear considerable risks to save the boy.

At the end of the movie, in cinemas in the affluent nations of the world,
people who would have been quick to condemn Dora if she had not rescued
the boy go home to places far more comfortable than her apartment. In fact,
the average family in the United States spends almost one-third of its income
on things that are no more necessary to them than Dora's new TV was to her.
Going out to nice restaurants, buying new clothes because the old ones are no
longer stylish, vacationing at beach resorts—so much of our income is spent
on things not essential to the preservation of our lives and health. Donated to
one of a number of charitable agencies, that money could mean the difference
between life and death for children in need.

All of which raises a question: In the end, what is the ethical distinction
between a Brazilian who sells a homeless child to organ peddlers and an   **661**

American who already has a TV and upgrades to a better one—knowing that the money could be donated to an organization that would use it to save the lives of kids in need?

Of course, there are several differences between the two situations that could support different moral judgments about them. For one thing, to be able to consign a child to death when he is standing right in front of you takes a chilling kind of heartlessness; it is much easier to ignore an appeal for money to help children you will never meet. Yet for a utilitarian philosopher like myself—that is, one who judges whether acts are right or wrong by their consequences—if the upshot of the American's failure to donate the money is that one more kid dies on the streets of a Brazilian city, then it is, in some sense, just as bad as selling the kid to the organ peddlers. But one doesn't need to embrace my utilitarian ethic to see that, at the very least, there is a troubling incongruity in being so quick to condemn Dora for taking the child to the organ peddlers while, at the same time, not regarding the American consumer's behavior as raising a serious moral issue.

In his 1996 book, *Living High and Letting Die*, the New York University philosopher Peter Unger presented an ingenious series of imaginary examples designed to probe our intuitions about whether it is wrong to live well without giving substantial amounts of money to help people who are hungry, malnourished, or dying from easily treatable illnesses like diarrhea. Here's my paraphrase of one of these examples:

Bob is close to retirement. He has invested most of his savings in a very rare and valuable old car, a Bugatti, which he has not been able to insure. The Bugatti is his pride and joy. In addition to the pleasure he gets from driving and caring for his car, Bob knows that its rising market value means that he will always be able to sell it and live comfortably after retirement. One day when Bob is out for a drive, he parks the Bugatti near the end of a railway siding and goes for a walk up the track. As he does so, he sees that a runaway train, with no one aboard, is running down the railway track. Looking farther down the track, he sees the small figure of a child very likely to be killed by the runaway train. He can't stop the train and the child is too far away to warn of the danger, but he can throw a switch that will divert the train down the siding where his Bugatti is parked. Then nobody will be killed—but the train will destroy his Bugatti. Thinking of his joy in owning the car and the financial security it represents, Bob decides not to throw the switch. The child is killed. For many years to come, Bob enjoys owning his Bugatti and the financial security it represents.

Bob's conduct, most of us will immediately respond, was gravely wrong. Unger agrees. But then he reminds us that we, too, have opportunities to save the lives of children. We can give to organizations like Unicef or Oxfam America. How much would we have to give one of these organizations to have a high probability of saving the life of a child threatened by easily preventable diseases? (I do not believe that children are more worth saving than adults, but since no one can argue that children have brought their poverty on themselves, focusing on them simplifies the issues.) Unger called up some experts and used the information they provided to offer some plausible estimates that include the cost of raising money, administrative expenses and the cost of delivering aid where it is most needed. By his calculation, $200 in donations would help a sickly two-year-old transform into a healthy six-year-old—offering safe passage through childhood's most dangerous years. To show how practical philosophical argument can be, Unger even tells his readers that they can easily donate funds by using their credit card and calling one of these toll-free numbers: (800) 367-5437 for Unicef; (800) 693-2687 for Oxfam America.

Now you, too, have the information you need to save a child's life. How should you judge yourself if you don't do it? Think again about Bob and his Bugatti. Unlike Dora, Bob did not have to look into the eyes of the child he was sacrificing for his own material comfort. The child was a complete stranger to him and too far away to relate to in an intimate, personal way. Unlike Dora, too, he did not mislead the child or initiate the chain of events imperiling him. In all these respects, Bob's situation resembles that of people able but unwilling to donate to overseas aid and differs from Dora's situation.

If you still think that it was very wrong of Bob not to throw the switch 10 that would have diverted the train and saved the child's life, then it is hard to see how you could deny that it is also very wrong not to send money to one of the organizations listed above. Unless, that is, there is some morally important difference between the two situations that I have overlooked.

Is it the practical uncertainties about whether aid will really reach the people who need it? Nobody who knows the world of overseas aid can doubt that such uncertainties exist. But Unger's figure of $200 to save a child's life was reached after he had made conservative assumptions about the proportion of the money donated that will actually reach its target.

One genuine difference between Bob and those who can afford to donate to overseas aid organizations but don't is that only Bob can save the child on the tracks, whereas there are hundreds of millions of people who can give $200 to overseas aid organizations. The problem is that most of them aren't doing it. Does this mean that it is all right for you not to do it?

Suppose that there were more owners of priceless vintage cars—Carol, Dave, Emma, Fred, and so on, down to Ziggy—all in exactly the same situation as Bob, with their own siding and their own switch, all sacrificing the child in order to preserve their own cherished car. Would that make it all right for Bob to do the same? To answer this question affirmatively is to endorse follow-the-crowd ethics—the kind of ethics that led many Germans to look away when the Nazi atrocities were being committed. We do not excuse them because others were behaving no better.

We seem to lack a sound basis for drawing a clear moral line between Bob's situation and that of any reader of this article with $200 to spare who does not donate it to an overseas aid agency. These readers seem to be acting at least as badly as Bob was acting when he chose to let the runaway train hurtle toward the unsuspecting child. In the light of this conclusion, I trust that many readers will reach for the phone and donate that $200. Perhaps you should do it before reading further.

Now that you have distinguished yourself morally from people who put their vintage cars ahead of a child's life, how about treating yourself and your partner to dinner at your favorite restaurant? But wait. The money you will spend at the restaurant could also help save the lives of children overseas! True, you weren't planning to blow $200 tonight, but if you were to give up dining out just for one month, you would easily save that amount. And what is one month's dining out, compared to a child's life? There's the rub. Since there are a lot of desperately needy children in the world, there will always be another child whose life you could save for another $200. Are you therefore obliged to keep giving until you have nothing left? At what point can you stop?

Hypothetical examples can easily become farcical. Consider Bob. How far past losing the Bugatti should he go? Imagine that Bob had got his foot stuck in the track of the siding, and if he diverted the train, then before it rammed the car it would also amputate his big toe. Should he still throw the switch? What if it would amputate his foot? His entire leg?

As absurd as the Bugatti scenario gets when pushed to extremes, the point it raises is a serious one: only when the sacrifices become very significant indeed would most people be prepared to say that Bob does nothing wrong when he decides not to throw the switch. Of course, most people could be wrong; we can't decide moral issues by taking opinion polls. But consider for yourself the level of sacrifice that you would demand of Bob, and then think about how much money you would have to give away in order to make a sacrifice that is roughly equal to that. It's almost certainly much, much more than $200. For most middle-class Americans, it could easily be more like $200,000.

Isn't it counterproductive to ask people to do so much? Don't we run the risk that many will shrug their shoulders and say that morality, so conceived, is fine for saints but not for them? I accept that we are unlikely to see, in the near or even medium-term future, a world in which it is normal for wealthy Americans to give the bulk of their wealth to strangers. When it comes to praising or blaming people for what they do, we tend to use a standard that is relative to some conception of normal behavior. Comfortably off Americans who give, say, 10 percent of their income to overseas aid organizations are so far ahead of most of their equally comfortable fellow citizens that I wouldn't go out of my way to chastise them for not doing more. Nevertheless, they should be doing much more, and they are in no position to criticize Bob for failing to make the much greater sacrifice of his Bugatti.

At this point various objections may crop up. Someone may say: "If every citizen living in the affluent nations contributed his or her share I wouldn't have to make such a drastic sacrifice, because long before such levels were reached, the resources would have been there to save the lives of all those children dying from lack of food or medical care. So why should I give more than my fair share?" Another, related, objection is that the government ought to increase its overseas aid allocations, since that would spread the burden more equitably across all taxpayers.

Yet the question of how much we ought to give is a matter to be decided 20 in the real world—and that, sadly, is a world in which we know that most people do not, and in the immediate future will not, give substantial amounts to overseas aid agencies. We know, too, that at least in the next year, the United States government is not going to meet even the very modest United Nations–recommended target of 0.7 percent of gross national product; at the moment it lags far below that, at 0.09 percent, not even half of Japan's 0.22 percent or a tenth of Denmark's 0.97 percent. Thus, we know that the money we can give beyond that theoretical "fair share" is still going to save lives that would otherwise be lost. While the idea that no one need do more than his or her fair share is a powerful one, should it prevail if we know that others are not doing their fair share and that children will die preventable deaths unless we do more than our fair share? That would be taking fairness too far.

Thus, this ground for limiting how much we ought to give also fails. In the world as it is now, I can see no escape from the conclusion that each one of us with wealth surplus to his or her essential needs should be giving most of it to help people suffering from poverty so dire as to be life threatening. That's right: I'm saying that you shouldn't buy that new car, take that cruise, redecorate the house, or get that pricey new suit. After all, a $1,000 suit could save five children's lives.

So how does my philosophy break down in dollars and cents? An American household with an income of $50,000 spends around $30,000 annually on necessities, according to the Conference Board, a nonprofit economic research organization. Therefore, for a household bringing in $50,000 a year, donations to help the world's poor should be as close as possible to $20,000. The $30,000 required for necessities holds for higher incomes as well. So a household making $100,000 could cut a yearly check for $70,000. Again, the formula is simple: whatever money you're spending on luxuries, not necessities, should be given away.

Now, evolutionary psychologists tell us that human nature just isn't sufficiently altruistic to make it plausible that many people will sacrifice so much for strangers. On the facts of human nature, they might be right, but they would be wrong to draw a moral conclusion from those facts. If it is the case that we ought to do things that, predictably, most of us won't do, then let's face that fact head-on. Then, if we value the life of a child more than going to fancy restaurants, the next time we dine out we will know that we could have done something better with our money. If that makes living a morally decent life extremely arduous, well, then that is the way things are. If we don't do it, then we should at least know that we are failing to live a morally decent life—not because it is good to wallow in guilt but because knowing where we should be going is the first step toward heading in that direction.

When Bob first grasped the dilemma that faced him as he stood by that railway switch, he must have thought how extraordinarily unlucky he was to be placed in a situation in which he must choose between the life of an innocent child and the sacrifice of most of his savings. But he was not unlucky at all. We are all in that situation.

WHAT DOES HE SAY?

1. Peter Singer begins with a description of a moral dilemma posed by a movie. Summarize this story and explain how Singer uses it to introduce the themes of his essay.

2. Summarize the other scenarios or case studies that Singer uses in this essay. How are they sequenced or ordered? How do they influence your thinking about Singer's argument?

3. Write out a list of all the questions that Singer asks in this essay, in the order in which they appear. Look at the list. Write a paragraph about the effect of reading these questions. How are the questions related to each other?

4. At the end of this essay, Singer makes a specific, concrete proposal in the form of a formula involving income and expenses for the average person. Write this formula out as an equation.

WHAT DO YOU THINK?

5. Make a list of three reasons why Singer's proposal is impractical, crazy, extreme, and wrong. Explain each of the reasons briefly. Then make a list of three reasons why Singer's proposal is practical, rational, balanced, and right. Explain these briefly as well. End by making sense of the contradictions.

6. Watch an hour of commercial television between 7:00 PM and 11:00 PM. Keep a log of all the commercials, including this information: the product or service advertised, the beliefs or values they assume viewers share with the commercial, and what information (if any) is given about cost. Based on this information alone, construct a profile of what Americans value and what Americans want. Then compare and contrast this profile with what "The Singer Solution to World Poverty" values and wants. End by explaining what is clearer to you as a result of these comparisons. Variation: Use as your source ten advertisements in the current issue of a general-audience magazine.

7. Apply Singer's formula to your own life, in specific detail. Calculate how much it costs for you to live each month—room and board, tuition, transportation, a little spending money. Subtract this amount from the money you actually take in each

month, from whatever sources. In light of these numbers, is Singer's proposal workable for you at this point in your life? Is it attractive? Explain.

8. Stretch this exercise into the future. What are your career goals after you graduate? What is the average starting income for people in your field? What is the average income for people in your field after ten years? Estimate in general terms: How much will it cost for you to buy an average house in the kind of community where you want to live? the kind of car you want to drive? food and other expenses? How much would be left over for giving to others? The question here is twofold: (1) Is Singer's plan workable? (2) If it is workable, is it desirable? How does it match or challenge your assumptions about your future?

WHAT WOULD THEY SAY?

9. Garrett Hardin, in "Lifeboat Ethics: The Case against Helping the Poor" (p. 130), clearly and sharply disagrees with all of Peter Singer's assumptions and proposals. These two thinkers couldn't be more different. Write an essay making these differences clear point by point. Frame the essay with your own views. Force yourself to take one side or the other (for the sake of the exercise). Which of these two extremes makes more sense to you, and why?

10. Compare "The Singer Solution to World Poverty" to the Dalai Lama's "The Need for Discernment" (p. 205) and Helen Prejean's "Executions Are Too Costly—Morally" (p. 614). The Dalai Lama and Prejean would clearly be sympathetic to Singer's arguments. Singer would clearly be sympathetic to theirs. But are their assumptions the same? Are they arguing in the same ways, for the same ends? In other words, what is the deepest connection among these writers? What is the deepest difference?

REBECCA SOLNIT

The Silence of the Lambswool Cardigans

In this brief essay, Rebecca Solnit (b. 1961) challenges readers to think about where their purchases come from. Everything we buy at a mall has ethical consequences somewhere in the world. But there's hope here, too; there's something to do: buy conscientiously, with critical awareness.

A much-published writer, critic, and activist, Solnit's books include Savage Dreams: A Journey into the Landscape Wars of the American West *(1994), A* Book of Migrations: Some Passages in Ireland *(1997), and* Wanderlust: A History of Walking *(2000). "The Silence of the Lambswool Cardigans" first appeared in the July 2003 issue of* Orion.

There was a time not so long ago when everything was recognizable not just as a cup or a coat, but as a cup made by so-and-so out of clay from this bank on the local river or woven by the guy in that house out of wool from the sheep visible on the hills. Then, objects were not purely material, mere commodities, but signs of processes, human and natural, pieces of a story, and the story as well as the stuff sustained life. It's as though every object spoke—some of them must have sung out—in a language everyone could hear, a language that surrounded every object in an aura of its history.

"All commodities are only definite masses of congealed labor-time," said Marx, but who now could dissolve them into their constituent histories of labor and materials, into the stories that made them about the processes of the world, made them part of life even if they were iron or brick, made them come to life? For decades tales of city kids who didn't know that milk came from cows have circulated, and the inability of American teenagers to find Iraq on a map made the rounds more recently, but who among us can picture precisely where their sweater or their sugar comes from?

I've been thinking about that because a new shopping mall has opened up at the eastern foot of the Bay Bridge, in what was once, according to the newspaper, the biggest shell mound in northern California (though the town I grew up in claimed the same distinction for the Miwok mound it bulldozed without excavation for a shopping center in the 1950s). From the 1870s to the 1920s, this place was Shellmound Park, an amusement park, racetrack, dance hall, and shooting range, but Prohibition put the pleasure grounds out of business and the mound was bulldozed for industry. The remains of seven hundred Ohlone people that an archaeologist snatched from the construction site in 1924 are still at the University of California at Berkeley. Meanwhile, the industrialized site hosted paint and pesticide factories that eventually made it into a wasteland so toxic that those venturing into it wore moon suits. It was reclaimed for shopping, and the cleanup disturbed the Ohlone remains that hadn't already been bulldozed.

The street that goes out there is still called Shellmound, but the mall itself hosts all the usual chains that make it impossible to know if you're in Phoenix or Philadelphia: Victoria's Secret, Williams-Sonoma, Express, all three versions of the Gap corporation, including Old Navy and Banana Republic, all laid out on a fake Main Street. Anti-Gap protestors haven't arrived yet, though they are frequent presences in downtown San Francisco, decrying both the Gap's reliance on sweatshop labor and the clear-cutting of old-growth redwood forests in Mendocino owned by the Gap's CEO (see Gapsucks.org). But the day the mall opened, activists from the International Indian Treaty Council handed out flyers protesting the desecration of a burial ground. As a substitute for protecting the actual site, the city of Emeryville has offered a Web site with information about it, as if a place could be relocated to cyberspace. The mall is a distinctly modern site, a space that could be anywhere into which commodities come as if out of nowhere.

In *The Making of the English Working Class*, Engels recounts the crimes   5 behind the production of everyday things — ceramics, ironware, glass, but particularly cotton cloth. He wrote in a time when objects were first becoming silent, and he asked the same thing that the activists from Gapsucks.org do, that we learn the new industrial languages of objects, that we hear the story of children worked into deformity and blindness to make lace, the story of the knife grinders with a life expectancy of thirty-five years, or nowadays the tales of sweatshop, prison, and child labor. These industrial stories have always been environmental stories too, about factory effluents, cotton chemicals, the timber industry, the petrochemical industry.

Somewhere in the Industrial Age, objects shut up because their creation had become so remote and intricate a process that it was no longer readily knowable. Or they were silenced, because the pleasures of abundance that all the cheap goods offered were only available if those goods were mute about the scarcity and loss that lay behind their creation. Modern advertising — notably for Nike — constitutes an aggressive attempt to displace the meaning of the commodity from its makers, as though you enter into relationships with very tall athletes rather than, say, very thin Vietnamese teenagers when you buy their shoes. It *is* a stretch to think about Mexican prison labor while contemplating Victoria's Secret lavender lace boy-cut panties. The Western Shoshone rancher and landrights activist Carrie Dann, whose own family graveyard has been flooded by a gold mine pumping out groundwater to get at the gold below, once remarked to me that everyone who buys gold jewelry should have the associated spent ore delivered to their house. At Nevada's mining rates, that would mean a hundred tons of toxic tailings for every one-ounce ring or chain you buy.

The objects are pretty; their stories are hideous, so you get to choose between an alienated and ultimately meaningless world and one that makes terrible demands on you. Most consumers prefer meaningless over complicated, and therefore prefer that objects remain silent. To tell their tales is to be the bearer of bad news—imagine activists as Moses coming down from Sinai but cutting straight to Leviticus, the forty thousand prohibitions: against shrimp (see <www.montereybayaquarium.org>), against strawberries (methyl bromide, stoop labor), against gold (see <www.greatbasinminewatch.org>), and on and on. It's what makes radicals and environmentalists seem so grumpy to the would-be consumer.

Maybe the real question is what substances, objects, and products tell stories that don't make people cringe or turn away. For the past half century the process of art making has been part of its subject, and this making becomes a symbolic act that attempts to substitute for the silence of all the other objects. But nobody lives by art alone. There's food from the wild, from your own garden, from friends, ancient objects salvaged and flea marketed, heirlooms and hand-me-downs, local crafts, and a few things still made with the union label, but it's not easy for anyone to stay pure of Payless and Wal-Mart. Good stores too—pricey organic and free-range and shade-grown food that is only available in the hipper stores of the fancier regions—can be a luxury.

Some of the enthusiasm for farmer's markets, which are springing up like mushrooms after rain, is of meeting objects that aren't mute, because you see the people who grew the produce and know the places they come from are not far away. This alternative economy feeds people who want to be nourished by stories and connections, and it's growing. Some farmer's markets are like boutiques with little bunches of peas or raspberries displayed and priced like jewels, but I go to an intensely multiethnic mob scene called Heart of the City Farmer's Market. The food, even some of the organic stuff, is pretty cheap and everyone is present, including the homeless who hang out in that downtown plaza all week anyway, and the locals who use the market to make up for the way supermarkets boycott poor neighborhoods. Seeing the thorn scars on the hands of the rose growers there was as big a step in knowing what constitutes my world as realizing that, in this town where it never snows, our tap water is all Sierra snowmelt.

What bothers me about the mall is its silence, a silence we mostly live in 10 nowadays; what cheers me are the ways people are learning to read the silent histories of objects and choosing the objects that still sing.

WHAT DOES SHE SAY?

1. Solnit's essay begins by recalling a time when the objects a person used every day—clothing, plates, furniture, and so on—were mostly made locally. Recall an object you or your family owned that was made by someone you actually knew. Write a paragraph about the extent to which it was unusual or unique.

2. As you read, copy out three sentences that disturb you or make you think.

3. Make two columns: in one, list the things, values, or attributes Solnit favors. In the second, list the things, values, or attributes she doesn't like.

WHAT DO YOU THINK?

4. Write an essay explaining how Solnit's "The Silence of the Lambswool Cardigans" is really a discussion about what we mean or should mean when we consider notions of cost and value. Then critique her analysis. Does it seem complete? incomplete? fair? unfair? accurate? inaccurate? Does it persuade you? Explain.

5. Do you or does your family own any objects that fit the description of "a time not so long ago" that begins "The Silence of the Lambswool Cardigans"? If so, write an essay explaining how they fit or don't fit with Solnit's sense of such things as "signs of processes, human and natural, pieces of a story."

6. Pick two pieces of clothing you own, each made in a different country outside of the United States. Research the companies that made that clothing, the laborers, and the working conditions under which it was made. Write a report that starts by describing the two pieces of clothing you selected. Then write up the process of your research effort, together with whatever useful information you gather at each step. End by explaining what your information tells you about what you should do when it comes time to replace those items.

WHAT WOULD THEY SAY?

7. Consider "The Silence of the Lambswool Cardigans" together with Kofi Annan's "Nobel Lecture" (p. 225). Explain what reaction you believe Annan would have to Solnit's essay.

8. Assume that Cornel West has read "Silence of the Lambswool Cardigans" and that Rebecca Solnit has read West's "The Moral Obligations of Living in a Democratic Society" (p. 123). Write a dialogue in the voices of West and Solnit. Begin with Solnit making a comment on West's essay. Make sure that your dialogue quotes often from both essays (the speakers can quote each other's essays and they can quote themselves). Make it clear in your dialogue how you think these two would find areas of agreement or disagreement.

WENDELL BERRY

Out of Your Car, Off Your Horse

*O*NE WAY TO MAKE A COMMUNITY SELF-SUFFICIENT, *environmentalist and essayist Wendell Berry (b. 1934) argues, is simply to drive a lot less. Written as a series of separate aphorisms or propositions, this essay summarizes the demand for concreteness, in living and writing, that is the basis of ethical thinking. The author of more than thirty books, Berry has lived on a small farm in Kentucky since 1965, where he writes poems, stories, novels, and essays arguing for the balanced way of life he maintains. His books include* Openings *(1968),* The Unsettling of America *(1977),* Home Economics *(1987), and* What Are People For? *(1990). "Out of Your Car, Off Your Horse" was first published in the* Atlantic *in 1991.*

I. Properly speaking, global thinking is not possible. Those who have "thought globally" (and among them the most successful have been imperial governments and multinational corporations) have done so by means of simplifications too extreme and oppressive to merit the name of thought. Global thinkers have been, and will be, dangerous people. National thinkers tend to be dangerous also; we now have national thinkers in the northeastern United States who look upon Kentucky as a garbage dump.

II. Global thinking can only be statistical. Its shallowness is exposed by the least intention to do something. Unless one is willing to be destructive on a very large scale, one cannot do something except locally, in a small place. Global thinking can only do to the globe what a space satellite does to it: reduce it, make a bauble of it. Look at one of those photographs of half the earth taken from outer space, and see if you recognize your neighborhood. If you want to *see* where you are, you will have to get out of your space vehicle, out of your car, off your horse, and walk over the ground. On foot you will find that the earth is still satisfyingly large, and full of beguiling nooks and crannies.

III. If we could think locally, we would do far better than we are doing now. The right local questions and answers will be the right global ones. The Amish question "What will this do to our community?" tends toward the right answer for the world.

IV. If we want to put local life in proper relation to the globe, we must do so by imagination, charity, and forbearance, and by making local life as independent and self-sufficient as we can—not by the presumptuous abstractions of "global thought."

V. If we want to keep our thoughts and acts from destroying the globe, 5
then we must see to it that we do not ask too much of the globe or of any
part of it. To make sure that we do not ask too much, we must learn to live
at home, as independently and self-sufficiently as we can. That is the only
way we can keep the land we are using, and its ecological limits, always in
sight.

VI. The only sustainable city—and this, to me, is the indispensable ideal and
goal—is a city in balance with its countryside: a city, that is, that would live
off the *net* ecological income of its supporting region, paying as it goes all its
ecological and human debts.

VII. The cities we now have are living off ecological principal, by economic
assumptions that seem certain to destroy them. They do not live at home. They
do not have their own supporting regions. They are out of balance with their
supports, wherever on the globe their supports are.

VIII. The balance between city and countryside is destroyed by industrial machinery, "cheap" productivity in field and forest, and "cheap" transportation.
Rome destroyed the balance with slave labor; we have destroyed it with
"cheap" fossil fuel.

IX. Since the Civil War, perhaps, and certainly since the Second World War,
the norms of productivity have been set by the fossil-fuel industries.

X. Geographically, the sources of the fossil fuels are rural. Technically, how- 10
ever, the production of these fuels is industrial and urban. The facts and integrities of local life, and the principle of community, are considered as little as
possible, for to consider them would not be quickly profitable. Fossil fuels have
always been produced at the expense of local ecosystems and of local human
communities. The fossil-fuel economy is the industrial economy par excellence,
and it assigns no value to local life, natural or human.

XI. When the industrial principles exemplified in fossil-fuel production are applied to field and forest, the results are identical: local life, both natural and
human, is destroyed.

XII. Industrial procedures have been imposed on the countryside pretty much
to the extent that country people have been seduced or forced into dependence on the money economy. By encouraging this dependence, corporations have increased their ability to rob the people of their property and their
labor. The result is that a very small number of people now own all the usable
property in the country, and workers are increasingly the hostages of their
employers.

XIII. Our present "leaders"—the people of wealth and power—do not know what it means to take a place seriously: to think it worthy, for its own sake, of love and study and careful work. They cannot take any place seriously because they must be ready at any moment, by the terms of power and wealth in the modern world, to destroy any place.

XIV. Ecological good sense will be opposed by all the most powerful economic entities of our time, because ecological good sense requires the reduction or replacement of those entities. If ecological good sense is to prevail, it can do so only through the work and the will of the people and of the local communities.

XV. For this task our currently prevailing assumptions about knowledge, in-   15
formation, education, money, and political will are inadequate. All our institutions with which I am familiar have adopted the organizational patterns and the quantitative measures of the industrial corporations. *Both* sides of the ecological debate, perhaps as a consequence, are alarmingly abstract.

XVI. But abstraction, of course, is what is wrong. The evil of the industrial economy (capitalist or communist) is the abstractness inherent in its procedures— its inability to distinguish one place or person or creature from another. William Blake saw this two hundred years ago. Anyone can see it now in almost any of our common tools and weapons.

XVII. Abstraction is the enemy *wherever* it is found. The abstractions of sustainability can ruin the world just as surely as the abstractions of industrial economics. Local life may be as much endangered by "saving the planet" as by "conquering the world." Such a project calls for abstract purposes and central powers that cannot know, and so will destroy, the integrity of local nature and local community.

XVIII. In order to make ecological good sense for the planet, you must make ecological good sense locally. You can't act locally by thinking globally. If you want to keep your local acts from destroying the globe, you must think locally.

XIX. No one can make ecological good sense for the planet. Everyone can make ecological good sense locally, *if* the affection, the scale, the knowledge, the tools, and the skills are right.

XX. The right scale in work gives power to affection. When one works be-   20
yond the reach of one's love for the place one is working in, and for the things and creatures one is working with and among, then destruction inevitably results. An adequate local culture, among other things, keeps work within the reach of love.

XXI. The question before us, then, is an extremely difficult one: how do we begin to remake, or to make, a local culture that will preserve our part of the world while we use it? We are talking here not just about a kind of knowledge that *involves* affection but also about a kind of knowledge that comes from or with affection — knowledge that is unavailable to the unaffectionate, and that is unavailable to anyone as what is called information.

XXII. What, for a start, might be the economic result of local affection? We don't know. Moreover, we are probably never going to know in any way that would satisfy the average dean or corporate executive. The ways of love tend to be secretive and, even to the lovers themselves, somewhat inscrutable.

XXIII. The real work of planet saving will be small, humble, and humbling, and (insofar as it involves love) pleasing and rewarding. Its jobs will be too many to count, too many to report, too many to be publicly noticed or rewarded, too small to make anyone rich or famous.

XXIV. The great obstacle may be not greed but the modern hankering after glamour. A lot of our smartest, most concerned people want to come up with a big solution to a big problem. I don't think that planet saving, if we take it seriously, can furnish employment to many such people.

XXV. When I think of the kind of worker the job requires, I think of Dorothy 25 Day° (if one can think of Dorothy Day herself, separate from the publicity that came as a result of her rarity), a person willing to go down and down into the daunting, humbling, almost hopeless local presence of the problem — to face the great problem one small life at a time.

XXVI. Some cities can never be sustainable, because they do not have a countryside around them, or near them, from which they can be sustained. New York City cannot be made sustainable, nor can Phoenix. Some cities in Kentucky or the Midwest, on the other hand, might reasonably hope to become sustainable.

XXVII. To make a sustainable city, one must begin somehow, and I think the beginning must be small and economic. A beginning could be made, for example, by increasing the amount of food bought from farmers in the local countryside by consumers in the city. As the food economy became more local, local farming would become more diverse; the farms would become smaller, more complex in structure, more productive; and some city people would be needed to work on the farms. Sooner or later, as a means of reducing expenses

------

Dorothy Day (1897–1980): Influential pacifist and founder of the Catholic Worker movement. [EDS.]

both ways, organic wastes from the city would go out to fertilize the farms of the supporting region; thus city people would have to assume an agricultural responsibility, and would be properly motivated to do so both by the wish to have a supply of excellent food and by the fear of contaminating that supply. The increase of economic intimacy between a city and its sources would change minds (assuming, of course, that the minds in question would stay put long enough to be changed). It would improve minds. The locality, by becoming partly sustainable, would produce the thought it would need to become more sustainable.

WHAT DOES HE SAY?

1. This isn't so much an essay as it is a series of numbered pronouncements. Pick two of them that you think you understand and turn each of them into open questions. That is, take what Berry asserts, and see if you can identify the questions he's answering.

2. Identify three of these numbered sections that seem to you to be closely related. Then write a paragraph briefly explaining those relations.

3. Which one of these sections really confuses you? Write three sentences explaining why.

WHAT DO YOU THINK?

4. "Out of Your Car, Off Your Horse" contains twenty-seven numbered sections. Rewrite, combine, and reduce duplication so that you end up with five sections that do their best to reflect the full range of the original twenty-seven.

5. Identify two related sections of Berry's essay, explain how they're related, and then open up the discussion by explaining to what extent—or not—those sections define their terms, account for complexities, and offer examples. End by explaining what you think of these two sections now that you have analyzed them more rigorously.

6. Pay attention especially to sections VI, VII, VIII, and XXVII. Apply the reasoning and the assertions you find in those sections to your city or town. Explain how your example challenges or supports what Berry asserts. (You may also use other sections.)

7. Critique the effectiveness or lack of effectiveness of "Out of Your Car, Off Your Horse." As you do so, make clear what you believe to be the purpose of the essay, as well as your criteria for judging it.

WHAT WOULD THEY SAY?

8. Explain how Rebecca Solnit's "The Silence of the Lambswool Cardigans" (p. 668) connects with one or more of the sections of "Out of Your Car, Off Your Horse."

Variation: Take this one step further by explaining how these two essays also connect with the Earth Charter (p. 158).

9. Read "Out of Your Car, Off Your Horse" together with Peter Singer's "The Singer Solution to World Poverty" (p. 661). Write an essay explaining how these selections agree or disagree. End by explaining what is clearer to you as a result of considering these two essays together.

10. Read "Out of Your Car, Off Your Horse" together with Joy Williams's "Save the Whales, Screw the Shrimp" (p. 146). Explain how these essays agree or disagree. End by explaining which one you think is more effective for you as a reader.

KATHLEEN DEAN MOORE
The World Depends on This

*A*FTER LEARNING *that her daughter has been jailed during a war protest, essayist Kathleen Dean Moore reflects on the relation between parents and children, public and private, violence and peace. Though a war protest can be seen as a futile act, in another sense, Moore concludes, on some important level, "the world depends" on these individual acts, these individual loves.*

A professor of philosophy at Oregon State University, Moore is director of the Spring Creek Project, which seeks to connect ideas, nature, and the written word. Her books include Riverwalking: Reflections on Moving Water *(1996),* Holdfast: At Home in the Natural World *(1999), and* The Pine Island Paradox *(2004). "The World Depends on This" first appeared in* Portland *magazine in 2003.*

The message machine was blinking when I got home from work: "First, I want you to know that your daughter is going to be fine." I braced myself for whatever would come next. "She was arrested during the antiwar demonstrations. They're holding her in the San Francisco County Jail."

Frank and I had been watching world news all day. Now suddenly, this wasn't about world news. It was about our daughter and a parent's fears. What will she eat? How can she sleep? Do the handcuffs cut her wrists?

The night before, I had been dreaming about Erin. She was one of the young people in an outdoor clothing catalog, striding out in autumn colors, her hair as bright as apricots. Wearing a skirt the color of pumpkins, she had leaned against the other young people, laughing. But she wasn't in some dreamy, sun-saturated place now; she was sitting in a small cube of light in a darkened jail.

I tried to picture a jail at night. Do the other inmates sleep splay-legged and heavy on their backs? Do they curl up as if they were babies? And our daughter?—surely she's sitting awake on a bench with her knees to her chest and her arms wrapped around them. She will be cold, in that dark place.

Babies startle if they are not wrapped tightly. We learned this in a child-care class before she was born. Their bodies twitch and their arms flail as they sleep, and if nothing is holding them, they are afraid. So you have to wrap a newborn baby. We held our daughter close and wrapped her in blankets, tight as corn in the husk.

We loved her so much and raised her so carefully, and isn't this what all parents do if they can? Piano lessons, art lessons, a hundred-dollar safety seat for the car. When she learned to drive, we tried to keep track of where she went and when she would be home. It never occurred to us that she would go to jail.

So here is the first thing she said when she called collect from the holding cell: "What can I say to keep you from worrying?"

To keep a parent from worrying?

Tell us you're home in bed, I cried, but Frank took the phone from my hand. She told him she was in a holding cell with dozens of other women. They are strong, amazing women, many of them mothers and grandmothers, many elegantly dressed in black, she said, and Frank thought that Erin's own voice was strong and amazing, more certain than he had ever heard.

To pass the time, the women are teaching each other to dance, she said. 10 They are placing calls to news agencies, but they can't get through. Bombs are falling, newspapers aren't answering their phones, injustice and environmental destruction tangle in nets of violence and profit around the world—and all these beautiful women are in jail.

The police released Erin at 2:30 AM. A friend came into the city to drive her home.

Don't all parents want the world for their children? *Fellow parents, tell me, wouldn't we do anything for them?* To give them big houses, we will cut ancient forests. To give them perfect fruit, we will poison their food with pesticides. To give them the latest technologies, we will reduce entire valleys to toxic dumps. To give them the best education, we will invest in companies that profit from death. To keep them safe, we will deny them the right to privacy, to travel unimpeded, to peacefully assemble. And to give them peace, we will kill other peoples' children or send them to be killed, and amass enough weapons to kill the children again, kill them twenty times if necessary.

We would do anything for our children but the one big thing: stop and ask ourselves, what are we doing and allowing to be done? I looked again at the shopping list where Frank scribbled notes as he talked on the phone: *Toilet paper / Bourbon / Flowers / County Jail / War protest / Inmate / Dave 415-516-6372.* How everyday and ordinary are our disastrous decisions. Frank and I go busily about, buying this or that, voting or not, burning up gasoline or jet fuel or split pine—on a small scale, in the short term, making things work for our children—forgetting that whatever is left of the world is the place where they will have to live.

What will our grandchildren say? I think I can guess:

> *How could you not have known? What more evidence did you need that your lives, your comfortable lives, would do so much damage to ours?*
>
> *Did you think you could wage war against nations without waging war against people and against the earth? Didn't you wonder what we would drink, once you had poisoned the aquifers? Didn't you wonder what we would breathe, once you poisoned the air? Did you stop to ask how we would be safe, in a world poisoned by war?*
>
> *Did you think it all belonged to you—this beautiful earth?*
>
> *You, who loved your children, did you think we could live without clean air and healthy cities? You, who loved the earth, did you think we could live without birdsong and swaying trees?*

And if you knew, how could you not care? What could matter more to you than your children, and their babies? How could a parent destroy what is life-giving and astonishing in her child's world?

And if you knew, and you cared, how could you not act? What excuses did you make?

And now, what would you have us do?

Two days after she got out of jail, we walked with Erin beside the ocean. 15 Under a steep headland, we came across a jumbled heap of fishing nets, string, nylon cord, and bullwhip kelp, intricately tangled. Buoys were smashed and buried beyond hope.

"This is what the world is," she said. She tugged at a rope in the nets gone to tangled ruin, drifted with sand.

"Yes. But you don't have to go to jail to say so. There are other ways," I said softly, knowing I should be still.

She answered as softly. "Then you need to show me those ways," she said. "Don't tell me. Show me."

Dear god. I don't know what to do: what to hope and what to fear, what to invest in and what to give up, what to insist on and what to refuse, how to go on with living in a time of death. All I know is how to hold my daughter, wrapping my arms tight around her shoulders. Right now, the world depends on this.

WHAT DOES SHE SAY?

1. Read the first paragraph and stop. What do you think Kathleen Dean Moore will say in the rest of this essay? What do you think the essay will be about? Are you sympathetic to Moore at this point, or are you resisting?

2. Read to the end of the opening scene, to the short paragraph that begins, "The police released Erin at 2:30 AM." Stop. Now what do you think Moore is up to in this essay? What is the theme of the essay? war? being a parent? Has the essay surprised you up to this point? Has your sympathy for the narrator changed or remained the same? Predict what will happen next.

3. Read to the end of the essay, and write a short paragraph telling the story of your response, in chronological order: what you first thought, what you thought next, and what you thought at the very end. Did the essay surprise you? Did it go where you thought it would? What is your reaction to the ending? Did you respond differently at different points? What, finally, is the real theme of the essay?

WHAT DO YOU THINK?

4. The letter that Moore imagines her grandchildren writing consists of nothing but questions. Write an essay answering at least three of these questions. Write it in the form of a letter addressed to your grandchildren.

5. Write a letter to your grandparents. Ask nothing but questions.

6. *"Fellow parents, tell me, wouldn't we do anything for them?"* What does Moore mean by this question? Note the series of parallel statements that follow it. What is Moore's point here? How does it relate to the point of the whole essay?

7. What, according to Moore, does the world depend on? Why?

WHAT WOULD THEY SAY?

8. Say that Moore has read Dan Baum's "The Casualty" (p. 232). What would she say? Say that Moore's daughter, Erin, and the young soldier that Baum profiles in "The Casualty" get together for coffee after reading each other's essay. What do they say to each other?

9. How would Moore respond to Garrett Hardin's "Lifeboat Ethics: The Case against Helping the Poor" (p. 130)? What, for example, would Moore do if her daughter, Erin, was in an overcrowded lifeboat about to sink?

10. Consider "The World Depends on This" together with Kofi Annan's "Nobel Lecture" (p. 225). How does reading one help you read the other—and vice versa? Write an essay that discusses the relationships you see between these two essays, and end by explaining what is clearer to you as a result. Variation: Add the Earth Charter (p. 158) to this discussion.

MARTIN LUTHER KING JR.

Letter from Birmingham Jail

*I*N THIS FAMOUS LETTER, *Martin Luther King Jr. (1929–1968) argues that one cannot stand by, ignoring injustice, as injustice in any community affects all communities, and those who are oppressed must take back their freedom. King was a Baptist minister when he achieved fame for his policy of nonviolent resistance as he actively tried to end segregation. In 1964, he received the Nobel Peace Prize. He was assassinated four years later, while supporting striking workers in Memphis. "Letter from Birmingham Jail" is a response to a letter published in a newspaper by eight local clergymen; King wrote it after being arrested for participating in a march for which no permit had been issued.*

April 16, 1963

My Dear Fellow Clergymen:

While confined here in the Birmingham city jail, I came across your recent statement calling my present activities "unwise and untimely." Seldom do I pause to answer criticism of my work and ideas. If I sought to answer all the criticisms that cross my desk, my secretaries would have little time for anything other than such correspondence in the course of the day, and I would have no time for constructive work. But since I feel that you are men of genuine good will and that your criticisms are sincerely set forth, I want to try to answer your statement in what I hope will be patient and reasonable terms.

I think I should indicate why I am here in Birmingham, since you have been influenced by the view which argues against "outsiders coming in." I have the honor of serving as president of the Southern Christian Leadership Conference, an organization operating in every southern state, with headquarters in Atlanta, Georgia. We have some eighty-five affiliated organizations across the South, and one of them is the Alabama Christian Movement for Human Rights. Frequently we share staff, educational and financial resources with our

AUTHOR'S NOTE: This response to a published statement by eight fellow clergymen from Alabama (Bishop C. C. J. Carpenter, Bishop Joseph A. Durick, Rabbi Hilton L. Grafman, Bishop Paul Hardin, Bishop Holan B. Harmon, the Reverend George M. Murray, the Reverend Edward V. Ramage, and the Reverend Earl Stallings) was composed under somewhat constricting circumstances. Begun on the margins of the newspaper in which the statement appeared while I was in jail, the letter was continued on scraps of writing paper supplied by a friendly Negro trusty, and concluded on a pad my attorneys were eventually permitted to leave me. Although the text remains in substance unaltered, I have indulged in the author's prerogative of polishing it for publication.

affiliates. Several months ago the affiliate here in Birmingham asked us to be on call to engage in a nonviolent direct-action program if such were deemed necessary. We readily consented, and when the hour came we lived up to our promise. So I, along with several members of my staff, am here because I was invited here. I am here because I have organizational ties here.

But more basically, I am in Birmingham because injustice is here. Just as the prophets of the eighth century B.C. left their villages and carried their "thus saith the Lord" far beyond the boundaries of their home towns, and just as the Apostle Paul left his village of Tarsus and carried the gospel of Jesus Christ to the far corners of the Greco-Roman world, so am I compelled to carry the gospel of freedom beyond my own home town. Like Paul, I must constantly respond to the Macedonian call for aid.

Moreover, I am cognizant of the interrelatedness of all communities and states. I cannot sit idly by in Atlanta and not be concerned about what happens in Birmingham. Injustice anywhere is a threat to justice everywhere. We are caught in an inescapable network of mutuality, tied in a single garment of destiny. Whatever affects one directly, affects all indirectly. Never again can we afford to live with the narrow, provincial "outside agitator" idea. Anyone who lives inside the United States can never be considered an outsider anywhere within its bounds.

You deplore the demonstrations taking place in Birmingham. But your statement, I am sorry to say, fails to express a similar concern for the conditions that brought about the demonstrations. I am sure that none of you would want to rest content with the superficial kind of social analysis that deals merely with effects and does not grapple with underlying causes. It is unfortunate that demonstrations are taking place in Birmingham, but it is even more unfortunate that the city's white power structure left the Negro community with no alternative.

In any nonviolent campaign there are four basic steps: collection of the facts to determine whether injustices exist; negotiation; self-purification; and direct action. We have gone through all these steps in Birmingham. There can be no gainsaying the fact that racial injustice engulfs this community. Birmingham is probably the most thoroughly segregated city in the United States. Its ugly record of brutality is widely known. Negroes have experienced grossly unjust treatment in the courts. There have been more unsolved bombings of Negro homes and churches in Birmingham than in any other city in the nation. These are the hard brutal facts of the case. On the basis of these conditions, Negro leaders sought to negotiate with the city fathers. But the latter consistently refused to engage in good-faith negotiation.

Then, last September, came the opportunity to talk with leaders of Birmingham's economic community. In the course of the negotiations, certain promises were made by the merchants—for example, to remove the stores' humiliating racial signs. On the basis of these promises, the Reverend Fred Shuttlesworth and the leaders of the Alabama Christian Movement for Human

Rights agreed to a moratorium on all demonstrations. As the weeks and months went by, we realized that we were the victims of a broken promise. A few signs, briefly removed, returned; the others remained.

As in so many past experiences, our hopes had been blasted, and the shadow of deep disappointment settled upon us. We had no alternative except to prepare for direct action, whereby we would present our very bodies as a means of laying our case before the conscience of the local and the national community. Mindful of the difficulties involved, we decided to undertake a process of self-purification. We began a series of workshops on nonviolence, and we repeatedly asked ourselves: "Are you able to accept blows without retaliating?" "Are you able to endure the ordeal of jail?" We decided to schedule our direct-action program for the Easter season, realizing that except for Christmas, this is the main shopping period of the year. Knowing that a strong economic-withdrawal program would be the by-product of direct action, we felt that this would be the best time to bring pressure to bear on the merchants for the needed change.

Then it occurred to us that Birmingham's mayoralty election was coming up in March, and we speedily decided to postpone action until after election day. When we discovered that the commissioner of public safety, Eugene "Bull" Connor, had piled up enough votes to be in the run-off, we decided again to postpone action until the day after the run-off so that the demonstrations could not be used to cloud the issues. Like many others, we waited to see Mr. Connor defeated, and to this end we endured postponement after postponement. Having aided in this community need, we felt that our direct-action program could be delayed no longer.

You may well ask: "Why direct action? Why sit-ins, marches, and so   10
forth? Isn't negotiation a better path?" You are quite right in calling for negotiation. Indeed, this is the very purpose of direct action. Nonviolent direct action seeks to create such a crisis and foster such a tension that a community which has constantly refused to negotiate is forced to confront the issue. It seeks so to dramatize the issue that it can no longer be ignored. My citing the creation of tension as part of the work of the nonviolent-resister may sound rather shocking. But I must confess that I am not afraid of the word "tension." I have earnestly opposed violent tension, but there is a type of constructive nonviolent tension which is necessary for growth. Just as Socrates felt that it was necessary to create a tension in the mind so that individuals could rise from the bondage of myths and half-truths to the unfettered realm of creative analysis and objective appraisal, so must we see the need for nonviolent gadflies to create the kind of tension in society that will help men rise from the dark depths of prejudice and racism to the majestic heights of understanding and brotherhood.

The purpose of our direct-action program is to create a situation so crisis-packed that it will inevitably open the door to negotiation. I therefore concur with you in your call for negotiation. Too long has our beloved Southland been bogged down in a tragic effort to live in monologue rather than dialogue.

One of the basic points in your statement is that the action that I and my associates have taken in Birmingham is untimely. Some have asked: "Why didn't you give the new city administration time to act?" The only answer that I can give to this query is that the new Birmingham administration must be prodded about as much as the outgoing one, before it will act. We are sadly mistaken if we feel that the election of Albert Boutwell as mayor will bring the millennium to Birmingham. While Mr. Boutwell is a much more gentle person than Mr. Connor, they are both segregationists, dedicated to maintenance of the status quo. I have hope that Mr. Boutwell will be reasonable enough to see the futility of massive resistance to desegregation. But he will not see this without pressure from devotees of civil rights. My friends, I must say to you that we have not made a single gain in civil rights without determined legal and nonviolent pressure. Lamentably, it is an historical fact that privileged groups seldom give up their privileges voluntarily. Individuals may see the moral light and voluntarily give up their unjust posture; but, as Reinhold Niebuhr° has reminded us, groups tend to be more immoral than individuals.

We know through painful experience that freedom is never voluntarily given by the oppressor; it must be demanded by the oppressed. Frankly, I have yet to engage in a direct-action campaign that was "well timed" in the view of those who have not suffered unduly from the disease of segregation. For years now I have heard the word "Wait!" It rings in the ear of every Negro with piercing familiarity. This "Wait" has almost always meant "Never." We must come to see, with one of our distinguished jurists, that "justice too long delayed is justice denied."

We have waited for more than 340 years for our constitutional and Godgiven rights. The nations of Asia and Africa are moving with jetlike speed toward gaining political independence, but we still creep at horse-and-buggy pace toward gaining a cup of coffee at a lunch counter. Perhaps it is easy for those who have never felt the stinging darts of segregation to say, "Wait." But when you have seen vicious mobs lynch your mothers and fathers at will and drown your sisters and brothers at whim; when you have seen hate-filled policemen curse, kick, and even kill your black brothers and sisters; when you see the vast majority of your twenty million Negro brothers smothering in an airtight cage of poverty in the midst of an affluent society; when you suddenly find your tongue twisted and your speech stammering as you seek to explain to your six-year-old daughter why she can't go to the public amusement park that has just been advertised on television, and see tears welling up in her eyes when she is told that Funtown is closed to colored children, and see ominous clouds of inferiority beginning to form in her little mental sky, and see her beginning to distort her personality by developing an unconscious bitterness toward white people; when you have to concoct an answer for a five-year-old

---

Reinhold Niebuhr (1892–1971): Theologian and professor of Christian social ethics. [EDS.]

son who is asking: "Daddy, why do white people treat colored people so mean?"; when you take a cross-country drive and find it necessary to sleep night after night in the uncomfortable corners of your automobile because no motel will accept you; when you are humiliated day in and day out by nagging signs reading "white" and "colored"; when your first name becomes "nigger," your middle name becomes "boy" (however old you are) and your last name becomes "John," and your wife and mother are never given the respected title "Mrs."; when you are harried by day and haunted by night by the fact that you are a Negro, living constantly at tiptoe stance, never quite knowing what to expect next, and are plagued with inner fears and outer resentments; when you are forever fighting a degenerating sense of "nobodiness"—then you will understand why we find it difficult to wait. There comes a time when the cup of endurance runs over, and men are no longer willing to be plunged into the abyss of despair. I hope, sirs, you can understand our legitimate and unavoidable impatience.

You express a great deal of anxiety over our willingness to break laws. 15 This is certainly a legitimate concern. Since we so diligently urge people to obey the Supreme Court's decision of 1954 outlawing segregation in the public schools, at first glance it may seem rather paradoxical for us consciously to break laws. One may well ask: "How can you advocate breaking some laws and obeying others?" The answer lies in the fact that there are two types of laws: just and unjust. I would be the first to advocate obeying just laws. One has not only a legal but a moral responsibility to obey just laws. Conversely, one has a moral responsibility to disobey unjust laws. I would agree with St. Augustine that "an unjust law is no law at all."

Now, what is the difference between the two? How does one determine whether a law is just or unjust? A just law is a man-made code that squares with the moral law or the law of God. An unjust law is a code that is out of harmony with the moral law. To put it in the terms of St. Thomas Aquinas: an unjust law is a human law that is not rooted in eternal law and natural law. Any law that uplifts human personality is just. Any law that degrades human personality is unjust. All segregation statutes are unjust because segregation distorts the soul and damages the personality. It gives the segregator a false sense of superiority and the segregated a false sense of inferiority. Segregation, to use the terminology of the Jewish philosopher Martin Buber, substitutes an "I-it" relationship for an "I-thou" relationship and ends up relegating persons to the status of things. Hence segregation is not only politically, economically, and sociologically unsound, it is morally wrong and sinful. Paul Tillich has said that sin is separation. Is not segregation an existential expression of man's tragic separation, his awful estrangement, his terrible sinfulness? Thus it is that I can urge men to obey the 1954 decision of the Supreme Court, for it is morally right; and I can urge them to disobey segregation ordinances, for they are morally wrong.

Let us consider a more concrete example of just and unjust laws. An unjust law is a code that a numerical or power majority group compels a minority group to obey but does not make binding on itself. This is *difference* made legal. By the same token, a just law is a code that a majority compels a minority to follow and that it is willing to follow itself. This is *sameness* made legal.

Let me give another explanation. A law is unjust if it is inflicted on a minority that, as a result of being denied the right to vote, had no part in enacting or devising the law. Who can say that the legislature of Alabama which set up that state's segregation laws was democratically elected? Throughout Alabama all sorts of devious methods are used to prevent Negroes from becoming registered voters, and there are some counties in which even though Negroes constitute a majority of the population, not a single Negro is registered. Can any law enacted under such circumstances be considered democratically structured?

Sometimes a law is just on its face and unjust in its application. For instance, I have been arrested on a charge of parading without a permit. Now, there is nothing wrong in having an ordinance which requires a permit for a parade. But such an ordinance becomes unjust when it is used to maintain segregation and to deny citizens the First-Amendment privilege of peaceful assembly and protest.

I hope you are able to see the distinction I am trying to point out. In no   20 sense do I advocate evading or defying the law, as would the rabid segregationist. That would lead to anarchy. One who breaks an unjust law must do so openly, lovingly, and with a willingness to accept the penalty. I submit that an individual who breaks a law that conscience tells him is unjust, and who willingly accepts the penalty of imprisonment in order to arouse the conscience of the community over its injustice, is in reality expressing the highest respect for law.

Of course, there is nothing new about this kind of civil disobedience. It was evidenced sublimely in the refusal of Shadrach, Meshach, and Abednego to obey the laws of Nebuchadnezzar, on the ground that a higher moral law was at stake. It was practiced superbly by the early Christians, who were willing to face hungry lions and the excruciating pain of chopping blocks rather than submit to certain unjust laws of the Roman Empire. To a degree, academic freedom is a reality today because Socrates practiced civil disobedience. In our own nation, the Boston Tea Party represented a massive act of civil disobedience.

We should never forget that everything Adolf Hitler did in Germany was "legal" and everything the Hungarian freedom fighters did in Hungary was "illegal." It was "illegal" to aid and comfort a Jew in Hitler's Germany. Even so, I am sure that, had I lived in Germany at the time, I would have aided and comforted my Jewish brothers. If today I lived in a Communist country where certain principles dear to the Christian faith are suppressed, I would openly advocate disobeying that country's anti-religious laws.

I must make two honest confessions to you, my Christian and Jewish brothers. First, I must confess that over the past few years I have been gravely disappointed with the white moderate. I have almost reached the regrettable conclusion that the Negro's great stumbling block in his stride toward freedom is not the White Citizen's Counciler or the Ku Klux Klanner, but the white moderate, who is more devoted to "order" than to justice; who prefers a negative peace which is the absence of tension to a positive peace which is the presence of justice; who constantly says: "I agree with you in the goal you seek, but I cannot agree with your methods of direct action"; who paternalistically believes he can set the timetable for another man's freedom; who lives by a mythical concept of time and who constantly advises the Negro to wait for a "more convenient season." Shallow understanding from people of good will is more frustrating than absolute misunderstanding from people of ill will. Lukewarm acceptance is much more bewildering than outright rejection.

I had hoped that the white moderate would understand that law and order exist for the purpose of establishing justice and that when they fail in this purpose they become the dangerously structured dams that block the flow of social progress. I had hoped that the white moderate would understand that the present tension in the South is a necessary phase of the transition from an obnoxious negative peace, in which the Negro passively accepted his unjust plight, to a substantive and positive peace, in which all men will respect the dignity and worth of human personality. Actually, we who engage in nonviolent direct action are not the creators of tension. We merely bring to the surface the hidden tension that is already alive. We bring it out in the open, where it can be seen and dealt with. Like a boil that can never be cured so long as it is covered up but must be opened with all its ugliness to the natural medicines of air and light, injustice must be exposed, with all the tension its exposure creates, to the light of human conscience and the air of national opinion before it can be cured.

In your statement you assert that our actions, even though peaceful, 25 must be condemned because they precipitate violence. But is this a logical assertion? Isn't this like condemning a robbed man because his possession of money precipitated the evil act of robbery? Isn't this like condemning Socrates because his unswerving commitment to truth and his philosophical inquiries precipitated the act by the misguided populace in which they made him drink hemlock? Isn't this like condemning Jesus because his unique God-consciousness and never-ceasing devotion to God's will precipitated the evil act of crucifixion? We must come to see that, as the federal courts have consistently affirmed, it is wrong to urge an individual to cease his efforts to gain his basic constitutional rights because the quest may precipitate violence. Society must protect the robbed and punish the robber.

I had also hoped that the white moderate would reject the myth concerning time in relation to the struggle for freedom. I have just received a letter from a white brother in Texas. He writes: "All Christians know that the colored people will receive equal rights eventually, but it is possible that you are in too great a religious hurry. It has taken Christianity almost two thousand years to accomplish what it has. The teachings of Christ take time to come to earth." Such an attitude stems from a tragic misconception of time, from the strangely irrational notion that there is something in the very flow of time that will inevitably cure all ills. Actually, time itself is neutral; it can be used either destructively or constructively. More and more I feel that the people of ill will have used time much more effectively than have the people of good will. We will have to repent in this generation not merely for the hateful words and actions of the bad people but for the appalling silence of the good people. Human progress never rolls in on wheels of inevitability; it comes through the tireless efforts of men willing to be coworkers with God, and without this hard work, time itself becomes an ally of the forces of social stagnation. We must use time creatively, in the knowledge that the time is always ripe to do right. Now is the time to make real the promise of democracy and transform our pending national elegy into a creative psalm of brotherhood. Now is the time to lift our national policy from the quicksand of racial injustice to the solid rock of human dignity.

You speak of our activity in Birmingham as extreme. At first I was rather disappointed that fellow clergymen would see my nonviolent efforts as those of an extremist. I began thinking about the fact that I stand in the middle of two opposing forces in the Negro community. One is a force of complacency, made up in part of Negroes who, as a result of long years of oppression, are so drained of self-respect and a sense of "somebodiness" that they have adjusted to segregation; and in part of a few middle-class Negroes who, because of a degree of academic and economic security and because in some ways they profit by segregation, have become insensitive to the problems of the masses. The other force is one of bitterness and hatred, and it comes perilously close to advocating violence. It is expressed in the various black nationalist groups that are springing up across the nation, the largest and best-known being Elijah Muhammad's Muslim movement. Nourished by the Negro's frustration over the continued existence of racial discrimination, this movement is made up of people who have lost faith in America, who have absolutely repudiated Christianity, and who have concluded that the white man is an incorrigible "devil."

I have tried to stand between these two forces, saying that we need emulate neither the "do-nothingism" of the complacent nor the hatred and despair of the black nationalist. For there is the more excellent way of love and nonviolent protest. I am grateful to God that, through the influence of the Negro church, the way of nonviolence became an integral part of our struggle.

If this philosophy had not emerged, by now many streets of the South would, I am convinced, be flowing with blood. And I am further convinced that if our white brothers dismiss as "rabble-rousers" and "outside agitators" those of us who employ nonviolent direct action, and if they refuse to support our non-violent efforts, millions of Negroes will, out of frustration and despair, seek solace and security in black-nationalist ideologies—a development that would inevitably lead to a frightening racial nightmare.

Oppressed people cannot remain oppressed forever. The yearning for 30 freedom eventually manifests itself, and that is what has happened to the

American Negro. Something within has reminded him of his birthright of freedom, and something without has reminded him that it can be gained. Consciously or unconsciously, he has been caught up by the *Zeitgeist*, and with his black brothers of Africa and his brown and yellow brothers of Asia, South America, and the Caribbean, the United States Negro is moving with a sense of great urgency toward the promised land of racial justice. If one recognizes this vital urge that has engulfed the Negro community, one should readily understand why public demonstrations are taking place. The Negro has many pent-up resentments and latent frustrations, and he must release them. So let him march; let him make prayer pilgrimages to the city hall; let him go on freedom rides—and try to understand why he must do so. If his repressed emotions are not released in nonviolent ways, they will seek expression through violence; this is not a threat but a fact of history. So I have not said to my people: "Get rid of your discontent." Rather, I have tried to say that this normal and healthy discontent can be channeled into the creative outlet of nonviolent direct action. And now this approach is being termed extremist.

But though I was initially disappointed at being categorized as an extremist, as I continued to think about the matter I gradually gained a measure of satisfaction from the label. Was not Jesus an extremist for love: "Love your enemies, bless them that curse you, do good to them that hate you, and pray for them which despitefully use you, and persecute you." Was not Amos an extremist for justice: "Let justice roll down like waters and righteousness like an ever-flowing stream." Was not Paul an extremist for the Christian gospel: "I bear in my body the marks of the Lord Jesus." Was not Martin Luther an extremist: "Here I stand; I cannot do otherwise, so help me God." And John Bunyan: "I will stay in jail to the end of my days before I make a butchery of my conscience." And Abraham Lincoln: "This nation cannot survive half slave and half free." And Thomas Jefferson: "We hold these truths to be self-evident, that all men are created equal. . . ." So the question is not whether we will be extremists, but what kind of extremists we will be. Will we be extremists for hate or for love? Will we be extremists for the preservation of injustice or for the extension of justice? In that dramatic scene on Calvary's hill three men were crucified. We must never forget that all three were crucified for the same crime—the crime of extremism. Two were extremists for immorality, and thus fell below their environment. The other, Jesus Christ, was an extremist for love, truth, and goodness, and thereby rose above his environment. Perhaps the South, the nation, and the world are in dire need of creative extremists.

I had hoped that the white moderate would see this need. Perhaps I was too optimistic; perhaps I expected too much. I suppose I should have realized that few members of the oppressor race can understand the deep groans and passionate yearnings of the oppressed race, and still fewer have the vision to see that injustice must be rooted out by strong, persistent and determined action. I am thankful, however, that some of our white brothers in the South have grasped the meaning of this social revolution and committed themselves to it. They are still all too few in quantity, but they are big in quality. Some — such as Ralph McGill, Lillian Smith, Harry Golden, James McBride Dabbs, Ann Braden, and Sarah Patton Boyle — have written about our struggle in eloquent and prophetic terms. Others have marched with us down nameless streets of the South. They have languished in filthy, roach-infested jails, suffering the abuse and brutality of policemen who view them as "dirty nigger-lovers." Unlike so many of their moderate brothers and sisters, they have recognized the urgency of the moment and sensed the need for powerful "action" antidotes to combat the disease of segregation.

Let me take note of my other major disappointment. I have been so greatly disappointed with the white church and its leadership. Of course, there are some notable exceptions. I am not unmindful of the fact that each of you has taken some significant stands on this issue. I commend you, Reverend Stallings, for your Christian stand on this past Sunday, in welcoming Negroes to your worship service on a nonsegregated basis. I commend the Catholic leaders of this state for integrating Spring Hill College several years ago.

But despite these notable exceptions, I must honestly reiterate that I have been disappointed with the church. I do not say this as one of those negative critics who can always find something wrong with the church. I say this as a minister of the gospel, who loves the church; who was nurtured in its bosom; who has been sustained by its spiritual blessings and who will remain true to it as long as the cord of life shall lengthen.

When I was suddenly catapulted into the leadership of the bus protest in 35 Montgomery, Alabama, a few years ago, I felt we would be supported by the white church. I felt that the white ministers, priests, and rabbis of the South would be among our strongest allies. Instead, some have been outright opponents, refusing to understand the freedom movement and misrepresenting its leaders; all too many others have been more cautious than courageous and have remained silent behind the anesthetizing security of stained-glass windows.

In spite of my shattered dreams, I came to Birmingham with the hope that the white religious leadership of this community would see the justice of our cause and, with deep moral concern, would serve as the channel through which our just grievances could reach the power structure. I had hoped that each of you would understand. But again I have been disappointed.

I have heard numerous southern religious leaders admonish their worshipers to comply with a desegregation decision because it is the law, but I have longed to hear white ministers declare: "Follow this decree because integration is morally right and because the Negro is your brother." In the midst of blatant injustices inflicted upon the Negro, I have watched white churchmen stand on the sideline and mouth pious irrelevancies and sanctimonious trivialities. In the midst of a mighty struggle to rid our nation of racial and economic injustice, I have heard many ministers say: "Those are social issues, with which the gospel has no real concern." And I have watched many churches commit themselves to a completely other-worldly religion which makes a strange, unbiblical distinction between body and soul, between the sacred and the secular.

I have traveled the length and breadth of Alabama, Mississippi, and all the other southern states. On sweltering summer days and crisp autumn mornings I have looked at the South's beautiful churches with their lofty spires pointing heavenward. I have beheld the impressive outlines of her massive religious-education buildings. Over and over I have found myself asking: "What kind of people worship here? Who is their God? Where were their voices when the lips of Governor Barnett dripped with words of interposition and nullification? Where were they when Governor Wallace gave a clarion call for defiance and hatred? Where were their voices of support when bruised and weary Negro men and women decided to rise from the dark dungeons of complacency to the bright hills of creative protest?"

Yes, these questions are still in my mind. In deep disappointment I have wept over the laxity of the church. But be assured that my tears have been tears of love. There can be no deep disappointment where there is not deep love. Yes, I love the church. How could I do otherwise? I am in the rather unique position of being the son, the grandson, and the great-grandson of preachers. Yes, I see the church as the body of Christ. But, oh! How we have blemished and scarred that body through social neglect and through fear of being nonconformists.

There was a time when the church was very powerful—in the time 40 when the early Christians rejoiced at being deemed worthy to suffer for what they believed. In those days the church was not merely a thermometer that recorded the ideas and principles of popular opinion; it was a thermostat that transformed the mores of society. Whenever the early Christians entered a town, the people in power became disturbed and immediately sought to convict the Christians for being "disturbers of the peace" and "outside agitators." But the Christians pressed on, in the conviction that they were "a colony of heaven," called to obey God rather than man. Small in number, they were big in commitment. They were too God-intoxicated to be "astronomically intimidated." By their effort and example they brought an end to such ancient evils as infanticide and gladiatorial contests.

Things are different now. So often the contemporary church is a weak, ineffectual voice with an uncertain sound. So often it is an archdefender of the status quo. Far from being disturbed by the presence of the church, the power structure of the average community is consoled by the church's silent—and often even vocal—sanction of things as they are.

But the judgment of God is upon the church as never before. If today's church does not recapture the sacrificial spirit of the early church, it will lose its authenticity, forfeit the loyalty of millions, and be dismissed as an irrelevant social club with no meaning for the twentieth century. Every day I meet young people whose disappointment with the church has turned into outright disgust.

Perhaps I have once again been too optimistic. Is organized religion too inextricably bound to the status quo to save our nation and the world? Perhaps I must turn my faith to the inner spiritual church, the church within the church, as the true *ekklesia*° and the hope of the world. But again I am thankful to God that some noble souls from the ranks of organized religion have broken loose from the paralyzing chains of conformity and joined us as active partners in the struggle for freedom. They have left their secure congregations and walked the streets of Albany, Georgia, with us. They have gone down the highways of the South on tortuous rides for freedom. Yes, they have gone to jail with us. Some have been dismissed from their churches, have lost the support of their bishops and fellow ministers. But they have acted in the faith that right defeated is stronger than evil triumphant. Their witness has been the spiritual salt that has preserved the true meaning of the gospel in these troubled times. They have carved a tunnel of hope through the dark mountain of disappointment.

I hope the church as a whole will meet the challenge of this decisive hour. But even if the church does not come to the aid of justice, I have no despair about the future. I have no fear about the outcome of our struggle in Birmingham, even if our motives are at present misunderstood. We will reach the goal of freedom in Birmingham and all over the nation, because the goal of America is freedom. Abused and scorned though we may be, our destiny is tied up with America's destiny. Before the pilgrims landed at Plymouth, we were here. Before the pen of Jefferson etched the majestic words of the Declaration of Independence across the pages of history, we were here. For more than two centuries our forebears labored in this country without wages; they made cotton king; they built the homes of their masters while suffering gross injustice and shameful humiliation—and yet out of a bottomless vitality they continued to thrive and develop. If the inexpressible cruelties of slavery could not stop us, the opposition we now face will surely fail. We will win our freedom because the sacred heritage of our nation and the eternal will of God are embodied in our echoing demands.

Before closing I feel impelled to mention one other point in your statement that has troubled me profoundly. You warmly commended the Birmingham police force for keeping "order" and "preventing violence." I doubt that you would have so warmly commended the police force if you had seen its dogs sinking their teeth into unarmed, nonviolent Negroes. I doubt that you would so quickly commend the policemen if you were to observe their ugly and inhumane treatment of Negroes here in the city jail; if you were to watch them push and curse old Negro women and young Negro girls; if you were to see them slap and kick old Negro men and young boys; if 45

---

ekklesia: The citizens' legislative body in ancient Athens; often used as a theological term (as here), as a synonym for "church." [EDS.]

you were to observe them as they did on two occasions, refuse to give us food because we wanted to sing our grace together. I cannot join you in your praise of the Birmingham police department.

It is true that the police have exercised a degree of discipline in handling the demonstrators. In this sense they have conducted themselves rather "non-violently" in public. But for what purpose? To preserve the evil system of segregation. Over the past few years I have consistently preached that nonviolence demands that the means we use must be as pure as the ends we seek. I have tried to make clear that it is wrong to use immoral means to attain moral ends. But now I must affirm that it is just as wrong, or perhaps even more so, to use moral means to preserve immoral ends. Perhaps Mr. Connor and his policemen have been rather nonviolent in public, as was Chief Pritchett in Albany, Georgia, but they have used the moral means of nonviolence to maintain the immoral end of racial injustice. As T. S. Eliot has said: "The last temptation is the greatest treason: to do the right deed for the wrong reason."

I wish you had commended the Negro sit-inners and demonstrators of Birmingham for their sublime courage, their willingness to suffer, and their amazing discipline in the midst of great provocation. One day the South will recognize its real heroes. They will be the James Merediths°, with the noble sense of purpose that enables them to face jeering and hostile mobs, and with the agonizing loneliness that characterizes the life of the pioneer. They will be old, oppressed, battered Negro women, symbolized in a seventy-two-year-old woman in Montgomery, Alabama, who rose up with a sense of dignity and with her people decided not to ride segregated buses, and who responded with ungrammatical profundity to one who inquired about her weariness: "My feet is tired, but my soul is at rest." They will be the young high school and college students, the young ministers of the gospel and a host of their elders, courageously and nonviolently sitting in at lunch counters and willingly going to jail for conscience's sake. One day the South will know that when these disinherited children of God sat down at lunch counters, they were in reality standing up for what is best in the American dream and for the most sacred values in our Judaeo-Christian heritage, thereby bringing our nation back to those great wells of democracy which were dug by the founding fathers in their formulation of the Constitution and the Declaration of Independence.

Never before have I written so long a letter. I'm afraid it is much too long to take your precious time. I can assure you that it would have been much shorter if I had been writing from a comfortable desk, but what else can one do when he is alone in a narrow jail cell, other than write long letters, think long thoughts, and pray long prayers?

James Merediths: James Meredith (b. 1933), won a court order in 1962 to become the first African American student to enroll at the University of Mississippi. [EDS.]

If I have said anything in this letter that overstates the truth and indicates an unreasonable impatience, I beg you to forgive me. If I have said anything that understates the truth and indicates my having a patience that allows me to settle for anything less than brotherhood, I beg God to forgive me.

I hope this letter finds you strong in the faith. I also hope that circum- 50 stances will soon make it possible for me to meet each of you, not as an integrationist or a civil-rights leader but as a fellow clergyman and a Christian brother. Let us all hope that the dark clouds of racial prejudice will soon pass away and the deep fog of misunderstanding will be lifted from our fear-drenched communities, and in some not too distant tomorrow the radiant stars of love and brotherhood will shine over our great nation with all their scintillating beauty.

Yours for the cause of Peace and Brotherhood,
Martin Luther King Jr.

WHAT DOES HE SAY?

1. Hard as it might now be to believe, the famous civil rights activist Martin Luther King Jr. wrote this letter after being arrested for parading without a permit in Birmingham, Alabama, in 1963. Even before you begin reading his letter, write a paragraph about what you think of civil disobedience: for example, how do you feel about those who peacefully break the law in order to make a point?

2. As you read, copy out five separate sentences that seem to you unusually eloquent or significant to King's argument.

3. Write a paragraph about how the idea of conscience finds expression in this essay.

4. Identify the single most powerful paragraph—in your estimation—in this letter. Then write your own paragraph paying attention to the writing you've identified. What methods of construction and what choices about content make the paragraph work so well?

WHAT DO YOU THINK?

5. Do a bit of research about the occasion that prompted the composition of "Letter from Birmingham Jail." Explain what you learn and then explain how, why, or in what ways you believe this letter is or is not dated—for example, no longer valid or useful. Make sure that your discussion includes mention of some current issue in the newspapers.

6. Use the notions of *logos*, *ethos*, and *pathos* to interrogate and analyze "Letter from Birmingham Jail." Based on your analysis, explain your judgment of its effectiveness.

7. Understanding that the first reader of a letter is always its author, write a letter in the spirit of "Letter from Birmingham Jail" addressing some injustice or inequality

that concerns you. As "Letter from Birmingham Jail" does, make your letter try to answer objections that you think your readers might have to what you say or to what you advocate. Quote "Letter from Birmingham Jail" at least once.

WHAT WOULD THEY SAY?

8. Read Kofi Annan's "Nobel Lecture" (p. 225). Then write an essay identifying and explaining any places in Annan's speech that seem to have been influenced by "Letter from Birmingham Jail." End your analysis by explaining what you think Martin Luther King Jr. would have said in response to Annan's "Nobel Lecture." Quote Annan at least once.

9. Read Studs Terkel's interview with C. P. Ellis (p. 568) together with Dr. King's essay. King's essay identifies many different individuals and many different kinds of responses to segregation. Where would C. P. Ellis fit in King's analyses? Explain this, quoting from both King and Ellis. End by explaining what King would have thought of Ellis and what Ellis would have thought of King.

10. Consider Joy Williams's "Save the Whales, Screw the Shrimp" (p. 146) together with "Letter from Birmingham Jail." What contrasts or similarities do you see between them? Write an essay discussing whatever seems clear to you as you consider these two essays together.

Why I Volunteer

In this brief newspaper article, published in the Atlanta Journal-Constitution *on December 24, 2003, five people talk about why they volunteer with refugee families and with people who have AIDS.*

'It's the children' who inspire
SARA ZUK, arbitrator

It's the children. Their laughter, their shy smiles, their eagerness to learn, their unfettered adoration, the way they blossom under the sunshine of my attention.

It's been a thrill to watch them each week as their ability to express themselves increases, both mentally and emotionally. And each day, as they acquire additional words and phrases, I am let into their worlds just a little more.

Yes, it's the children—all six of them. They're what's had me fall so deeply in love with the Bostan Ali family.

When we were matched in late May, I stood in the three-bedroom apartment in Clarkston and looked at the smooth, round faces of a refugee family from Afghanistan.

They were strangers. I read the information that I was given about   5
Afghan culture and hoped that I would be a good family mentor who could keep up with bimonthly visits and teach them well. Now, seven months later, I have trouble tearing myself away from my visits, and often feel as though I'm the student.

However, I am clear that I make a difference in their lives—from helping the children with their homework, to driving them to visit Afghan friends, to showing them how to make Easy Mac and Instant Quaker Oatmeal. The smiles and the laughter are unending.

My choice to volunteer came easily—I have always been fascinated by different cultures. It is inspiring to me to see just how similar people actually are, despite our obvious outer differences.

I am filled with hope for the future when I see people who come from different cultural, religious, and socioeconomic backgrounds sharing moments of joy and aliveness. As this occurs more and more, it seems inevitable to me that we will learn to live with increasing compassion, realizing that there is often more than one "right" way to live.

697

'A source of . . . inspiration'
Eliza Heery, student

Like many people these days, I have a tendency to get caught up in the chaos of our current surroundings: the large bustling shopping malls, drive-through Starbucks coffee shops and massive, fluorescent-lit grocery stores.

The culture of consumption seems so all-encompassing that in the course of a normal day, it would be very easy for me to forget that other ways of life even exist.

I began volunteering at Refugee Family Services a little over a year ago. My initial training was eye-opening, as I learned for the first time of the plight of refugees and political-asylum seekers within the United States. But my respect for these experiences only truly developed when I began tutoring and interacting with refugee youths on a weekly basis.

Their life stories were more complex than I could have ever imagined. And yet, like children from every culture or background, these students brought with them an enthusiasm and joy that has re-created my definition of resilience. I volunteer with them because they are a source of continuous inspiration. They help me step back from my routine environment and strive to value some of the more basic joys of life.

After spending a good deal of time at Refugee Family Services last year, I am even more convinced that local action can further the progress of human rights around the globe. The world has a responsibility for its people, and whether that responsibility is fulfilled affects all of us in some way or another.

I work with these children in the hopes that my support will make their process of adjustment a bit easier. At the same time, they help me contextualize and encourage the coexistence of my American culture and the rest of the world.

'Making a difference'
Gwen Wernersbach, student

There are several reasons why I volunteer regularly. Most important, I volunteer because I care about people. There is nothing better than the look on someone's face after you have made a small difference in their lives, whether it was helping an AIDS patient by providing transportation to the hospital or tutoring children in an after-school program.

Volunteering does not have to cost anything or be inconvenient, time-consuming, or something that you do out of obligation. In fact, it's quite the opposite of that. You just have to find something that you are interested in and feel very passionately about, and then put yourself out there with fervor and dedication toward your cause. Being involved in making a difference will become the most precious thing in your life.

For as long as I can remember, I always knew that I wanted to make a difference in people's lives. Helping people to help themselves is the best feeling in the world, and it is the greatest gift imaginable. Most of my volunteer experience in the past has been with patients living with HIV or AIDS. I have made a lifetime commitment to working in the field of HIV/AIDS prevention, particularly in sub-Saharan Africa, where AIDS is most rampant.

Even if just one life has been spared through prevention, then I have done my job. When people tell me that it is futile to even attempt to put a dent in this scourge, I simply reply that although I am just one person, and there is only so much that I can do, one person is all it takes to make a small but meaningful difference.

I believe that we each have something unique to contribute. Volunteering is a wonderful learning experience. It is a constant reminder that there will never come a time when kindnesses are no longer needed as long as people are still suffering.

'Always close to my heart'
JAHAN ARSHID, engineer

I believe that human beings have certain inherent characteristics. Helping 20 your neighbors is one of them. Each person, not only as a citizen of a country but as a citizen of the world and member of the human race, must look within themselves and act upon their civic duty to help those in need. I feel that no matter where you are in your journey of life, whether you are at a personal high or low, there are always those who can use your help and compassion.

Volunteering has always been something that is very close to my heart. No matter where I've been in life, I have always found the desire and the need to help those that could use my help. Recently I volunteered to help Lutheran Immigration and Refugee Service raise awareness of refugees and their plight at the Lutheran Youth Congress, which was held in Atlanta this year. I also regularly volunteer to help refugees on an individual basis through Lutheran Services of Georgia.

I have translated for Farsi-speaking refugees at job interviews and trainings, assisted refugees with college enrollment and by letting them know of various educational programs, and also by keeping refugees in my community informed about their legal obligations to the Citizenship and Immigration Services Bureau (formerly the INS).

Most people find satisfaction in different ways, some through hobbies or by challenging themselves somehow. I find satisfaction from helping others: the simple gratification of knowing that what I do, however small, can possibly improve another person's life, even for a few short moments. Knowing that my assistance could possibly inspire another to do the same.

'Putting feet to one's faith'
MARGARET SHUMAN, homemaker

Our story of working with refugee children starts back when my husband, the son of a pastor, was quite young. He enjoyed hours of listening to stories from folks who had lived in other countries and then "passed through" his family home in Pittsburgh.

Though my early home in Mississippi was also frequented by many 25 guests, they were mostly from the same community. It was my husband's love for internationals and their stories that spilled over into our life. Early in our marriage, we were inspired by the international outreach of Intown Community Church and decided to share our duplex in Virginia-Highland with college students from other countries.

We enjoyed having a guest, often for up to three years, stay in our extra bedroom—a Taiwanese actuarial student at Georgia State University, a Japanese education major at Georgia Tech, a Ukrainian PhD in math from Emory. After we moved to Clarkston and had a son, we still had as many as two students staying with us at a time.

Our twelve-year-old son, Perry, has grown up hearing the words of the Bible that are very clear about putting feet to one's faith. He understands that serving those in need is "how we know what love is: not to love with [only] words, but with actions and in truth." When he became old enough, it seemed natural to search out a place where our whole family could serve in a very tangible way. We found Georgia Mutual Assistance Association Consortium: a program that helps refugee children transition into their new communities.

We have marveled at how smart these kids are, often having survived quick escapes from war-torn countries, and not just learning one new language along the way, but often three or four.

Coming to an understanding of our new friends' perspectives has built respect and love for them. We are glad to be part of their lives, even in such a small way. We serve because we want to share God's love with them, and we are also very blessed along the way.

WHAT DO THEY SAY?

1. As you read these five short pieces, write a brief paragraph summary for each one.

2. Several of these volunteers work with refugee families. What is the picture that you get of these families?

3. Why do these people volunteer?

WHAT DO YOU THINK?

4. Based on these accounts—and on any volunteer experience you have had— explain why volunteering is a selfless act, a selfish act, a waste of time, or any combination of these.

5. Interview someone who volunteers on a regular basis. Find out what this person does and why, where, how often, and who benefits. What's the most surprising aspect of their volunteer work? Also ask that person to relate a significant story about their experience of volunteering. Write up your interview results carefully, and quote often. End by giving your own reaction to having conducted this interview.

6. Consider the idea of volunteering as part of a spectrum. At one end of the spectrum would be activities or jobs that you would do a lot to avoid. Someone would really have to pay you a lot of money to do these activities or jobs on a regular basis. At the other end of the spectrum would be activities or efforts that you would choose to do because they're a pleasure. Identify the two ends of the spectrum—the work or activity you'd try hard to avoid and the work or activity you'd seek out and do often because you like it so much. Between these two extremes, identify something you'd like for a paid job and that you have a reasonable chance of landing. Also, identify something you'd volunteer for if you didn't have to worry about finances. Write an essay explaining how and why you've identified each of these four things.

7. Write about a time when you learned something significant from an experience outside of a classroom. Write about this experience and about what you learned, and give attention to the contributions other people—either paid or unpaid— made to this learning experience. End by discussing the ways you have tried to show your gratitude for this lesson.

WHAT WOULD THEY SAY?

8. Read Adrienne Rich's "Claiming an Education" (p. 608) together with these stories of volunteering. Explain how these stories relate—in any way—to two particular parts of Rich's speech.

9. Assume that you are Stephen L. Carter, author of "Welcoming the Stranger" (p. 111). Write an essay (in Carter's voice, saying what you think Carter would say) in response to "Why I Volunteer." Make sure that you quote "Welcoming the Stranger" at least once.

BRENDA UELAND

Tell Me More

BRENDA UELAND *(1881–1985) argues that our failure to listen to each other is the source of much trouble in the world. The opposite is also true: the world can be changed, conversation by conversation, when we silence ourselves and open our minds to someone else. Ueland was a well-known writer, memoirist, and writing teacher. She published three books, including* If You Want to Write *(1938) and* Me *(1939). This selection is reprinted from* Strength for Your Sword Arm: Selected Writing *(1993).*

ON THE FINE ART OF LISTENING

I want to write about the great and powerful thing that listening is. And how we forget it. And how we don't listen to our children, or those we love. And least of all—which is so important too—to those we do not love. But we should. Because listening is a magnetic and strange thing, a creative force. Think how the friends that really listen to us are the ones we move toward, and we want to sit in their radius as though it did us good, like ultraviolet rays.

This is the reason: when we are listened to, it creates us, makes us unfold and expand. Ideas actually begin to grow within us and come to life. You know how if a person laughs at your jokes you become funnier and funnier, and if he does not, every tiny little joke in you weakens up and dies. Well, that is the principle of it. It makes people happy and free when they are listened to. And if you are a listener, it is the secret of having a good time in society (because everybody around you becomes lively and interesting), of comforting people, of doing them good.

Who are the people, for example, to whom you go for advice? Not to the hard, practical ones who can tell you exactly what to do, but to the listeners; that is, the kindest, least censorious, least bossy people that you know. It is because by pouring out your problem to them, you then know what to do about it yourself.

When we listen to people there is an alternating current, and this recharges us so that we never get tired of each other. We are constantly being re-created. Now there are brilliant people who cannot listen much. They have no ingoing wires on their apparatus. They are entertaining, but exhausting, too. I think it is because these lecturers, these brilliant performers, by not giving us a chance to talk, do not let us express our thoughts and expand; and it is this little creative fountain inside us that begins to spring and cast up new thoughts, and unexpected laughter and wisdom. That is why, when someone has listened to you, you go home rested and lighthearted.

702

Now this little creative fountain is in us all. It is the spirit, or the intelli- 5
gence, or the imagination—whatever you want to call it. If you are very
tired, strained, have no solitude, run too many errands, talk to too many
people, drink too many cocktails, this little fountain is muddied over and covered with a lot of debris. The result is you stop living from the center, the
creative fountain, and you live from the periphery, from externals. That is,
you go along on mere willpower without imagination.

It is when people really listen to us, with quiet fascinated attention,
that the little fountain begins to work again, to accelerate in the most surprising way.

I discovered all this about three years ago, and truly it made a revolutionary change in my life. Before that, when I went to a party I would think anxiously: "Now try hard. Be lively. Say bright things. Talk. Don't let down." And
when tired, I would have to drink a lot of coffee to keep this up.

Now before going to a party I just tell myself to listen with affection to
anyone who talks to me, *to be in their shoes when they talk*; to try to know them
without my mind pressing against theirs, or arguing, or changing the subject.
No. My attitude is: "Tell me more. This person is showing me his soul. It is a
little dry and meager and full of grinding talk just now, but presently he will
begin to think, not just automatically to talk. He will show his true self. Then
he will be wonderfully alive.

Sometimes, of course, I cannot listen as well as others. But when I have
this listening power, people crowd around and their heads keep turning to me
as though irresistibly pulled. It is not because people are conceited and want
to show off that they are drawn to me, the listener. It is because by listening I
have started up their creative fountain. I do them good.

Now why does it do them good? I have a kind of mystical notion about 10
this. I think it is only by expressing all that is inside that purer and purer
streams come. It is so in writing. You are taught in school to put down on
paper only the bright things. Wrong. Pour out the dull things on paper too—
you can tear them up afterward—for only then do the bright ones come. If
you hold back the dull things, you are certain to hold back what is clear and
beautiful and true and lively. So it is with people who have not been listened
to in the right way—with affection and a kind of jolly excitement. Their creative fountain has been blocked. Only superficial talk comes out—what is
prissy or gushing or merely nervous. No one has called out of them, by wonderful listening, what is true and alive.

I think women have this listening faculty more than men. It is not the
fault of men. They lose it because of their long habit of striving in business, of
self-assertion. And the more forceful men are, the less they can listen as they
grow older. And that is why women in general are more fun than men, more
restful and inspiring.

Now this nonlistening of able men is the cause of one of the saddest
things in the world—the loneliness of fathers, of those quietly sad men who

move among their grown children like remote ghosts. When my father was over seventy, he was a fiery, humorous, admirable man, a scholar, a man of great force. But he was deep in the loneliness of old age and another generation. He was so fond of me. But he could not hear me—not one word I said, really. I was just audience. I would walk around the lake with him on a beautiful afternoon and he would talk to me about Darwin and Huxley and higher criticism of the Bible.

"Yes, I see, I see," I kept saying and tried to keep my mind pinned to it, but I was restive and bored. There was a feeling of helplessness because he could not hear what I had to say about it. When I spoke I found myself shouting, as one does to a foreigner, and in a kind of despair that he could not hear me. After the walk I would feel that I had worked off my duty and I was anxious to get him settled and reading in his morris chair, so that I could go out and have a livelier time with other people. And he would sigh and look after me absentmindedly with perplexed loneliness.

For years afterward, I have thought with real suffering about my father's loneliness. Such a wonderful man, and reaching out to me and wanting to know me! But he could not. He could not listen. But now I think that if only I had known as much about listening then as I do now, I could have bridged that chasm between us. To give an example:

Recently, a man I had not seen for twenty years wrote me: "I have a fam- 15
ily of mature children. So did your father. They never saw him. Not in the days he was alive. Not in the days he was the deep and admirable man we now both know he was. That is man's life. When next you see me, you'll just know everything. Just your father all over again, trying to reach through, back to the world of those he loves."

Well, when I saw this man again, what had happened to him after twenty years? He was an unusually forceful man and had made a great deal of money. But he had lost his ability to listen. He talked rapidly and told wonderful stories and it was just fascinating to hear them. But when I spoke—restlessness: "Just hand me that, will you?...Where is my pipe?" It was just a habit. He read countless books and he was eager to take in ideas, but he just could not listen to people.

Well this is what I did. I was more patient—I did not resist his nonlistening talk as I did my father's. I listened and listened to him, not once pressing against him, even in thought, with my own self-assertion. I said to myself: "He has been under a driving pressure for years. His family has grown to resist his talk. But now, by listening, I will pull it all out of him. He must talk freely and on and on. When he has been really listened to enough, he will grow tranquil. He will begin to want to hear me."

And he did, after a few days. He began asking me questions. And presently I was saying gently: "You see, it has become hard for you to listen."

He stopped dead and stared at me. And it was because I had listened with such complete, absorbed, uncritical sympathy, without one flaw of boredom or impatience, that he now believed and trusted me, although he did not know this.

"Now talk," he said. "Tell me about that. Tell me all about that."   20

Well, we walked back and forth across the lawn and I told him my ideas about it.

"You love your children, but probably don't let them in. Unless you listen, people are wizened in your presence; they become about a third of themselves. Unless you listen, you can't know anybody. Oh, you will know facts and what is in the newspapers and all of history, perhaps, but you will not know one single person. You know, I have come to think listening is love, that's what it really is."

Well, I don't think I would have written this article if my notions had not had such an extraordinary effect on this man. For he says they have changed his whole life. He wrote me that his children at once came closer; he was astonished to see what they are; how original, independent, courageous. His wife seemed really to care about him again, and they were actually talking about all kinds of things and making each other laugh.

For just as the tragedy of parents and children is not listening, so it is of husbands and wives. If they disagree they begin to shout louder and louder—if not actually, at least inwardly—hanging fiercely and deafly onto their own ideas, instead of listening and becoming quieter and quieter and more comprehending. But the most serious result of not listening is that worst thing in the world, boredom; for it is really the death of love. It seals people off from each other more than any other thing. I think that is why married people quarrel. It is to cut through the nonconduction and boredom. Because when feelings are hurt, they really begin to listen. At last their talk is a real exchange. But of course, they are injuring their marriage forever.

Besides critical listening, there is another kind that is no good: passive, 25 censorious listening. Sometimes husbands can be this kind of listener, a kind of ungenerous eavesdropper who mentally (or aloud) keeps saying as you talk: "Bunk...Bunk...Hokum."

Now, how to listen? It is harder than you think. I don't believe in critical listening, for that only puts a person in a straitjacket of hesitancy. He begins to choose his words solemnly or primly. His little inner fountain cannot spring. Critical listeners dry you up. But creative listeners are those who want you to be recklessly yourself, even at your very worst, even vituperative, bad tempered. They are laughing and just delighted with any manifestation of yourself, bad or good. For true listeners know that if you are bad tempered it does not mean that you are always so. They don't love you just when you are nice; they love all of you.

In order to learn to listen, here are some suggestions: try to learn tranquility, to live in the present a part of the time every day. Sometimes say to yourself: "Now. What is happening now? This friend is talking. I am quiet. There is endless time. I hear it, every word." Then suddenly you begin to hear not only what people are saying, but what they are trying to say, and you sense the whole truth about them. And you sense existence, not piecemeal, not this object and that, but as a translucent whole.

Then watch your self-assertiveness. And give it up. Try not to drink too many cocktails to give up that nervous pressure that feels like energy and wit but may be neither. And remember it is not enough just to *will* to listen to people. One must *really* listen. Only then does the magic begin.

Sometimes people cannot listen because they think that unless they are talking, they are socially of no account. There are those women with an old-fashioned ballroom training that insists there must be unceasing vivacity and gyrations of talk. But this is really a strain on people.

No. We should all know this: that listening, not talking, is the gifted and great 30 role, and the imaginative role. And the true listener is much more believed, magnetic than the talker, and he is more effective and learns more and does more good. And so try listening. Listen to your wife, your husband, your father, your mother, your children, your friends, to those who love you and those who don't, to those who bore you, to your enemies. It will work a small miracle. And perhaps a great one.

WHAT DOES SHE SAY?

1. Brenda Ueland says that there is a "little creative fountain" inside of all of us. Explain what she means and how this relates to the act of listening.

2. Explain what Ueland means by effective listening. What are we supposed to do as listeners? What are we to avoid doing?

3. What is the effect of good listening according to Ueland? What does it accomplish?

4. Why do we include this essay in a chapter called "What Should You Do?" How does Ueland answer that question? What ethical good can listening do?

WHAT DO YOU THINK?

5. Pair up with a classmate. Decide who goes first. Then for three minutes have one person talk about Ueland's essay—thoughts, reactions, questions—while the other person listens, never interrupting, not adding anything. Just listening. Then switch roles: the listener talks and the talker listens.

6. Step back and reflect on the listening exercise in question 5. How does it illustrate Ueland's point? Was your experience at all like the experience that Ueland describes?

7. Relate Ueland's idea of listening to your experience in classrooms at the university. Does listening in this sense happen very often in this setting? In your experience,

who usually listens to whom? In what way? Who doesn't get to talk? Who doesn't get to listen?

8. Write an essay arguing that listening in Ueland's sense is the key to university education. An educated person, you'll argue, knows how to listen. And to arrive at this point, to achieve this level of education, it's necessary for students to spend a good deal of their time at the university actively and creatively listening—and being listened *to*. In your analysis reflect on what would have to change in university education for this model to be achieved.

9. Write an essay reflecting on a time when you were listened to—really listened to, long and hard and deep. Use Ueland's essay to interpret this experience.

WHAT WOULD THEY SAY?

10. How would Parker Palmer in "The Community of Truth" (p. 627) respond to Ueland's essay? How does the idea of listening correspond to the idea of the community of truth? Explain.

11. Expand the topic in question 10 to include Adrienne Rich's "Claiming an Education" (p. 608) and David Denby's "Passion at Yale" (p. 593). Use all four of these essays—by Rich, Denby, Palmer, and Ueland—to develop a theory of university education.

12. Apply Ueland's idea of listening to Sarah Vowell's "Shooting Dad" (p. 29), Maxine Hong Kingston's "No Name Woman" (p. 45), and Winona LaDuke's "Voices from White Earth" (p. 72). Argue that all of these writers are good listeners in Ueland's sense and that all three are urging us to listen, too, whether to other people or to the earth itself.

13. Think back on any essay that you've read in this book. Write an essay arguing that one or more of these writers fails to listen in Ueland's sense: fails to listen to others, fails to listen to the subject, fails to listen to life.

For Community Learning and Research

1. Visit your campus career center or volunteer center, interview someone there, and on the basis of your interview and any other information available, write a profile of three volunteer opportunities that would especially benefit from greater student involvement. If possible, include interviews with students who already volunteer in these programs. Assume that you're going to be able to print this essay in your campus newspaper.

2. If there are sorority or fraternity organizations on your campus, contact the volunteer coordinator for one of those houses. Find out what that organization has done in the last three years in terms of volunteer service to the community. If you're impressed by what you learn, write an essay—assume it's for your school paper—that promotes these efforts and that announces the next one. If you're less than impressed, write an open letter to the president of the organization explaining what you've learned and why you're not impressed. End it by challenging that organization to improve their local volunteer record.

3. Using the essay "The Singer Solution to World Poverty" (p. 661) as inspiration, write a one-page brochure or pamphlet that could be posted and distributed on campus in order to encourage students to donate money or food to address local hunger concerns. Before you write this document, contact some local food banks or other local programs that regularly help those who need food. Determine the local need, and use some of your information, together with the Singer essay, as part of your effort to motivate students to help.

4. Ask around your campus or town to find a local person whose efforts and characteristics are similar to those of Paul Farmer ("The Good Doctor," p. 645). This person need not be a doctor, but she or he should be someone who has a strong record of working for the betterment of others. Once you've identified this person, interview her or him; if possible, follow this person around for a day. On the basis of what you learn, write a profile that could be an extended feature article in your local or campus newspaper. (One possibility: Ask your alumni office if they know of a local alum who might fit this description. If you're successful finding such an alum, see if your alumni publication is interested in your profile.)

5. Interview someone in your local American Civil Liberties Union office about what the ACLU thinks of civil disobedience of the sort that Martin Luther King Jr. speaks of in his essay "Letter from Birmingham Jail" (p. 682). What issues provoke civil disobedience now? Is the ACLU involved in any such cases? What does the ACLU think of the right to dissent? On the basis of your information gathering, write a letter to your campus newspaper urging students either to support the ACLU or to understand why it's not worthy of such support.

6. Identify a group on your campus that is not really heard or well known to others partly because their views seem outside the mainstream. Go to a meeting of this group, identify yourself and your reasons for being there, and then find out all you can about why this group exists, what they want or would hope for, what they find objectionable—anything that helps you understand why they might not be well understood. Prepare a five minute speech for your class explaining what

you've learned about this group and what you think others ought to know. (Variation: Do this as a group project, with a group report lasting fifteen minutes.)

7. Identify five items of clothing that most students need to buy on a regular basis. Then go to a local Wal-Mart or similar store and check the stock of these items. Make note of where these clothing articles are made. Then see if you can locate a store that sells similar items of clothing made closer to where you live or that sells similar clothing secondhand. Find out what you can about the working conditions in the countries that made the Wal-Mart stock. Find out what you can about the working conditions for those who made similar items closer to home. Or, if no such items are made closer to home, find out who benefits from the secondhand clothing store. On the basis of your investigation, write a brochure that could be distributed to students so that they could make informed decisions about where to purchase clothing locally.

Richard Rodriguez. "The Achievement of Desire." From *Hunger of Memory* by Richard Rodriguez. Copyright © 1982 by Richard Rodriguez. Reprinted by permission of David R. Godine Publishers, Inc.

Benjamin Saenz. "Exile: El Paso Texas." From *Flowers for the Broken* by Benjamin Saenz. Copyright © 1992 by Benjamin Saenz. Reprinted by permission of the author.

Scott Russell Sanders. "Looking at Women." From *Secrets of the Universe* by Scott Russell Sanders. Copyright © 1991 Scott Russell Sanders. Reprinted by permission of Beacon Press, Boston.

Eric Schlosser. "What We Eat." From *Fast Food Nation* by Eric Schlosser. Copyright © 2001 by Eric Schlosser. Reprinted by permission of Houghton Mifflin Company. All rights reserved.

Jenefer Shute. "Life-Size." Excerpt from *Life-Size* by Jenefer Shute. Reprinted by permission of the author.

Peter Singer. "The Singer Solution to World Poverty." Originally published in the *New York Times Magazine*, September 5, 1999. © 1999. Reprinted by permission of the author.

Rebecca Solnit. "The Silence of the Lambswool Cardigans." Originally appeared in *Orion*, July 2003. Copyright © 2003. Reprinted by permission of the author.

William Stafford. "Traveling through the Dark." From *The Way It Is: New and Selected Poems* by William Stafford. Copyright © 1962, 1998 by the Estate of William Stafford. Reprinted with permission of Graywolf Press, Saint Paul, Minnesota.

Brent Staples. "Just Walk on By: Black Men and Public Space." Reprinted by permission of the author.

Peter Steiner. Copyright © *The New Yorker* Collection 2001 Peter Steiner. From cartoonbank.com. All Rights Reserved.

Andrew Sullivan. "The Pursuit of Happiness: Four Revolutionary Words." First published in *The New Yorker*, 2001. Copyright © 2001 by Andrew Sullivan. Reprinted with the permission of the Wylie Agency, Inc.

Studs Terkel. "C. P. Ellis." From *Race: How Blacks and Whites Feel about the American Obsession* by Studs Terkel. Copyright © 1980 by Studs Terkel. Reprinted by permission of Donadio & Olson, Inc.

Sallie Tisdale. "We Do Abortions Here." Reproduced by special permission from the October 1997 issue of *Harper's Magazine*. Copyright © 1997 by *Harper's Magazine*. All rights reserved.

Brenda Ueland. "Tell Me More." From *Strength to Your Sword Arm: Selected Writings* by Brenda Ueland. Copyright © 1992 by the Estate of Brenda Ueland. Reprinted by permission of Holy Cow! Press (Duluth, Minnesota).

Lindsy Van Gelder. "Marriage as a Restricted Club." First published in *Ms.* magazine, 1984. © 1984 by Lindsy Van Gelder. Reprinted by permission of the author.

Sarah Vowell. "Shooting Dad." From *Take the Cannoli* by Sarah Vowell. Copyright © 2000 by Sarah Vowell. Reprinted with the permission of Simon & Schuster Adult Publishing Group.

Alice Walker. "Am I Blue?" From *Living by the Word: Selected Writings 1973–1987*. Copyright © by Alice Walker. Reprinted by permission of Harcourt, Inc.

Bill Watterson. "Calvin and Hobbes." Copyright © 1993 Bill Watterson. Reprinted with permission of Universal Press Syndicate. All rights reserved.

Henry Wechsler, Charles Deutsch, and George Dowdall. "Too Many Colleges Are Still in Denial about Alcohol Abuse." Originally published in the *Chronicle of Higher Education*, April 15, 1995. Reprinted by permission of Henry Wechsler.

Cornel West. "The Moral Obligations of Living in a Democratic Society." From *The Good Citizen* by David Batstone and Edwardo Mendieta, editors. Copyright © 1999 by David Batstone and Edwardo Mendieta. Reproduced by permission of Routledge/Taylor & Francis Books, Inc.

Joy Williams. "Save the Whales, Screw the Shrimp." First appeared in *Esquire*. Copyright © Joy Williams. Reprinted by permission of International Creative Management.

Terry Tempest Williams. "Two Words." Originally appeared in *Orion*, Winter 1999, as "Where There's Hope: Two Words" by Terry Tempest Williams. Copyright © 1999 by Terry Tempest Williams. Reprinted by permission of Brandt and Hochman Literary Agents, Inc.

Naomi Wolf. "The Beauty Myth." From *The Beauty Myth* by Naomi Wolf. Copyright © Naomi Wolf. Reprinted by permission of HarperCollins Publishers, Inc.

Index of Authors, Titles, and Terms